AF507440

Once Upon a Time

in the

American Revolution

Directed by
Bishop Neil R. Coombs, Ph.D.
Dean of Students, California State Institute of Social Sciences

Contributing editor
Ellen D. Kiehl, Ph.D.
Assistant Executive Director Government and Industry Affairs
(Retired)

Proofread by
Shirley A. Albright, CPIA, CISR
Director of Industry Resource Center

Jacqueline A. Schrom
Industry Resource Center Administrative Assistant

> *"Who Shall Write The History of the American Revolution? Who can write it?" Thus wrote, John Adams on 30 July 1815 to Thomas Jefferson. "Nobody," Jefferson replied from Monticello on 10 Aug. 1815, "except merely its external facts.... The life and soul of history must be forever unknown."*

Rev. Gordon R. Hackel D.H.L.

Statement of Author

The true events written in this story were recorded in family Bible records, diaries and journals, which had been passed down in the family from the Prussian Wars in Germany and the American Revolution till the present time. This author spent 45 years of his life verifying and thoroughly documenting the chronological order in which these events took place. This author spent years going to the Genealogical Library in Salt Lake City, Utah and also went to the National Archives in Washington DC, where hundreds of correspondences on Captain John KEMPER were on file. There were also many records on his brother, Colonel Daniel KEMPER.

There was also a file on their brother, Captain Jacob KEMPER, but it was empty. This did not make a lot of sense since the pension law was enacted in 1832 and Daniel and John's brother, Jacob, died young in the year 1800. The apparent reason for his file was that he had descendants that were putting in for his benefits on land bounty rights. This author had them all copied and he brought them back home to New York to transcribe them for easy reference.

There were hundreds of correspondences on John KEMPER's life during the American Revolution, extending over a twenty-year span; this author arranged them in chronological order, along with his family Bible records, diaries and journals. In addition, other members of his family like, his cousin Colonel Sebastian BEAUMAN and niece Eliza Susan (Morton) QUINCY are reflected upon. The following story is the result of one month shy of forty-seven years of painstakingly hard work.

In the beginning, when this author began collecting diaries and journals from his family—there was never any intention of writing a story; he did not know that there was one. Its only intent was to gather enough documentation in order to ascertain what went wrong. Captain KEMPER had discovered he was being underpaid and requested the procedures to follow to correct the deficit. Consequently, his service under General George WASHINGTON was then inappropriately reclassified civilian, instead of military to answer for the shortage; therefore, he was ineligible to continue receiving his military pension. Hence, it was suspended.

The author needed to examine the discrepancy between family records and ones found in the National Archives. Through this process, he uncovered a hornet's nest. He discover that Captain KEMPER's original declaration had been thoroughly investigated and given credence by the Department of War and a voucher was signed by Lewis CASS, secretary of war and James L. EDWARDS, commissioner of pensions. The evidence that brought the Department of War to its conclusion was available at the time but has since disappeared. This discovery compelled this author to delve further into the realm of suspicion.

All through this process of gathering documentation, supporters would often encourage this author to write Captain John KEMPER's biography. It was not until the year 2013 when so much documentation had been gathered, that it was now possible. Hence, we began formatting the life events into story form.

This process opened up new doors of complications. Since this author had only categorized most important events with the record, volume number, page numbers, footnotes etc., we would have to go back forty-five years when it all began and recover all the citations used. This author, or his supporters, would have another forty-five years to see it to fruition. In addition, it would take another volume to record all materials covered.

Worse than that, this author was able to obtain support and advice from other authors, who had gone through the process and, having previous stories stolen, brought to our attention, how some publishers steal your work. If you give all your work to a publisher, even when they only need three chapters, and go out the next day and get hit by a truck, then the story is theirs.

Some publishers will try to get all your work, rather than just the three chapters that are required. They will then, change the characters' names, confirm the volume and page number of the sources, re-titled your story, copyright it, and bingo! Your story has been stolen. All authors must remember, all publishers are bankrupt unless authors give them business.

Therefore, after thorough consideration by all involved, we decided to camouflage our source material, listing sources consulted only, leaving out volume and page numbers, but accurately recording all of the facts. Now, they would have to do the same forty-five years of hard research in order to steal our work. No one is going to do that.

The final attempt to make the story gel was to contact the New York State Archives to obtain copies of all the correspondences of New York State agent of veteran's affairs, Giles F. YATES, Esq. He had given over ten years of his life to have Captain John KEMPER's rank and military status under General George WASHINGTON restored.

He had many correspondences with other veterans, including Captain KEMPER's brother, Colonel Daniel KEMPER. When we contacted the state archives, they informed us that, *those veterans' records were destroyed many years ago.*" This was a slap in the face. Totally unbelievable, that New York State would destroy such important documents on the birth of our country.

In order to put a close on this case, it was this author's intention to contact President George W. BUSH (1946-?) for a Presidential Medal of Freedom for Captain John KEMPER-then, to contact senatorial and congressional representatives to, appropriately do up a congressional resolution commemorating Captain John

KEMPER's service to our country. However, during this period of time, we were at war. It was decided by this author not to interrupt or distract our Government officials from the defense of our country.

In the memory of my grandfather, Basil G. K. Wilcox (1888-1968) for planting the seeds of knowledge and wonder about the role of his third great grandfather in the birth of America from the struggles of the American Revolution ... and to my dear friend, colleague and mentor, Bishop Neil R. Coombs, Ph.D. (1927-?), for inspiring me to delve into the world of genealogy and history and for his continued support throughout my lifetime.

Thirdly, to my aunt Gwen (Lyons) Lane (1917-1992), who started this author in our family history, by relating all her knowledge she had remembered throughout the years. Aunt Gwen knew more about the family history than all the rest of our family members combined. Finally to New York State agent, Giles Fonda Yates, Esquire, for giving the best ten years of his life in a non-stop battle to win for Captain John Kemper, a pension increase based on the part he played as captain and wagon master in the Continental Army under General George Washington. Without Yates' work this author would not have had the motivation to continue where he had left off and finally win justice.

My final and most important dedication is to Jacqueline "Jackie" A. Schrom, Industry Resource Center administrative assistant; the lady with a heart of gold. This author first met Jackie in June 2013 at Selkirk, New York. She encouraged this author to write this story from all the documented evidence accumulated over a lifetime. She volunteered to proofread. Because of her involvement, others from her company PIA (Professional Insurance Agents) came on board like, Ellen D. Kiehl, Ph.D., assistant executive director of Government and Industry Affairs (retired); Shirley A. Albright, CPIA, CISR, director of Industrial Resource Center; and attorneys Matthew Guilbault and Bradford Lachut who gave legal advice.

Contents

Preface

On 6 December 1953, a Sunday, my grandmother Bertha WILCOX (1882-1953) came over for a celebration. The party was for the birthday of my younger sister, Bertha Gwendolyn Dianthus PROPER (1950-?) who had been named after her, along with my own. Bertha was born on December 4th, while I was born on December 8th and my mother was celebrating both of our birthdays on December 6th with Grandma.

During her visit, it became apparent that she had become very ill. Knowing that she was soon going to die, she had my mother, Dianthus May (Wilcox) PROPER (1920-1985) (named after my grandmother's favorite flower), take her little red wagon (my mother did not drive) and make several trips to pick up Grandma's personal belongings. She wanted the family belongings to remain with my mother after she passed on.

Among all the possessions she retrieved were four metal trunks (footlockers). They measured 40 inches long by two feet wide by eighteen inches deep. All edges and corners were re-enforced with brass stays. Inside was a four-inch deep wooden tray with sections. In these trunks were things like a silver pocket watch that opened up and chimed. Inside on the left was a picture of a person, but I cannot remember who it was.

There also was a uniform and a sword that belonged to my grandmother's father, Frederick Woodruff COX (1837-1897), from the Civil War. The sword had been placed diagonally at the bottom of the chest. It was silver, in a black leather sheath, protected at both ends by metal. There also was a locket that once belonged to my grandmother's mother, Charlotte E. BOGARDUS (1844-1917). Inside the locket on the right side was a picture of her husband, Frederick W. COX. This locket is still in the possession of this author today.

There were wooden Dutch shoes, along with a couple of dozen tintypes (pictures), small oil paintings and other family memorabilia. There was a music box six by eight inches long and four inches deep; when you opened it, a doll popped up in a white gown and danced to a tune. You wound it up with a brass butterfly key at the bottom of the music box. There also was a gold necklace that once belonged to my grandfather's mother, Minnie Florence WILCOX (1863-1925). This was a gold medallion with a lion's head on the front. We were forbidden to go into these trunks; but, whenever mom was away, Bertha and I would rummage through the trunks with delight. What a treasure trove we had discovered. The significance of the family heirlooms did not come into focus until years later.

In 1958, while living in Albany, New York, my sister Linda WILCOX (1945-2007) told me that my grandfather, Basil WILCOX (1888-1968), wanted to see me. Even though I have pictures taken with my grandfather when I was a young child, I did not remember him at this time. We went to Central Avenue and down to a downstairs apartment under a stone staircase. We knocked on the door, my grandfather opened it and we entered. My sister then said, *"Here he is."* My grandfather seemed to be a stout stature of a man; tall and medium build. One of the things I remember most clearly is that his eyes seemed to be sunken, like those of an owl. One of the things that I remember about his apartment is that it was always so hot. We were there just to say hello, sit and have cookies and milk.

On later visits, my grandfather started reading to me from Captain KEMPER's books titled, *Wagon Master* and *US Naval Affairs.* They were exciting stories and I was enthralled by the military presence within them. I would relive them in my playtime, pretending I was Captain KEMPER. At that time, I was unaware of the importance of these as official military records; to me they were just stories. The importance did not come into focus until later years when they came into my possession.

As time went on, he would read from the KEMPER family Bible records and the journals and diaries of his third great grandfather Captain John KEMPER (1757-1842). He also read from a diary of John's daughter, Elizabeth KEMPER (1798-1867), which was in shambles. He randomly took pages out to read them and then placed them back when he finished. These pages were very old and brittle, that many were torn and some were in pieces. Unknowingly to me at that time, a family history was being implanted in my brain that could never be forgotten.

Some of the stories were so full of life and opened your eyes, while others made you feel sad. Many of the pages were so mixed up and scrambled it was difficult to arrange them all back in order correctly. Consequently, it was difficult to properly chronologically arrange his memoirs. In reality, I was not there for the stories, but, in fact, the goodies; sometimes candy. However, if I wanted the goodies I had to listen to the stories. Grownups, they always make you work hard and listen for the good stuff.

One of the stories that really opened my eyes was about the soldiers at camp at Valley Forge. They were encamped there for the winter, regaining their health and strength when the ground began to tremble with the thunderous sound of hundreds of horses' hoofs and the clanking of steel, as the noise grew closer and louder. All the soldiers at camp perked up their ears; General Anthony WAYNE (1745-1796) grabbed his spyglass for observation at a distance, and sent an officer for General WASHINGTON (1732-1799). Everyone feared that the entire British army was coming in to finish them all off. Grandpa then shocked me with the finish!

Another one of my grandfather's stories, that was memorable, was when Captain KEMPER came upon a British party, buying supplies from a local farmer. He raided the farm, captured all the supplies, and their horses, and left everyone standing in their underclothes in mid-winter. The British commander, who had a curly mustache stood with his arms folded across his chest, shivering and smoking a cigar. Captain KEMPER grabbed the cigar, stuck it in his own mouth and rode off with all the goods. I can still remember asking my grandfather, *"Well, how did the British finally get home, grandpa?"*

My grandfather was laughing when he replied, *"I have no idea!"*

In 1970, when I was on leave from the US Army, I visited my close, dear friend, Neil R. COOMBS, (1927-?). He showed me oil paintings he had of his ancestors in his apartment and his certificate as a member of the Sons of the American Revolution.

I exclaimed, *"I am too, my grandfather told me the story."*

Roger replied, *"Here is my certificate proving my descent; where is yours?"*

I answered, *"I do not have one yet,"*

"Aaaaaaaaaaaaaaaaaaaaaah," Roger replied. Then, Roger showed me his certificate as a member of the descendants of the *Mayflower.*

I again responded, *"I am too, my mother told me the story."*

Roger again replied, *"Here is proof of my line of descent; where is yours?"*

I answered, *"I guess I have something to prove."*

Roger responded, *"Really?"*

Although some of you who are reading this, may think that Roger was intimidating. The fact is, he was quite the opposite; Roger was a very warmhearted individual who always gave anyone a helping hand that needed it. He always cheered up a party or special event and made everyone laugh. Roger was in the Korean War when the one million Chinese crossed over the border. The American Army was on the right and retreated. The Korean Army was on the left and retreated. The Marines, who were in the middle, not knowing that the American and Korean Armies retreated, stayed!

The one million Chinese surrounded the marines; their only way out was to fight their way out. Roger is a living emblem of American bravery that we all look up to. Roger was also responsible for helping me find the path to my destiny. I have been very fortunate to have him in my life and honored to be able to call him a friend.

After I received my discharge from the US Army on 7 June 1971, I again visited Roger, who took me to the genealogy library in Los Angeles, California. This is where my journey began. At this particular time in my life, I was only out to prove my line of descent from my ancestors, Reverend Everardus (1607-1647), and Anneke Jans BOGARDUS (1605-1663); and Captain John KEMPER, and try to find out what happened to him during the American Revolution. I was in for the shock of my life!

Unbeknownst to this author, I was headed deep into the heart of the birth of America. I was soon to find out that my ancestor, John KEMPER, who was a captain in the Continental Army, joined the United States Navy afterward and became a lieutenant. While a lieutenant in the navy, he was on board the American war ship, *Hector*. They met up on the Delaware River with the HMS (His Majesty's Ship) *Iris,* a thirty-two-gun ship, where they did battle.

They were captured by the British, tortured in the various prison ships, tortured again by the Provost Marshal, Captain William *"Bloody Bill"* CUNNINGHAM (1756-1791) in the Provost Prison in New York City and then again, in Mill Prison, England.

Everywhere I researched, Captain KEMPER was in the middle of everything during the American Revolution. Where was this story headed?

However, the most severe heartache came in the final years of Captain John KEMPER'S life, during his seventies and eighties, when he was psychologically tortured to his death by the very country he loved and adored, *"America!"* Truly unbelievable, until I had taken the next fourteen years gathering all documentary evidence, finding out what happened and proving his case. Now, would America be everything it has advertised to be over generations, a land of justice? Would they right the wrong that was committed against Captain John KEMPER of the Continental Army and Lieutenant John KEMPER of the United States Navy? We would soon find out. …

In July 1984, I contacted James (Jim) S. CALVIN (1950-?), a reporter for the *Register Star* newspaper in Hudson, New York. He started out his full-page story on me, in his words, *"All my irons I have in the fire."* He started out by covering my history, where I was born and grew up, graduated, etc. He then began covering my various projects, my spending years copying all the stones in the Old Hudson City Cemetery, my letter to the Veterans' Administration requesting a monument for Captain John KEMPER, and especially, the new national magazine I had been working on, *the US Genealogist,* being mentored by my dear friend, William (Bill) WORRALL (1936-?), owner and editor of *Keyboard World* magazine, and friend of Valentio LIBERACHI (1919-1987).

After Mr. CALVIN's article was published, everyone was drawn to Captain John KEMPER'S story and the *US Genealogist* magazine went on the back burner. A friend of mine, Bob THORSEY, gave the name and number of a friend of his, Tito GRENCI, who had connections up in the state Capitol. He was sergeant-at-arms in the New York State Senate, and former body guard to Governor Nelson Rockefeller (1908-1979).

I called Tito and told him Captain John KEMPER's story. I then asked him, *"I'll send you a package on Captain KEMPER'S history and if you feel it is worth while, may I use your name to try to get additional support?"*

Tito replied, *"It sounds like this project needs to be brought to the attention of the State."*

My eyes opened wide and my jaw dropped; I was totally speechless. After I sent him the package and he went over everything thoroughly, he did just what he said, and brought everything to the attention of the State.

After the State received all the documentation, they drew up a resolution commemorating Captain John KEMPER's service to our country. His story then launched across America reaching all levels of government—from Congress to the Pentagon, to the White House, picking up support and awards from all. The reconstruction of Captain KEMPER's history, backed up by thorough documented sources, became mandatory as his story was going to all levels of government and had to be 100 percent correct. There could be no room for error.

However, the resolution reflects some of my personal history inaccurately. I was baptized when I was a child in a Lutheran church, but I was ordained in the Evangelistic Church of Christian Dynamics. The newspaper article unintentionally combined the two events into one stating that, I was ordained as *"a minister with the Evangelistic Lutheran Church of Christian Dynamics."* There is no such church!

Introduction

The KEMPER family name is derived from the ancient German tribe of Cimbri. The Cimbri were responsible for defeating CEASAR's (100B.C.-44B.C.) legions of 120,000 soldiers back in 113 B.C. This was one war the Roman soldiers were marching into from which they would not be returning home. The Cimbri descendants adopted the family name of CIMBER, KIMBER and KEMPER. Other variations of the family name were CAMP and KEMP. The KEMPER family also was responsible for starting the Kempen Village in North Rhine-Westphalia, Germany. This location is in the western central part of Germany, near the French border. Captain John and Colonel Daniel KEMPER's family descend from this line and location.

Since Kempen Village was so close to the French border, there was a constant flow of French troops across the border to raid nearby German villages. Many of the Kempner families moved inland along the Rhine River for safety. From this location they could easily travel up and down the Rhine to other major cities in Germany. It is from this location Johann (Johannes) KEMPER (1657-1712) inherited his right in his military career. After attending Heidelberg University, Johann took military school, joined the Imperial Army, was given the rank of colonel and entered the Prussian Wars.

Frederick William I "the Great Elector" tightly restricted enrollment in the officers corps to Germans of noble descent. Even though Colonel Johann KEMPER'S line of noble descent came down on his mother's side, he still became a favorite of both the *"Great Elector"* and his son, Frederick III. Later on in his military career, he gained the personal attention of the Emperor of the Holy Roman Empire, Leopold I (1640-1705), himself, while fighting for him against the Turks.

On 17 September 1680, the Great Elector sent Colonel KEMPER on board the frigate Wappen *von Brandenburg*, a forty-four-gun ship to the Gold Coast of West Africa. He was sent as an overseer to assist in searching for a locality suitable for colonization and make sure everything went right. He was then to help establish trade with local African tribes and get a contract so that they could build a fortress. They reached Guinea in January 1681. They sold a barrel of brandy to three local Alhanta-Hauptlingen African chiefs, Pregate, Sophonie and Apany Zu Schlieben, which put smiles on their faces.

What the three African chiefs wanted in return was, military protection for their trade, themselves and from their enemies. The Europeans, the chiefs exclaimed, had fire power that the Africans did not. Some ivory was traded for, but little gold could be found. What the African chiefs were pushing was an endless amount of slaves. This commodity, they claimed, was worth more than gold, as we could build an empire on free labor.

Colonel Johann KEMPER reported back to the Great Elector that, illnesses ran rampart in Africa, like malaria and other diseases. The vast majority of everyone who came to build the colony and fortress were all bed ridden, including the commander of the project, Major Otto VON DER GROEBEN (1657-1728), who had to be replaced by Philipp Peterson BLONCK, until he recovered in August 1683 when he returned to Prussia. Mr. BLONCK was the commander of the frigate *Morian,* a thirty-two-gun ship. He later became the first Governor of the colony.

Even though Major Otto VON DER GROEBEN was unable to complete the task that he was sent to the Gold Coast to undertake, he was given full credit by the Great Elector for getting it started. Philipp Peterson BLONCK made sure everything was completed. The stone fortress was built on a hill overlooking the coast. Cannons were aimed out at sea in the event enemy ships threatened the area. You had a clear view of the ocean pounding the shores on the sand beach.

Colonel KEMPER periodically sent forth various captains from Prussia to the Gold Coast, to replenish supplies and transporting trade goods, until everything was set and under control. He continued his report that, he believed the African chiefs created the gold hoax as a method to lure Europeans to the Gold Coast for their valuable trade items and protection. Even though the slaves offered free labor, he foresaw that their health costs would be immense in order to maintain their longevity. In addition, Africans had no skills in European construction or fighting methods. They would all have to be trained. The Africans even traded or sold their own children.

The construction of the fortress was led by Major Otto Friedrich **VON DER GROEBEN**. After its completion on 1 January 1683, drums pounded and ship guns fired as captain of the frigate *Churprintz*, a twelve-gun ship, Mattheus DE VOS, paraded the huge Brandenburg flag from the ship to the fort. It was received by all armed soldiers and hoisted on a high flagpole. Otto named the fortress Grob friedrichsburg, after himself and his great elector, the Overlord. This stone fortress can still be seen today, 2016. This was just one of many great adventures that Colonel Johann KEMPER was sent on by both the Great Elector and his son, Frederick III.

In September 1683, the Great Elector sent Colonel KEMPER and other valuable contingents to help the emperor of the Holy Roman Empire on his second front against the Ottoman Turks, who were invading Europe. On 11 September 1683, Colonel KEMPER fought the Turks at the second Siege of Vienna. The Turks were becoming a menace; they were killing the men and raping women and children everywhere. Leopod I was going to have to build a huge army to rid Europe of these villains.

Colonel Johann KEMPER served under "the Great Elector's" head general of the Imperial Army, Prince Charles LEOPOLD I of Lorraine (1643-1690). Sometimes he served under Field Marshall George VON DERSSLINGER (1606-1695). There was always strict competition to get him in their army.

Because of his bravery in battle and supplying security for *"the Great Elector"* he quickly rose in rank to an oberst (full) colonel, under Frederick William I, "the Great Elector" (1620-1688) and maintained that rank under his son, Frederick I (1657-1713), king in Prussia. Colonel Johann KEMPER and his *"illustrious cuirassiers,"* an elite regiment of dragoons, became deeply depended upon by General LEOPOLD I and became one of his chief regiments for attack, defense and security.

Colonel Johann KEMPER was born around and lived in the area of North Rhine-Westphalia and later Königsberg, Brandenburg, Germany. As he served in the Prussian wars under Frederick William I, "the Great Elector," and his son, Frederick I, king in Prussia, he continued to receive wounds from, sword, knife and musket. None of these early wounds could slow down the colonel in battle. However, after continual battles and additional wounds, they began to take their toll on the Colonel. His final battle was in the War of the Spanish Succession, under Emperor Leopold I.

The colonel had too often led his *"illustrious cuirassiers"* into battle, thereby becoming a main target. This information was recorded in the KEMPER family Bible kept by Johann's grandson, Johannes (John) KEMPER, who was his namesake and is the focus of this story. John had recorded everything from his father, Jacob, and his family Bible; and added to his own research.

Johannes also recorded that his grandfather had earned his rank in knighthood, not only from his bloodline on his mother's side, but also from actual heroics witnessed by General Charles

Leopold I and both, Frederick William I, *"The Great Elector"* and his son, Frederick I, king in Prussia. A knight was a military servant of the king or other feudal superior as a mounted man-at-arms.

On 16 June 1684, Colonel KEMPER accompanied Charles Leopold I and the Imperial Army of eighty thousand men on their first siege of the fortress of Buda. This siege lasted for 109 days and finished on 30 October 1684. Unsuccessful they would return two years later with a larger army. The Turkish Muslims had a foothold in Europe and would rather die fighting to keep it, than give it up. The Turks truly believed they were in honey heaven.

In June 1686, Colonel KEMPER once again, accompanied the imperial army on their second siege of Buda. This time, the imperial army consisted of between 65,000-and 100,000 troops. On 27 July 1686, the imperial army stormed Buda, slaughtered over 3,000 Turks and captured over another 6,000.

On 12 August 1687, Colonel KEMPER once again accompanied Charles Leopold I and participated at the Battle of Mohács. Back in 1526, the French had aligned themselves with the Ottoman Empire, encouraging them to enter Europe and help conquer the Holy Roman Empire. This was one of the main reasons both the KEMPER and ERNST families hated the French, besides their incursion into the Rhine River Valley murdering many German families.

On 14 January 1688, he helped defeat the Turks at Munkacs. For this action, he received the medal "Ordre de la Generosite" (the Order of Generosity). This award was originally established back on 20 May 1667 by the "Great Elector." This order was primarily reserved for royal princes, like Charles LEOPOLD I. In 1685, it became a secular military and civil order; open to an unlimited number of knights. Colonel KEMPER received both the breast star and sash badge. Medals continued to adorn the chest of Colonel KEMPER from kings and emperors. When in dress uniform, all eyes were on him.

On 30 July-6 September 1688, he fought at the battles that captured Belgrade. On 17-22 June 1689, his troops helped capture Kaiserworth and participated in the Siege of Bonn in October 1689. On 8 September 1690, he fought at the siege of Belgrade. On 19 August 1691, he participated in the Battle of Slankamen, which also defeated the Turks. On 24 July 1692, he fought in the Battle of Steinkerk. On 29 July 1693, he fought at the battle of Neerwindem. On 4 October 1695, he fought at the Battle of Marsaglia in the Netherlands. On 11 September 1697, he fought at the Battle of Zenta, which, likewise, defeated the Turks.

The Siege of Stahleck Castle

On 11 October 1688, while Colonel Johann KEMPER was fighting in the Prussian wars up north, drums began to pound, while alarms bellowed out from Stahleck Castle. They were informing the residents of Bacharach that a large French fleet of war ships were approaching. The town's people ran to the castle's front gate where they were let in to gather in the castle courtyard for their protection. After the war ships anchored off the coast, they began their bombardment of the town of Bacharach.

The castle still stood some distance back and at an elevation of about one thousand feet above the river bed. After the bombardment had finished, the French began unloading their cannons and started hauling them up through the center of town towards the front of the castle gates. Arrows began to pour down from the sky by the hundreds, like rain, from both the castle and its guard towers and walls. As the arrows fell, French guards held their shields up to protect the ones hauling the cannons. Some received arrows in their arms or thighs, while others dropped like flies.

Musket rifles fired from the walls of the castle that led to the Rhine River. Cannons likewise, fired relentlessly at the French troops and their ships anchored off shore. This was a major assault ordered by Louis IVX (1638-1715) "the Great," king of France to sack Stahleck Castle at all costs. The French troops took far more casualties on this siege than the Germans, but they came with enough forces to sustain the attack.

Eventually the French cannons were in distance of the front gates to the castle, and began to bombard it. The town's people began to scream and flee in panic, out from the draw bridge to the southwest and the rear entrance to the north. Women and children, who were unable to escape, were grabbed by the French soldiers, pulled to the side and ravaged in the midst of battle. Any soldiers who were found wounded were finished off, while the French attended to their own soldier's wounds. Overwhelmed by French forces, the German troops began to retreat.

Finally, Commandant VON DACHENHAUSEN surrendered the castle to the overwhelming French forces. What Louis IVX wanted was, for the Rhine River to be the border between France and Germany as it had been during the Roman Empire; thereby cutting the German territory in half and adding it to the French Empire. He made constant raids on the German castles along the Rhine, but he could not conquer the Holy Roman Empire.

After the smoke cleared and things began to settle down, the French troops began to strip all the armor from the fallen soldiers. They buried their own dead and carried the corpses of the Germans and tossed them into the Rhine River for a quick and easy disposal. The French soldiers then took over the guard positions of the former German knights and began to celebrate their victory. However, they would not be able to hold the castle for long, for they were in the heart of Germany.

This was the territory of Leopold I, emperor of the Holy Roman Empire. The French ended up abandoning the castle in the following year 1689. The castle had been besieged, retaken and rebuilt eight times. Leopold I would inevitably put the castle in the hands of one of both his and Frederick I's, king in Prussia's, most gallant and heroic knights, Colonel Johann KEMPER.

Colonel Johann KEMPER had achieved what he had pledged to his king, chivalrous conduct. Frederick William I, "the Great Elector," had bestowed knighthood upon Colonel KEMPER as a gallant knight—courageous, courteous, honorable, and readiness. Most knights were tenants, holding land in the promise to serve their king. Colonel Johann KEMPER had received not only land for his incredible heroics during the Prussian wars, but was awarded Stahleck Castle by Emperor Leopold I, as well. Colonel KEMPER was a knight all others looked up to and tried to mimic.

Because Colonel Johann KEMPER's bravery in battle and the many wounds he received because of them, "the Great Elector" bestowed many grand gifts upon Colonel Johann KEMPER. One of which was a grand sword for his gallantry against the Turks, under Emperor Leopold I, which he proudly displayed in his castle. His wife, Sophia, later passed it down to their son, Jacob, who took it to America with him. After he started his tavern, he proudly displayed it before all who entered.

The *"Great Elector's"* son, Frederick I, king in Prussia, followed in suit rewarding Colonel KEMPER for his continued service under him. Colonel Johann KEMPER'S dress uniform had become embellished with so many medals. The Prussian wars provided Colonel Kemper with the fuel that nourished his fever for battle. The upcoming War of the Spanish Succession would be the colonel's final battle.

During this period of time, the Germans had a point system in place for obtaining medals. One of the medals Colonel KEMPER received in the mid-1680s was the "Pour le Merite" (Blauer Max/ Blue Max). This medal was inaugurated back in 1667 and was awarded to Prussian officers who had accumulated a minimum of one thousand points and having over ten victory points.

On 15 January 1701, Oberst Colonel Johann KEMPER traveled to Königsberg, Germany on a royal invitation sent to him by Frederick III to attend his coronation. After his arrival he was escorted with honors into Königsberg Castle where he was given quarters until the ceremony. The castle was bustling with flamboyant activity in preparation for the day. For the next couple of days he enjoyed the hospitality of the castle. After this ceremony, Frederick moved the capital from Königsberg to Berlin.

The upcoming coronation was approved by, Holy Roman Emperor Leopold I, Archduke of Austria who allowed Prussia to be elevated to a kingdom. This agreement was ostensibly given in exchange for an alliance against King Louis XIV (1638-1715) of France in the War of the Spanish Succession. Frederick III had a huge army, the fourth largest in Europe, and was victorious in many battles. This was a most valuable transaction for the emperor. It gave him an edge in the upcoming war. Colonel Johann KEMPER would be in his glory.

Upon this agreement, Leopold I personally requested the service of Oberst Colonel Johann KEMPER. He related that he had grown fond of this dashing, daring and gallant officer in his earlier battles with the Turks, when loaned to him by his father, the *"Great Elector."* Frederick I granted the Emperor's wish with an earnest request, *"Colonel Johann KEMPER has been with the family for a very long time. He has helped the Imperial Army win many battles. This battle hardened officer has lived through more musket, knife and sword wounds than any other officer in the Imperial Army, and still lives to talk about them; please return him!"*

On 18 January 1701, Oberst Colonel Johann KEMPER attended the coronation of Frederick III, who after his installation was granted the title, Frederick I, king in Prussia. Festivities followed, however business did not cease, as on this same date, Frederick I established the "Orden das Schwarzen Alder" (Order of the Black Eagle). The "Order of the Black Eagle" was the highest chivalry order in Prussia.

In order to obtain this medal, one had to have accumulated a minimum of two thousand points and having achieved over twenty victory points. During the War of the Spanish Succession, Colonel Johann KEMPER was one of the first officers to receive the new *"Order of the Black Eagle."*

After the coronation, Colonel Johann KEMPER, along with generals and other officers were invited to Emperor Leopold I's court. For the next few days, they would go over battle plans for the upcoming War in the Spanish Succession.

Shortly thereafter, the War of the Spanish Succession began (1701-1714). Frederick I, siding with Austria, sent forth eight thousand troops of the Imperial Army into another war. Colonel Knight Johann KEMPER thrust forward with his regiment of *"illustrious cuirassiers"* of dragoons into battle.

During these battles, Colonel KEMPER became severely wounded, which shortened his military career. This was the last war in which the colonel was able to participate. Colonel KEMPER was up for promotion to general, but because of his many battle wounds, was constrained in his mobility. The War of the Spanish Succession had taken its toll on the colonel. He received his fourteenth and final wound. It was a musket shot in his upper right chest, near his shoulder blade. The musket ball had such impact that it knocked him right off his horse.

Because of his incredible heroics and disabilities from battles, during War of the Spanish Succession, Frederick I adorned Colonel KEMPER with yet another medal, the new "Order of the Black Eagle." He further awarded the governorship of Bacharach and hereditary military commander of Stahleck Castle, as ordered by Emperor Leopold I of the Holy Roman Empire. Colonel Johann KEMPER's gallantry in the War of the Spanish Succession was witnessed and noted by all officers in the field and reported to Emperor Leopold I.

The castle was one of the enclaves (territories) the Emperor received on the Lower Rhine. Stahleck Castle sat on a huge cone hill of rock above Bacharach. Some heights reached as high as one thousand feet. Stahleck, in German, meant "Impregnable castle on the Craig." Along with the seat in Bacharach, Frederick I awarded the colonel a comfortable pension for his remaining days. After his death, his pension was turned over to his widow, Sophia for her remaining days.

The grand castle of Stahleck had twelve towers that protruded up into the sky. Two large fortified walls extended from the castle down to the Rhine River on both sides of the town of Bacharach, connecting it to the stronghold. From the guard towers you could clearly see both north and south on the Rhine in the event any war ships approached. Cannons were set up on the walls and in the castle for its defense and the defense of the town of Bacharach. The northern wall was a shield wall to enhance the castle's defense from arrows in the event an army approached from the upper mountain overlooking the castle. A northern ring wall encircled the keep.

The main entrance to the castle for visitors and couriers was by a set of stone stairs that descended from the center of the castle through the town of Bacharach down to the Rhine River. To the southwest corner of the castle was the draw bridge, which was slowly lowered over a moat by chains whenever troops, knights or artillery were being received, after a mission that they had been sent on. They would then gather in the courtyard. Wagons and carts carrying weapons, ammunition or food, used this same entrance. There was a rear entrance to the north and in the back of the castle.

Frederick William I, "the Great Elector" and his son, Frederick I, king in Prussia, had become fond of Colonel KEMPER during the Prussian wars. Colonel KEMPER was bold, brave and always one of the first to launch his regiment of cuirassiers dragoons into the heat of battle in defense of his King, fearing no army. This was the kind of officer cherished by "the Great Elector" and his son, Frederick I. They flooded the Colonel with many gifts. They also paid to have oil paintings done of the Colonel with them. His oil paintings were passed down in the family to this author.

One portrays "the Great Elector," along with his son, Frederick III, awarding the *"Grand Sword"* to the Colonel, while another portrays Colonel Johann KEMPER at the coronation of Frederick III, (Frederick I) king in Prussia, at Königsberg Castle. Still another portrays the Colonel on horseback, leading his dragoons of *"illustrious cuirassiers"* into battle during the Prussian wars.

On 20 April 1704, while in Prussia, he married Sophia KODTSTADT (ca.1683-aft.1740) in which Frederick I attended their marriage ceremony. They started a family and had three sons and one daughter. His oldest son, Philip was born in 1705; being his first born son and following the naming traditions, was usually named after the father, but not in this case. Colonel Johann KEMPER later took a ship down the Rhine to Bacharach, Mainz-Bingen, Rhineland-Palatinate in the heart of Germany. Sophia's maiden name, KODTSTADT, comes to us from her marriage record. Her middle name, Hypolita, comes to us in a baptismal record in Kaub.

He then assumed his new position as hereditary military commander of Stahleck Castle on a rise of a hill just above Bacharach, while still serving under Frederick I, king in Prussia. After Leopold I had awarded Colonel KEMPER his accommodations in Bacharach, both Frederick I and Leopold I requested that he only remained involved by training their officers for war.

Colonel Johann KEMPER sailed his ship down the Rhine River to Bacharack. He anchored his ship off the shore and gazed at his new castle in awe. He then took a skip into shore to tour the town. He soon sent for an artist in Königsberg to come and paint a picture of him with his castle as a setting in the back-round. He had the artist cover up the damage done from the previous siege by the French. This painting is the only true way the castle actually looked before it was rebuilt in later years.

Because Colonel KEMPER's children were so young when he died, he was unable to pass on the tradition of knighthood to his three sons, Philip, Jacob and a third son, mentioned in family records but not named. When they were kids, they used to run throughout the castle yelling and screaming, while playing hide-and-seek. Half of the time, Sophia did not know if they were just having fun or a ghost was chasing them.

There was another son born in 1709, no name mentioned but recorded to have finished school. Johann Jacob was recorded in the KEMPER family Bible as being born on 7 December 1707 in Bacharach, Mainz-Bingen, Rheineland-Pfalz, Germany. However, after searching the church records in Bacharach, they reflect no such birth. Possibly they were born at home or in the castle. They had a daughter (possibly Sophia) born in 1711, likewise not named but mentioned frequently. She married and settled near Königsberg, Germany. Colonel KEMPER now needed a cane to steady him.

Sophia injected into her children, that even though their father was much older, he was everything a young girl dreamed of, a knight, serving a king and an emperor and being awarded a castle. In addition, he was appointed governor of Bacharach, a town on the Rhine. Not an inland town, but one on a major travel route through Germany. Leopold I wanted control of the Lower Rhine area in the hands of loyal subjects.

Life would be made a lot easier for young girls who married into knighthood and for the children that they would bear for them. Sophia added, *"Prussian women are hot-blooded and love nothing less than a brave knight. Many young girls wanted and competed heavily for your father, but I was the one who won his affection. What enchanted your father most and often brought him comfort was when I played my harp for him. The sweet sounds were as if they had come from the heavens."*

"Frederick I, when traveling down the Rhine, would often stop in to see your father. They would wonder off to the castle, if not meeting there, for whatever business they had to discuss. No one ever knew what they talked about, and I knew better than to ask. If your father had something to say, he would say it; you would not have to ask. Your father had given a lifetime of loyal service

to the Great Elector, his son Frederick I, and Emperor Leopold I. He was always shown the greatest respect by all. Sometimes they would stroll through town, with guards, while all the town's folks stood starry-eyed."

"Your father," Sophia exclaimed, *"had many battle wounds and scars all over his body from the various wars he fought for in Prussia and for our Emperor Leopold I against the Turks. He had one wound in his side that he received from a bayonet charge; he had his pistol drawn so was able to shoot the culprit down. However, if he had not moved to the side, he would have been stabbed in his belly. He then leaped back up on his horse, laughing hysterically, 'he, he, he, he thought he was going to drop me.' There are just so many stories of this battled-hardened knight."*

Now that life had slowed down for the colonel in his retirement at Stahleck Castle, memories never left his heart and mind of Prussia. Prussia was the prime real estate in Germany, as it extended from the North Sea all along the Baltic Sea, and bordering Russia. It was where all the action was that Colonel KEMPER still hungered for.

Colonel Johann KEMPER's oldest son, Philip, after he attended Heidelberg University, went to work for his uncle in Leyden, Holland. He was in a sea-going business which carried him to the East Indies. When he returned, he settled in Leyden, South Holland, near the mouth of the Rhine River that empties into the North Sea. Here he had easy access to the shipping business.

Since all of Colonel KEMPER's children were so young when he died, none could remember him other than from stories told to them by their mother, Sophia Hypolita KEMPERIN. By 1737, all of Colonel KEMPER's children were married and moved to various parts of Germany, except Jacob, who stayed close to his mother. Because of this, Sophia made sure that the hereditary military commanding rights of Stahleck Castle were passed onto her son, Jacob.

Eventually, all these records were passed onto their grandson Johannes' (John's) daughter, Elizabeth KEMPER. Johannes had been named after his grandfather, Johann (Johannes), and never let anyone forget it. In the final years of his life, all he would have left would be his memories.

There are more families who have lost their history than those who have preserved it. This family felt that it was important to pass down their story to the next generations. It is because of this commitment that this family and American history have been kept alive. Each generation managed to find someone who cherished these important documents and kept them safe. Elizabeth played an instrumental role in this family's heritage.

It is because of Elizabeth's diligence that she was able to create such a database of information. This author has continued to carry on his family heritage and has expanded upon it with his own research and devotion as well.

Elizabeth continued collecting records on the family history from many members of the family, including her uncle Colonel Daniel KEMPER and cousin, Colonel Sebastian BEAUMAN. Elizabeth was preparing the first lawsuit against the pension department for robbing her father of his pension as captain and wagon master under General George WASHINGTON. She claimed they were responsible for her father's death in the final years of his life, when they should have been there to comfort and protect him.

While all this was going on, Captain John KEMPER's niece, Eliza Susan (Morton) QUINCY, was likewise collecting family history from all members of the family on her father and mother's side. She contacted her uncle John for anything he could remember. She reached her uncle John at a good time in his life, when he had already completed their family history. He had been currently corresponding with a Peter H. KEMPER (1780-1867) of Fauquier County, Virginia in 1826. They were sharing their KEMPER connection in Germany and the history on John's grandfather, Colonel Johann KEMPER in complete detail.

Captain KEMPER sent his niece, Eliza S. QUINCY, a copy of this letter filled with the early history of their family in Germany. Eliza kept this letter all her life, and it was still in her possession in 1878. It is unknown if it was passed on in the family; however, she did record parts of it in her memoirs. Eliza accidentally sent this letter to her editor on her memoirs; he recorded parts of it.

Out of all the thousands of descendants of Colonel Johann KEMPER, none was ever able to figure out where his family came from. While they remained in the dark, this author and genealogist cracked the riddle. In reality, it was quite simple as Colonel Johann KEMPER's grandson, Captain Johannes (John) KEMPER, the focus of this history, kept good records. He had put together a comprehensive profile of his grandfather's history and recorded it in the KEMPER family Bible, kept up by his wife, Eliza (Hopper) KEMPER (1764-1826).

Furthermore, Captain KEMPER had written a letter, depicting the early history of the KEMPER family in Germany, to a distant cousin, Peter H. KEMPER, in Virginia. They exchanged their pedigree charts with each another. They were conferring their pedigree charts with their common ancestor in Germany. He sent a copy of this letter, along with other KEMPER family records, to his niece, Eliza Susan (Morton) QUINCY in Boston, Massachusetts.

In addition, Captain KEMPER had recorded various parts of his grandfather's history in his journals that he kept while serving under General George WASHINGTON during the American Revolution. He also recorded parts of his history in his book, "*Wagon Master.*" He had shared his grandfather's history with many of the officers in the Continental Army with whom he had grown close, including General George WASHINGTON, General Baron Frederick Wilhelm VON STEUBEN (1730-1794),

General Peter MUHLENBERG (1746-1807), General Marquis DE LAFAYETTE (1757-1834) and Colonel Alexander HAMILTON (1757-1804), just to name a few.

Captain KEMPER shared many of these stories around the campfires while at Valley Forge and at his wagon-train camp. These records enabled this genealogist to uncover Colonel Johann KEMPER's ancestors back to where the KEMPER name began, and far beyond, into the 1300s.

In 1736, Johann Jacob KEMPER married Maria Regina ERNST of Mannheim. Her father was Reverend (Johannes?) ERNST (1680-1752). He was a minister of the Reformed Church in that city. Her mother, Maria Ursula (1685-aft.1752), was a woman of rank and fortune (high social and economic standing). Maria's parents owned an eloquent mansion with plush gardens. This entire estate was managed and groomed by hired help. This included a butler who welcomed guests and a steward who managed the outside grounds.

On the stone path that led up to the mansion, there stood a fountain in its entire majestic. Its heavenly sounds enchanted the area as if a harp was being played from the heavens, enticing everyone to come in. When the sun shined, a rainbow would seemingly sparkle up from the mist that the fountain made. There were female Roman statuettes circling the fountain, pouring water from their vases. Vines encircled the pillars and statuettes. The whole estate seemed magical. Anyone who was visiting the grounds glared in amazement and wonder. How could one family be so creative?

Although the location of the mansion was well known to family members at the time, for whatever reason, it was never recorded in the family Bible or records. It can be speculated that the mansion probably sat in Mannheim, as this city appears to have been the center of Reverend and Maria Ursula ERNST's family. All references to the ERNST family end up in Mannheim.

In 1737, Johann Jacob KEMPER (1707-1794) and Maria Regina ERNST (1712-1789) moved to Koblenz (old spelling Coblenz) where their first daughter, Anna Gertrude (1737-1786) was born. Koblenz was southeast of Kempen Village, which was named after the KEMPER family. Since Koblenz was a Roman-Catholic city, as recorded in the family Bible, Mrs. KEMPER was not allowed to depart until her child was, baptized by the Pfarrer (clergy) at St. Kastor, with the ceremonies of that church. The sponsor of the child was her godmother, Anna Gertrude, for whom she was named.

Their second daughter, Maria Sophia, was born on 21 May 1739 and baptized on 24 May 1739 at Pfarrhaus, Kaub-Pfalz, Germany. The sponsors, Frau (Mrs.) Sophia Hypolita KEMPERIN and Maria Ursula ERNESTIN von (from) Kirn-Becherbach were the child's grandparents. Maria Sophia was given the names of both of her grandparents. By this date, Maria Ursula and Reverend ERNST, who was living in Mannheim, were now divorced. Kirn-Becherbach was just west of Meisenheim and southwest of Kaub and Bacharach, Germany; a short distance for Sophia to visit her son in Bacharach.

The KEMPER family Bible records that Jacob KEMPER and Maria Regina ERNST were married in Kaub (old spelling Caub). However, this author had the Lutheran church records searched diligently and there were no records of any KEMPERS or ERNSTS being married there. It is possible that they were married at the Roman Catholic Church, St. Kastor, in Koblenz where their first child, Anna Gertrude was baptized. When this author's German researcher was in Koblenz, the pastor was on leave, and therefore she was unable to view those records.

Further excerpts from Jacob KEMPER's family Bible, which was passed down on Colonel Daniel KEMPER's side of the family, and copied over to his brother John's records, state that Colonel Johann KEMPER, because of the many battles in Prussia in which he was involved, was wounded fourteen times during his military career. Under the recommendation of his king, Frederick I, he was obliged to retire and live off his pension. John also transferred this information over to his family Bible records thus expanding to the many records he already had collected.

Johann survived many years off his pension, dying in 1712, after a lingering illness from his battle wounds. He died while sitting in his easy chair on the ramparts of Stahleck Castle viewing the breath-taking scenery over Bacharach and the Rhine River. This easy chair was fit for a king, having a carved lion's head protruding from each arm of the chair. This chair was part of the furniture in Königsberg Castle, until Frederick I, king in Prussia, gave it as a gift to Colonel Johann KEMPER, who always favored it whenever visiting Frederick I at Königsberg Castle. Colonel KEMPER had it converted into a rocker by a local carpenter in Bacharach.

Upon his death, Frederick I, king in Prussia, made sure his widow, Sophia, was still allowed to receive his full pension, which enabled her to give each of their three sons a liberal education. All attended Heidelberg University. After school, they all went off in different directions, except Jacob. Some went to Mannheim and Königsberg, Germany, while Philip went to Leyden, Holland to work for his uncle. The following year in 1713, Frederick I, king in Prussia, likewise, passed on.

Interestingly enough when Johann died on the ramparts of Stahleck Castle, he was guarding the gates to its partial ruins. Stahleck Castle had been under siege and sacked by a French fleet of war ships back on 11 October 1688, while Colonel KEMPER was fighting in the Prussian wars in Northern Germany, and remained in partial ruins. It was turned over by the Treaty of Ryswick in 1697 back to the Palatinate, where it remained into the late eighteenth century and had not yet been fully restored.

Johann was like a ghost guarding the gates to a castle of the past as he slowly rocked back and forth in his elegant, high-back, easy chair as it creaked; a truly haunting scene! If a real army had approached while he was brandishing his sword, they might have run in fear, fearing they were seeing a castle ghost, as Stahleck Castle was often covered in a heavy fog. Further research for records on Kaub and Bacharach can be found at Stadt Archives in Koblenz.

Some descendants continued carrying the name *"VON"* from the KEMPER family Bible, inferring nobleness, which led other descendants down a blind alley to a dead end. This reference appears to have blossomed from a letter John KEMPER wrote in 1826 in Hudson, New York, to Peter H. KEMPER, in Virginia. In this letter he stated that, *"since all officers that served in the army under the 'Great Elector' were noblemen, he must have been a man of rank."* This assumption was correct.

The fact is the KEMPER family in Germany never went by the name, VON KEMPER. In addition, this author's ancestor, Johannes (John), who was named after his grandfather, Johann, kept his oil paintings and passed them down in the family. On the back of the oil painting, it clearly says, *"Colonel Johann KEMPER."* Furthermore, Captain John KEMPER's wife, Eliza, kept a diary in which she recorded some of the history on his grandfather, again naming him only as Colonel Johann KEMPER. He had an ebony cane with an eagle carved on its crown.

Finally, this author's ancestor, John recorded in his journals that he and his brother, Colonel Daniel KEMPER (1749-1847) spoke with General Baron Frederick Wilhelm VON STEUBEN, after his arrival at Valley Forge, about their grandfather Colonel Johann KEMPER, who fought in the Prussian wars, the same location from where the baron had come.

The name change from KEMPER to VON KEMPER occurred only in the KEMPER family Bible. On 28 October 1902, Lewis Hoffman KEMPER (1865-1951) filled out his application to join the Sons of the American Revolution. In his application he states that he was the second great grandson of Colonel Johann Jacob VON KEMPER and Maria Regina ERNST. Two mistakes were made here. First, Johann Jacob KEMPER was never in the military, therefore, never a colonel. Second, Johann Jacob VON KEMPER only went by von in the KEMPER family Bible, never by any records in Germany.

Lewis then went on to say that, he was the third great-grandson of Colonel Johann VON KEMPER, commander of Stahleck Castle, Bacharach, Germany. He further spread this virus of wrong information to a KEMPER family in Virginia working on the KEMPER records. They printed this information without verifying the source. Now the whole world has access to the wrong information.

Another reference states that, Colonel VON KEMPER descended from an earlier knight VON KEMPER in Franconia. He served in the service of Elector Palatine Frederick III (1515-1576).This author and genealogist has traced all the KEMPER families in Germany, and none descended further back than the beginning of the KEMPER name in the mid-fifteen hundreds, after a cross-over from another name.

What Lewis did not have access to, outside of Captain John KEMPER's 1826 letter to Peter H. KEMPER in Virginia, was this author's ancestor Captain John KEMPER's full records. He was the brother of Lewis' ancestor Colonel Daniel KEMPER. He reported and answered solely to General George WASHINGTON. He kept complete diaries and journals under General WASHINGTON. He was a recorder of events.

In addition, because he was his grandfather's name sake, he had done far more documented research on the KEMPER family in Germany and after their arrival in America, than the rest of the entire family combined. He has the oldest recorded history on his grandfather, Colonel Johann KEMPER's service under the "Great Elector." Likewise, he gives the best detailed description of Stahleck Castle in world history. The result of all that hard work is this publication, *"Once upon a Time in the American Revolution."*

John KEMPER had recorded how his father, Jacob, had often shared their family heritage in Germany. Jacob recorded how after he had sold his hereditary rights to Stahleck Castle, his mother, Sophia, was happy, saying, *"It was a dingy old castle anyway and only brought back haunting memories."*

"Your father, Sophia exclaimed, was an old 'stick-in-the-mud'," She claimed, *"I can still see and hear your father, harnessed in his gallant uniform of a colonel, brandishing his dress sword, while creaking back and forth in his easy chair on the ramparts of Stahleck Castle. He would often un-sheath and raise his sword as if ready to attack anyone who tried to enter its gates and then re-holster it."*

Sophia continued, *"Your father was a stubborn man and refuse to allow anyone to help him get around. I would often bring him a jug of his favorite wine from the wine cellars at Bacharach, while he rested on the ramparts of the castle. Since he was the governor, we got our wines for free. It was a steep climb and I often wondered how he made it on his own. When I would approach while stepping on rubble, your father would ask, 'Is that you Frederick?'"* [King in Prussia]. *It seemed so sad to see such a gallant knight so helpless. He was fortunate to have lived as long as he had. War always brings about tragedy."*

"On other occasions he would say, 'I can still see my enemy; I can feel my blood rush through my body as I thrust into battle. I can see everything as clearly as if it happened yesterday. Why do I hunger for war? Everyone wants my castle! Why does the Rhine [River] *seem so peaceful when so much war has revolved around it?'"*

Sophia stated, *"His statements appeared to be clearly broken and leading nowhere."* She continued, *"He seemed to be quenching in old melancholy memories. He had acquired a nickname, 'the Flaming Knight'. It had something to do with carrying a torch on night raids, either in Prussia or against the Turks; I can no longer clearly remember, maybe both. He always kept two torches burning at the entrance to the castle. Then on his final day, the torches were out. I felt something was wrong."*

Sophia closed by saying, *"Then one day as the heavy fog was beginning to dissipate, I was approaching your father with a jug of his favorite wine, but his easy chair was not creaking. In his lap he held his sword, but as I got closer, I knew he had passed on. There was stillness in the air and a kind of haunting feeling. Chills ran through my body as I was shaking with a scary feeling. I immediately threw the jug of wine to the ground, left the area and reported the incident to the constables."*

"The constables ordered a team to take a stretcher and remove his body for burial. He was given full military honors as ordered by our King, Frederick [I], who likewise, comforted me as well. There was a huge turnout for his funeral, but I had such a numb feeling at the time, I cannot remember them all. Your father could not see that his time was running short; he always had to remain in battle, rather real or imaginary. He could have lived a lot longer if he could have seen the writing on the walls. The following year, our King passed on as well and joined him."

Colonel Johann KEMPER had personally served and was favored by Royalty all of his life. He dealt personally with Frederick William I "the Great Elector," his son, Frederick I, king in Prussia and Leopold I, emperor of the Holy Roman Empire. Little did he know that, two of his grandsons would likewise, deal personally with royalty in a new land far, far away, in a new country being formed called ... America!

After Colonel KEMPER's death and all his children finished school, his widow, Sophia moved to a more peaceful village, Kirn-Becherback, to be near her sister-in-law, Maria Ursula ERNST.

Sophia stated that, *"When your father took over the castle, it had been inhabited by bats and birds. Whenever you went through the corridors, you could see and hear the birds quickly flutter to take flight. After things calmed down, you could hear the birds singing to one another. Small animals would scurry everywhere."*

"At night," Sophia exclaimed, *"was a different story. Bats would exit the castle by the hundreds, looking like a large dark cloud, only to return by dawn. Grapevines grew everywhere; Nature had definitely taken over. I use to like to climb the spiral staircase up to the bird's nest; a location so called because of its high perch overlooking the castle."*

Sophia went on to say, *"Stahleck Castle was entrenched in death. You could hear haunting sounds, screams, howls and clanking of metal echoing through the castle at night. It was as if men were sword-fighting. When the wind blew through the castle, the whooshing sounds increased your fears, making you imagine things, whether real or not. There were seldom peaceful nights at Bacharach."*

Sophia closed by saying, *"There was a strange, eerie presence that lurked in Stahleck Castle. Whenever you toured the dark halls with a torch, all of a sudden, torches on the walls or candle-lights in the rooms would automatically ignite. When you walked by a fireplace, there would be a 'poof,' then all of a sudden there was a fire as if someone had just lit it, but there was no one there. Old oil paintings that once hung on the walls, lit up, and then slowly faded away. You did not want to tour the castle alone. Things only seemed to happen when few were around, as if trying to tell a story."*

After receiving many correspondences from his brother-in-law, Mattheus ERNST in America, Jacob informed his mother that he was contemplating on joining Mattheus in America. Sophia pleaded with her son, Jacob, to stay in Germany, because his sister was married and lived far away up north, near Königsberg, Germany and there was no one left in the family who lived close by, other than Maria Regina ERNST. Jacob tossed this idea around in his mind, over and over again. He had to get away, he needed a new start.

Other members of the family lived in North Rhine-Westphalia, Germany. Jacob replied, *"Mom, Pop has been gone for 29 years, why do you not come with us?"*

Sophia answered, *"Because, Germany is my home!"*

Jacob closed by saying, *"I am sorry, Mom, I hear a calling and I must follow. I have a different destiny than my father."*

Knowing that her son had been raised without a father, and hungered for a destiny in America, did not make his leaving any less hard on her.

Jacob KEMPER's brother-in-law, Johann Mattheus ERNST/ ERNEST (1706-1780), had gone to America sometime prior to 1734. He had written to his sister, Maria Regina and her husband, Jacob, repeatedly inspiring them to join him in America for greater opportunities. Mattheus had been living on and off in New York City and Germantown, Columbia County, New York.

Although his ship passenger list had not survived, when he joined the Dutch Reformed Church in New York City it was recorded that, Mattheus ERNST, of Meisenheim, in the district of Zweibrüken, Germany, and his wife, Anna Maria BOMPER (1708-aft.1783), joined on 31 August 1753. This was the small village Mattheus was living in prior to his migrating to America, but not where he was born.

Other strong references show his father's home as Mannheim, Germany, including family Bible records. However, this author had the church records in Mannheim searched extensively and there were no recordings of either Reverend ERNST/ERNEST (1680-1752) or the KEMPER family recorded. Perhaps the German genealogist checked the wrong church, as there are many in Mannheim. The family Bible records that Reverend ERNST was a minister in the Reformed Church there.

Chapter I
From a Castle in Germany to a
Farm in America

Further Bible excerpts show that Johann Jacob studied at Heidelberg University, Duchy of Baden-Württemberg, Germany. His mother had bought a small sailing vessel for him to ply up and down the Rhine, transporting goods and people. As its master and captain, he transported freight for his own account to the various cities along the Rhine River, including Amsterdam.

Jacob's wife received numerous letters from her brother Johann Mattheus ERNST, urging them to join him in the States. Jacob was further induced by, a company of men called Newlanders, who were employed by the ship-owners in Holland to persuade Germans to immigrate to America. This was a profitable business and since Germany had no sea-going vessels capable of sailing the vast oceans, they had to depend on other countries for transportation.

The Newlanders painted a beautiful picture of this new land called America. It was the perfect arcadia, a land laced with milk and honey. There were mines filled with gold and silver just waiting to be discovered. It was not a crowded land like Germany; it was a vast new land filled with wilderness, rivers, lakes and mountains filled with many caves and other mysteries. European mines had been emptied eons ago. The German's eyes would swell.

Johann Mathias ERNST was the son of Reverend (Johannes?) ERNST/ERNEST, who after his divorce, stayed in Mannheim,

Baden-Württemberg, Germany. Reverend ERNST's wife, Maria Ursula, moved to Kirn-Becherback. Mannheim was where Jacob KEMPER first met Maria Regina, daughter of Reverend ERNST. Mathias had sneaked away and left for America prior to 1734 and settled in Germantown, New York, without ever informing his father.

Her marriage to Mr. ERNST/ERNEST had offended her parents because he had been her tutor (private teacher). They never forgave him for having taken advantage of their daughter when he was supposed to have been teaching her. Once a year they sent for their daughter and her children to visit them at their splendid mansion, but excluded Reverend ERNST; and when her father died, sometime after 1741, his grandchildren in America shared in their mother's portion of the estate.

When Mattheus ERNST and Anna Maria (Bomper) SCHERP met, they were both living in Germantown, Columbia County, New York. He did business with her husband Jacob SCHERP. Anna Maria had already had a few children by Jacob SCHERP. Mattheus later established himself as a merchant at a place in Rhinebeck, New York.

Rhinebeck got its name from the settlers having come from the Rhine River in Germany and from the name of the proprietor BEEKMAN, thus Rhinebeck. When Mr. ERNST was in a German community, he went by his German name, Johann Mathias ERNST. When he was in a Dutch community, he went by the Dutch spelling, Mattheus. When he was in an English environment, he went by the English spelling, Matthew.

On 18 May 1734, Zenger's Weekly Journal recorded that … *"we hear from Livingston Manor that one Mr. Jacob Scherp, a noted trader and farmer there, on 16th of Feb. last, had the misfortune to be drowned in Livingston's Creek, by the stumbling of his horse. His body was found some days after by his own son* [Johann Peter SCHERP (1710-1782)] *on a small shoal* [sandbar] *in the mouth of the creek.*" Johann Mathias ERNST, who was a friend of the family, comforted Mr. SCHERP's wife, Anna Maria BOMPER. They later became close and started courting.

On 7 April 1736, Johann Mathias ERNST married Anna Maria BOMPER at Germantown, Columbia County, New York. They started having children born and baptized them at the Germantown Reform Church. Anna Maria BOMPER had already had three children born there with her late husband, Jacob SCHERP. Both were comfortable and accustomed to the large German Palatine settlements of the area. They later moved to Rhinebeck where Mr. ERNST's in-laws, Jacob and Maria Regina (Ernst) KEMPER later joined them from Germany.

There were repeated correspondences between Jacob KEMPER's wife Maria Regina with her brother Mattheus ERNST requesting that they join him in the states. They finally decided that, moving to America would be a good venture. After Jacob agreed, Maria Regina's face lit up like a campfire. She quickly got a letter out to her brother Mattheus that they were going to join him in America.

Jacob then cleaned out Stahleck Castle of all the family's personal belongings, including the Königsberg easy chair, the statuette of a knight in shining armor, and his father, Johann's Grand Sword, with trunks of his father's military memorabilia and family oil paintings. He then sold his rights as hereditary military commander of Stahleck Castle in the commission of the governor of Bacharach for 600 rix-dollars (dollar of the realm, formerly of Germany, any of several silver coins worth about one dollar). This money they converted into over thirty pounds of gold and held it in reserved for their passage and new start in America.

After receiving his sister, Maria Regina's letter, Mattheus excitedly responded with a request, *"Please ask your husband* [Jacob], *if it would be possible to bring our sister, Christina, with you? I would gladly refund her passage after all of you arrive in America; or I can send you her passage ahead of time."* After receiving Mattheus's letter, Jacob answered it personally, saying, he had plenty of money from the sale of his castle and would not need compensation. He had enough gold to live off for many years without having to work and would be able to invest some into business.

Since Christina was both Mattheus's and Jacob's wife, Maria Regina's sister, she was therefore, family. It would be an honor for them to bring Christina along with them to join him in America. Many Europeans were already speaking of America as a country, even though, in reality, it was not yet. However, the KEMPER family would play an important role in making it a country. Since Jacob's mother Sophia was still living comfortably off their father's pension, Jacob did not fear leaving her destitute.

On 23 September 1741, while living in Bacharach, Germany, Joh. Jacob KEMPER applied for papers for emigration to Philadelphia for himself and his wife, Maria Regina ERNEST, daughter of Reverend ERNEST (Reformed Evangelical) from Mannheim. They embarked with other Palatines on the ship, the *Marlborough*, Thomas BELL, master from Rotterdam, Netherlands. Jacob's age was listed as thirty-two, making him born in 1709 and not 1707 as recorded in the family Bible. Which date is right?

On their passage to America, they landed in England on a stopover. After the *Marlborough* had landed in England, its crew's stay was lengthened by many months, for they tarried for some time as a pastime with other passengers, taking advantage of the new sights and things to buy, which was common. After the ship's captain and crew had had their fill on the sights in England, they returned to their original heading, America!

After they got back at sea, during their passage to America, Jacob's daughter Maria Sophia was seized with the symptoms of the small pox. The captain, who had never had the disease, which was then so dreaded and often fatal, though a humane man, said,

"I must insist that she should be thrown overboard. If I should get sick and die the passengers would be left in the midst of the ocean with no one capable of commanding the ship and of conducting them to the land to which they destined; and what was the value of the life of a child of two years, compared with all on board?"

Jacob, appalled and disheartened, combated his insistence by arguing, *"We paid well for these accommodations. Our cabin separates us from other passengers."* Mrs. KEMPER pleaded, *"I will shut myself up in our cabin and use only the supplies from our sea store until the danger is passed. We are not even truly sure if our daughter has the small pox."* This action and acceptance changed history, for if Maria was dumped overboard, then she would not have grown up to marry John MORTON, who ended up being the wealthiest contributor to both General George WASHINGTON and the Continental Congress. He became the most powerful in-law to marry into the family.

The parents successfully combated these arguments. The *Marlborough* was exclusively for the wealthy. Everyone on board had money and paid well for their passage and special accommodations. They consisted of young married people, with their children. No passengers were wealthier than Jacob and Maria Regina KEMPER. Most of the ships that transported immigrants were crowded with people who had little to nothing and had sold everything just for the passage to the new land in hopes of a better life. As it turned out, Maria Sophia had not been affected by the small pox. If she had been thrown overboard, history would have been changed for the upcoming American Revolution!

Upon their eventual arrival in Philadelphia, they took the oath of allegiance to the American government in the courthouse, and decided to enjoy the sights, before moving on to meet Mattheus. They had landed two hundred miles southwest of her brother Johann Mattheus ERNST, whom they had come so far to meet. In their possession they had a folio Bible in the German language and many books, fine additions of that day, handsomely bound and ornamented with prints. The folio Bible stood about fifteen to sixteen inches tall by ten to eleven inches wide, printed on 100 percent rag cotton linen sheets.

They also brought trunks and chests of household linen, clothing and many articles of furniture. Weighing heavily in their trunks was over thirty pounds of gold and silver left from the sale of their castle in Germany. This was an equivalent in today's market of over $633,600. They had spent some gold for their first-class passage to America, which included their own cabin.

As soon as the KEMPERS disembarked from the vessel, a German agent quickly appeared on the scene, as if from out of nowhere to befriend them. Having been from the same country, he welcomed his greeting in German, putting them immediately at ease.

They spoke joyfully with one another. He induced Mr. KEMPER to exchange his gold and silver for depreciated paper money, which he represented by saying, *"It is of equal value and more convenient to carry, as it was the currency of the country and paper instead of carrying around this heavy gold."* As Jacob unpacked his gold and silver placing it on the agent's scales for exchange for an equal paper currency, the German agent's eyes began to swell in excitement.

When Jacob reached New Brunswick, he met with an honest German resident whose name was Johann Jacob DILLIDINE (1684-?) and his wife, Catharina JUNG (1786-?), to whom he exhibited his funds. Mr. DILLIDINE dutifully informed him, *"I am afraid, my friend, that you have been defrauded by a sharper* [scammer]." Mr. DILLIDINE had immigrated to America in 1709 with the German Palatines.

Jacob KEMPER, who had sold everything for his start in America, and had enough gold to live off for many years, was now almost penniless. Jacob looked at Mr. DILLIDINE and then at Maria and asked, *"How will our family survive?"* He would have to start all over again, with nothing, a stranger in a strange land.

Mr. KEMPER's journey of eighty miles from Philadelphia, Pennsylvania, to New Brunswick, New Jersey had exhausted all his other expenses since he left Germany, from the use of the depreciated paper money. All they had left was enough currency to afford passage on a sloop to New York City and then on up the Hudson River to Rhinebeck where they were greeted with great enthusiasm by Jacob's wife, Maria Regina's brother, Mattheus ERNST. Mattheus was happy Mr. KEMPER trusted in him and came to America, and was ready to help him get started.

After hearing of Jacob's misfortune, Mattheus warmly grabbed him about his shoulders and walked him over to a location where he could talk to him in private. When they were apart from the rest of the family, Mattheus stuffed a roll of something soft into Jacob's left pocket. When Jacob went to pull it out, Mattheus whispered, *"Stop! Look at it later and I do not want to hear anything more of it."*

After Jacob was by himself, his curiosity got the best of him. He pulled out the item Mattheus stuck in his pocket; it was a roll of money. Mattheus was compensating Jacob for the cost of his sister's passage. Jacob exhausted a breath of air, feeling saddened that he had been forced into accepting any money from a family member.

Jacob then slowly strolled over to where Mattheus was standing and put his hand gently upon his right shoulder, and as Mattheus turned to face him, Jacob said, *"Thank you my friend."*

Mathias replied, *"For what? I have not done anything yet."*

Jacob softly grinned and nodded but gave no further remark. This was the kind of man Mattheus ERNST was, one who always went out on a limb for his family and dear friends and knew when they were going through tough times. He asked very little and gave so much more in return.

They passed the ensuing winter at his hospitable abode speaking of the old land and making plans for their future. Mattheus was seasoned in the new land and was able to advise and assist Jacob when he was down on his luck. Jacob was fortunate to have had family in America; otherwise, he and his family would have been out on the streets with no place to go and with someone else ready to take advantage of their misfortune.

In 1740, Mattheus (Matys, as called by his friends) ERNST was listed as a deacon with the Dutch Reformed Church in Rhinebeck, New York. On 5 November 1743, Matys is still with the church, but for whatever reason, he never had any children baptized there.

In the spring of 1742, Jacob KEMPER's brother-in-law, Mattheus (Matys) ERNST advised him, *"Take command of a sloop, which I own, or buy one for yourself, to ply up and down the Hudson River between Rhinebeck and New York City. It is a profitable business, which you know well from having been employed in it back in Germany. Your family can then remain near us. I am family and more familiar with the new country. There also is the advantage of a church and school in our own language."*

Mr. KEMPER did just that; and began transporting passengers back and forth from New York City and Rhinebeck. However, Mr. KEMPER's heart became heavy, yearning to venture into this new, strange wilderness and become a farmer. After all, the Indians were all they had to worry about. How bad could that turn out to be. Europeans were the dominant factor in the settlement of the new land.

On 22 September 1742, Jacob and Maria Regina KEMPER had a daughter Catharina born and baptized in their house at Bachmay. This event was recorded by the pastor in the Lutheran

Church, New York City on 5 October 1742. Sponsors were Philip Solomon and daughter, Catharina FLAGLER who had become close friends with the KEMPER family. Mr. FLAGLER coached Jacob into coming up to Beekman where he would help him with his dream of becoming a farmer, but beware of Indians.

Mr. KEMPER then insisted with Mattheus on going back in the country on the *"New-land"* he had heard so much about to become a farmer. He thanked Mattheus and replied, *"I left Germany with farming in mind and nothing can divert me from my goal."*

Mr. ERNST finally assisted Mr. KEMPER in obtaining a farm on a patent of Robert A. LIVINGSTON (1708-1790) on a lease of three lives. Jacob and Maria Regina KEMPER's children, Anna Gertrude, Maria Sophia and Catharina (1742-1764) were the three lives, as they were expected to outlive their parents.

In this part of Dutchess County, was the town of Beekman, sixty miles below Rhinebeck and twenty miles east of the Hudson River. On this farm, there was a small house and a barn, with some land cleared for a garden; the rest was wilderness and uncultivated.

In 1745 they had relocated to Beekman. The family, who had been brought up in cities with a fast pace, was now established in the wilderness and they were ignorant of the best modes of clearing and cultivating the ground and obtaining daily comforts. Mr. KEMPER's ignorance of the English tongue made his start even more difficult, as business was carried on in that language. The going started out rough but then eased up as neighbors acquainted them with farming procedures.

Mr. KEMPER's nearest neighbor, Philip Solomon FLAGLER (1701-1766) and wife Margaretha (Grietje) DOPP (1692-1764), along with Mr. Johann Theobald (Dewald) BRILL (1698-1763) and wife, Catharina BECK/PICK (1703-1790), and Mr. Martynus WILTSIE (1722-1755) and wife, Jannetje SUDAM (1722-1794) instructed and assisted him in the management of his farm.

While Jacob was learning farming, Catharina was teaching his wife Maria Regina how to put up preserves.

The most difficult change was being away from the abundance of people that they were accustomed to in the various cities along the Rhine River, Germany. In addition, there was no castle; they were now in complete wilderness, under the threat of Indian raids. Mr. KEMPER cleared many acres of land; planted an orchard, grew wheat, corn and owned cattle and other stock. His business slowly became profitable, while his name continued to grow.

Christina ERNST remained with her brother Matthew and his family. Matthew ERNST continued to assist the KEMPERS by every means in his power. He visited them several times a year and brought them coffee, tea and sugar, sixty miles over almost impassible roads. He traveled on horseback with his saddlebags loaded with things for the family.

There was always joy to his occasioned arrival. The children ran out to see what was in the saddlebags. Everyone was always excited; sometimes there would be surprises. Mr. ERNST had worked very hard to make his start in the new land; now he was helping his sister and brother-in-law to do the same. Unlike Mr. KEMPER who was getting help, Mr. ERNST had had no one to help him; he had had to go through the hard knocks, alone.

In 1745, when Maria Sophia was six years old, an event happened to her on the farm that she retold time and time again throughout the years. She claimed that, *"she was accustomed to eating her bowl of rice and milk after dinner while seated on the sill of the house-door. She was heard to speak of 'die schon Schlange,' who came and ate her rice."* Her mother watched to see what these words meant.

To her surprise and consternation, she saw a large rattlesnake with its head in the bowl, eating with the child, who, when her visitor took more than its share, tapped it on the head with her spoon. It went quietly away when the meal was finished. This intimacy was too dangerous to be allowed and Mr. Jacob KEMPER killed the snake. The rattle, a very large one, with eleven or twelve rings, was preserved for some years. It was lost when the family removed from Livingston Patent.

This story of the rattlesnake is obviously slightly exaggerated (far-fetched); however, Maria KEMPER told this story the same way to her family throughout all of her life. Therefore, this story has become part of the family history. It is most likely that Jacob killed the snake on the spot when everyone first saw it. For those of us who have accidentally come across a rattlesnake in the wilderness, like this author, knows, that the rattlesnake begins his rattle warning far before anyone gets close to it. In fact, you do not even have to be in biting distance before it springs to attack. It immediately coils up in preparation for the attack on any creature threatening its space.

Soon after this occurrence, the women and children were secured in a stockade from an alarm fearing the attack of Indians, which happily proved groundless. The next year, Mr. KEMPER's daughter, Maria Sophia, was playing in jumping *"the beautiful snake,"* when she slipped, fell and broke her arm. Mr. KEMPER's neighbor, Philip Solomon FLAGLER instructed his son, Zacharias, (1726-1799), *"Quickly, take the horse. I know it is upward of 20 miles for the nearest surgeon, but go now. Be careful, be aware of Indians, but make haste."*

The surgeon did not arrive for twenty-four hours and was obliged to wait a day and night for the swelling to reduce in the arm before he could set it. All these German families had their children baptized either in the Lutheran or Reformed Churches in New York City, or one of the Reform Churches in Rhinebeck, Fishkill or Poughkeepsie, Dutchess County, New York.

Mattheus had a couple of children baptized at the Reformed Church, Kingston, Ulster County, New York. They were always taking a sloop to and fro for supplies and staying for a short time in each location. One of his children he had baptized there was Johannes. Since none of the sponsors of the child had that name, it is believed by this author/genealogist that, he named this son after his father in Germany.

In circa 1745, Maria Christina ERNST (1722-1786) met John Coenraat WETZELL (1721-1785) of New York, who had been traveling through the area and stopped to buy goods. They fell in love and then married. Christina then removed with Mr. WETZELL to the city (New York) to live. Matthew ERNST, likewise, removed to New York, so that he could remain close to his sister.

On 24 July 1746, Jacob and Maria Regina KEMPER had a son, Solomon (1746-ca.1748) baptized at the First Reformed Church, Fishkill, Dutchess County, New York. He was born on the farm in Beekman and named after his friend and neighbor, Philip Solomon FLAGLER. Philip was proud of his middle name, Solomon, and always used it. Jacob, therefore, honored him with a son after that name. Solomon KEMPER died young on the farm ca. 1748, and was interred there, before they left for New Brunswick, New Jersey.

Mr. ERNST, on his last visit in the autumn proposed, *"Come Jacob, make plans to sell your lease, quit the farm and remove back to New Brunswick, I will provide a place for you so that all the family can remain close."*

Something else was bothering Jacob, his children were growing up in the country without schools. These changes eventually persuaded Jacob KEMPER to start planning to leave his farm in the wilderness, which was starting to get the best of him, and return back to civilization. Mr. Mattheus ERNST was definitely the dominant leader in the family, but he did it lovingly and tactfully.

In 1748, Mr. KEMPER sold the lease, and in the spring of 1749 they left the farm and the improvements of three years to the great regret of their kind neighbors, who assisted them in getting to Rhinebeck, where they could catch a sloop down the Hudson River to New York City. By the sale of his lease, farm and implements, Jacob KEMPER was able to repay his brother-in-law, Matthew ERNST, for an excellent stone house on Albany Street in New Brunswick, New Jersey.

Mr. KEMPER engaged in a profitable business as a merchant; in addition, Jacob had built a sloop so that he could carry passengers and customers back and forth from New Brunswick and New York across the South River. He once again returned to the trade he had become familiar with while on the Rhine River in Germany; Jacob had climbed out of the cellar.

In 1751, while at New Brunswick, New Jersey, Jacob, once again, had a son, whom he named after his friend, Philip Solomon FLAGLER. He was also named after his older brother, Philip KEMPER in Leyden, Holland; thus Philip Solomon KEMPER was born.

Because of the distance between the brothers they had lost contact. However, in later years, Philip's grandson, Professor John Melchior KEMPER (1776-1824), began researching his paternal line as being related to him by his father, Joann (John) Hendrik KEMPER (ca. 1750-1786). He knew that part of his early family had moved to America.

Professor KEMPER having seen the article on Eliza Susan (Morton) QUINCY's memoirs recording her early KEMPER family in Germany, made contact with the publisher who was handling the story. His interest had been piqued because his grandfather Philip the older brother of Eliza's grandfather, Jacob KEMPER had been mentioned. Family histories were exchanged and they tried to match up their coat of arms, but Jacob KEMPER's had been lost during the Revolution.

About 1752, while the **KEMPERS** continued to prosper in New York City, Matthew **ERNST** made a fortune and resolved to visit his father in Mannheim, Germany. Matthew had sneaked away from his parents' home twenty years earlier without their knowledge when he was just a young man. He had written them a letter after he was settled in America letting them know where he had gone and that he had married Anna Maria **BOMPER/ POEMBER** (1708-aft.1783), a widow of fortune, left to her by her late husband, Captain Jacob **SCHERP/SHARP** (1680-1734).

In July 1752, upon Matthew's arrival in Mannheim, Germany, he was unfortunately too late to see his father. His father, a minister of Mannheim, was burned at the stake for his religious beliefs one-month prior. Matthew was able to visit his mother, Maria Ursula **ERNST** in Kirn-Becherbach, and his sister, Johanna Catharina (Ernst) **HOFFMAN**. Mr. **ERNST** then learned of his sister, Susan's demise. She was married and resided on the banks of the Rhine River.

A fierce, summer storm had approached and torrential rains drowned the mountainside of the Rhine. By the sudden bursting of a water-sprout against the mountain at her residence, a tremendous flood descended to the river, carrying death and destruction to all in its course. Her home was washed into the Rhine. She was last seen standing outside her front door with an infant in her arms. Her neighbors looked on from across the river in dread. No help could reach her and her desperate, piercing screams could be heard as she perished into the river with all her family.

Matthew knew his sister, Johanna Catharina **ERNST** (1719-aft.1784), was heartbroken by her father's murder, and the loss of their sister, Susan. He assured her by saying, *"You and your husband, Michiel/Michael* [**HOFFMAN** 1715-1776]*, can accompany me to America with your two sons. There you can escape the horrors of prosecution for religious beliefs and have a* *new start in the new land.*" Like their KEMPER in-laws, Mattheus helped them get started.

Catharina/Catherine was pregnant with another child. They brought workmen with them on their voyage to America from Germany. After their arrival in America around early March 1753, they proceeded to set up a glass factory six miles from the city (New York).

On 25 March 1753, Michael HOFFMAN and his wife, Catharina ERNST had a daughter, Christina (1753-?) baptized at the Dutch Reformed Church in New York City. She was named after Catharina's sister, Maria Christina.

Mr. ERNST was a huge advocate for encouraging and supporting family members in Germany to immigrate to America for a new life. From one civilization to another, America continued to grow. However, this venture failed and supporting the glass factory had cost Mr. ERNST a great deal of his fortune. However, he did not let it get him down and continued to go forward in helping his family.

By 1754, the French had started their incursion into the Ohio frontier, setting up camps and building forts in the wilderness. They went to locations unoccupied by the British, although claimed. They wanted to carve out a piece of the real estate for themselves, over confident that the British would not intercede by sending forces deep into the vast, dense and uncharted wilderness to take back what was theirs. They were dead wrong!

The British made Major General Edward BRADDOCK (1695-1755) commander-in-chief of the British forces in the states. They sent him to America to organize forces to march on the French forts and take back what was theirs.

In February 1755, General BRADDOCK arrived in Virginia and started preparing for his expedition to the French Fort Duquesne.

He acquired Lieutenant Colonel George WASHINGTON as his aide-de-camp. His chief scout was Lieutenant John FRASER ((1721-1773). He continued to build his army. His march was called Braddock's Expedition.

Colonel WASHINGTON had some previous experience in battle with the French at Fort Necessity in 1754. He lost over one third of his men and was forced to evacuate in order to regroup and rebuild his army.

Benjamin FRANKLIN provided a hundred and fifty wagons and many other supplies. Among the wagoner's were Daniel BOONE (1734-1820) and Daniel MORGAN (1755-1821). Later they became legends in American history.

Commanding officers were Colonel Sir Peter HALKETT (1695-1755) of the 44th foot; Colonel Thomas DUNBAR (1732-1767) of the 48th foot; Colonel Nicholas MERLWETHER (1736-1772); Lieutenant Colonel Thomas GAGE (1719-1787). Captains included Horatio GATES (1727-1806) of New York; Thomas RUTHER-FORD (1729-1804) of New York; William MERCER (1726-1777); Roger MORRIS (1727-1794); Robert ORME (1725-1790); Charles LEE (1732-1782); Robert STEWART/STUART (1710-?) of Virginia. Ensigns, William CRAWFORD (1722-1782); Charles SCOTT (1737-1813).

Each company was allowed to have two women and some children to accompany them on their march as maids and cooks. In all, there were fifty some women.

On 29 May 1755, General BRADDOCK set out from Fort Cumberland in Maryland heading for Fort Duquesne at Monongahela River to the far west in the Ohio frontier. Being that the dense wilderness was so thick, he had to cut through laying eighty-five miles of road, so that he could haul his convoy of one hundred and fifty wagons along with his artillery.

On 8 July 1755, prior to crossing the Monongahela River, General BRADDOCK separated his army. He left Colonel Thomas DUNBAR in charge of the slower moving support train, to set up camp.

General BRADDOCK took his remaining army and proceeded to cross the Monongahela River. Colonel Thomas GAGE led the advance guard of 300 German grenadiers. The drummers played the grenadier's march.

On 9 July 1755, after crossing the river, General BRADDOCK's army accidentally ran into the French and Indians as they were advancing. Both parties surprised each other and battle was engaged.

The British Army was used to parading out in the open, in columns, in the European theater of battle. In the wilderness, the French and Indians hid behind trees and other cover, ambushing their enemies. When they fired, the larger number of British soldiers, dropped like flies. Many of the troops were either wounded or killed from friendly fire, as the army panicked and shot in all directions.

General BRADDOCK was shot off his horse and mortally wounded. The British quickly retrieved his body and started their retreat. The Indians came in with their knives and tomahawks, while whooping and hollering, to take the scalps of the dead and wounded. Some women and children were murdered and scalped. However, the French and Indians did not have a large enough party to pursue the larger British Army who had panicked and ran.

The dead, the dying, the groans, lamentations, and cries of the wounded for help, pierced the hearts of all those in retreat. Twelve of the British, who were captured by the Indians, were stripped naked, tied to their horses and dragged back to Fort Duquesne. During the night, they were tortured to death at the river-side, where their bodies could easily be disposed of. Of the fifty or so women who accompanied the British columns, only four returned with them. Half were murdered and half were made captives with not so pleasant fates. .

On 17 July 1755, Colonel DUNBAR arrived at Fort Cumberland. Here they rested temporarily and refurbished their supplies. Major General William SHIRLEY (1694-1771) was made the new commander-in-chief of the British forces in the states.

On 2 August 1755, Colonel DUNBAR left Fort Cumberland and marched towards Philadelphia, hoping to set up winter quarters. When in Philadelphia, he received orders from General Sir William SHIRLEY, dated 6 August 1755. He ordered him to march to Albany, New York and set up winter quarters outside of town and wait for further orders.

Before leaving for Albany, General SHIRLEY ordered Colonel DUNBAR to leave officers from each regiment in Pennsylvania, Maryland and New Jersey to recruit new soldiers to replenish the ones lost in the Battle of Monongahela River.

As General BRADDOCK's wretched defeated army passed through New Brunswick, two of Colonel DUNBAR's German Grenadiers, BURNS and KAUN, were told to break off to recruit new soldiers. Once they were noticed by Jacob KEMPER, they are given free quarters in his home. The rest of the army which was headed to Albany, were transported across the water.

After the grenadiers got settled in, they all sat down at the table together. While Jacob's wife, Maria Regina, served food and drink, they began talking to Jacob in German. They told him about the carnage in Monongahela River that they had recently experienced, and how General BRADDOCK lost his life.

Jacob's wife Maria Regina, listening in on the conversation, gasped. She clearly remembered the terror that the French inflicted on the German families in the Rhine River Valley. Jacob and Maria Regina's daughter, Maria Sophia, who was now eighteen, over heard the conversation and was horrified. Jacob, not realizing that his daughter was present asked her to go to another room so as not to upset her.

The grenadiers likewise, did not realize that a young girl was in the room and apologized. Jacob replied, *"It is taken care of."* Mr. KAUN told Jacob that they needed to recruit new soldiers to fill the ranks of all the regiments, because so many that was lost. They told Jacob that they would need to get across the river to the city later on, and offered to pay him to ply them across.

Jacob answered, *"That is not necessary, this one is on me. Just let me know when you are ready to go. In the meantime, relax; enjoy your stay, food and drink."*

Jacob closed by saying, *"The French seem to be everywhere, they constantly inhabit territories of other countries that are not theirs. They can never seem to find anything on their own to settle. Therefore, they try to intimidate and terrorize other lands into submission to their empire. One day, not soon enough, they will all be driven from our lands. Eventually, there will be no new land for the French to settle, and they will become insignificant in world affairs. Their hearts filled with so much jealously will finish them off. They will be forced to retreat to their small country that no one else wants."*

The grenadiers thanked Jacob and his family for their hospitality, and anxiously went into their rooms. They were grateful for a home-cooked meal and a comfortable, safe night's rest in a real bed back in civilization. Soon enough, they would be heading back into the wilderness where haunting sounds of animals and howls of owls at night stretched their imaginations.

The family had hitherto resided in a settlement where only German was spoken; the children knew only that language. By attending a school where the services were in Low Dutch, the prevalent language of the town, and an English Presbyterian church, they soon acquired both languages. After the family had resided for about ten years in New Brunswick, trade suddenly turned to new channels. The town declined and Mr. KEMPER was obliged to seek a new abode (house). He sold the vessel he had built to ply (sail back and forth) between New Brunswick and New York and all the property he could dispose of without sacrifice.

His real estate was retained two years when it was sold at a reduced price. With the proceeds he entered into business in New York where Matthew ERNST was a prosperous merchant. The removal from New Brunswick in 1756 was very heartbreaking to the family, especially to his children. Their hearts were grieved to leave their dear friends who lamented their departure with tears, and whose kindness they took every opportunity to return. However, Mr. KEMPER's affairs continued to prosper and he was able to afford fine educations for his five sons and four daughters. Prosperity and good fortune followed him everywhere he went.

On 1 October 1757, after Jacob and Maria Regina (Ernst) KEMPER had returned to New York City from New Brunswick, New Jersey, they had their last child, Johannes (John) born on 29 September 1757 baptized at the Lutheran Church in New York City. He was named after Jacob's father, Colonel Johann (Johannes) KEMPER. The baby in the family would become a giant in the American Revolution.

In 1758, after Jacob KEMPER moved to New York City, he acquired a license to open a tavern, which he would name after himself, *"Kemper's Tavern."* Jacob used the money he had been saving from taking people back and forth across the water, from New Brunswick, New York City, and other locations. It would be in the middle of prime real estate in downtown New York City at Spring Garden on Broadway.

Jacob's tavern would be like none other before it. This would not be someone else's creation, but in fact his very own. It would take him ten years to complete the construction.

Later in her diary, Elizabeth covered her grandfather's tavern in quite great detail. She explained how this was a soldier's paradise filled with military memorabilia going back to the Prussian Wars. Before entering the tavern, to the left of the front door, stood a wooden Indian which was life-size. Inside, next to the indoor fireplace, on the left side as you look at the hearth, stood a knight adorned in tarnished and dented, shining armor, placed there in honor of her father's grandfather.

The knight's right hand was resting in a position relaxed on the hilt of his sword, which extended down to the floor. Some patrons, over the years, would ask, *"Whose sword is that?"* Others asked, *"Where did you get that?"* The children who accompanied their parents for dinner at the tavern would often be heard saying *"Is that real?"* Above the oak mantel hung an oil painting of her father's grandfather, Colonel Johann KEMPER, in his splendid Prussian uniform on horseback leading his regiment into battle during the Prussian Wars.

The oil painting that caught everyone's attention and was the talk of the tavern, as well as the towns-people, was the one behind the bar of Colonel Johann KEMPER attending the coronation of Frederick I, king in Prussia at Königsberg Castle. This is the one the family was most proud of. Many other oil paintings were hung around the tavern and in the back room where special entertainment occurred. Being in the downtown area on Broadway, the tavern was always bustling with activity. Kemper's Tavern became the most active tavern in New York City.

1. The Goose That Laid the Golden Eggs

On 28 August 1760, John KEMPER's sister, Maria Sophia married in New York City, a wealthy Irish banker, John MORTON (1729-1782), who had been employed in the British Army in the commissary department. He became a banker at No. 9 State Street, New York City facing the Battery along the southwestern tip of New York City. He became an incredible asset in the *"birth of America."* He was of amiable and cheerful disposition and acquired the nickname, *"Handsome Johnny." "He would be "the Goose That Laid the Golden Eggs"* for General WASHINGTON and the Continental Congress.

Soon after their marriage, Mr. MORTON relinquished his position in the commissary department and went into business for himself as a merchant and soon acquired a large estate. Mr. MORTON made two voyages to home (England) to arrange correspond-dences with merchants and with manufacturing establishments, who were excited about conducting business in the new land. The possibilities were endless. America was growing and anyone conducting business in it, would likewise, grow.

Mr. MORTON bought a large, red brick house on Water Street, New York City, in which he resided. This property lay along the East River (also called the South River). Behind his home was a wharf, which extended below the low-water mark. His ships used to unload in his spacious warehouse situated on the wharf, which also served as a flaxseed store—a branch of trade in which he was largely engaged in shipping to Ireland.

When war later seemed inevitable, Mr. MORTON joined the American cause and quickly began financing his KEMPER in-laws, General WASHINGTON and the Continental Congress. The British became so enraged. *"The Rebel Banker,"* Mr. MORTON became a leading target by the British, who wanted to disrupt his financing of the American Revolution. Bags of gold were common in his safe. Mr. MORTON was one of the richest men during the Revolution and everyone knew it and wanted him on their side. Mr. MORTON certainly had more than two gold pieces to rub together.

John MORTON loved gold and knew how to make it easily. In his home, everyone had gold; jewelry, watches, necklaces, trinkets, ornaments, etc. Mr. MORTON fought in the American Revolution with a weapon mightier than the sword and pistol. His was mightier than the artillery of war, but with the mightiest weapon of all, *"gold dollars."* He lavishly spread his gold on his brother-in-law, Captain John KEMPER and his wagon-train, General WASHINGTON and the Continental Congress. Much like a person spreads butter on bread and loved doing so.

After the Revolution, Captain KEMPER would instill in his family the importance of carrying on the MORTON name, constantly reminding them that Mr. MORTON was one of the real heroes of the American Revolution. Unfortunately, Mr. MORTON was never credited for it. John KEMPER and John MORTON were truly *"The Johnny-in-laws."*

During this period, Mr. MORTON had extensive importations from England, Scotland and Ireland and his customers were very numerous. Because of this, Mr. MORTON liked to look presentable; therefore, he had a hairdresser, employed daily. He wore powder in his hair, which was arranged in one long curl around the back of his neck; this gave him a handsome appearance.

His store was unusual, consisting of a great assortment of dry goods, mirrors, frames, pictures from London, carpets, carpeting, tea in boxes, so forth. Mr. MORTON also had a seal made with the initials JM (John MORTON) for stamping all his documents. It was made of silver with an ebony handle.

Mr. MORTON made sure all his profits went into his loan office for the Continental Army and Congress. Mr. MORTON became the only hero of the Revolution who fought without a sword, but in fact, with a more damaging weapon, gold dollars, while generals like Lord STIRLING, who were using their own money to supply shoes and clothing for their regiments, had their funds quickly become depleted.

The generals had to contend with war, and were not able to concentrate on making money. Mr. MORTON's financial support for General WASHINGTON and the Continental Congress was the only means that was sound and steady.

Mr. MORTON also had a storehouse three stories high with machinery for cleaning and preparing flaxseed for exportation. This work was done in the winter season in preparation for extensive shipping to Ireland. For some years, this work was directed by, Mr. P. W. (Peter Wallace) GALLAUDET (1755-1843).

They received the seed from coasting vessels in a rough state, cleaned and prepared it to be sent on board and often turned out and sent off to different vessels. They processed one hundred hogsheads or casks of seven bushels each in a day—all in new casks, coopered and marked in the spring and autumn. Mr. MORTON had everything he needed to make money and he knew it.

Whenever John's older brother, Daniel, would find out something had happened to his younger brother, he would quickly approach his brother and ask, *"Why did you not tell me something was wrong, so that I could help you?"* Or, *"Why did you not let me know you needed help?"* Or, *"Is everything okay?"* John would always reply, *"Nothing was wrong!"* Or, *"I did not need help."* Or, *"Everything is just fine!"* Daniel, knowing otherwise, would just shrug and shake his head. How was he going to help his little brother if he continued to evade his questions, caring more for others than he did for himself?

While the brothers were growing up, John was the silent one. When friends or family would hear about something, the whole neighborhood would know. When John heard about something, it never went anywhere else. Again, Daniel would come to John and ask, *"Why did you not tell me?"* John would reply, *"There was nothing to tell."* Being deeply concerned, Daniel would just look at his brother intensely finally realizing that he was just going to have to look after his younger brother without his consent.

Because of Daniel's deep concern for John, these brothers formed a close bond, one that was unbreakable. Daniel stood by his brother's side his entire life, including the final years of John's life, during his battle with the pension department. John died at eighty-five; Daniel continued to fight to restore his brother's dignity and integrity until he died at ninety-eight.

Being the kind of young man John was, other kids from the neighborhood admired him and wanted his attention, but did not know how to acquire it. One day while at school, Daniel at the head of the conversation with his brothers, was boasting about something to his friends, when the neighborhood bullies came upon John alone, knowing he was the youngest and smallest, and targeted him, saying, *"What was Daniel bragging about? Tell us little Johnny boy or we will beat it out of you!"* John of course, pretended ignorance.

They later ambushed him after school and dragged him into the woods on the east side. They gave him one last chance to tell the secret that they felt he and Daniel shared. John denied knowing what they were talking about and would rather endure their beating than reveal any knowledge that might hurt his brother.

Daniel, upon hearing about this episode from neighborhood gossip, knew better than to go to his brother and ask why he did not come to him for help. This time, Daniel took things into his own hands and went with his brothers, Matthew (1744-1824) and Jacob (1753-1800) and took care of the neighborhood bullies themselves. When John heard about what Dan did, he went to his brother and asked, *"Why did you not tell me what you were intending on doing so I could help?"* Daniel replied, *"There was nothing to tell!"* John chuckled and laughed until he cried, then the brothers embraced.

On 8 May 1762, Johan Jost PETRIE (1695-1775) had recorded in his papers that, he had purchased a number of goods from the merchant Jacob KEMPER. Mr. KEMPER was still prospering as a merchant in lower New York City while he was building his tavern. During this time, his wife Maria Regina attended to all their children's wants and needs. She often described the cities, rivers, mountains and people of the old country, beyond the great ocean. She would relate the many dangers and great sacrifices the family had made to get where they are now.

On 15 July 1764, Elizabeth HOPPER was baptized in the Dutch Reform Church in New York City. She was the daughter of Mattheus HOPPER (1742-1776) and Agnietje Christina CALSJER (1739-1795). She would learn to play the harpsicord and sing and dance at Kemper's Tavern. She would become the child-hood sweetheart of John KEMPER, and when he returned from the Revolution, they would get married.

In 1765, Matthew and Daniel KEMPER took their sister Anna Gertrude (1737-1786) and her two children back to Königsberg, Brandenburg, Germany to be with her husband, Dr. Christian MILLER. Dr. MILLER had previously returned to Germany on request of his family stating that, he was due to inherit a small fortune. After he arrived, his father forbade him to return to America; it appeared to have been some sort of entrapment in order to get their son to return to Germany. However, Mr. MILLER had left his family in America expecting to return; now they had to come to join him.

Matthew ended up staying in Germany and settling near his sister and brother-in-law, Dr. Christian MILLER. Matthew tried to persuade Daniel to stay with him, but Daniel declined, his heart was in America and so he returned to the States. After Daniel arrived back home and told his parents that Matthew (Matt) had stayed behind, their mother, Maria Sophia, lowered her head and sobbed. When she left Germany, she had left behind all her dear friends that she felt a great loss for, and that she knew she would never see again. Now she feared that she would never see her son, Matt, again.

After Matthew remained in Germany, his father, Jacob, now realized how his mother felt when he left her. Daniel returned to join his other two brothers, Jacob and John KEMPER who had remained and enjoyed living in the new land. While growing up in the city of New York, with the population of about twenty thousand, surrounded by a vast wilderness, including swamps, they experienced a constant influx of immigrants. The island began to shrink as the city continued to swallow up the wilderness.

On 1 June 1769, Jacob moved into the house of the late William BURNHAM (?-1765) and his wife Isabella, along New Road, about a mile out of New York City and finally opened his tavern on Broadway, named after himself, *"Kemper's Tavern."* At the time, none of them realized how important the tavern would be to the community and the cause of the Revolution.

Jacob's tavern was located at Spring Garden, across the street from St. Paul's Chapel at 206 Broadway. At this time, New York City was in the middle of the island. New Road turned into Post Road and then into Route 9 into Hudson, New York. As his wealth grew, he bought an estate in New Greenwich, just northwest of the city.

Now that Jacob's tavern was finally going to open, it was time for a big celebration. Everyone in the city had been hearing about its construction, wondering if it was ever going to be completed. Now it was time to find out if it was going to be everything that was advertised, a place for friends and family to meet for love, drinks, good food, and song and dance. Jacob's son-in-law, John

MORTON, had donated a harpsicord for music to be played on stage in the back room. Fireworks were set off everywhere.

Outside the tavern in back, Jacob KEMPER had built a pit. Here, Jacob would have a bonfire where crowds could gather and enjoy the evening. If it started raining, the crowds could move inside to the room in the rear of the tavern, where the main lines of entertainment were song and dance. On many occasions, Jacob's wife, Maria Regina, would sing, and enchant and their audience with her lovely voice.

On this same date a venue was advertised to be held, to raise funds to pay overdue debts. Things were definitely booming for Kemper's Tavern; there were always smiles, laughs and excitement in the smoky crowds at Kemper's Tavern. Maria Regina, with her charming voice, always enchanted their audience. Business was so good in the downtown area. How could anything go wrong?

On 18 March 1770, at the celebration of the Stamp Act Repeal, Sergeant William CUNNINGHAM and a companion made an assault upon the Patriots and gathered around the liberty pole. They were driven off and CUNNINGHAM, who had been a liberty boy himself before joining the army, was severely whipped.

That whipping was clearly paid for in the lives of eleven thousand American prisoners who died during the British occupation of the city under the treatment of the vengeful provost-marshal, Captain William CUNNINGHAM. One of the earliest of his acts after the occupation of the city by the British, in September of 1776, was to order the liberty-pole leveled to the ground. It probably seemed to him a visible reminder of the humiliation of the whipping he had received.

By October 1770, posters were seen throughout the city offering good times, food and drink in Kemper's tavern at Spring Garden. It was located opposite St. Paul's Chapel on the west side of

Broadway, where George WASHINGTON used to worship, and Ann Street. Later they would be changed to Fulton and Vesey Street, extending with its church yard to Church Street. Downtown business was booming and Kemper's Tavern was blossoming in the middle of it all. Maria Regina would be humming and singing as she delivered drinks and dinners to their customers at the tavern.

Mr. KEMPER later acquired a fortuneteller, who set up a booth under the overhead outside to the right of his tavern entrance. This would help his business to continue to grow. People would come from all around to have their fortunes told and as word spread, the crowds would grow larger. After people had their fortune told, they always needed a drink and to discuss their fortune.

The diary of John KEMPER's daughter, Elizabeth, was not like the diaries of today; hers was leather bound, tied together with string that fell apart over the years. As she would record her family history, she would date it, then, place the new pages in her diary. Some of her diary pages however are not dated and it is not clear whether they were part of a previous dated event or not. These pages were obviously scrambled over succeeding generations by family members when taken out to read, and then accidentally replaced back in the wrong order.

Elizabeth's world revolved around her father, as he meant the world to her. If not for Elizabeth, much of the important history in the birth of America would have been lost forever. She had enjoyed listening to her father's yarns (stories/tales) and recorded so many. After her father's battle with the pension department and eventual death, she began collecting more of his history, much the same way her cousin Eliza Susan did for her father, John MORTON.

Excerpts from Elizabeth's diary were placed in chronological order along with her father's journals and other documented sources. Other memories she gathered from her family after her father's death. The family could not always remember when the event took place, these she placed as best she could. She gathered as many stories on the family history as she could, regardless of whether they had to do directly with the Revolution, or not. She started with her father growing up as a young boy in New York City, his life experiences, his service directly under General WASHINGTON, and finally, the mysteries that surrounded his life up to and including his death. This is her story ...

"In 1769, when my father was a young boy of twelve, he had built a fort high in a tree in the woods at the edge of the swamp, east of the city. He had named it the Eagle's Nest because of its high perch. From this position, he could view the swamp and anyone approaching. This is where he used to play soldier with his friends and family. He often loved to sleep in the fort enjoying the musical sounds of frogs and crickets. At night he would gaze over the hundreds of buildings and homes throughout the city, which were all lit up from the many flickering lamp lights. He wondered if anyone ever went to sleep, as he watched the fireflies blink on and off throughout the night."

Elizabeth recorded, one of her favorite stories of her father, which was about the hornet's nest. In said story, her father was a young boy of about twelve or thirteen. Her father was out building a snowman one winter's day, when all of a sudden, he spotted a hornet's nest up in a tree. Since there were no hornets flying around, he thought it had been abandoned and it would surely make a nice trophy. John climbed the tree and broke off the branch where the hornet's nest was attached. He brought the beehive home that afternoon and placed it on the mantle of the fireplace. He planned on mounting it just above the mantle the following day after he got home from school.

During the night the beehive came back to life. Close to morning, John was startled awake by screams throughout the house and got up to see what was wrong. The entire house was buzzing with hornets! His sisters and mother were running from one room to another to escape being stung by the bees. Finally, his sisters ran out the door barefoot and in their nightgowns into the freezing cold, as they frantically slapped the bees off themselves.

As all the male folk were trying to kill the bees, John threw his hands out asking, *"How did all the bees get in here?"*

John's dad replied, *"John! We could use a little help!"*

John grabbed a branch from out of the fire and swung at the bees, which smoked up the house in the process. John then grabbed the beehive with his right hand and while curling his left hand to his mouth coughing, then smoked the rest of the hive while the remaining members of the family ran outside coughing to escape the smoke.

When everything was thought to be under control and most everyone was outside freezing, John's dad grabbed the branch with the hornet's nest on it and shook it in front of John's face saying, *"This is mine! Be grateful I do not beat you to a pulp with it or make you eat it."*

As Jacob shook the nest, a couple more hornets flew out.

John's mother yelled, *"Stop shaking that damn nest, there are still some bees in there."*

Everyone got stung that day except John.

John's dad said, *"If you ever do this again, I am going to crown you with the hive. Did you not know that bees hibernate in the winter?"*

John's mother yelled, *"If you are going to bring home bees, bring honey bees they are sweeter, these were aggressive and huge!"*

His family never let him live that day down.

Jacob later mounted the hornet's nest above the entrance to the back room in his tavern, where community events and entertainment took place. It was still attached to the branch it was fastened to, before being broken from the tree. When Jacob's customers would ask, *"How did you get that hornet's nest?"* Jacob would only reply, *"You do not want to know!"*

In the back room, there hung an oil painting of Colonel Johann KEMPER. This one was of him with Frederick I, king in Prussia in his splendid Prussian dress uniform adorned with the many medals he had received. There was still another that hung depicting his final days, resting in his easy chair on the ramparts of the partial ruins of Stahleck Castle. All these oil paintings were passed down in the family to this author. The back room was where dancing and other entertainment took place. Crowds would often gather here for dinners and refreshments.

One day while playing soldier with his friends and neighbors in the woods, when John was about thirteen or fourteen, the opposite team was hot on his trail trying to catch him. Within a moment of being captured, John jumped over a fallen tree on a ridge, slipped and fell. He then noticed a space under the fallen tree and quickly rolled under.

Two of the boys who were chasing him said, *"We got him now, he is just over the ridge, he can run, but he cannot hide."* They then came to the fallen tree and, stood on it while they looked for John.

One said to the other, *"Where is he?"*

The other boy replied, *"I saw him run over this bank, he has to be here."*

John, who lay just eighteen inches below them, feared for sure he was going to be found. However, the boys had frozen. There was no John anywhere! He was like a genie, *"poof"*, and he was gone.

The two boys continued to look over the vast wilderness, but as the area was only about fifty feet across, with a slight slope going down about fifteen or twenty feet, there was just no one here or anywhere to hide. On this day John learned a very valuable lesson; the best place to hide from your enemies was right under their noses. Using this same tactic in the future would save his life from real soldiers.

While growing up, John had created a coding system, giving code names to his friends, family, obstacles, locations and adventures. John was always observant about everything that was going on around him. He would often keep records of things or events that seemingly were unimportant to others. When asked why he did it, he would just look at the inquirer without trying to intimidate him, but gave no answer. John appeared to be a loner but was not afraid of anyone. He was a young man of few words but many actions. He would often take action without giving any warning of his intent.

When John was not outside playing, he enjoyed listening to his father telling the tales of his grandfather's heroics during the Prussian Wars. He lived vicariously through his grandfather's adventures. Since John's family had a vast history of military service in Germany, he had visions of one day upholding those military standards of being honorable, devoted and trusted. He wanted to go down in history as honorable as his grandfather had.

However, John was not sure how he was going to do that, since the country in which he lived had no army or castles and in fact, lived under British rule. What and how long would it take for this opportunity to present itself to John? He did not want to have to return to Germany to fulfill his destiny. Some kind of change would have to happen soon, in the land he was in.

John, as a young man growing up, would never give up on a task. When confronted by obstacles he would find a way around them. When challenged by others, he would use his charm and wit, rather than brawn, to bring his opponents to submission. He would often manipulate them into feeling ashamed if they did not meet their moral obligations.

John enjoyed staying in the shadows, rather than the limelight as a target. He often made his challengers feel superior thereby defusing their intended violent acts. Since John never threatened them physically, they did not know how to deal with him, so just avoided him when they could. However, at times when they could not avoid him, knowing that he would never challenge them, would approach him peacefully.

Among the many regulars who came to the Tavern were Jacob's son-in-law, John MORTON and good friend, Mattheus/Matthew HOPPER (1742-1776). His wife, Agnietje (Anna) (1739-1795) and their children would often accompany him. Mattheus died from injuries sustained from the bombing of New York City by the British man-of-war, *Asia*, in early 1776. He had planned on joining the Revolution.

From 1759 to the start of the American Revolution in 1775, there were many references of naturalizations in New York City, witnessed by Jacob. After the war broke out, emigrations came to a halt, because of the dangers involved. Mr. KEMPER would ultimately have to move his family to New Jersey for safety. The good times at Kemper's Tavern would thus come to an end.

On 1 October 1770, another venue was advertised at Kemper's Tavern to raise funds to pay overdue debts. What was going on during this period of time was, our system had been set up which enabled everyone to go into debt with no way out. Venues would be set up at locations visited by many in hopes of helping each other. Later on in 1800, Congress was pressured to enact legislation to help people overburden by debt erase it so that they could get a chance at a new start in life. Laws continued to be adapted to our new way of living and continued growth in civilization.

Matthew **HOPPER**'s oldest daughter, Elizabeth (Eliza) (1764-1826), likewise kept a diary. In the early part of her diary she mentions her favorite doll, later her childhood crush on John and the many trips she took with her father and mother to the tavern of John's father. There, Eliza would flirt with John and, duck her head in and around her father, mother, Agnietje (Anna) Christina (Calsjer) **HOPPER** and the customers at the bar. She would whisper, while pointing her finger at John, saying that he was hers and that he better wait for her to grow up.

In 1773, Alexander **HAMILTON**, at age 16, moved to New York City. He attended King's College (Columbia University) and was befriended by Daniel **KEMPER**, who likewise had gone to the same school and often visited old friends and teachers. Alexander told Daniel, *"I am recently new to the City, and my mother sent me here to attend school. I know few people and have not made any friends yet."*

Daniel replied, *"Not any longer, my friend. Let me bring you back to my father's tavern where our family and friends meet, and introduce you to our family."*

"My brother John," Daniel continued, *"is your same age and has an embedded dream of becoming an officer and soldier in a great war; much like our grandfather was in the Prussian Wars."*

"Aaaah!" Alexander replied, *"It sounds like we have something in common already."* Alexander, likewise, had a dream of becoming an officer and soldier in a great war.

Daniel, hoping that his brother John and Alexander, because of their same age, would form a friendship and bond, did as he said and took Alexander to his father's tavern. At the tavern he introduced him to his family. As Daniel was hoping, the friendship and bond forged between these two men became unbreakable and remained throughout their lifetime.

Chapter II
The Fortune-teller

On 16 July 1774, it was a warm, pleasant Saturday and a busy weekend for Mr. KEMPER as he was celebrating a new business venture with fireworks. There was a small inquisitive crowd of people huddled around a gypsy fortune-teller woman named, Madam Ursula. She had set up her booth to the right of the front door, but still under the roof overhang, of KEMPER's Tavern. She bargained with Mr. KEMPER, *"Let me sit here and tell fortunes and I will give free readings to your family and personal friends in exchange. Being in a downtown area, both of us will benefit."*

Some fortune-tellers told fortunes by the hand, tarot cards and tealeaves in a jar, but this one had a crystal ball. Mr. KEMPER invited his family to take advantage of this free service and in hearing of this, Jacob's son, John, a young lad struggling with what his future would hold, jumped at the idea, besides she was German and pretty besides.

Madam Ursula wore an elegant gold and dark-green fabric over her head and the same fabric for her long-flowing skirt. She wore a dark-red cape, and silver-and-turquoise wrist bracelets and armbands. On her forehead she wore some sort of a triangle jewel, which appeared to glisten with rubies, diamonds and emeralds. Her earrings hung from her ears with three or four strings of diamonds or crystals. Her short-sleeve blouse was some sort of white knitted material, with fancy gold and green trim, that you could see her skin through. Her chest was open with the lower part of her blouse, which was the same color as her gown, covering the lower part of her breasts, but you could still faintly see her feminine features beneath the fabric. Her hair was golden, and her eyes were a piercing green. Her hands and long nails were folded under her chin while she rested her elbows on the table, waiting for her next customer.

Along the side of the tavern she parked her horse and carriage. She had a special headdress for her horse, feathery gold, which caught everyone's attention as she drove down the street. On each side of her coach, she had a lantern, which she used for night driving. As she rode down the street, her jingle bells chimed. Around the roof of her coach was gold draping like curtains. Her carriage was so eloquent that it looked fit for Queen Cleopatra (69BC-30BC) of Egypt.

Jacob took John over to the gypsy and introduced him to Madam Ursula as his son. Madam Ursula slowly cocked her head, opened her right arm out, and with her palm facing the sky, softly said, *"Please, have a seat."* John nervously excited, sat down in front of the table at the booth she had set up outside his father's tavern. On the table in front of the gypsy sat a crystal ball, which lay on a deep-maroon cloth, which was draped over the table and embellished with gold braid. The booth, likewise, was enclosed with maroon drapes. The drapes above John in front of the booth were laced with gold braid and strings of crystals. How could something so elegant be set up outside his father's tavern?

Madam Ursula placed her hands around the crystal ball, and, *"poof!"* A mist began to spill out from beneath the crystal ball. *"I see a storm cloud coming in, war is headed your way; but your family is used to it, as they descend from many wars in the fatherland. There will be a courageous and fearless leader, mounted on a white horse, which will come forth to lead you; trust in him. You will witness much pain, suffering and death. You will be personally involved with many powerful figures; you will be sent out on many missions and always bring back good results. You are the silent one; you avoid confrontation but always end up in the middle of things, although never planned. I see an air about you, a mystery of secrecy and danger."*

As she gave a little chuckle, she laminated that John, as a young boy, had been involved with a swarm of bees, but was never stung. Her face scrunched in a slight frown as she continued, *"You were not stung as a young boy, although many thought you should have been, but be aware that you might get stung later in life by an unexpected source. This sting will come not from what you have done, but from what you have not done."*

John squinted his eyes and thought to himself, *"Where are we going with this?"*

Madam Ursula continued, *"You will be loved, you will be hated. I also see a cigar, but I am not sure of the meaning. Likewise, I see a halo of stars; again, the meaning is unclear, but it is followed by love, hate, war and death. I see a great fire; I also see a sword on fire. I see you looking around in a dense jungle, you are lost!"*

As the mist continued to flow out from her crystal ball, and her eyes peered back and forth, she said, *"I see your childhood sweetheart; oh, she is a pretty thing. She will become increasingly significant in your life. Always be aware of your surroundings, stay close to family and trust those who support and back you. Stay in touch with those who love you."*

"I see several important figures in your life, one man in particular being your mentor or hero. Wait! No, not just a man, your brother, who will seemingly appear from out of nowhere, like a genie when you are in dire need of help. He will be by your side, either in body or spirit, to the end of your days and beyond."

"There will be treachery and deception along your journey, but also great loyalty from your family and dear friends for many years to come. Generations of your descendants will cherish your memory. Although others will try to erase it, you will not be forgotten by those who love you!"

"I see you traveling on a vast ocean into darkness. I also see you riding into the sunset; these are different journeys. You will meet two Indians who will be argumentative and competitive with each other, but loyal and trustworthy to you. There will be an endless loss of trusted and loved ones during your lifetime and there will be a struggle to understand the mystery that surrounded them. Some of these losses will be within a short time frame. You will end up living off your memories."

"These things will never be completely discovered . . . some because they were either, hidden, lost or deliberately destroyed for the good of all; and still others because of the secrecy I spoke of. You will come out of a cloud of smoke undamaged, yet you will be surrounded by treachery and deception. You will find yourself among murderers and cutthroats and must blend in. Your heroics will be camouflaged; however, you will go down in history!"

The gypsy closed by saying, *"Take care my young friend and follow your path to your destiny, but watch your back!"*

As John walked away, he was completely flabbergasted! The crowd, who had been watching and listening, was left bewildered. Was this really a fortune-teller, or was she some kind of a witch? John later recorded that this event could not have been for real; it had to be some kind of a joke. Was this gypsy just trying to make money off the customers from their business, or were some of her predictions really possible? Time would certainly tell.

"How could she know about the bees? Dad must have told her. The part about sailing on a vast ocean is dead wrong! I am not a sailor, nor am I ever going to be one; neither am I going to be sailing to my parent's homeland in Germany. I certainly am not going into any jungle. Indians? Hmmmm, what could I possibly do with Indians? War, if there was going to be war, it could not happen soon enough." All in all, John felt that her predictions were well worth his time; after all, she did shine a light of hope into his destiny.

John then accompanied his father, Jacob, into their tavern. John, thinking that his father had told the gypsy about the bee's nest said, *"Thanks, Dad."*

Jacob, thinking John was thanking him for the fortune-telling said, *"My pleasure."*

Jacob continued, *"You know John, there was quite a crowd out there; I truly believe she is going to help bring business to our tavern. After everyone speaks to her, they are going to want to have a drink and one for the road."*

John replied, *"Dad, I think you are absolutely right, besides, we are in the middle of the downtown district."*

Jacob then asked, *"How about you John?"*

John answered, *"Dad, you know I do not drink."*

Jacob offered, *"How about a mug of cider or carbonated water? It is the newest thing and selling like hotcakes!"*

John took his right hand and threw it into the air in the shape of a gun pointing towards his father, winked his eye and said, *"That I will gladly have, thanks, Dad."*

As Jacob fixed John his drink and pushed it towards him, he then threw out his hands and said, *"You know what I just cannot figure out?"*

John inquired, *"What Dad?"*

Jacob answered, *"How in the hell she knew about the bees."*

John looked at his father intensely in shock and said, *"What?"*

Jacob repeated, *"The bee's nest, how in the hell would she know about the bees?"*

John answered, *"Oh my God!"*

Jacob gasped, *"What?"*

John said to his father, *"Listen Dad, I have had a big day and I need to go home and digest everything that has happened."*

Jacob replied, *"I understand; you came to the city with me in my carriage, would you like to take one of my horses tied out back to ride home?"*

John answered, *"No Dad, I think I need to walk this one off. Greenwich is just a couple of miles north, I could use the exercise."*

Jacob replied, *"Okay John, can you move the barrels to the back room for me before you leave?"*

John answered, *"Of course."* John moved the barrels and left the tavern.

Other regulars who came to the tavern who were intrigued by the new fortune-teller were, William DUNLAP, Alexander HAMILTON and Anthony MAXWELL, among many others. As John stepped out the door, the bell rang at St. Paul's Chapel, across the street. For a moment, things were going in slow motion; he glanced to his left at Madam Ursula, who glanced back with a smile. John then headed up Broadway to Canal Street, headed west, and then crossed on over to the road leading to Greenwich along the Hudson River, and continued walking north.

After John had traveled a mile out of the city, still tossing around in his mind everything the fortune-teller had told him, he heard the sound of jingles bells as a single-horse carriage pulled up alongside of him and stopped. As John looked up to see who it was, to his surprise, it was Madam Ursula. She looked down at John, softly smiled, and then asked, *"Would you like a ride?"*

John smiled back and answered, *"Why not? Thank you Madam."*

As Madam Ursula was driving John home, John would periodically look over at her, and then back at the road. Finally he got up enough courage to ask her, *"Madam Ursula, how did you know about the bees?"*

Madam Ursula turned to John, softly smiled, and answered, *"John you are headed on a vast journey into your destiny, you will have good times, you will have bad times, take heed."* Madam Ursula then finished driving him to his estate and dropped him off.

John thought to himself, *"Adults, they never answer your questions and always leave you with more riddles."*

As John stepped down from the carriage, Madam Ursula was looking around. John thanked her again, and

Madam Ursula replied, *"You have a beautiful home, John."*

John thanked her and said, *"It is my parent's."*

Madam Ursula replied, *"I know."*

They both looked at each other for a moment, then, Madam Ursula softly smiled, turned her horse and carriage around, and headed back down the road to the city (New York).

John tossed his head about then kicked a bucket as hard as he could, while asking himself, *"Why do adults never answer your questions and close with a more confusing statement? When in the hell am I going to grow up? If only I was just ten or twelve years older."*

Meanwhile, back at the tavern, Mattheus and Anny Christina (Calsjer) HOPPER's daughter, Eliza, had become a favorite of many of the guests that attended the various festivities. When she was not singing with Maria Regina **KEMPER**, she was singing and dancing on stage in the back room to the music of the harpsicord.

John and Maria Sophia **MORTON** had become fond of young Eliza; they showed special favors to her and bought costumes for her show. They often referred to her as Mattheus and Anny's darling little daughter. They often teased John about her crush on him. She was already being considered as part of the family.

On 16 September 1774, after both John and his wife, Maria Sophia **MORTON** had become close to Mattheus **HOPPER** and his family at the tavern, they decided to name a daughter after her and Maria's sister, Susan; Thus, Eliza Susan **MORTON** was born. Hopefully, she would turn out to be a singer and performer like the young Eliza **HOPPER**.

On 19 April 1775, because of the Siege of Boston by the British Army, the Continental Congress adopted a resolution to raise military units from the thirteen states in defense of the colonies. It was as if, *"Poof!"* all of a sudden, we had a country. Wait a minute now, where did this unity of the thirteen states come from? What is happening? The need for a defense of the states, are we a country now? Oh my goodness, is this what John **KEMPER** was hoping would happen? Would we now have a country he could fight for? Why is everything taking so long?

In 1775, John **MORTON** placed the greater amount of his extensive property in the land office for the use of the colonies. For this act he was dubbed, "the Rebel Banker" by the adherents (loyal followers) of King George. This was the beginning of Mr. **MORTON**'s love for the new land he was in and his attachment would continue to grow. Soon enough, he would begin to be recognized by General **WASHINGTON** and the Continental Congress. Their attachment would become a strong bond.

On 12 June 1775, Elizabeth recorded the following event in her diary. After flirting with John as usual, she jumped up on the bar and slowly waltzed down to a position in front of John, while smiling. Eliza's father, Mattheus HOPPER, sitting on John's right, softly nudges his left elbow into John's ribs. John's brother, Daniel, sitting on his left, likewise nudges John softly in the ribs with his right elbow. John's sister, Maria Sophia, was standing off to his left, smiling her life away.

Maria's husband, John MORTON, came up from behind John, clutched him on his shoulders and shook him softly, while saying, *"Wake up John, your girl is about to put on a show for you. Can you not hear the music of the harpsicord picking up?"*

Eliza had informed the harpsicord player to pick up the beat when she jumped up on the bar. John started blushing while pounding his fists on the bar; this was all planned. He then took his two hands and covered his face, while he bowed his head to the bar trying to hide his blushing.

Eliza began singing and dancing while exuberantly swishing her skirt from side to side. Customers in the tavern cheered exclaiming, *"That is what you get at Kemper's Tavern, a song and a dance while having a drink with your dinner."*

When her dance was finished, John lifted her off the bar, kissed her on her cheek, winked at her and set her down. Eliza giggled as she scurried away.

Eliza's father, Mattheus, remarked, *"You know John, we never know what tomorrow will bring to any of us."*

John answered, *"I know Matt; I am learning fast."*

There was dancing; there were cheers; and there was laughter at Kemper's Tavern, while the piano played in the back room, where community events were held. However, there was a storm coming in and smoke would soon cover the scene. Immigration to America would come to a halt. Baptisms in the Dutch Reformed Church in New York City, which was the largest in America, would come to an end.

Refugees, in fear of their lives, would flood to the nearby localities, like New Jersey, Pennsylvania and Upstate New York. No one ever took kind to refugees, as they were a strain to whatever location they escaped to. Kemper's Tavern would just become a memory.

Elizabeth would often ask John, *"What do you want to be when you grow up?"*

John would always reply, *"An officer in a great army!"*

Eliza grinned, but understood, knowing that he came from a military family. She then said, "Everyone is saying that war is in the air."

John replied, *"Yes it is."*

Eliza replied, *"I know you are excited, but it is scary at the same time."*

Once John joined the Continental Army, she thought he was so handsome she became starry-eyed. She was falling in love with a man in uniform. She would write and wait for John to return from the Revolution.

On 14 June 1775, Congress created a resolution to coordinate the military efforts of the thirteen colonies in their revolt against the rule of Great Britain. The Continental Army was born! Now the country that the KEMPER family lived in had an army; John's mind was racing and going places. How could he play a part? Things were now moving along fast; everyone anxiously looked over, every bit of news that was coming forth. What was going to happen next?

On 15 June 1775, the Continental Congress having George WASHINGTON in front of them in full uniform and ready to fight, were totally impressed with the confidence that he showed. He was gutsy and just what they felt they needed. Recognizing he was someone just as courageous as they were, they appointed him commander-in-chief of the Continental Army—The bond was created!

George WASHINGTON was the best choice for this position because he was the one with the most military expertise and tenure from the French and Indian Wars. In the past, he had been under other commanders; now, he was put in charge of the outcome of the war! He would end up making the Continental Congress the power of the land for making him who he was; jumping him in rank from a lieutenant colonel to a three-star general.

John asked his family, *"Who is this man George WASHINGTON?"*

They replied, *"We have no idea!"* -Nobody had a clear answer, yet anyway.

On 29 June 1775, Simon SARTWELL (1722-1790) at Cambridge, Massachusetts, is listed in Captain Seth MURRAY's (1736-1795) company, in Colonel Benjamin Ruggles WOODBRIDGE's (1739-1819) regiment. He would become an important part in enlisting recruits for the Continental Army.

On this day, business for Kemper's Tavern was bustling; the tavern was filled with noisy, excited crowds. Jacob asked John to watch the bar as he went to the back room. Then, all of a sudden, screeching echoed out from the back room as if a baby was dying. Jacob yelled, *"John!"* John rushed to the back room. When he arrived, his father was jabbing a pole into an empty grain barrel. The sound that was coming from the barrel was a high *Screeeeeeeeeeeeeeech!* Then the screaming stopped, and Jacob told John to get a glove.

After John put on the glove, he went over to the barrel, and his father said, *"Do not touch it! Pick it up with your gloved hand, take it outside and throw it in the pit."*

It was a rat!

"Pop!" John exclaimed, *"How could something sound so horrible?"*

Jacob replied, *"I have no idea that is the first time I ever heard a rat scream. Chills ran through my body and made me feel as if I was doing something dreadfully wrong; a terrible haunting feeling. I had to first back up and rethink of what I was doing. As I was jabbing it, I got the impression I was killing a human baby."*

John remarked, *"It sounded just like you were beating a human baby."*

Jacob, *"I know, I know."*

In the tavern, most of the customers had stood up, terrified as to what was going on in the back room. One female patriot yelled out, *"It sounds like a baby screaming for help."*

Jacob quickly returned to the tavern and softly motioned with his hand to calm down the crowds, then exclaimed, *"It was a rat that had jumped into an empty barrel of grain and could not get out."*

One patriot inquired, *"That was a rat?"*

Jacob, *"Yes it was."*

The crowd slowly sat back down in relief of knowing that such a haunting sound was just a rat.

On this morning, John was helping his father prepare for the day; Jacob had opened the cigar box to find only a few cigars left.

Jacob exclaimed, *"John, can you rush down to the trade store and pick me up a couple more boxes?"*

John replied, *"Sure, Pop."*

John, who was loading wood for the fireplace, was finishing up as his father handed him some money. He said, *"Dad, I have some money from some jobs I did for Mr. [John] MORTON."*

Jacob replied, *"It does not matter, that was for you, this is for me. If you see anything else interesting, pick that up as well and put it on my bill."*

John took the money and headed out the door to the trade store.

When John entered the trade store, the clerk was arguing with a Mohegan Indian over the amount of furs he was trading in for some supplies. The clerk kept saying, *"Not enough, not enough!"*

The Mohegan said, *"My furs blessed by great spirit. These are top grade beaver and bear furs, my furs worth more than other Indian furs."*

The clerk replied, *"Maybe to you, but not to me."*

John slowly walked over to the two arguing and asked, *"How short is he for the supplies he needs?"*

The clerk replied, *"It is a lot of money, John."*

John continued to stare at the clerk, waiting for an answer. The clerk then said, *"Okay, okay. Everything comes to about three dollars, including the beaver and bear furs he is trading in."*

John replied, *"It looks like he has a lot of furs there, why do they not cover the cost?"*

The clerk answered, *"The beaver and bear traps he wants are no big cost, but this crossbow, John, this is a mighty fine crossbow. He wanted to trade his bow in for it; I have no use for an Indian bow."*

After slowly and carefully looking over the supplies the Mohegan wanted, John replied, *"I will cover the difference."*

The clerk quickly gasped, *"John!"* Then, he slowly shook his head and said, *"Okay, okay. I will probably be banned from the entertainment center at Kemper's tavern if I do not cooperate."*

The clerk grabbed the furs and carried them to the back room. John waved his right hand to the Mohegan, motioning him to take his supplies.

The Mohegan glared at John with uncertainty, in shock that he had helped him pay for his supplies.

John repeatedly waved his right hand, motioning the Mohegan to take his supplies and leave. The Mohegan, finally nodding in gratefulness, picked up his supplies and headed out the door.

The clerk returned from the back room and asked, *"Is there anything else I can do for you, John?"*

John answered, *"Yes, I need a couple of boxes of cigars."*

The clerk pulled out a couple of boxes from under the counter and placed them on top.

He then asked, *"Is there anything else, John?"*

John answered, *"Not right now, thanks. Here is the money for the cigars, put the balance owed on the crossbow on our bill."* John paid the clerk and headed out of the trade store.

As John exited the store, standing in the middle of the street, and looking like a wooden Indian stood the Mohegan. John slowly walked up to him, and the Mohegan introduced himself. *"I am 'Lone WOLF,' given this name by my chief, Bald EAGLE, because I am mighty warrior and need no braves behind me."*

John smiled and said, *"I am John KEMPER, I am not a mighty warrior, but wish to be one, and all I have behind me is my family."*

Lone WOLF replied, *"Wrong! Now you have the mighty Lone WOLF."*

Lone WOLF began his story, *"Great Spirit come to me in my dreams and spoke of this day; the day I would meet a great white warrior dressed as a gent (gentleman). He will become close to the 'Great White Chief.' Trust in him and follow his path. He will need a mighty warrior and good scout."*

John smiled profusely, as he shook his head from side to side and said, *"Lone WOLF, you sound just like my fortune-teller."*

Lone WOLF asked, *"Was she a wise woman?"*

John uncurled his smile and asked, *"How did you know she was a woman?"*

Lone WOLF just glared at John.

John continued, *"Listen, WOLF, if this time comes to be when I will become close to my great White Chief, I am surely going to need a mighty warrior and good scout. I will definitely make sure that you fill that position."*

Lone WOLF smiled and turned to walk away.

John asked, *"How will I find you?"*

Lone WOLF, turned back to face John and said, *"I will find you!"*

Lone WOLF paused for a moment, and then asked, *"You wouldn't happen to know where I can find a good horse, would you?"*

John answered, *"Sorry WOLF, not at the moment."*

Lone WOLF then led his *painted pony* off with his supplies.

After John returned from the trade store, he told his father, *"Well Pop, I did find something else interesting to add to our bill."*

Jacob replied, *"Good, what was it?"*

John answered, *"An Indian and his supplies."* Jacob gasped, *"An Indian!"*

John, trying to settle his father down, said, *"I will work it off, Pop."*

Jacob responded, *"I cannot wait to hear the rest of the story on this one."*

In July of 1775, Admiral Samuel GRAVES (1713-1787) sent their Man-of-War HMS *Asia*, a British sixty-four-gun ship commanded by Captain George VANDEPUT (?-1800), loaded with 480 men, into the East River, opposite John MORTON's house. Knowing that he was so financially powerful and had been successful for them and had married an, American woman, Maria Sophia KEMPER, they feared that he would turn his attention to his wife's side of the war.

Not knowing that John MORTON had already chosen the American side, they were hoping that he feared the Rebels. They promised him protection against any American retaliation on his business and family. However, they threatened to open fire on the city if he did not remain a loyal and quiet subject.

Mr. MORTON and his family, fearing the threat of further British action, started the preparations for the removal of their goods to a safer location. Philadelphia was a much safer location to transport his stores, but for how long? Being a smart businessman, Mr. MORTON took one step at a time and planned accordingly, for he never intended on deserting the American cause he had joined.

The order to threaten Mr. MORTON had come down the chain of command from King George III, himself. His intelligence had informed him that one of his previous employees, John MORTON, married an American woman, Maria Sophia KEMPER, and left his service. Threats of retaliation did not force Mr. MORTON to surrender, and he became one of the main targets of the British Empire.

Meanwhile, the HMS *Asia* continued to periodically bomb New York City, sending its residents fleeing in panic. Many refugees went to Upstate New York, Connecticut, New Jersey, or Pennsylvania. John KEMPER's childhood sweetheart, Elizabeth HOPPER's father, Matheus, was one of the casualties of these bombings in the spring of 1776. He never got a chance to join the Revolution. Many families fled in different directions, hoping to reunite later on.

In July 1775, a vessel belonging to Mr. MORTON arrived from England, laden with valuable merchandise. Most of the goods in his warehouse were hastily packed and added on board this ship, which, with its cargo, was ordered round to Colonel John BAYARD's (1738-1807) counting-house in Philadelphia, Pennsylvania.

At this time, this area was considered out of reach of the British. The stores were put under the care of Mr. P. W. GALLAUDET, the confidential clerk of Mr. MORTON; these were where the goods were sold at high prices and the money deposited in the loan office. This money was then used to fund both the Continental Army and Continental Congress.

When Mr. MORTON's brother-in-law, John KEMPER, arrived in Philadelphia, he would be the go-between for Mr. P. W. GALLAUDET, Colonel John BAYARD and Mr. MORTON, in addition to his own duties. Captain KEMPER's association with Mr. MORTON was not only family, it was a necessary and intricate part of making all the dealings work between Mr. MORTON, General WASHINGTON, and Congress.

Both General WASHINGTON and the Continental Congress, in order to fulfill his duties, had given him carte blanche. Because John KEMPER was Mr. MORTON's brother-in-law, General WASHINGTON put him in a position where he became invaluable to Mr. MORTON, General WASHINGTON himself, and the Continental Congress. They all never looked a gift horse in the mouth.

Mr. GALLAUDET worked for Mr. MORTON from 1774 through July 1775, when he went into the counting-house of Colonel John BAYARD. He then went around with Colonel BAYARD, attending the sales of Mr. MORTON's goods. The monies were then deposited in Mr. MORTON's loan office. In the winter of 1777, Mr. GALLAUDET, after having learned the ropes of a businessman, went into business for himself.

After the British took Philadelphia, he had to relocate, then returned to Philadelphia once they evacuated. After the Revolution, President WASHINGTON appointed Mr. GALLAUDET as his personal secretary. What was good enough for Mr. MORTON was good enough for President WASHINGTON. In addition, this appointment gave President WASHINGTON inside information as to what John MORTON and his successful business was all about.

Mr. MORTON's property was further diminished by the depreciation of the paper money issued by Congress, in which currency he was obliged to receive all debts due him. The partial interest allowed by Congress for the money deposited in the loan office, after the French loan was negotiated, was paid in specie (coin instead of paper money). This, together with merchandise taken out of New York and sold or exchanged for articles needed by the family, furnished their means of support during the war.

Because Mr. MORTON was the wealthiest contributor to the American Revolution, General WASHINGTON and the Continental Congress would need a direct link to him. Mr. MORTON'S brother-in-law, Captain John KEMPER, became that link. Mr. MORTON's other brother-in-law, Lieutenant Daniel KEMPER, while at Morristown, was bucked up to colonel, aide-de-camp to General WASHINGTON, and deputy clothier-general of the Continental Army. Like his brother John, Daniel stuck by General WASHINGTON's side throughout the Revolution, and became invaluable, especially when at camp.

Chapter III
The Kemper Brothers join the Revolution

Shortly after George WASHINGTON became the commander-in-chief, recruitment posters started pouring off the press. One day a Continental officer entered Kemper's Tavern impressively all dolled up in a new Continental uniform. He walked up to the bar and said, *"Mr. KEMPER, we have been informed that you and your family are favorable for our cause of the Revolution. We were wondering would we be permitted to hang recruitment posters up in your place of business?"*

Mr. KEMPER, for a moment, was mesmerized, and then replied, *"Absolutely! Put one up above the fireplace mantle as you enter. Stick another one up on the venue board, hand me some for the bar."*

The officer thanked Mr. KEMPER then began hanging posters.

Mr. KEMPER added, *"Do not forget to hang one up in the back room; in fact, why not set up a recruitment center in there? It can be accessed by the side door. That is where our crowds gather and entertainment takes place, so a lot of men would have a chance to join. Also hang one outside the front entrance next to the wooden Indian, announcing the recruitment center in the back room. Hang one outside the side door so they know where to enter."*

The recruitment poster read …

TO ALL BRAVE, HEALTHY, ABLED BODIED, AND WELL
DISPOSED YOUNG MEN,
IN THE NEIGHBORHOOD, WHO HAVE ANY INCLINATION TO JOIN THE
TROOPS,
NOW RAISING UNDER
GENERAL WASHINGTON,
FOR THE DEFENCE OF THE
LIBERTIES AND INDEPENDENCE
OF THE UNITED STATES
AGAINST THE HOSTILE DESIGNS OF FOREIGN
ENEMIES

TAKE NOTICE

Now, with the fortune-teller, Madam Ursula out front, the back room of Kemper's Tavern was the recruitment center, where people came from all over. With the already-good entertainment and the good food, the tavern became, even more of a bustling center in the city of New York, especially being down-town. After the Revolution, Kemper's Tavern became a tourist attraction. As the breeze blew the leaves around the old tavern, like everything, it later slowly faded away with time. Eventually it was replaced by new structures.

When the Revolution started, John MORTON joined the American cause. Because of his wealth, his huge loans to the Continental Congress, and helping to outfit soldiers who joined the Continental Army, the British became even more furious over the "Rebel Banker." He paid for his brothers-in-law, Daniel, Jacob and John KEMPER, who also became favored by General WASHINGTON and the Continental Congress, to be outfitted for the Revolution.

Whoever was close to the KEMPER brothers, remained close to money. Mr. MORTON further declared that, *"he would pay to those who could fight, the last farthing he possessed."* Captain John KEMPER and his sister, Susan (Kemper) JACKSON named children after John MORTON. Because Captain KEMPER became so close to Mr. MORTON, his descendants carried on the MORTON name for generations.

Kemper's Tavern had become a place where Continental soldiers would come to answer questions for the young recruits who gathered there. They would meet, have a drink and share their stories. John and his brothers, Daniel and Jacob, met there to discuss plans to join the American Revolution. When not at the bar being served by their father, or at a table having one of their mother's specials, they often sat in front of the stone fireplace discussing family situations. In the pot that hung in the fireplace, there was always something cooking. However, on this day, John recorded that *"something new was brewing,"* their participation in the Revolution.

This day was different, this was a private meeting called by their father, Jacob. Their father began, *"No matter what country the KEMPER family lives in, we are not going to be able to escape war. This is our country now and it is calling us. You are all full-grown men; whatever decision you make you will have to live with for the rest of your lives. I also have enough money to help with getting you started."*

Daniel replied, *"We can do one of two things, either sit around and complain about rough times like the Tories/Loyalist and side with the enemy, or stand up and be counted like real men; let us honor our grandfather!"*

Jacob replied, *"I am ready!"*

John sighed, and then took a deep breath, gazing into the crackling fire. Although he was no longer looking at his family, he could feel them all looking at him with pride. Then he replied, *"This is what I have been waiting for, let us get started! I was not named after my grandfather for nothing."*

Their sister, Maria Sophia, and her husband, John MORTON, were present, likewise, to assist in any way they could. *"Money will not be an issue,"* assured Mr. MORTON, *"I will make sure it is no problem, all will be outfitted with the best! No job is too big, no task is too small."*

On 15 September 1775, the three KEMPER brothers, Daniel, Jacob, and John joined the Revolution in Brooklyn in Kings County Light Horse—Captain Adolphus WALDRON (1720-1802) of the New Jersey Line—as a company of minute men for service in the militia; Colonel Rutgert VAN BRUNT (1722-1812); Lieutenant Colonel Nicholas COWENHOVEN (1744-1793); Major General Charles LEE (1732-1782).

In his declaration to the War Department in 1832, Colonel Daniel KEMPER stated that his brother John enlisted in the New Jersey militia. After 15 Aug. 1776, this regiment reported to Major General Nathanael GREENE (1742-1786). All this information was recorded in the KEMPER family Bible; Captain Jacob KEMPER (1753-1800) added precise information on this event in his application when he helped organize and became an original member of the Society of Cincinnati after the Revolution.

1. Continental Celebration

This was a special evening of celebration being set up by the Continental officers of the recruitment center in the back room. The outside and inside posters read, "Tonight's starting entertainment will be performed by the stunning Maria Regina KEMPER, and the young and talented, Eliza Hopper. Songs will include, "My Days Have Been So Wondrous Free," by Francis Hopkinson [(1737-1791)]; "Yankee Doodle," by Dr. Richard Schuckberg [(?- 1773)], and their closing rendition of "Free America'," by Dr. Joseph Warren [(1741-1775)]. There will be free drinks and plenty of hors d'oeuvres for all those in attendance. Sponsored by, John Morton."

Some of the other family and friends who were attending the celebration were, Sebastian BEAUMAN, Alexander HAMILTON, William DUNLAP, Anthony MAXWELL, Mattheus and Anna Maria ERNST, Michael and Johanna Catharina HOFFMAN, John and Maria Sophia MORTON, John and Maria Christina (Ernst) WETZELL, Mattheus and his wife, Anny, and daughter, Eliza HOPPER. The tavern was filled with crowds of people from wall to wall. Noisy chatter and excitement was everywhere.

As everyone was busy intermingling, John was temporarily caught alone. While looking over the crowds at the tavern, Eliza quickly took advantage of the situation and moved in. She started playing with the buttons on his uniform, and, while softly and sadly looking up at John, said, *"I would like to have an audience with you, mister. Can we talk in private for a moment?"*

As John was inquisitively looking down at Eliza, he replied, *"Of course, Eliza, you have addressed me as a princess would have addressed a knight in shining armor; your request is granted, my lady. Let us step outside by the pit for a moment."*

After they went outside, Eliza, once again, started playing with the buttons on his uniform. While sadly looking up at John, trying to get up the courage to say what she wanted to say, she finally started, *"You have always been excited when talking about our descent from Royalty on my father's side. If you will wait for me to grow up so that you can marry me, I will make you my King."*

John, while softly smiling and moving his head from side to side, while looking up at the sky, replied, *"Now that is the most eloquent offer I have been given since I joined the Continental Army; I always wanted to know what it felt like to become a King; however, I am going to need you to agree to a pact of my own."*

Eliza quickly inquired, *"What?"*

"I am going to need you to agree to wait for me until I return from the Revolution. At that point in time, I am going to need someone who cared enough to wait for me."

Eliza, while blushing, quickly responded, *"Agreed!"*

After both John and Eliza embraced and caressed each other, they exchanged kisses on the cheek. John then closed by saying, *"Now that the most important business has been settled, let us return to the party inside, surely our family and friends are going to be missing us."*

Eliza quickly burst out, *"Yeeeeeeeeeeeeeees!"* Everyone outside looked over to see what was going on.

Now that the whole family had agreed to be part of the Revolution, they all began to celebrate with other Continental soldiers at the tavern. Jacob addressed the family who were all clustered together, *"My mare is about ready to have another foal, and I sure wish I could sell that extra horse, Sandy, I have out back. Would anyone happen to know anyone interested?"*

All the family just slowly shook their heads.

Excited noisy chatter was everywhere. All of a sudden, the chatter became hushed. Everyone was looking at the entrance of the tavern. As John and his family looked over, a Mohegan Indian was standing in the entranceway; it was Lone WOLF.

Jacob being startled remarked, "Whooooa, what is going on here?"

John MORTON answered, *"Maybe he came for John's scalp."* John's sister, Maria Sophia, just burst out laughing.

Eliza placed her hands on her hips, looked up at Mr. MORTON and said, *"That was not very nice Mr. MORTON,"* while he continued to laugh.

John then exclaimed, *"Wait just one minute!"*

Jacob inquired, *"What is it, John?"*

John replied, *"That horse!"*

Jacob asked, *"What about it?"*

John answered, *"Hold on a minute!"*

John got up from his seat, walked over to the WOLF and asked, *"How did you know I was here?"*

Lone WOLF replied, *"You not remember? The trade clerk feared you would band him from Kemper's Tavern."*

John softly smiled, bowed his head, looked back up at Lone WOLF and said, *"Yes he did, you would not still happen be looking for a good horse, would you?"*

Lone WOLF's eyes opened wide as he answered, "Yes I am, do you know where I can find one? Indians do not have horses to sell. We must get them from white man who bring them across Great Ocean."

As John softly smiled and bobbed his head up and down, he said, *"How do you like the name, Sandy?"*

Lone WOLF said, *"Is that the name of a squaw?"*

John said, *"Come on over, let me buy you a drink and introduce you to my family and friends."*

"Drink!" Lone WOLF exclaimed, *"Drink sound good; meet family and friends sound good, too. You have whiskey?"*

John answered, *"Absolutely!"*

Lone WOLF replied, *"Me like whiskey, whiskey good for spirits."*

Once the tavern's crowd saw that the Mohegan Indian was John's friend, the chatter began to pick back up once again. John brought Lone WOLF over and introduced him to his father, Jacob, running the bar; his brothers Daniel and Jacob; his sister, Maria Sophia and her husband John MORTON. John then said, *"And this is my sweetheart, Eliza, her father Matt and mother Anny HOPPER."*

The WOLF looked down at Eliza, who was all dolled up in her show clothes and said, *"Hmm, and awfully young squaw."*

Eliza looked up at the WOLF with a crooked grin.

John then said, *"Dad, the WOLF would like a whiskey."*

Jacob replied, *"I heard."* Jacob poured a shot of whiskey and pushed it towards Lone WOLF. The WOLF gulped it down.

"Eaaaaaasy," said John's father, *"We do not want to be carrying you out of here."*

Mr. MORTON then said, *"John is just trying to buy the Mohegan with a whiskey so that he does not take his scalp."* Both Mr. MORTON and his wife die laughing.

Eliza, once again, came to John's defense, crossed her arms, looked back up at Mr. MORTON, and while tightening her facial expressions, said, very slowly and seriously, *"Mr. MOOORTON."*

Lone WOLF jumped in and said, *"Your Mr. MORTON very funny guy. Me see him in dream try to ride moose instead of horse and get the horns, ha, ha, ha. Maybe me take his scalp and make him laugh more. He look real funny then."* Lone WOLF seemed to instantly blend in with the family.

Now, Eliza burst out laughing. She then playfully took her right hand and swatted Mr. MORTON on his left arm and said, *"There, that will teach you."*

Mr. MORTON just looked down at Eliza, while still laughing. Everyone was having a good time, but with war in the breeze, how much longer could it possibly last?

John then added, *"The WOLF is also looking for a good horse."*

Jacob replied, *"Now, that we can help him out with as well. John, take Lone WOLF out back and show him our horse, Sandy."*

John showed Lone WOLF out to the stables to see the horse.

Lone WOLF softly patted the horse on its neck while opening his mouth to check out its health and age. He remarked, *"Nice horse, Sandy; well fed and groomed. How much does your father want for him?"*

John answered, *"Let us go back in and find out."*

As both John and Lone WOLF returned to the bar, Jacob poured another shot of whiskey and slid it towards the WOLF and said, *"This one is on me."*

Lone WOLF gulped it down and while licking his lips, looked earnestly at John's father and said, *"Good whiskey! Good horse, too. Me have furs on painted pony outside to trade for more whiskey and maybe horse as well."*

"Furs," Jacob exclaimed, *"What kind of furs?"*

The WOLF replied, *"Me get em, be right back."*

While the WOLF headed out of the tavern to retrieve his furs, John said to his family, *"I am really beginning to like this guy."*

Daniel remarked, *"You know, John, we may end up needing an Indian scout soon."*

John replied, *"So our fortune-teller says."* He then said, *"Dad, I know your horse is worth a lot more than your whiskey. I just hope that you can offer some sort of exchange to even the difference."*

Jacob replied, *"We will work something out."*

John warmly replied, *"Thanks Dad."*

When the WOLF returned with the furs, John's father said, *"Bring them behind the bar."*

After looking over the beaver and bear furs, Jacob replied, *"These are nice furs. These are good for all you can eat and drink for three days at Kemper's Tavern. If you get smashed, there is a straw bed out in the back stables where you can sleep, it is better than sleeping out in the streets or the swamps. However, these are not going to fully compensate for the horse. Now if you do not mind a little work, I have a lot of jobs that need to be done around the tavern, you can work off the balance. Free meals and stay come with the jobs."*

Lone WOLF's eyes opened wide as he excitedly replied, *"Me make you happy you help Lone WOLF, me work hard for you."*

Jacob remarked, *"Good enough."*

The WOLF inquired, *"Me buy drinks for family and friends, too?"*

Jacob answered, *"Anything you want."*

As everyone got situated, John's brother, Jacob, ordered a beer, Daniel ordered a whiskey.

John MORTON said, *"Thanks, I will have a glass of wine."* John then said to his sister, *"And how about you Sis?"*

Maria Sophia, smiling profusely, said, *"I will have the same as my husband, thanks WOLF."*

Matt had a beer; Anny had a glass of wine, while Eliza had a mug of cider.

WOLF then said, *"Give whiskey to young squaw, maybe she grow fast."*

Eliza then placed her hands back on her hips, looked back up at Lone WOLF with another crooked grin, and said, *"Ha, ha, ha WOLF, you are so funny. Maybe you will get lucky and a bear will eat you alive in the woods."* Everyone at the bar burst out laughing. Mr. MORTON spilled his glass of wine all over himself. Maria Sophia's jaws were getting sore from laughing.

As everyone settled down, Lone WOLF replied, *"Spunky little squaw, If me catch bear in woods, me eat him."*

John then said, *"I do not normally drink a lot, but this time I think I will have a whiskey with the WOLF."*

The WOLF glared down at Eliza, then stared at John and said, *"You look good in uniform. You look like mighty soldier with long knife* [referring to sword]. *No one can get close to one with long knife. One day soon, we will look good together."*

John responded, *"Thanks WOLF, you can count on it; but beware of the bear in the woods. There are lions there as well."*

Lone WOLF then gazed around the tavern and said, *"Me see many soldiers, you planning war party?"*

John answered, *"Not yet WOLF, we are celebrating our joining the Continental Army."*

Lone WOLF replied, *"I hear Red Coats come."*

John answered, *"You hear correct."*

The WOLF said, *"You will need mighty warrior and great scout."*

John replied, *"Yes we will. When that moment arrives, we will look for you."*

The WOLF quickly nodded and gulped down another whiskey.

On 24 September 1775, Ethan ALLEN (1738-1789), who was no part of any military organization, gathered a bunch of men together and called them the "Green Mountain Boys." He played military cowboy and led his men in an attack on the British stronghold at Fort Montreal, Canada, and consequently, he was captured. Because of the length of time he spent as a prisoner of war, he became an American status symbol.

Years later General WASHINGTON negotiated his exchange and rewarded him by granting him the rank of colonel. The British always kept Fort Montreal at peak defense, fearing both American and French raids. Many American and French assaults were made on Montreal, but all failed. The British never used Fort Montreal as a base to attack from, for it would expose their troops and leave the fort vulnerable to attacks from other directions.

Montreal, Quebec, was the only attempt by the French to settle North America. They were off their turf and in British territory, which quickly and easily captured their two small bases, assisted by their general Charles LEE in 1759 and 1760. This was one of the main reasons for the French involvement in the American Revolution; they were hoping for the Americans to assist them in doing what they could not do, recapture Montreal. However, all hope was in vain. These were not major settlements, but more like a couple of small duck ponds.

By the time the French had decided to sail to the Western Hemisphere, it was too late; the Spanish and English had claimed everything. Later the French acquired an island off of South America, which they named, "Devil's Island." This island became notorious for executions conducted by the French; other than that, this was the extent of any French involvement in the Western Hemisphere.

On 17 October 1775, John MANLEY (1733-1793) was appointed captain of the schooner *Lee*, (named after General Charles LEE), by General George WASHINGTON. He assumed command on 24 October 1775 with a crew of fifty men from Colonel John GLOVER's (1732-1797) Marblehead Regiment, near Boston, Massachusetts. Because of Captain MANLEY's bravery at sea, he became invaluable to General WASHINGTON.

On 2 November 1775, Johann George Frederick WILLHEIT (1723-1792) joined as a corporal in Captain Henry FISTER's company, Colonel Nicholas HAUSSEGGER's (1729-1786) Eighth Maryland German Regiment. He fought at the Battles of Long Island (27 August 1776) and White Plains (28 October 1776). He went on to cross the Delaware with General WASHINGTON on Captain John KEMPER's flatboats and participate in the Battle of Trenton (26 December 1776).

On 4 November 1775, the Continental Congress adopted a resolution ordering an increase in the Army to 20,372 soldiers and standardized regimental size. Each regiment (battalion) was to contain 728 men divided among eight companies. Each company was to contain one captain, two lieutenants, one ensign, four sergeants, four corporals, two fifers or drummers and seventy-six privates. Congress gave the authority to raise a larger army, but where was the money going to come from?

Some companies had a larger contingency of men. Captain Aaron AORSON's (1740-?) Fifth Company in Colonel Peter GANESVOORT's (1749-1812) Third Regiment of the New York

State Line had 190 men. Captain John KEMPER's company had 170 men. Furthermore, Captain KEMPER had 150 wagons under his command. Each wagon had one additional man riding the left horse nearest the wagon in order to steer them. They were called wagoneers. This comprised a total of 320 men under Captain John KEMPER's command. As of June 2016, Captain KEMPER still held the record for the largest contingency of a company of men in the history of America; and for a very good reason, which will be made clear shortly!

He also fought in the Battles of Assunpink Creek (2 January 1777), Princeton (January 3, 1777), Brandywine (11 September 1777) and Germantown (4 October 1777), and then wintered at Valley Forge (December 1777-18 June 1778). He then fought in the Battle of Monmouth (28 June 1778), served in Sullivan's Expedition (18 June 1779–3 October 1779), under General Edward HAND (1744-1802) against the Indians. He was present at the Siege of Yorktown (19 October 1781) and retired as a major. Having a German bond, he and Captain KEMPER would end up becoming good friends.

What would become crazier than the friendship that was established between Major Johann WILLHEIT and Captain John KEMPER is what would happen in the future. Major WILLHEIT's fifth great-grandson, John GRIMES (1936-?), would become Director of National Security Telecommunications, and then Deputy Assistant Secretary of Defense, under Secretary Richard (Dick) CHENEY (1941-?).

In 1985, he would end up backing Captain KEMPER'S fifth great-grandson, the Reverend Gordon R. PROPER in restoring John KEMPER's rank of captain which was wrongfully taken from him during his turbulent pension years. They would be successful. At this particular time in history, neither one knew that their ancestors were close and that there was a mysterious bond.

On 9 November 1775, Captain MANLEY sailed from Marblehead flying the new pine tree flag from the main truck (a nautical term for a wooden ball at the top of the mast) above the crow's nest.

On 28 November 1775, Captain MANLEY captured one of the most valuable prizes of the American Revolutionary War—the British brig, *Nancy,* carrying much ordinance and military supplies for British troops in Boston which proved invaluable to General George WASHINGTON's army. By the end of 1775, Captain MANLEY captured several additional prizes (ships) carrying cargoes of food, rum, coal and dry goods, all badly needed by the Continental forces.

On 1 January 1776, after Captain John MANLEY proved his bravery on the seas, in addition to his *"great vigilance and industry,"* General WASHINGTON made a New Year's resolution and appointed Captain MANLEY as America's first commodore in charge of the US fleet. Captain MANLEY had forged on the seas like Captain John KEMPER did on land.

Commodore MANLEY, honored by his new rank, continued his aggression on the seas. It was as if Commodore MANLEY had been injected with some sort of steroids; he quickly became bolder and braver. He had drawn the attention of the Royal Navy who were by now, fed up with hearing about his exploits against them. He had to be stopped, even if the Royal Navy had to send out everything they had against him! First, they had to find him.

On 10 January 1776, Colonel Daniel and Captain John KEMPER's brother Jacob was listed as an ensign in the regiment of Colonel Lord STIRLING (1726-1783) of the second company, which was commanded by, Captain Silas HOWELL (1746-1812). One lesson that the KEMPER brothers quickly learned was, whenever something bad happened to an officer of the Continental Army or Continental Navy, the news spread fast like wildfire. All Revolutionary soldiers stood together to the end.

On 19 January 1776, the Second Continental Congress drew up a resolution for clothes for the troops:

"That it be recommended to the assemblies and conventions of the United Colonies, forthwith to cause a suit of clothes, of which the waistcoat and breeches may be made of deer leather, it to be had on reasonable terms, a blanket, felt hat, two shirts, two pairs of hose and two pairs of shoes. To be manufactured, or otherwise procured at reasonable rates; in their respective colonies, for each soldier of the American Army, enlisted therein for the present campaign, and that the same baled invoices, and stored in suitable places, to be delivered to the order of Congress, or the commander-in-chief of the American Army.

Chapter IV
The British are coming!

In February 1776, General WASHINGTON delegated Major General Charles LEE to fortify New York City from British invasion. General LEE ordered Captain Adolph WALDRON (1720-1802) of King's County Light Horse, to fortify the city in preparation for General WASHINGTON's arrival. Captain WALDRON was German and a friend of the KEMPER family. All three KEMPER brothers, Daniel, Jacob, and John, had joined his company. They would all be waiting to see who this man named, General George WASHINGTON was.

By 14 March 1776, after rallying a large number of recruits, Lieutenant Alexander HAMILTON founded the Provincial Artillery Company in New York City and is commissioned a captain. Captain HAMILTON was now feeling his oats; he was quickly being rewarded for his hard work. Action would come soon to the City and everyone would be as ready as they could.

On 29 March 1776, Mathias HOPPER died in New York City. Mathias HOPPER was a politician and ran for various offices in the city of New York. After he passed away, people ran around the city yelling, *"Mathias HOPPER has died!* These statements were published in the New York Genealogical and Biographical Record. After hearing of Matt's death, John rushed over to Eliza's house to comfort her.

After arriving at the HOPPER residence, John rushed up to the door and softly knocked.

Eliza's mother, Anna, answered, *"Come in."*

As John entered, the three girls were huddled around their mother, grieving their father's death. When Eliza saw that it was John, she rushed into his arms. As John held Eliza he said, *"I am so sorry, I can only repeat some wisdom that your father told me at the tavern a short time ago, 'you know John, none of us ever know what tomorrow has in store for any of us.'"*

On 4 April 1776, after a few days' grieving, Mathias HOPPER was laid to rest. Many of his friends, family, and the town's-people attended the funeral. In two more months, the British would be in town, so everyone except the Tories/Loyalists had to start planning for their escape. Things were happening fast, and even though the family was in a mental fog, grieving had to be cut short. They knew they had to move fast or they could be joining Mathias.

Eliza recorded in her diary, that after the death of her father (Mathias), in the spring of 1776, her mother was left with no man to take care of her and her children. After the British captured New York, they pillaged and ravished women and children everywhere. Tories/Loyalists capitalized on this confusion, joined in on these exploits, as well as helping to loot the stores. She went on to explain how her mother, Anna, had fled the city [New York] in fear with her and her two sisters, Anna (Anny) (1767-1817) and Mary (Polly) (1770-1848).

They went across the bay to the Dutch community of Hillsborough and New Millstone, Somerset, New Jersey to escape the war, and there, hopefully her mother could find a new husband. Eliza also explained how her younger sister, Anny, became the first to marry, young at just the age of sixteen, to John VAN NOORTWICK (1762-1828).

After periodical bombing of New York City by the HMS *Asia*, Lieutenant Alexander HAMILTON took his position of defense on the battery. Later he was promoted to captain.

In the spring of 1776, residents began to flee after receiving news that the British Royal Navy was headed to New York City to capture its ports and harbors. John, along with his parents, Jacob and Maria Regina KEMPER, crossed the border to Elizabethtown, New Jersey. This is where John's older brother, Daniel, (who was head of the household by this time), had purchased a residence to try to distance his family from the war. Daniel already had obtained teams (horses and wagons) to move the family's personal belongings.

Mr. MORTON had his furniture and personal affects follow them as they fled across the North River (Hudson River) to Elizabethtown, New Jersey. Here he purchased a large house with a garden adjacent. After abandoning their beautiful home and all their real estate, the British took possession of their pleasant dwelling and appropriated everything that was left behind that the MORTONS did not have room to take, for their own use during the seven succeeding years of war. Jacob KEMPER and his family, likewise, abandoned their home and tavern then fled to Elizabethtown, where the family would all get together to decide what to do next.

In 1776, while in Elizabethtown, New Jersey, John MORTON had a son born whom he named Washington MORTON (1776-1810), after their commander-in-chief, General George WASHINGTON. Washington MORTON was the first child born in the world named after General WASHINGTON; hundreds of others would follow. Mr. MORTON truly believed General WASHINGTON was the right man for the job and named a son after him, proving his beliefs early on. General WASHINGTON would often stop in to see Mr. MORTON and greet his namesake. Anyone donating countless thousands of dollars to their cause, always got General WASHINGTON's and the Continental Congress's personal attention, with many favors that followed.

John and Daniel's older sister, Maria Sophia MORTON, was staying with her uncle and aunt Michiel (Michael) and Johanna Catharina (Ernst) HOFFMAN and their youngest children. Catharina had been incidentally detained in New York, because of some confusion, until the time of departure had gone by. Because of this, the British authorities did not allow her to follow her eldest son and daughter to Elizabethtown, where they had gone to prepare for their arrival.

Mr. HOFFMAN was viewed by, the British, as someone who was trying to escape. He was accused of being favorable to the American cause and was imprisoned by the Hessian officers. An illness he contracted because of his sufferings while in prison, ended in his death, and he never saw his family reunited. His widow remained in New York until she could reunite with the rest of the family. After Mr. HOFFMAN'S death, his 178 acres of land southeast across the river from New York City, near Allendale, New Jersey, was left to his widow, Johanna Catharina (Ernst) HOFFMAN.

Mr. MORTON later removed to Basking Ridge, while Jacob and Maria Regina KEMPER removed fourteen miles further inland to Germantown, New Jersey. The house Mr. MORTON purchased in Basking Ridge was two stories, situated on the high road, about half-way down a hill. On one side, the parlor windows were even with the ground; on the other, was a high porch with seats, the steps of which led to the second story.

In front was a small courtyard, enclosed by pales (stakes); and on the side down the hill, an excellent garden. It was a comfortable, convenient house; and the furniture, plates, books, pictures, and mirrors brought from New York, gave it the appearance of a gentleman's residence. Any Continental officers in the area always stopped by and received Mr. MORTON's generous hospitality.

The American troops were constantly passing to and fro, and Mr. MORTON's house was frequently filled with officers, who were always received and treated with hospitality. All were freely given shelter, food, and relief for the sick and wounded. Their horses were given shelter and fodder (corn stalks, hay, or straw) in the stables out back. There was also a blacksmith available if their horses needed new shoes or hoof care.

Since Mr. MORTON was so hospitable, many Continental officers would often detour to make sure they would be able to stop there for comfort on their journey. Who would not want to be in Mr. MORTON's company?

Later in history, a similar sort of occurrence took play in Germany, when Oskar SCHINDLER (1908-1974) wined and dined in order to gain favor with top Nazi leaders, who ended up depending on him and showed him many favors, in return. He needed these favors in order to capitalize on the opportunities: the power, the money, and prestige that they afforded. However, Oscar SCHINDLER used the Jews as workers for the German army and was not in control of the outcome of their fate. He later bought the freedom of 1,200 Jews.

John MORTON worked with and for the Continental Army and their cause. They never tried to control him. He fed, clothed and hospitalized them and never used them to make money or gain power. Mr. MORTON made money from his own business but donated all of it to the American Revolution. He was a more polished and generous benefactor as his heart and soul were truly behind the American cause. There was nothing for him to gain, except feeling good about himself for helping a worthy cause, which seemed hopeless. The overwhelming power of the opposition never shook him.

The residence of Mr. MORTON on the high road and near headquarters exposed them to great expense, fatigue and labor. As a party of hungry soldiers would pass by, Mr. MORTON would call to them saying, *"Come eat, rest."* They would be given a loaf of bread and another prepared. These also would be called for and bestowed in the same manner, together with beer and cider, with whatever other provisions the house afforded.

The seat of General Lord STIRLING, called by the country-people, "the Buildings," was two miles' distance. It was designed to imitate the residence of an English nobleman. The stables, coach-houses and other offices, ornamented with cupolas (a look out, a widow's walk on top of a building) and gilded vanes, were built around a large paved court behind the mansion. The front, with piazzas (porch), opened onto a fine lawn, descending to a considerable stream called "the Black River." A large hall extended through the center of the house. On one side there was a drawing room with painted walls and a stucco ceiling.

Lord STIRLING had grown close to Mr. MORTON and the KEMPER brothers. When all else failed, all they had left were themselves. The Continental bond was strong. It is important to show how the continuity of the Continental officers interwove and how they always came together as one, including any interruption of treachery.

William Alexander, "Lord STIRLING," (Earl of Stirling), had married Sarah (1725-1805), daughter of Colonel Philip LIVINGSTON (1686-1749) and sister of Governor William LIVINGSTON (1723-1790), one of the signers of the US Constitution. After Sarah had married Lord STIRLING, she became known as "Lady Sarah." They had two daughters, Lady Mary ALEXANDER (1749-1820) and Lady Kitty (1755-1826).

Lord STIRLING's stepmother, Madam (Mary Sprat) ALEXANDER (1691-1760), owned a large establishment in New York City and acquired property by trade. Lord STIRLING, having inherited a large fortune from his father, had become a very wealthy and prominent man. He used his own money to outfit his troops and, like Mr. MORTON, contributed much of his fortune to the cause of the Revolution. He and Mr. MORTON were like two peas in a pod; their bond became strong.

Because Lord STIRLING was a heavy drinker, he enjoyed stopping by at Mr. MORTON's for a taste of his fine wines. He often attended General WASHINGTON's visits and enjoyed the company of Mr. MORTON's in-laws, Colonel Daniel and Captain John KEMPER, besides working closely with them in the army.

At a distance of about a half of a mile from Mr. MORTON's residence, in two farmhouses lived the family of Colonel Elias BOUDINOT (1749-1831), who had retired there from his elegant seat in Elizabethtown, New Jersey. Continental officers everywhere surrounded Mr. MORTON, including his brothers-in-law. In this case, instead of Rome, all roads led to Mr. MORTON. Colonel BOUDINOT, likewise, became a close friend of Mr. MORTON's and his in-laws', Colonel Daniel and Captain John KEMPER. Lord STIRLING often seemed to lodge with the MORTON's.

Also, in 1776, Daniel and his two brothers, Jacob and John, being in the New Jersey Line, participated in America's first battle in Brooklyn. Jacob went on to become a captain in the artillery of the New Jersey Line for most of the Revolution. Daniel became colonel, aide-de-camp to General WASHINGTON and deputy clothier-general of the Continental Army. Daniel later helped procure his brother, John's, appointment as captain and wagon master. Later John served directly under General WASHINGTON and was ordered to become a lieutenant in the US Navy for hidden reasons.

On 4 April 1776, the same day as the funeral for Mathias HOPPER, General WASHINGTON left Cambridge, Massachusetts with nineteen thousand Continental troops and marched to Lower Manhattan in defense of New York City. Once he arrived in the city, he had to position his army at various locations surrounding the city until he learned where the British's general Sir William

HOWE (1729-1845) was going to land. He could then regroup his army for defense of the city.

The **KEMPER** family Bible records that all three **KEMPER** brothers were in this army that ended up fighting in the Battle of Brooklyn. This would be the first battle that the **KEMPER** brothers would light their matchsticks on. John was in his glory as he was now a soldier, his dream fulfilled. One small detail was being overlooked here; the British could bombard the Continental Army with little risk to their troops. They could keep them on standby to finish off General **WASHINGTON**.

On 8 April 1776, Simon **SARTWELL** Jr. (1722-1790) is listed as a lieutenant in the Continental Army. He ended up crossing the Delaware on Captain John **KEMPER'S** flatboats for General **WASHINGTON**'s march on Trenton (26 December 1777). He also participated in the Battles of Princeton (3 January 1777), and, Saratoga (19 September–7 October 1777), spent the winter at Valley Forge (18 December 1777-18 June 1778), and participated in the Battle of Monmouth (28 June 1778) and Sullivan's Expedition (18 June–10 October 1779). On 21 March 1780, he was promoted to captain and was on duty with his regiment at West Point.

On 13 April 1776, after General **WASHINGTON** had arrived at Captain **WALDRON**'s fortification he met the **KEMPER** brothers for the first time, mounted on horseback in their dazzling uniforms as his welcoming committee. John **KEMPER** finally saw who this man, George **WASHINGTON** was. Here was a man who rode a white horse and sat tall in his saddle; he reminded John of his grandfather—bold, brave and unafraid of anything.

When General **WASHINGTON** got off his horse, John's eyes began to swell, as General **WASHINGTON**'s presence quickly took center stage. General **WASHINGTON** looked down on everyone, as he stood well over six-feet tall. Likewise, he had so many thousands of troops behind him. How could we possibly lose? Something else was going on here; John was seeing a vision of his fortune-teller in a fog, a white horse.... John's dream of following in his grandfather's footsteps was about to come true ... or was it?

General WASHINGTON was always kept abreast of who was who, in and for the Continental Congress and Continental Army. He was informed that John MORTON, who had been labeled as a "Rebel Banker" by the British, was their wealthiest contributor to their cause. He was informed that, because of Mr. MORTON's marriage to Maria Sophia KEMPER, he had outfitted his three brothers-in-law, Daniel, Jacob, and John KEMPER, among many others. However, family always got the best. Mr. MORTON favored whoever favored them.

Soon, General WASHINGTON would meet other congressional suggestions and other recruit recommendations by Benjamin FRANKLIN (1706-1790) like General Marquis DE LAFAYETTE, General Count Casimir PULASKI (1745-1779), and General Baron Frederick Wilhelm VON STEUBEN (1730-1794). As always, General WASHINGTON had the final decision on how these recruits were to be used. They would all advance on their own merit. Mr. FRANKLIN hauled in three big fish for General WASHINGTON, while in Paris.

The only question now was would General WASHINGTON be able to defeat the mightiest army and navy on earth? The answer would come through his recruitments. Could this be John's dream of following in his grandfather's footsteps coming true? Would he have the chance to be heroic? Although something was missing here, what was it? A flag! Every country has a flag. Where was ours? What would it look like?

On 17 April 1776, Commodore John MANLEY because he remained an apple of General WASHINGTON's eye (high standards, cherished above all others), was given command of the Continental battleship, USS *Hancock,* named after the President of the Continental Congress, John HANCOCK (1737-1793). This battleship was America's best. No honor could have been higher for this new commodore.

In May 1776, with news spreading fast like wild fire of the British Royal Navy heading for New York City, Anthony MAXWELL (1754-1825), after reading the fliers he picked up at Kemper's Tavern, quickly joined the Continental Army. He entered as a private in Captain William WEEKS/WICKS's (1755-1843) Company, Colonel William MALCOLM's (1745-1791) Regiment. Anthony, likewise, became instrumental in enlisting recruits and volunteered for foraging excursions with Captain John KEMPER, while stationed at Valley Forge.

On 6 June 1776, the Hessian troops entered and captured Elizabethtown. John KEMPER was in the process of helping his brother, Daniel, move their family belongings to Morristown, New Jersey, when he grabbed his grandfather's royal sword. It was a good thing that he had, for they were unable to get away with more than two teams in moving their belongings before the Hessians captured their home. The family had been fortunate enough to have moved their most important artifacts (oil paintings) and treasured belongings in the first two loads.

John and Daniel's father, Jacob KEMPER, stayed at the Elizabethtown residence to protect their valuables. When the Hessians seized control of the KEMPER home, they did not detain Jacob because he was German and spoke the language as fluently as they did; however, they would not allow him to take anything with him. Even though they had gotten away with two loads, many of the KEMPER family's personal belongings and treasures were still lost at this time. Daniel, alone, estimated his loss to be around $3,000, a considerable amount at that time in history.

On 20 June 1776, after the British fleet had headed for New York, Major General Artemas WARD (1727-1800) wrote a letter to General WASHINGTON reporting that Lieutenant Colonel Archibald CAMPBELL (1739-1791) had been captured at sea by the Patriots. Colonel CAMPBELL, who was sent to join the British fleet off the coast of Massachusetts, was not notified that Vice Admiral Sir Richard HOWE (1726-1799) had taken the entire Royal British fleet to New York City. Therefore, Colonel CAMPBELL was easily captured with no protection. Though not intentional, miscommunication takes place in every war.

On 4 July 1776, delegates from the thirteen states got together to declare their independence from Great Britain and democracy was born. America had now been declared an independent nation by, its leaders. It would continue to grow and get better organized as time went on. After Benjamin FRANKLIN assisted in drafting the Declaration of Independence, he was elected as America's first Ambassador to France.

On 9 July 1776, the Patriots tore down the statue of King George III (1738-1820) in New York City. They melted parts of it down to make bullets to use against the British, how ironic. Shortly after, the British landed on Staten Island, New York.

In early July 1776, 427 British battle ships, loaded with countless thousands of troops and commanded by General Sir William HOWE, landed on Staten Island, New York. General HOWE unloaded thirty-two thousand troops on Long Island. Watching the British unload thousands of artillery, wagons and troops, had a stunning, paralyzing effect on all who looked on in amazement. General WASHINGTON's entire navy could not take on one British man-of-war battle ship; therefore, he would have to draw General HOWE inland away from his superior navy.

The relentless sound of steel cannons and guns clanking could be heard echoing everywhere as they unloaded the ships. After the long sea voyage across the Atlantic, the British were antsy and ready for action! The men were like the cows coming out of the barn in the spring, excited and full of energy after the long confinement. General WASHINGTON, after hearing of the landing, prepared for the defense of the city.

Counting on this show of force, General HOWE offered a pardon to all Rebels. General WASHINGTON retorted, *"Those who have committed no fault want no pardon."* Clouds were moving rapidly overhead, as if a storm was coming in, but the storm had already arrived. The British troops came on like an endless army of ants. They were like a devastating infestation or plague of locusts, devouring everything in sight. They were everywhere, pillaging, raping women and children. There was no doubt that when this force met General WASHINGTON and the Continental Army, this war would be over fast ... wrong!

After General HOWE had arrived, the Tories/Loyalists quickly swarmed and informed him that all he needed to put a smile on any Indian's face and win them over to his side was to offer, steel knives, rifles, whiskey, and tobacco. General HOWE smiled and replied, *"All these items and much more are in my specialty."*

On 17 July 1776, at reveille, General WASHINGTON's army was informed that the enemy had landed in Elizabethtown, New Jersey. Troops were ordered to march to that town for its defense. On their arrival at 2:00 p.m., they discovered that it had been a false alarm.

This was part of one of the problems during the Revolution; the people were scared, jittery and jumped easily to conclusions. They often drew troops away from the main body because of fear that they were going to be under attack. On other occasions, Tories/Loyalists manufactured these stories as a diversion, as to assist the British by confusing the Rebels.

The Continental Army, being in the vicinity of the British Army, decided to cross over to Staten Island that night to visit General HOWE's troops, but a hurricane made landfall, which prevented their embarkation. After the storm and torrential rains had cleared, it was ascertained that they would have been cut off had they landed.

General HOWE's brother, Vice Admiral Richard HOWE (1726-1799), was in command of the naval forces that stood waiting in the harbor for orders. He was the back-up force for his brother. The sight of the 427 battle ships was just astounding. They spread across the vast seascape. According to witnesses of the colonists at the time, because of the towering mass of masts jutting into the sky, it looked like a vast forest on the ocean.

The KEMPER brothers, among other colonists watching from across the bay, looked on in wonder. One of the colonists who was witnessing this astounding sight turned toward the KEMPER brothers and remarked, *"How in the hell are you going to defeat that?"* The brothers answered only with a silent glare.

On 14 August 1776, a deserter from the British Army said, that they had about twenty-five thousand troops on Staten Island who were preparing to embark, attack, and capture New York City. General WASHINGTON was well aware that the so-called British deserter was, in fact, a British agent. He had been sent over by General HOWE to get behind enemy lines and feed the Americans what General HOWE wanted them to know in order to intimidate them. In turn, he would inform the British of how the Americans reacted and what they were planning. This action gave General WASHINGTON new ideas.

General WASHINGTON played along; he had ideas of his own on sending agents behind British enemy lines. The "I spy" game was played heavily by both sides during the Revolution. However, General WASHINGTON would later be forced to incorporate a new ingredient into the "I spy" game, which included Captain John KEMPER. Neither side before had ever tried this new idea. Would it work? They had to wait and see!

Since need is the mother of all inventions, ideas, and schemes, something was about to happen that General WASHINGTON would desperately need answers to. However, this would not be the regular routine of an agent being sent behind enemy lines like a deserter, for answers. A new plan would have to be devised to find out what General WASHINGTON and the intelligence committee needed to know. It meant devising a plan to enter into the confines of the mightiest army and navy in the history of the planet earth, even mightier than the Roman Empire and still making history. The Romans could transport troops around the Mediterranean Sea, while the British could transport troops around the world.

He would need to send an agent deep into the heart of the British Empire without suspicion, but how could he do that? Whenever an American deserted to the British lines, it was generally because he was hungry and needed clothes. These kinds of deserters were always under suspicion and in the spotlight. How could General WASHINGTON get an agent in without suspicion? The answer would come later under a cloud of mystery, and General WASHINGTON would become the master of intelligence during the Revolution. Superb intelligence would make America strong, but it also would take daring.

On 15 August 1776, General WASHINGTON placed Major General Nathanael GREENE in charge of the Continental Army on Long Island. However, General GREENE fell sick and was unable to participate in the upcoming first battle of the American Revolution. General GREENE stationed his army at Fort Washington's sister fort, Fort Lee, across the Hudson River at the foot of the Palisades.

Fort Lee was formally named, Fort Constitution and renamed to honor General Charles LEE, who had fled from the British Army to join the American Army. General LEE was put second-in-command under General WASHINGTON. The British released information that General LEE was a traitor and would be hunted down, but was General LEE really a traitor, or was he just another agent placed behind enemy lines to infiltrate the Continental Army? Time would tell!

On 17 August 1776, General WASHINGTON received intelligence that the British had struck their tents and were getting ready to attack. He immediately issued a proclamation for all women, children and infirm people to leave the city (New York) until after the engagement. All troops were closely inspected with regard to their arms and ammunition. All troops rested on their arms all day and night so that they would not be taken by surprise.

On 21 August 1776, torrential rains and severe thunderstorms were pounding the city of New York. A bolt of lightning struck the Continental camp and killed one captain, one lieutenant and one ensign. The Continental Army not only had to worry about the invading army, but being struck by Mother Nature as well. Whose side was Mother Nature on? She would strike again!

On 27 August 1776, the first major battle of the American Revolution, known as the Battle of Brooklyn, also known as the Battle of Long Island, was fought. The victory quickly went to General HOWE. Whatever General HOWE looked at and desired was his for the taking and it happened fast.

As the Continental Army was retreating from the overwhelming number of British forces, the enemy squeezed between them and the fort. As the Rebels were being driven from place to place till 3:00 p.m., they resolved to die rather than being taken prisoner. They were now stopped at Mill Pond, the last location for escape. As they attempted to swim across the pond, weighed down by all their heavy gear, many died by drowning, the way they preferred.

Also on this day, *"256 Maryland troops were killed in the assaults in front of the Old Stone House and fewer than a dozen made it back to the American lines. General WASHINGTON, watching from a redoubt* [stronghold] *on nearby Cobble Hill said to Major General Israel 'Old Put' PUTNAM* [1718-1790], *'Good God, what brave fellows I must this day lose!'"*

On 28 August 1776, Brigadier General Lord STIRLING boldly held off the British, allowing for General WASHINGTON and the remaining Continental Army to evacuate. While escaping by boat to the Island of Manhattan, they slowly faded from view through the heavy night fog. General Lord STIRLING, who was now surrounded by the British, refused to stoop to being captured by them and instead he broke through the British lines and surrendered to the Hessian troops commanded by Leopold Philip DE HEISTER/VON HEISTER (1707-1777).

During the Battle of Long Island, General HOWE's trophies of the day included capturing Brigadier General Lord STIRLING and Major General, John SULLIVAN (1740-1795), amongst many others. General STIRLING was several months a prisoner on parole in New York City and exchanged later in the year for Royal Governor Montfort BROWNE (ca.1740-?). General HOWE's ego continued to rise, feeling that his incursion into the States was going to be a cake-walk. Nothing put more glee and smiles on his face than high anticipation of capturing America's best, General WASHINGTON.

On 30 August 1776, General HOWE called for a flag of truce, offering an account of American officers that had been captured and now held prisoner. He then offered an exchange for British officers being held by the Americans.

General HOWE paroled General SULLIVAN and made him believe that he was being sent to the Continental Congress to deliver a message of peace. A formal request from General HOWE was sent to Congress via captured American general John SULLIVAN. A committee made up of Benjamin FRANKLIN, John ADAMS (1735-1826) and Edward RUTLEDGE (1749-1800) met with General HOWE on the 6 September 1776. Discussions immediately halted when General HOWE announced, *"If you lay down your arms, all Rebels may await the generosity of the British Empire."*

The committee then returned to Philadelphia and reported to Congress that, *"General HOWE has no propositions to make us and America is to expect nothing but total unconditional submission."* This committee might have exaggerated the outcome of this meeting in order to maintain animosity toward the British. This author could not find the disposition claimed by this committee. General HOWE did not publish an account. The British just commented, *"They met, they talked, they parted; and now nothing remains but to fight it out."*

General WASHINGTON and his army was no match for the well-trained British Army and a dominant conquering world naval power, but he had to let his presence be known. In other words, he was mystically saying, *"Here I am; come and catch me if you can!"*

On 22 September 1776, Major General John SULLIVAN was exchanged for British General Richard PRESCOTT (1725-1788), who had been captured on 17 November 1775 at Quebec.

On 27 September 1776, at camp Mount Washington, Lieutenant Simon SARTWELL turned in a receipt for pay for enlisting recruits. The Revolution had become a serious part of Lieutenant SARTWELL's life and he was working as hard as he could to acquire new recruits. He had become an intricate part of General WASHINGTON's needs. Paymaster Benjamin HEYWOOD (1745-1816) was one of many who were assigned to pay officers for bringing in recruits for the Continental Army.

After September 1776, Benjamin FRANKLIN was sent to Paris to assume his new duties as ambassador to France. The French subsequently transported him to Paris. During his nine-year stay in France (1776-1785), Mr. FRANKLIN was able to acquire three recruits who would make a big difference during the Revolution: Captain Marquis DE LAFAYETTE, Count Casimir PULASKI, and Frederick Wilhelm VON STEUBEN. He eventually obtained France's full support, and then the war had a new front.

After General HOWE quickly took Brooklyn from America's main army, the British knew the war was over. Or was it? General HOWE waited for General WASHINGTON to surrender ... and waited and waited ... Finally, he sent an officer with his team under a flag of truce to negotiate their surrender. The officer quickly returned, yelling, *"General WASHINGTON is gone!"*

General HOWE froze in his saddle in amazement, his face expressing total disbelief as he jerked his horse's head back and forth with its reins. Then he paused for a moment, gave a slight grin, bobbed his head and then responded, *"The fox is on the run! It does not matter, I just wiped out the best he could put together, the war is all over; it is just a matter of time!"* After the Battle of Brooklyn, General WASHINGTON and the Continental Army quickly regrouped.

What General HOWE was unaware of was that General WASHINGTON was fully aware of the terror that this mighty super-power could bring down on any country. General WASHINGTON did not intend to defeat General HOWE but, instead, to outlast him on WASHINGTON's own turf. Sooner or later, General HOWE would have to go home. He needed to draw him inland away from his navy, and he did so. Now, the playing field was a little more even.

General HOWE continually laughed about the size of General WASHINGTON's forces, as they continued to dwindle away, through either mass desertions or being killed in action. However, whenever General WASHINGTON lost 15,000 or more troops to either of these reasons, he could always hope for recruits as replacements. He constantly had men working at that. General HOWE could not; he already had all the troops the British Empire or Germans could offer. Therefore, when one of his soldiers died, he was surely dead. The only hopes he had for replacements, could only come from either desertions of General WASHINGTON's army or Tories/Loyalists; both of whom were loyal to no one other than themselves.

General HOWE would only use a small force of 15,000 troops and 1,500 wagons and artillery when he was going to conquer a city, in addition to having the availability of naval bombardment. Whatever small force General HOWE picked was indeed, larger than anything General WASHINGTON could imagine putting together. Even if he had the troops, he still could not match the artillery or naval power. General WASHINGTON's troops were spread thinly around the outskirts of the British-occupied territories, supplying intelligence to General WASHINGTON of all their movements.

If needed, General HOWE could call into service thousands of additional troops, wagons and artillery, which he had stationed at his home base in New York City, New York. However, he needed to maintain them at that location if he intended to hold that island. This was a strategic location with access to the mouth of all waterways of the area, making it extremely effective for control of the region.

He also had military posts stationed in various strategically available localities, like Long Island and New Jersey. Furthermore, he had additional troops and artillery on board his brother's ships, but one day the ships would have to return home and they would be needed to sail the vessel. General HOWE was much like Julius Caesar (100BC-44 BC) in the days of Ancient Rome, *"He came, he saw, he conquered!"* More importantly, he was hungry for more!

Since General WASHINGTON could not defeat General HOWE in battle, would there be any way that this master general of the British Empire could be removed, without having to face him in battle? The answer would come soon, early on in the Revolution in Philadelphia. Then, just maybe, the fighting plane could be leveled.

General WASHINGTON was like a ghost whenever he and his Continental Army would appear for an attack. Upon strong resistance, he would seemingly disappear and reappear at a new location ready to resume his attack. Wherever the British were, General WASHINGTON was always on their heels and attacking them at every chance he got; however, he always left an exit with backup not far away.

Whenever General WASHINGTON's army was advancing or retreating, Tories/Loyalists harassed them. They were a nuisance to smaller companies of troops while attacking and fleeing like mosquitoes; Tories were a constant threat. Smaller companies of troops would often have to take detours around towns to avoid encountering them. The majority of all cities and towns were for the Crown, occupied mostly by Tories/Loyalists.

General WASHINGTON was beyond clever but he had something else up his sleeve. The only question was would it work? If successful, General HOWE and the British Empire would be caught completely off guard by not knowing how to battle this new tactical warfare—nor, that it was even going on. It would not come into full blossom until 22 December 1778, when Congressman Henry J. LAURENS (1724-1792), president of the Continental Congress, called him to Philadelphia.

He would bring Captain John KEMPER permanently on board his entourage to test the waters. Moreover, how could he maintain its secrecy? If its operatives could not maintain secrecy, his new operation would be shut down permanently! Was his new idea worth the gamble on just one man? He would have to find the right man who could stand up to interrogation. We would soon find out …

On 15 September 1776, Major General Sir William HOWE captured New York City. Captain KEMPER's cousin, Captain Sebastian BEAUMAN (1739-1803), who was assisting in the evacuation, was the last to leave New York City. John's dream of following in his brother Daniel's footsteps to King's College (Columbia University) collapsed all around him. It looked and felt like the British were here to stay. General WASHINGTON was never too ashamed to retreat in order to save his army so that he could regroup, rather than sacrifice them.

Some never learn from history, like General George Armstrong CUSTER (1839-1876), who sacrificed his entire company of men to a massacre at Little Big Horn (25-26 June 1876). Two other companies of cavalry that he sent in advance to meet up with him were smart enough to retreat. Entering the Indian Nations in that particular time and location in history was like entering a mad hornet's nest. All his company suffered some of the most bizarre torture in American history, regarding genitals, far too graphic to portray here!

On 16 September 1776, the Continental Congress ordered an additional 88 regiments for the duration of the war. They appointed them among the following states: Maryland, 8; Massachusetts, 15; New Hampshire, 3; New Jersey, 4; New York, 4; North Carolina, 9; Pennsylvania, 12; Rhode Island, 2; South Carolina, 6; and Virginia, 15. As General HOWE continued to conquer, the Continental Congress continued to build their army, but where would they get the money to pay these additional soldiers?

Civilian and military leaderships are generally different and rightfully so. General WASHINGTON, when possible, always gave the Continental Congress a chance to make the dominant decision in hopes they would match his by suggestion. General WASHINGTON respected the civilian-constituted authority but did not appreciate them interfering in military affairs especially when, they were not present in the field.

Chapter V
Who Burned New York City?

After General HOWE captured New York City, Congressman John JAY (1745-1829) and several senior officers, including General Nathanael GREENE, suggested that they burn the city to the ground so that the British could not benefit from the fruits of the hard labors of the colonists. General WASHINGTON submitted this idea to the Second Continental Congress, who not agreeing with their colleague John JAY replied, *"It should in no event be damaged."*

After General WASHINGTON read Congress's response to his senior officers, they all stared with a blank glare. After studying General WASHINGTON and the American Revolution for the past forty-five years, and majoring in psychology, a half way decent psychological analysis of what event took place next is as follows:

Either 1 General WASHINGTON directly told his senior staff to send officers in under sealed lips to take care of this matter themselves and burn the city, or most likely he 2. After reading Congress's response to his senior officers stated, *"Well, you heard what Congress thinks of our idea, but if some patriotic Americans were to take this matter into their own hands and burn this city to the ground, there is nothing we can do about it."*

On 21 September 1776, fire broke out in the City starting at the Fighting Cocks Tavern near Whitehall Slip. About seven hundred buildings were burned including the Trinity Church (Madam Ursula's great fire?). General WASHINGTON wrote to John HANCOCK in Congress denying charges of arson. The following evidence supports this author's analysis.

General Sir William HOWE sent a message to London suggesting the fire was deliberately set, *"A most horrid attempt was made by a number of wretches to burn the town."* The British were so upset because their army needed the supplies they lost in the fire to live off, that they decided to start the city's first fire department to prevent this kind of incident from reoccurring.

Royal Governor William TRYON (1729-1788) suspected that General WASHINGTON was responsible and wrote that, *"many circumstances led to conjecture that Mr. WASHINGTON was privy to this villainous act"* and that, *"Some officers of his army were found concealed in the city."*

Finally, General WASHINGTON himself wrote to his cousin Lund WASHINGTON (1737-1796) about the fire. *"Providence or some good honest fellow has done more for us than we were deposed of doing for ourselves."* General WASHINGTON might have believed that since he was writing his family, this letter would never be released. There is a lot more evidence from eyewitness reports that could be released on this case, but it would take away from the purpose of this story.

The French were our allies but remained behind the scene for several years before they were officially declared as such. They were waiting for an opening to their advantage. By the fall of 1776, a trading firm was the front for the French assistance. Through this fictitious shipping firm, they supplied to the Rebels *"nearly 300,000 pounds of gunpowder, 30,000 muskets, 3,000 tents, more than 200 pieces of artillery, and clothing for 30,000 soldiers."* Politics was already starting to play a role!

On 11 October 1776, a barge of General WASHINGTON's was coming down the Hudson River when it was taken for one of the enemy's by the engineers at Fort Washington, who fired an eighteen-pounder at it, killing three men on board. Friendly fire takes place in every war, especially when nobody knows where the enemy is or where they are coming from. Everyone was fearful, with a high anxiety and trigger-happy. So many were scared, antsy and wanted to play safe. This was indeed, the first major war in America. Most did not know how a war was supposed to go.

On 28 October 1776, General WASHINGTON and the Continental Army took another major defeat and were once again sent on the run after their loss at White Plains. At this time, the main part of the Continental Army mass deserted and went home. Everyone at this point thought the Revolution was over. Nothing good was becoming of General WASHINGTON's army. They were losing everywhere! Many truly believed that the cause was lost and General WASHINGTON and the Continental Army were finished. Was there anyway any new life and hope could come out of all these loses?

Those who stayed on had nowhere else to go. However, General WASHINGTON was about to pull another rabbit out of his hat in August 1777, while in Philadelphia. General WASHINGTON always looked at every day as a new day, a beginning, not a failure, just like in the birth of a human being.

Chapter VI
The Headless Horseman
(A Legend Is Born)

Something else happened at the Battle of White Plains that would be talked and written about forever in the hearts of Americans. General William HEATH (1737-1814) sent Colonel William MALCOLM's regiment, along with Lieutenant Ephraim FENNO (1734-1820) of artillery and one field piece to be stationed on Merritt Hill. Lieutenant FENNO fired a cannonball at the advancing British and Hessian troops. It decapitated a German Hessian artilleryman. Anthony MAXWELL, who was in Colonel MALCOLM's regiment, personally witnessed this event and talked about it for years to come. Lieutenant Daniel KEMPER and Captain Alexander HAMILTON, likewise, fought there.

Shattered remains of the Hessian's head were left all over the battlefield, while his comrades hastily carried his body away. He was later buried just nine miles west of White Plains in the graveyard of the Old Dutch Church in Sleepy Hollow, on the eastern banks of the Hudson River. Every Halloween night he rises as a malevolent ghost, furiously seeking his lost head. Originally he was known as the Headless Hessian; later it was changed to the Headless Horseman.

On 9 November 1776, at Fort Ticonderoga, New York, Captain John KEMPER's brother Jacob was appointed first lieutenant of the third Regimental Continental Corps of Artillery—Colonel John CRANE's (1744-1805)—and assigned to Captain John WINSLOW's (1701-1778) company.

After the Revolution Jacob helped his brother Daniel organize the Society of Cincinnati and they became two of its original members (OM). They tried to get their brother, John, to help them, but he was busy settling the affairs of their late brother-in-law, John MORTON, with General WASHINGTON and Congress.

Colonel Daniel and Captain Jacob KEMPER planned for the regulations to read that, all officers would have to prove three years solid service in the Continental Army or navy in order to become a member. This would eliminate all the many thousands of deserters that could not prove this length of time. Most deserters were non-officers anyway, but some were high-ranking, like Major General Benedict ARNOLD.

For some unknown and fully unrecorded reason, Jacob and Daniel had a serious difference of opinion at the Society of Cincinnati. Jacob later separated from the family. He strolled off to himself, sort of like the "black sheep" in the family. Something terrible must have happened to distance him from his family, but the family anywhere did not note it. It was as if he had disappeared off the face of the earth. Jacob died young in 1800, no reason recorded, not even by his own family.

Chapter VII
The British capture Washington!

On 16 November 1776, General HOWE surrounded Fort Washington (named after General WASHINGTON) and closed in on General WASHINGTON and the remainder of his Continental Army. Eight thousand British troops faced the remaining 2,900 plus troops left after the mass desertion. This was General WASHINGTON's last stronghold on the Island of Manhattan. Not being able to stand fast and stay in control was sort of like General Armstrong CUSTER's last stand.

General HOWE called for their surrender, but was refused. A bombardment followed from British batteries across the Harlem River. The British and Hessian troops then closed in from the north, east and south, while massacring 2,900 Continental soldiers. General WASHINGTON's Continental Army was decimated. What would he do now? Ironically, this would be the only *"Washington"* that the British would ever capture throughout the entire Revolution. General WASHINGTON learned quickly and would never allow himself and his Continental Army to ever be cornered again.

General WASHINGTON retreated west across the Hudson River to Fort Lee, located on the crest of the Hudson Palisades. The Palisades are an incredible sight, a line of over twelve miles of steep cliffs along the western side of the lower Hudson River that jetted nine hundred to one thousand feet up into the sky and are about three hundred feet wide. There was lush forest on both the top and bottom of the cliffs, but this was no time for sightseeing, the army had to get to safety where it could regroup.

Lieutenant Daniel KEMPER, who also was made an adjutant (a staff officer who serves as administrative assistant to the commanding officer), aided in the evacuation of Fort Lee as they trampled through the wilderness, west as they headed for the Delaware River. From this location, General WASHINGTON had quick and easy access for making assaults on British posts, wherever they had quickly been set up. His defeat at Fort Washington taught him to steer clear of the mighty British navy. He needed to draw General HOWE inland away from his navy.

What was unknown at the time was that, after the Battle of Long Island, Daniel KEMPER, in anticipation of the worst, sent his brother John to camp out on Malta Island, near New Hope with access to his specialty, wagons, wagon boats and flatboats should they be needed for their escape. All John needed was the authority. This location was within a minimal distance from America's capital, Philadelphia. Many decisions had to be made quickly, rather right or wrong, only time would tell.

John had been passing back and forth knowing that his brother, Daniel, was likely still in battle. John was anxiously waiting for the opportunity to prove his expertise in wagons and flatboats and his worth to both his brother and his commander-in-chief. All he needed was for something to break the ice. That something was about to happen. Finally then, he could meet his destiny.

General Lord CORNWALLIS (1738-1805) took four thousand troops six miles north of Fort Lee and marched south to put the squeeze on General WASHINGTON, but General WASHINGTON had already left. By the time General CORNWALLIS reached the fort, he found that General Nathanael GREENE had hastily abandoned it and marched his army to join General WASHINGTON at Hackensack, New Jersey. In his rush, he left behind fifty cannons, huge stores of flour and ammunition and vast quantities of other supplies. General CORNWALLIS then went in pursuit of General WASHINGTON's army.

On 30 November 1776, the American Army, already in meager condition, was further depleted when more than two thousand militiamen from Maryland and New Jersey reached the end of their enlistment terms and went home. General WASHINGTON sent repeated pleas to General Charles LEE (1732-1782) to bring help and join him. General LEE ignored his requests, refusing to help and hoping for General WASHINGTON's defeat and his own ascent to command, since General LEE was already second in command. Everyone was forgetting that General LEE was a British deserter, or was he?

General LEE had previously commented, *"WASHINGTON was not fit to command a sergeant's guard."* General LEE was a legend only in his own mind. General LEE had married a squaw, a daughter of a Mohawk Indian chief. Because of General LEE's temper and intemperance, the Mohawks nicknamed him *"Ounewaterika"* (Boiling Water).

On 11 December 1776, after General WASHINGTON continually marched the depleted Continental Army across New Jersey, managing to stay one step ahead of General CORNWALLIS, he finally reached the Delaware. They started collecting a small flotilla of boats along the banks and burned the rest they could not use, so that the British could not follow them. Everywhere they went looked like the end of the road. Nobody seemed to be able to run far and fast enough to escape the terror of the mighty British Army. Would the British run the Americans down forever?

They then began crossing the river into Pennsylvania. The British and Hessians, who had just entered and captured Trenton, watched the boats burning on the shore, while the last Americans were quickly rowing for their lives. They all began laughing hysterically. They were confident that their victory in the States was going to be a quick and easy one, a real cakewalk.

General CORNWALLIS so sure of having defeated General WASHINGTON returned to camp and ordered his personal belongings to be placed aboard an England-bound ship preparing to go home. What the British were about to find out was, that General WASHINGTON was more deadly after a defeat, than he was after a victory. Could that really be possible? We would soon find out.

After they crossed the river, Adjutant Daniel KEMPER reported to General WASHINGTON that, *"his brother John has access to flatboats, should they be needed for his transportation."*

General WASHINGTON quickly jerked his head to the right to face Daniel as he glared at him intensely. General WASHINGTON then slowly asked, *"How many flatboats does your brother have access to?"*

Daniel replied, *"As many that are needed to transport our entire army, its horses and artillery faster down river instead of trampling through the wilderness. He is camped out on Malta Island, your Excellency. He also knows where to obtain larger flatboats for transporting Conestoga wagons if need be; all he needs is the authority."*

General WASHINGTON continued to glare at Daniel for a moment then, slowly turned back to refocus on what needed to be done next.

General WASHINGTON, in one of his rare moments of doubt, wrote to his favorite cousin, Lund WASHINGTON in Virginia, expressing his distressing situation. After his men continued to surrender to General HOWE on their own, looking for food and shelter, he commented that, *"I am in dire need of new enlistments. If this fails, I think the game will be pretty well up."*

On 12 December 1776, General Charles LEE spent the night at Widow White's Tavern, in Basking Ridge, New Jersey with ladies of the evening. Loyalists (seemingly) quickly gave his location to the British who sent Lieutenant Colonel William HARCOURT

(1743-1830) and Cornet Banastre TARLETON (1754-1833) from New Brunswick, New Jersey to capture General LEE.

They brought a troop of cavalry to watch General LEE's movements. A detachment of seventy light horse surrounded the tavern. Shots were exchanged and General LEE surrendered while still in his dressing gown. He was, subsequently, taken into custody. How interesting that these two officers, who had formerly threatened to hunt him down when he left the British to join the Americans, were the ones who showed up to capture him.

The strategy that General LEE used, by ignoring General WASHINGTON, hoping that General WASHINGTON would be captured or killed, seemingly backfired on him and he was captured instead. It was later uncovered that General LEE might have had this event staged in order to get intelligence to the British, making General WASHINGTON think he was captured.

Since General LEE was British, he sat on the fence, jumping over to whatever side fancied him at the time. He was a real scoundrel in his own right. He always got his jollies by endangering General WASHINGTON, hoping that he would either be killed or removed from command; thereby, General LEE who was second in command, would take his place. The British would be victors.

John KEMPER's brother-in-law, John MORTON, whose hospitality was top-shelf, was always accommodating to Continental officers with fine wines and dinners. He had invited General LEE for breakfast the following morning. When General LEE had not arrived, Mr. MORTON headed out to meet him. As he was heading up the hill to White's Tavern he encountered many of the country people running in great consternation (great fear or shock), exclaiming, *"The British have come to take General LEE!"* How would so many of the town's-people, be privy as to General LEE's whereabouts?

Mr. MORTON hurried on and saw General LEE, who had lost his hat and cloak while seemingly being hastily captured, was being forcibly mounted and carried off by a troop of horse. It appeared the British did not want to waste a lot of time in this capture. What General WASHINGTON was unaware of was that, they had captured a treacherous officer, whom General WASHINGTON would end up paying dearly for in the end. Mr. MORTON, who welcomed all officers, was in the dark as well.

General John SULLIVAN took command of General LEE's two thousand troops, who were well outfitted and did what General LEE refused to do. He headed to reinforce General WASHINGTON at his camp at McKonkey's Ferry on the Delaware River. General WASHINGTON had a surprise in store for everyone. The war was not over, and it had just begun!

Unknown at the time, General LEE, while in his plush accommodation as prisoner, being served fine foods and wines in his three rooms by his personal servants, was drafting battle plans for the British to defeat General WASHINGTON and the Continental Army. General LEE cared for no one other than himself and did not respect any superior authority, including his commander-in-chief's, the Continental Congress, or even the British for that matter.

General LEE was in fact, a double agent giving of himself to whichever side treated him best at the time and never doing anything in exchange but offers of false promises. He would use anyone he could for his own selfishness. Everyone was wrong, but he was always right. He never even cared if he was caught doing wrong. He always had his mouth to back up his actions, attacking everyone verbally, expecting withdrawal.

Chapter VIII
Fire and Sword

Refugees from New York City continued to flood the shores of New Jersey. There were repeated alarms of the British arriving with *"fire and sword,"* (torches blazing for the purpose of burning down innocent families' homes and using sabers to cut down the residents). During these alarms, woman and children were often sent in wagons to cottages among the hills, several miles away. Could this be Madam Ursula's sword on fire?

On one such occasion in November of 1776, there was an alarm at Basking Ridge. Captain KEMPER's brother-in-law, John MORTON, had his children sent at night to a Mr. GOBIES' in the woods. They were placed on their beds in the wagons and well covered up, as it was very cold. They were driven by BELFAST (a young Negro servant, a mode of securing services by wages), who cheered and encouraged them in their dark-some expedition.

After treading a steep and dangerous road, at the risk of their lives, they finally reached their place of refuge. They were received, very kindly, by the good woman of the cottage who gave them some bread and milk and spread their beds on the floor. Great to their astonishment were the arrangements she had made for her own children. She had raised some boards in the corner of the only room in the house under which was a bed of dry leaves, where the children were placed and covered with their clothes and a blanket. Eliza MORTON was scared that they were going to place her there. However, BELFAST comforted her by saying that; he would take care of her by sitting up all night by the fire with her, which he did do, along with the hospitable owners of this humble roof.

On 20 December 1776, another six thousand troops from General Horatio GATES' (1727-1806) division arrived at camp. Soon after, another one thousand militia arrived from Philadelphia under Colonel John CADWALADER (1742-1823). Before long, as more troops began to arrive, General WASHINGTON soon had seven thousand troops fit for duty. General WASHINGTON then informed Daniel that his brother, John, now had the authority he awaited and a dispatch was immediately sent to John's location.

However, Daniel was now just a little confused. Why would General WASHINGTON continue to build his army if he was intending on further retreat; unless, he needed a larger army for defense, after retreating to safety? General WASHINGTON always kept his intentions secret until the moment arrived. That way, he never had to worry about being betrayed.

As General WASHINGTON remained camped out on the banks of the Delaware River, their campfires were blazing to keep the men warm and signify their location for John KEMPER's flatboats. Then it began, from out of the dark of night, blazing torches and lanterns swinging signifying the arrival of John KEMPER and his long line of flatboats. They were coming down the choppy icy Delaware in blizzard condition, through sleet and snow. The flatboats followed close together while his men steered them as they followed KEMPER's lead.

As they got closer to the shores of the Delaware where they were camped, the troops threw their hands up in the air in cheers that their means of transportation had finally arrived. John's brother, Daniel and good friend, Captain Alexander HAMILTON saluted with glee as if they were about to have a small family reunion. However, General WASHINGTON was about to reveal his secret plans for their next mission. It would drop everyone's jaws.

1. Crossing the Delaware!

When John KEMPER arrived with the flatboats for transporting General WASHINGTON, his horses, troops and artillery from Malta Island near New Hope, Daniel KEMPER later informed his brother how General WASHINGTON curled his fist up with joy, as if ready to punch with excitement. Things were quickly coming together nicely and General WASHINGTON was excited. It was as if a troop of cavalry had just arrived to back up General WASHINGTON. John hid the flatboats behind Taylor Island at McKonkey's Ferry (Taylorsville) as General WASHINGTON had ordered.

The British (Red Coates) were everywhere, occupying all major towns, bridges and ferry flatboat crossings; intending on crippling General WASHINGTON and the Continental Army.

Generally, ferry crossings were at a location where boats could neither go further up-river or they had to avoid a waterfall or other natural hazard. They were important for the need in a particular area, for the population to cross.

Boats that transported troops would have to avoid these areas as well, so as not to interfere with the ferry traffic. Also, they had to avoid heavily populated areas so as to keep their crossings more secure and undetected, as they were constantly under surveillance by British patrols.

At wider locations like at West point or Fishkill Landing on the Hudson River, John KEMPER would often have to use his pettiaugers (long flat-bottom boats) for towing chain across the river. Its purpose was to provide a sound means of transportation for troops, stores and equipment on his wagon or flat boats so that they would not be carried down-river by the current. Afterwards, the chains would have to be hauled in so as not to interfere with shipping on the river.

Because of the KEMPER brother's quick thinking and action, General WASHINGTON was now able to plan his first top secret mission. He could now be transported around British check points and surprise their armies wherever they were posted. He would be successful; and the KEMPER brothers would not be forgotten.

John KEMPER, who had a small boat attached to his flatboat, untied it and went to shore to receive General WASHINGTON's new orders. General WASHINGTON told John to have some of his men bring his flatboats to shore to load up his army, horses and artillery for crossing the Delaware.

General WASHINGTON had additional troops stationed at bridge crossings, further north and south of his camp. He sent dispatches to their location, informing them to meet him on the other side of the Delaware at the appointed time. General WASHINGTON then prepared 2,400 troops for his march.

Just when the Continental Army was relieved for now having speedy transportation to flee the area to safety, General WASHINGTON announced, *"We are going back!"* Everyone's eyes open wide and they froze in their tracks. Everyone's mouths just dropped; they silently glared at one another, shrugged their shoulders and then looked back at General WASHINGTON to find out where. General WASHINGTON announced, *"We are going to attack Trenton."* Although what was left of the Continental Army, before being refurbished, was ready to continue their retreat, the new troops who had marched to join General WASHINGTON had energized everyone.

Let us stop and pause for a moment; now, let us go back in time to the Battle of Actium (2 September 31 BC) and some little known historical facts. Hollywood did not portray the movie Cleopatra quite the way it really happened. Marcus ANTONIUS (Mark ANTONY) (83BC-30BC) and Cleopatra (69BC-30BC) had gone to Actium to prepare for battle against Augustus OCTAVIAN (63BC-14AD). If Mark ANTONY had marched his legions into Rome against OCTAVIAN, as Julius CAESAR did against Pompey "the Great" (106BC-48BC), history would surely have changed.

After Mark ANTONY and Cleopatra arrived at Actium, Senators left Rome to join ANTONY's side, feeling that the war was going to be over quickly since he was Julius CAESAR's cousin and head general. However, ANTONY was blinded by his love for Cleopatra and tried to coax and entice OCTAVIAN to their field of choice for the final battle. Fortunately, OCTAVIAN was scared, since many of the senators had already abandoned him. Over the course of a year, ANTONY's thousands of legions had to forage the countryside until there was nothing left to eat.

During this period of time, since ANTONY was taking no action, the Senators started deserting ANTONY and went back to Rome to join OCTAVIAN's side. Furthermore, his top generals and troops likewise, began to desert. One of his head German generals wanted action but sat around doing nothing for over a year. He started dreaming of the Black Forest back in Germany; then one morning, as the sun began to rise, he was gone! At the Battle of Actium, ANTONY defeated himself. The important historical message here is, *"Do not put off to tomorrow what you can do today. Otherwise, you could lose everything!"* Later on in the Revolution, we will be returning to this time zone once again, and for a very good reason.

Whenever John KEMPER transported troops and artillery across a river, depending on the roughness of the weather, and the width of the river, everyone and everything would generally get drenched. Sometimes equipment, stores or artillery would break lose and be lost in the river.

On 25 December 1776, at 11:00 p.m. General WASHINGTON crossed the Delaware heading for Trenton, New Jersey. Every battle that George WASHINGTON had fought in, from the French and Indian Wars up until this point in time, had been lost. He had had enough of losing and on the 26 December went forward with the code words, *"victory or death!"* to battle the British, allied Hessian troops stationed there.

This would be one Christmas party no one would ever forget. This event would go down in history. They were going to celebrate Christmas in Trenton and make the British and Hessians pay for their party. This action would bring about a comment to General WASHINGTON by John KEMPER, that he would never forget, *"Boy! What a Christmas party."*

One of the many who crossed the Delaware with General WASHINGTON on this day was, Captain Silas BINGHAM (1758-1840). This was the first time that he and John KEMPER had become acquainted. Silas had joined the Army when he was sixteen years old as a minuteman in Colonel Seth WARNER's (1743-1784) regiment as part of the Massachusetts Militia. Silas quickly bumped up to become captain of a company of Green Mountain Boys and was with the army when they invaded Canada. He had accompanied General WASHINGTON leading his nineteen thousand Continental soldiers from Cambridge, Massachusetts to New York.

It was recorded that, *"Silas was full of anecdote and humor, social and kind in his feelings, a man of excellence sense and a terror to evildoers. He had great energy, stern integrity, and high morals; He was a strict disciplinarian. Though, not a member of any church, his religion consisted in carrying out the Golden Rule* [Do unto others as you would have them do unto you] *and inculcating* [persistent urging] *sound precepts of morality and a firm adherence to principal."*

When John KEMPER transported General WASHINGTON, his army, horses and artillery, the horses were put in a separate part of the flat boats and had to be held steady, as they were known to wobble when the wagon or flatboats rode the waves.

The troops were placed in another part of the flat boats and had to remain seated or knelt, so as not to lose their balance. Artillery and equipment had to be tied down, in yet another location, from iron rings that skirted the flat boats.

After taking all night crossing the Delaware, General WASHINGTON had found that his other re-enforcements had not arrived at the appointed time; the British guarded the bridges, so those forces encountered combat and were unable to make it. He now had to make a drastic decision, with little time to spare; should he turn back or go forward? He decided to proceed as planned.

This was a tentative decision made by General WASHINGTON at this time. All he had to rely on was what information his intelligence could supply him with. General HOWE had maps of all cities, towns and strategic locations in the states. These maps also included all major bridge and ferry boat crossings. Since seventy-five percent of civilians in the states were behind the Crown and not the Revolution, he had to guess on what a greedy general might do. His guess would be correct.

General HOWE ordered minimal forces to march in and occupy all major towns and bridge locations in order to lockup General WASHINGTON and the Continental Army. When the British and Hessian troops marched into any town, they were instantly cheered on by its residents and it automatically became theirs, without ever having to fire a shot. When the British locked up bridge and flat boat crossing areas, the Continental Army was crippled.

Since General HOWE's military strategies took troops away from the main army, thereby weakening it, this gave General WASHINGTON the edge he needed. He could then attack any of General HOWE's many armies and do sever damage. This action would infuriate General HOWE where he would have to eventually hunt down General WASHINGTON and the Continental Army.

Another soldier who would play an important role at Valley Forge was, James MATHERS (1744-1811). In 1775, James had married Mary MAXWELL (1753-1805), who was the sister of Anthony MAXWELL and William MAXWELL (1759-1836). The MAXWELLs had come from Maxwelton (named after the family), Dumfries, Scotland. James was a private in Colonel James McCLAUGHRY's (1722-1790) Second New York Regiment, First Regular Ulster County Regiment and Second Ulster County Regiment, New York militia.

Elizabeth recorded how they crossed the Delaware with their torches blazing through the uncommonly severe, stormy and extremely harsh winter conditions. Rain, sleet and slabs of ice that formed, quickly broke up on the rapid-flowing Delaware River. Elizabeth told how her father had used these same wagon or flatboats to supply General WASHINGTON whenever he camped by a river, so as to save much wear and tear on the animals, as well as quickly replenishing General WASHINGTON. Her father also used these flatboats to re-supply General Thomas MIFFLIN (1744-1800) (intelligence chief) at Fort Mifflin on Mudden Island after the British evacuation from Philadelphia.

The British had confused General WASHINGTON's retreat from Fort Washington and Fort Lee with cowardice. The purpose was to regroup so that he could launch a counter-attack against the British outposts, since they no longer had the forces to go up against General HOWE's main army. This time he led the offensive. They were about to find out what kind of stuff General WASHINGTON was really made of. The kind of stuff that would rot his opponents' bones and rattle their cages. General HOWE would begin having nightmares about General WASHINGTON.

General WASHINGTON continued to burn the night lamps and candle-lights at General HOWE's camp. How could a man who just had his army wiped out, lost everything, leaving behind all their artillery at Fort Washington and Fort Lee, and who lost what few men were left through mass desertions, dare counterattack the Great British Empire and win ... with nothing? This just was not possible! What in the hell was going on here?

John KEMPER had come through for General WASHINGTON in a big way, in time for him to win his first battle of the Revolution. He would not be forgotten! General WASHINGTON never forgot anyone who came through for him, like Brigadier General Lord STIRLING, whom he promoted to a major general, for sacrificing himself to save General WASHINGTON and the Continental Army.

He approved Daniel KEMPER's increase in rank from adjutant to colonel when made deputy clothier-general of the Continental Army and made him aide-de-camp. He would later have something very special in store for his brother, John KEMPER.

As recorded in the diary of John's daughter, Elizabeth KEMPER, both her father and Uncle Dan (Colonel Daniel KEMPER) were present for this crossing. Daniel also covered this crossing in his declaration to the United States Senate and the United States Congress on 9 April 1842. General WASHINGTON would now be attacking the very town the British and Hessians had recently occupied, as they laughed hysterically watching the Americans row for their lives.

This would be one battle that the British and Hessians were unprepared for. They were fully relaxed, truly believing that General WASHINGTON fled in fear. They were barely recovering from their premature celebration when all hell broke loose. In reality, General WASHINGTON had just circled around and had prepared to attack. Who would do something like this, other than a fool or a mad man? Afterward, no one uttered a word. General WASHINGTON's shocking strategy had humbled them. No one was laughing now!

On 26 December 1776, at 7:00 a.m. General WASHINGTON arrived at Trenton. He had Generals, Nathanael GREENE and John SULLIVAN begin the attack, which lasted until 9:00 a.m. They had James MATHERS guarding the stock, which resulted in him getting wounded in the shoulder. The Americans killed and wounded upward of a hundred and took 1,014 prisoners. They mortally wounded "Oberst" Colonel Johann Gottieb RAHL/RALL (ca. 1726-1776), whom General WASHINGTON visited before his death as a manner of honoring his rank.

The prisoners were moved inland to Newtown, Bucks County, Pennsylvania. General WASHINGTON allowed the Hessians to retain their baggage, ordering that they be treated with favor and humanity. This conduct, so contrary to their expectations, excited their gratitude and veneration (to look upon with deep, great respect) for their admirable conqueror that they styled, *"a very good rebel."*

Shortly after the capture of six Hessian field officers in Trenton, General WASHINGTON proceeded to contact General HOWE and offered an exchange of these officers for General Charles LEE. General HOWE responded, *"Only an offer of equal rank can be accepted."* General WASHINGTON's attempt to negotiate for LEE's exchange went on for months.

Here was a general who was ready to turn General WASHINGTON over to the wolves; however, General WASHINGTON did not take it personally and tried to save him, not knowing that, in reality he was a traitor. In addition, General HOWE was inflamed that General WASHINGTON had dared turn back and captures his army at Trenton. He was supposed to have been preparing for his surrender. What kind of man was he? He was defeated! Was he mad or what?

The prisoners would discover the shocking and unbelievable; that they would be treated with respect and humanity, as ordered by General WASHINGTON, while many American prisoners would be tortured to death. This kind of treatment that General WASHINGTON started is still carried on today. No matter how bad or evil other countries are when captured, they are still allowed to maintain their dignity, rather real or imaginary.

As recorded in John KEMPER's journals and his daughter Elizabeth's diary, countless stories were told to her about this event by both her father and Uncle Dan. Her father, John KEMPER, managed the flatboats to transport General WASHINGTON, the Continental Army, and all their artillery and their horses for their surprise attack in Trenton. This was General WASHINGTON's second encounter with John KEMPER, brother-in-law of the "Rebel Banker" John MORTON. The *"Johnny-in-laws"* were involved in everything. This might have been one of the reasons General WASH-INGTON later wanted him to command his special convoy. Good financial backing could not hurt General WASHINGTON's plans, but could only help them blossom.

In addition, after John KEMPER's escape from Mill Prison, England, General WASHINGTON wrote him a letter, delivered by his brother, Daniel, which welcomed him back home and asked if he remembered Trenton. Anytime something important or critical happened, John KEMPER always seemed to be in the middle of things. Most of the time his involvement centered around his brother-in-law, Mr. MORTON in his dealings with General WASHINGTON, his senior staff and the Continental Congress. After the Revolution, John stated he never planned it that way, it just happened.

On 27 December 1776, Congress, in fear of losing everything, authorized General George WASHINGTON to raise *"from any and all of these United States, sixteen battalions of infantry, in addition to those already voted on by Congress."* Whenever General WASHINGTON received authorization from Congress, he always fulfilled it to the best of his ability, feeling cooperation begets cooperation. Furthermore, General WASHINGTON desperately needed recruits.

Congress always attempted to meet General WASHINGTON's needs the best that they could. They also empowered him to appoint a clothier general in hopes of alleviating that need. He never had enough food, clothing and money for his troops, but he never gave up.

Another important part of these companies that were raised was a couple of companies of artificers. These consisted of civilian or military mechanics and artisans employed by the army to provide necessary services. An artificer company included blacksmiths, carpenters, coopers, harness-makers, nailers and wheelwrights. In order for the army to maintain control, a captain was always in charge of these companies.

On 1 January 1777, New Year's Day, General WASHINGTON returned to Trenton with an army of five thousand to lure British forces south. General HOWE, sick and tired of hearing about General WASHINGTON's aggression against the British Empire sent his leading general, Lord CORNWALLIS, with 5,500 troops to Trenton to halt the ridiculous antics of this clown. General CORNWALLIS left 1,200 men under Lieutenant Colonel Charles MAWHOOD (1729-1780) in Princeton, while he marched southwest to meet General WASHINGTON in Trenton.

After he arrived on the following day, they both exchanged fire in minor skirmishes testing each other's strength. As night fell, General CORNWALLIS relented for the day, overly excited about the next morning when he was intending on finishing General WASHINGTON off, thinking he had trapped him. He then stated, *"I will catch the Fox in the morning."* But he could not bag the fox. General WASHINGTON created a diversion by leaving five hundred men at camp to keep the campfires burning as he executed a daring night march to capture Princeton. He was intending on taking back all British outposts back to New York City, but his men were becoming weary from constant combat.

General WASHINGTON then had his army tie burlap around the horses' hoofs and wagon wheels to muffle the sound. They then silently slipped away in the night, while General CORNWALLIS and the British Army watched the campfires burn off in a distance, having full intention of putting out General WASHINGTON's fires in the morning. They were so excited about the next day they were having trouble sleeping. They were over excitedly dreaming of finishing off General WASHINGTON.

Meanwhile, General WASHINGTON continued his silent march to Princeton, as if ghost riders were coming in from the night. This was a haunting march, indeed, as he was getting ready to terrorize the British in Princeton. Would General HOWE ever forgive him? After all, he was supposed to stay in Trenton so that General CORNWALLIS could turn his lights off for him.

What General WASHINGTON was intending on doing was to take back all the posts General HOWE's army had occupied without a fight. Now, they would have to fight to keep it. All General HOWE had to do was to march his army into any town or city in the thirteen states and the jurisdiction was automatically his. All its residents were filled with Tories/Loyalists backing the Crown.

It is to be noted here that the only Americans in the thirteen states, for the most part, were with the Continental Army or Congress, who were constantly on the move. General HOWE could not capture a town or city and capture America. He had to defeat General WASHINGTON! General WASHINGTON would constantly pick away at General Sir William HOWE's and General Sir Henry CLINTON's (1730-1795) army, or keep them chasing him or bottled up throughout the Revolution.

On 3 January 1777, General WASHINGTON and the Continental Army, seemingly coming from out of nowhere, arrived in Princeton, surprising everyone. After General WASHINGTON captured over three hundred prisoners that day, he left Princeton in good order. General WASHINGTON intended to make for New Brunswick, but his army was exhausted, and the British were too close behind. Instead he moved north to Morristown reaching there on 6 January 1777. The American Army finally went into winter quarters having inflicted two embarrassing blows on the British.

Great was their surprise, when, at dawn, they discovered that the American campfires were still burning, but the army had departed. General CORNWALLIS could hear what he thought was rumbling of distant thunder, but Sir Lieutenant General William ERSKINE (1728-1795) realized that it was indeed the sound of artillery, and explained, *"To arms General! WASHINGTON has outgeneraled us. Let us fly to the rescue at Princeton!"* It was more productive to attack a British outpost, rather than General HOWE's main army, with what small forces they had left.

The British, who were utilizing the very institution of slavery, offered all slaves in the thirteen states their freedom if they would continue to serve and fight on their side. Thousands of slaves joined the British ranks, believing like two-thirds to three-quarters of the population of the States at that time did, that the British were surely going to win. After General HOWE offered the slaves their freedom, General WASHINGTON's senior staff asked him if he thought he should do the same. General WASHINGTON replied, *"No! Let us wait and see what happens."* General WASHINGTON never followed or copied his enemy's tactics; he just listened and observed.

Down in Virginia, the last royal governor, John MURRAY (1730-1809) fourth Earl of Dunmore, organized Lord DUNMORE's Ethiopian Regiment. They were led by British officers and sergeants and white Loyalist militia recruited in the colonies. Twenty-five thousand slaves fled South Carolina to join the British to help fight against the Americans. Another thirty thousand slaves joined from Virginia, while 25 percent of Georgia's slaves joined in as well.

With 66 to 75 percent of the population of the thirteen states being Tories/Loyalists, who were helping the British defeat the Americans, how could General WASHINGTON, the Continental Army and Congress possibly survive? However, what this new regiment soon found out was, wherever the Europeans went, they carried communicable diseases with them. Smallpox quickly set in and killed off most of them, even as they assembled.

Since so many slaves had joined the British cause in the States, a discussion came up in Parliament whether to arm them or not, since they outnumbered the British Army. Because of their natural cultural differences, they harbored hostile, violent tendencies. Edmund BURKE (1729-1797), after discussing the matter with its members, announced in the House of Commons, *"The horrible consequences that might ensue from constituting 100,000 fierce barbarian slaves to be judges and executioners of their masters."*

Thus, they were given remedial jobs like digging ditches, cleaning latrines, carrying supplies, etc. In reality, they were still slaves, as the British clearly believed they remained their masters. The slaves did not comprehend that they were being manipulated. The Indians had the best description of the Europeans, *"White man speak with forked tongue!"*

General WASHINGTON had some slaves, like Harry, who joined the Loyalists and fought for the Crown. Titus CORNELIUS, an escaped slave from Quacker, John CORLIES (1745-1786), and thousands more, taking advantage of the confusion, deserted, running anywhere. However, General WASHINGTON held higher standards for the military than he did civilians. If a soldier deserted and fled over to the British ranks, if he was ever captured, he was executed; civilians were not.

Slaves, during this period of time, were the property of the British Empire. They truly believed that their masters were going to win the war and wanted to be on the winning side. General

WASHINGTON knowing that slaves were Loyalists to the Crown, later **barred** them from joining the American Revolution, since they could not be trusted and had no fighting skills anyway. They were a tribal people from the continent of Africa who were familiar with bows and arrows and spears only. They had no knowledge or training in European battles or fighting skills and techniques. For the most part, Africans, like the rest of the world, were terrified by European technology.

One slave in particular, Titus (Tye) CORNELIUS (ca.1753-1780), who had escaped and fled to the British ranks, joined Dunmore's Ethiopian Regiment and was made a private. Tye enjoyed making constant raids against helpless families in the New Jersey countryside, taking anything he wanted, but knew better than to face off with the Continental Army. They murdered who they claimed were patriots or patriot sympathizers, whether they really were or not. Most, who were not part of the Continental Army, just wanted to live in peace.

Over a hundred years after the Revolution, it was claimed that the British had made Tye an honorary colonel to torment and mock the Americans, after the Battle of Monmouth. However, this author could not confirm this claim. There was no documented source, whatsoever. The British never gave any rank, honorary or otherwise, to slaves, nor were they given any weapons in fear that they would turn on their British masters.

In January 1777, at winter quarters, Morristown, New Jersey, General WASHINGTON began rebuilding his army and announced general orders that one wagon drawn by four horses or oxen would be allowed to each eighty men. General WASHINGTON continued to closely supervise the preparation of wagon transportation. He also directed that wagon masters give strict orders to waggoneers (a person who drives wagons), forbidding them from riding army horses too hard, regardless of the circumstances.

The quarter-master-general was in charge of securing all wagons. A wagon master-general had five wagon masters under his command. A regimental wagon master was allowed between seven and nine wagons, depending on the size of his regiment (battalion), which was generally around 728 men but sometimes as low as 585 men.

On 10 January 1777, General WASHINGTON appointed James MEASE (1740-1785), a Philadelphia merchant, clothier general of the Continental Army, but he was given no military rank himself and did not question it. However, Mr. MEASE, as clothier-general, was given the authority to assign rank as high as a colonel, but had to be okayed by General WASHINGTON. General WASHINGTON informed James MEASE that he would receive $150 per month and any assistant $50 per month and would have to accompany the main army in order to fulfill his duties properly.

In February 1777, James MEASE arrived at camp in Morristown ready to assume his duties. He received recommendations from several officers that Daniel KEMPER, who had attended King's College (1766-1768), would make a good deputy clothier-general. At this time, Daniel was in the sick-bed in the hospital located on his brother-in-law John MORTON's estate.

The hospital was a long, low, log building, situated on a rising ground in the meadow; a brook ran in front of it and supplied the inmates with water for cooking and washing. General WASHINGTON often made trips to Mr. MORTON's hospital to visit his ailing soldiers. Mr. MORTON continued to amaze General WASHINGTON with his support. Whatever the Continental Army needed, Mr. MORTON was in the middle of it all.

Mr. MORTON splurged his wealth on the needs of General WASHINGTON, the Continental Army and the Continental Congress, who continually basked in his overwhelming generosity. They would never look a gift horse in the mouth. What would they do without him? How could they reward him?

Dr. James TILTON (1745-1822), the director of the medical department, along with Dr. STEVENSON, DR. COVENTRY, and other physicians, had rooms in Mr. MORTON's house; and a small schoolhouse was converted into an apothecary's (pharmacy) shop. Daniel was being taken care of by army physicians, Doctors William SHIPPEN Jr. (1736-1808), John COCHRAN (1730-1807), BOND and others. James MEASE met Daniel and informed him that he came with good recommendations from his fellow officers as someone who would make a good deputy clothier-general. If he was interested, he would wait until he recovered, Daniel agreed.

Daniel had an impressive start from the very beginning of the Revolution in 1776. He served in Colonel Nicholas JASPER's (1752-1827) regiment, Brigadier General Charles SCOTT's (1739-1813) brigade and under Brigadier General William MAXWELL's (1733-1796) command. He fought at the Battles of Scotch Plains (26 June 1776), Long Island (27 August 1776), White Plains (28 October 1776), Trenton (26 December 1776; and was with General WASHINGTON when he crossed the Delaware River (25 December 1776). Mr. KEMPER was just the man Mr. MEASE was looking for, someone dedicated to the Revolution! Besides, Mr. MORTON was his brother-in-law. Everyone knew who was who!

After the remaining nineteen thousand Continental troops were crushed at the Battle of Fort Washington, General WASHINGTON started all over again to rebuild his army. However, the British continued building their forces as well, intending on crushing the Rebel resistance. The only question now was how could General WASHINGTON and his small armies stand up against the mightiest army and navy on earth? He had few supplies and uniforms, an insignificant navy, no allies and no bank account and treachery surrounded him. The answer would come soon through his recruitments.

On 19 February 1777, General WASHINGTON promoted General Lord STIRLING to major general because of his heroics and selfless acts of sacrificing himself in order to allow his commander-in-chief and the Continental troops to escape to safety and recoup.

On 21 February 1777, because of his incredible influence in the region, Congress appointed John Peter MUHLENBERG (1746-1807) of Virginia a brigadier general and ordered him to put together as many men as was possible from his popularity in his area and march to join General WASHINGTON in Morristown, New Jersey. General MUHLENBERG quickly assembled his German regiment and marched to Morristown.

Formerly, he had been a Lutheran minister, but in his last sermon to his congregation, he exclaimed, *"To everything there is a time and a season . . . a time of war and a time of peace. This is a time of war."* He then tore off his clergy robe to reveal a colonel's uniform. To everyone's astonishment, this was the beginning of his military career. After the Revolution, he never did return to the clergy.

On 28 February 1777, after hearing about the mistreatment of their prisoner of war, Colonel Archibald CAMPBELL, General WASHINGTON wrote the Massachusetts Council, testing his authority, referring to Colonel CAMPBELL's confinement as being, *"shocking to humanity."* General WASHINGTON also wrote to Congress complaining about these tactics; they were unacceptable! General WASHINGTON did not want the enemy to be able to claim that Americans mistreated their prisoners just because the British did. General WASHINGTON did not measure right and wrong from what others did or did not do. He would observe, but keep silent as to his thoughts.

On 1 March 1777, Captain Alexander HAMILTON was promoted to lieutenant colonel and aide-de-camp to General WASHINGTON. He had fought at the Battles of Long Island, White Plains and Trenton, along with his personal friend, Daniel KEMPER. General WASHINGTON remembered very well, that he, himself, once held the rank of lieutenant colonel in the French and Indian Wars. It was time he promoted those who were dedicated to the Revolution.

On 1 March 1777, Captain Benjamin TALLMADGE (1754-1835) was put in charge of espionage, but he had, as of yet, no men under him. They would have to be carefully selected by General WASHINGTON and the intelligence committee of the Continental Congress, with some suggestion by Mr. TALLMADGE in order to fulfill his needs. However, Mr. TALLMADGE only held the rank of captain, the rank required for all intelligence agents. In order for him to be respected by the same rank, he would have to be promoted. Afterward, he would acquire Captain John KEMPER.

Generally, a paymaster was set up to pay a soldier for enlisting recruits; however, if a soldier was able to enlist many recruits, he was honored for doing so by being given a choice of money or rank. Rank was always what a soldier preferred, if he desired to work hard enough to obtain it; and in the long run, it meant more money. A good example of this procedure was when Anthony MAXWELL had enlisted enough recruits he was offered the rank of ensign; he accepted, making him an officer in the Continental Army, every soldier's dream.

In March 1777, after Daniel's recovery, he went to see James MEASE and was appointed deputy clothier-general of the Continental Army. He received a colonel's pay and was given six rations, with a horse's forage. General WASHINGTON approved of his new rank and appointed Daniel aide-de-camp. He was a designated special assistant aide at the Battles of Germantown (4 October 1777) and Monmouth (28 June 1778), in company with

Lieutenant Colonel John LAURENS (1754-1782), aide-de-camp to General WASHINGTON.

After the crossing of the Delaware, Daniel climbed the ladder fast. Daniel, fluent in German, was a great asset, as he was able to serve as an interpreter between the many Germans who served on both sides of the Revolutionary War as well, including Major General Wilhelm von STEUBAN (1730- 1794).

Now that Daniel was deputy clothier-general and aide-de-camp to General WASHINGTON, he was instrumental in procuring his brother John's appointment as *"master"* wagon master. He officially introduced his brother to General WASHINGTON at that time. Daniel explained to General WASHINGTON John's expertise in wagons and reminded him of John's participation in crossing the Delaware, when John had managed the flatboats used for transporting his troops, artillery and horses when crossing the river on his march to Trenton.

However, General WASHINGTON had never forgotten, but a new light went on in General WASHINGTON's head and he realized that he needed a way of supplying the army that he was rebuilding and a means of camouflaging the operations he had planned for John KEMPER. John, who was adept at wagons and wagon-boats, would be the expert General WASHINGTON would put in charge of procuring and delivering supplies for his troops. In addition, because of John's background and his family connection to John MORTON, there was another task that General WASHINGTON was considering that no one could ever know about, except those in the intelligence circle.

On 7 March 1777, Daniel and John's brother, Jacob, was listed as an ensign in the seventh company under Captain Abraham PIATT (1741-1791) in Colonel John NEILSON's (1745-1833) regiment. This battalion left Albany, New York on this date and marched to Morristown, New Jersey, where it was discharged.

Jacob was now with his brothers, Daniel and John for a short time, before receiving his new orders.

After the Revolution, Daniel was issued the Badge of the Society of Cincinnati, after its foundation by General Marquis DE LAFAYETTE. The Society of Cincinnati was a small exclusive club of officers, who served three years or more on the Continental Line, and they were the only ones eligible to join. This is the *"cream-de-la-crème"* of all organizations in America, in which all members were responsible, in some part, for the founding of our great nation.

Both Daniel and Jacob KEMPER were among the original founders of the Society of Cincinnati. The first meeting of the society was held in May of 1783. Daniel with his brother Jacob, rallied to have George WASHINGTON elected the first president general of the society, serving from December 1783 until his death in 1799. Both Daniel and Jacob were listed as original members (OM) and often sat at the meetings together.

On 22 March 1777, General John Peter Gabriel MUHLENBERG, who led the eighth Virginia German-American regiment, joined General WASHINGTON's main army in the north at Morristown, New Jersey. When General WASHINGTON saw all the troops accompanying General MUHLENBERG, he was immediately promoted to major general. He quickly became acquainted with the KEMPER brothers and formed a natural bond because of their German heritage. In fact, Captain John KEMPER, after he escaped from Mill Prison, England and returned to Philadelphia in November of 1781, finished his Revolutionary service under him.

On 7 April 1777, Captain Benjamin TALLMADGE's rank was remedied by being promoted to major, just because of the position he held. For the next few months the framework for General WASHINGTON's espionage ring was being organized, with the guidance of General WASHINGTON and the intelligence committee of the Continental Congress.

Within two years after Major TALLMADGE had become adept at espionage, he, along with General WASHINGTON and the intelligence committee came up with a master plan to infiltrate the British Empire; it was bold, it was daring, and Captain John KEMPER would play a major role in this operation. *"Necessity is the mother of all inventions!"*

On 1 May 1777, after fighting at the Battles of Long Island (17 August 1776), Harlem Heights (16 October 1776) and White Plains (28 October 1776), Anthony MAXWELL was promoted to sergeant in Captain John SANTFORD/SANDFORD's (1724-1785) company, Colonel William MALCOLM's regiment.

On 9 May 1777, at camp Morristown, New Jersey, Mr. KEMPER received a letter from Charles YOUNG (1757-1842), clerk and deputy clothier-general under James MEASE, stationed at Philadelphia. In this letter Mr. YOUNG stated,

> *Sir, since the foregoing, Mr. MEASE has yours by the post, and he directs me, positively to forbid the fine goods being given out at Morristown, but to those of the general's family alone, say 20 or 30 shirts and 3 or 4 dozen hose. He tells me, they cannot be viewed as clothing for the Army; that he particularly directed them to serve his own friends and he chooses himself to issue them; I am afraid you speak too freely of their coming.*

After receiving Mr. YOUNG's letter, Mr. KEMPER was furious, knowing personally that General WASHINGTON appointed James MEASE to represent the Continental Army, not himself. He turned Mr. YOUNG's letter over to General WASHINGTON. General WASHINGTON, likewise, was infuriated and wrote the foregoing letter to Mr. MEASE.

Sir:

The following extract from Mr. Young's letter, one of your clerks in Philadelphia, to Mr. Kemper, I transmit for your consideration.

P.S. Since the foregoing, Mr. Mease has yours by the post, and he directs me, positively to forbid the fine goods be given out at Morristown, but to those of the Generals family alone, say so or 31 shirts and 3 or 4 dozen hose. He tells me, they cannot be viewed as clothing for the army; that he particularly directed them to serve his own friends and he chooses himself to issue them; I am afraid you speak too freely of their coming.

Sir, this proceeding surprises me much and requires but few comments. Those goods are certainly public property, purchased by public agents and were transported at public expense and risk. The Army is in great need of them and will want all articles of the kind you can procure, so that they cannot be applied, upon any principal, to the purposes of private emolument [payment] or private friendship. Supposing those intended to be favored with them, should be of the Army, yet, if a preference is due to any, it is certainly to the officers and men who have been longest in service and to those earliest in the field; but the postscript does not hold forth an interpretation so favorable. I trust another instance of the sort will never happen, nor can I bring myself to believe, upon this occasion, that Mr. Young has not take[n] up a wrong idea of your directions. I am Sir, Yours &ca

G. WASHINGTON

> **P.S.** *I am convinced, that we shall experience many inconveniences, from our soldiers being dressed in red; I therefore wish, to have all the clothes now on hand in that color dyed, I don't care what the color is.*

Now that the Continental Army had gotten back up to strength, Colonel Daniel KEMPER inquired to

General WASHINGTON, *"Do you think we are strong enough to take back New York City?"* General WASHINGTON replied, *"Out of the question! The city is a fly trap. Our intelligence has informed us that all of the British most powerful artillery is entrenched around the perimeter of the city. In addition to naval bombardment, any attempt would be suicide. We need to draw General HOWE inland away from his navy."*

Let us stop and pause for a moment, once again, and go over some more little known historical facts back into that time zone of Mark ANTONY and Cleopatra. After ANTONY and Cleopatra fled from the Battle of Actium, ANTONY did not return to Alexandria with Cleopatra as the movie portrayed. He, in fact, went to a lone island in the Egyptian delta, soaking over the incredible blunders he had just made in deserting his army at Actium. He had so quickly lost his empire and was totally dazed. He sat and glared out at the ocean as his hair and beard began to grow. He remained on this island over the course of a year, while a loyal officer brought him food and water.

While ANTONY had accepted his loss, even though embarrassed and ashamed, he could not figure out what he had done wrong. When Julius CAESAR was around, he did what he was told, but after CAESAR was gone, things had changed; he found out it was not so easy being a CAESAR after all. Some people it comes natural to, others have to work harder at it. The important historical message here is, after ANTONY had lost all his legions at the Battle of Actium, he gave up. General WASHINGTON, after losing all his troops at the Battle of Fort Washington, did not. He started all over again and rebuilt his army to go back up against the mightiest army and navy on earth.

Even though Mark ANTONY had lost his empire, his descendants went on to rule the world. By the year 1900, Europeans owned, ruled or occupied the entire planet, including China, India, and the entire continent of Africa, with the exception to the Congo—only because nobody wanted it. It was filled with malaria, other diseases, and unbearable temperatures. Not to mention, the entire western hemisphere as well. How were Europeans able to conquer, capture, or control the entire world? They had invented weapons that the rest of the world knew nothing about and were terrified of.

Over the next hundred years, all nations of the world would try to buy in or steal European inventions and technology as they continued to develop. A new trend would develop where third-world people would begin migrating to European nations and settlements to enjoy better living conditions and new opportunities. Without them, they would remain in the jungles and sands where they had originated for thousands of years. New hostilities would develop because of natural cultural differences ordained by God.

This author descends from dozens of different lines of Mark ANTONY through both of his wives, Octavia and Cleopatra. Thousands of years have since passed since the reign of Mark ANTONY and Cleopatra, yet their memory remains distinct in the world population. Some have learned the significance between love and war; many have not. What was the magic between these two who were so madly in love, and why have they captured the curiosity of the world population forever? The biography of Mark ANTHONY and Cleopatra is currently be written by this author.

Chapter IX
A Halo of Stars in a Blue Field

On 14 June 1777, Congress adopted a resolution designating an official flag to represent their dream, America. The resolution read, *"Resolve that the flag of the thirteen United States be thirteen stripes. Alternate red and white, that the union be thirteen stars, white on a blue field, representing a new constellation."* They gave the order to have this new flag made to a colleague of theirs, Francis HOPKINSON, who was from New Jersey. However, others would try to claim credit for his incredible invention of our flag ninety-three years later.

He was chairman of the Continental Navy board's middle department, a signer of the Declaration of Independence and judge of the admiralty of Pennsylvania. He also helped design the Great Seal of the United States for government, along with designs for other seals, symbols and currency of the United States. He also was the treasurer of loans during the Revolution handling the loans from John MORTON to the Continental Congress. Francis HOPKINSON was a genius in his own time and he was a personal friend of General WASHINGTON. He also was credited with being the first American composer.

This resolution, like all adopted by Congress, was adopted for the sole purpose of strengthening the Continental Army, which they had created, and the new country that was being established, by implementing a symbol to set them apart from the rest of the world—something that was their own. It was their hope that this symbol would inspire and give a reason for the army's existence. Congress later became ecstatic about the greatness that this new flag had become. In addition, what was it that Madam Ursula saw in the halo of stars?

Furthermore, the Continental Army was Congress' only line of protection; if they did not make it strong, they would not have a strong defense. The British Army could then move in and arrest all members of Congress. The British now had a new army to contend with. They were not interested in capturing Congress, a civil force that they did not recognize as a threat; an army is only trained to contend with and to fight another army.

Francis HOPKINSON made various versions of the new flag, but the most commonly accepted by both General WASHINGTON and the members of the Continental Congress was the circular design representing a halo. Upon completion of the new US flag and other seals for government by his team, Francis submitted a letter to the Continental Board of Admiralty regarding his designs asking, *"Whether a quarter cask of the public wine would not be a proper and reasonable reward for these labors of fancy and a suitable encouragement for future exertions of a like nature?"* His request was turned down because Congress regarded him as a public servant.

Congress was more flabbergasted by conjuring up the creation of the military, during this period of time, than it ever had been in the entire history of America. The Continental Army was organized and formed by Congress, for the purpose of protecting the allegiance of the newly formed nation and civilian-constituted authority, the Continental Congress. If not for the army, Congress would not have succeeded in running the country.

Therefore, when Congress adopted this resolution, the order to have this new flag made was given to a government official and not to a regular civilian. The only orders given to the civilians by the Continental Congress, were to comply with the Continental Army's needs, providing, at a reasonable cost, food stuff, clothing, cloths, artillery, horses, wagons, weapons, etc.

Since no reasonable costs were defined, some merchants were so greedy and invented charges to inflate the overall cost.

Congress had made many important and wise decisions during this period of time, but the most important one of all was appointing George WASHINGTON as its commander-in-chief of the Continental Army. They did not realize how much so, until the end of the Revolution. Although General WASHINGTON lost more battles than any other leader in American history, he sent a new and definitely clear message heard all around the world, *"You can defeat a man who surrenders, but you can never defeat a man who refuses to give up!"*

After the close of the Revolution, Congress turned over its powers of recruiting and promoting military personnel to the president of the United States. Likewise, Americans learned of General WASHINGTON's greatest intuition; with the military might to take over the country, he bowed to the civilian-constituted authority and surrendered his sword, thereby disbanding the Continental Army—one of the most honorable debuts in world history.

This separation between civilian and military was essential to establish the democracy we enjoy today. General WASHINGTON then became the first and only uncontested president in the history of America, realizing first-hand the importance of civilian authority. Military might is important in a time of war, as long as it is balanced and controlled by a civilian-eminent authority. However, politics always seems to play a main role in controlling it.

On 1 July 1777, Anthony MAXWELL, because of his success in enlisting many recruitments, was boosted up in rank to an ensign in Captain John SANTFORD's (1724-1785) company, Colonel William MALCOLM's regiment. He was now an officer in the Continental Army.

In early July 1777, Benjamin FRANKLIN, while in Paris, recommended Count Kazimierz (Casimir) PULASKI (1745-1779) of Poland, to General WASHINGTON. The count had been previously captured by the Russians and only released if he promised not to attack them again. Benjamin FRANKLIN, hearing of his heroic cavalry assaults on the Russians, offered the count a better deal, by setting him up directly with the commander-in-chief of the States, where he could attack anyone he wanted, as long as they wore a red coat. Count PULASKI was, *"an officer renowned throughout Europe for the courage and bravery he displayed in defense of his country's freedom."*

The count thought to himself for a moment, *"Humph... Red, gee, I love that color, especially if it means action."* The count replied, *"As soon as my transportation is set up, I will be ready to leave."* The French Navy ended up transporting him to the States. The count turned out to be a pearl to General WASHINGTON who was generally attracted to rebels who feared no one.

On 7 July 1777, the USS *Hancock* captured the HMS *Fox*, a twenty-eight-gun ship. Commodore John MANLEY took its captain, Patrick FOTHERINGHAM (1712-1781) on board with forty of his men as prisoners. The remaining prisoners were taken on board the other American ship, *Boston*, commanded by Captain Hector McNeill (1728-1785) who was assisting in the capture.

Other British battle ships soon arrived and joined in the pursuit of the *Hancock*. This was finally one of the British dreams come true; they had found Commodore MANLEY and the USS *Hancock*. Now, all they had to do was catch him. However, that was not going to be as easy as they thought. What kind of ship did Commodore MANLEY command? It was like a flying fish on the sea. Whatever it was, the British wanted it and were not about to give up until they captured it.

On 8 July 1777, in the early morning, after a thirty-nine-hour chase, the *Hancock* was fleeing in the blind; after zigzagging and their flanks constantly being cut off by other British ships, they no longer knew their location or heading and began slowing down. This enabled the British to get within striking distance. The forty-four-gun ship HMS *Rainbow* began to score with her bow chasers and followed with a series of broad sides. The *Hancock,* with a total of 239 men on board, including officers and crew, was forced to strike her colors.

Commodore MANLEY slowly bent his head in sorrow, but there was no shame here. Commodore MANLEY had fought as boldly and bravely as any commander could, he was just vastly out-numbered by a larger superior navy. After their surrender, Captain Patrick FOTHERINGHAM and the other forty British prisoners on board, immediately threw their fists and arms wildly up in the air, while shaking them about and screaming, *"Yeeeeeeeeeeeeeeeeeeeeeeeah!"*

On 10 July 1777, the Americans, once again, captured British General Richard PRESCOTT (1725-1788) while he was sleeping in his bed, while lodging at Rhode Island. General PRESCOTT took living in America too casually; he acted as if the country was already theirs and that he could go and stay anywhere he wished without fear of being captured. General WASHINGTON now had a British general that he could offer in exchange for General Charles LEE. After the British confirmed General PRESCOTT' capture, they began to negotiate the exchange. However, would this end up being a drastic mistake, unknowingly bringing a traitor back into his ranks? General WASHINGTON always gave the benefit of a doubt.

On 23 July 1777, Count PULASKI arrived in Marblehead (near Boston), Massachusetts via, a French transport The count wrote General WASHINGTON, stating, *"I came here, where freedom is being defended, to serve it, and to live or die for it."* Little did Count PULASKI know, but General WASHINGTON desperately needed his kind of man; someone fearless, a real rebel, just like General WASHINGTON and the Continental

Army were labeled by the British. Count PULASKI would prove an incredible addition to General WASHINGTON's army.

One of General WASHINGTON's chief concerns, during the beginning of the Revolution, was in the clothier-general's department. Since all British and French officers and regular soldiers had full uniforms and the Continental Army did not, he had to make concessions. He would give priority to having uniforms made for his officers first, along with the proper cockades (a knot of ribbons with a circular or oval shaped symbol of distinctive color, worn in the American Revolution as a form of rank insignia).

These improvements would make them more easily identifiable to the rest of the Continental force. Most of the regular soldiers wore their hunting clothes, never really feeling like part of the unit. Many of the Continental soldiers, who survived the war, retired never having had a uniform or a paycheck. Many did not even have a wife to go home to; then, their life had to begin ... with nothing!

Elizabeth recorded how both her father and uncle Dan (Colonel Daniel KEMPER) repeatedly told her while growing up, how her uncle was finally able to convince her father by pleading with him for some time to transfer his service to his department. Daniel needed someone he could trust and depend on by his side and knew his brother, John, would serve him well. This bond was shown again in more recent history, in the era of the KENNEDY brothers, when President John F. KENNEDY (1917-1963) pulled his brother, Robert (Bobby) F. (1925-1968) over to his side to be attorney general.

After Daniel was appointed deputy clothier-general of the Continental Army and aide-de-camp to General WASHINGTON, he was in a position to make a difference for his brother. After Trenton, Daniel continually reminded General WASHINGTON of his brother, John's expertise in wagons. However, General

WASHINGTON never forgot and was already making plans for John.

In addition, after learning about John's stone silence since he was a child and his coded names for childhood friends, General WASHINGTON had something else very special and far more important for John to handle. He needed someone to fill a new office he was contemplating, someone who, if captured by the enemy, could not be broken!

Even though General WASHINGTON had his own vision on the outcome of the American Revolution, it coincided with the Continental Congress as well. All his recruitments and appointments would make the difference between success and failure. Only years later, after the Revolution, would historians be able to look back and wonder, how in the hell was he able to do so much right, when so much treachery and deception surrounded him. In addition, he always gave the benefit of a doubt.

Chapter X
Preparing the Intelligence Web

General WASHINGTON was deeply involved in secret intelligence committees. Congress set up many such committees. General WASHINGTON retained full authority, from beginning to end, over all Continental Army and navy intelligence.

The intelligence committee's chief heads appointed by Congress were such men as Benjamin FRANKLIN (1706-1790), Robert MORRIS (1734-1806), and Robert LIVINGSTON (1746-1813), among others. The heads of these committees got together, with General WASHINGTON, to decide what kind of men would be best suited for the intelligence circle. They would have to be young, bold, brave, cunning and able to keep their mouth shut if the enemy captured them. Most importantly, their country would have to be rated top-shelf; nothing could come before it. They would have to be willing to make a sacrifice if their country called for it.

General George WASHINGTON could not possibly win the war on *"battle power"* by any means. His army and navy were nowhere near the size, or a match for the British forces who were the largest in the world. To that end, General WASHINGTON relied heavily on his trusted, specially designated officers and aides to help him gain intelligence and assist him in conducting intelligence operations. General WASHINGTON's first officer to assume this role was Colonel Joseph REED (1741-1785); Colonel Alexander HAMILTON (1757-1804) followed Colonel REED.

Because of intelligence failure at the Battle of Long Island in 1776, General WASHINGTON found it necessary to specify an *"elite detachment"* dedicated to reconnaissance. These specially handpicked officers were sent on a variety of covert operations, far too dangerous and too vital for regular troops to handle. ***"They were to report to him directly!"***

In 1778, General WASHINGTON appointed Brigadier General, Charles SCOTT (1739-1813) *"intelligence chief."* Succeeding him was Colonel David HENLEY (1749-1823), who served only temporarily, until Benjamin TALLMADGE (1745-1835) took the post.

Since intelligence officers held the rank of captain or higher, some of the officers listed were, General Thomas MIFFLIN (1744-1800), Captain Charles CRAIG, Captain Eli LEAVENWORTH (1748-1819), and Captain Nathan HALE (1755-1776). After Mr. HALE was captured and hung as a spy, General WASHINGTON revised his intelligence circle. Some officers' names, depending on their importance, were kept so top secret that their names were never revealed! They were only known by, General WASHINGTON and the intelligence committee.

General WASHINGTON needing to fund his efforts sought and obtained funding from the Continental Congress through a ***"secret service fund."*** Paper money was worthless, partly because the British were counterfeiting our money. General WASHINGTON addressed Congress by saying that he preferred *gold* to paper money, stating, *"I have always found a difficulty in procuring intelligence by means of paper money, and I perceive it increases."* There was only one person they could rely on for the gold, John MORTON!

In instructing his officers, General WASHINGTON stated, *"Leave no stone unturned, do not stick to expense in gathering intelligence."* He further commanded those employed for these intelligence purposes that their duty be *"upon those whose firmness and fidelity we may safely rely."* Now, where could General WASHINGTON and the Continental Congress obtain gold from, since their paper money was worthless? Why, John "the Rebel Banker" MORTON, of course. He was the only means. Captain KEMPER would help obtain the gold for a worthy cause, once again.

Secrecy was of utmost necessity in order to keep the flow of intelligence. General WASHINGTON could not afford for his suppliers to be identified. In his journals, he alluded to this by saying, *"The names of persons cannot be inserted."* Congress likewise made it known that secrecy was top priority by resolution, stating, *"Withholding the names of the persons they have employed, or with whom they have corresponded."* Congress, apart from the public journals that they kept on public file, recorded separate *"secret journals"* on these agents and operations. After the American Revolution, those journals mysteriously disappeared.

Now all General WASHINGTON had to do was pick who his **top secret agent** would be. It would have to be someone who was naturally silent and knew how to keep his mouth shut—someone who would not be interested in boasting of his deeds, one who would be quiet as a mouse, yet stood solid as stone. Somehow, General WASHINGTON would have to clear his path directly to him without throwing suspicion, with either friend or foe, as to his true identity.

General WASHINGTON would have to *camouflage* this agent's activities, so as to blend in with another service where none of his other officers, except those in intelligence, would know or suspect anything out of the ordinary. This individual's role would have to be so top secret that his true identity could never be revealed, even after the Revolution was over. America's first *secret service* was about to be born, along with its first *top secret agent!*

"Army Intelligence spearheads all branches of America's future intelligence offices, the FBI (Federal Bureau of Investigation), CIA (Central Intelligence Agency) and NSA (National Security

Agency), which became the best in the world!" Other nations looking on pondered as to how a country so young rocketed into the future ahead of other countries thousands of years old. Master intelligence was one of the main reasons.

America soon became the hot bed of some of the greatest inventions in the history of the world, from the creation of the nuclear bomb to the landing on the moon. In the twenty-first century, Americans began planning the first manned mission to Mars. Other nations became envious. Countries of evil, fostering the greatest hatred on the planet, generally harness jealousy. Other countries try to steal or buy into our secrets, knowing there is no other way to obtain them. Other nations continue to reach into our intelligence circle and try to shut it down, or expose it!

Whenever you become the number 1 power in the world, like Rome, or the number one builder in the world, like Egypt, all other nations want what you have and will die to get it. Security on the world's most dangerous weapon invented by Americans was not placed high enough. Russians soon found an American family involved with the bomb, who was more interested in the risk of gaining more money than they were their own country.

By AD 646, Prophet Muhammad's (570-632) Muslim forces, led by General Amr ibn al-As (585-664), had conquered all of Egypt. Eventually what little was left of the Egyptian race, culture and language, was finished off. Egypt was a now a land of a new people, Arabs in an Egyptian land, grabbing all its wealth for themselves. Arabs were described by the Egyptian people for thousands of years, as the desert dwellers who came, robbed, and then fled. Now, they were living here! Other world powers, like Rome, Macedonia or Persia, who either conquered or controlled Egypt, allowed its people to maintain its culture and language; the Arabs wiped it out!

There is a very valuable lesson to be learned here from history; and it is the prediction of this author that, if America does not maintain a strong defense, then we will lose it all, like Rome and Egypt. It is also the prediction of this author that, if America does fall, it will be done from within, with the influence of outside evil forces lurking in the shadows of darkness, waiting to assist, but appearing to be innocent. They will also seek the highest offices in American government in order to bring it down. The worst massacres in world history have always been committed under the name of God.

By the year 2000 new arrivals came on the scene, hoping to compromise and dislodge America's judicial position on world order. By this time, that country had become the richest in the world because it had more slaves than all other countries in the history of the world combined. They used their puppet countries to harass Americans, while it gained a foothold on world dominance. They had also given the nuclear bomb to West Pakistan in order to put India on the defensive and North Korea, to put South Korea and America on the defensive.

Russia, in need of money, ended up selling its very soul to that country, which was a former adversary. Russia sold them all their space and naval technology. This country likewise gave loans to America hoping to gain its technology and anything else they could obtain, under the reason of, debt owed. What that country has not yet learned, over all the thousands of years of its history, is, ***"You cannot rule the world by slavery!"*** Both Egypt and Rome failed trying. Furthermore, this country has the worst kind of slavery, its own people.

Great Britain, who was one of the last world powers to utilize slavery by transporting slaves from Africa to all its colonies around the world, likewise, discovered it could not continue; therefore, they freed all their slaves. This is one of the main reasons they have been able to remain a world power to this very day. What the British started would have an everlasting chain-reaction throughout the world.

Captain John KEMPER, throughout the entire American Revolution, never had any financial problems. He always seemed to have money and is one of the few Continental officers who never put in for back pay. Why? Even his brother, Colonel Daniel KEMPER, put in for 6,600 plus dollars owed to him in back pay, for his services during the Revolution; but, like other Continentals, never got paid.

What did Daniel know about his brother, John, as alluded to by him, which only General WASHINGTON, Colonel Alexander HAMILTON, Colonel Benjamin TALLMADGE, and Benjamin HARRISON (1726-17910) knew? Colonel TALLMADGE, Colonel Daniel KEMPER, and Captain KEMPER reported directly to General WASHINGTON for a very good reason.

Chapter XI
Final Preparation for War

On 24 July 1777, while in Philadelphia, Colonel Daniel KEMPER, aide-de-camp, wrote his final letter of appeal to his brother, John, who was staying on and off at their home in Morristown, New Jersey. *"Please come to Philadelphia and help bring this madness that is ravaging our land to an end. I have acquired a most important position for you to fill from your regular routine."* A new revitalization was becoming of the Continental Army. Who would play the important roles?

> *General WASHINGTON has just created a special convoy and the only main line of support for the entire Continental Army. Because of my recommendation and after becoming better acquainted with you after crossing the Delaware and at Morristown, he has left this ticket open for you to fill. You will be in charge of a 150 wagons, with a captain's guard of 170 men to protect the transports, and 150 wagoners, comprising a total of 320 men under your command. This number will fluctuate when Continental Dragoons or a regiment are added for your escort. You will maintain General WASHINGTON's 'Special Protection' from any interference of his other officers with your command, providing a clear path through all guards and sentinels.*

> *Your appointment in the Clothier-General's Department is a deception; in actuality, you will be under the direct command and control of our Commander-in-Chief, General George*

WASHINGTON, himself. All messages between General WASHINGTON and you at Philadelphia or your wagon-train camp will be sent sealed. If any of these seals is ever broken, the incident is to be reported directly to General WASHINGTON, immediately, and the agent or courier involved will be held accountable. We cannot risk the enemy discovering General WASHINGTON's or your location, or the war is over. Your other close contact, besides me, will be our friends, Colonel Alexander HAMILTON or Major Benjamin TALLMADGE [intelligence officers]. General WASHINGTON wants this to be like a tightly knit family; Beware of Tories/Loyalists!

General WASHINGTON, after becoming better acquainted with you at our winter quarters in Morristown, is the one who gave me the nudge to bring you on board, hoping your country's need, will make the difference in your involvement. General WASHINGTON was impressed with my story and explanation of your stone silence since you were a young boy, your coded names for your childhood friends and your perseverance over your childhood demons. It is time to meet with General WASHINGTON and Colonel Alexander HAMILTON for more details, see you in Philadelphia. As we have previously discussed, everything must remain confidential. Whenever you need me I will be there for you. After you have read this letter, please burn it!

Dan

John's dream had always been to be in command in a combat situation like his grandfather, but that was slowly slipping away. When we join the service, it is not up to us, but to the men in charge as to where they feel they need our special abilities most. Hearts may be broken, but the decision is best.

Elizabeth recorded, *"Even though my father was supposed to have burned this letter, he did not, and kept it buried in a secret location in Morristown. I have recorded it as it was. When Uncle Dan had sealed my father's loyalty to General WASHINGTON in Morristown, he was just the man General WASHINGTON had been looking for, and when his new project was completed, my father would be in charge."*

All John had to do was pack up and move to Philadelphia; everything was ready. And then he had a meeting to attend. John brought both of his journals with him, one for regular recordings in the wagon master department and another one for something else. Unbeknownst to John, these journals would become the historical recordings in the *"birth of America."*

John MORTON, after learning of John KEMPER's new deployment to join his brother Daniel in Philadelphia, informed him, *"After you get to Philadelphia and everything is set, you contact me immediately and I will make sure you have the best of everything for your new position. Depending on your needs at the time, I will obtain what is quickly available and follow up with your other needs as time goes on."* Because of this close attachment between John MORTON and John KEMPER, they became quickly known as the *"Johnny-in-laws."*

In closing, Mr. MORTON presented John with a gold pocket watch and an additional horse. The purpose of the two horses was, when one was not being used, it would be tied to the rear of the lead wagon. When the horse John was riding got tired, it would be exchanged for the fresh one. John who had named his current horse, Johann, after his grandfather, now named the new horse, Eliza, after his childhood sweetheart, Eliza HOPPER.

On 27 July 1777, a young nineteen-year-old French aristocrat Captain Marquis DE LAFAYETTE arrived in Philadelphia, Pennsylvania and offered to serve without pay. Congress appointed him major general of the Continental Army. General LAFAYETTE met General WASHINGTON on 1 August 1777. General LAFAYETTE came to play a major role in the American Revolution. He very quickly became acquainted with the brothers, Colonel Daniel and Captain John KEMPER, while marching with them in a parade in Philadelphia, serving with them at Valley Forge and thereafter.

Captain LAFAYETTE was sympathetic to our cause and came to America against the wishes of his father-in-law who refused to supply a ship for his transportation. Captain LAFAYETTE then bought his own ship. He was overwhelmed by the rank of major general being bestowed upon him by the Continental Congress. He had no idea it was going to go that far, especially since he had little prior military experience. He also was concerned that other Continental officers thought that he was there to teach, when he was there to learn.

Elizabeth continued by saying her father stated, *"That General LAFAYETTE was sincere in his endeavors to help Americans win their liberty and establish a new nation, but because of his French connection, they had their own agenda."* Her father further stated that, *"General WASHINGTON always kept General LAFAYETTE under his wing, much like a school teacher does* with *a special student. He attempted to conceal from other Continental troops what the Marquis* [DE LAFAYETTE] *knew little about, military protocol!"*

The Marquis (nickname given to General Marquis DE LAFAYETTE by Captain John KEMPER) learned fast and without fear of dying, put his life on the line a couple of times for our liberty, even to the extent of being wounded in the Battle of Brandywine. The Marquis had an odd egg-shaped head disfigured from a difficult birth. Her father closed by saying,

"General LAFAYETTE quickly became a figure that other Continental officers began looking up to."

Elizabeth recorded many of her father's descriptions of George WASHINGTON, whom he knew personally, having been so often by his side. She recorded how her father had shared with her over the years, how General WASHINGTON would sometimes get enraged, as well as being warmhearted. He would get exhilarated and he would either place his hand on your shoulder, or warmly grab your arm in order to comfort you, realizing the stress you were under. He would often verbally share his own hardships in trying to hold the army together, while other officers likewise, were under stress trying to get their offices to function correctly.

Elizabeth went on to record how her father clearly stated, *"General WASHINGTON was not a womanizer. Even though he and Martha were married, if you did not know about it personally, you would not have been able to guess it when you saw them together. There were never any romantic gestures* [on either side]. *Theirs was a marriage entered into for personal advantage of economic and political reasons. He would never fraternize with other women, regardless if they were beautiful or shapely. Other officers thought of this as kind of odd about him; because of his position, he could have had anyone he wanted."*

She continued expressing how her father repeatedly shared stories with her over her lifetime, how *"General WASHINGTON was a perfect gentleman, until his feathers were ruffled, but soon calmed down; however, he never held personal grudges. He was fully aware of other officers who wanted his position, but never took it personally, or allowed it to interfere with his judgment or leadership."*

The month of August had arrived and General WASHINGTON had revitalized the Continental Army. He added, among others, three major military personnel, Major General Marquis DE LAFAYETTE, Count Casimir PULASKI and Captain John

KEMPER, who would all come through, in a big way, with major contributions in the spirit and outcome of the war. Just who were these three recruits, and how would they be able to change the outcome of the war? Like General WASHINGTON, all would play their part to the hilt! Let the journey begin and their stories unfold.

Elizabeth recorded that her mother, Elizabeth (Eliza) HOPPER, John KEMPER's childhood sweetheart, presented her father John with a journal to record his memoirs. He took this journal with him when he went to join his brother Daniel in Philadelphia. However, something else was going on here; somewhere along the way, Captain KEMPER either acquired or started two new books; one, *Wagon Master*, and two, *US Naval Affairs*.

It was originally assumed that, John started writing the book, *US Naval Affairs* after he joined the US Navy, but after diligent research, this author could not verify this supposition. After the Revolution, the Congress destroyed all the secret journals they kept, not wanting anyone to ever know who was in them and what their missions were. Neither did Congress want anyone in the world to know the inner dealings except resolutions passed. Therefore, there were no records left or notes taken, just *"word-of-mouth."* Because of this need of secrecy, John, therefore, had to be very diligent in keeping his journals in code and hidden. Elizabeth or this author was unable to decipher Many of these coded entries. Many questions and mysteries continued to accumulate in the family.

On 2 August 1777, Colonel Marinus WILLETT (1740-1830), commander at Fort Stanwix, New York, wrote, *"The fort never had been supplied with the new flag. The necessity of having one, upon the arrival of the enemy, taxed the invention of the garrison, and a decent one was soon contrived. The white stripes were cut out of ammunition shirts furnished by the soldiers; the blue out of the camlet cloak taken from the enemy at Peekskill; while the red stripes were made of different pieces of stuff procured from one another and the garrison."*

Apparently, Colonel WILLETT, who had attended King's College as Colonel KEMPER and Colonel HAMILTON had, had no means of putting stars into the blue field. The waiting for the new flag was driving everyone absolutely mad. Everyone knew about it, but it just was not happening soon enough. Fort Stanwix was situated on the banks of the Mohawk River on the western frontier of New York. It was constantly considered by the British, as a base for an invasion into Canada.

In early August 1777, after being concerned that the USS *Hancock* was way overdue, a local commander at Boston, Massachusetts, sent a dispatch to General WASHINGTON expressing their concerns for Commodore John MANLEY. They feared that he might have been either, captured or killed.

After the *Boston* returned to port reporting on the fate of the *Hancock,* a new dispatch was sent to General WASHINGTON. General WASHINGTON, after reading the dispatch, lowered his head in concern, took a deep breath, and then exhaled. Would there be any way he could find out if Commodore MANLEY was still alive and a prisoner of war or deceased?

General WASHINGTON would try to get answers the only way he knew how, through the intelligence network he had already set up, but all attempts were negative. He would have to quickly revise his intelligence web to accommodate this new challenge. Need would once again become the mother of inventions, ideas and schemes.

Chapter XII
Master Wagon Master

After John KEMPER arrived in Philadelphia, he entered into the meeting with General WASHINGTON, his brother, Colonel Daniel KEMPER, Colonel Alexander HAMILTON, Major Benjamin TALLMADGE and a couple of members of the Continental Congress. Little is recorded in Captain KEMPER's journals of this meeting other than who was involved, excluding the names of the members of Congress who had attended the meeting. However, Captain KEMPER did record General WASHINGTON's words of wisdom, after the meeting was finished, *"Look for friends where you expect to find enemies, and enemies where you expect to find allies, and learn to expect what least is expected."* Captain KEMPER would become known as the ghost who appeared, then disappeared.

Little did John KEMPER know, but General WASHINGTON's words of wisdom would end up haunting the both of them until the very day they died. Captain KEMPER recorded that, *"General WASHINGTON generally knew what was going to happen before it happened, like some kind of prophet, but always gave the benefit of the doubt. Sometimes that doubt cost him dearly."* Captain KEMPER tried to mimic General WASHINGTON's wisdom the best that he could but ended up paying dearly for it in the final years of his life, during his pension years.

After their meeting with General WASHINGTON and the members of Congress, Colonel Daniel KEMPER, Colonel Alexander HAMILTON, Major Benjamin TALLMADGE and John KEMPER hurdled up together outside. Colonel Daniel KEMPER took the lead, *"Okay, we all know what we have to do.*

John, both you and Alexander are going to have to see to matters in Philadelphia."

Colonel **HAMILTON** said, *"John, you are going to need some Indian scouts for your army, do you know of any?"*

John bowed his head, shaking it from side to side and said, *"Not really."*

Major **TALLMADGE** peered around Captain **KEMPER's** shoulders and said, *"Well, there is one right behind you, maybe you can get him."*

John slowly turned around, his eyes opened wide, his jaw dropped; it was Lone WOLF, standing like a statue in the middle of the street with his horse.

John walked up to Lone WOLF and asked, *"Where in the hell did you come from?"*

Lone WOLF glared at the captain and said, *"The time has come."*

John paused for a moment, and then replied, *"Yes it has and I intend on fulfilling my promise to you; I need a mighty warrior and good scout, you will now be part of my army."*

Lone WOLF was standing tall and proud, showing internal strength, as if a great destiny had finally been met. John then turned to his comrades, curled his fist in the air, acknowledging success. John's brother, Daniel, was smiling as he remembered Lone WOLF from the tavern.

Captain **KEMPER** then glanced over at the horse, Sandy, that his father had sold to Lone WOLF. Hanging upside-down from a leather strap wrapped around his horse's neck on its right side, was the crossbow. John nodding, while smiling, looked back at Lone WOLF and remarked, *"That is a mighty fine looking crossbow you have their, WOLF."*

Lone WOLF responded, *"A mighty white warrior helped me buy it."*

Captain KEMPER continued to smile, holding his lips tight, while nodding.

From this point on, Captain KEMPER and Colonel HAMILTON's friendship continued to grow, as their involvement became closer. They would often meet at City Tavern to discuss business under a more relaxed atmosphere. They had their favorite corner, under lamplight. This atmosphere reminded both Alexander and John of his father's tavern where they established their friendship and made them feel comfortable.

On 7 August 1777, John headed to the clothier-general's department, where he entered into the service of the United States under James MEASE, clothier-general of the Continental Army. His brother, Colonel Daniel KEMPER, was deputy clothier-general at camp with General WASHINGTON, while Charles YOUNG was deputy clothier-general and first clerk to James MEASE, stationed in Philadelphia. James YOUNG (?-1780) was wagon master-general.

Everything was kept low-keyed, and John KEMPER was appointed wagon master by James YULE (1755-1832), deputy wagon master-general, and received a captain's pay and rations and the same for his horse. Captain KEMPER was engaged in convoying the massive Conestoga wagons with essential transports to General WASHINGTON and the Continental Army, among other duties directed solely by General WASHINGTON.

After John KEMPER got out of his meeting with General WASHINGTON, his brother Colonel Daniel KEMPER, Colonel Alexander HAMILTON, Major Benjamin TALLMADGE and members of Congress, their strategy began. Once John was appointed captain and wagon master, he informed Mr. MORTON of his deployment. This new development was John MORTON's dream come true. He now had a direct channel through his brother-in-law to his commander-in-chief and the Continental Congress. General WASHINGTON and the Continental Congress needed this connection as well.

Mr. MORTON spent everything he could throughout the Revolution to try and keep Congress and General WASHINGTON afloat. He began by fulfilling his promise to his brother-in-law by furnishing and supplying uniforms and the best equipment he could muster for Captain John KEMPER's army. In addition, he was able to obtain three extra Conestoga wagons and 18 horses to be added to Captain KEMPER's wagon-train, a great feat.

Before leaving Philadelphia, Captain KEMPER had his men carve names on boards and had them placed on the side of the wagons Mr. MORTON supplied; one was named, *"Morton's Supply,"* while another, *"The Johnny-In-Laws."* For the third wagon, he had a board carved with the name *"KEMPER"* fastened to the rear of the lead wagon. The lead wagon always remained empty so as not to slow down the rest of the convoy, and pave the way for other wagons, especially during the winter months. On the right forward side of each of the three wagons was fastened a brass plate.

On each side of the front of the three wagons was placed a brass ring for holding torches. On the left rear of the lead wagon, as well as the wagons marked, "Morton's Supply" and "The Johnny-in-Laws," another brass ring was set for holding the flag of the United States. Finally, a brass ring was placed on the rear of the last wagon in his convoy of 150 wagons. Captain KEMPER loved his flag.

One of the other purposes of the lead wagon was to make night runs during the full moon. In one of General WASHINGTON's dispatches to Captain KEMPER, he was warned that, if the night was cloudy, preventing the light of the full moon from illuminating the countryside, he was to wait for new orders. Captain KEMPER's lead wagon was used when General WASHINGTON gave him special assignments. Horses cannot see well at night, so special missions were planned during a full moon.

When General WASHINGTON had stopped by one of Captain KEMPER's wagon-train camps, he observed Captain KEMPER's carvings on the three wagons; he then slowly turned towards Captain KEMPER, bowed his head and said, *"Identification job well done."* Apparently everything had been discussed prior to completion.

The two wagons marked *"Morton's Supply"* and *"The Johnny-in-laws"* were always parked alongside the tent of Captain KEMPER's officers' when at camp and specially guarded. General WASHINGTON was always kept abreast of Mr. MORTON's continued contributions and support for both, the Continental Army and Congress, through his direct involvement. Financial support was the hardest to come by during the Revolution and was quickly rewarded with special favors by both, General WASHINGTON and the Continental Congress.

The two wagons were specifically named for a reason. The wagon, which had the boards on both sides carved *"Morton's Supply,"* was specifically for General WASHINGTON. The wagon with the boards carved, *"The Johnny-in-Laws,"* was specifically for the Continental Congress. Prior to these wagons being specifically named, the idea was submitted to both General WASHINGTON and the Continental Congress and accepted. The contents of the boxes, barrels, crates and other carefully packed and sealed containers were labeled in code that John KEMPER had developed when he was a young boy, and likewise, accepted by both General WASHINGTON and the Continental Congress.

Benjamin FRANKLIN was in the meeting involved in making these decisions on intelligence with Congress in the beginning, before he went to Paris. The purpose of the coding was so that no one would know the contents of the shipment but the packer and receiver. All shipments had to be stamped by Captain John KEMPER's seal, which was *"JK"*, surrounded by a halo of thirteen stars, paid for by his brother-in-law, John MORTON, and developed by Francis HOPKINSON.

Like Mr. MORTON's, Captain KEMPER's was made of silver but had an ivory handle instead of ebony. Mr. KEMPER had put a special request into Mr. MORTON to have his initials surrounded in a halo of 13 stars. Mr. MORTON said, *"It was tricky,"* but he was able to get the job done through Francis HOPKINSON. Depending on how supplies were transported, sometimes crates would be marked with both Mr. MORTON's and Mr. KEMPER's seal.

Since both of the wagons were named accordingly, shipments would be delivered to either General WASHINGTON or Congress as designated. On one occasion, Captain KEMPER recorded in his book, *"Wagon Master,"* that as he was preparing a shipment for Congress, when General WASHINGTON stopped by his wagon-train camp with General LAFAYETTE, escorted by Continental Dragoons. He had brought some crates of his own to be added to the shipment.

Although this was a surprise visit and out of the ordinary from what was agreed upon at the original meeting, he did not question His Excellency because of who he was. General WASHINGTON and General LAFAYETTE, along with the Continental Dragoons, then accompanied him to the commons (Independence Hall). Captain KEMPER's convoy would become known as the invisible wagon-train, for whenever it faded away in the wilderness, it would seemingly disappear. Neither the British, nor anyone else for that matter, could ever locate it. The only ones who were kept abreast of its exact location were General WASHINGTON and the Continental Congress.

It was always pleasant to have General Marquis DE LAFAYETTE in company, he was often very helpful, always asking how he could help, never being forceful because of rank. He was polite, non-confrontational and non-competitive, a real gentleman. He often accompanied Captain KEMPER on his runs because the French were so deeply involved in support. They were secretly supplying arms, ammunition, powders, tents, uniforms and other supplies. All these operations were conducted under the cloak and dagger of the clothier-general's department. At the time, only the top brass and Congress knew what was going on.

General LAFAYETTE became the go-between of the French and the Americans. He even returned to France to obtain an additional six thousand troops, who were used in the Siege of Yorktown and the ultimate surrender of Lord CORWALLIS.

After the Revolution, Captain KEMPER told countless stories to his children as they were growing up, on how their uncle John MORTON was one of the heroes of the Revolution, not through combat, but through the thrill of the only profession he knew how—by making money to finance its cause. He related how both of their uncles, John MORTON and Colonel Daniel KEMPER, continued to back him up and make sure that he succeeded during the Revolution. While Daniel did it with gold braid, Mr. MORTON did it with gold dollars.

Captain KEMPER related how he and John MORTON had become so close because of being brothers-in-law and of his business dealings in financing the Revolution, that they were given the nick name, *the Johnny-in-Laws.* Mr. MORTON had given him a gold pocket watch as a keep-sake. John had placed a picture of Eliza inside the cover of the watch. After the Revolution, he was bound and determined to name a son after Mr. MORTON, especially after his needless way of dying.

Captain John KEMPER instilled the importance of the MORTON name into his children, who carried on the name for generations.

Captain KEMPER's son Daniel, named after his brother, had a son named George Morton KEMPER, who, likewise, named a son, Morton *"Mortie"* John KEMPER (1872-1937). It is not clear why John's brother Daniel never named any children after Mr. MORTON, probably because the *"Johnny-in-Laws"* were closer.

Captain KEMPER was the direct go-between of Mr. MORTON, General WASHINGTON, and the Continental Congress. Daniel did name a son after their brother-in-law, Dr. David JACKSON (1747-1801), who had married their sister, Susan KEMPER; thus, David Jackson KEMPER. Even Susan named a son after her father, Jacob and brother-in-law, Mr. MORTON; thus, Jacob Morton JACKSON (1791-1874). However, their son Jacob never married, so the name never was carried on like her brother John's children had.

On 10 August 1777, General George WASHINGTON appointed General Marquis DE LAFAYETTE aide-de-camp, on recommendation in a letter he received from Benjamin FRANKLIN. General LAFAYETTE reminded General WASHINGTON that he was there to learn, not teach, as he had little military training or experience since he was so young. In fact, he was the exact same age as Captain John KEMPER, both being born in the same month and year of September 1757.

Later at a campfire discussion at Valley Forge, General LAFAYETTE had invited Captain KEMPER to his residence for a more relaxed conversation. He told John that when he was jumped up in rank from a captain to a major general, he was dazed, a little confused and somewhat scared. He was afraid of being given a general's task, without ever learning the ropes up to that rank.

On 20 August 1777, Count PULASKI met with General WASHINGTON at his headquarters in Neshaminy Falls, outside Philadelphia. At that time, the Count was waiting for Congress to assign him an official rank; Benjamin FRANKLIN was rallying for him.

Throughout the American Revolution, General WASHINGTON continued to visit Mr. MORTON at his estate in Basking Ridge, New Jersey. He enjoyed his hospitality and always made sure to thank him for his continued financial support for both the Continental Army and the Continental Congress. General WASHINGTON often brought his suite (members of his senior staff) along on his visit. Before leaving, he always asked Mr. MORTON if there was anything else he could do for him to keep things running smoothly.

General WASHINGTON always remembered to inform Mr. MORTON as to the well-being of two of his brothers-in-law, Colonel Daniel and Captain John KEMPER, who served directly under him. He also informed him that, although his brother-in-law, Jacob KEMPER did not serve directly under him, he bumped into him from time to time and he was doing just fine in the field of his choice, artillery.

Anytime General WASHINGTON made a visit to Mr. MORTON, he was always favored with two pipes (250 gallons) of Madeira wine (Portuguese) brought from Mr. MORTON's stores in New York City. This fine wine always contributed to the refreshment of the beloved commander-in-chief. General WASHINGTON would always bow upon entrance and exit of Mr. MORTON's estate. General WASHINGTON also assigned a personal courier to Mr. MORTON in the event he needed to get quickly through to General WASHINGTON, regarding supplies or hospital care for his troops. General WASHINGTON left no stone unturned.

Whenever Captain KEMPER was in Philadelphia, his means of getting mail to his family in Morristown, New Jersey, was through Mr. MARTIN. Mr. MARTIN was an old man who carried the mail between Philadelphia and Morristown, New Jersey, and was called *"the Postman"* (one who delivers mail). He wore a blue coat with yellow buttons, a scarlet waistcoat, leathern small clothes, blue yarn stockings, and a red wig and cocked hat, which gave him sort of a military appearance. Mr. MARTIN generally traveled in a sulky (two-wheeled cart), but sometimes in a chaise (carriage) or on horseback, according to the season of the year or the size and weight of the mailbag.

Mr. MARTIN was also a great means of communication between Basking Ridge, Philadelphia, and Princeton. He always stopped at Mr. MORTON's house to refresh himself and his horse, tell the news and bring packets. Mr. MARTIN was especially good at delivering live messages from Captain KEMPER to his friends and family in Basking Ridge and Morristown, New Jersey, while Captain KEMPER was in Philadelphia. Everyone in the family knew the Postman, who traveled over hills, rivers by ferry and wilderness country to deliver the mail. Mail, during this period of time, was the most important means of communication; everyone looked forward to it.

When roads were in poor condition, the horse-drawn wagons made slow progress going only about eight to ten miles per day and an even slower progress when drawn by teams of oxen. The oxen were stronger and were used for hauling artillery. When the roads were in good condition, a wagon master could travel as far as twenty miles per day. When a wagon-train was en route, often many wagons would, unintentionally, have to break away from the convoy to avoid getting stuck in ruts or they would be thrown off-course when they encountered bad road conditions.

One of the wagon master's duties was to travel back and forth among their convoy to make sure all wagons were moving in good order. Wagon masters would often stop at taverns along the way to ease the stress and fatigue of the waggoneers and troops who guarded the transports. This also allowed time for the animals to rest. The major problem Captain KEMPER had wherever he held up was, he had to remain vigilant as to Tories/ Loyalists giving away his location. Consequently, he could not tarry there and had to remain constantly on the move.

It also was up to the wagon master to determine the best time and place to make camp, pitch their tents, have lunch, and feed and water the horses. It was up to the wagon master to direct the parking of wagons before setting up camp. Camp almost always was set up near a stream, creek, or river, so the men could acquire fresh water before watering the horses, which would quickly turn the water muddy.

Tents were set up for the troops who protected the transports. An officer's tent was set up as headquarters to receive dispatches from General WASHINGTON and Congress, as well as scouting reports on British routes, troop movements, and potential foraging targets. Setting up camp was never complete until the new American flag had been hoisted on a flag pole erected just left to the entrance of the officer's tent. It was as if a ceremony in itself was taking place. All of Captain KEMPER's troops would salute their flag as it was raised.

During the Valley Forge encampment, Captain KEMPER's wagon-train camp was safely set up in a location just southeast of Lancaster and northwest of Valley Forge, at Conestoga Creek, strategically and completely out of reach of British patrols.

Captain KEMPER had recorded in his book, *"Wagon Master"* that, when he set up camp at Conestoga Creek, he had backed half of his 150 wagons to the creek, while he backed up the other half on the other side, leaving a road through the center to the officer's tent. The horses were un-harnessed, watered, and fed forage before the men could rest. On each side in front of the wagons, 80 tents were set up for his 320 troops, two men to a tent. The wagons labeled *"Morton's Supply"* and *"The Johnny-in-Laws"* were placed on each side of the officers' tent.

There was an additional six tents set up around the officers' tent in the rear in a horseshoe type fashion, housing twelve Continental Dragoons, which were responsible for security and escorting the special wagons, *"Morton's Supply"* to General WASHINGTON, and *"The Johnny-in-Laws"* to the Continental Congress. Captain Henry *"Light Horse Harry"* LEE (1756-1818) often accompanied them. Guards were always posted, no matter if they were safe from British patrols or not. Latrines were always set up outside of camp so that the odors would not offend the troops or visitors.

Captain KEMPER was ordered by General WASHINGTON to keep a logbook of all those officers who visited his wagon-train camp for supplies by his consent only, or other business. The time and supplies had to be listed as to what the officers picked up or his suppliers, like John MORTON, dropped off. While at camp, Captain KEMPER's army was often entertained by *"Crazy Legs,"* the Shawnee dancing Indian.

Among the many officers, Congress or businessmen who visited Captain KEMPER's camp on one or more occasions were, generals, (George WASHINGTON, Marquis DE LAFAYETTE, Anthony WAYNE, Lord STIRLING, Count Casimer PULASKI, Thomas MIFFLIN, Charles SCOTT, Nathanael GREENE, Peter MUHLENBERG, John SULLIVAN, and Baron Frederick VON STEUBEN); colonels, (Daniel KEMPER, Alexander HAMILTON, Elias BOUDINOT, and Benjamin TALLMADGE); captains, (Henry *"Light Horse Harry"* LEE and Sebastian BEAUMAN); a congressman (Benjamin HARRISON); and a businessman (John MORTON). Some officers often came in company with General WASHINGTON.

General George WASHINGTON was now confident that he had put together the best possible contingent for his attack and his support unit's success, through his new enlistments. General WASHINGTON was ready to put America's best before the British Empire. First, he had to find General HOWE. Where could King George's (1738-1820) genie of a top general be in the States?

Trying to conceal General HOWE's thousands of troops, dressed in red, in a dense green forest, was like trying to conceal bright-red decorations on a green Christmas tree. They were always bobbing throughout the countryside, searching everywhere for General WASHINGTON as well. Neither side knew where the other one was. Intelligence would play a big part on both sides. Both sides were being hunted by each other.

Wherever General HOWE led his magnificent army, it was like leading a stream of *"bright red cherries,"* as they bobbed through the countryside. What was more frightening about this army was that the thunderous sound of their approach could be heard miles before they ever got close.

The marching of thousands of troops as they hauled hundreds of heavy artillery, clanking as their fifers played and their drummers pounded, echoed throughout the countryside. Wildlife scattered in all directions in terror, unsure of which way to run for safety. They just ran in the opposite direction of the sound. *"General HOWE was not so hard to find after all!"*

On 22 August 1777, General WASHINGTON's web of intelligence informed him of General HOWE's location; he had landed his troops on the shores of Chesapeake Bay, leaving General Sir Henry CLINTON (1730-1795), second-in-command, in charge of New York City. General HOWE was now in the southwest, just past Philadelphia and marching northeast.

General WASHINGTON sent rush orders to General John SULLIVAN to march from eastern New Jersey *"with all convenient speed"* to rejoin the main army, which was to march *"tomorrow morning very early toward Philadelphia and onwards."* General WASHINGTON had a surprise for General HOWE, a new army.

The Continental Army then marched to meet the British Army, like two locomotives heading on a collision course. Battle after battle would be fought until the British retired in Philadelphia and the Americans retired at Valley Forge.

Chapter XIII
Grand Parade

On 23 August 1777, at 0400, General SULLIVAN left his camp on the Neshaminy River and reached Germantown (an outlying community five miles north of Philadelphia) that evening. During this period, 35 percent of the population of the thirteen states was German. There were Germantown settlements everywhere throughout the States. When General SULLIVAN's forces joined the main Continental Army, all the troops began to blossom with excitement and anticipation as their army continued to grow.

General WASHINGTON's senior officers suggested that he march in a parade through Philadelphia, which was on the way, to show off their strength to Philadelphians and Congress. At first General WASHINGTON was reluctant; then he thought better of it, as this was a chance to show Congress just how badly equipped his army was. The parade through Philadelphia was scheduled for Sunday morning, 24 August. General WASHINGTON sent a message to John HANCOCK in Congress, informing him that he would be marching the Continental Army through Philadelphia the following morning.

General WASHINGTON directed that his men *"burnish your arms and wash your clothes so that you will show our best appearance before the citizens and Congress."* Some of the soldiers were so impoverished that they wore British uniforms that they had taken off dead British soldiers. He also directed that each soldier wear a *"green sprig, emblem of hope"* in his hat. The best part of the preparation for this parade was about to take place. General WASHINGTON was going to unfurl the new flag of stars and stripes for the first time during this special event, instead of in battle as originally planned.

Francis HOPKINSON had made sure that General WASHINGTON received the first flag. The long anticipation for its arrival was over! The flag and what it stood for boosted the morale of the entire Continental Army. Everyone looked at the halo of stars as a guardian angel; everyone truly believed that the heavens were shining down on them.

General WASHINGTON commanded, *"The army is to move precisely at four in the morning, if it should not rain—the division commanded by Genrl [Anthony] WAYNE is to take its proper place in the line (to wit, between Lord STIRLING's and Genrl STEPHEN's division). The divisions march as follows—[Nathanael] GREENE's, STEPHEN's—LINCOLN's, Lord STIRLING's—"*

"The following Order of March is to be observed. First—A sub: and twelve light horse—200 yards in their rear a complete troop, a residue of [Theodoric] *BLAND's (1741-1790) and* [George] *BAYLOR's (1752-1784) Regiments—100 yards in the rear of these, a company of pioneers, with their axes &c. in proper order—One hundred yards in the rear of the pioneers, a regiment of MUHLENBERG's Brigade; and close in the rear of that regiment, all MUHLENBERG's field artillery—the brigade followed by* [George] *WEEDON's (1734-1793),* [William] *WOODFORD's (1734-1780) &* [Charles] *SCOTT's, in order with all their field artillery in their respective fronts3—*

"The park of artillery, and the artificers belonging thereto, in the center—[Benjamin] *LINCOLN (1733-1810) and* [William Alexander] *Lord STIRLING's (1725-1783) divisions following, with all their brigade artillery in the rear of their respective brigades—A regiment of Lord STIRLING's division for a rear guard, and to be 150 yards from Genrl* [William] *MAXWELL's Brigade—*[Elisha] *SHELDON's (1741-1805) and* [Stephen] *MOYLAND's (1737-1811)*

horse 150 yards in rear of this regiment, and a troop of 150 yards in the rear of the regiments of horse."

Grand parade! What the heck would a parade be doing going on in the middle of a war? General WASHINGTON, all his senior staff and Congress were all in the same location at the same time. There would never be another time in the entire history of America when all officials would be so exposed. However, the rest of the world did not have a clear picture of what was going on.

There were torrential rains, rumbles of violent thunder and bolts of lightning flashing and striking all over Philadelphia from the heavens; they could be seen and heard for miles. It was as if the Lord was christening the birth of a new nation under him. The entire Continental Army stood in awe! John ADAMS wrote a letter to his wife, Abigail (1744-1818), describing the current events.

On 24 August 1777, this morning would be like none before or after it. The day started out fair but soon torrential rains began to pour down and the army was now worried about getting soaked and feared their show would be spoiled. *"The previous evening, there had been very loud, sharp and violent thunder gusts, followed by lightning and heavy rains. The lightning struck in several locations; it struck the Quaker Alms House on Walnut Street, between Third and Fourth Streets, not far from Captain Matthew DUNCANS' [1750-1807] place. They were smart enough to have placed an iron rod upon the top of the steeple, for a vane to turn on, but had provided no conductor to the ground. It also struck on Fourth Street, near Mrs. CHEESMANS'; nobody was hurt."*

General WASHINGTON gathered all his troops a mile out of town, northeast of Philadelphia, along the Delaware River. He then began emphatically instructing them on parade procedures, so that the line of march through the city might be as little encumbered as possible, *"Only one ammunition wagon is to attend the field piece [cannon] of each brigade and every artillery park. Each brigade is to be preceded by their own drummers and fifers and a tune for the quickstep rhythm played but to such moderation that the men may step to it with ease. The baggage-wagons containing all clothing and other necessaries and spare horses were to file off to the right, to avoid the city entirely, and move onto the bridge at the middle ferry, and there, halt."*

General WASHINGTON continued mandatory orders, *"It is expected that every officer, without exception, will keep his post in passing through the city, and under no pretense whatever leave it; and if any soldier shall dare to leave his place he shall receive thirty-nine lashes at the first halting place afterwards."*

On 24 August 1777, Sunday morning, General WASHINGTON decided to unfurl the new American flag for the first time for their march through Philadelphia. Officers and soldiers alike were keyed up with anticipation as General WASHINGTON unfurled the new flag and then attached it to a flagpole. They were ecstatic. They twisted and bobbed their heads to catch a glimpse; all the while, chattering, *"Can you see it? What does it look like? Can you see the stars? Why is it taking so long? . . . Oh, how grand it looks!"* After General WASHINGTON had made the new flag visible, it appeared to sparkle, as if the sun were shining down from the heavens on it alone. The entire Continental Army hummed in silence and trembled in its awe.

Captain John KEMPER's daughter, Elizabeth, recorded in her diary the stories her father had shared with her on this event. She said that her father had told her that Francis HOPKINSON, whom the Continental Congress had delegated to make the new flag, made sure General WASHINGTON received the first one. General WASHINGTON had originally intended to display the new flag in battle before General HOWE and the British Army that had landed at Chesapeake Bay. This occasion changed his mind.

Then it ended—the torrential rains stopped, leaving the roads muddy. While the sun broke through the clouds on this eighty-degree day, it appeared to *"magically illuminate"* their new flag of broad stripes and bright stars, which had just been unfurled for the first time and now proudly displayed. Wherever this flag was flown, everyone's eyes were always on it.

General George WASHINGTON, mounted on his white horse, led his grand parade of sixteen thousand troops. As they proceeded into town, all his mounted officers followed directly behind, with the sounds of drummers and fifers echoing throughout the city. General WASHINGTON had already replaced sixteen thousand of the nineteen thousand Continental soldiers he had lost on the Island of Manhattan, through new enlistments. He was continually able to replenish his loses on his own soil while General HOWE was not. If General WASHINGTON fell when he clashed with General HOWE, he would die hard!

This grand parade of sixteen thousand soldiers was a spectacular sight. Each brigade was led by their drummers, fifers and flag carriers, their show of artillery and then soldiers marching in rows of twelve men wide. If the men had marched alone, that would have been 1,333 rows, but with the addition of their musicians, artillery, and wagons, its expansion was ten miles long. It commenced at 0700 and concluded after 1000 (7:00 a.m. to 10:00 a.m.).

All the officers joined in this parade with pride and inspiration. There was magic in the air and everyone was feeling goose bumps. The green sprigs the soldiers were wearing in their hats seemed to give a deeper meaning to their cause. To prevent the audience from interrupting the parade, Captain Henry *"Light Horse Harry"* LEE rode guard on the left of the procession. No one could foresee the hardships they would encounter in establishing the liberty of the new nation they were forming. It was like one big happy family; they would all meet together again at Valley Forge.

They started south down Front Street along the Delaware River. As they reached Market Street, from the Coffee House

Corner, Captain Alexander GRAYDON (1752-1818), among others, watched the parade. Loyalists, who were watching from the same location, snubbed their noses at the procession. The parade continued to Chestnut Street, then onward west on up past Fifth Street and Independence Hall, where Congress was conducting business. This brought a halt to business as usual. Some members of Congress peered out of windows, while others, like John HANCOCK and John ADAMS (1735-1826), went outside to watch. This was the day they had been waiting for, to look upon their creation.

Officers rode guard along the procession preventing the army from being crowded by the onlookers. Cheers of extreme excitement were abundant everywhere; some were seen crying with joy. Others were seen raising their fists in the air, showing signs of euphoria, hope and confidence, as if a great victory had already been won! Tories/Loyalist continued to snub their noses in the air, but knew better than attack the army. The Continental troops were surrounded by mixed emotions.

Although Congress had heard that General WASHINGTON had rebuilt their army, they had not seen its magnificence until today. All they could remember was that, their army was wiped out on the Island of Manhattan. The Tories, likewise, were totally amazed, they had hoped that General WASHINGTON and the Continental Army would have been crushed, but now they began to worry.

Many people got caught up in the excitement of the parade, as mentioned in Captain KEMPER's journals. One civilian was marching alongside the parade on Captain KEMPER's left, as they proceeded up Chestnut Street toward the commons (Independence Hall). He wore a white shirt and black over-alls, had no weapons, but was grinning profusely, with his hands curled into fists as if ready to fight. His arms and fists swayed to and fro as he glared straight ahead, while proudly marching alongside the parade. It looked as if he was ready to start off running. It was unclear why this individual was so energized or why he did not just join the army. The Continental Army needed men like this who shared in their belief and displayed themselves proudly.

The formation was such that leading the grand parade were five men. At the center of the front line was a soldier holding the new flag in a leather flag belt. To each side of the flagman was a drummer, and on the outside of each drummer was a fifer. The fifer on the left, as the parade was headed toward the commons (Independence Hall), had a wooden leg. His pant leg was curled up to the knee joint, exposing the peg leg.

Captain KEMPER later recorded in his journals that he never knew if the man with the peg leg actually belonged to a company or was just marching in the parade. Was General WASHINGTON just grabbing anyone he could get, or was it that everyone just wanted to play a part? Everyone just looked at the peg leg, then at each other in a silent glare, which was self-explanatory. Very few questioned what was going on during this period of time; most just went along with the flow, like a river that travels one-way and never turns back. The man with the peg leg was never seen again; it was as if he had disappeared in a fog or the excitement of the glory of a special moment in time.

Next in the formation came all the officers on horseback, leading the troops as they marched. Note that all the officers on parade were a tightly knit unit. Everyone knew one another, but to the world, they were not yet of any importance. Everyone knew who all the Continental officers were; they were always at the front of everything that was going on, drawing everyone's attention and standing out prominently. General WASHINGTON always wanted his officers to be easily recognizable and their American audience to be envious of them. The officers looked beautiful and glorious in their new uniforms that Captain KEMPER was responsible for supplying and the cockades signifying their rank. Even they themselves were not aware they would become the founding fathers in the birth of America.

As it was noted in Captain KEMPER's journal, General Marquis DE LAFAYETTE was on the right of General WASHINGTON and to General WASHINGTON'S left was General Nathanael GREENE. Riding in the next line in the formation were General John Peter MUHLENBERG, Count Casimir PULASKI, who was not yet in uniform because he was still waiting for his rank to be issued by Congress, and Major General Anthony WAYNE.

In the next line were Colonel Alexander HAMILTON, Captain John KEMPER and Colonel Daniel KEMPER. All other officers, like Lord STIRLING, were also there, but Captain KEMPER could not remember their exact location for his journal, because there was so much going on that day and everyone was in such high spirits and greatly excited from the event. Everyone in the crowds was constantly changing their positions. Crowds of people everywhere, cheering! Where were the Tories/Loyalists and neutralists? Were they playing a part in this audience?

As they approached the commons (Independence Hall), all eyes were on General WASHINGTON. Congressman Benjamin HARRISON (1726-1791), who was standing outside, watching the parade approach, pointed his finger in the direction of Colonel Alexander HAMILTON and Colonel Daniel and Captain John KEMPER, offering a soft, warm. The three returned the soft nod. Ambassador Benjamin FRANKLIN was in Paris during this period of time, or he certainly would have been watching this parade.

Major General John MUHLENBERG dropped back and motioned for Colonel Alexander HAMILTON to also drop back for a moment, so that he could get close to John KEMPER. General MUHLENBERG grabbed John KEMPER's left arm, reached over, and whispered something into KEMPER's ear in German, then went back into formation. This moment was always known as *"the whisper."*

"The whisper"—what was it all about? What was said? We will never know what the significance of the whisper was, but it was noted by Captain KEMPER that he felt it should not be entered in his journals. This event was also mentioned in Elizabeth's diary.

After the parade, General WASHINGTON sent Captain John KEMPER to his station in Philadelphia, while the rest of the army marched southwest toward Chesapeake Bay to meet up with General Sir William HOWE. Colonel Daniel KEMPER, aide-de-camp, followed along. Because of Daniel's continued loyalty and readiness, at the Battle of Brandywine and helping General LAFAYETTE to safety, he made Daniel special assistant aide, along with Colonel John LAURENS at the Battle of Germantown.

Elizabeth again mentioned her father recalling the time the count made his grand appearance as he marched with him in the parade, through the streets of Philadelphia. He stated, *"The Count was a wretched sort of character, which made General WASHINGTON leery. That he was peppy, vivacious and always looking for battle. He was brave, always out front and never feared of being outnumbered. He would always be one of the first to volunteer for or assist in any task, no matter how difficult, especially if there was a chance of meeting up with the enemy and the color red."*

After the parade was finished, which took over three hours to complete, General WASHINGTON led the Continental Army as they marched to meet General HOWE, who was pushing northeast toward Philadelphia. Captain John KEMPER was ordered to take his troops and proceeded to join his wagoners at their post on Front Street, along the Delaware River, to await further orders from General WASHINGTON. Colonel Alexander HAMILTON, along with Colonel Daniel KEMPER, likewise, went with General WASHINGTON's army to Chesapeake Bay. General WASHINGTON always favored trusted backup in preparation for the worst.

On 3 September 1777 what everyone had been waiting for happened. The new American flag, which the Second Continental Congress had ordered to be made by Francis HOPKINSON back on the fourteenth of June, was hoisted up at Independence Hall. Francis HOPKINSON had made sure Congress and other commanders were some of the next to receive a new flag. The KEMPER brothers, Daniel and John looked on in marvel with the rest of the audience. You could never see enough of it.

Independence Hall was the home base for Congress and where the "Constitution of the United States" was written and signed. This was that special moment they had been waiting for. Their own flag replaced the Grand Union flag and flew over their capital. Captain John KEMPER already had had a leather holster strapped on the right chest of his horse in anticipation of holstering this new flag on his journeys.

Francis HOPKINSON was mass-producing the new American flag and making sure all Continental officers who led a unit, or were stationary as in a fort, received one. While the new flag was being hoisted over Independence Hall, General William MAXWELL was displaying it in battle for the first time on this very day, in the skirmish at Cooch's Bridge (Newark, Delaware).

Colonel Marinus WILLET—who had been going mad waiting for the new flag, so made his own—now received his. Colonel WILLETT stared at the new flag in a daze; it was so different than the one he had made, —it was the real thing! This special moment was shared with Captain John KEMPER on one of his routine gathering of officers, along with Colonel WILLETT, after he had returned from Fort Stanwix, and a prisoner of war.

Throughout the American Revolution, Colonel Marinus WILLETT became close to the KEMPER brothers. He continued that closeness after the Revolution and during his membership in the Society of Cincinnati. Colonel WILLETT went on to furnish a certificate on the integrity of Colonel Daniel KEMPER later on after the Revolution. Colonel Daniel KEMPER reflected on Colonel WILLETT's certificate in his declaration to the United States Senate and United States Congress given on 9 April 1832; it also is covered in his brother, John's journals.

Before the collision of the two armies, General HOWE was momentarily mesmerized by the appearance of the new American flag, leading the advance of General WASHINGTON and the Continental Army. Now the Americans had a symbol to represent their cause. This symbol gave them faith and hope; General HOWE was enraged! How did it ever get to this?

What was more startling was, where in the hell did General George WASHINGTON get his new army? General HOWE had wiped out his army a year ago at Fort Washington: he was not supposed to rebuild it, and he was supposed to have surrendered. Just what was wrong with this man called General WASHINGTON? Did not anyone ever tell him that the superior British Army was here, that he was supposed to have surrendered and the war was supposed to be over?

This was one of the military blunders General HOWE made. By not running down General WASHINGTON and finishing him off, he allowed him a chance to rebuild his army. Whenever General HOWE lost any troops, they were gone permanently; he had all he could get from home (England) and Germany. However, General WASHINGTON was like a genie playing a video game in the twenty-first Century and resurrecting his army. Now, General HOWE really had a serious problem: he had to try to wipe out General WASHINGTON's new army all over again, at the cost of losing many more thousands of troops in return. What kind of war was this going to turn out to be?

The new American flag was just another one of General HOWE's nightmare coming to life, an emblem of unity, strength, and pride; this could give an army faith. This new flag would become an emblem of freedom and justice and perpetuate fear into all evil countries around the globe, even into the twenty-first Century. On this same date, Congress had started moving to Lancaster because of mounting fears that the British would capture Philadelphia—and would love to capture them as well.

On 11 September 1777, after several skirmishes between the two armies, each trying to figure what the other was going to do, finally the two locomotives collided at Brandywine in the heavy fog. Colonel Daniel KEMPER, witnessing General LAFAYETTE being shot off his horse, immediately ordered troops to carry him to safety. Since the wound was not that severe, he was able to recover.

General LAFAYETTE would never forget Colonel Daniel KEMPER's life-saving orders. After the Revolution, General LAFAYETTE, being grateful, petitioned the society for the privilege to be able to award Colonel KEMPER the Badge of the Society of Cincinnati, citing his bravery and commitment to his fellow officers; it was granted by President George WASHINGTON.

General WASHINGTON was forced to retreat, and because all his artillery horses were killed, he was forced to leave all his artillery behind as well. Killing the horses that hauled the artillery was one of the first objectives by the British in order to immediately disable the American Army and obtain their firepower, which further disabled them.

This magnificent emblem representing freedom and justice steadily launched America into the future. America quickly evolved into a leading nation on many fronts. In the early 1800s, we jumped into the Industrial Revolution. In 1969 we not only landed on the moon, we proudly planted the American flag, as the whole world watched in awe.

Other countries, filled with jealousy and envy of the accomplishments of our young nation, would repeatedly strike our colors in the only manner possible, by burning it on their own soil, in order to to try and disgrace us, knowing better than to face-off with the army it represented anywhere in the world. America ended up leaving many other countries behind in the deserts and jungles, where they had remained for thousands of years. The magic of the American flag never disappears, only grows more intense.

On this same date of 11 September 1777, while General WASHINGTON's main army was fighting General William HOWE's main army, Ensign Anthony MAXWELL, who was in John SANTFORD's company, Colonel William MALCOLM's regiment, was in the battle of Hackensack, New Jersey. Somehow, Colonel MALCOLM's regiment got separated from General WASHINGTON's main army and was not able to participate in the parade. Colonel MALCOLM would later march his regiment to join General WASHINGTON's army at Valley Forge.

On 15 September 1777, Congress appointed Count Casimir PULASKI brigadier general of the Continental Army, recommended by Benjamin FRANKLIN. He reformed the cavalry and wrote the first regulations on formation, gaining recognition as *the father of the American cavalry.*" Things were continuing to come together for General WASHINGTON.

On 18 September 1777, General WASHINGTON sent a dispatch to Colonel HAMILTON that General HOWE was capturing everything in his path on his march to Philadelphia. He then ordered Colonel HAMILTON to destroy a flour warehouse on the other side of the Schuylkill River in Valley Forge before the advancing British troops could capture it. Colonel HAMILTON took eight cavalrymen, including Captain Henry LEE, to Valley Forge to burn the flourmill. Unbeknownst to Colonel HAMILTON, Loyalists had already given its location to the British Army, who had sent British Dragoons there to protect it for their own use.

The British had camped at Tredyffrin, a small village three miles southwest of Valley Forge. There they found a magazine (a military supply depot) filled with a treasure trove of American supplies: 3,800 barrels of flour, soap and candles; 25 barrels of horseshoes: several thousand tomahawks and kettles and entrenching tools; and 20 hogsheads of resin in a barn.

After they had arrived at the river crossing, Colonel HAMILTON posted two sentries on the hill overlooking Valley Creek to keep watch. He then used the flatboat attended by two civilians to cross over the river. After Colonel HAMILTON and Captain Henry LEE had crossed and proceeded to the warehouse, Colonel HAMILTON's sentries spotted British Dragoons and fired warning shots. Colonel HAMILTON and four cavalrymen re-boarded the flat boat and pushed off. Captain LEE, being at a further distance, did not want to get trapped, so he took off on horseback with two cavalrymen in the direction they were heading.

The British Dragoons fired numerous volleys at Colonel HAMILTON and his party as they were attempting to re-cross the Schuylkill River on the scow (flat boat), attached to a cable to keep it from being washed down river. The muskets wounded one cavalryman and killed one civilian; Colonel HAMILTON's horse was shot out from under him, and he had to swim across the Schuylkill River to the other side for safety. The wounded horse was swept down the river by the current.

Colonel HAMILTON doubled up on a horse with one of the other soldiers who had made it across. Upon escaping, Captain Henry LEE wrote General WASHINGTON of the results of their attempt and that he was concerned as to the fate of Colonel HAMILTON. The dispatch reached General WASHINGTON about the same time as Colonel HAMILTON arrived at General WASHINGTON's headquarters in Potsgrove.

After reaching safety, Colonel HAMILTON realized that the heavily armed British cavalry were only the preliminary to what was to follow, the main British Army. General WASHINGTON ordered Colonel HAMILTON to return to Philadelphia and clean out the city. He informed John HANCOCK, president of the Second Continental Congress, to abandon the capital for Lancaster and to apprise other members that the main British Army was on its way.

Wherever Congress moved became America's new capital; so Lancaster was now the new capital. Colonel HAMILTON then ordered Captain John KEMPER to remain vigilant and be ready! Captain KEMPER replied, *"I am always ready!"* By 19 September 1777, all remaining members of Congress had fled to Lancaster.

On 20 September 1777, General Anthony WAYNE was ordered by General WASHINGTON to harass the enemy baggage train from Malvern, Pennsylvania, near Palio, to slow down the British approach to Philadelphia so General WASHINGTON could get in a better position for defense. However, some of his troops deserted and fled to the British lines, informing them of his location. Upon receiving this information, the British commander, General HOWE ordered General Charles GREY (1729-1807), to prepare his regiments for battle.

During the Revolutionary period, the musket rifle had no rifling (grooves) in the barrel; therefore, it was inaccurate. You could be shooting at someone in front of you and hit someone else off in another direction, or no one at all. General GREY, knowing this, ordered his men *"not to fire or they would be considered Rebels."* He ordered his men to use their swords, bayonets (a spiked-shaped sword that fits underneath the muzzle) and firearms and to charge in and hack and pound the Americans to death. During this brutal attack and slaughter on the Americans as they were loading their muskets, the British commander earned the nickname, General Charles "No Flint" GREY.

General Anthony WAYNE's forces were taken by surprise by an overwhelming number of enemy troops; with no reinforcements, they were forced to make a hasty retreat, leaving behind much-needed weaponry and supplies. Because of this slaughter, General WAYNE lost 158 men. He was so ashamed that he requested his own court-martial; but after careful review, it was not accepted. His Excellency, General WASHINGTON, approved.

Chapter XIV
Captain Kemper's Indian Scouts

During the American Revolution, both sides used Indian scouts heavily. Indians constituted over one-fifth the population and lived naturally in the dense forests surrounding the colonial settlements. Some of those used by General WASHINGTON's army were the Mohawk and Mohegan of New York; Delaware of New Jersey; Iroquois, Shawnee, and Susquehannock of Pennsylvania; and Cherokee from the Southern states, like North and South Carolina, Virginia, and others.

Being from New York City, Captain KEMPER favored the Mohegan (Mahican, Mahigan, Mohigan, Mohican). *"Mahican"* comes from the word Muheconneok, *"from waters that are never still"* (the Hudson River). The Mohicans was also known as *"the River Indians."* Other Indian scouts Captain KEMPER had in his service were the Delaware, Iroquois, Lenape, and Shawnee. Captain KEMPER recorded in his journals that whenever they were at camp, these Indian scouts would generally go off to themselves and smoke their tobacco pipe, waiting for further orders. As John prepared his army by adding Indian scouts, visions of his fortune-teller continued to come into focus.

Captain John KEMPER had grown particularly close the Mohegan scout named Nusuwi Muks (Lone WOLF), since their meeting at the trade store and because of their displacement and forced migration to Westport, Connecticut, at the start of the Revolution. Therefore, he made Lone WOLF his chief scout. Upon being chosen as chief scout, Lone WOLF took a bear-claw necklace that he had made and attached it around Captain KEMPER's neck for the honor he had bestowed upon him. Captain KEMPER kept this bear-claw necklace all his life and upon his death his daughter, Elizabeth, made sure it was buried with him.

While Lone WOLF rode with Captain KEMPER on his lower right, Bouncing BEAR traveled with the rear guard. A lieutenant rode a little to the rear on Captain KEMPER's left, alongside the team of horses pulling the front wagon. Another lieutenant rode midway with the wagon-train.

Bouncing BEAR was Captain KEMPER's Lenape Indian scout. His name was derived from an incident that took place when he was a young boy. As a young boy, he found a bear cub lost in the woods and brought it back to the tribal camp as a pet. The young boy and the bear cub would bounce playfully around the tribal camp. Not long after, its mother came looking for her cub and caused quite a ruckus; the tribe had to kill the angry sow (mother) bear. The tribe called the boy by the name of *"Bouncing BEAR"* from then on. The tribe smoked the bear meat, made a blanket from its fur, then made a bear-skull fur hat for Bouncing BEAR.

Since the prime area in which the American Revolution took place was in the heart of the Lenape Indian territory, Bouncing BEAR played a major role as one of Captain KEMPER's leading scouts. Bouncing BEAR and Lone WOLF would become rivals.

Bouncing BEAR always wore his bear-skull fur hat, which had a tail of bear fur that trailed down his back. As he walked, the tail of fur would waggle back and forth. Bouncing BEAR would always bolster, *"Me hairy scary like big bear."*

Lone WOLF would reply, *"You hairy, not scary like little bear."*

Bouncing BEAR bantered back, *"Me no longer share your corncob pipe."*

After this incident, Lone WOLF's corncob pipe went missing.

The two Indians were always competitive with one another, but very seldom got physical. On one occasion, there was a wrestling match near their campfire, WOLF pulled out his knife. Captain KEMPER yelled, *"Stop! No weapons!"*

WOLF replied, *"Me just gonna shave the sides of his head, he not miss it. Then he look good like Mohegan."*

Captain KEMPER answered, *"Let us call this even; our enemy is out there dressed in red, not in camp."*

BEAR replied, *"You save his skin, Captain! I was just about to take that knife of his and stick it up where the sun don't shine!"*

Captain KEMPER yelled, *"Enough!"*

On another occasion, when Captain KEMPER was preparing his troops for a raid, Lone WOLF stated, *"Me do war dance, bring good luck on raid."*

Bouncing BEAR replied, *"No Indian dance like Lenape. We invented Indian dance."*

Lone WOLF said, *"Crazy Legs might disagree with you."*

The BEAR said, *"Crazy Legs is bow-legged. The only other thing those legs are good for, besides dancing, is riding a horse."*

This is the way life was at camp or on the trail. Whenever one made a comment, the other countered it. Even though Captain KEMPER's troops always got a laugh out of the confrontation, he knew how serious it could end up if he did not take control of the situation.

In Philadelphia, the largest city in the States at that time, with a population of about thirty thousand surrounded by hundreds of miles of dense wilderness, was the heartbeat of America. The houses were very crowded together; the streets full of people, hurrying to and fro; the throng (crowd) of carriages, carts and wagons were making noises everywhere. Philadelphia was definitely a busy city, but something big was about to happen that would go down in history.

Captain KEMPER recorded in his journal a fact that was well known by all Continental officers, that many Philadelphians hated General WASHINGTON and wanted him captured and hung. He was regarded as the *"ringleader"* of a band of rebels, also commonly known as whigs (outlaws) according to Tories/ Loyalists, and who were the majority of the population in the thirteen states, amounting to about 65 percent. Congress also was considered a *"band of racketeers"* for allowing the Continental Army to take whatever it needed for their cause.

On 22 September 1777, General WASHINGTON, being unable to stop General Sir William HOWE's advance, sent an emergency dispatch to Colonel Alexander HAMILTON, informing him of General HOWE's march toward Philadelphia with fifteen thousand troops and artillery. General WASHINGTON always strategically placed reliable officers in key locations, readily available for backup and support. General WASHINGTON learned fast and did not want General HOWE to capture all the stores in Philadelphia as he had done in New York City. Nor did he want to have to burn America's capital to the ground to avoid its supplies being overtaken. General WASHINGTON's letter states as such:

> *Sir, the distressed situation of the army for want of*
> *blankets, and many necessary articles of cloathing is*
> *truly deplorable; and must inevitably be destructive*
> *to it, unless a speedy remedy be applied. Without*
> *a better supply than they at present have, it will*
> *be impossible for the men to support the fatigues*
> *of the campaign in the further progress of the*
> *approaching inclement season. This you will know*
> *to be a melancholy truth. It is equally the dictate of*

common sense and the opinion of the Physicians of the army, as well as every officer in it.

No supply can be drawn from the public magazines. We have therefore no resource but from the private stock of individuals. I feel, and I lament, the absolute necessity of requiring the inhabitants to contribute to those wants, of which we have no other means of satisfying, and which if unresolved would involve the ruin of the army, and perhaps the ruin of America. Painful as it is to me to order and as it will be to you to execute the measures, I am compelled to desire you immediately to proceed to Philadelphia, and there procure from the inhabitants contributions of blankets and cloathing, and materials to answer the purpose of both, in proportion of the ability of each.

This you will do with as much delicacy and discretion, as the nature of the business demands; and I trust the necessity will justify the proceeding in the eyes of every person well affected to the American cause, and that all good citizens will cheerfully afford their assistance to the soldiers, whose sufferings they are bound to commiserate, and who are eminently exposed to danger and distress, in defense of everything they ought to hold dear.

As there are also a number of horses in Philadelphia both public and private property, which would be a valuable acquisition to the enemy, should the city by any accident fall into their hands, you are hereby authorized and commanded to remove them thence into the Country to some place of greater security, and more remote from the operations of the enemy. You will stand in need of assistance from others to execute this commission with dispatch and propriety,

*and you are therefore empowered to employ such
persons as you shall think proper to aid you therein.*

On 23 September 1777, General WASHINGTON sent an
emergency dispatch to Colonel Alexander HAMILTON stating
that, *"the British Army, commanded by Major General Sir William
HOWE, was marching towards Philadelphia with 15,000 troops."*
It ordered Colonel HAMILTON to go to Philadelphia and *"find
who he trusted to evacuate said city and have all the supplies of the
stores cleared out with everything that he could carry, before the
British got possession of the city."* Colonel HAMILTON went
to Philadelphia and set up temporary headquarters on Walnut
Street. He quickly sent for Captain John KEMPER to report to
him immediately to fulfill this emergency necessity!

After Captain KEMPER arrived, Colonel HAMILTON
informed him that, he had received an emergency dispatch from
General WASHINGTON and with a smile on his face he pushed
the letter forward on his desk for Captain KEMPER to read.
Captain KEMPER, knowing something was up because Colonel
HAMILTON was smiling profusely, began to read the dispatch.

Captain KEMPER knew that General WASHINGTON was
always a very serious man, but that he could also be a very funny
guy at times.

> *As I was reading, I uncontrollably burst out laughing;
> I had found the part Colonel HAMILTON was
> chuckling about. General WASHINGTON was
> issuing orders for us to make military acquisitions
> of all the private stock in the city held by the civilian
> population, as contributions to the American cause,
> including their mode of transportation, horses.
> General WASHINGTON continued that all good
> citizens would cheerfully afford their assistance.*

> *As I passed General WASHINGTON's letter back to Colonel HAMILTON, he continued smiling, then said, 'Here are your orders of march Captain, please go out there and get those contributions.' As I left Colonel HAMILTON's office, I was still smiling and laughing, while shaking my head."* Colonel HAMILTON finalized by saying, *"Remember Captain, use as much delicacy and discretion as possible. Before we are finished, Philadelphians are surely going to love us. General WASHINGTON is just making sure we will be remembered in history. When you are finished, please return.*

Since the British were on their way, Captain KEMPER had to make haste. You would be able to hear the thunderous sounds of thousands of troops marching to the beat of drums and fifers, along with the hauling of their heavy artillery, far before they ever reached Philadelphia. Captain John KEMPER's part in the birth of America had now reached its **grandeur.** He now had to sign many certificates to be given for the many generous donations by the citizens of Philadelphia.

Captain KEMPER put his Indian scouts on high alert and fanned them out to the southwest of Philadelphia to watch for General HOWE's advance. Lone WOLF stayed with Captain KEMPER; he then took his army of 320 men and quietly and strategically placed them throughout Philadelphia at all the locations of the stores in preparation for a timed-military acquisition. His prime target area was High Street (Market Street), which started at Front Street along the Delaware River and ran west through Philadelphia to the Schuylkill River.

This street was in the heart of Philadelphia and was where all the markets had flourished. He did not want to start confiscating supplies at one store, while the rest got news of what was going on and try to conceal their goods. What no one knew at the time was that, General WASHINGTON, Colonel HAMILTON and

Captain KEMPER had all planned for this moment, should it arrive. That is why when General WASHINGTON was battling General HOWE's army, Colonel HAMILTON and Captain KEMPER remained vigilant in Philadelphia.

Captain KEMPER quickly rode to the docks to warn all the navy captains that the British were on their way. They were instructed to load as many supplies as quickly as they could and leave the vicinity to a safer location so that their ships could not be captured.

Meanwhile, Captain KEMPER's uncle and aunt, Matthias and Anna Maria ERNST were living in Philadelphia. While Captain KEMPER's men were getting ready, he quickly rode off to his uncle's house. He then jumped off his horse, ran to his uncle's house and urgently rapped on the door. Matthias opened the door and said, *"John! What a pleasant surprise."*

John hurriedly addressed his uncle, *"The British are on their way, quickly gather what belongings you can without drawing too much attention to yourself. I have to clean out the city, beware of Tories/ Loyalists!"*

Matthias replied, *"I understand."*

John remounted his horse while Matthias said, *"Thanks, John!"*

John replied, *"Hurry!"* He then galloped off. Matthias told his wife to start packing while he headed to the docks to hire a sloop to transport their furniture and personal belongings to Trenton.

Captain KEMPER had men stationed at street corners so that when he gave the signal. they would start confiscating all the supplies. He also sent a party to the stables to confiscate all the horses from the public domain. He then seized all the horses of private citizens in the city. When it was time to leave, he had the horses attached to the rear of his wagons. When everyone was ready, Captain **KEMPER** gave the command to empty all the stores with due diligence and it took the next two days to fill his wagons with all the goods, leaving the shelves at each store empty.

As he accompanied his men to the various stores, the store clerks raised their hands while backing off from so many rifles being pointed in their direction. The military baring their arms in excessive force alarmed most of the clerks. They knew something big was about to happen, since this was the military, not a run-of-the mill robbery, but did not question the action. For those who did question as to the reason, Captain **KEMPER** just answered with a silent glare.

As the noise picked up all over the city and Continental soldiers were seen and heard galloping, while hustling and bustling throughout the city, fear began to set in the residents as their horses, wagons and carts were hauled away. While the army was emptying all their stores, citizens began rushing to the windows and doors yelling, *"What is going on?"* Field cannons were being rushed off, while guns were being pointed in every direction.

Residents could be heard yelling, *"They are taking our horses and wagons. What are we going to use for transportation?"*

Still others exclaimed, *"They are taking our food as well! What are we going to eat?"*

While others yelled, *"They are taking everything!"*

Philadelphia now was really a hectic city! Anger was everywhere; blood daggers were in their eyes! The collection of *"contributions"* to be picked up, ordered by General **WASHINGTON**, was well under way.

Another resident yelled, *"Captain, your army is cleaning out our whole city. Do you think you are going down in history as a hero? How can you not have a conscience for what you are doing? What are you looking for as a reward, captain, chocolates? Only General WASHINGTON is going to give them to you. Although you probably already robbed the candy store."*

After Captain **KEMPER**'s officers started reporting in on their completion of the tasks given them, they informed him of the discontent of the citizens of the city and asked if he was sure they were doing the right thing?

Captain **KEMPER** replied, *"No time to go over our feelings, we must hurry!"*

Chapter XV
The Introduction of Certificates

Since the Continental dollar had collapsed, General WASHINGTON had certificates made up and given to all officers in the field who dealt with civilians. The purpose of these certificates was to be given in exchange for goods to civilians if they refused to cooperate. They could be redeemed for full cash value of their goods in the future, when the economy was better. Captain KEMPER was about to introduce these certificates for the very first time in the American Revolution.

At the wet and dry goods store they were able to requisition all the camping supplies including utensils, tents, blankets and other various needed equipment. The blacksmith shop yielded supplies such as hammers, needed to keep the horses' hoofs and wagons in good condition. While the blacksmith was shoeing a horse, one of Captain KEMPER's men took the hammer right out of his hand and then led the horse away as well.

As the bewildered smithy watched his tools and supplies being loaded, he growled, *"What the hell is going on?"*

Captain KEMPER replied, *"We are just picking up your contributions."*

Further confused the smithy said, *"Contributions! What contributions?"*

Grinning to himself, Captain KEMPER answered, *"Contributions General WASHINGTON said you would be cheerfully willing to donate."*

Further angered, he replied, *"Why, that no good-for-nothing! Hang the beggar, I say!"*

Each shop's specialty had something that General WASHINGTON needed and made sure if his troops had enough, which was rare, Captain KEMPER would receive his fair share for his wagon-train and men's upkeep. The dozens of certificates that were left behind for the shop owners and citizens showed General WASHINGTON's generosity and Captain KEMPER made sure that he left them at each location in exchange for the goods seized. All in all, it was truly believed they would be fully redeemable in the future. No one knew of Congress' constant struggle for funds.

One clerk, in particular, at the weapons shop, smirked at Captain KEMPER. John then threw a handful of certificates in the air and watched them float slowly to the counter. The gunsmith's smirk quickly turned to a scowl, and he grumbled, *"We heard about General WASHINGTON's introduction of these certificates as a means of stealing our goods. How dare you graffiti my store with them."*

He continued, *"I just cannot wait until the British capture you!"*

Captain KEMPER just glanced at the clerk, but said nothing.

The clerk continued, *"Your reputation precedes you Captain; everyone knows who you are, so you can run, but you cannot hide."*

As Captain KEMPER turned to leave, the clerk stated, *"Everyone says that you are a gentleman Captain, but I do not see that. Regardless of orders, all I see is another crook, like all Rebels. The time in your immaculate, glorious Continental uniform, which is obviously for show, will be short lived. The British, along with all us Loyalists to the Crown, are surely going to win this war; this is our country, not yours! More importantly, Captain, you are going to need to prepare your plot. Do you like carnations?"*

Captain KEMPER answered, *"Yes I do."*

The clerk bellowed out, *"What are you, a wise guy?"*

John got on his horse, secured his pistol in his britches and cocked the American flag in its holster; as he slowly raised it to an upward (vertical) position. For a moment there was a feeling of mystical magic in the air. John looked down at the clerk, who started laughing and asked, *"Do you really believe that flag is going to make a difference?"*

Captain KEMPER answered with a slight smirk, *"It already has!"*

John then saluted the clerk and rode off with his guards as the flag waved in the wind, as if saying good-bye.

The clerk yelled, *"What is wrong with you? Is that all you have to say about that? Cat got your tongue? I am not finished with you. Get back here!"*

Under his breath, as John continued to fade away in the distance, he said, *"Idiot!"* There would never be any warm reception to receiving certificates instead of cash.

The gunsmith then turned to leave for home, as he had nothing left to sell. As he strolled along his way, he began to mumble, *"God! I hate Rebels, they steal anything they want and call it law; they never even say thank you. I bet that bastard Captain KEMPER is probably going to open up a shop of his own, or fence Philadelphia's finest wares, mine! He will then line his own pockets with what should have been my gold. Rebels are good for nothing; string them all up! Where is the British army when you need them?"*

As the clerk faded away in the distance, so did his mumbling ...

Captain KEMPER's uncle and aunt, Mattheus and Anna Maria ERNST had finished loading the sloop they hired to transport their furniture and personal belongings, and they headed for Trenton in a horse and carriage by land. The captain of the sloop, as soon as he got out on the Delaware River, did a quick about-face and headed to the British lines to turn all Mattheus' belongings over to the British, looking for favor.

When Mattheus and his wife reached the docks in Trenton, they found that the sloop had never arrived. The captain of the sloop had turned around and turned everything over to the British, looking for favor. Even though they had been warned of Tories/ Loyalists by their nephew, Captain KEMPER, Mattheus, and his family had lost all their family belongings including heirlooms and oil paintings of the family. All they had left was the money they carried with them.

Even though Captain KEMPER had warned his uncle, there was no way to tell whose side any of the civilians were on. Mattheus and his wife then went to Morristown, New Jersey to live with friends and family until his death, three years before peace was declared. Mattheus never got a chance to know that their struggle was successful. He died being torn apart for all his family's losses to the Tories.

Captain KEMPER's Conestoga wagons, with six and a half tons' capacity, were one and a half tons empty, five tons loaded. The cover length was twenty-eight feet. Box bottom length was seventeen feet, while the rear wheel height was five feet. With 150 wagons, Captain KEMPER was able to clear out all of Philadelphia, the capital of America. This was the first time in American history that this necessity was called for.

On 25 September 1777, in mid-afternoon, Captain KEMPER finished loading all his wagons with the stores' supplies. The horses were now tied to the rear of the wagons and lined up all along Front Street heading north. He then reported to Colonel Alexander HAMILTON that he was ready to go.

He asked Colonel HAMILTON if he wished to accompany him to General WASHINGTON's camp, or leave separately. Colonel HAMILTON replied, *"I will be accompanying you, I would not miss General WASHINGTON's expression on his face that, he has finally beat General HOWE at something!"*

Captain KEMPER smiled, then they went to the head of the wagon-train on north Front Street at the edge of town. Captain KEMPER then left Philadelphia with 150 wagons under his command and a *"captain's guard"* of Continental Dragoons to protect the transports.

Captain KEMPER had Lone WOLF recall his Indian scouts and headed north on the road to White Marsh, then northeast to General WASHINGTON's headquarters at Potsgrove. The wagons were laden with all the *"contributions"* they had loaded. The food, clothing, cloths and arms were all conveyed to the headquarters (General WASHINGTON's camp).

As they left town, John looked at his gold pocket watch, then at Colonel HAMILTON and said, *"Good timing and not bad for a couple of days of hard work."* Colonel HAMILTON looked back at Captain KEMPER, smiled, and blew out air with relief that they were getting out of the city in time with little time to spare, but none-the-less, in time. Every time Captain KEMPER opened his pocket watch, there was something special on the inside cover, a picture of his childhood sweetheart, Eliza HOPPER. Would she still be waiting for him to return after the Revolution, as promised?

When Captain KEMPER's Indian scouts returned, they informed him that, General HOWE's thunderous approach of drums, fifers, and artillery, could be heard off in the distance, echoing throughout the countryside and were about a half-day's march from Philadelphia. Captain KEMPER's wagon-train hurried on.

Captain KEMPER now proudly displayed something very special he had been looking forward to for a very long time— he was one of the first officers to boldly display America's new flag of broad stripes and bright stars while supplying General George WASHINGTON and the Continental Army. Colonel HAMILTON accompanied Captain KEMPER to General WASHINGTON's camp, where the arms and other *"contributions"* were unloaded.

General WASHINGTON greeted both Colonel HAMILTON and Captain KEMPER with a warm grin, showing his tarnished teeth. Captain KEMPER saluted and bowed, offering a soft nod of his head.

General WASHINGTON returned the salute then replied, *"Good job men! If General HOWE stays in Philadelphia this winter, he will finally know what it is like to struggle."*

Captain KEMPER replied, *"I have a feeling it is going to be a long winter, your Excellency."*

General WASHINGTON answered, *"Yes, indeed!"*

General WASHINGTON then ordered Captain KEMPER to hide the extra horses inland away from British patrols, under security, and to convey the cloths to Lancaster so that they could be stitched into uniforms for the Continental Army. Patriotic women made some 1,200 shirts for the soldiers at Valley Forge. For a short moment in time, General WASHINGTON felt wealthy in supplies from *"contributions"* from the citizens in Philadelphia.

First and utmost, General WASHINGTON ordered Captain KEMPER to start the Continental Army's first military warehouse in Lancaster, from all the abundance of supplies he had confiscated at gunpoint from all the stores in Philadelphia. He ordered Captain KEMPER to post guards so that no civilians, especially Tories/Loyalists, could acquire supplies to transfer to the enemy; a new horizon had come!

On other occasions, depending on the importance of the shipment, General George WASHINGTON, as well as other senior staff, such as Major General Marquis DE LAFAYETTE, Major General John Peter MUHLENBERG, General Lord STIRLING, Colonel Daniel KEMPER and Colonel Alexander HAMILTON, was known to accompany Captain KEMPER. Whenever senior staff would accompany Captain KEMPER, the troops would be augmented, but Captain KEMPER was still the man in total command, reporting solely to General WASHINGTON. Even Captain KEMPER's brother-in-law, Mr. MORTON would accompany him on some runs.

When Captain KEMPER cleared out all the stores in Philadelphia so the British could not capture them, its citizens were enraged; Since Captain KEMPER was spearheading both General WASHINGTON's and Colonel HAMILTON's orders, he became the immediate target of Tories/Loyalists, who would never forget what he had done. Now that General WASHINGTON had drawn General HOWE inland away from his Royal Navy, what did he have in store for him?

However, residents knew that General WASHINGTON was ultimately responsible for the orders; therefore, they no longer wanted General WASHINGTON hung—they now wanted him skinned alive! Their feelings would not have been hurt if Captain KEMPER were added to the menu as well. After all, he was the one who carried on General WASHINGTON's dirty work. He was just one more, good-for-nothing rebel!

The colonists were well aware of a pending action and their senses were heightened. They were now on high alert since Captain KEMPER had confiscated at gunpoint all the goods from all the stores in Philadelphia. Captain KEMPER had been as busy as an agitated beehive. Residents knew something big was about to happen, but were puzzled as to exactly what. Then they heard the thunderous sound of General HOWE's marching advance—his massive troops, wagons and artillery, which made them quiver with pure tension. They wondered, now what?

As the procession came into view, anyone who witnessed it no longer wondered; they could now see what they had only heard, the advance of Great Britain's main army, led by General Sir William HOWE. General HOWE's procession was followed by 1,500 wagons and artillery and 15,000 battle-hardened troops, ready for war. All Philadelphians could do was stand and look in awe! The Tories/Loyalists were grateful that their hero had finally arrived; this was a good day. Now! Catch that Captain KEMPER guy!

In contrast, General WASHINGTON had only a main force of 150 wagons under Captain John KEMPER's command, and still, he was able to supply the entire Continental Army. The difference between the two—General HOWE's convoy of 1,500 wagons and artillery was a wagon-train on the march, while Captain KEMPER's was a convoy (wagon-train) on a gallop. All that was needed was the right man, in the right place, at the right time in history.

On 26 September 1777, General HOWE entered and captured Philadelphia. He set up his artillery in defensive positions all around the city's entrances and exits. The Tories/Loyalist hurriedly huddled around and smothered General HOWE with smiles and gratitude and they wasted no time filling him in with all that happened just prior to his arrival. They informed him about Captain KEMPER's confiscation at gunpoint of all the supplies and livestock in the city. They told General HOWE that Captain KEMPER had only a half-day lead. Following him, would likely lead the British right into General WASHINGTON's camp.

General HOWE immediately sent out British patrols to locate Captain KEMPER's wagon train. After all, how difficult could it be? He had 150 wagons. Where could he possibly hide from the great British Army? Besides, Captain KEMPER had an entire city of such wonderful supplies that the British Army so desperately needed. He would have to stash them in a cache somewhere. Where could he store an entire city of supplies?

After the British patrols returned, they all had the same answer; they could not locate Captain John KEMPER and his wagon train. Although they did lead to General WASHINGTON's camp, afterwards his wagon tracks somehow seemingly disappeared into the deep and dark wilderness. All that could be heard were the haunting sounds of animal cries' everywhere and the hungry growls of their own stomachs.

However, General HOWE, now that he had captured America's capital, Philadelphia, was once again looking for a surrender that he expected to get from General WASHINGTON. Once again, it never came! General WASHINGTON's refusal to surrender was becoming very annoying. Frustrated, General HOWE left Philadelphia in pursuit of General WASHINGTON and his army at Potsgrove.

With their hero in town, Tories/Loyalists became bolder and braver. They would grab clubs, rakes, shovels, or pitchforks and chase Continental troops at any chance they got. They never feared of being shot, and of course, they never were. However, they would often have to be arrested if they continued their pursuit.

On 30 September 1777, Congress moved to York County Courthouse, York, Pennsylvania. Congress could do little except sit back, try to meet their Continental Army's needs and wait for something to unravel. Congress, frustrated by not being in the heart of the action, was in the dark most of the time until they received word from one of General WASHINGTON's couriers that something good had happened. Unfortunately, most of the time, whenever they received a dispatch from General

WASHINGTON, it regarded the many hardships the army was going through and their dire need of money, food and clothing, which they needed so that they could continue.

Whenever Captain KEMPER was in Lancaster or York, he was ordered by General WASHINGTON to fill Congress in on any progress, hardships or needs of the army. Captain KEMPER was always a good emissary to Congress, for wherever they were became Captain KEMPER's home base of operations for the Continental Army, which was the only military security for Congress. This role was one of the main reasons he had the largest contingency of a company of men in American history. During the Valley Forge Encampment, Congress quickly knew Captain KEMPER as the bearer of bad news. Most importantly, he was the brother-in-law of John MORTON, so he always received carte blanche treatment. In addition, Congress always needed him to relay their needs to Mr. MORTON.

Captain KEMPER is the only officer in American history to have carried a *"shield of protection"* by his commander-in-chief, General WASHINGTON from detention or interference from any superior officers. This protection was never abused! Its purpose was to make sure that any correspondence or intelligence from Congress, or other sources that Captain KEMPER carried, got directly to General WASHINGTON without interruption. General WASHINGTON's undying trust in Captain KEMPER always proved fruitful.

Whenever Captain KEMPER arrived at General WASHINGTON's camp, everyone knew who he was as he had an automatic clearance through all guards, sentinels, and superior officers. All they would do was, salute him and either clear his path or escort him directly to General WASHINGTON. Often times, Continental Dragoons escorted Captain KEMPER when on special missions. Dragoons were much like the marines are today; among America's best. All Dragoons were eloquently uniformed and mounted on the army's best steeds.

Whenever Captain KEMPER was at the headquarters, everyone's eyes were always on him, although he would never acknowledge that he knew. Captain KEMPER generally avoided conversations with regular officers, as they were always trying to get information out of him. He would often bow in acknowledgment of their welcome or hello then, nonchalantly, head on his way.

Captain KEMPER's supplies, as well, were handled just as delicately so that they got to General WASHINGTON for proper distribution to the Continental Army. It is highly speculative that General WASHINGTON's senior staff advised him of this action to ensure proper delivery and distribution. Proper reception of supplies was always one of General WASHINGTON's priorities.

If General WASHINGTON had not been on his toes that very day, then General Sir William HOWE would have captured Colonel Alexander HAMILTON and Captain John KEMPER and history would surely have changed. Instead of Captain KEMPER clearing out all the stores in the city of Philadelphia, the British would have captured them and General George WASHINGTON and his Continental Army would have undergone more suffering at Valley Forge. General WASHINGTON's special and only convoy to supply the Continental Army would have been captured.

Captain KEMPER's major fear, as portrayed in his journals and the diary of his daughter, Elizabeth KEMPER, *"was that he would be captured before he was able to flee Philadelphia with all its supplies."* As it turned out, with Captain John KEMPER miraculously emptying all the stores in Philadelphia and escaping on that afternoon before the British captured the city, the British Army was now deprived in Philadelphia. General HOWE was infuriated.

General HOWE's rush to capture Philadelphia and its supplies was only partially successful. He had missed the opportunity of capturing a couple of General WASHINGTON's top officers,

Colonel Alexander HAMILTON and Captain John KEMPER and the coveted supplies by one-half day.

General HOWE was then faced with a dilemma; all he had was what he brought with him. He had expected to live off the supplies of Philadelphia as his troops were doing in New York City. In addition, he had to feed and clothe the many Tories/Loyalists who filled the city. His constantly repeated requests for transports, food and supplies went continually unanswered. The outlook was bleak; he ended up competing with Captain KEMPER and other foragers in the countryside. The capture and occupation of Philadelphia ended up being meaningless. In reality, Captain KEMPER seriously wounded General HOWE without ever firing one shot.

Before General HOWE captured Philadelphia, he was led to believe that he would be greeted by *"friends* [Loyalists] *thicker than woods."* As it turned out, *"he was greeted by women and children,"* who amounted to 75 percent of the population left in Philadelphia. Many of the homes had been evacuated, some by Loyalists out of fear they might be misidentified as working with the Continental Army. Instead of Philadelphia being a busy and bustling city, it was now quiet and partially abandoned; there was no livestock left to move anything or for consumption. Would General HOWE be able to help? After all, there were mostly Tories left who were on his side.

As General HOWE's troops began plundering the city, he had them disciplined for their actions. This response to his countrymen led to negative feelings in England, as it was well-known that General HOWE was sympathetic toward the colonists and was only fighting because that was what he was ordered to do. General HOWE and his officers' biggest battles were with Captain KEMPER in the countryside, where they were often taken by surprise.

From New York to Philadelphia, and all villages in between, captured by the British, American women became courtesans to the British soldiers so that they could live. Many other women were taken and ravished anyway. Many of the American women ended up having British children not by choice and many little girls as young as eight years old were raped.

After taking Philadelphia, General HOWE—because all the stores had been cleared out by the Continental forces, leaving no means or supplies available for his troops, wrote to England, reporting an urgent need for transports and provisions. All requests went unanswered. King George was upset with General HOWE for going to Philadelphia when he was supposed to have joined General John BURGOYNE (1722-1792) and General Barry St. LEGER (1733-1789) at Albany, New York.

Because Colonel Daniel KEMPER was becoming a reliable aide-de-camp, and rescued General LAFAYETTE at the Battle of Brandywine, General WASHINGTON made him special assistant aide, in conjunction with Colonel John LAURENS, at the Battle of Germantown.

On 4 October 1777, General HOWE and General George WASHINGTON clashed in Germantown. The British victory ensured that Philadelphia remained in British hands throughout the winter of 1777-1778. Now part of the city of Philadelphia, in 1777 Germantown was an outlying community northeast of the city.

Most importantly, who was this man called General WASHINGTON? Did he not know that when outmatched by a superior force that had captured the capital of his country, it was time to surrender? General WASHINGTON was a new kind of commander that General HOWE was not familiar with. He just could not figure out how to deal with a man who refused to give up, lay down his arms and surrender to a superior force.

By this point in time, General HOWE and the British Army had quickly taken control of pretty much everything in the States, with the exception of three entities only!, The Continental Congress, General WASHINGTON, and the Continental Army. How could just three entities possibly win the Revolution? If General HOWE was chewing gum, he would have blown bubbles bigger than a house, being so excited about his victories in the States.

On 23 October 1777, Captain Silas TALBOT (1751-1813) of the Continental Army was severely wounded at Fort Mifflin (named after General Thomas MIFFLIN), while fighting to defend Philadelphia.

On 27 October 1777, as the remaining deep-red, orange-and-brown oak leaves fell to the ground, Captain KEMPER looked up into the dark-gray, cloudy skies. Winter was vastly approaching, and preparation for it was on everyone's mind. Captain KEMPER's Indian scout, Bouncing BEAR, took them on a small journey. His squaw (wife), Song BIRD, so named because she always sung with birds since she was a little girl, now was a medicine woman. At the request of her warrior husband, she had made a special gift for Captain KEMPER.

This journey began northwest of Philadelphia and southeast of Lancaster and continued across the Schuylkill River. As they crossed the Schuylkill heading northeast, Bouncing BEAR exclaimed, *"This is the 'Tool-Pay Hanna* [Turtle River]." This was the Lenape name for the Schuylkill River. When on Front Street in Philadelphia, Bouncing BEAR would look out at the Delaware River and say, *"This is the Len-Api Hanna* [People like Me River]."

This journey could have been very dangerous, as they needed to travel through dense forest filled with lions and bears. However, Captain KEMPER brought a small force of twenty-five men with him; the wildlife steered clear of their advance. This area was surrounded by, sharp cliffs, swamp and caves, filled with scary surprises. As a heavy mist surrounded the men, eerie sounds were about everywhere! This story was not about how the Europeans and the Indians did not get along, but in fact, how they chose sides they believed in and how they blended in with Captain KEMPER and the Continental Army.

This forest was where the young men of Bouncing BEAR's tribe went for training to become warriors. Only Bouncing BEAR knew the way through; Captain KEMPER's chief scout, Lone WOLF, accompanied him. As they traveled deep into the forest, they came upon a huge boulder alongside of a tall pine tree, which stood in front of steep shale cliffs. There was a stream that ran alongside. Bouncing BEAR suggested that they fill their canteens here, for there would be no more fresh water until they got to Spider's Creek.

While on their journey, as recorded in Captain KEMPER's journals, Bouncing BEAR described the locality to Captain KEMPER as they approached his tribal camp. They advanced through a storm of sleet and hail, on up through Thunder Pass, so called because of the many rock landslides that were common in this area. Along the cliffs, around Dead Man's Swamp (quicksand) and into Whispering Pines they went, as the breeze fed them its perfumed scent.

The weather had since calmed down and allowed for more comfortable travel. They then entered Hidden Valley; off to the left stood Climate Peak, which emerged out from Spider's Creek. High and to the right stood Rainbow Point, a beautiful sight and very bright as the sun glistened off the running waters. Along its side gleamed Sunshine Falls, which fed the land below. They were now at Bouncing BEAR's tribal camp.

Upon their arrival they were greeted by the tribal chief, Big EAGLE. The Indians exchanged words in their own language as the chief glared at the flag Captain KEMPER was holding in place, set in the leather holster he had made on the right-hand side of his horse's chest. This bold flag of broad stripes and bright stars was something new the white man was carrying that the Indians had not seen before; what did it mean?

Bouncing BEAR's tribe lived in a cave on a bluff that seemed to protrude from out of nowhere. It stood about 50 to 75 feet high, 75 feet wide by 350 to 400 feet long. It looked like the shape of a large whale, land bound. The entrance was pyramid-shaped, about 8 feet high at its point and about 10 feet wide at its base. Inside was a large natural cavern about 30 feet wide by 70 feet long by 12 feet high. Half way-up the walls and the ceiling, you could see where generations of Indians had made hundreds of scoops, carving it out smoothly to remove the sharp edges.

About 150 feet in front of the cave was Spider's Creek. It was about 15 feet wide and a couple feet deep. It was clear and ran rapidly and smoothly, with plenty of fish constantly breaking water. Captain KEMPER's chief scout, the Mohegan Lone WOLF, was envious and homesick as it reminded him of his tribal home along the Hudson River in the state of New York. The tribe had been busy shaping arrow and spearheads when they looked up at the new arrivals who accompanied Bouncing BEAR.

Bouncing BEAR's squaw, Song BIRD, knew what everyone was there for and brought out their gift of a fur coat that she had been working on for Captain KEMPER. This fur coat was made out of half lion hide and half bear hide. A full bear coat was far too heavy, but half lion with bear fur sewn in for the shoulders and back to keep the important parts warm was just right.

While Bouncing BEAR was visiting with friends and family in the tribe, Captain KEMPER and Lone WOLF stood by the creek, watching the fish jump for bugs. In a shallow pool was a large swarm of minnows flowing about. All of a sudden, from out of nowhere, something burst into the center of the cloud of minnows. The minnows shot out in all directions from its center;

a water snake, which had grabbed one of them, was whipping its body back and forth while trying to subdue it.

After the snake got control, it rose to the surface and slowly swam into shore to consume it. Lone WOLF turned to Captain KEMPER and said, *"Me have to work lot harder to catch my fish."*

Captain KEMPER chuckled then responded, *"So do I."*

Captain KEMPER, who had not come empty-handed, made a gift of a saber and knife and a couple of bottles of whiskey for the chief and the tribe and a mirror for Song BIRD. While the Indian warriors were busy gazing eagle-eyed on the long knife given to their chief, the squaws, scared at what they first saw, soon became delighted in seeing their reflection in the mirror.

Before leaving, as they sat around the campfire in the moonlight smoking the tobacco pipe, everything seemed so calm and peaceful. They could hear the eerie sounds of wolves howling off in the distance, while various groups of men chuckled over different stories. If only things could remain this way, but war was calling. They could not stay long.

In the morning, as they were preparing to mount and depart, Lone WOLF quickly jumped up on his horse and said, *"We no longer need Bouncing BEAR, he can return to rear guard, I know way out."*

Bouncing BEAR headed to the rear.

Captain KEMPER cut in, *"BEAR, you do not need to go to the rear."*

Bouncing BEAR replied, *"It okay, Lone WOLF good scout, and this give him chance to show how good in new environment."*

Lone WOLF turned to Captain KEMPER with a broad smile on his face, from cheek to cheek, and said, *"You see, the BEAR knows what good for him."*

Captain KEMPER then threw his right hand into the air, with his two fingers pointing to the sky, then thrust them forward, while saying, *"Let us go."*

As Lone WOLF led them deep into the forest, they finally reached the spot they had stopped at for water earlier, by the huge boulder, next to the tall pine, by the steep shale cliffs. Lone WOLF immediately exclaimed, *"You see, I told you I know way."*

They continued on and about after an hour, they arrived right back at the same location. The men began to groan while Lone WOLF jerked his head in all directions to figure out where to go.

One of the men requested, *"Captain, can we please have the BEAR lead us out of this mess?"*

Lone WOLF threw his arms up in the air, saying, *"Go ahead."*

In no time at all, Bouncing BEAR had quickly led them out of the forest and back across the Schuylkill River.

Lone WOLF exclaimed, *"You see, I knew we were close."*

After everyone was on the road, ready to head back to camp at Conestoga Creek, Bouncing BEAR said, *"This good lesson for you, Captain, is best Bouncing BEAR be made chief scout; and throw Lone WOLF back to the wolves in the rear."*

Lone WOLF immediately threw his fists in the air in front of his chest, grumbling and growling, while showing every kind of facial expression you can imagine. Bouncing BEAR burst out laughing, and continued chuckling all the way to the rear as he assumed his position. He had won that verbal battle!

Lone WOLF turned to Captain KEMPER and said, *"The BEAR thinks he funny guy, but he not. He think he tell big joke, but he don't. He boasts because he in Lenape country. If I take him to Mohegan country in Hudson River Valley, his head spin."*

As the party headed west, Lone WOLF looked back one more time at the BEAR, who was still laughing so hard his shoulders were shaking. Lone WOLF jerked his head forward to follow the trail and no longer intended on even looking at Bouncing BEAR.

On 15 November 1777, the Articles of Confederation were drafted and served as the first Constitution of the United States. All politicians at this time were known as Federalists. George WASHINGTON, when he became the first President of the Unites States of America, was a Federalist.

On 18 November 1777, the British now realized that they were going to need the Delaware River cleared so they could transport supplies to Philadelphia. This situation created a new problem; they needed to capture a couple of forts on the Delaware in order to safely move transports. For three days, General HOWE had his navy bombard Fort Mifflin on Mudden Island and Fort Mercer (named after General Hugh MERCER [1726-1777]. By 21 November 1777, both forts fell to British control. The occupants had retreated across the river to Fort Mercer and onward.

On 21 November 1777, General WASHINGTON wrote Francis HOPKINSON. This would be one of many correspondences between these two gentlemen over the years, extending at least until 13 March 1789. Both General George WASHINGTON and Francis HOPKINSON were well acquainted with each other, as well as to the Continental Congress.

On 26 November 1777, Congress resolved to recommend that the States, *"exert their utmost endeavors to procure"* additional clothing for the army to be distributed *"at such reasonable prices as shall be assessed by the clothier general or his deputy, and be in just proportion to the wages of the officers and soldiers, charging the surplus of the cost to the United States."* Because of the inflated costs that the civilian merchants had been charging, Congress now defined the cost to be set by the clothier-general.

Congress further resolved that, *"all clothing hereafter to be supplied to the officers and soldiers of the Continental Army out of the **public stores** ... shall be charged at the like prices."* At this particular time in history, this was the only means of supplying the Continental Army, from the public stores. Transportation of supplies from public stores had already been in process; on this date, Congress decided to make it law.

On this same date, while Congress was making new laws to strengthen the Continental Army, General HOWE was going mad in Philadelphia. Since Captain KEMPER had cleaned out the entire city, its stores and livestock, General HOWE had nothing left for his army to live off during the upcoming long winter months, other than what he brought with him. He sent out General Lord CORNWALLIS with four thousand troops to ravish the countryside of Gloucester County and forage everything he could for his army back at Philadelphia.

General WASHINGTON, hearing of this, immediately sent out a troop to disrupt General CORNWALLIS. However, before General WASHINGTON's troops had arrived, General CORNWALLIS had already confiscated all the livestock and returned to Philadelphia.

Chapter XVI
Valley Forge

On 30 November 1777, General WASHINGTON held a conference with his generals to discuss the best location for their winter quarters, as winter would shortly be upon them. Their strategy, most importantly, was to locate a site that allowed them adequate ability to monitor the movements of the British so that they could defend against enemy attack.

About twenty miles northwest of Philadelphia, then America's capital, was Valley Forge. Valley Forge afforded them that defensive position, as well as other necessities like rivers for water and fishing, forests for hunting and wood. General WASHINGTON then sent a dispatch to Captain KEMPER at his wagon-train camp at Conestoga Creek, to inform him as to where winter quarters were being set up. Trees were to be cut down around the perimeter of Valley Forge for security.

On 4 Decembe 1777, General Sir William HOWE led a sizable contingency of troops out of Philadelphia in one last attempt to destroy General WASHINGTON and the Continental Army before the onset of winter. Between December 5 and December 8, a series of skirmishes took place between the British and the Continental Army, but General WASHINGTON had become too strong. General HOWE needed his Royal Navy for bombardment, but they could not sail inland. Had the playing field been leveled?

General HOWE was forced to call off the attack and return to Philadelphia. No matter what action General HOWE chose, it was just never enough to stop General WASHINGTON. General

HOWE would have to wait until spring before he could launch an all-out assault against General WASHINGTON. However, King George had other ideas in store. General WASHINGTON then marched his troops to winter quarters at Valley Forge.

On 16 December 1777, because merchants were demanding and charging exorbitant prices and lack of transportation prevented the moving of clothing and rations when they could be obtained, coupled with the lack of funds, Clothier-General, James MEASE sent in his resignation to General WASHINGTON. However, since there was no one to take his place and since General WASHINGTON was busy with trying to set up winter quarters for the Continental Army, his request was ignored. James MEASE continued trying to do the job expected of him with little financial support from Congress and no means of getting supplies from the East, like Massachusetts; his difficulties lingered on.

On 18 December 1777, General WASHINGTON and his hard-pressed Continental Army staggered into Valley Forge. As it was recorded, *"It was a cold, cloudy, windy day, with light snow falling."* There were eleven thousand ragged, hungry men, whose clothes were filthy and in shreds; their shoes were barely staying on their feet, as they were falling apart at the seams. They were all cold and exhausted from their defeats at Brandywine (11 September 1777), Paoli (20 September 1777) and Germantown (4 October 1777).

General William HOWE almost trapped them in a surprise attack at White Marsh (5 Dec. 1777). The Continental Army's warning of this pending attack was credited to a known American spy – a patriotic, Quaker housewife, Lydia Barrington DARRAGH (1728-1789).

Along with the troops were camp followers, which consisted of the wives, children, mothers and sisters of the soldiers. The camp followers often served as laundresses, cleaning and mending the clothing of the soldiers and nursing them when necessary. These women and children also provided emotional support to the army, encouraging them to remain at camp and continue training and soldiering during the winter months. Women were allotted half the rations and wages of a soldier, as well as a half pension after the war—if they had done enough work. Children would receive a quarter ration if enough work was done.

After General WASHINGTON was set up at camp, he ordered a large team to cut down the forest surrounding Valley Forge. He needed to prevent General Sir William Howe from staging a massive surprise attack and finish off General WASHINGTON and the Continental Army. General WASHINGTON had once again out foxed General HOWE for he had surely planned to finish General WASHINGTON off. He later sent a force to survey General WASHINGTON's camp in preparation for an assault.

An officer of General Sir William HOWE's staff wrote, *"For a quarter of a mile in front of the American camp was the thickest abates* [barricade] *of felled trees I ever saw. We reconnoitered* [continued to survey the region on the enemies position] *for nine miles around the camp to see if we could find an opening; but it was all equally strong."* It was an impenetrable fortress.

General WASHINGTON then sent for one of his slaves, named William *"Billy"* LEE (1750-1828), who was his personal valet. Billy attended to General WASHINGTON's needs at various camps like Valley Forge. Because he was his body servant and favorite slave, he referred to him as his *"black shadow."* He was the only slave freed outright in General WASHINGTON's will. Billy had been purchased along with his brother, Frank LEE, from Colonel John LEE's (1724-1767) estate. Frank was made a butler at Mount Vernon.

On 31 December 1777, the commissary department complained that they had difficulty in buying supplies and could not forward what they did purchase; hence, General WASHINGTON was forced to order his cavalry, commanded by Polish Brigadier General, Count Casimir PULASKI, to Trenton, New Jersey, where sufficient forage could be obtained.

General WASHINGTON had been pretty much on the run since the start of the Revolution. When the British navy arrived, they had overwhelmed General WASHINGTON with over thirty thousand troops—he did not stand a chance. General WASHINGTON had earned a nickname, *"Fox on the Run!"* The British were not happy about General WASHINGTON retreating, but were apprehensive about pursuing him through a dense, unknown wilderness. This was one grave mistake the British made, *"for a man who runs away lives to fight another day!"*

Being overwhelmed by superior forces never disheartened General WASHINGTON, nor slowed him down. He remained on the offensive and, afterwards took a defensive position, and then returned to the offensive—much like a lantern is turned on and off.

However, the most dangerous mistake the British made was underestimating their enemies. With Great Britain being the world's largest and most powerful military and naval force, minor naval powers like France, Spain, Portugal and Holland were ready to jump on board and take anyone's side in order to tip the scales in their favor. In addition, all these minor naval powers had taken a beating on the seas by Admiral Sir George Bridges RODNEY (1718-1792) of the Royal Navy.

Later on in the Revolution, the tide would quickly change when countries like France, Spain and Portugal would declare war against Great Britain. Now, with the British main naval force in the States, they would have to worry about an invasion in their homeland. They would now have to re-think their plans for the States. Was it really worth the fall of their country? This war was becoming very costly and stressful to all countries involved— England, France and America.

Elizabeth KEMPER recorded in her diary how amazed her father had become over the years, about how many officers at Valley Forge had become founding fathers. She stated that when her father was at camp, everyone was more concerned about where their next meal was coming from and staying alive. Their major fear, according to her father, was that, *"the British army would launch a major assault on their camp and wipe out everyone while they were down on their luck."*

Continuing he said, *"After the Revolution, the only ones other than those who served in Congress, who qualified for political office and to be called **Americans**, were the ones who rebelled against the Crown and fought to create **America**."*

Elizabeth continued to explain, *"That when her father was at camp, he claimed there were never any political aspirations on who was going to prosper after the Revolution."* He stated that, *"Everyone was a comrade in arms, who had formed a strong bond and alliance and were ready to give anyone a helping hand that needed it. Everyone was on edge, they were cold and hungry, but all had to remain vigilant!"*

Elizabeth further stated that her father said, *"that of the few conversations he had with Lieutenant Colonel Aaron BURR [1756-1836], there was never any indication, whatsoever, that he would end up becoming vice president of the United States. Mr. BURR was a fill-in when Colonel William MALCOLM was absent. It never appeared that he was going to amount to anything."*

Aaron BURR, after becoming vice-president, ended up killing his friend and comrade General Alexander HAMILTON in an illegal duel, just because he used his influence to prevent him (BURR) from becoming governor of New York State. Her father clearly stated, *"The war was not supposed to be with ourselves!"*

General WASHINGTON was cut off from both New York and Philadelphia. He had few supplies and was having more difficulty than he had had the winter before at Morristown, New Jersey holding his ragged regiments together. Most importantly, Mr. MORTON did not travel with the main army as he was not military, therefore, he was not readily available with his generous hospitality as he had been in Morristown. General WASHINGTON's number one priority was always the supplies for his troops. The troops often were subjected to starvation.

Captain KEMPER recorded that *"General WASHINGTON is about to start the long winter at camp* [Valley Forge] *and rogue officers already are interfering with my supply train."* This was partly due to the confusion caused by their commissaries who were interrupting the transportation of supplies from the quartermasters and forage-masters.

General WASHINGTON issued special orders, "No other officers, including Major Generals, were to detain or interfere with Mr. KEMPER's command." All supplies needed to come directly to him for proper distribution.

Constantly, he needed to reiterate his orders to remind his officers against interference. What was really going on here?

Since the clothier-general's department was failing under James MEASE, not from his own doing, but because of little cooperation, General WASHINGTON acted as his own clothier-general throughout most of the war. This made it necessary to rely more heavily on his assistant, Colonel Daniel KEMPER, who unlike James MEASE, remained at camp with the army and by General WASHINGTON's side. This was just one more way Captain John KEMPER continued under the direct command of his commander-in-chief himself.

However, General WASHINGTON continued to grace the ground he walked upon and never removed Clothier-General MEASE from his post, but allowed him to stay in that office until his death in June 1785. Even though others like, General James

WILKINSON (1757-1825) who came and went, James MEASE stayed on and, right before he suddenly died, was working on settling Colonel Daniel KEMPER's accounts.

When Captain KEMPER was removed from his stint in the clothier-general's department and placed out in the open before the Continental Army under General WASHINGTON's personal command and control, his duties were modified. Captain KEMPER was sent out on foraging excursions into the countryside and, military raids against British foraging parties and as courier to Congress and other missions that were essential to the survival of the Continental Army. Who really was Captain John KEMPER?

While the British remained in Philadelphia, Captain KEMPER's supply route was from Lancaster to General WASHINGTON's headquarters at the Park (Valley Forge). When food and clothing supplies got low in Lancaster, Captain KEMPER was often sent out on foraging excursions. When Captain KEMPER's convoy was transporting supplies in the vicinity of the enemy or within the battle zone, he tied burlap around the horses' hooves and around the wheels of the wagons to muffle the noise. This was the standard procedure for all wagon masters. Captain KEMPER's wagon-train camp, during the Valley Forge encampment, was maintained at Conestoga Creek, just southeast of Lancaster, Pennsylvania.

Although Captain KEMPER's convoy had 150 wagons, they were not used on military raids or foraging expeditions as they would slow down his company of men far too much. This large convoy was used primarily to transport large quantities of supplies from military warehouses and public stores between cities like Philadelphia and Lancaster to General George WASHINGTON's headquarters on necessity, wherever he was camped in the Northeast.

The contingency of his company had two first lieutenants, one second lieutenant, one volunteer (one rank under lieutenant), two ensigns, eight sergeants, six corporals, one drummer and two fifers. This was the basic company used on patrol. In addition, he had 170 cavalry and 150 wagoners steering the wagons, amounting to 320 men under his command.

In addition to this main force, Captain KEMPER had three special additional wagons obtained for him by his brother-in-law, John "the Rebel Banker" MORTON. One wagon was marked *"Morton's Supply"* and was scheduled solely for General WASHINGTON. Another wagon was marked, *"The Johnny-in-Laws,"* and was scheduled specifically for Congress. The third was simply marked *"Kemper"* on the rear of the wagon that led the convoy.

When at his wagon-train camp, these wagons were parked so that one was on each side of his officer's tent. Continental Dragoons strictly guarded both of these wagons. Whenever Captain KEMPER was delivering supplies in one wagon or the other to its perspective recipient, solely Continental Dragoons escorted them. No one but Captain KEMPER, Mr. MORTON and their perspective recipients knew what they contained. All crates and barrels were stamped with both Mr. MORTON's and Captain KEMPER's seals. Only the recipients could break the seals.

When Captain KEMPER was transporting supplies on a high priority from public, military stores, and the warehouse in Philadelphia or Lancaster to General WASHINGTON's base, he maintained a *"captain's guard"* (Royal Guard). This company of 170 men was different than a regular army on the march, in which only officers rode horseback; all Captain KEMPER's men rode horseback to protect the transports on the way to the Continental Army. It was truly magnificent to witness the sight and sound of Captain KEMPER's convoy arriving at camp, *"Thunderous with the earth shaking, like an earthquake and metal clanging from the horses' harnesses being attached to the metal strips at the front of the wagons."*

Because Captain John KEMPER's headquarters for supplying the Continental Army was in the same locality as that of Congress, he was the most secure means of delivering General WASHINGTON's messages to Congress as a courier, as he had an entire company to ensure safe deliverance. Depending on the importance, he also had Continental Dragoons at his disposal. Captain KEMPER was also the only means of evacuating and escorting the Continental Congress. He had the only army in the immediate vicinity of Congress.

When out on military raids and foraging expeditions, Captain KEMPER would use his company of men along with a minimal number of wagons, depending on the situation, generally only a few. Captain KEMPER would use his Indian scouts to locate potential targets and then park his wagons before taking his cavalry in on military raids and foraging excursions. Usually, foragers had between twelve and twenty-five men and one wagon.

Captain KEMPER's unit was the largest General WASHINGTON could put together for this purpose and for transporting supplies. There were just no more wagons to start other units. That is why Captain KEMPER had 320 men under his command to protect General WASHINGTON's largest convoy with the largest assembly of men possible for this occasion.

The Valley Forge entrenchment was far from being easy street for the soldiers. When available, the usual camp menu, whether it was breakfast, lunch or dinner, consisted of *"fire cake and water."* Fire cake was the camp name for bread baked in front of the campfire. Luxuries like sugar, tea, liquor, vegetables or chocolate were not available. The men were constantly subjected to hunger, fatigue, inclement weather and unhealthy living conditions and their clothes were lacking and what they had were shabby.

The hundreds of campfires that were needed for cooking and staying warm kept them *"smoked out of their senses."* The soup, if you could call it that was often filled with burnt leaves and dirt that filtered down into it from the air around the fires. They were surrounded by shameful conditions that became worse day by day. There was no pay and there was no free lunch; everyone was expected to pull his or her own weight. Captain KEMPER's Indian scouts complained that, there was too much smoke at camp (Valley Forge); they had all the smoke they needed from their pipes (corncob smoke pipes).

Most of the soldiers' meals were a result of their own hunting and fishing skills. Fortunately, during this period of time, the vast wilderness that surrounded them was filled with plenty of wildlife and game. In addition, there were plenty of springs, streams and rivers; therefore, there was no shortage of fish or water. Because the area surrounding Valley Forge was being thoroughly hunted by thousands of Continental troops, their hunting grounds had to be constantly extended. The end result was as if the entire area surrounding Valley Forge had been ravished by a massive army of foragers. When they left camp it appeared desolate.

In late December 1777, Colonel William MALCOLM's (1745-1791) regiment marched to join General WASHINGTON's army at Valley Forge. Bewildered troops continued to pour into winter quarters at Valley Forge from all over the country. There was nowhere else to go; Tories/Loyalists were targeting small groups, while the British were picking them off. Over twenty-five thousand Tories/Loyalists fought on the side of the British.

Many times, when the Tories were in large numbers, they attacked small parties of the army themselves. Both Americans and British were killing each other's foragers; some were taken prisoner. Dire conditions were mounting because of increased numbers in need of food and clothing. Camp was quickly becoming very overcrowded—campfires and clouds of smoke everywhere! It was as if camp was constantly smoldering.

After General WASHINGTON got situated at Valley Forge and a perimeter of defense set up, he needed to be alerted if a surprise attack was in progress. He ordered Major Benjamin TALLMADGE to take a detachment of Continental Dragoons as an advanced corps of observation, between the American Army and the British in Philadelphia. The duty was strenuous as the British light horse continually patrolled the intermediate grounds around Philadelphia, fearing the same action from General WASHINGTON. It was unsafe to permit the Dragoons to unsaddle their horses for even an hour and they rarely stayed through a night in the same place.

General WASHINGTON then sent a dispatch, ordering Major TALLMADGE to go to a tavern near the British lines to meet up with a country girl. She had been instructed to go to Philadelphia to sell eggs in order to obtain intelligence regarding the enemy. She was then instructed to meet up with Mr. TALLMADGE at the tavern.

Accordingly, he left his corps at Germantown and, with a small detachment proceeded toward the British lines. The tavern sat in a valley. Major TALLMADGE left his troop on the brow of the hill to escape observation, alighted at the tavern, in full view of the British outposts, with only a few horsemen whom he stationed on guard.

The girl soon came. While she was giving Major TALLMADGE the intelligence she had acquired, one of his guards dashed into the room, exclaiming, *"The British light-horse are advancing!"*

Going to the door, he saw them coming at full speed, chasing his patrols. He instantly mounted; but was stopped by the girl, who fell on her knees in great terror, crying, *"They will kill me! They will kill me! Don't leave me!"*—

"My child, they will kill me if I stay here; but can you ride?'—

"Yes, anything to save my life."—

'Then jump up behind me and hold on to my belt.'"

Major TALLMADGE then rode off with his men, with the British in hot pursuit, firing at him. Major TALLMADGE wheeled and returned fire. Alternately charging and retreating, they reached their detachment on the hill. The girl behaved with great courage and never expressed any fear; though, when the bullets whistled past them, he felt her cling closer to him. He then took her three miles to Germantown, where she dismounted in relief.

What was going on was that the young girl, who was being a spy for General WASHINGTON, was spotted as such by the British, but they kept quiet and just followed her at a distance so that she would not notice them. When they were confident that she had made her contact, the British charged full steam ahead for Major Benjamin TALLMADGE and his guards. The spy game was not going well for General WASHINGTON; he had lost Captain Nathan HALE and now he had almost lost this young lady. However, General WASHINGTON would never have sent his head of intelligence on a mission of this sort; he would have sent a lower subordinate.

This story was released by Colonel TALLMADGE after the Revolution and after the death of President WASHINGTON. It was never acknowledged by General WASHINGTON or confirmed by any other source that this event ever took place.

General WASHINGTON would once again have to revise his intelligence circle. In addition, he still did not know the status of Commodore John MANLEY and it remained weighing heavily on his mind as to whether he was dead or still alive. If he was alive, why was he not put up for exchange? How could he get a spy behind enemy lines to find out, without them becoming suspicious?

Whenever a unit of the Continental Army marched through a city or town, they were always surrounded by huge gatherings of Tories/Loyalists. Often many would have to be arrested or captured when they hailed them with hatred. There was no one else to trust other than their own fellow Continental troops. Danger lurked around every street corner; eyes were always on the Continental officers.

1. Harsh Conditions

Supplies were short despite Captain KEMPER's expeditions into the countryside. Transport wagons also were in short supply, and their teams and artillery horses were dying from lack of hay. Most men were unfit for duty because of lack of shoes, stockings, shirts, breeches and coats. Some men had to make their clothes out of their blankets. The soldiers' shirts and breeches were hanging in mere shreds of cloth. Sometimes as many as three men had to share one blanket. The look on the men's faces portrayed them as forsaken and discouraged; many were crying with despair—hundreds deserted!

Men would load wood and provisions on their backs to carry to their campsite. Soldiers would huddle up by any one of the hundreds of campfires to stay warm. Clouds of thick smoke that burned everyone's eyes floated over Valley Forge. These were the darkest days for the Continental Army. If seen from the heavens, it could have been said that Satan had covered it over so that the Lord could not witness the human suffering. Would they survive?

In mid-December, General WASHINGTON instructed Major General John SULLIVAN to build a bridge across the northern section of the Schuylkill River (which he named after himself, *"Sullivan's Bridge"*). This bridge was made exclusively of logs, sat close to the water, and was about twelve feet wide. This location was at a ford (a shallow crossing over the Schuylkill in a foot-deep water). This ford was used by Captain KEMPER to supply General WASHINGTON prior to the bridge being built but was difficult to cross with his heavy wagons. It was used to expedite the collection of provisions on the northern side of the river by foragers of the Continental Army.

As the month of December rolled into the month of January, the lack of food and clothing got worse; sickness increased with exposure and the number of effective soldiers ready for combat was dramatically reduced. This sparked General WASHINGTON to write to Congress, *"I am convinced beyond a doubt, that unless some great and capital changes suddenly take place . . . this army must inevitably be reduced to one or other of these three things. Starve, dissolve or disperse, in order to obtain subsistence in the best manner they can."*

His intelligence had informed him that the British had sent out a large detachment of soldiers from Philadelphia on a foraging expedition toward Darby, which was about five miles southwest. General WASHINGTON ordered a few *"small raiding parties"* to keep an eye on and torment the enemy. Foraging parties were sent out to confiscate everything the army could possibly use, before the enemy seized it. When under duress, Captain KEMPER asserted his force to maintain the Continental Army.

As the month of January flowed in with blizzards, diseases and starvation, plus low troop morale, General WASHINGTON was forced to make alterations. General WASHINGTON took General Marquis DE LAFAYETTE, Colonel Daniel KEMPER, Colonel Alexander HAMILTON, with a couple of wagons and an escort of Captain Henry *"Light Horse Harry"* LEE and his Continental Dragoons and headed to Captain John KEMPER's wagon-train camp for supplies.

After General WASHINGTON arrived at Captain KEMPER's camp, he dismounted while tucking a bundle under his left arm.

They all then went into the officer's tent for a meeting, while all eyes at camp were following them.

While in late January, at one of Captain KEMPER's wagon-train camps in the woods, just southeast of Lancaster, at Conestoga Creek, he received a dispatch from General WASHINGTON that he was needed to go on foraging excursions for the army. On this occasion, he called his army for inspection and informed them of the new mission. Lone WOLF, as usual, started painting up his face with war paint, in preparation for his powwow (dancing and singing).

Whenever he did this, he would look so scary; he could just glare at the British and terrorize them into submission.

On this day John laughed while shaking his head stating jokingly that, *"You are just one 'ugly and deadly' Lone WOLF."*

The whole camp around the main campfire outside the officer's tent burst out laughing.

Bouncing BEAR jumped in, exclaiming, *"You received nickname and it fits."*

Lone WOLF smiled until he was beet red.

Lone WOLF's nickname stuck throughout his service under Captain KEMPER. Whenever there was difference at camp in which Lone WOLF was involved, he would remind his opponent, *"Remember my nickname!"*

Captain KEMPER recorded, *"I always considered my Indian scouts as part of the Continental Army and they were always treated as equals. Even though they were a tribal people, they were highly industrious, self-sufficient and brave warriors, fearing nothing and extremely loyal to me!"*

Captain KEMPER had been put on *"special assignment;"* General WASHINGTON authorized him to conduct military raids on British foraging parties and go out on scouting and foraging expeditions at his own discretion. General WASHINGTON feared that if over one hundred supply wagons were crowded into camp at Valley Forge, men would try to sneak in the middle of the night and steal supplies.

These operations were ordered to take place from Captain KEMPER's wagon-train camp, northwest of Philadelphia along the Conestoga Creek, and southeast of Lancaster, out of sight from British transport and supply routes. If John needed any further troops, they were to be sought after from volunteers at camp, who needed something to do to stay busy. *"The need was great! The time was short!"*

Ensign Anthony MAXWELL and his brother-in-law, Private James MATHERS, was a couple of these volunteers.

As General WASHINGTON turned to leave with his staff, he turned back while removing the bundle he had under his left arm. He said to Captain KEMPER, *"I almost forgot, this is for you,"* and handed the bundle to Captain KEMPER, saying, *"It will help to keep you warm and more easily recognizable,"* and then turned to leave.

Captain KEMPER unfolded the bundle to find a forest-green cloak, with red inner lining; he then nodded his head to himself and put it on, adding it to his wardrobe.

Elizabeth added a special entry in her diary, *"My father always told me repeatedly over the years that, General WASHINGTON, unlike some members of the Continental Congress, was so warm hearted that he would often place his hand on your shoulder or arm to comfort you whenever he had to ask you to give that extra mile. He was compelled to assure you that he would always be there by your side through thick and thin, good or bad, if he favored you, and you obeyed orders."* You then became invaluable. My father also said, *"Because I was so close to General WASHINGTON, other officers would try to use me in order to get to him or find out information. I would pretend to pay attention or shrug my shoulders then carry on."*

2. His Excellency, General George Washington Is Enraged!

Elizabeth recorded how her father stated that *"General WASHINGTON, was referred to by his officers as 'His Excellency.' General WASHINGTON was often enraged and could be heard yelling at his officers as they entered and exited the door to his headquarters."* Some of his officers complained, *"Everything WASHINGTON did was a disaster and that he could not win a battle if he wanted to."* While General WASHINGTON claimed that, *"He did not have enough officers with enough military experience who could win a battle."* In addition, General WASHINGTON had to worry about deserters, traitors and Tories/Loyalists.

John KEMPER's sons Charlie (1793-1869), Daniel (1803-1870) (named after his uncle Colonel Daniel KEMPER), and John Jr. (1807-1862) remembered that their father had told them that General WASHINGTON very seldom smiled. When he did, his teeth were so discolored that they had to often look away as respectfully as they could, feeling uncomfortable. They related that their father repeatedly told them, over their lifetime, that during the Revolution, there were good times and bad times!

As a young boy, General WASHINGTON had had a disease called small pox, which scars the human body for life. John's children said their father had told them that General WASHINGTON looked like a cat had clawed him, leaving pores in his face. In the summer, when it got hot and General WASHINGTON began to sweat, the powder that he put in his hair (which was customary at the time) would drip down into the pores of his face so he resembled a ghostly figure.

Officers would again have to look away as respectfully as they could so as not to offend *"His Excellency."* After the Revolution, oil paintings were done of General WASHINGTON covering these pores to make his scarred appearance look less repulsive.

General WASHINGTON's senior officers were content because they already held as high a rank as could be obtained. Some of his junior officers only stood by his side hoping for an increase in rank. Still others, like Colonel Alexander HAMILTON, verbally discussed and conspired against him by writing letters to members of Congress like John HANCOCK, or other members of Congress, complaining that General WASHINGTON was the cause of everything that went wrong.

Captain KEMPER recorded: *"General WASHINGTON and Colonel HAMILTON did not always get along, but they were not each other's enemies either."*

The junior officers suggested that General WASHINGTON be removed and replaced with whoever they thought would do a better job, but all their letters were in vain. No one could understand why Congress kept General WASHINGTON at the head of the Continental Army. No matter who said what, General WASHINGTON's position did not change. Part of the reason could have been that the Continental Congress had granted General WASHINGTON total command of everything. He was the only one who knew all the top secret agents and all intelligence for the Continental Army, Continental Navy and Continental Congress.

Congress could not afford to let him go because of someone's misunderstandings and whims. General WASHINGTON's junior officers had no way of knowing of his total involvement in intelligence, nor were they entitled to. Furthermore, it would be like letting go one of their own. It would also have been devastating to transfer leadership in mid-stream, for all top secret intelligence that General WASHINGTON knew would have to have been transferred as well. Then there would be no more secrets as they would have spread like wildfire.

Out of everyone who was available to Congress, General WASHINGTON had the most military experience. The choices of all his military strategies and the positions he appointed men to turned out to be incredibly effective. It was to the advantage of Congress that they had kept him in command, as the democracy of today benefited from it, including the life of Congress. It was as if they were protecting one of their own. In reality, they were; he was America's first congressional general, but no one questioned it at the time because he was in uniform.

General WASHINGTON's main fear, during this period of time, was that the British Army commanded by General HOWE, living easily in Philadelphia, was well fed and ready for battle and, would launch a major assault on him and the bewildered Continental Army entrenched at Valley Forge. This action could finish off the last of America's hopes and reserves before they were allowed to re-strengthen themselves. Throughout the entire winter encampment this fear overshadowed the soldiers' spirits and concerns.

Elizabeth continued through the years to record in her diary some of the stories her father shared with her about his adventures in the Revolution. One of these stories took place in January 1778, when her father and General LAFAYETTE were having a discussion about their birth dates while under the soft, warming light of a campfire at Valley Forge. They smiled about how they were both born in the exact month and year of September 1757 and wondered if it was their destiny that they had met.

When at camp (Valley Forge), Captain KEMPER would often be seen sitting on a rock, log or stump, wrapped in the American flag. When asked why he did it, John would reply, *"It keeps me warm!"* Everyone had their own spot at Valley Forge; when at camp, John's was away from the crowded section, off on a *"gray stone,"* as he waited for orders or was just having peace of mind. Lone WOLF always remained close by, waiting for his orders.

Civilian agents such as farmers, although they did not participate in military operations, were urged to establish a market for their business in camp. They were reminded that a resolution of Congress made them subject to military penalties. The agents who did establish their markets in camp eased only the concern of where they were and to whom they were selling their wares. The wares that they had quickly dwindled and were far from enough to sustain the constant demand of the huge numbers in camp that were constantly mounting as other regiments that had been sent out on other assignments were now being recalled by General WASHINGTON to rejoined the main army.

While in the service as wagon master, Captain KEMPER was not exclusively assigned to the clothier-general's department, but more often under direct command and control of General WASHINGTON, himself. His position in the clothier-general's department was, in fact, a cloak-and-dagger cover. Captain KEMPER was often sent out on foraging excursions. His special assignment was to superintend the convoy bringing food and clothing supplies from foraging excursions and from Lancaster to General WASHINGTON's headquarters at the Park (Valley Forge).

Captain KEMPER carried out the tasks assigned to him, crashing through the ice and snow, leading his convoy on military raids, short trips in search of food, clothing, hay for the horses and other essential provisions to maintain the Continental Army. When snow covered the ice, horses would slip and fall quite frequently. When the snow got deep, Captain KEMPER would send several empty wagons to the front to open and beat down the road for the rest of the convoy.

By the time Captain KEMPER's convoy reached the camp, the horses were so exhausted that they had to have time to regain their strength or be replaced by fresh teams prior to further foraging expeditions. For this reason, foragers often took turns.

Over the course of the winter, General WASHINGTON sent several requests to Clothier-General James MEASE to set up his headquarters at camp (Valley Forge). All these requests were ignored by James MEASE, pretty much the same way his resignation request went ignored by General WASHINGTON. There just was no one who wanted the job.

On 6 January 1778, after Colonel John CRANE (1744-1805) marched to join General WASHINGTON's Army at Valley Forge with 206 men fit for duty, he wrote a letter to a minister that he was now in WASHINGTON's camp. Camp continued to be overcrowded. Anytime a new regiment marched into camp, they were stunned in awe. There were thousands of troops and campfires everywhere; it was like walking through a dense, thick fog of smoke, constantly coughing while rubbing their burning eyes. It was often more comfortable to lie on the ground, avoiding breathing as much smoke as possible.

On 8 January 1778, Count PULASKI arrived in Trenton as per General WASHINGTON's orders to obtain forage. General WASHINGTON needed to have a constant flow of forage coming into camp, no matter how small of an amount.

Because of the harsh conditions in the month of January, General WASHINGTON was forced to take drastic measures. He had all available wagons collected and ordered Captain KEMPER and other foraging parties to seize privately owned goods for the army's needs. However, he gave strict orders that certificates were to be left behind with the farmers for their goods that could be fully redeemed for cash in the future. These certificates were valued at the army's best estimate, instead of the bumped-up charges that the civilians were constantly making.

In January 1778, as conditions continued to get worse Captain KEMPER went out to purchase goods from the farmers. Since the economy had collapsed, the Continental currency was worthless; the farmers would not accept Continental dollars. They were considered as made-up money; certificates were given as redeemable for cash in the future. The farmers still did not like this alternative, but Captain KEMPER had the army.

After the Revolution when the farmers tried to redeem the certificates, they proved worthless as Congress still had no money even to pay the Continental soldiers' claims. The Revolution was a drain on everyone; lucky it succeeded.

As the month of January lingered on, conditions got worst and desertions increased, many more deserting their posts. General WASHINGTON overwhelmed by various departments not being able to fulfill their obligations, sent a courier with sealed orders to Captain KEMPER's wagon-train camp northwest of Valley Forge at Conestoga Creek.

Upon receiving General WASHINGTON's orders, Captain KEMPER called his army for inspection. He ordered a general beat and tents were struck. He separated 250 troops, furnished three days cooking provisions, and thirty rounds of ammunition. He then ordered the remaining men to lie under arms (stand ready) until his return.

He then led his army down Lancaster Road toward Valley Forge and stopped at the Spread Eagle Tavern, about six miles outside General WASHINGTON's camp. Here he had his men set up camp and pitch their tents. The ground was frozen with eight inches of snow and it was difficult to pound stakes. The weather was cold with blizzard conditions. Setting up camp during the winter was always difficult.

The following morning Captain KEMPER had his army search the surrounding countryside around General WASHINGTON's camp, looking for deserters. Upon capturing any, he was then to report to Major TALLMADGE on the Island of Barbados.

Barbados was a large island just north of camp on the Schuylkill River. For some unknown reason, the name of the officer whom Captain KEMPER was supposed to report to was partially inked out but could still be read, possibly because much of it had faded over time. After Captain KEMPER's army had scoured the countryside surrounding General WASHINGTON's camp, they had found and captured four regulars (British officers), forty Tories, and twenty-three deserters. Did they miss anyone? What could all this have been about?

For some reason, which was not recorded in Captain KEMPER's journals, a special base had been set up on the island of Barbados. After turning the prisoners over on the island of Barbados, Captain KEMPER repaired to headquarters (General WASHINGTON's camp). Upon entering camp, his brother Daniel greeted, mounted and accompanied him. Continental Dragoons escorted him directly to General WASHINGTON's headquarters, while being saluted by senior officers, hoping for good news. All of General WASHINGTON's senior officers were lined up for a meeting called by General WASHINGTON.

As both Captain John and Colonel Daniel KEMPER rode through, all of General WASHINGTON's staff who separated to allow them through while saluting them. Captain KEMPER brought his right hand up to his right eyebrow and held it there until he reached headquarters. It was easier than saluting each officer individually. He and Daniel then entered General WASHINGTON's headquarters and reported his results.

General WASHINGTON replied, *"Something very big was about to happen here. Maybe we will find out exactly what when we get answers from Barbados."* He then posted extra guards around the batteries at camp.

After reporting to General WASHINGTON and visiting with his brother, Daniel, Captain KEMPER had his men pull up stakes and they headed back to their camp at a safe location along Conestoga Creek. Here they were safe from British Patrols.

By 24 January 1778, Colonel Edward STEVENS' (1745-1820) regiment, who marched to join General WASHINGTON's army at Valley Forge, put in for his resignation. STEVENS had 442 men assigned, but only 175 were fit for duty. Colonel Daniel and Captain John KEMPER's brother, Jacob KEMPER was a first lieutenant in STEVENS' battalion of artillery. All three brothers were now together again. Jacob would volunteer in his brother, John's company on foraging excursions. When you were Continental, you eventually bumped into and got to know everyone, sooner or later.

On 24 January 1778, Charles YOUNG, born in Prussia, Germany, and close friend of Captain KEMPER because of their German heritage, wrote a letter to General WASHINGTON. In it he stated,

> Sir:

> *Mr. Mease being much indisposed has directed me to acquaint your Excellency of the arrival of a quantity of linens, cloths &c. from Virginia. They were long detain'd at the Susquehannah, and with much risqué and difficulty, were brought over on sleds, Thursday last. The chief of goods from which in unloading, were greatly injured by being wet; indeed their situation is beyond description bad. The linen particularly were all under water, and many of the woolens, and before their getting to Lancaster were so frozen that to this time we are not enabled with safety to do anything with them, as by the last opening or removal they cracked like burnt paper.*

We are preparing a large building with a stove to receive them this day, & Mr. Mease would be happy to know your pleasure respecting the piece goods, as he conceives it cannot be eligible, to send to camp such a quantity of linens and cloths that might so soon be manufactur'd here. When their situation will admit; the blankets, shoes, and hosiery, would have been sent on before, but could not procure teams, are promis'd them Monday next, when they will be sent together some shirts &c. to Mr. Kemper. In behalf of Mr. Mease, I have the honor to be—Your Excellency's most Obt. Hble Servt.

Cha. Young

Mr. YOUNG told Captain KEMPER that, since Mr. MEASE constantly avoided conversing with His Excellency, he often had him handle his affairs for the department and cover for him, which made Mr. YOUNG feel very uncomfortable. Whenever His Excellency contacted him personally, he obeyed his commander-in-chief.

3. Wagon Tracks in the Snow

On 25 January 1778, on one of the foraging expeditions Captain KEMPER went on, he came upon some wagon tracks in the snow. Captain KEMPER's Indian scout, Bouncing BEAR, reported, *"There is a farm just over the ridge."*

Captain KEMPER then sent Lone WOLF up ahead while his company continued to follow the wagon trails. The scout came to a hill, heard chatter, got off his horse, tied it to a tree, and crouched down while moving quietly to the top of the hill. He looked over and saw a British convoy of seventy-five to one hundred men purchasing supplies from a local farmer and loading them on four wagons. This was just one of the many disloyalties that were taking place under the noses of the starving troops at Valley Forge.

After Lone WOLF reported back, Captain John KEMPER immediately sent his lieutenant with a company of men to the left and a second company of men with his ensign, Anthony MAXWELL, to enter from the right. He had his second lieutenant stay with his remaining troops for backup. Captain KEMPER grabbed his flag and said, *"Let's scramble some eggs,"* and with his main company of men, waving his hand forward, led the frontal assault.

The British, caught off-guard while loading supplies and confused about which way to fire, froze. Their commander, who saw that they were vastly outnumbered, yelled, *"Halt!"* He then pulled a white handkerchief out of his pocket and waved it above his head, around in circles, surrendering. The commander then reluctantly surrendered his sword. Although he was humiliated, the worst humiliation was about to take place, one that he would never forget and one that made him seek vengeance. He would hunt down Captain KEMPER to the end of his dying days.

4. Captain Kemper Leaves the British Troops in Their Underclothes in Mid-winter

Captain KEMPER confiscated all the British commander's money, horses, arms, and wagons already loaded with supplies. He cleaned out the farmer's supplies as well, including his livestock, so he could not sell anything more to the British. Captain KEMPER's chief scout, Lone WOLF turned to Captain KEMPER and said, *"Kukumotumun,"* (We [I and you] steal?)

Captain KEMPER turned slowly to Lone WOLF, smiled, and nodded.

Lone WOLF smiled back and said, *"Wikun"* (It is good.)

Captain KEMPER, while mounted and facing the farmer, thrust his right hand out slowly, opening his palm as he released a handful of certificates while watching them float slowly to the ground. Captain KEMPER then stated, *"Because of General WASHINGTON's generosity, even traitors are allowed these for their goods. They are fully redeemable for cash value in the future."* The farmer quickly picked them up before the wind blew them away, and nodded.

Heavy snow was falling, while blizzard conditions whistled throughout the forest and countryside. The farmer, after being stared in the eye by Captain KEMPER, replied, *"I have to eat too!"*

Captain KEMPER responded, *"It looks like you had more than plenty to eat!"* He then left the British troops standing in their underclothes in mid-winter, along with the farmer.

The British commander, who had a curly mustache, stood with his arms crossed, shivering and smoking a cigar, then stated, *"You sure have one ugly Indian scout!"* As he talked, his tongue twisted his cigar. Lone WOLF quickly lunged forward, not believing what he heard. The British commander hastily backed up exclaiming, *"Aaaaaaaaaaaaaah!"* fearing Lone WOLF wanted his scalp.

Lone WOLF always carried a tomahawk stuck in his waistband, which was easily visible and accessible. While Lone WOLF looked down, staring at the British commander in the eye, Captain KEMPER whisked by, grabbed the cigar out of his mouth, stuck it in his own and rode off. Captain KEMPER's troops took the British wagons filled with supplies with some of their horses tied to the rear of the wagons and followed. Captain KEMPER's troops led off the remaining British horses by their reins.

As Captain KEMPER and his troops rode off with their generous donations from the British Army, Lone WOLF, hysterically laughing said, *"Me sure glad me your pal and not dressed in red coat. Sure be no fun hopping home in winter blizzard in underwear, he, he, he."*

The British commander, who was not only numb from the cold, but being caught with his pants down, now had fire in his eyes and was red hot. It was as if the snow and ice around him was sizzling. He steadily watched having the captain in his sights, as if aiming a rifle. Captain KEMPER slowly faded away in the distance. Was Captain KEMPER untouchable now, or would the British commander hunt him down?

How would all the British troops get back to Philadelphia in their underwear and no horses? It must have been quite a sight to see the British troops arriving back in Philadelphia jumping and rubbing their arms in the freezing cold. The rest of the British troops stationed at Philadelphia must have had the laugh of their life. *"What in the hell happened to you guys?"* You can be sure the situation brought anger and laughter for years to come. The commander was sure to never forgive or forget and to hunt Captain KEMPER down, but how could he find him in such a dense wilderness?

After Captain KEMPER's departure, the British commander asked the farmer, *"Who in the hell was that man?"*

The farmer replied, *"Why that was Captain John KEMPER, sir; everybody knows who he is."*

The British commander seething with anger yelled, *"So that is Captain John KEMPER!"*

The farmer replied, *"Yes sir! He has some kind of special protection under General WASHINGTON and does all his dirty work for him."*

The British officer then responded, *"Yes, I have heard of this man. Our intelligence has informed us of him, he is one of the in-laws of that 'Rebel Banker,' John MORTON! He is also the one responsible for cleaning out Philadelphia so that we are forced to forage in order to survive. He is a menace! Do you know what that protection is for?"*

The farmer replied, *"I do not know, sir, but he comes and goes as he damn-well pleases! He also takes what he wants, as you have just witnessed personally. As for these certificates, they are probably worthless, but I have nothing else to hope for."*

In response, the commander replied, *"Well, well, he may have General WASHINGTON's protection, but not from me! That bastard stole my cigar, my sword and left me and my men in our underwear in mid-winter. Only a Rebel would do something so humiliating and cruel! I would rather have been shot! He has not seen the last of me. When I catch him, I am going to wring his neck for him. I will make sure he never forgets this day!"*

The British commander closed by saying, *"I think it is time we cleaned up General WASHINGTON's dirty work for him. It sure is not going to be any fun getting home with a winter blizzard coming on. Do you have any burlap?"*

The farmer replied, *"Yes! It is in the barn."*

The British commander then called his lieutenant, *"There is some burlap in the barn, go fetch it so we can start preparing for our long march back to Philadelphia and our embarrassment."*

Lieutenant, *"Yes sir!"*

The lieutenant turned to go to the barn, then abruptly stopped, looked back, and asked, *"Where in the barn?"*

The farmer replied, *"I will show you."*

This would not be the last time these two men would meet; perhaps they would meet again to share another cigar. After the Revolution, this farmer would boast about this encounter with the *"Master Forage Master,"* and ghost, Captain John KEMPER.

Bouncing BEAR always rode his donkey he called "Sasafras." It did not have the speed of a horse and would not be able to escape a British assault, so he always kept a horse tied to the rear of the wagon on the rear guard in the event he needed to convert over for speed.

As Captain KEMPER and his army rode on, Bouncing BEAR, who always rode rear guard, quickly galloped to catch up with Lone WOLF, who always rode on Captain KEMPER's lower right, yelling, *"Lone WOLF! WOLF! Hold up!"*

As Lone WOLF looked to his right as Bouncing BEAR was catching up, Bouncing BEAR said, *"I told you, I told you WOLF, your nickname so true, even the British know it and they never met you before, ugly, yeeea! But deadly, noooo! Definitely not scary! Ha, ha, ha."*

Lone WOLF answered, *"Bouncing BEAR, you so funny guy, almost as funny as your donkey, hee haw, hee haw. Now I give you good nickname; you now, 'Rear guard' Bouncing BEAR, or maybe hee haw Bouncing BEAR; ha, ha, ha."*

Bouncing BEAR continued to bellow out laughter as he held up on the reins of his donkey and turned to head to the rear guard as they caught up.

Captain KEMPER asked, *"Can you braves please try and keep it down?"*

Lone WOLF replied, *"He started it. Bouncing BEAR jealous because British commander afraid of me. Commander never take second look at him. Bouncing BEAR never make it as Mohegan brave, we too ferocious; it best he remain bouncing around little cubby bears. I also believe the BEAR one who stole my corncob pipe! Just other day, the BEAR offered to help me find corncob pipe, but want one painted pony if he finds it. No corncob pipe worth one painted pony, no less anything. Should be good deed. Only Lenape Indian that crazy."*

"Now I ask you Captain, what is wrong with the BEAR?"

Captain KEMPER replied, *"I have no clue WOLF, what is wrong with the BEAR?"*

Lone WOLF, *"I'll tell you what's wrong, the BEAR knows where my corncob pipe is. Now if the Captain would give me consent to search his wigwam* (domed *move-able* shelter) *I find corncob pipe and the BEAR can give me, one painted pony."*

Captain KEMPER, after hearing about the lost corncob pipe ever since it went missing, softly said, *"Please WOLF, please, I have heard enough about your corncob pipe. I will gladly buy you a new one the next time we go to a town."*

The WOLF answered, *"White man's corncob pipe not as good as Mohegan. Not even Lenape pipe as good, that's why the BEAR steal Mohegan corncob pipe."*

Captain KEMPER responded, *"Arrrrrrrrrrrrrrrrrrrrrrrrrrrrrrrrgh."*

Lone WOLF said, *"but when in town, you can pick up some chocolate, me like chocolate."*

Lone WOLF went on, *"Once had Mohawk chief offer me a choice of three daughters and his favorite tomahawk; I just laughed inside. He dreamin' having Mohegan grandson, but not by this great warrior."* He closed by saying, *"There three kinds of Indians, brave warrior Indians like Mohegan, not so bad Indians like Mohawk, and not so good Indians like Lenape; Bouncing BEAR Lenape, iye,*

iye, iye, iye. Just other day, the BEAR have nerve to call me baldy; he heap big trouble!"

Lone WOLF started on his history, *"Mohegan owned both sides of Hudson River, from city* [New York] *to what you call Albany, before white man come. Even Mohawk feared us."* Lone WOLF bolstered, *"All Indian tribes wish they could be Mohegan; we bravest and most magnificent looking warriors. All other Indian squaws dream of having Mohegan brave, but only best get one of us. All Mohegan squaws are daughters of some other chief's tribe. It take three Lenape to equal one Mohegan. When we get back to camp* [Valley Forge] *of the Great White Chief, Lone WOLF no longer need pipe, there plenty of smoke for everyone!"*

Lone WOLF continued to lecture Captain KEMPER on the history of the Mohegan Indian as they rode along. Captain KEMPER just smiled and shook his head as they rode on.

On 27 January 1777, at the headquarters at Valley Forge, General WASHINGTON responded to James MEASE's letter. In it he states,

Dear Sir:

I last night recd Mr. YOUNG's letter of the 24th *informing me of the unlucky accident that had befallen the Virginia cloathing. I have consulted the Brigadiers what is best to be done in their present situation, and they think that the cloths and linens proper for soldiers, to be made up agreeable to the directions given by Genl. Scott to Lieut,* [James] *Gamble (1753-1813) regimental quartermaster],* who *will remain at Lancaster and receive the cloathing as it is made up and forward it to camp. All the stockings shoes hats and ready made shirts to be sent off immediately, if not already done—Threads and*

trimmings to be sent with the fine cloth and linen.
I am &ca.

Go. Washington

On 27 January 1778, Captain KEMPER sent a dispatch to General WASHINGTON advising him that he had his wagons filled with supplies for the troops at camp. He requested an additional escort and for the special path to be cleared for his arrival at camp. Furthermore, he had some additional wagons he had captured from a British detachment party.

After General WASHINGTON received Captain KEMPER's dispatch, with a map and directions to his wagon-train camp, he requested volunteers for his escort. Many volunteered, but Captain KEMPER's personal friends—General LAFAYETTE, Colonel HAMILTON, and Captain Henry "Light Horse Harry" LEE—and his Continental Dragoons were approved by General WASHINGTON. They prepared an escort detail and headed for Captain KEMPER's wagon-train camp.

He then ordered the special path to be cleared for their arrival. General WASHINGTON, when preparing camp, had the forest cut down and crisscrossed around the perimeter as a barrier of protection against invasion. He left one special area designated for easy removal for supplying his own troops. Captain KEMPER was like a genie from an Aladdin's lamp, appearing and disappearing.

On 29 January 1778, General WASHINGTON wrote to the Continental Congress Camp Committee regarding the mandatory character of men to be appointed wagon masters, *"They should be plain, sober, diligent men, acquainted with the management of horses and wagons, and untainted with the absurd fancies of gentility, [men] who would understand the end and design of their appointment, and not to consider the means of making themselves useful as a degradation* [degrading in rank] *of their imaginary dignity."*

5. An Army Approaches Valley Forge! (The Spyglass Incident)

Out of the many dozens of trips Captain KEMPER made, transferring supplies from Lancaster to General WASHINGTON's headquarters at Valley Forge, as recorded in his journals, this one was the most memorable. He would laugh and tell this story throughout his life to all his friends and family. His brother Colonel Daniel KEMPER and friend Captain Anthony MAXWELL, likewise, never forgot it. This story seemed to enrich family and friends on the history of the birth of America.

On Thursday, 5 February 1778, everything at camp seemed calm and routine. Then it began—off in the distance, the sound of rumble and thunder, getting closer and closer, metal was clanging as if artillery was being moved. General Anthony WAYNE (1745-1796) perked his ears up. Everyone in camp went silent in fear, as if they had just seen a *"Mad Ghost!"*

What was happening? What was that sound? Why was the earth shaking? Could this be it? Could this be the final day at Valley Forge that General WASHINGTON so dreadfully feared? Had the British spies witnessed the clearing of the path for Captain KEMPER and launched an all-out assault on the Continental Army? There was no time to wonder—action had to be taken quickly! Camp quickly became as busy as a beehive!

General WAYNE sent for General WASHINGTON and ordered all barricades re-inforced, all able-bodied men and guns to the front. The officer galloped off, whipping his horse, and arrived at General WASHINGTON's headquarters. General WASHINGTON was already coming out, placing his hat on his head, as he was alarmed by the thunderous sound of the advance of what sounded like the entire British Army. The officer rapidly saluted General WASHINGTON and yelled, *"Sir, the entire British army is on its way."*

General WASHINGTON mounted his white horse and was hurriedly escorted by the officer to General WAYNE's location.

As General WASHINGTON arrived at the barricade, all non-able-bodied men, likewise, were crawling to the front. If this was going to be their last day, they wanted to die fighting. Cannons ready to fire, the ground trembling like an earthquake as the noise continued to grow closer.

General Anthony WAYNE climbed onto a cannon for elevation, as all other officers and troops in camp rushed to the scene. With his hand in the air, while looking through his spyglass, ready to give the order to fire everything they had, he said, *"Ready! Ready! . . . Oh my God!"*

Everyone in camp froze, *"What is it? What is happening? What is going on? Are there a million of them?"*

General WAYNE slipped and fell, yelling, *"Stop! . . . It is Captain KEMPER!"*

"Are you sure?"

Both Colonel Alexander HAMILTON and General Marquis DE LAFAYETTE had accompanied Captain KEMPER on this occasion, providing additional troops to protect the transports on this very special day. Everything Captain KEMPER could acquire—from magazines, foraging, hunting, and fishing—was in this shipment, but it had to be dispersed in increments by General WASHINGTON. John had asked for an escort and got it; the arrival was breathtaking, nerve-racking, and earth-shaking!

The soldiers quickly scrambled to remove the barricade so Captain KEMPER could enter with his convoy of over a hundred wagons filled with much-needed supplies of food and clothing for the Continental Army. The soldiers were still shaking, but this time, they were crying with joy, *"Food! Clothing! Blankets!"*

General WASHINGTON's response was, *"Good timing!"*

As Captain KEMPER, Colonel HAMILTON, and General Marquis DE LAFAYETTE entered camp through the dismantled barricade, they were momentarily immobilized in awe as they stared at all the hundreds of guns and cannons pointed in their direction. The camp was prepared to fire with everything they could muster in preparation for what all thought would be their last battle. Surprising Captain KEMPER turned out to be a ghost of a chance.

After everyone in camp chuckled over what almost happened, General WAYNE gulping as he prepared his explanation, commented to Captain KEMPER, *"You are so lucky I cleaned my spy-glass this morning!"*

Captain KEMPER replied, *"When I am not in control of a situation, I depend on luck; that is why I display our flag proudly!"*

John's brother Daniel smiled with glee. All officers laughed for a while, as recorded in the KEMPER journals, Elizabeth's diary, and Uncle Dan' (Colonel Daniel KEMPER's) recollection of the event.

What was unknown at WASHINGTON's camp at the time was the difficulty Captain KEMPER had gone through prior to his arrival. Halfway on the trail between Lancaster and Valley Forge, four of his wagons broke down, while a fifth got stuck in a ditch. Captain KEMPER had to halt his wagon-train so that repairs could take place.

General LAFAYETTE quickly rode up to Captain KEMPER and nervously exclaimed, *"We are sitting ducks."*

Captain KEMPER replied, *"This sort of situation happens all the time, we are fully prepared. We have five wagons filled with nothing but wagon parts for this occasion. In addition, we have a special team of wheelwrights prepared to quickly repair the wagons."*

General LAFAYETTE continued, *"What about British foraging parties?"*

Captain KEMPER answered, *"This is the wilderness; the British do not like traveling in it any more than they have to, besides they are content with traveling the main roadways and making headquarters in large cities."*

The *"Marquis"* who had started this campaign with little military experience in the wilderness of a new country was learning fast!

Captain KEMPER first had his Indian scouts put on alert; he then had a team detached from one of the wagons and attached to the wagon stuck in the ditch so as to help pull it out. He then dispatched his wheelwrights and repair teams to the broken-down wagons, while Colonel HAMILTON helped organize the parties.

Although there was no threat from British patrols, these procedures had to be followed anyway. Captain Henry "Light Horse Harry" LEE and his "Continental Dragoons" had accompanied them. Since these repairs were going to take some time, the men asked Captain KEMPER if they could start a campfire in order to warm themselves. He granted it and added that some coffee be made for the troops. *"Good idea, Captain!"*

When Captain KEMPER led his convoy, he always flew the American flag from the leather holster attached to the right side of his horse's chest. When stationary, or leading his horse to a particular location, he would have the flag strapped alongside his horse on its right side.

Over the years, Captain KEMPER would chuckle with his friends and neighbors over how General *"Mad"* Anthony WAYNE's spyglass (field glass) saved his life from friendly fire, when General WAYNE finally saw the American flag that Captain John KEMPER always displayed proudly on his journeys. Besides Elizabeth KEMPER recording this story from her father and family, she also collected various versions of the same story from friends and neighbors after her father's death.

On 8 February 1778, Bouncing BEAR went into his wigwam and came out just as quickly as was possible and so angry he was spitting nails, yelling, *"Captain!, Captain!"*

Captain KEMPER responded, *"Yes BEAR, what is wrong now?"*

The BEAR continued, *"Someone stole my furs! He did it while I was away checking my traps. Now, someone stole my moccasins while I was asleep. This had to be another Indian who wants to see the mighty BEAR go barefoot."*

Lone WOLF injected, *"I be glad to help you find them, but if I do, I would like one painted pony or if you are so lucky to find my corncob pipe, we will call it even."*

Frustrated, the BEAR, while shaking his fists in the air, said, *"This not funny WOLF,"* and growled, *"Grrrrrrrrrrrrrrrrrrrrrrrrrrrrrrrrrrrr."*

On 9 February 1778, General WASHINGTON, concerned that Captain KEMPER's supplies would be depleted fast, because so many were needed immediately, ordered General WAYNE to take several hundred troops into New Jersey and continue foraging for much-needed provisions. General WASHINGTON ordered this to maintain a constant flow of supplies.

However, General WAYNE was in such desperate need of clothing and shoes for his troops that he strayed out of his jurisdiction in the direction of the clothier-general's department in Lancaster, thinking his rank might give him privilege. However, he bumped heads with James MEASE, clothier-general of the Continental Army; unsuccessful, General WAYNE headed on his way.

General WAYNE discovered that Captain KEMPER's job was not so easy after all. It took General WAYNE about two months to obtain a small portion of what Captain KEMPER could acquire in a couple of weeks with a company of 320 men. In addition, Captain KEMPER had his brother-in-law, Mr. MORTON on his team. General WAYNE soon relished the thought of returning to camp, where he could plan for his specialty—battle!

On 14 February 1778, Captain KEMPER had recorded that Sullivan's Bridge had been completed. Immediately upon completion of the bridge, Captain KEMPER and other foraging parties were able to ride or march across it into the countryside, confiscating everything that was not nailed down so the army could survive. Local farmers whose premises had been raided severely protested these desperate measures taken by the army.

On 15 February 1778, the Continental Congress planned a trip to Valley Forge to witness the hardships and needs of General WASHINGTON and the Continental Army and to go over military strategy. They sent a dispatch to Clothier-General James MEASE requesting his presence. James MEASE replied that he was too ill to make the trip and sent along a copy of the resignation that he had sent to General WASHINGTON, which he had ignored. The thousands of troops and the desperate conditions they endured overwhelmed Congress. They were not in shape to do anything but they needed to keep the men's hope up by letting them know they cared and were trying to help in any way they could.

After the Congressional Committee returned to York, they tried repeatedly to find someone to take over as clothier-general. However, everyone they offered the position to, declined claiming, *"The salary annexed is by no means equal to the post."*

By 16 February 1778, construction of the two thousand huts that had begun in December of 1777 for living quarters was now completed. The army was starving and made ill by typhus, smallpox, pneumonia and other diseases. General WASHINGTON's army continued to barely exist.

Men had been on half rations for weeks; there were periods of four or five days when the camp was without bread or meat. Clothing was in such short supply that uniforms were shared to maintain an appearance of military routine. The huts were better than the tents but still left a lot to be desired in comfort. They were small and crowded but gave better shelter from the elements.

There was a major concern that the army would be wiped out by disease, battle, mutiny or mass desertions. Morale was low, and the situation in camp was potentially explosive. The British, who were sitting in occupied Philadelphia, were in higher spirits, living in homes, and sleeping on beds with American women. Most of the Continental soldiers had to sleep on a layer of hay on the ice-cold ground with no one to love them. The British seemed to remain content to lie about, with no fear of coming under attack, enjoying the fruits of their victories.

As the month of February rolled on, the horses were beginning to starve. There was no more hay, and the horses were trying to eat the soldier's bedding. Colonel Tench TILGHMAN (1744-1786), aide-de-camp to General WASHINGTON, wrote, *"But if some* [forage] *is not got in soon, it will come too late as I fear we shall not have a horse left alive to eat it."*

Whatever direction General WASHINGTON turned, times were hard, tempers were short, and supplies were few. The Continental Congress could not keep up with the growing needs of the Continental Army. Had Congress created more than they were capable of handling? Had they bit off more than they could chew? They kept ordering increases in the army, but had no substance to offer them, which became evident when they visited Valley Forge.

General WASHINGTON continued to maintain privileges for Captain KEMPER as well as he could. Since Captain KEMPER had over eight hundred army horses in his convoy, including the ones ridden by the troops, hay was stored in his wagons for their consumption. If he did not make it back to camp, the Continental Army was finished!

Since both American and British foraging parties had ravished the countryside, Captain KEMPER and other foraging parties could not bring back a sufficient quantity of hay for the horses at the camp. In addition, another problem arose: the quartermaster and commissary departments failed, preventing the arrival of those much-needed supplies in camp. The quartermaster-general, Major General Thomas MIFFLIN, aide-de-camp to General WASHINGTON, was unable to maintain control of that department.

Meanwhile, Captain KEMPER continued combing the countryside in search of food and clothing, trying to hold the army together. Local farmers continued to sell their produce to the British for hard cash. This made Captain KEMPER furious! He would seek out these farmers and confiscate their supplies before they could be sold to the enemy. Many of these farmers would protect their grain and cattle with firearms and burn it before they would sell it to their fellow Americans, even knowing that they were starving at Valley Forge.

Cornmeal, hay and other products were often confiscated at the point of bayonet. Captain KEMPER would search the woods for horses and livestock hidden there by the farmers. Upon locating the livestock, he brought it to the attention of the closest farmer. He informed them that he had found the animals hidden in the woods and asked them if the animals belonged to them. The farmers, being afraid of retaliation, denied any ownership.

Captain KEMPER informed them that because of General WASHINGTON's generosity, he had certificates for the owners of livestock confiscated that were fully redeemable for full-cash value in the future. The farmers, feeling that they were being tricked, continued to deny ownership. Finally, Captain KEMPER asked, *"Are there any farmers that would like to take credit for the animals so that I can offer these certificates for them?"* The farmers quickly threw up their hands, like excited school children and in exhilarated voices yelled, *"I will be glad to take credit!"*

Captain KEMPER then drove the herds back to Valley Forge for the army's consumption. The army was so hungry that when Captain KEMPER arrived at camp with the herds, the soldiers were often ready to eat them alive! They were ready to eat anything on a hoof, including horses. Captain KEMPER always found a way to try to work around the farmer's fears. He truly believed, at this point in time, that the certificates were going to be fully redeemable.

In Philadelphia, General HOWE called for one of his most treacherous officers, Captain William *"Bloody Bill"* CUNNINGHAM (1756-1791), provost marshal in New York City, to take charge of Bridewell City Hall Prison at Sixth and Walnut Streets in Philadelphia. While he was marshal in Philadelphia, Captain CUNNINGHAM slowly starved the American prisoners to death. One prisoner, driven to the last extremes of hunger, ate his own fingers to the first joint from the hand before he died.

Others ate the mortar and stone that they chipped from the walls while some were found with pieces of wood and balls of clay in their mouths, which in their last moments of life, they desperately sucked on in hopes of obtaining some nourishment that might sustain their lives for a few short moments longer.

One day the prisoners were returning to the prison from the yard; many of them were so sick they could hardly walk. Captain CUNNINGHAM repeatedly beat them with his rattan (whip). When the last prisoner staggered in, Captain CUNNINGHAM gave him a blow with a large key belonging to the gaol (prison) made of brass and measuring around ten inches long. The blow knocked the man down dead. Hundreds of prisoners, who suffered death through torture and starvation from Captain CUNNINGHAM, were piled in holes twenty to thirty feet square in "Potter's Field" (Washington Square). This location later became known as, "the City of the Dead."

Captain CUNNINGHAM would boast, *"I am as absolute in my prison, as General HOWE is at the head of his army."* He also boasted that *"he killed more Rebels with his bare hands than had been killed by all of the King's forces in America."* Most of the Americans who entered into captivity were strong, healthy, and able-bodied young men. By the time they got out, if they got out, they were weak, frail, deranged, ghostly-looking creatures. Hundreds of prisoners left their names in graffiti records on the prison walls. All prisoners were surrounded by fear, torture, starvation, intimidation, and slow, painful death.

In February, General WASHINGTON, angered by these reports, dispatched his commissary-general of prisoners, Colonel Elias BOUDINOT (1749-1831), to Philadelphia to investigate. Colonel BOUDINOT secured the evidence from both Americans and a British officer, whose stomach was turned by Captain CUNNINGHAM's torture. BOUDINOT reported to General WASHINGTON, who, in turn, sent a letter to General HOWE threatening retaliation against British prisoners in his custody if this matter was not corrected by a certain date.

General HOWE compliantly replaced Captain CUNNINGHAM with Tory, Henry Hugh FERGUSON (1747-?), and returned Captain CUNNINGHAM to New York City as provost marshal. General WASHINGTON probably had little to no prisoners, but the threat got results.

Little did Captain KEMPER know at that time, that, he would end up in the clutches of this "Monster," Captain CUNNINGHAM! Later on, he would be captured by the British, imprisoned and tortured on the *Scorpion* and *Jersey* prison ships off the coast of New York City. He was thence flipped from the frying pan into the fire as he was transferred to the provost marshal, Captain William *"Bloody Bill"* CUNNINGHAM, in New York City, where the mistreatment continued.

He was then transferred to Mill Prison, Plymouth, England, by order of Admiral Sir George Bridges RODNEY. The British always transferred officers to their country, where there was no chance for escape, to barter in exchange for the release of their own officers.

On 23 February 1778, Baron Frederick Wilhelm VON STEUBEN of Prussia, who was recruited in Paris by Benjamin FRANKLIN, arrived at Valley Forge to begin drilling the troops. He was appointed major general of the Continental Army. He taught the soldiers military routine, battle tactics and discipline. Finally, the Continental Army was learning to work together as a unit and learning new techniques in order to survive. General VON STEUBEN only knew German, so he had to have an interpreter. Although he spoke no English, he quickly picked up the curse words.

Shortly after Baron VON STEUBEN's arrival at Valley Forge, the brothers Colonel Daniel and Captain John KEMPER, who spoke German as fluently as he did, greeted him. The KEMPER brothers informed General VON STEUBEN that their grandfather, Colonel Johann KEMPER had served in the various battles in the Prussian wars under Frederick, "the Great Elector," and his son Frederick I, king in Prussia. They had awarded to him the governorship of Bacharach on the Rhine for his bravery in battle. He moved from Königsberg to Bacharach to take his new position. He then assumed the hereditary rights of command of Stahleck Castle, which was passed down to their father, Johann Jacob KEMPER.

They continued by telling the baron that their grandfather Colonel Johann KEMPER was wounded fourteen times in the various battles during the Prussian wars and was provided a comfortable pension for his retirement. Then their grandfather died from a lingering illness while sitting in his easy chair (rocking chair) on the ramparts of Stahleck Castle from the wounds he had received in battle.

Their grandmother continued to receive his pension, which afforded a good education for their father, Jacob, at Heidelberg University, Duchy of Württemberg, Germany.

General VON STEUBEN, being familiar with the Prussian Wars replied, *"Obviously, you gentlemen are not going to need my training, perhaps you might consider assisting me, I always need another good interpreter."*

On 27 February 1778, Ensign Anthony MAXWELL walked into a tent to find Lieutenant Frederick Gotthold ENSLIN (1740-?) attempting to sodomize Private John MONHORT. Ensign MAXWELL reported the incident to his superior, whereby Lieutenant ENSLIN responded that Ensign MAXWELL had slandered his good name. Ensign MAXWELL was then arrested and brought before a brigade court-martial charged with *"propagating a scandalous report prejudicial to the character of Lieutenant ENSLIN."*

Colonel Aaron BURR was president. *"The court after mature deliberating upon the evidence produced, could not find that Ensign MAXWELL had published any report prejudicial to the character of Lieutenant ENSLIN, further than the strict line of his duty required and do therefore acquit him of the charge."*

His Excellency, the commander-in-chief, approved the foregoing sentences and ordered Ensign MAXWELL to be discharged from his arrest.

On 28 February 1778, after Ensign Anthony MAXWELL was cleared of any wrong doing, and because of his constant volunteering in Captain John KEMPER's foraging excursions, he was promoted to second lieutenant in Captain John SANTFORD's company, Colonel William MALCOLM's regiment. Anyone assisting in bringing much-needed food and supplies into camp for the Continental troops was always noticed and never forgotten.

Lieutenant Anthony MAXWELL later fought at the Battles of Monmouth (28 June 1778) and Springfield (23 June 1780). He was promoted to a captain-lieutenant (the second officer of a colonel's company of every infantry regiment) in General William MAXWELL's brigade under Major General John SULLIVAN's Expedition (18 June 1779–3 October 1779) into the Finger Lakes region of Wyoming County, Western New York.

The purpose of the expedition was to combat the Indian raids on the American settlers. All would be shocked to discover the heinous crimes committed by the Indians on the American settlers. Captain-Lieutenant Anthony MAXWELL finally retired on 1 January 1781 in Stony Point, New York.

On 1 March 1778, General WAYNE confiscated some 90 cattle and 35 horses from the farmers in New Jersey. They, in turn, reported his activity to the British patrols. The patrols set out in pursuit of General WAYNE, who had immediately sent for Brigadier General Count PULASKI from Trenton. Count PULASKI came to back him up with fifty horsemen. Even though the cavalry had arrived to assist and escort General WAYNE, they still lost over half of the stock on the trip back while encountering minor British skirmishes.

On 3 March 1778, Lieutenant Frederick Gotthold ENSLIN was brought to trial before a court martial. Colonel Benjamin TUPPER (1738-1792) was president. Lieutenant ENSLIN of Colonel William MALCOLM's regiment, was tried for attempting sodomy with Private John MONHORT; secondly, for perjury in swearing to false accounts. On March 10, 1778, he was found guilty of the charges exhibited against him; being breach of fifth Article eighteenth Section of the Articles of War and do sentenced him to be dismissed the service with infamy.

"His Excellency, the commander-in-chief approves the sentence and with abhorrence & detestation of such infamous crimes orders Lieutenant ENSLIN to be drummed out of camp [Valley Forge] *tomorrow morning."* The next day would be remembered and reiterated by the entire Continental Army for years to come.

On 15 March 1778, Lieutenant James MC MICHAEL (1761-1845) recorded the sentence in his diary being carried out. *"I this morning proceeded to the grand parade, where I was a spectator to the drumming out of Lieutenant ENSLIN of Colonel MALCOLM's regiment. He was first drum'd from right to left of the parade, thence to the left wing of the army, from that to the center, and lastly transported over the Schuylkill with orders never to be seen in camp in the future. This shocking scene was performed by all the drums and fifes in the army — the coat of the delinquent was turned wrong side out."*

On 21 March 1778, General Sir Henry CLINTON, who had been put in charge of New York City by General HOWE, was quickly bucked up to lieutenant general by King "George William

FREDERICK," to intimidate, shame and replaced Major General Sir William HOWE in Philadelphia as commander-in-chief.

This order was given by King George III (1738-1820), who had been upset with HOWE for disobeying his orders to take his army to Albany, New York and meet up with General *"Gentleman"* Johnny BURGOYNE. This ultimately caused his surrender. Instead, he went to Philadelphia, overly anxious to capture General WASHINGTON and America's capital, in the hopes of ending the war fast. General HOWE, being reprimanded and humiliated, retired and returned to England.

What King George did not know at the time was that he had made his last and final huge mistake; by replacing General HOWE with his subordinate General CLINTON. General CLINTON was not half the man General HOWE was. After the evacuation of Philadelphia, General CLINTON quickly ran from General WASHINGTON for safety in British-controlled New York City. He ran so fast that it was as if he was holding up his skirt as he was running through the mud puddles.

General CLINTON continued to send his minions into the Jersey countryside, burning down homes of families with fire and sword, but never once took the main army, like General HOWE did, and to pursue General WASHINGTON. Things had reversed, and this war was over; it was just a matter of time.

The last real general that King George had in the States was Lieutenant General Sir Lord Charles CORNWALLIS (1738-1805); however, he was not the commander-in-chief and had to follow orders from a general, who, in fact, was a real coward. General CLINTON was the cause of General CORNWALLIS' downfall at Yorktown by ordering him to dig in instead of having him return to the city for safety as he, himself had done.

General CLINTON always sent out others to do his dirty work for him. Upon Lord CORNWALLIS' surrender, King George had no real generals left in the States, and the last war in the Revolution had been fought and lost to the Continental Army. All that would remain would be minor skirmishes by Tories/Loyalists, who would end up paying dearly for their support of the Crown.

King George was not a military man and, therefore, did not know military order, nor was he able to climb down from his high horse and re-evaluate the situation. He made a couple of serious military misjudgments; one, King George should have sent his entire army and navy to the New York City area instead of having them split up over the entire thirteen states, staging his power. He should have sent all his forces after General WASHINGTON and the American capital, Philadelphia.

If he had sent seventy-five thousand troops after General WASHINGTON at Fort Washington, he would have surrounded General WASHINGTON on all sides and there would have been no place for General WASHINGTON to retreat. The war would have been over fast in favor of the Crown. General HOWE knew what he was doing; King George did not! He also made a mistake on the three-prong attack in Albany, New York. Once again, he should have sent his entire force to back General HOWE up instead of splitting them up and dividing the power for show.

On 24 March 1778, Major General, Nathanael GREENE was appointed quarter master general and General WAYNE returned to rotation at Valley Forge.

On 26 March 1778, John's brother, Colonel Daniel KEMPER, deputy clothier-general at Valley Forge, gave his report to General WASHINGTON, showing that some food and supply improvements had been achieved. By May, as the mud dried on the roads and green appeared in the fields, the army was now receiving good daily rations of meat, fish, etc.

During the bleak winter of 1777-1778, over 2,500 Continental soldiers died at Valley Forge by disease, or starvation, while others froze to death. Now the hills were colorful again with the blooms of dogwood and other spring blossoms; everyone was in high spirits. The Continental Army was now ready for battle, both physically and mentally! Since General HOWE was unable to launch a major assault on Valley Forge during the winter hardships, because of General WASHINGTON's insights to build a perimeter of felled trees, it was now, too late!

On 17 April 1778, from the headquarters at Valley Forge, General WASHINGTON wrote James MEASE,

> *In a word your absence, & the incompetency of a Clerk, to answer the various applications that are daily making, throws a load of business upon me which ought to be the burthen of your own Shoulders—& which were you present you would become more intimately acquainted with & know better how to provide for. For these reasons if you mean to continue in the office I am obliged to insist that you shall reside with the Army or so near it, that I can, upon every application to me, for matters in your department, receive proper information from you.*

> *I should suppose that an active deputy at Lancaster could superintend the making of the clothing at that place . . . I cannot get as much cloth as will make Cloaths for my Servants, notwithstanding one of them that attends my person and Table, is indecently, & most shamefully naked and my frequent applications to Mr. KEMPER (which he says he has as often transmitted to you) in the course of the last two months.*

It is to be noted here that, General WASHINGTON was speaking the same language as Captain KEMPER used in later years when filling out his declaration to obtain a pension. Revolutionary expressions were the same among all Continental soldiers.

On 6 May 1778, Colonel Archibald CAMPBELL had been given in exchange for Ethan ALLEN. General WASHINGTON had written a letter to Colonel CAMPBELL, congratulating him on his exchange and apologizing for his mistreatment. Ethan ALLEN, after he returned home, was finally given a rank of lieutenant colonel with no military training. He was given his rank because of his bravery in the battle and status he received as a long time prisoner of war.

6. The French Alliance

On 8 May 1778, cannon smoke clouded the field while a roar of muskets crisscrossed the grand parade. Thousands of double-ranked troops performed a feu de joie ("fire of joy"), a precision-timed firing of muskets through the ranks. The army was celebrating the new alliance with France, a very powerful ally and world power, which had come to Valley Forge to announce and celebrate the new alliance.

The French had no love for the American Revolution, but they had ulterior motives. The French were so jealous of the British Empire that they were easily excited into helping another cause to dislodge a part of it, and they used the colonists to try to help them get Quebec back, which had been taken by the British back in 1759. Their man, General Marquis DE LAFAYETTE, would lead this army of American soldiers.

France showed its true colors after the Revolution during the Napoleonic Wars in the late 1790s. Napoleon BONAPARTE (1769-1821), in need of money to finance his war, demanded payment in full for the outrageous charges the French had made for their assistance during the Revolution. America refused, claiming that the debt was owed to the Crown, not to the monarch who overpowered them. France then went to war against the United States, capturing over three hundred merchant ships and sinking many more. The British, at this point in history, took our side; old rivals were at it again.

On 8 May 1778, the same date of the celebration, General Charles LEE had been exchanged for General Richard PRESCOTT. General LEE had been absent a year and a half as a supposed prisoner of war. What General WASHINGTON and the rest of the Continental Army did not know at the time was that General LEE had been living under plush conditions with servants. Did General LEE possibly have something up his sleeve? British intelligence filled General LEE in on the size of General WASHINGTON's army before releasing him.

On 12 May 1778, the Oath of Allegiance ordered by Congress to be administered to all officers of the army at Valley Forge took place. Each officer had to put his hand on the Bible and swear allegiance to the United States before their commander-in-chief, major general, or brigadier general. This had to be done before the opening of the campaign. Everyone was excited; the army was rebuilt and ready.

By 15 May 1778, General WASHINGTON received intelligence that the British were preparing to evacuate Philadelphia. General HOWE ordered for all American vessels in the vicinity of the Delaware River to be burned and launched British foragers and marauders to the outskirts of Philadelphia to strip the countryside and take everything with them that they could confiscate.

General WASHINGTON detached General LAFAYETTE with 2,100 men and five cannons to restrain British foragers and marauders who were plundering the countryside. General LAFAYETTE crossed the Schuylkill River and took post on Barren Hill, about halfway between Valley Forge and Philadelphia.

On 16 May 1778, General WASHINGTON again wrote James MEASE, enclosing a duplicate copy of a previous letter sent to him, to whom Clothier-General MEASE had not responded, and giving him *"a positive and peremptory injunction immediately to repair to Head Quarters."* James MEASE was still not at camp when he replied on 23 May, 1778, claiming that the original letter had *"somehow miscarried."* James MEASE was letting General WASHINGTON know, in uncertain terms, in a roundabout way, he wanted nothing more to do with this department.

On 20 May 1778, General Charles LEE arrived at Valley Forge to assume service. The only question by some was, General LEE was treacherous to General WASHINGTON once, and would it happen again? It would not take long for that question to be answered. After General LEE had arrived, the thousands of troops General WASHINGTON had accumulated mesmerized him. The last General LEE had heard, General WASHINGTON's Continental Army was decimated at Fort Washington. British intelligence had given General LEE the wrong information on the size of General WASHINGTON's army. He was now in dreadful fear that General WASHINGTON might be strong enough to over-take General CLINTON.

General WASHINGTON then held out the Bible for General LEE to place his hand upon, and then began reading the Oath of Allegiance to the United States. As General WASHINGTON began reading, General LEE quickly withdrew his hand. When General WASHINGTON demanded a reason for his conduct, General LEE replied, *"As to King George I am ready enough to absolve myself from all allegiance to him; but I have some scruples about the King of Wales."* Since the entire Continental Army's eyes and ears were on him, he eventually subscribed to the oath. However, his heart was not in it, and he would soon show his true allegiance again, through treason.

On 30 May 1778, in addition, all officers stationed at Valley Forge, including General George WASHINGTON, who were present and not off on a mission, were given the right to sign the Oath of Allegiance to the United States of America.

On 8 June 1778, Captain KEMPER delivered his last supply to camp Valley Forge. This was different, as it contained weapons, powders and ammunition. This early June day had begun with a brief, light shower. As the skies cleared, rainbows burst into a brilliant show of colors, bringing with them renewed hope and a sense of joyfulness. A new strength to move forward was gained. Shortly thereafter, General CLINTON evacuated Philadelphia and General WASHINGTON was hot on his heels. There would be no more retreating!

There was something mystical about Captain KEMPER's wagon-train that began to raise eyebrows of other Continental officers. It was more like a large armored baggage train carrying supplies of weapons, tents, Indian corn, clothes, blankets, and yes, even champagne and whiskey for the Continental officers. Captain KEMPER was with the clothier-general's department; what was really going on here? Since he had General WASHINGTON's personal protection, all were satisfied.

On 18 June 1778, the British Army, now under the command of its new commander-in-chief, Lieutenant General Sir Henry CLINTON, evacuated Philadelphia, taking three thousand Tories/Loyalists with him, leaving most of the city in shambles. They feared that the French fleet would block the Delaware River and thus bottle them up. The British Army left with a long convoy of 1,500 wagons and artillery, extending for miles, crossed the Delaware, marched northeast toward New Jersey, and headed for Sandy Hook. Here the Royal Navy was waiting to transport them to British-controlled New York City, where they could reinforce their stronghold and be safe. Trailing this long convoy was another twelve-mile-long baggage train. It was a long march and—somebody was following them!

General WASHINGTON could have had the bridge crossing the Delaware River destroyed during the winter, thereby preventing the escape of the British Army from Philadelphia. He might have kept it intact in fear of enraging the British Army commanders into retaliating by decimating the Continental Army at Valley Forge before they were able to re-strengthen and rebuild themselves. In addition, he needed the bridge in place for their use when foraging and transporting supplies.

The British Army was well content with their confidence of world dominance. In addition, Great Britain had some of the most beautiful and well-trained marching troops on the planet. Other world powers like France and Spain knew better than to underestimate this beauty, for it could be just as deadly. The British, in their global dominance, had acquired quite a bit of resentment and jealously from other European powers. The sun never set on its empire!

However, the British had a weakness; whenever they overwhelmed and conquered cities like New York and Philadelphia, they had no problem sitting back, taking it easy, and enjoying the fruits of their victories. They were well aware that the Continental Army was in no shape to take back anything they had captured, especially with all the artillery and firepower they brought with them. All they had to do was sit back, enjoy life and wait until better weather arrived so that they could continue their military dominance in the States.

General WASHINGTON was well aware that the best time to attack the British was when they were on the march, which extended for miles. Their hundreds of wagons filled with supplies, and the artillery slowed them down dramatically. When the British were in camp, they were all set up and ready to repel any force with devastating results. Now, they had broken camp; this was just what General WASHINGTON and the Continental Army had been waiting for. This time, things would be different!

General WASHINGTON immediately sent out six brigades, glowing with fire in their eyes and revenge in their hearts. They were sent out to head off General Sir Henry CLINTON and the British Army at the pass at Sandy Hook. Their objective was to get to the British escape point in advance and wait for General WASHINGTON and the main Continental force. They would then put the squeeze on General CLINTON and pin him down, making him regret the very day he decided to come to this new land now called America!

On 19 June 1778, General WASHINGTON ordered Major General, Benedict ARNOLD (1740-1801), with a minimal army, to march back to secure Philadelphia and take over as military governor. After General ARNOLD arrived in Philadelphia, the remaining Loyalists who had not fled pretended to blend in. General CLINTON had declined to fulfill the Loyalists' request to leave a couple of thousands of troops for their protection. With just a mere couple of thousands of Loyalists, they were helpless against the Continental Army once again.

On 21 June 1778, General WASHINGTON put together the remaining Continental Army. They gathered all the arms they were capable of carrying from Captain KEMPER's timely supply. General WASHINGTON left Valley Forge via Sullivan's bridge, crossed the Delaware River, and pursued the enemy into New Jersey. General WASHINGTON was no longer "the Fox on the run," but, in fact, *the hound on the chase!*" General HOWE or CORNWALLIS could never bag the fox.

7. Escort of the Continental Congress

On 24 June 1778, after the British evacuated Philadelphia, Congress voted to convene back in Philadelphia. Captain John KEMPER, waiting for orders from General WASHINGTON, cleared the way for the clothier-general and the Continental Congress to be able to return.

In preparation for the upcoming battle, General WASHINGTON offered a command to General LEE, who declined. General WASHINGTON then offered the command to General LAFAYETTE who accepted. Once General LEE saw that General LAFAYETTE was going to lead the charge, he rebutted and offered to take command. It appeared that General LEE was jealous of someone else getting the command for this big event. In reality, he was in fear of General WASHINGTON crushing the remaining British forces. General LAFAYETTE honorably stepped aside. Because of his continued faithful service, Colonel Daniel KEMPER was made special assistant aide at the Battle of Monmouth.

On 28 June 1778, the two armies met at Monmouth County Court house and engaged in battle. General LEE, as soon as his eyes met his comrade General CORNWALLIS', immediately let him know he was on his side and in control of almost half of the Continental Army. He ordered his 5,440 troops to retreat. The troops who were ready to engage with enthusiasm were confused with General LEE's order to retreat, but they had to obey orders.

General LAFAYETTE, along with Colonel Daniel KEMPER, witnessing the cowardly actions, was stunned. General LAFAYETTE said, *"What in the hell is going on here?"*

Colonel Daniel KEMPER answered, *"He is retreating and there are no British chasing him."*

General LAFAYETTE sent a dispatch immediately to General WASHINGTON reporting on General LEE's cowardly retreat.

General WASHINGTON, who was leading the advance of the main army, ran smack into the retreating General LEE. He scolded him in front of his subordinates using foul language. General LEE, in turn, sprang back at General WASHINGTON in the same manner. General WASHINGTON needed those additional 5,440 men to finish off General CLINTON. General

LEE, once again, made sure his army was not going to help General WASHINGTON win this battle. The British were his family and where his loyalty resided.

General CLINTON, after just receiving his new command, was afraid of losing his first battle and being reprimanded by his king; therefore, he slipped away when night fell. General LEE's treachery had cost this victory. General LEE had only been back in service one month when he let General WASHINGTON and the Continental Army down, once again, big-time! It was later discovered that General LEE had been on the side of the British all along. He gave battle plans on how to defeat General WASHINGTON and the Continental Army, while a suspected prisoner. This was just another staged measure taken by General LEE to make sure General WASHINGTON did not win.

It is the firm belief of this author that General Charles LEE was King George's first planted deserter sent in as an agent to infiltrate the Continental Army and take control. Being a top British general deserter would guarantee automatic clout. In fact, it landed him the position of second-in-command under General WASHINGTON. Therefore, if anything happened to General WASHINGTON, he would then be the commander-in-chief and the British would be in full control. All that would be left to do was, to make sure General WASHINGTON was either captured or killed. This process of having deserters act as spies was constantly used by both sides.

General WASHINGTON had hoped to stop the British Army at Monmouth, preventing them from escaping back to British-controlled New York City and safety. General WASHINGTON had done his best, but the British boats had been waiting to transport them.

General CLINTON, while on board the ship, gazed into the night totally amazed at General WASHINGTON. Did he not realize that he was supposed to have surrendered years ago?

What the hell was going on here? General WASHINGTON was a *"mad man!"* He just was not a normal human being.

Let us stop and pause for a moment. What was really going on here? Had the British lost their focus? Did they not come to the States to conquer the rebel resistance? This was the moment General HOWE had hoped for, dreamed of, to face-off with General WASHINGTON and the entire Continental Army, thereby finishing them off. Why is General CLINTON running from them? Had General WASHINGTON's resilience crushed the British spirit? Everything General HOWE saw, he captured; everything General CLINTON looked at, he ran from. How could two leaders be so different? Had King George made a bad exchange? Where was this war headed?

What was unknown at the time was, King George had ordered General Sir Henry CLINTON to evacuate Philadelphia and return to strengthen their control in New York City. If he could not hold the city, then he was to further his retreat to Montreal. King George was no longer planning on his victory in the States but, in fact, his retreat!

On 1 July 1778, after General WASHINGTON had General LEE arrested for cowardice and fleeing from the enemy, General LEE's court-martial began at New Brunswick, New Jersey. General Lord STIRLING presided. General WASHINGTON had reported the incident to the Continental Congress, who sanctioned the court-martial. General LEE was charged with three counts: (1) Disobedience in orders in not attacking the enemy. (2) misbehavior before the enemy in making, an unnecessary, disorderly, and shameful retreat. (3) disrespect to the commander-in-chief.

General LEE was found guilty on all counts. General LEE was a traitor, and during this period of time, traitors were hung. General WASHINGTON had confused General LEE's loyalty to the Crown with cowardice in battle. However, General LEE had not been labeled a traitor at this point.

After General LEE was found guilty, he contacted Congress to try to get the results of the charges revoked. Unsuccessful, General LEE then began slandering General WASHINGTON. Colonel John LAURENS, taking personal offense in having his commander-in-chief slandered, challenged General LEE to a duel, in which General LEE was wounded in his thigh. General LEE then turned and limped off in shame. Subsequently, other officers loyal to General WASHINGTON, including General Anthony WAYNE, challenged General LEE to many other duels. General LEE suddenly got cold feet. Now in fear of his life, he cowardly declined all, naming one excuse after another.

Meanwhile, back at Captain KEMPER's wagon-train camp, Lone WOLF approached the Captain and said, *"General LEE heap big mouth but no action. He run from battle like squaw run from raiding party. He should be nicknamed, 'Big mouth talk too much'."*

As Captain KEMPER laughed, Lone WOLF continued, *'Why not great white chief* [General WASHINGTON] *send Captain to challenge him to duel? Me be proud to be by your side when you kill him."*

As Captain KEMPER chuckled, he answered, *"Because General WASHINGTON has ordered me never to take part in anything life threatening unless ordered to do so directly by him only."*

As Lone WOLF blew circles of smoke rings from his tobacco pipe, he grumbled, *"Hump! Great White Chief weak in knees."*

John's daughter, Elizabeth KEMPER, recorded that *"my father always told me that, he never liked General LEE and always thought he was a bad apple, deliberately sent over from England to spoil the whole bushel."* How true that ended up being.

When General Charles LEE came over from the British to join the American cause at the start of the American Revolution, he was flooded with honors. General WASHINGTON had a schooner named after him, which Captain John MANLEY commanded. General WASHINGTON, likewise, renamed Fort Constitution at the foot of the Palisades on the west bank of the Hudson River, after him. General LEE was made second-in-command of the Continental Army under General George WASHINGTON. Lee, Massachusetts; Lee, New Hampshire and Leetown, West Virginia were named after him as well. General LEE's loyalties remained with Great Britain, which named nothing after him; they knew his true worth.

From the beginning to the end of the Revolution, General LEE's heart was filled with deception, treachery, hatred and jealously, the key ingredients to anyone's downfall, including Adolph HITLER's (1889-1945). HITLER's worst mistake was when he turned on his strongest ally, Russia, and invaded them. General LEE loved neither God nor man, only himself. Why were these names not changed after General LEE showed such extreme treachery toward the United States? Because man accepts changes, whether good or bad, as a memory of what went right or wrong.

General WASHINGTON always sent his orders to Captain KEMPER sealed. If any of these seals was ever broken, he was to report the incident to General WASHINGTON and the courier or dispatcher involved would be held accountable. General WASHINGTON could not risk revealing the location of the Continental Army or Captain KEMPER's wagon-train camp to the enemy.

After the British evacuated Philadelphia and escaped General WASHINGTON's pursuit, General WASHINGTON sent orders for Captain KEMPER to break camp and move closer to Philadelphia. He further instructed Captain KEMPER to escort members of the Continental Congress back to Philadelphia. Captain KEMPER ordered his men to strike their tents.

While breaking camp, Lone WOLF commented, *"The BEAR's canoe has hole in it and not fit for use, why not leave it behind or cut it up for firewood. No use continuing to haul it around in our wagons."*

Captain KEMPER replied, *"Because the BEAR said he is going to patch it."*

The BEAR jumped in saying, *"Me not have to patch it if someone not make hole in it hoping to sink my canoe in the Turtle River with the mighty BEAR in it. It must have been another Indian, anyone have any ideas who?"*

As the camp burst out laughing, Captain KEMPER repeated, *"Let us break camp, men."*

On 2 July 1778, Captain John KEMPER, after receiving General WASHINGTON's orders, took his 320 troops and escorted members of the Continental Congress back to Philadelphia.

Captain KEMPER then established a military warehouse system in Philadelphia. He filled it with transports and other supplies brought back from Lancaster. The goods that were confiscated and not used, were returned to the stores.

Now that Philadelphia had been re-occupied, Fort Mifflin and Mudden Island, which had been ransacked by the British, had to be re-occupied and re-supplied as well.

After returning to Philadelphia, Captain KEMPER quickly became the target of hatred. Cries came out from the residents, *"What do you know; the big, bad wolf is back in town!"*

One man elbowed his companion and sneered, *"What are you going to take from us now Captain, our breeches?"*

Another asked, *"Captain, how would you like a bunch of new recruits; we would all love to catch you alone in the dark somewhere, just to give you one last big hug. The British have things right, all Rebels have got to go."*

Captain **KEMPER** continued to ride on, ignoring the ill-content, while they continued slandering him, *"Captain, do not ride away, we want to talk, we love you so much,"* screaming out, *"Snake in the grass!"*

What the residents did not realize was, General **WASHINGTON** had ordered Captain **KEMPER** to carry the stores back again with what supplies were left. He had his wagons stop at the appropriate store of their transports, which had been marked. The goods that were not used were quickly unloaded and delivered back to the store clerks, who momentarily stood in shock. They then quickly grabbed the supplies and put them back on the shelves before anyone changed their mind.

The citizens of Philadelphia stood stone-faced total in silence; this was just unbelievable! Why would a crook bring back what he took? The city of Philadelphia was in shambles from the British and Loyalists' exit, but at least, they had some of their stores back that the Continental Army had not used. In addition, Captain **KEMPER** failed to ask the clerks to return their certificates, so they were delighted in thinking they would get double their value. They just kept silent hoping that he would not remember the certificates, which he did not; or was it deliberate?

As Captain **KEMPER** rode off, everyone looked on in wonder. General Benedict **ARNOLD** was riding around like a bump on a log, appearing to have no destination in sight and going nowhere. He seemed to be on some kind of a tour. General **ARNOLD** stopped as Captain **KEMPER** was passing by and addressed him, *"I understand you were ordered to escort members of Congress back to town, good job! Where is your new wagon-train camp being set up?"*

Captain KEMPER, as he was slowly passing General ARNOLD jerked his horse's reigns back to face General ARNOLD.

He then replied, *"I thought you were close to General WASHINGTON."*

General ARNOLD ex-claimed, *"Well, I am, why do you suppose he made me the Governor of Philadelphia?"*

Captain KEMPER responded, *"Then why did he not tell you?"*

General ARNOLD froze and trembled in his saddle, angered by the captain's answer. How could a captain dare speak to a general like this? Since nothing more was being said, Captain KEMPER nodded and departed.

Captain KEMPER rode on to the headquarters of Congress, whom he had just escorted back. He reported to Henry LAURENS, president of Congress and told him that all the stores had been carried back as ordered. Mr. LAURENS thanked him and invited him in for a moment; there was something they wanted to discuss with him. Congress had their own mess to contend with before things were going to be back to normal at Independence Hall.

From Philadelphia, Captain KEMPER continued to serve in his duties as wagon master, supplying General WASHINGTON and the Continental Army wherever they camped in the great Northeast. His duties remained pretty much the same. He was constantly kept abreast by scouts, couriers, and dispatchers of General WASHINGTON's plans on movement and where he was setting up camp. General WASHINGTON always kept everything *"top secret"* between himself and Captain KEMPER.

What General WASHINGTON, Captain KEMPER, and Congress did not know was that, the military governor of Philadelphia, Major General Benedict ARNOLD, appointed by

General WASHINGTON, was also a traitor and was filling the British in on all intelligence regarding military and congressional movements. He just could not locate the location of Captain KEMPER's wagon-train camp. That was between General WASHINGTON, Captain KEMPER, and Congress alone. Others who were kept abreast when needed were, Colonels, KEMPER, HAMILTON, and Major TALLMADGE.

What General ARNOLD did not always know, was Captain John KEMPER's exact location, as it was kept secret between him, General WASHINGTON and Congress alone. General ARNOLD also had no authority to order or question Captain KEMPER, under any circumstances. General WASHINGTON was constantly surrounded by, Tories/Loyalists and traitors. It was truly amazing that he won the Revolution at all, since the deck always seemed to be stacked against him.

Elizabeth KEMPER recorded in her diary one of her father's stories he shared with the family. Her father stated that, *"after he escorted the Continental Congress back to Philadelphia, he and General Benedict ARNOLD would occasionally exchange eye contact, with seldom little said other than good day. Sometimes he* [General ARNOLD] *would give sort of a silent stare, or glare at him* [Captain KEMPER], *with little expression other than, a stone-faced, kind of empty look. At this time, no one knew he* [General ARNOLD] *was a traitor—just that there was something odd about him."*

Her father said that, *"at the time, he just thought that General ARNOLD might have been jealous of his 'special protection' and service under General WASHINGTON and the fact that he could never interfere or intervene with his* [Captain KEMPER's], *command."* Years later he thought something else had been on his mind.

Likewise, Captain KEMPER's brother-in-law, John MORTON, returned to Philadel-phia to clean up his shop and set it up again for business. Mr. MORTON stopped in to see Captain KEMPER and asked, *"Is it possible, John, outside of your regular duties, that you could keep an eye on my shop?"*

John replied, *"It has already been ordered so by General WASHINGTON and Congress!"*

Mr. MORTON exhaled in a sign of relief, realizing that he was entitled to some special treatment.

Mr. MORTON was always shown special privileges by General WASHINGTON and Congress, who always treated him as preciously as a gem. Throughout the Revolution, the *"Johnny-in-Laws"* would be deeply involved in continuing to fund money into the loan office (bank) for General WASHINGTON and the Continental Congress' use.

While Captain KEMPER was stationed in Philadelphia, along with James MEASE, clothier-general, and his deputy clothier-general, Charles YOUNG, he was often sent out on errands to pick up supplies, as he was their only means of transportation. During this period of time, Captain KEMPER and Charles YOUNG became close. When not on duty, they would often sit down and enjoy a game of chess together. While focusing on the game, they cleared their minds of the stress of supplying General WASHINGTON and the entire Continental Army.

On many occasions, depending on the location of General WASHINGTON's headquarters, Captain KEMPER would often had to cut his own road through the dense wilderness so that he could haul his convoy of one hundred and fifty wagons through. He would try to chart his route through so that he could pick up on another road on the other end to his destination. This was very time consuming, for the trees had to be cut and cleared for his continued journey. His Indian scouts were always put on alert.

On other occasions, since Charles YOUNG was born in Prussia, Captain KEMPER often shared stories on his grandfather,

Colonel Johann KEMPER. He related how his grandfather served under Frederick William I, the *"Great Elector,"* and his son, Frederick I, king in Prussia; as well as Leopold I, emperor of the Holy Roman Empire. As Mr. YOUNG stared intensely at Captain KEMPER as he told his stories, you could see stars in his eyes, as he was carried back in time to the father-land.

Captain KEMPER recorded in his journals, *"On one day, in particular, I had just finished checking in with Mr. MORTON, to make sure everything was going okay. As the sun began to set and the shadows were leaving the city, I was riding down Front Street, when all of a sudden I noticed a figure on horseback standing still in the middle of the street, near Market Street, as if he was waiting for someone. As I approached, I saw that it was General Lord STIRLING. I stopped about ten feet short of him and wished him, good day."*

Lord STIRLING replied, *"Well! If it is not the invisible master, 'dragon' master. The British stands a ghost of a chance to catch you; and you very seldom have the protection of the main army."" Lord STIRLING slowly grinned while bowing his head. I did the same, but was a little confused as to his reference to 'dragon,' but I did not want to sound ignorant so I did not ask what he meant by his remark. Lord STIRLING had a way of looking at me, not in any means of intimidation, but admiration, without ever speaking a word. We would often meet at my brother-in-law's, John MORTON. I knew that I would see him there again, sooner or later."*

"As I rode on, the reference to dragon continued to bother me; so I looked back to see where Lord STIRLING had gone, and to my surprise, he had turned to watch me ride north up Front Street. He was still mounted in the middle of the street, as if he was a stone statue. I rode on to finish my rounds, but never did know what he meant."

"When not on duty, Lord STIRLING and I often bumped into one another at my brother-in-law, John MORTON's estate. I would be

there on business for General WASHINGTON and the Continental Congress, why he would be there with other officers like General WASHINGTON for comfort and lodging. Sometimes I was ordered by General WASHINGTON to meet him at Mr. MORTON's, as it was convenient and inconspicuous." This action permitted Captain KEMPER another chance to visit his family.

Major General Thomas MIFFLIN, aide-de-camp, was in charge of Fort Mifflin on Mudden Island. Captain John KEMPER, awaiting orders from General WASHINGTON, stood ready to utilize the wagon-boat system to re-supply the fort. The wagon-boats measured fifteen feet wide by fifty-four feet long and had to be transported over land on special wagons built specifically for this purpose. These flatboats could carry as many as eighty men. The largest could accommodate four Conestoga wagons as well. The use of wagon-boats was established to utilize the river system where road travel was limited. The wagon-boat usage was more practical, as it saved considerable time and stress on the animals.

On 8 July 1778, General George WASHINGTON arrived with the Continental Army at Fort West Point, where he proceeded to set up his new headquarters. Captain John KEMPER's new route for supplying the Continental Army now lay from Philadelphia to West Point, an easy route north along the western side of the Hudson River in New York, away from British supply routes. This new headquarters would relieve a lot of stress from Captain KEMPER's concern about being detected by the enemy, for the most part.

Captain KEMPER recorded, *"On one of our trips to West Point to supply General WASHINGTON's army, we came upon a party of about a 100 British Dragoons. I was in attendance of my full troop of 320 men; we originally thought they were going to attack, but then they thought better of it and backed off on a ridge. I halfway through a salute, waving nonchalantly, not in a way as to intimidate them, but in a friendly manner of respect, knowing they had their own cause as well. The rest of my troops followed in suit and waved as well. The British Dragoons likewise, raised their hands and arms in the air waving back and forth, pretending they were cheering us on, Yeaaaaaaaaaaaaaa! Or maybe they were."*

"They watched our wagon-train, which went on for miles. I gave Lone WOLF his iye, iye command, who always gave his Indian cry, iye, iye, iye, iye, iye, while whipping the back of his horse, back to wait for the rear guard. In the event they tried to attack, we would immediately turn around and return the attack. Lone WOLF had Long FEATHERS race to the rear guard to apprise the BEAR of the possible threat. However, the British Dragoons never made a move on us and watched us slowly fade away."

"Long FEATHERS derived his name from refusing to conform to the tribal head dress of the Delaware Indians, so was cast out from the tribe. The tribal headdress feathers were never long enough for him. He always liked to add an extension. The story that he told me [Captain KEMPER] was, 'He was hunting one day when he caught a rabbit in his sights, and then, all of a sudden, a Bald Eagle swooped down from out of the sky and grabbed it. As he was ascending in slow motion, because of the weight he was carrying, he plucked it out of the sky with one arrow."

"The rabbit, badly injured by its claws, fell to the ground bouncing around. He then went over, stabbed the rabbit with his knife, carried it over to where the eagle laid, picked it up and went over to a stream to clean his game. He then started a fire and had lunch. He then had the white tail feather attached as an extension to his eagle feather, which spread out like a white fan.'"

"Lone WOLF, after over an hour waiting for the rear guard to catch up to his position, was waved on by Bouncing BEAR who was riding his donkey, letting him know it was okay to leave, he would take over. The BEAR always rode alongside the rear wagon while his canoe with a hole in it, stuck out of the back wagon. The BEAR then turned his head to the Dragoons, opened his mouth

wide and growled, while shaking his head. Then Lone WOLF, while constantly watching the British Dragoons, rode to return to his position by my lower right side as the sun began to set."

On 12 July 1778, while in-route to refurbish supplies General WASHINGTON used at the Battle of Monmouth, to part of his army now stationed at West Point, Captain KEMPER did not have his full wagon-train at this time. He fanned out his Indian scouts to warn him of any dangers from British activities or troop movements. Bouncing BEAR reported to him that there was a large British patrol nearby, but was unsure of the number, as they could only be heard off in the distance.

Captain KEMPER then had his army tie burlap around all the wagon wheels, the horses' hooves, and all metal that made contact to prevent clanging. He then ordered his Indian scouts to stay alert to the British activity as he continued on his route. After they arrived at West Point, Captain KEMPER stopped in to see his cousin, Captain Sebastian BEAUMAN and friend, Lieutenant Anthony MAXWELL.

On 21 July 1778, while at headquarters at White Plains, after being informed that Charles YOUNG had requested teams to transport clothing to Philadelphia, General WASHINGTON wrote to Mr. YOUNG.

> *Sir, being informed that you have applied for teams to transport clothing to Philadelphia, I would be glad to know for what purpose it is to be sent away when it is so much wanted here, or the propriety of doubling the course of carriage, and burdening the continent with the unnecessary expense.*
>
> *Mr. KEMPER has a large quantity of shoes at Morristown; you will be pleased to direct him to have them brought forward to the army immediately.*

He has some shirts and overalls, which he will send with the shoes. I am &.

Go: WASHINGTON

On 21 July 1778, at Post Fishkill, New York, Charles YOUNG responded to General WASHINGTON's inquiry.

Sir,

I have your Excellency's favor of this morning, and am to acquaint you, that on my coming here last Thursday, I found in different places at this post, 94 Hogsheads of clothing. My instructions on my leaving Mr. MEASE were, to forward all stores on to Philade [lphia]. I thought necessary that I might meet on the road or find here. On examining these, I found 85 packages were appropriated to particular regiments, & marked or addressed to the commanding officers of such. This occasioned my concluding to continue them here, & immediately wrote Mr. MEASE what I had done; the teams I applied for, were to remove the remaining 9 Hhds [Hogs heads] to FishKill Landing, 5 of which I wrote the Qtmr [Quartermaster] on the other side to prepare teams for, to send to Phila [delphia].

The other 4 were to have been sent from the Landing to Tarry Town by water, addressed to Mr. KEMPER. The invoice of the 9 Hhds is herewith enclosed, that your Excellency can judge the propriety of my proceedings. How such a representation could have been made your Excellency, I cannot conceive, it was really for my design to execute. Your Excellency's favour will procure me the teams so long applied for, in the morng [morning]. So that some good is like to arise from this misinformation.

A Mr. [George] MEASAM [17?–1783] has come to this post from Albany, [New York] by order of Genl. GATES, at a time Mr. MEASE's assistant was acting here, on which account the latter resigned. Mr. MEASAM is a Gent:, who does not view himself accountable to Mr. MEASE for his proceedings. Three Hogsheads of blankets came this day from Boston [Massachusetts] to him. Tho' I did not expect attention would be paid to my request, I thought my duty to acquire his assistance, he being [mutilated] to send them on their coming to receive them, & immediately acquaint Genl. GATES, who would direct their distribution, & from which he could not alter.

Your Excellency may be assured that during my stay here, I shall forward all on to the army of Cloathing Kind, that comes to my Knowledge. I have the honor to be your Excellency's most Obt. Hble Servt.

Cha. Young D.C.G.

In August 1778, Francis HOPKINSON wrote a letter to the board of admiralty regarding his design for that board's seal as well as the design of *"the flag of the United States of America"* and other seals and currency designs. He asked for $2,700 compensation. There was no dispute over his charge; however, there was no money available for these labors either. Congress decided to sit on it for a couple of years, perhaps hoping that he would forget about it and let it slide.

In late August 1778, Captain KEMPER received a dispatch from General WASHINGTON at his wagon-train camp along the Macoby Creek. It instructed Captain KEMPER to bring a troop of Continental Dragoons and meet him and Lord STIRLING at Mr. MORTON's estate with two wagons at the specified time.

After Captain KEMPER had arrived at his brother-in-law's, General WASHINGTON instructed him to have his men load the crates on his wagons that Mr. MORTON had had stacked, and accompany Lord STIRLING to the *"Doll House."* Upon diligent research by this author, including searching WASHINGTON's papers, he could find no reference to what or where the *"Doll House"* was, other than in Captain KEMPER's book, Wagon Master. Was this another coded entry to keep the meeting place a secret?

In September and October of 1778, Captain KEMPER recorded that this was a busy time for him. He had been giving special supplies for Colonels Marinus WILLETT, (something to do with his exchange as a prisoner of war); and John LAURENS; and Generals John SULLIVAN, Lord STIRLING, and Nathanael GREENE, all cleared by General WASHINGTON.

He again received another dispatch by General WASHINGTON that, General LAFEYETTE would be arriving at his wagon-train camp, just west of Philadelphia along the Macoby Creek, to pick up supplies that would be arriving at dock in Philadelphia. It instructed Captain KEMPER to assist General LAFAYETTE by all means necessary, including accommodations. Captain KEMPER recorded that he always kept his wagon-train camp at a distance from any possible British naval landings.

He was to have the supplies loaded on his wagons marked, "Morton's Supply" and "The Johnny-in-Laws" for delivery to headquarters. Two wagons would be enough for this shipment. General LAFAYETTE would be accompanying him with an escort of Continental Dragoons. Captain KEMPER recorded that something was definitely going on here. General WASHINGTON appeared to be planning something big, but nothing ever leaked out, nor did he hear of any action taken. What all these special supplies and security were for was never known about or at least, recorded.

Meanwhile, Mr. MORTON continued to work overtime to make sure his brother-in-law, Captain KEMPER remained stocked with the best supplies he could raise. Since Mr. MEASE and the clothier-general's department were failing, Mr. MORTON was General WASHINGTON's last hope. Mr. MORTON was under no obligations or commitments, yet he came through for the Continental Army's needs endlessly.

The supplies he delivered to General WASHINGTON were separate from the supplies he sold to the general public, which he used to make money for the other supplies. Mr. MORTON's brother-in-law, Captain John KEMPER, who had a direct link to General WASHINGTON and the Continental Congress, was made the go-between.

On 8 October 1778, General WASHINGTON ordered Colonel Daniel KEMPER to attend Elisha SMITH's court martial. The actual text is as follows:

> *At a General Court Martial held at Bedford the 8th of October 1778, by order of General* [Charles] *SCOTT, whereof Lieutt. Colo. BLACKDEN 27 was President, Elisha SMITH, a Private of Captn.* [Josiah] *STODDARD's* [1747–1779] *Company, in the 2nd Regiment of Light Dragoons was tried for deserting to the Enemy last August, for piloting the Enemy in an Incursion into and against the Troops of these States, defrauding the Public by selling his horse, Arms, Accoutrements, Furniture and Cloathing in a treasonable manner to the Enemy and for Mutiny in insulting and menacing his Officers while a Prisoner with them, found guilty of breaches of the 1st Article, 6th Section and of the 3rd Article of the 12th Section of the Articles of War and sentenced to suffer Death."* [Note: Lieut. Col. Samuel BLACKDEN (BLAGDEN), of the Second Continental Dragoons]

His Excellency, the commander-in-chief, *"approves the sentence and orders said Elisha SMITH to be executed next Monday the 12th inst. 11 o'clock in the forenoon at or near Bedford [N.J.] as General SCOTT shall direct."*

On Friday, 9 October 1778, Headquarters, Fredericksburgh, General WASHINGTON issued general orders,

> *Particular Brigade returns to be made to the orderly Office on Monday next agreeable to form, which will be given by the Adjutant General. Regimental returns to be delivered in the same day by the Brigade Majors containing every Article of Cloathing in Possession of the non-commissioned Officers and soldiers discriminating the good and serviceable from the bad and unserviceable; these returns are to be as exact and complete as possible.*

> *All Commissaries and Cloathiers in and near the Army to make returns on the same day and in the same manner of all the Cloathing and Materials for cloathing in their hand, respectively, distinguishing State from Continental Cloathing, and if any Quarter Masters have Cloathing of any kind in their possession they are to do the same.*

> ***Mr. Kemper*** *will take particular care to communicate this order to the Commissaries and Cloathiers and the Quarter Master General to his Assistants and Deputies.*

It is important to note here, that General WASHINGTON, out of all his top brass, authorized his aide, Colonel Daniel KEMPER to be in charge of delivering all his orders to the three main departments of the Continental Army. General WASHINGTON had lost his faith in most of his department heads, which all just seemed to be failing everywhere, including Clothier-General James MEASE.

He put his trust in Daniel, who was always at camp by his side. The KEMPER brothers had become invaluable; when all else failed, the KEMPER brothers always came through, as in *"Johnny on the spot."*

On 15 October 1778, Captain KEMPER was sent on a hunt, inland to a secluded location by General WASHINGTON to meet up with *"the Cobbler."* Since timing had to be precise, he set his pocket watch by the camp sundial. He then informed his chief scout Lone WOLF that they were going on a hunt.

Lone WOLF inquired, *"Who gonna be in hunting party?"*

Captain KEMPER answered, *"Just you and me."*

Lone WOLF replied, *"Wise decision, the BEAR can stay behind and watch camp and maybe patch his canoe, he he."*

Captain KEMPER recorded, *"As we arrived at General WASHINGTON's designated location near a glade, which was marked, all appeared silent. There was a rustle in the bushes, but it was just an animal."*

The foliage this time of year was just beautiful, deep bursting colors of red, gold, orange and yellow, mixed in with the pine trees. There was a babbling brook nearby a rocky ledge which fed into the glade, where they filled their canteens with fresh water and watered their horses.

"We decided to get some shut-eye until the appropriate moment. After a couple of hours, we were awoken by a sharp, high-pitched spurting sound. A gray squirrel that had been jumping trees, started down one about 20 feet in front of the party when it caught sight of

them. It started screeching and then, bang! The squirrel fell to the ground without its head."

As John looked up, Lone WOLF was lowering his rifle saying, *"Too noisy!"* He then went over and picked up the squirrel by its tail in his right hand, raised it in the air to Captain KEMPER and said, *"Lunch!"*

Captain KEMPER just smiled and shook his head.

Lone WOLF did not know that after they had reached their location, at the appropriate time, they were to signal their presence with a rifle shot. Although Lone WOLF was early, there was no harm done. They decided to start a campfire and cook the squirrel for lunch. Captain KEMPER told Lone WOLF to listen for the sound of a horn. This was a meeting that no other details were given on, other than General WASHINGTON ordering Captain KEMPER to go on a hunt and meet *"the Cobbler."*

All of a sudden, the sound of a horn bellowed throughout the countryside; *"the Cobbler"* had arrived. It appeared that Captain KEMPER kept regular journals up until this point when he met with *"the Cobbler"*, then stopped recording. No name was recorded for *"the Cobbler."*

After they returned to camp, Lone WOLF replied, *"Some kind of hunt, all we got was a squirrel; I was hoping for a lion or a bear which are everywhere. Probably that stupid horn scared them away. Probably the BEAR didn't fix canoe either."*

By November 1778, the British had built their army to 121,000 troops, of whom 24,000 were Hessians, while 40,000 were militia. In addition, they had over 500,000 Tories/Loyalists in the states, along with over 100,000 slaves, totaling over 721,000 angry men prepared to crush the Rebel resistance. What chance could General WASHINGTON and his small armies of 15,000 troops have?

On 5 November 1778, Captain John KEMPER's brother Jacob was promoted to captain-lieutenant (the second officer of every colonel's infantry regiment) in Colonel Edward STEVENS' regiment. On 2 December 1778, this battalion became part of the third Continental artillery under Colonel Ebenezer STEVENS (1751-1823).

On 11 December 1778, General WASHINGTON set up headquarters in the WALLACE house, Middlebrook, New Jersey; troops spent the winter at Watchung Mountains in Middlesex, New Jersey. His men began building huts to live in which were completed by February. By spring, General WASHINGTON had to change his supply tactics. In addition, he had new ideas on Captain KEMPER's deployment and needed to deactivate his station, with reason that would not be questioned.

The Continental Army could march straight across country to reach a British camp or outpost. Captain KEMPER's wagon-train could not. He had to take roundabout roads to either reach General WASHINGTON directly, or get close enough to his camp so that he could easily supply them, or General WASHINGTON would have to send wagons to obtain supplies from wherever Captain KEMPER's wagon-train camp was set up. If General WASHINGTON was camped by a river, then Captain KEMPER could use his wagon-boats.

Unfortunately, General WASHINGTON still had no status report on his commodore, John MANLEY. During this time in history, there was really no one else to take his place; there just was no one as daring, brave, and courageous on the seas as Commodore MANLEY. General WASHINGTON now had a new idea in the works on how to find out if Commodore MANLEY was still alive so that he could barter for him (offer an exchange).

What if he was to have an officer not desert over to the British lines but, instead, set up to be deliberately captured? He would never end up under suspicion. He would end up in the same track of prison channels that Commodore MANLEY went into, if he were still alive. He would end up at his same locality as a bartering chip of exchange for captured British officers, but why was he not listed for exchange? The answer would come soon!

On 22 December 1778, Congress called General WASHINGTON to Philadelphia. General WASHINGTON spent the next six weeks there as a guest of Henry LAURENS, president of Congress, to discuss crucial matters. General WASHINGTON's wife, Martha (1731-1802) joined him in the city. After the meeting, General WASHINGTON summoned Captain KEMPER to his residence to discuss future plans. He informed Mr. KEMPER that the clothier-general's department was being restructured and that eventually he would need him in another location.

He informed Captain KEMPER of his plans and asked him if he thought he could handle it. Captain KEMPER replied, *"I can handle anything your Excellency!"* He informed Mr. KEMPER that Mr. [Major Benjamin] TALLMADGE would be in contact with him with further details on the plans of the operation.

General WASHINGTON then closed by saying, *"Remember what happened to Mr.* [Captain Nathan] *HALE* [captured and hung]. *You must remain invisible! The plan is daring, if at any time you feel that you want to pull out, we will not hold it against you."*

Captain KEMPER closed by saying, *"Anything new to try will throw the British completely off guard. We will finally catch the British in the dark, let us finish this up!"* General WASHINGTON then closed by saying, *"When you return, all will be as if it never happened, apart from memories, some good, some bad."*

General WASHINGTON then took his right hand, placed it warmly on Captain KEMPER's left shoulder, looked him softly in his eyes and said, *"Please go into the heart of our enemy as your grandfather would have done, and thank you, Mr. KEMPER."*

Captain KEMPER replied, *"I intend on it, your Excellency!"*

This process that General WASHINGTON had started in locating MIA's, would set its prints and follow the American tradition throughout its history.

John recorded this part of his summon in his journals. He also mentioned that their discussion was entered in his other book (probably the one entitled *Wagon Master,* or *US Naval Affairs*). However, this author could not find any entries, but there were pages missing. In closing Captain KEMPER stated, *"I see Madam Ursula all over again. She continues to constantly haunt me."*

On 9 February 1779, General WASHINGTON returned to Middlebrook, Somerset, New Jersey. His wife, Martha, joined him.

After Captain KEMPER's meeting with Major Benjamin TALLMADGE, he recorded little about the mission, only Major TALLMADGE's advice and warning. He informed Captain KEMPER that, they were currently working out the plan, so he still had time to pull out if he wanted to. Captain KEMPER replied, *"I did not join the Revolution to pull out."*

Major TALLMADGE answered," *Okay then, let us begin. You will need to enter captivity as a lieutenant, not a captain, but still an officer. There will be no problem getting you behind enemy lines, but once there, we would not be able to assist or rescue you. Nor would we be able to offer an exchange for your release, as we are not supposed to know of your capture; we cannot allow any suspicion to arise. You may find other matters of interest of which were unexpected; be sure to log everything mentally only, as usual, until you are safe. Most importantly, you must remain invisible as to your true objective. You must remain a saddened, captured prisoner of war."*

He continued, *"You will be surrounded by death and mayhem, that the normal human being would not be able to stomach. You will have to find the location of the information General WASHINGTON and the Intelligence Committee needs to know, as it is unknown. If successful, you would then need to find a way of getting that information home, as well as finding your own way home. Do not do anything to draw attention to yourself, remain quit as a mouse; leave no stone unturned. As in the past, you will need to use your cunning to survive."*

Captain KEMPER continued recording in his book, *"US Naval Affairs"* that, Ben [TALLMADGE] had informed him that he would need very little candy (gold?) on this mission, just enough to open the British officer's eyes and get him into the same channels that were needed to arrive at the same location as his target, if indeed the major target did still exist. If not, then he was to locate other targets. Many missions were entered, but for some unknown reason were never finished as being concluded. It was as if he needed the notes for his recollection only.

On 3 March 1779, at the headquarters, Colonel Tench TILGHMAN sent a letter to Colonel Daniel KEMPER. In this letter he stated,

> *"Sir: I spoke to his Excellency respecting the great quantity of clothing upon your hands. He thinks all the uniforms except about 1,500 suits of blue and red and about half that quantity of brown and red had better be sent to Philada. Directed to the Board of War as I believe Mr. MEASE has given up the clothing department.*
>
> *You must apply to the quarter master general for the benefit of the return wagons to Trenton from whence it will go immediately down by water. A conductor should accompany each division of wagons to attend the contents and see them delivered to Philada. Otherwise they will lay at Trenton and be damaged or lost. Endeavour to make the number of coats, vests and breeches equal. If you have any fine thin*

> *linen in the store be pleased to send about two yards.*
> *His Excellency wants it to paste some maps upon*
> *it."* I am your most obedt. Servt, Tench Tilghman

Colonel Daniel KEMPER followed regular procedure and had his brother, Captain John KEMPER go to Trenton to pick up the supplies for the board of war in Philadelphia. After Captain KEMPER picked up the supplies, he had his wagons loaded onto his flatboats and sailed down the Delaware River to Philadelphia. Once in Philadelphia, he unloaded all his wagons and delivered the supplies to the board of war.

In March 1779, Anthony MAXWELL was listed as a lieutenant and captain in Colonel Oliver SPENCER's (1736-1811) fifth battalion (regiment) of the New Jersey line. Anthony had become close friends with Captain KEMPER when volunteering for foraging excursions while at Valley Forge. He later was called to assist Captain KEMPER in Hudson, New York, and this was where their families intermarried. This author descends from three different lines of Captain Anthony MAXWELL's children.

On 23 March 1779, Congress enacted its first ordinance for regulating the clothing department, adopting General WASHINGTON's suggestions that each state should be in charge of clothing for all their regiments. Regimental clothiers would report to their state, which, in turn would report to the Continental clothier. This was General WASHINGTON's way of relieving the pressure on James MEASE and putting it in the rightful hands of the regiments and states, which were on location and knew first-hand their own needs. General WASHINGTON's insightfulness again showed what a compassionate leader he was, instead of taking action of a punishment against Mr. MEASE.

On 5 April 1779, while General WASHINGTON continued restructuring the clothier-general's department, Congress authorized the salary of the clothier-general at $5,000 per annum. Congress was hoping that the new salary would develop new interest in fulfilling the post. However, anyone who took on the new post always had the same problems and quickly became dissatisfied with the position.

In May of 1779, after General WASHINGTON was confident that his smaller regimental wagon trains of seven to nine wagons would suffice and that he would no longer need a huge convoy of wagons, Captain KEMPER was released. General WASHINGTON had restructured the clothier-general's department so that Captain KEMPER could be released without suspicion.

Captain KEMPER's invisible wagon train, which the British could never find, was then dismantled and evenly distributed throughout the various regiments in the Continental Army. He now had to go and see his friend and comrade, Charles YOUNG for separation from the Continental Army. Mr. YOUNG wished Captain KEMPER good luck and hoped that they would meet again someday, after the Revolution, under better conditions. After the war, Captain KEMPER named a son after Charles YOUNG and his brother-in-law, John MORTON; thus, Charles Morton KEMPER (1793-1869) was born.

Captain KEMPER was released by Charles YOUNG, deputy clothier to James MEASE, clothier-general of the Continental Army, stationed in Philadelphia. Since John was now cleared in this capacity, he was able to join the United States Navy, in Philadelphia, Pennsylvania. To others, this was because the revolutionary blood was flowing in his veins, when actually General WASHINGTON was sending him on another mission, but why in the navy? Captain KEMPER closed in his journals on this department by saying, *"Madam Ursula, you have cursed me! How could all this be possible?"*

Because Captain KEMPER and Charles YOUNG had become so close, not only because of their German heritage and bond, but because of their close connection in the clothier-general's department, their friendship remained intact. Mr. YOUNG was always sending Captain KEMPER out to pick up supplies for the army, as there were no others. Sometimes it was problematic, since he was mainly under General WASHINGTON's control; therefore, he would often have to secure teams elsewhere. This action would often put him under stress, because of General WASHINGTON's scrutiny.

Captain KEMPER started discharging his army and Indian scouts on Front and Market Streets in Philadelphia. Bouncing BEAR headed west down Market Street to Suetts Ferry to cross over the Schuylkill River.

Lone WOLF, sitting on his horse, stared at Captain KEMPER intensely. He then asked, *"Have you seen young squaw lately?"*

Captain KEMPER answered, *"No, but we stay in touch through our letters."*

Lone WOLF continued, *"She probably all grown up now."*

Captain KEMPER replied, *"I know."*

Lone WOLF sadly said, *"You miss many good years."*

Captain KEMPER closed by saying, *"The best years will follow."*

Lone WOLF slowly nodded.

Lone WOLF then swung his right leg over the neck of his horse and slid off. He slowly strolled over to Captain KEMPER and stopped directly in front of him. He sadly grinned and then drew his knife. Captain KEMPER thought for a moment, *"Is Lone WOLF going to stab me for having to discharge him?"*

Lone WOLF transferred the knife to his left hand, held his right hand up and cut his palm diagonally from his forefinger to the heel of his palm. He then turned the knife butt first and handed it to Captain KEMPER. Captain KEMPER now knew what Lone WOLF was offering. He accepted the knife in his left hand, held up his right hand and likewise, cut his hand diagonally. They then grabbed each other's right hands and squeezed tightly.

Lone WOLF then said, *"We now blood brothers."*

Captain KEMPER replied, *"Yes we are!"*

As Lone WOLF turned to leave, Captain KEMPER yelled, *"Wait!"*

The WOLF looked back as Captain KEMPER said, *"I have something for you. Something that will help keep anyone from getting too close to you."*

Lone WOLF being puzzled, exclaimed, *"Huh?"*

Captain KEMPER slowly untied, what appeared to be a pole wrapped in black velvet cloth, strapped to the side of his horse.

He then handed the item to Lone WOLF. As Lone WOLF grasped it and slowly pulled it out halfway, he saw that it was a long knife (sword). Lone WOLF quivered as tears began to fall from the eyes of this battle-hardened brave.

Lone WOLF then sadly said, *"But I have no gift for you."*

Captain KEMPER responded, *"You have already given me a gift from your heart, your bear-claw necklace, a great tribal achievement."*

Lone WOLF softly grinned, then nodded as he turned to leave.

While Captain KEMPER began wrapping his hand, Lone WOLF climbed back on his horse, looked down at Captain KEMPER, saluted him one last time, took his right heel and bucked the rear of his horse. He galloped north up Front Street, yelling, *"Iye, iye, iye, iye, iye!"* It was as if the WOLF knew that his mission had been fulfilled.

Hardly above a whisper, Mr. KEMPER said, *"Good-bye my loyal friend,"* as he watched him depart. Soon he was gone from the city. He reached under his shirt and rubbed the necklace Lone WOLF had given him, and rode off himself. Captain KEMPER was going to miss his chief Indian scout, who had become a good, loyal friend.

During this period of time, Captain KEMPER's sister, Susan, was married to Dr. David JACKSON of Philadelphia. Captain KEMPER managed a furlough to attend the wedding at their parents' in Germantown, New Jersey; and informed Susan that he would be joining the US Navy in Philadelphia, so would accompany them to the city.

Upon reaching Philadelphia, John wished them well and said he would stop by to see them whenever he was in port. He then headed for the docks. Later, their sister, Maria Sophia (Kemper) MORTON, sent her daughter, Eliza Susan, to live with her aunt Susan JACKSON in Philadelphia, so that she could attend school. However, Eliza threw a fit, wanting to return home rather than go to school in Philadelphia, being terrified by the sounds of the big city.

Eliza Susan MORTON returned home with the postman Mr. MARTIN in his carriage and then moved in with her grandparents Jacob and Maria Regina KEMPER in Germantown, New Jersey. There she attended school under Master LESLIE. He was a strict disciplinarian, but was more lenient on the girls. She contended with the necessities of her young age but felt more comfortable in the German community of Germantown, rather than Philadelphia, Pennsylvania.

Chapter XVII
John Kemper joins the US Navy

In May 1779, immediately after receiving his discharge from the Continental Army, Captain KEMPER joined the United States Navy in Philadelphia, Pennsylvania. He entered on board the corvette ship, *General* (Nathanael) *Greene*, in capacity of first midshipman (student in training to become an officer), commanded by Captain James MONTGOMERY (1747-1808); Samuel CARSON was first lieutenant and Jacob DEHART second lieutenant.

When Captain KEMPER reached the docks at Chestnut Street Wharf, Captain MONTGOMERY said, *"I received a dispatch that you were going to be arriving; however, I cannot understand why a captain in the Continental Army would want to be demoted in rank to join the Navy."* John replied, *"I want to become a naval officer and need to learn the ropes."*

"Okay, Captain," Captain MONTGOMERY replied, *"Come on board and I will start teaching you. Change into your new uniform in my cabin. I will make you first- midshipman, which is the best I can do."* Mr. KEMPER replied, *"Thanks, Captain, let us get started!"* He spent six months cruising along the coast protecting our country's capital, Philadelphia, while learning the ropes. He was discharged in November 1779.

Now that General HOWE was gone and General CLINTON was locked down in New York City, the Revolution started to go slowly stagnant. General CLINTON was skeptical about pursuing General WASHINGTON as General HOWE had done.

He felt more comfortable staying in the city where he was well protected.

This opportunity gave General WASHINGTON a chance to focus on other important matters. He put together a huge army of three thousand Continental troops for General SULLIVAN to be sent on another mission. He planned another one thousand troops to rendezvous up with General SULLIVAN at another location.

On 18 June 1779, General WASHINGTON sent General John SULLIVAN to Upstate New York to Fort Niagara. The purpose of this mission was to interrupt the six Indian Nations raiding of frontier settlements. The Indian and Tories/Loyalists were crippling the Continental Army by depriving it of food and manpower, spreading terror by murdering and taking prisoners, while raping women and children. This campaign was named, *"Sullivan's Expedition."*

There were 5,036 Indian warriors stationed at the British Fort Niagara, led by Seneca chief CORNBREAD (1760-1836) and the Mohawk warrior chief THAYENDANEGEA (Joseph BRANDT 1743-1807). These Indian chiefs were, in turn, led by the British Colonel John BUTLER (1728-1796) with his Tories/Loyalists. They were manipulating the Indian chiefs into believing they could keep their lands that the Americans were settling, if they sided with them. All they had to do was to help the British and their Tories/Loyalists kill the American settlers, and it did not matter how it was done.

On 24 July 1779, the Continental Congress finally found someone to take James MEASE's place and appointed Brigadier General, James WILKINSON (1757-1825) clothier-general of the Continental Army. General WILKINSON liked the position and pay but did not like the work that went with it. He was very seldom at his post and left his assistant in charge, most of the time, to carry on the affairs of his department. General

WILKINSON's assistant went through the same problems trying to acquire supplies that James MEASE did. In addition, Congress did not pay General WILKINSON promptly, so he resigned his commission on 27 March 1781.

On 29 August 1779, General SULLIVAN's chief scout Lieutenant Thomas BOYD (1756-1779) was successful in destroying the crops in the neighborhood of Newtown. Lieutenant Thomas BOYD always scouted up ahead of the army. Knowing that SULLIVAN's army was behind him, he became over-confident and strayed too far ahead of the main army. Consequently, he and his men were ambushed and captured.

By the time General SULLIVAN had reached the Indian village of Geneseo, the town was abandoned, and he found his lieutenant next to a tree dead. General SULLIVAN had Geneseo burned to the ground.

On 5 September 1779, after successfully spearheading General WASHINGTON's espionage ring and launching Captain KEMPER to infiltrate the heart of the British Empire, Major Benjamin TALLMADGE was promoted to colonel.

On 17 September 1779, because of his successful fighting afloat for the Continental Army, Congress made Captain Silas TALBOT a captain in the Continental Navy. Congress had no suitable war ship, so they put him in command of the privateer *General Washington* in August of 1780. He was still on board when he was captured by a British seventy-four-gun ship *Culloden*.

On 30 September 1779, after other engagements in various towns, General SULLIVAN sat down and wrote a letter to His Excellency John JAY, Esq., in Congress, describing the heinous acts of torture and murder of Lieutenant BOYD and his companion. *"It appears that they had whipped them in the most cruel manner, pulled out Mr. Boyd's nails, cut off his nose, plucked out one of his eyes, cut out his tongue, stabbed him with spears in sundry* [various] *places, and inflicted other tortures* [genitals] *which decency will not permit me to mention.*

A witness to this event later told how they then cut open his stomach, pulled out his intestines, and tied them around a tree. They then chased him around the tree, whippinmg him with briers, until all his intestines had run out. Lastly, they cut off his head, and left his body on the ground with that of his unfortunate companion."

The Indian scouts kept an eye on General SULLIVAN's huge army from a distance. Whenever he began to approach a village, the scouts would warn the chiefs to evacuate. Consequently, whenever General SULLIVAN arrived at an Indian village; he had no opposition when he burned down the Indian villages along with their crops.

General SULLIVAN, who had destroyed over forty Iroquois villages, along with their crops, had originally intended on marching forward to attack Fort Niagara, but changed his mind and decided to return to the east. This turned out to be a wise decision, for the Indians stationed at Fort Niagara well out numbered his army, and they all could have met the same fate as Lieutenant BOYD. With no crops, the Indians were going to have a tough time this winter. This put an end to *"Sullivan's Expedition."*

On 11 October 1779, Brigadier General Count Casimir PULASKI died from a wound he had received in his thigh in battle during a cavalry charge on 9 October 1779 in Savannah, Georgia. He never regained consciousness because of the amount of blood he lost. This event fulfilled his promise that he made to General WASHINGTON after his arrival in America. In his letter, he had stated that, *"he would fight, defend and live or die for our freedom."*

In November of 1779, after John was discharged from his six-month tour in the navy, he recorded that, he went to settle accounts with John MORTON and pick up new business, but did not say what that new business was. Whatever business he was performing for his brother-in-law seemed to have taken about four months, at which point he re-enlisted in the navy for another six-month tour. Whenever working for Mr. MORTON, General WASHINGTON or Congress, John KEMPER always kept a low profile. Somehow, John KEMPER seemed to be deeply involved and in the middle of everything that was going on during the American Revolution, and shortly thereafter, as well.

In March 1780, after four months unaccounted for, John KEMPER entered the brig *Fair American* as a volunteer (rank just under lieutenant), under Captain Stephen DECATUR (1751-1808). This was a brig of sixteen guns. John KEMPER again spent another six months cruising along the coast. By this time, there still was no British activity on the Delaware, but that was about to change. A sixteen-gun ship was no match for a British thirty-two-gun ship, or a man-of-war, which was a sixty-four-gun ship. Anytime an American vessel stumbled upon a British war ship, after a short resistance or a brief failed attempt to escape, a white flag went up immediately! The battle was over before it began. However, Mr. KEMPER was learning the ropes and moved up in rank on each tour.

On 25 May 1780, Francis HOPKINSON submitted another letter to Congress, requesting compensation for the following works and designs that his team had completed ...

- the flag of the United States of America;
- seven devices for the Continental currency;
- a seal for the board of treasury;
- ornaments, devices, and checks for the new bills of exchange in Spain and Holland;
- a seal for the ship papers of the United States;
- a seal for the board of admiralty;

- the boarders, ornaments and checks for the new Continental currency now in the press, a work of considerable length; and
- a great seal for the United States of America, with a reverse.

"For these services I have yet made no charge nor received any recompense. I now submit to your honors' consideration whether a quarter cask of the public wine will not be a proper & reasonable reward for these labours of fancy and a suitable encouragement to future exertions of a like nature."

"I sincerely hope that your honors will be of this opinion & am with great respect, gentlemen. Your very humble servant," Frans HOPKINSON wrote.

Please note Francis HOPKINSON's charge for the item, Continental currency in the press. This was one of the primary difficulties that the Continental Congress and Continental Army had in paying their debts. According to the British and their Loyalists, these rebels were just a bunch of thugs (outlaws) running off their own money, which had no backing. After the money was run off the press, it was worthless, pretty much like Monopoly game money is today (easy money, but worthless!).

Farmers and merchants refused to accept the made-up Continental dollars representing the rebel resistance; however, both Congress and General WASHINGTON forced them to accept notes for payment in the future. General WASHINGTON ordered seizure of all goods and supplies for which merchants refused to accept the Continental dollar, but made sure certificates were left behind for their claim.

On 17 June 1780, the British advanced on the farms at Elizabethtown, New Jersey. One soldier, who was watching the premises, saw Mrs. Hannah (Ogden) CALDWELL (1733-1780) go into her house at Connecticut Farms to comfort her children.

She was sitting with her infant in her arms when the soldier stuck his rifle in the window, took deliberate aim at her and discharged his musket. She received the ball in her heart and died instantly.

1. The Spirit of 1776

At the earnest request of Captain CHANDLER, (who was in the British service and a son of the Episcopal clergyman of Elizabethtown), the body of Mrs. CALDWELL was carried with her children to a house at a greater distance. They then burned her house and all the property it contained. The British burned about twelve other houses and the Presbyterian Church that day and then marched back to Elizabethtown.

On 23 June 1780, the British advanced to Springfield. They burned forty dwelling houses and the church. Except for four houses, the whole village was reduced to ashes. The British pursued by the militia, who were enraged by the conflagration they had just witnessed, again retreated to Elizabeth Point, New Jersey and crossed the same night to Staten Island. When morning came, families began to scrape up what things could be recovered. They raked through the ashes of their former dwellings for nails, hinges and other ironwork for use in the erection of new habitation.

Upon the approach of the British with five thousand infantry, a large body of cavalry, and fifteen or twenty pieces of artillery, the women and children fled from town. They collected together on the brow of a hill about a mile distant, in full view of the conflagration. As one house after another caught fire, they called out, *"There goes your house!"*

One woman, whose husband had just built a fine large house and shop adjacent, was among them; and, as she seemed to have the most to lose, was observed the most.

One of her companions called out to her, *"There goes yours! A beautiful new house!"* She replied, *"Well, let it go, we can live in the shop."*

A few moments after, smeone said,—*"There goes the shop too!"* *"Well, let it go, they can't burn the ground it stands on, and there is wood enough to build another, when they are all beaten and driven away."*

In July 1780, General Benedict ARNOLD was put in command of the fortress at West Point. What no one knew at the time was, General ARNOLD had already turned-coat with the British. He had developed a scheme to surrender West Point to them. He quickly sent word to Lieutenant General Sir Henry CLINTON stationed in New York City.

2. Battle on the Delaware with the British Frigate, Iris

On 11 September 1780, John KEMPER entered the brig *Hector*, as second lieutenant, under Captain James SLOVER (1759-aft.1795); Thomas JUSTICE was first lieutenant; and Charles LYNN and John CONNOR were midshipmen. This ship was named after the warrior HECTOR of the Trojan War. The *Hector* was a brig of fourteen guns. It weighed eighty tons and carried seventy men.

Before entering on board, Lieutenant KEMPER recorded in his book, *US Naval Affairs* that, *"the pigeon was in the area and he was hiding his books in a secured location."*

Mr. MORTON saw his brother-in-law off and reminded him, upon his return, to please be sure to stop by and see him on further business. He handed him a letter for Eliza. What business was Mr. MORTON talking about and why was he seeing him off? He was not military. Although Lieutenant KEMPER had recorded this event in his book, *"US Naval Affairs,"* he did not comment on it further or give any details.

It appears that the code word, pigeon, was intended for the British war-ship HMS *Iris*, the former USS *Hancock*. Had General WASHINGTON's intelligence web kept him informed of its constant location? Was this some sort of hideous, scary, spooky plan devised by General WASHINGTON and the intelligence committee of the Continental Congress, or what?

Lieutenant KEMPER sailed from Philadelphia in the morning. By evening, they encountered the British frigate *Iris*, the former USS *Hancock*, commanded by Commodore John MANLEY; a thirty-two-gun ship now commanded by Captain George DAWSON—and battle ensued. Their fourteen-gun ship was no match for the British thirty-two-gun ship and was quickly overcome. They were forced to strike their colors (surrender their flag). John KEMPER's naval career seemed to be short-lived, or was it?

The *Iris* was previously known as the Continental war ship USS *Hancock*, commanded by Commodore John MANLEY (1733-1793), before the British captured it on 8 July 1777, over two years prior. She had been named after John HANCOCK, president of the Continental Congress. The ship was so fast that it took the British thirty-nine hours to capture it.

The British boasted that they now had the fastest ship in their fleet. It was quickly converted and renamed the *Iris*. An American vessel that the British had felt was superior enough to be added to their own arsenal had in fact captured Lieutenant John KEMPER. Was this all a coincidence, or was there something else going on here? Was the same thing that happened to Commodore MANLEY going to happen to Lieutenant KEMPER?

By nine that night, the British who were not interested in capturing such a small armed vessel were ruthless in their bombardment. After their ship became disabled and started to sink, they were forced to surrender their colors. As the British prepared to board their ship in order to disarm and take prisoners, Lieutenant KEMPER unsheathed his sword and stood steadfast.

Captain SLOVER responded, *"Sheath your sword, lieutenant, it is over. The British have the rifles aimed at you; the accuracy of a musket is not that good. They could be shooting at you and the musket ball could hit me instead."*

Lieutenant KEMPER replied, *"Sorry sir, a bad habit I picked up from my grandfather; he would often un-sheath his sword, whether ready for combat or not."*

Captain SLOVER stared at Lieutenant KEMPER silently as he was still holding his sword steadfast. Captain SLOVER, forcing himself to remain calm, then asked, *"If I address you by your true rank of captain, would you then consider sheathing your sword?"*

Then Lieutenant KEMPER replied, *"Sorry Sir,"* then sheathed his sword. The British, who had their rifles trained on Lieutenant KEMPER, in the event they had to use them, lowered their arms.

The British commander Captain DAWSON stared at Lieutenant KEMPER for a moment, but said nothing. The British then lowered their gangplanks (a narrow moveable platform/ramp) and entered the *Hector* and confiscated all their weapons (swords). Lieutenant KEMPER additionally had a pistol stuck in his breeches, which when one of the British officers removed, and held it up at various angles, admiring it. The British then returned to the *Iris* while admiring the newly confiscated weapons.

Officers and crew were taken on board their conquering vessel and put in irons. They were taken to the port of New York and had their irons knocked off at Crane-Wharf; from there they were transported on board the schooner *Relief* to the prison ship *Scorpion*. After Lieutenant KEMPER was on board for a short while, he was transferred along with other *Iris* prisoners to the old sixty-four-gun prison ship, the *Jersey*. His new experience as a prisoner of war became frightening! This fear was later recorded in the Kemper family Bible records, even though he was prepared for it by Colonel TALLMADGE. War was fine if you were out in the open and was able to have cover, but not when you were helplessly under someone else's control. This is when the really bad things take place.

Now that Lieutenant KEMPER had been launched into the heart of the British prison system, all General WASHINGTON, Colonel TALLMADGE, and the Congressional Intelligence Committee could do, was sit back, and wait until Lieutenant KEMPER located his targets, and was able to break free and get a message back to His Excellency, General WASHINGTON. If the status of the targets were still alive, why were they not on the list for exchange? Lieutenant KEMPER would soon find out.

On 20 September 1780, General Sir Henry CLINTON sent his favorite aide, Major John ANDRE (1750-1780), up the Hudson River aboard the sloop-of-war *Vulture*, a fourteen-gun ship, to confer with General ARNOLD and pick up his plans.

On 22 September 1780, while the ship was anchored off-shore, waiting for Major ANDRE to complete his mission, it was spotted by American troops stationed across the river at Verplank's Point. They brought it to the attention of their commander, Lieutenant Colonel James LIVINGSTON (1747-1832), who ordered it to be fired on. The ship took several hits before it was forced down river without Major ANDRE.

After General ARNOLD finished his business with Major ANDRE, he had a couple of his men transport Major ANDRE in their row-boat to the eastern side of the Hudson River. General ARNOLD then brought Major ANDRE a horse, a set of civilian clothing and a passport, under the name of John ANDERSON.

On 23 September 1780, after being en route back to New York City, Major ANDRE was stopped near Tarrytown by three armed militia men, John PAULDING (1758-1818), Isaac VAN WART (1762-1828), and David WILLIAMS (1754-1831). Major ANDRE, seeing one of the men wearing a Hessian soldier's over coat, inquired, *"Gentlemen, I hope you belong to our party."*

One of the men inquired, *"What party?"*

Major ANDRE answered, *"The lower party,"* (meaning the British).

"We do," answered one of the men.

Major ANDRE, now being more comfortable, commanded, *"I am a British officer and must not be detained!"*

They then surprised Major ANDRE when they told him they were Americans and he was now their prisoner. After Major ANDRE's jaw dropped, they searched him from shoulders to toe. In one of his boots, they found six pages proving the defection of a high American officer over to the British lines.

Commandant Colonel John JAMESON (1751-1810) was planning on sending Major ANDRE to General ARNOLD, not realizing he was involved; however, Major Benjamin TALLMADGE arrived and took control of the prisoner. Colonel JAMESON immediately sent the captured pages of treason to General WASHINGTON.

Colonel JAMESON decided that he should notify General ARNOLD of the incident and that they had uncovered a conspiracy of a high officer defecting to the British. General ARNOLD was at breakfast with his officers when he received the dispatch. He made an excuse to leave the room and was never seen again. He quickly made his escape and fled down the Hudson River and boarded the British sloop-of-war *Vulture*. He notified the British that Major Andre had been captured and their plans foiled.

General WASHINGTON arrived at West Point a day or two later and ordered General Benedict ARNOLD arrested. However, it was too late: he had made his escape. General WASHINGTON offered General Sir Henry CLINTON an exchange of Major ANDRE for General Benedict ARNOLD. Even though General CLINTON despised General ARNOLD, he refused General WASHINGTON's offer of exchange. Major John ANDRE became the sacrificial lamb.

On 2 October 1780, after Major John ANDRE had been found guilty and since the British refused an exchange of General ARNOLD for him, he was scheduled for execution. Major ANDRE requested a firing squad. However, he had to be hung the same way that their spy, Captain Nathan HALE was when he was captured. The execution took place in Tappan, New York.

Chapter XVIII
Prisoner of War (Conditions)

The prison ship *Jersey* was commanded by, Captain David LAIRD. His crew consisted of two mates, one steward and a dozen sailors—a guard of twelve invalid marines, and about thirty soldiers drafted from the British and Hessian troops on Long Island. The officers' cabin and sailors' steerage (quarters) were under the quarterdeck. The northwest chamber on the second floor was devoted to officers and civilians of highest rank and was called, in ridicule, Congress Hall. The *Jersey* contained an average of about one thousand American prisoners, sometimes as many as 1,500. The prisoners were fed rotten beef and pork and worm-eaten bread. This decayed food had been condemned on board the British ships of war and thus sent to the *Jersey* for the prisoners' consumption. There was never anything to look forward to here. The smell of the rotten food was hardly appetizing!

Water, which was transported from the city on board the schooner *Relief,* had a scent that smelled worse than any odor to which the prisoners had previously been subjected. The British kept hogs that they raised for their own consumption in pens on the upper gun deck of the *Jersey.* The stench and refuse (excretion) of the hogs seeped through to the lower decks. Sometimes the hogs were fed the husks of grain from wheat, rye, oats, etc. The prisoners, whenever they could sneak up to the deck undetected by the sentries (guards), would take their tin pots, scoop the hogs' food from their pens and eat it as greedily as the hogs did.

The British guards harassed the prisoners and often addressed them, *"You damn'd Yankee,"* or *"You Rebel,"* or *"You damn'd rebellious Yankee rascals or you worthless Whigs."*

The prisoners had no berths or bunks. Many of the prisoners, during the harshness of winter, seldom had enough clothes to cover their bodies. In order to stay warm, they had to either remain in their hammocks or stay active—otherwise they would have died from the cold. Many prisoners, a few minutes after eating, would buckle over in the agonies of death. They had been poisoned. Many prisoners just plain, starved to death. Others lost their toes from frostbite.

The ship portholes, where the prisoners were held, were closed tightly and locked, cutting off fresh air. As recorded in the prisoner's diaries, only one prisoner at a time was allowed on deck at night for the purpose of breathing fresh air. (This obviously is exaggerated, as it is mathematically impossible.) One night, while many prisoners gathered at the hatchway, waiting their turn to go on deck, one sentinel shoved his bayonet down among them repeatedly. In the morning, twenty-five of them were found wounded and stabbed in the head. The wounded who had been left to suffer, died slowly. On several mornings, from five to ten prisoners were found brutally slaughtered by the same means.

Disappointment, fever, madness and loss of hope overcame the prisoners and filled their quarters with filth, disgrace and horror. New prisoners were brought on board about as fast as the old ones were dying, replacing the bloodthirsty guards' amusement. Men would be dead for days, smelling wretched, before the guards would take them out and either throw them like dead dogs into the shallows of Wallabout Bay or bury them in its banks.

On 27 October 1780, after repeated requests questioning why Francis HOPKINSON was not paid for his services, the treasury board reported to Congress that the reason they turned down Francis HOPKINSON's request for payment was because, *"HOPKINSON was not the only person consulted on those exhibitions of fancy, and therefore, cannot claim the sole merit of them and* [is] *not entitled to the full sum charged."*

Here we go a mass manipulation of words; Francis HOPKINSON had made it perfectly clear in his first request for payment for his **team** that he asked only *"whether a quarter cask of the public wine could not be a proper and reasonable reward for these letters of fancy and a suitable encouragement for future exertions of a like nature?"*

Wow! Francis HOPKINSON's request for a quarter cask of public wine, as payment for his team, was sure to break their piggy bank. The exact same thing that happened to Francis HOPKINSON here by Congress, happened to Captain John KEMPER in the final days of his life during his pension years, when Commissioner James L. EDWARDS (1787-1867) would try to erase everything he had done in the birth of America. All the top statesmen and members of Congress, who came behind Captain KEMPER, would not be able to bring about a resolve. That did not happen until 150 years later.

Unbeknownst to Francis HOPKINSON, he would die after finding out, like all Continental officers did, that Congress had no money to pay anyone for their struggles, hardships and contributions in the birth of America. In addition, something worse happened to Francis HOPKINSON; about a hundred years after his magnificent blueprint for the first flag of the United States of America, another family tried to steal his thunder. Since he and all those who knew of his painstaking design had passed on, would there be anyone left alive to defend his honor and his miraculous creation? A true wonder—in the birth of America! The further forward in time we advance, the hazier history becomes.

Almost a century after the first American flag was made, since no one ever boasted about any ancestor's involvement, Betsy ROSS' (1752-1836) pretentious grandson, William J. CANBY (1822-1897), jumped out like a jack-in-the-box, claiming, *"It was my grandmother!"* Her grandson knew that anyone could claim an ancestor's involvement back during this period of time without being contested, since everyone was dead. So he, in fact, did just that! Unbeknownst to him, there was evidence recorded in the journals of Congress that it was, indeed, Francis HOPKINSON who had created the flag of the United States of America, among other seals and symbols. No one was aware of this at that time, so the myth was born and uncontested.

Her grandson William J. CANBY went one step further in causing one of the biggest ruckuses in American history. He actually went out and tried to acquire affidavits from anyone he could but could only acquire them from his family. This included three aunts, as if they were privy to this belated secret, when they were not even born when the flag was made. They claimed that they had heard the stories from their mother, but they temporarily forgot. A niece also recollected the stories she had heard told. As we all know, anyone can tell a story! The reality is that no one else wanted to partake in this incredible fraud, a product of hearsay! Families will often stick together whether right or wrong.

Knowing that his grandmother used to make flags, but not American, CANBY contrived stories to support his lies. He claimed that General WASHINGTON actually visited his grandmother, Betsy ROSS. Contrary to popular belief, it was not Betsy ROSS who sewed the first flag! However, people wanted answers and were willing to accept anyone; consequently, over time, as new oil paintings were created to support the lie, the belief grew stronger! All these oil paintings were created over a hundred years after the alleged events actually took place.

Then, all of a sudden, more oil paintings started popping up everywhere, portraying *"a"* Betsy ROSS sewing the first American flag. Then, a second oil painting showed General WASHINGTON meeting with Betsy ROSS to see the results of the first flag. They are all just one incredible hoax! Betsy ROSS, in fact, never had anything to do with the American Revolution! If she had anything to do with it at all, it would have been on the opposing side only. When Philadelphia was evacuated, all that remained were Loyalists. There is no record, whatsoever, that Betsy ROSS ever left Philadelphia.

Something else was going on here that has been missed in history. Betsy ROSS was born and raised and died in America's capitol, Philadelphia. Philadelphia was also the capitol of Tories/Loyalists during the time of the American Revolution. Betsy ROSS might very well have been a Loyalist. Now that America was both sound and solid, her grandson William CANBY might have been trying to clear both her and their family's name by manufacturing this incredible hoax. Betsy ROSS, who was long gone and buried, had no clue as to what her grandson would contrive.

What William CANBY did not know was that Francis HOPKINSON, the actual designer of the first American flag, along with the seal of the United States of America, was in the journals of the Continental Congress. He had put in for pay for his team who he had designed the first American flag and the seal of the United States, among other works he was in charge of. If Mr. CANBY had known this, his plans would have been foiled from the start. Now that we can go back in time, we can shed light on those who were truly involved in the birth of America and rightfully return their contributions that were stolen so easily from them, after their demise.

The fact is: General WASHINGTON never knew of Betsy ROSS in his lifetime. If he had, you can be rest assured that she would have been mentioned in his journals or one of his hundreds of correspondences, like with Francis HOPKINSON, as someone very special. She would have been mentioned by many others who had to do with the birth of America; those leaving behind diaries, journals, or declarations would have mentioned her in their records.

Furthermore, there was never any correspondence between General WASHINGTON and Betsy ROSS or Congress and Betsy ROSS in regard to the flag, or any other circumstances. However, there were between Congress and Francis HOPKINSON on his creation of the flag and between Francis HOPKINSON and General WASHINGTON on many subjects.

Charles Willson PEALE (1741-1827), who was responsible for painting the only pictures of General WASHINGTON from life, would have indeed captured this special moment, not some other artist over a hundred years later, after the fact, by creating it.

Furthermore, Betsy ROSS died without being concerned about who made the first flag. If it had been her, she would have been like any other American, very proud from the beginning, admitting it instead of taking it as a secret to her deathbed, relying on her grandson to reveal our flag's origin. In addition, all her friends, neighbors, and family would have known its origin and bragged about it constantly. It would not have taken almost a hundred years to come about. They would not have kept the whole nation wondering about its origin. Betsy ROSS's involvement was just a figment of someone's imagination—her grandson's!

Most importantly, the Continental Congress knew better than to trust civilians with such an important task, as they were well aware that far too many civilians were Loyalists to the Crown. Many civilians were feeding the British all the information they could in hopes of felling the Continental Congress and Continental Army under the same pretense and label that the British had given them, *"Rebels!"*

Many civilians truly believed that this mighty super power, Great Britain, was going to win the war. General Benedict ARNOLD shared in this belief! Many wanted to earn favor and be on the side they were confident was going to prevail. Others did not care; they just wanted the war to be over so they could live in peace.

As far as oil paintings go, it is obvious that at the Battles of Monmouth, Germantown, etc., General WASHINGTON did not stop the battles to have the oil paintings done, which took several months to finish. Likewise many oil paintings done depicting Valley Forge were all done after the fact.

A German, Emanuel Gottlieb LEUTZ (1816-1868), who, in his excitement of Americas' struggle for liberty during the American Revolution, portrayed a wrong setting. In his oil painting done of General WASHINGTON crossing the Delaware, he portrayed General WASHINGTON boldly standing in a rowboat filled with troops on choppy, icy waters, surrounded by small icebergs. In order to find icebergs, you need to go to either the north or south poles.

There were a couple of other things wrong about this oil painting. It also showed the flag of thirteen stars and stripes, which had not been designed by the time of the crossing but, in fact, a year later by Francis HOPKINSON. In addition, General WASHINGTON never went anywhere without his horse. When John KEMPER transported General WASHINGTON and the Continental Army across the Delaware on his flatboats, his horse went with him.

In reality, General WASHINGTON ordered this author's ancestor John KEMPER to bring his flatboats for transporting his troops, artillery, horses, and wagons across the Delaware for their march on Trenton. They would not have been able to have been transferred in a row-boat. Mr. LEUTZ had not researched the heart in the birth of America. This oil painting of an inaccurate account of the crossing of the Delaware has been planted all over the world—and never corrected!

However, all these events are well documented, and there is nothing wrong with putting together an oil painting from *"well-documented"* evidence. Historically trusted sources such as Bible records, diaries, correspondences, journals, and declarations are reliable testimonies. They respectfully represent these events, showing the many hardships and detailed accounts endured at specific locations, along with all those who were involved.

What is heartbreaking is when oil paintings are developed to support a fabrication of an event that never occurred, implicating an involvement of a new generation of Americans who, in reality, knew little to nothing about the time line in the birth of America. This was a very sad time in American history when record keeping was in its infancy. There was always someone who was ready to take advantage of this situation and manufacture their own records for their own personal gain. In retrospect, it was much like when this author was a union organizer; everyone was afraid to get involved, but once we were successful, they all wanted to play a part and claim that they had something to do with it.

Our founding fathers, like General WASHINGTON, General MUHLENBERG, General WAYNE, Colonel HAMILTON, Colonel Daniel KEMPER, and all those who dealt with them personally, like Captain KEMPER, took so much for granted. They all knew each other personally and what each had contributed to the birth of our nation and left it at that. They did not realize the historical significance it would mean to future generations of Americans, leaving the door wide open for others to romanticize the Revolution.

What should have happened was for General WASHINGTON and all his senior staff to have had record keepers at their side recording everything, pretty much as the record keepers documented the siege of Troy. These records were plagiarized by, HOMER along with his coverage of the Journey of ULYSSES (Odysseus) (1220BC-aft. 1180BC), which took place during the twelfth century BC. Record keeping, however, was not on any one's mind; trying to stay alive against the mightiest army and navy on earth was.

Many, like Captain KEMPER, kept diaries or journals, which were either later published or passed down in the family. However, some of the most important diary entries recorded was made by John's daughter, Elizabeth, from stories shared with her by both her father and uncle Dan (Colonel Daniel KEMPER) while growing up. Today, records are kept on everyone who does either civil or military service and, what their contributions and/or awards were.

By November 1780, the prisoners on the prison ships no longer were subjected to the extreme heat. The cooler days and frosty nights contributed to the lower average of ten deaths per day. Their conditions were still deplorable, and many prisoners would talk to themselves while wringing their hands; others would walk in circles in their small, cramped quarters. Some could be seen crying. Others just shook in a condition of nervous breakdown. Many others prayed for salvation, and others were just empty vessels of once-vibrant humans, now appearing ghost-like.

Eugene L. ARMBRUSTER (1865-1943), author of an article published in the *American Advertiser,* a newspaper of Fishkill, New York, later reported from a diary of Mr. William HEATH (1737-1814) recorded on 8 May, 1783, *"There were 11,644 American prisoners who suffered death, by the inhuman, cruel, savage and barbarous usage on board the filthy and malignant British Prison Ship, 'Jersey.' It also mentioned that many of the men's legs and feet were frozen. Let this news go to every paper throughout the land, in every country throughout the world; let the tragic incidents never be forgotten."*

When the Revolution was over, human bones could still be seen bleaching on the shore of Wallabout Bay and daily exposure by the low tide revealed a deplorable sight; it demonstrated that the *Jersey* had been more devastating than any battlefield during the American Revolution. The sight demonstrated how bad things could get and how costly wars are.

These men were some of America's first *"missing in action"* (MIA's). Many other MIA's were never discovered, their fate never known; thousands had just simply vanished. The Revolution was just the start of the MIAs in America. For all wars after, they would continue to be put at the top of the list for investigation on what possibly happened to them. Were they deserters or just killed in action and disappeared?

Meanwhile, Eliza HOPPER, who was living with her mother and two sisters in the small town of New Millstone, Somerset, New Jersey, had not heard from John since August and was becoming scared. She coaxed her mother, Anny, to obtain a horse and carriage on loan so that they could go to Basking Ridge to see John's sister, Maria Sophia MORTON, who lived in the same state, not far away.

Upon their arrival, Maria welcomed them in and offered them some refreshments. Eliza said, *"Maria, I have not heard from John since August and I am afraid for him."*

Maria responded, *"I am afraid I do not have good news to report."*

Eliza said, *"Noooooooooooooooo."*

Maria replied, *"The last we heard was that John was at battle on the Delaware with a British frigate, their ship was sunk and their crew was captured. Their fate is unknown."*

Eliza said, *"Nooooooooooooo."*

Maria replied, *"I am sorry, Eliza."* She tried to ease Eliza's pain and said, *"You need to remain strong, Eliza, and not give up hope. John will make it through this."*

Eliza said, *"How do you know?"*

Maria replied, *"Because I know my brother, he knows how to handle stress well. There is very little more I can tell you, Eliza, other than he worked closely with my husband, General WASHINGTON and Congress. However, my husband does not tell me everything, but he did say he saw John off when he boarded the Hector, but has not seen or heard from him since."* She finished by saying, *"As soon as we hear more, we will contact you."*

She then said, *"I almost forgot, I have a letter from my brother for you. He had given it to my husband when he saw him off at the docks in Philadelphia. We have to apologize; he had been carrying it around with him and forgot about it."*

Eliza's eyes opened wide as she said, *"Oh boy!* As she tore open the letter and began reading, she said, *"oooooooooooh, he signed it with hugs and kisses. I wish Mr. MARTIN could deliver our mail to New Millstone."*

Maria said, *"Your town is too small, Eliza. How many families do you have in Millstone, 50 to 100?"*

Eliza answered, *"Something like that, I know we have to go into Hillsborough for anything major."*

Eliza's mother, Anny, confirmed everything her daughter's broken heart was spilling.

Eliza's mother, Anna HOPPER, then spoke, *"Maria, thank you so much for your hospitality, along with the KEMPERs, it has always been top-shelf. Most importantly, thanks for the update on John's status. It is too bad that the war had to separate our families from all the good time we used to have at your father's tavern. All that are left are good memories."*

Maria closed by saying, *"Anny, we all miss you and your family dearly, especially Matt; he was a good man. Good friends are so hard to come by."*

Anna replied, *"Thank you Maria, he was a good man. I feel just terrible that his three daughters have to be raised without him. I hope this never happens to you."* They all embraced, and then the HOPPERS left the MORTON's residence, fully content with their trip.

1. The Provost Marshal Captain William "Bloody Bill" Cunningham

After a time, Lieutenant John KEMPER, along with seventy-one other officers, was transferred from the prison ship to the provost prison in New York City, under the provost marshal Captain William "Bloody Bill" CUNNINGHAM (1756-1791), where he was confined for three weeks. Lieutenant KEMPER was then in the clutches of the *"monster"* who reigned over the American prisoners in Philadelphia. Being under the provost for three weeks was like being in *"hell"* for three years. Very few were fortunate enough to get out alive; only officers were moved.

Captain CUNNINGHAM's quarters were in the provost prison, on the right-hand side of the main door. To the left of the hall was the guardroom. Within the first barricade was the apartment of his assistant, Sergeant O'KEEFE. Two sentinels guarded the entrance day and night; two more were stationed at the first and second barricades, which were grated, barred and chained. When a prisoner was led into the hall, the whole guard was paraded, and he was turned over to Captain CUNNINGHAM or his deputy, and questioned as to his name, age and rank, as well as his size and how he was captured; this data was entered into a record book.

When Americans were taken prisoner, they were stripped and robbed of their clothes and personal belongings and their papers confiscated, which identified their service to their country. Because of the confiscation of their records, it became difficult for some of the soldiers to prove their service to their country in the future and to account for where they were during this period of time. Many froze to death from lack of clothing and blankets. More men were packed into provost prison than its quarters could provide; sleeping like sardines had become part of the torture. When they lay down on the floor to sleep all in a row, they had to turn over at the same time at the call, *"Turn over! Left! Right!"*

The prisoners' rations were two pounds of hard bread and two pounds of pork per week usually spoiled and uncooked; many prisoners starved. They were given muddy and impure water to drink, but never a sufficient quantity to sustain life. Other times, water was brought to the men in the tubs they used in their rooms, which they drank from or perished; the effects of the water caused much sickness. If a man asked for more, or for clean water to drink, he was thrown into the dungeon on half rations without seeing fire or candlelight. Some men were kept in the dungeon for as long as fourteen weeks.

If Captain CUNNINGHAM had a grudge against any prisoner, that prisoner was not entered in LOSSING's field book of prisoners of war; consequently, they would not be known about or exchanged. Searing irons and secret whippings tortured whatever prisoners displeased the provost marshal. Anyone making the slightest complaint would be beaten unmercifully with his rattan, knocked down, and then consigned to the dungeon. Other prisoners heard sounds in the night, footsteps of someone walking around and heavy breathing. Was it a ghost of a dead prisoner, or was it as they feared, Captain CUNNINGHAM coming for one of them for his slaughter, which excited him more than his orgies with American women?

Captain CUNNINGHAM had no pity or mercy; he persisted in his inhuman treatment of the prisoners' physical and mental health. He thirsted for the Americans' blood and took an eager delight in their slaughter. Many of his captives were hung in the gloom of night without a trial or any hope of justice. Captain CUNNINGHAM sold the prisoners' provisions and exchanged the good for spoiled food in order to provide for the drunken orgies, which usually took place after his dinner; he even poisoned some prisoners.

One night, about midnight, a guard was dispatched from the provost to the upper barracks to order the men on the line of march to close their window shutters and put out their lights.

Then the guards gagged about 250 prisoners, took them out of confinement and led them to be hung in the gallows just behind the upper barracks. Their gags were removed so Captain CUNNINGHAM could hear their shrieks of agony while they begged for mercy, appealing to God for justice.

Then they were hung without ceremony, simply to gratify Captain CUNNINGHAM's bloodthirsty mood. About half a dozen men were hung each night, until women in the neighborhood petitioned General HOWE to have the practice discontinued, pleading that the men's shrieks and piercing cries for mercy were haunting and made them quiver to the bones. These stories were continually told and recorded in the diaries or journals of the prisoners of war who survived. While Lieutenant KEMPER was under duress, he had to maintain his focus on his mission.

Captain CUNNINGHAM would leave messages outside the prisoners' door, saying that, *"Three other prisoners had a rope concealed in a bag in one of the rooms in order to make their escape;"* so Captain CUNNINGHAM could murder them, claiming they tried to escape. Every day at least a dozen corpses were dragged out and dumped into the ditches and swamps beyond the city. Dying men were denied visits from their wives and friends; they were not allowed the services of a doctor. Prisoners' wives who came to the prison to see their dying husbands were beaten by the guards and thrown off the premises. No pen, ink, nor paper was allowed which prevented their treatment from being made public.

2. The British Commander Returns to Share His Cigar

One night while Lieutenant KEMPER was sound asleep, all of a sudden, footsteps could be heard descending the stairs to the dungeon where the prisoners were held. Lights could be seen flickering through the cracks of the door to the prisoners' quarters. At the bottom of the stairs, an officer ordered, *"Stop!"* He was then heard pulling something out of his waistcoat then said, *"Give me a light."* A new sparkle of light flared up as the door slowly squeaked open, and the men entered. Everyone pretended to be asleep, fearing that Captain CUNNINGHAM was coming to grab one of them for his amusement.

Lieutenant KEMPER was then abruptly awakened by a kick in the head from the leather boot of Captain CUNNINGHAM. Captain CUNNINGHAM yelled, *"Wake up Lieutenant KEMPER! Or is it Captain? I am totally confused! But you have a visit from a very old friend."*

Lieutenant KEMPER squinted his eyes as he tried to focus in the lamplight. As he looked up, he saw the figure of a British commander with a curly mustache, standing with his arms crossed, pretending to be shivering and smoking a cigar. The British officer then took the cigar out of his mouth and blew out circles of smoke as he looked down at Lieutenant KEMPER lying on the floor, shackled in irons and chains.

"Your gold was turned over to Admiral RODNEY; he always shows special favor to those who donate so generously to the Royal Navy. I suspect that he will soon be sending you closer to the King. Geeez, I cannot even get close to him. Gold just seems to buy everything; perhaps Mr. MORTON can buy your way free.

Lieutenant KEMPER replied, *"Freedom has a price everyone must pay!"*

The British commander paused for a moment and then said, *"Indeed! Before I leave, Captain, please! Have one of my cigars,"* He then took his cigar and forced it into Lieutenant KEMPER's mouth, saying, *"Just thought I would drop off one of my famous cigars that I know you enjoy so well, please have a good night! After all, here in the dungeon you live in a 24 hour night."*

The British commander then slowly strolled off with the provost marshal, who kept looking back chuckling at Lieutenant KEMPER. After the British officers had left, one of the prisoners lying next to Lieutenant KEMPER said, *"Please Captain, you would not mind sharing that cigar, would you?"* Lieutenant KEMPER then spit the cigar out near the prisoner, who quickly grabbed it up with his teeth, straightened it out with his tongue, and puffed away with a smile on his face. There was no other way to get any smokes down here in this cold, and dingy dungeon.

Lieutenant KEMPER rolled over on his back and looked up into darkness as Madam Ursula reappeared in a mist. Lieutenant KEMPER later recorded that, for a moment, he could not figure out how in the hell the British commander would have learned of his capture, until he later spoke to other prisoners. They informed him that, whenever a British officer had a grudge against a particular rebel, he would give his name to the heads of all prisons so that in the event he was captured, it would be brought to their attention.

When John KEMPER retired as captain and wagon master for General George WASHINGTON he was given new orders for deployment by General WASHINGTON, after he was called to Philadelphia to meet with members of Congress. He then joined the US Navy and went about a slow promotion to lieutenant. Since Lieutenant KEMPER had been captured and made a prisoner of war, he had gone from being in total control to being under someone else's total control.

He later recorded in his book, *"US Naval Affairs"* that he was overwhelmed with the feeling of helplessness and worried he would not be able to fulfill his mission. He closed by saying, *"In the event I fail, there would be no body to retrieve; for I had vowed I would sacrifice my very life for my commander-in-chief, my Congress and my country."* He never recorded what that mission was.

As General WASHINGTON always had scouts and spies out supplying him with a constant feed of intelligence on British troop movements, etc., so did the British regarding General WASHINGTON's movements. In addition, the British had something that General WASHINGTON did not—a constant flow of deserters into their ranks, feeding them with intelligence on who was who in General WASHINGTON's army.

Could the deck of cards have been stacked any worse against General WASHINGTON? However, what the British did not know was that General WASHINGTON was head of intelligence for the Continental Army and navy. Just how much so, was not known until later years, because everything had to be and was kept *"top secret."*

In the winter of 1780, fifth-teen prisoners made their escape and crossed a bridge of ice that had formed over the East River. Captain CUNNINGHAM tightened his security.

On 1 January 1781, at Major General Anthony WAYNE's winter quarters at Mount Kemble, New Jersey, his regiments began to mutiny. They had reached their limit due to lack of food and clothing and not having seen a paper dollar within a year. Many of the soldiers had families at home for whom they could no longer provide. Conditions got so bad there was no other recourse. General WAYNE tried to stop them, but was warned that he would be executed if he tried.

Two thousand battle-hardened troops marched out of camp, in battle readiness, with six field guns (cannons). General WAYNE sent several wagons of rations to the mutineers to show that he cared. He also dispatched couriers to General WASHINGTON, the area commanders and Congress. General WASHINGTON could have ridden to the front of the troops and said, *"Let us get them men, let us get our money!"* However, being the kind of man General WASHINGTON was, he insisted they all meet in Princeton for negotiations.

He defused the tension by offering certificates to the mutineers that were supposedly redeemable in the future for full cash value; they were accepted. After the Revolution, it was impossible for

Congress to meet any of their promises and commitments, for their vaults were still empty.

3. Mill Prison, England

On 11 January 1781, Lieutenant John KEMPER, along with about seventy other officers, *"were committed to Mill Prison, Plymouth, England,"* by order of Admiral Sir George Bridges RODNEY. They were taken on board the *Old Yarmouth*, a sixty-four-gun ship, and conveyed to Plymouth, England, where they were charged with piracy and high treason. All officers, who were now thousands of miles away from home and on an island, felt helpless, with no hope of escape. How would Lieutenant KEMPER get out of this one? Before, all he had to worry about were British troop movements, of which his scouts kept him fully informed, and he could fight his way out.

Upon their arrival in England, they were confined to Mill Prison. An imposing structure located on a hill between Plymouth and Plymouth Dock, jutting into the sea, it was fitted for four hundred prisoners. The keeper of Mill Prison, William COWDRAY, as portrayed in the pages of many prisoners' diaries, was a wretched character. Corrupt and unprincipled, he stole money and other valuables from them. Some of the other officers who were in prison with Lieutenant John KEMPER were, Commodore John MANLEY (1733-1793), Captains Gustavus CUNNINGHAM (1744-1819), Silas TALBOT (1751-1813), Joshua BARNEY (1759-1818), James SLOVER, and John KEMP (1723-1795)—a host of officers who fought for America on its waters.

Here was Commodore John MANLEY, General WASHINGTON's first and only commodore, who commanded the USS *Hancock* when the British captured it. After its capture, the British changed its name to HMS *Iris*. While under this new name, it captured the ship *Hector* while Lieutenant John KEMPER was on board.

It was now clear why Commodore John MANLEY and Captain Silas TALBOT were not put on the list for exchange. They both were constantly escaping and thrown in the *"black hole."* Consequently, they both were put at the bottom of the list for exchange, so no one knew their whereabouts and whether they were alive or dead.

Was this a coincidence, or was this what General WASHINGTON wanted Captain KEMPER to locate and, thus, be deliberately captured so he could enter into the British prison system unsuspected as an enemy agent? He could then verify the status of other officers held prisoner, their location, in hopes of an offer of exchange. Hopefully, he could find out if Commodore MANLEY was still alive and where he was being held.

Finally, one day Commodore MANLEY and Captain TALBOT were seen talking alone; Lieutenant KEMPER slowly and cautiously approached them and intensely glared at them. Commodore MANLEY asked, *"Is there something we can help you with lieutenant?"*

Lieutenant KEMPER then softly replied by naming both of the officers' family members. Both, officers' eyes opened wide while backing up and stumbling into each another. They quickly looked to see who, if anyone was watching.

Commodore MANLEY softly motioned Lieutenant KEMPER to nonchalantly join them in the corner. There was nothing else clearly recorded in his book, *US Naval Affairs* other than *"the pigeon must come home."* Since Lieutenant KEMPER had not taken his book with him, as his captors would have confiscated it, he must have recorded this incident after he returned home.

All new prisoners' names and ranks were entered into Mill Prison's logbooks and then released to the rebels to negotiate for exchange of captured British officers. Mill Prison was a prison mostly for officers only, which could be exchanged for

British officers captured by the Americans. Depending on their importance, some seamen were imprisoned as well.

The British were not about to waste the expense of transferring midshipman or lower-ranking sailors, whom they considered worthless. They were kept in the prison ships off the island of Manhattan, in New York City, or under the provost marshal, William CUNNINGHAM, where the bodies could be disposed of easily. The British wanted to maintain control over their captured officers on their own soil where no escape was possible; even so, many foolishly tried, but there was no-where to run.

Therefore, when Lieutenant John KEMPER's ship, the *Hector* was captured, the only officers qualifying for transfer were Captain James SLOVER, First Lieutenant Thomas JUSTICE, and Second Lieutenant John KEMPER. Midshipmen Charles LYNN and John CONNOR, along with all lower-ranking sailors, were kept in the various British prisons in the New York City area. Was anyone's new place of residence going to be better than the others?

All this data on Lieutenant John KEMPER and other officers transferred to Mill Prison is backed up by British prison records, which also have been published in the New York Genealogical Biographical Record. However, the British did not release these records until years later. Since all prisoners' papers were confiscated when they were taken prisoner, it made it very difficult for the veterans to verify their service until then. Other military records, after being gathered and put in one location, were burned in a mysterious fire at the War Department in later years.

American prisoners were to receive one pound of bread, one quart of beer, three-quarters-a-pound of beef, except on Sunday when it was replaced by cheese, and one-half pint of peas or greens five times a week. However, under Captain COWDRAY's administration, the beer was watered down until almost tasteless. So tainted was the beef that maggots fell off it as it was handed to the prisoners and the cheese was green with mold. Captain COWDRAY also kept about two hundred hogs where coal was stored, feeding the hogs the prisoners' rations while some of the prisoners starved.

Meanwhile, back in the States, during the spring, General WASHINGTON and Colonel Alexander HAMILTON had a falling out. Colonel HAMILTON was so frustrated that he resigned his position as aide-de-camp. However, General WASHINGTON never held grudges against his officers. Later in 1799, he insisted that President John ADAMS appoint Colonel HAMILTON major general of the army. President ADAMS reluctantly agreed. Captain KEMPER recorded that *"Whenever Colonel HAMILTON stood his ground with General WASHINGTON it often looked like he was the one in charge. General WASHINGTON and Colonel HAMILTON did not always get along, or see eye-to-eye, but they were not each other's enemies either."*

Captain COWDRAY was a man who sought vengeance, drank heavily, and was often known to have tantrums, according to reports from the prisoners. Those who attempted escape but were recaptured could face a term of up to forty days in the *"Black Hole."* The *"Black Hole"* was a small dark cell separate from the other prisoners. Often they were restricted to half rations and put on the bottom of the list for exchange. Since most of these officers were constantly trying to escape, their existence or status was never known about in the States. Therefore, unless General WASHINGTON knew of their status and location, he was unable to barter for their exchange.

Freedom was unquestionably more desirable than the *"Black Hole"* and the other punishments that were doled out by William COWDRAY in Mill Prison. In their desire to be free, some prisoners went over the wall, and some tunneled under the wall. Others, like Captain Joshua BARNEY, bribed guards, who let them disguise themselves in British officer's uniforms and walk out undetected. Others found a convenient method of escaping like hiding in a coffin, pretending to be a corpse. Treachery and deception was everywhere. Many secretly cooperated with local citizens in an effort to escape, only to be betrayed by them and brought back again to collect the five pounds' reward.

If all these methods failed and their dream of being exchanged seemed hopeless, there was but one last resort: to join the Royal Navy in hopes of increasing their chances of escape. First, the officers had to wait for the royal pardon before they could be released. For some unknown reason, Lieutenant KEMPER kept a low profile, never doing anything to excite or challenge the guards. Was he waiting to make a move?

William COWDRAY had written a letter to Parliament stating that the prisoners were exceedingly riotous and abusive and attempting to escape every chance they could. He could not understand why they wanted their freedom, since he was such a *"nice guy."* In fact, at the end of hostilities, Captain COWDRAY had the gall to take a petition for the prisoners to sign, stating that he had treated them kindly. The prisoners reported, *"It was immediately torn up!"*

Both Captain Joshua BARNEY and Captain Silas TALBOT discussed escaping over the wall or tunneling under it, but Lieutenant John KEMPER disagreed. If they were to use this method, they would still remain stuck on an island with no means of escape. In dire need of food and water in order to survive, there was no one they could trust. When a lieutenant gave suggestions to a captain, it was like going in one ear and right out the other. Captains did not want to appear inferior to subordinates.

Captain Joshua BARNEY escaped on 18 May 1781; Captain Gustavus CUNNINGHAM escaped on 4 June 1781, but both were recaptured once again. Captain Silas TALBOT was pardoned for exchange along with Commodore John MANLEY on 16 October 1781, after Lieutenant KEMPER escaped and arrived home. Hardly a coincidence!

Up until this point in John's life, his brother Colonel Daniel KEMPER had always been there for him—before the Revolution, during his stint in Philadelphia, at Valley Forge, and while picking up supplies at his wagon-train camp for the Continental Army. Daniel was John's hero, confidant, and guardian angel—the one who was always there to give him the right advice. Somehow, Daniel would always appear like *"poof,"* from out of nowhere, like Aladdin's lamp. It was as if someone from the heavens waved a *"magic wand"* whenever John needed him most.

This time was different; Daniel was not able to get to him. John had to figure his way out of this *pickle* (predicament) on his own. John could not get reckless; he had to be cunning in order to fool the British officers and return home to his brother, his country, General WASHINGTON, and his sweetheart, Eliza HOPPER.

After being confined a long time and continually being cruelly treated, Lieutenant John KEMPER, met together with Captain James SLOVER who believed in the same action as he did. They decided that they had been there long enough, as there appeared to be no hope for exchange anytime soon. In addition, captains always had priority over lieutenants in being exchanged. Nothing was going to happen unless they took matters into their own hands. Besides, Lieutenant KEMPER's mission was complete; it was time for the pigeon to come home.

Since Commodore John MANLEY had been found alive and well, outside of being cruelly treated, Lieutenant KEMPER needed to get that intelligence back to his commander-in-chief.

Both Lieutenant KEMPER and Captain SLOVER planned on joining the Royal Navy to increase their chances of escape out in the open, rather than locked up in prison. Since they were both captured on the same ship, they felt that it would be too conspicuous and suspicious if they applied for the royal pardon together.

They both agreed that Lieutenant KEMPER would apply for the royal pardon first. As things winded down and if everything went well, Captain SLOVER would follow suit shortly thereafter. If both of their escapes were successful, they planned on meeting back up in Philadelphia.

After a while, they obtained a little indulgence. In the spring of 1781, Lieutenant KEMPER, along with other officers, carefully planned for their escape. They accomplished this by manipulating their captors into believing they would enter on board their British vessels and fight for them. All they had to do was to wait for a royal pardon and take their chances when the British ships moored on an island or land for supplies. Lieutenant KEMPER left his graffiti on the prison walls, *"Lieutenant John KEMPER was here, but now he is where?"*

On 20 March 1781, Lieutenant John KEMPER was pardoned for the Royal Navy. On 27 March 1781, he then petitioned to go into the Royal Navy and entered into service on 25 April 1781. This vessel was headed toward the island of Jamaica; in his passage, he would have to devise a plan of escape with other American prisoners.

In May of 1781, Captain James SLOVER was pardoned for the Royal Navy. On 5 June 1781, he entered the Royal Navy. What the British thought they were doing was breaking the American spirit. What they did not realize was, once you're an American your spirit cannot be broken. Now, all that Lieutenant KEMPER and Captain SLOVER had to do was, escape so that they could meet back in Philadelphia as planned.

On 22 June 1781, General WASHINGTON wrote a letter to Daniel and John's brother, Captain Jacob KEMPER.

"Sir you are to proceed to Sussex County agreeable to the orders which will be given to you By Genl. [Henry] KNOX (1750–1806) to endeavor to procure 12 Barrels of Oil—If the owners of that Article will not except the terms of that payment which the Quarter Masr General will authorize you to make, you are hereby directed to seize the above mentioned Quantity and bring it with you to the post—If you are under the necessity of making a seizure, you will give them Receipts for the Quantity. I am Sir Yr most obt Servt. G. Washington.

Chapter XIX
The Great Escape
(the island of Jamaica)

On 10 August 1781, after the British had arrived and docked on the island of Jamaica, they proceeded to pick up supplies and drop off new ones. They always used the American prisoners to perform most of the hard labor, while pretending to treat them as equals. Lieutenant KEMPER, along with some other officers, planned their escape. Lieutenant KEMPER was permitted to go ashore to drop off supplies and pick up tobacco, sugar cane, and other cargo, but was strictly watched.

Tobacco and sugar cane products were the prime exports of this tropical island oasis. The British had a regular routine system of stopping at Jamaica to drop of supplies for their colony and slaves, and pick up cargo for their return trip to England. They would load up their ships with these supplies and head back home for dispersal, sale, and trade to other countries.

One night, when Lieutenant KEMPER slowly strolled back as if to re-board the ship, one of his fellow prisoners distracted the guards by *"accidentally on purpose"* dropping a keg of gun-powder, so that John could make his escape. The British commander yelled, *"You idiot!"* He then ordered him tied to the mast and given nine lashes.

Lieutenant KEMPER quickly ran over by some barrels near a turned-over boat, looking for cover. There was a colored woman, who was one of the British slaves on the island. She was working the fishing nets for the British. Seeing the lieutenant trying to escape, she then motioned him to hit the ground. She then threw a mesh of fishing nets over his body, concealing him. She then went on with her business as if nothing had happened. The smell of fish was just terrible; bees and flies were hovering, but it was better than being captured. Here, Lieutenant KEMPER did what he learned to do as a young boy: hide right under his enemies' noses.

After the American officer got scolded and punished for dropping the powder keg, the British refocused on their mission, picking up supplies, while dropping off others for future pickups. One British officer yelled, *"Where did Lieutenant KEMPER go?"*

One guard exclaimed, *"He was just here getting ready to board and pick up more supplies, I saw him."*

The captain yelled, *"Fan out!"*

The British, who thought John got farther away from them than he actually had, passed right by him, checked under the boat and continued their search.

After the last British patrol returned, they remarked, *"We do not know where the hell he went, but he is gone! This is a big island, he could be anywhere or better yet, maybe one of the jungle animals got him."*

The captain looked at the man who had dropped the powder keg, whom they had tied to the mast with ropes, and ordered him sent to the dungeon. He then replied, *"Okay, we have been here long enough, let us continue our supply route."*

Not wanting to waste any further time, they decided to leave.

The British were skeptical in returning to the war zone with prisoners of war. There they could easily blend in with their countrymen, quickly escape, and end up back in the ranks of the army against them. Instead, they used them on supply runs where they had better control and observance. However, this one got away.

John had to remain concealed for some days. Under the hot tropical sun without food or water, he quickly became dehydrated. During this time, Lieutenant KEMPER forgot that the human body needed to excrete certain bodily fluids daily. His location was quickly becoming a smelly situation. This was one experience John did not learn when he was a young boy.

Once they were clearly away, the colored woman led Lieutenant KEMPER to a safer location. He then dove into the ocean to wash off the stink. The colored woman then directed John to the other side of the island where American vessels sometimes moored for supplies. John then cautiously moved about the island, looking for something to drink. He found that he was in a tropical heaven; coconut trees were everywhere. He found a branch on the ground and broke it to size then continued to throw it at the coconuts until he knocked one down. After one of the coconuts fell, he proceeded to peel it with his knife and then stabbed a hole in it so he could drink the coconut milk.

Although he was more thirsty than he had ever been in his life, he knew better than to drink too much too fast; otherwise, he could become sicker than he already was. John grabbed a rock and broke the coconut open and proceeded to dig out the coconut with his knife so he could eat it.

Now it was time to find something else to eat, not knowing for sure how he was going to get back home or how long it would take. After all, he had just escaped. His new habitat was also filled with luscious tropical forest, and there were swamps everywhere. John had never been to the tropics and was now surrounded by beautiful scenery and vines filled with fruit that he had never seen before at any market. He began picking bananas, mangoes, pineapple, and other fruits and started eating.

As John was looking at the vast jungle, he froze his eyes and mouth opened wide and he yelled out, *"Nooooooooooooooooooooooooooooooooo! Madam Ursulaaaa!"* As his screams echoed throughout the jungle, the wildlife returned sirens of their own sounds. John was now in the vast jungle Madam Ursula had predicted he would be looking around in and lost. Now, he had to find his own way home. Where and how would he begin?

Lieutenant KEMPER found out that surviving in the tropics was not going to be a problem; however, there were bugs everywhere, which wanted him for lunch, besides other creatures as well. Beautiful tropical sounds were everywhere. They could easily lull you into a deep sleep at night, providing you with a safe location where some critters would not be able to join your company.

Meanwhile, how was the Revolution going? John was overly excited about getting back in the middle of it, but first, he had to find a way home. How was that going to be possible? Did he get off the wrong boat? Was he here to stay; only to watch other British ships come and go? Would he have to turn himself back in order to get off the island? John was totally unfamiliar with this new atmosphere. Everywhere he looked, there appeared to be no escape and he was surrounded by the unknown.

John started moving toward the swamp trying to figure out how he was going to get through or around it. John noticed that one of the logs in the swamp appeared to be moving slowly toward him. It was covered with moss and swampy grass. However, something was definitely wrong here. How could a log be moving when the water it was in was not? John moved closer to try to get a better idea as to what was going on here.

Then other logs started moving slowly in his direction as well. Waaaaaait a minute! John's eyes opened wide fast; these logs had eyes! John quickly backed up. These were not logs at all; these were crocodiles, and they were just as hungry as he was. This was the first time John had encountered a crocodile and had only heard that they were ambush predators, afraid of nothing, always hungry and ready to eat anything, especially if it had meat on it.

The tropics were certainly a nice place to visit, but not to live in. John was now going to have to find another way off the island so that he could return back home. He wanted to get out of a British uniform and back into a Continental one. The first night, after freeing himself from his hiding place, was kind of scary. With jungle sounds all around and rustling noises in the shrubbery, he feared he was being stalked, and he was afraid to go to sleep.

He was out in the open and all alone in a dense wilderness. All he had to defend himself was a knife that the British allowed him to have for cutting the burlap bags. They would not allow him to have a sword. He eventually fell to sleep, and upon awaking in the morning to the loud hooting of a bird, he had to refocus on where he was and how he was going to get off the island. Was he stuck here for life?

Lieutenant KEMPER began wandering about the island in the opposite direction of the British port. He then met another colored woman as she was retrieving fresh water from a spring. He told her that, even though he was in a British uniform, he was an American officer and needed to find a way home. She then assisted him by showing him where to get aboard *the Mosquito,"* an American merchant ship, supposing that was moored on the other side of the island, but who and what did they supply?

"Just follow the coast," she said. The *Mosquito* was a supply ship commanded by Captain Hendrick BOGART (1752-?), who was a Dutchman. The supply ship also had a dark side, which Lieutenant KEMPER would soon discover. The natives of Jamaica did trading with both the British and the Americans. The slaves had been brought over by the British for the same reasons they were taken to America. What he was about to find out was that he would be with his own kind, once again, literally!

1. American Vessel Homeward Bound

The Americans knew that the British moored on the island of Jamaica for supplies as well, so they were on constant guard. Both sides were always raiding the other's supplies when left vacant or attended by a minimal guard. When Lieutenant KEMPER approached the American vessel, he was still in a British uniform. One of the crew yelled, *"Captain! A British officer is approaching."*

The Americans aimed their rifles in an attempt to capture him until he explained who he was. He was easily identifiable by voice as he had a German-American accent, not British.

He was then warmly greeted and given a bath, food to eat and a change of clothes. They were all excited about his escape and wanted to know about his captivity. The American vessel was not a naval war ship but a supply vessel. They had been there to pick up supplies, goods, and fruits to bring back to other ports of trade in the islands and along the coast in the States while picking up other supplies in various ports along the way. Captain BOGART had developed quite a profitable business.

After Lieutenant KEMPER filled them in on his captivity and on who he was, the captain and ship's crew then filled him in on what was happening in the Revolution. As they continued talking, Captain BOGART left the deck for a moment; when he returned, he was carrying what appeared to be a pole wrapped in cloth. He, in turn, handed the item over to Lieutenant KEMPER while saying, *"An officer is truly naked without one of these."*

As Lieutenant KEMPER took and unwrapped the item. He found that it was a sword. As he pulled it out of its sheath and was admiring it, he slowly looked up at the Captain, with tears in his eyes, and said, *"Thank you."*

The captain replied, *"My pleasure."* The British had not allowed Lieutenant KEMPER to carry more than a knife to cut burlap with, but he was strictly watched to make sure he did not try to grab another British officer and put the knife to his throat.

Lieutenant KEMPER told Captain BOGART that he had to get a message to his commander-in-chief and asked if he had any means of having a message delivered.

The captain shook his head and replied, *"Not here, but in Havana, on our next stop, we have a message system set up where we can get your message sent out while we finish up our trading route."*

Mr. KEMPER replied, *"That will work just fine."*

The captain continued, *"However, the courier may end up reading your message."*

Mr. KEMPER answered, *"It will not matter, and it will be in code."*

The Captain smiled, nodded and replied, *"I understand."*

Although not a war ship, which Lieutenant KEMPER was used to sailing on, it would do just fine for getting home. Besides, being a supply ship, it was less conspicuous and proved to be a safer mode of travel. They now departed the West Indies and headed north, then west around the southwestern island of Cuba toward Havana.

After they docked, Lieutenant KEMPER gave his message to the captain to hand over to his courier. The captain said, *"Your message will be sent to our courier in Philadelphia, who will make sure it gets to its destination."*

They unloaded supplies while taking on new ones, including arms for the Continental Army. Up until this point in time, John had been in the heart of the Revolution, directly under General

WASHINGTON; now he was on the outside witnessing other countries who were supporting their cause.

The American Revolution had become the number 1 interest of all civilized countries around the world. Everyone could not wait to hear the latest of what was happening and if the American cause was still alive. Everyone was for the underdogs, the Americans. As the captain took the supplies on board, he looked at Mr. KEMPER, smiled, and said, *"We all have had to be vigilant and extra careful when helping others. You never know when there might be a spy among us."*

Lieutenant KEMPER smiled profusely as he bowed his head while shaking it and answering, *"I truly understand!"*

Captain BOGART replied, *"I thought you might."*

All laughed for a moment.

After finishing unloading and loading new supplies in Havana, they sailed east, then northeast toward other destinations along the eastern coast of the United States. They had stops, commitments, and other obligations, all the while trying to avoid the Royal Navy. The captain of the American vessel promised Lieutenant KEMPER that they would drop him off on his native shore but wanted to steer clear of New York City as it was under British control and there were always war-ships cruising the rivers.

Lieutenant KEMPER replied, *"I understand perfectly! If you can drop me off on the coast of New Jersey, I can find my own way home."*

Captain BOGART replied, *"We will try to get you as close to New Brunswick as possible. We will drop you off on the shores of the bay just east."*

On their voyage back, Lieutenant KEMPER strolled up on deck during one evening, just to sit and look at the thousands of stars that twinkled in the night. John recorded that because of his careful planning of his escape from being so long a prisoner of war, now he felt as if the weight of the world had been lifted off his shoulders. He was experiencing the joy of being free again.

He was content with being homeward bound but wondered about his comrades back at Mill Prison. He started making a list of other officers he shared quarters and exchanged stories with while at Mill Prison. He would turn everything over to General WASHINGTON when he got home, but what was in that message that he had sent to General WASHINGTON? He did not record it in his journals.

His thoughts also went to his family and Eliza. They must be worried sick not having heard from him in such a long time. Hopefully, he would be home soon. Eliza too was thinking of John, not knowing if he was dead or alive. She reread his letters over and over until she knew them all by heart and they were tattered from the constant handling.

In August 1781, the French Army stopped in Basking Ridge, New Jersey, to refresh themselves with water from the spring, before they continued on to Yorktown, Virginia. Everyone in town ran to the windows and doors to catch a glimpse of our new allies coming to help us defeat the British. Jacob and Maria Regina KEMPER, who were visiting, retired to their room while Maria broke down in tears, remembering the cruelty of the French Army on the Germans in the Rhineland. Jacob comforted his wife. Jacob and Maria knew first-hand that the French could be just as cruel as the British. The feelings were bittersweet.

Maria Regina, while sobbing, replied, *"After the French help us get rid of the British, they will then turn on us."*

Jacob responded, *"They will never get that chance; there are too many Germans in our country that hate the French. The English cannot stand them as well. The French are just trying to get even with the British for driving them out of North America during the French and Indian Wars. This is only temporary; the French will never be allowed to maintain a military base on our soil. One day, Germany will get its revenge on the French."*

Maria Regina, *"I hope you are right. The French definitely cannot be trusted, they dog everyone."*

Chapter XX
Siege of Yorktown

In early September of 1781, General Lord Charles CORNWALLIS found himself trapped on a peninsula in Yorktown. He had managed to get an emergency dispatch out to the British headquarters in New York City. General CLINTON ordered General CORNWALLIS to dig in. However, before help could arrive, he found himself being closed in by American and French troops on land and a large fleet of French war ships encircling the peninsula from the York River.

On 9 September 1781, while Lieutenant John KEMPER was on his way home, the British war ship HMS *Iris*, loaded with a crew of 290 men including officers, headed to Yorktown to back up General Lord Charles CORNWALLIS. As they approached the vicinity, they were taken by surprise by a fleet of French war ships that were waiting for them. The *Iris* was captured by the French frigate *Heron* which was commanded by Captain Jean Baptiste Marquis DE TRAVERSAY (1754-1831).

At the battle at the southern part of Chesapeake Bay, she was forced to strike (surrender) her colors (flag). The Americans and the French continued to build up forces surrounding Lord CORNWALLIS, while not allowing any help in.

The *Iris* (formerly USS *Hancock*) was never turned back over to the Americans but, in fact, kept by the French as a prize for themselves, as they were covetous for America's best, which almost out-ran the British war-ships (nice allies).

In addition, General LAFAYETTE had just arrived from France with an additional six thousand troops (good timing). General CORNWALLIS' eyes opened wide, and his heart beat fast; he knew he was in a pickle (deep trouble) now. Was it possible that one of Great Britain's greatest generals was about to fall? The British had sent a ship of 6,000 additional troops to assist General CORNWALLIS, but once they saw the large fleet of French war ships, which had recently captured the *Iris*, they turned around and headed back to British-controlled New York City. General CORNWALLIS' heart dropped; he knew that his stay was all over. He rested his left hand on his dress sword, knowing he would soon have to surrender it.

On 25 October 1781, the American vessel dropped Lieutenant KEMPER off on his native shore of the Raritan River which emptied into the Raritan Bay, just east of New Brunswick, New Jersey. He then caught a ride from a fisherman on his boat up the river to New Brunswick. On the road north leading out of town, he picked up a ride from a man in a horse and carriage who was headed to Morristown.

Once he arrived in Morristown, John found his way to his brother Daniel's house. John's sister-in-law, Jane (Branson) KEMPER (1750-1783), opened the door and exclaimed, *"John!"* John's parents, Jacob and Maria Regina KEMPER, were there visiting. Overjoyed with tears of relief, they embraced the son they thought they would never see alive again.

They sent for Daniel, along with their sister, Maria Sophia, and Mr. MORTON, and they notified Eliza HOPPER that John had escaped and returned home. They then began to nurse John back to health, which he needed because of the many hardships and sufferings he had undergone while in captivity.

Eliza HOPPER, after receiving her message from the courier, overly excited, stole a horse and carriage, left New Millstone, and quickly galloped northeast toward Daniel's house. She raced through Hillsborough (Hillsboro), New Brunswick, and then was on her way to Morristown. As she rode along, she could feel nothing; it was as if time was at a standstill.

Jacob began to fill his son John in on the events that took place in the American Revolution while he was a prisoner of war. Jacob informed John that the British Army commander Lieutenant General Lord Charles CORNWALLIS had recently surrendered on 19 October 1781 in Yorktown. Jacob closed by saying, *"There is now light at the end of the tunnel for our new country we have been fighting so hard for."*

John smiled and replied, *"I hope I am not too late for the finish."*

Mr. MORTON and Maria Sophia arrived shortly thereafter. Mr. MORTON nodded at John, saying, *"I feared I had lost my Johnny-in-law."*

John answered, *"No chance! I was just visiting the tropics."*

Mr. MORTON replied, *"Oh, sort of like a vacation?"*

John chuckled, *"Sort of. Sometimes one has to be careful not to be eaten alive on a vacation."*

Mr. MORTON then stated, *"We will talk about that another time; remember John, once your health is restored, we have business to attend to."*

John answered, *"Yes we do!"*

And then all of a sudden, the door burst open wide, and in rushed Eliza HOPPER. Quickly looking in all directions to see where everyone was, she ran into the room where John was in bed. She wrapped her arms around his neck, hugging him dearly, while kissing his cheeks and forehead all over.

John, while gasping for air, said, *"Now who could this be? It seems that someone is all grown up. It appears that she was someone worth waiting for."*

Eliza was blossoming with smiles and drenched in tears. She then stood upright and, while proudly promenading her figure, swirled around so John could see it all. Maria, while smiling, winked at Eliza.

This was the moment Eliza had dreamed and hoped for, remembering when they went to his father's tavern, and she flirted and pointed her finger at him, saying, *"You are mine! You better wait for me to grow up!"* How could a home-coming be any sweeter? John did not have to go to war in order to always be Eliza's *"knight in shining armor!"*

Then Maria Sophia and Eliza made eye contact. While smiling, Maria nodded, silently acknowledging and reminding Eliza that, she knew her brother would make it through his ordeal. It was a warm homecoming, and everyone was excited. It was good to see family once again.

Colonel Daniel KEMPER was the next to arrive home, and while exuberantly greeting his brother, he informed John that he had been with General WASHINGTON, General John MUHLENBERG, and Colonel Alexander HAMILTON when he received news of his escape and safe return.

After Daniel had broken the news of his brother's escape, all at camp hoorayed him as one of their own who finally made it home. General WASHINGTON was elated and wrote a personal letter to John. He then handed it to Daniel and excused him so that he could deliver it, along with the good tidings of other officers at camp.

Daniel started out; Colonel HAMILTON sent wishes for a rapid recovery and said, *"He will be glad to share a glass or two at city tavern on 2nd and Walnut Street, like days of old; on him."*

He said, *"He needs to go over 'certain circumstances' of which we both are familiar with and will know what he is talking about. If there is anything he can do to hasten your recovery and further assist, just let him know."*

John just nodded in acknowledgment.

Daniel respectfully asked their parents and Eliza for a moment alone with John and John (Mr. MORTON). They agreed and stepped out of the room. John slipped a note into Daniel's left hand, and in turn, Daniel slowly slipped it into his vest pocket. Daniel then took his left hand and placed it softly on John's right shoulder, saying, *"You have been a good soldier, a loyal and trusted friend to all—General WASHINGTON, myself, Congress and our country. I am very deeply honored to be able to call you my brother."*

Mr. MORTON added, *"I second that, as your brother-in-law and, your Johnny-in-law."*

Daniel continued informing John on other recent news of the Revolution. He stated that, Commodore John MANLEY and Captain Silas TALBOT, who were in Mill Prison with him, had recently been pardoned for exchange and should be home soon.

John took a deep breath, slowly exhaled, and replied, *"I am pleased it was well worth it, then."*

Shortly after their return, they met with John once again to show their gratitude for his sacrifice.

Commodore MANLEY exclaimed, *"We all know what you went through for our cause, Captain."*

Captain KEMPER answered, *"We likewise know what you went through for our cause. In the Revolution, one hand washes the other."*

Captain KEMPER then saluted Commodore MANLEY and Captain TALBOT, who both returned his salute. They then all moved on with their lives. After the Revolution, Captain TALBOT, likewise, went on to become a commodore in the US Navy.

Daniel then stated, *"General MUHLENBERG said, he is in need of a good soldier at Fort Mifflin on Mudden Island, on the Delaware River, when your health is restored. General WASHINGTON asked me to deliver his letter to you personally."*

He informed John that when he rejoined the Continental Army under General MUHLENBERG, his former rank of captain would be retained, as previously discussed. Daniel assured John that nothing had been lost in his absence.

Daniel went on to explain other ongoing events in the Revolution. He told his brother that he was fortunate he was an officer and had been sent to Mill Prison as a bargaining chip for captured British officers. The rest of his crew who had been captured along with him did not fare so well. They were all sent either to the gallows or to various prison ships and never heard from again. John bent his head in sorrow for a moment, as if saying, *"Sorry, my friends."*

John opened General WASHINGTON's letter and began reading. Even though John KEMPER's rank at this time was officially a lieutenant, General WASHINGTON always addressed his colleagues as Sir or Mr. This author's grandfather Basil WILCOX was still in possession of this letter from General WASHINGTON in 1958. He showed it to this author and expressed that it had been passed down in the family for generations. Eventually, somewhere along the line, it was either lost or stolen. Thankfully, if not for Elizabeth writing it in her diary, the contents would have been lost forever.

In this letter, General WASHINGTON started out by asking a question,

Sir, May I bow to you commemorating your service to our country in both the army and navy of the Revol.? Even though you have been gone, you have not been forgotten. We have lost many a good soldier in your absence; a good friend of ours, the Count [PULASKI] had passed on as heroically as any soldier could in combat, just prior to your capture. He left fulfilling the promise he had made to me when he reached our country, 'That he would fight, defend and live or die for our freedom,' a most honorable man. General [Marquis] LAFAYETTE, who has been deeply concerned about your well-being, has just arrived and been told of your fortitude. Remember Trenton? I can still recall the words you had to say . . . 'Boy! What a Christmas party!' All are cheering your escape; we all look forward to greeting you once again. I am Yr Most obt Servt Go. Washington.

How was General WASHINGTON privy to John's capture just after the count's death? Had General WASHINGTON unintentionally slipped in his letter to John, as he had in his letter to his cousin, Lund WASHINGTON, just after the fire in New York City? Lieutenant KEMPER had been sent on board the *Hector* to be deliberately captured so that he could infiltrate the heart of the enemy's prison systems.

John was looking for the officers who went missing in action, who General WASHINGTON suspected had been captured and were now prisoners. General WASHINGTON and the intelligence committee wanted their commodore back. John had made quite a tour of all the main British prisons, from New York City to England, never knowing for sure what targets would be located.

1. For He Is a Jolly Good Fellow!

After a much needed but short recovery at his brother Colonel Daniel KEMPER's home in Morristown, New Jersey, John quickly returned to Philadelphia, arriving in early November 1781. John and his brother Daniel joined Alexander HAMILTON at City Tavern for a glass or two, toasting for John's return—for he's a jolly good fellow! They all began sharing their stories. Colonel HAMILTON explained how General Lord Charles CORNWALLIS made a serious military blunder and got trapped on the peninsula in Yorktown.

They spoke of how the British frigate *Iris*, which captured the *Hector*, was captured by the French fleet on their way to rescue General CORNWALLIS. John then shared his prison experiences. They went on to discuss *"certain circumstances."* If Elizabeth knew what those circumstances were, she did not record them.

After they were done and said their farewells, John headed to see his brother-in-law Mr. MORTON, to pick up new business. He informed him that his new post would be at Fort Mifflin on Mudden Island located on the Delaware River and that he would be operating from that base in the meantime.

He was ready to enter into the service of his fellow comrade and officer with whom he had marched through the streets of Philadelphia and served at Valley Forge, joining the German-American regiment of General John Peter Gabriel MUHLENBERG. During this stay, he would resume being the leg-man for his brother-in-law, Mr. MORTON, who was the major financial backing for both General WASHINGTON and the Continental Congress. The *"Johnny-in-Laws"* were together once again.

After receiving a dispatch that Captain KEMPER would be returning to service, General MUHLENBERG had his guards meet and greet him at the gate to Fort Mifflin. They escorted him directly to General MUHLENBERG's headquarters, where Captain KEMPER was warmly welcomed back home and issued new orders.

General MUHLENBERG informed Captain KEMPER that he was not sure how much longer he would be in command before receiving new orders. It appeared as if things were in status quo during his service under General MUHLENBERG. However, John appeared to have gone invisible once again. There was no recorded activity. Why? We would not have known of his service under General MUHLENBERG if not for Colonel Daniel KEMPER's declaration and Elizabeth's diary entry.

Since John KEMPER was back in the army, he retained his rank as captain and served until General WASHINGTON disbanded the Continental Army on 13 June 1783. John, like so many others, joined the regular army, which was apparent as he did not appear in any civilian capacity until after returning home to New York City in February 1784; but not for very long, for in 1786, he was right back in the army as a captain, but there was no indication if he ever left the service. It is unclear if this was a military transfer or a re-enlistment in the army, as John KEMPER was clearly appointed captain over Captain Thomas LEE (1739-1814), who was demoted to John KEMPER's vice and later declined.

Captain Thomas LEE had been a captain in Company Eight of the Fifth New York Continental Regiment of infantry. Captain KEMPER's appointment solidified his importance over a captain of infantry because of his special service under General WASHINGTON and Colonel Alexander HAMILTON's recommendation and sealed orders.

On 24 November 1781, Reverend James "the Soldier Parson" CALDWELL (1734-1781), widower of the late Hannah of Connecticut Farms, was stopped at a checkpoint by an American sentry, James MORGAN (?-1782). Reverend CALDWELL was carrying a package that Mr. MORGAN ordered to have inspected.

When Reverend CALDWELL refused, Mr. MORGAN shot him. Mr. MORGAN was then arrested and found guilty of murder. It was later learned that Mr. MORGAN was bribed to find a means to kill Reverend CALDWELL. Friends and neighbors raised Reverend CALDWELL's nine children.

One of Captain John KEMPER's friends and comrade from Valley Forge, Colonel Elias BOUNDINOT, was one of the volunteers who raised the children. Colonel BOUDINOT was also a close friend and neighbor of Captain KEMPER's brother-in-law, John "the Rebel Banker" MORTON. Reverend CALDWELL also had named one of his children Elias Boudinot CALDWELL (1776-1825).

In the winter of 1781, some New Jersey law officers detained an eccentric soldier by the name of Jemmy. Jemmy, trying to get himself out of the jam he was in, told the constables that he was a good friend of Anthony WAYNE and that he should be released from jail. When a messenger addressed General WAYNE with the situation, General WAYNE became angry, refused to help Jemmy and went so far as to say if the incident was ever repeated he would order *"29 lashes well laid on."*

Jemmy replied with, *"Anthony is mad. He must be mad or he would help me. Mad Anthony, that's what he is, Mad Anthony Wayne."* Soldiers in the ranks and around the Continental campfires repeated this humorous event. Anthony WAYNE did have a temper that flared and the name "Mad" seemed appropriate and stuck as a nickname.

On 29 January 1782, James MORGAN was hung for the murder of Reverend James CALDWELL. General WASHINGTON, General Marquis DE LAFAYETTE and General Benjamin LINCOLN helped out other children of Reverend CALDWELL's, whom Mr. MORGAN orphaned. General LAFAYETTE adopted and took Reverend CALDWELL's oldest son, James Edward CALDWELL, back to France and educated him there.

Revolutionary and Continental soldiers stuck together to the end. They always went out of their way to help those who helped them make it through the difficult times and their sacrifices were never forgotten. The easiest to remember were men like Mr. MORTON, who gave his all in food, shelter, hospitalization and money. He was always there when others failed.

In her diary, John KEMPER's daughter, Elizabeth continued to cover some of the many stories her father shared with her about the Revolution. One of these stories took place when her father was in his final days under General MUHLENBERG. He was back home with friends and was no longer being controlled by others; he was free again to make his own decisions.

His tour of duty appeared to have been to stand ready to protect Philadelphia from British vessels coming up the Delaware to attack, even though the Revolution was winding down. Her father stated, *"General MUHLENBERG was as warmhearted as General WASHINGTON if you were loyal, trustworthy and sincere; making you feel wanted, needed, important and protected. General MUHLENBERG also favored German heritage and this was why he had formed a German regiment."*

Captain John KEMPER's niece, Eliza Susan, was only eight years old when her father, John MORTON, died in Basking Ridge, Somerset, New Jersey. When Eliza became a young woman, she began collecting the history on her family and started writing her memoirs. From the best of her recollection, and that of her family, she recorded that her father had died on 4 February 1782, but this was incorrect. Likewise, no one in their family could remember their father's exact birth date.

Another descendant of John MORTON's had recorded that Tories/Loyalists had caught him, but there were no British patrols in the area that they could turn him over to, so they just outright murdered him. He was then buried in an unmarked grave. Colonel Daniel KEMPER had always warned his brother

John about Loyalists; they were as deadly as the British. However, after prudent research, this author could not confirm one story over the other as to the true method of death or grave site of Mr. MORTON, other than he said, she said, until a newspaper article was found by this author that covered the story. *The Brick Academy* newspaper covered the story completely.

On 22 April 1782, as the newspaper recorded that between the hours of 11:00 p.m. and 1:00 a.m., Captain John KEMPER's sister, Maria Sophia (Kemper) MORTON, had put in for the night at their house in Basking Ridge, New Jersey. Everyone was resting peacefully, when all of a sudden a bunch of masked hoodlums forcibly broke open their front door. Three robbers entered the house; the chief, whose face was blackened and disguised by a handkerchief tied around his head and brought down to his eyes, first demanded all their keys and gold watches.

A bayonet was presented at every window and door when escape was attempted, and thus surrounded, they had no choice but to submit. They knew right where to go for the iron safe in the closet, where they removed thirty pounds of gold and silver, which had been from the sale of their home in Elizabethtown. The robbers took two hours ransacking the house and bagging everything of value.

Upon leaving, the robbers threatened to come back and burn their house if they did not remain silent. The following morning when they reported the incident to their father, John MORTON, he took his friend, Colonel Elias BOUDINOT, along with a couple of neighbors and went in pursuit of the thugs. After following their trail, they discovered that they had tied their horses to a tree and taken a boat back to British-controlled New York City.

Apparently, a team of Tories/Loyalists on the New Jersey side, including a previous employee of Mr. MORTON's, met a team from New York City. They showed them where Mr. MORTON's home was and where he kept his safe, in the closet. There was no mention whether the iron safe was one that required a number combination or a key.

Mr. MORTON was enraged over the amount of gold stolen, over $633,600 in today's money. This loss did not affect the gold Mr. MORTON had deposited in the loan office for General WASHINGTON and the Continental Congress. However, he shook with anger.

On 22 April 1782, after Mr. MORTON returned, he composed a notice to the newspaper offering fifteen gold coins for the capture of the villains. Mr. MORTON was more upset for the robbery because he had it set aside for commitments to both, General WASHINGTON and the Continental Congress. He then sent out an emergency dispatch to his brother-in-law, Captain KEMPER, and asked him to relay the current event to General WASHINGTON and the members of Congress, asking for forgiveness and a short period to rebuild the additional funds he had promised.

2. Who Killed The Goose That Laid the Golden Eggs?

A few days later, on 27 April 1782, Mr. MORTON, under stress and fatigue, had an attack of apoplexy (stroke) and died. The funeral was conducted by the Reverend Samuel KENNEDY (1720-1787) of the Presbyterian Church. The end result was that the British had finally dislodged a thorn in their side; they had killed the goose that laid the golden eggs. The British put a feather in their hat by finally getting one of their own, which boosted their ego; however, the last battle of the Revolution had been fought in Yorktown, and the war was over.

What Maria's friend Anna HOPPER had wished would not happen to her, in fact, did. Now Maria's children had to go on in life without their father, as the HOPPER family did. All families, in some way, had casualties due to the American Revolution.

After Mr. MORTON's death, the same messenger who was sent to notify General WASHINGTON, was sent to notify Mr. and Mrs. Jacob and Maria KEMPER in Germantown, New Jersey. Mr. and Mrs. KEMPER left Germantown to reside with their daughter, Maria Sophia MORTON and attend the funeral. Dr. David and Susan (Kemper) JACKSON came in from Philadelphia to join the family. Dr. KENNEDY performed the services at the funeral; and the procession, attended by a concourse of people, proceeded to the burial ground on the hill, near the church of Basking Ridge. Colonel Elias BOUDINOT, Maria Sophia, and her oldest son, Jacob MORTON (1761-1836), from Princeton, were appointed executors to Mr. MORTON's will; and the last two fulfilled the trust.

After diligent research into the interment records of the Presbyterian Church, by this author, found no record of John MORTON's interment. However, there was a record of Reverend Samuel KENNEDY's interment. Whenever a researcher is trying to verify an account in history, it can often become difficult, especially if a person or a newspaper accidentally records some wrong information. This happened to this author as well when the press was covering his story. It is obvious that Reverend KENNEDY conducted the funeral, but somehow, the press accidentally recorded that he was interred in the Presbyterian Church cemetery, but in fact, it was not recorded there.

It was later determined that the British had sent a bunch of Tories/Loyalists to rob *"the Rebel Banker,"* John MORTON, in order to interrupt his funding of the Continental Congress and Continental Army. Mr. MORTON had loaned hundreds of thousands of dollars (in today's money) to the Continental Congress, in addition to outfitting his brothers-in-law—Daniel, Jacob, and John KEMPER. Mr. MORTON also spent his own money to outfit many other Continental soldiers who were willing to fight. Mr. MORTON had become a thorn in the British side and had to be removed as he was making the war last longer than it should have.

On 7 August 1782, from his headquarters at Newburgh, New York, General George WASHINGTON issued the following order:

"The General ever desirous to cherish virtuous ambition in his soldiers as well as to foster and encourage every species of Military merit, directs that whenever any singularly meritorious action is performed, the author of it shall be permitted to wear on his facings over the left breast, the figure of a heart in purple cloth or silk, edged with narrow lace or binding. Not only instances of unusual gallantry, but also of extraordinary fidelity and essential service in any way shall meet with due reward.

Before this favor can be conferred on any man, the particular fact, or facts, on which it is to be grounded must be set forth to the Commander-in-chief accompanied with certificates from the Commanding officers of the regiment and brigade to which the Candidate for regard belonged, or other incontestable proofs, and upon granting it, the name and regiment of the person with the action so certified are to be enrolled in the Book of Merit which will be kept at the orderly office. Men who have merited this last distinction to be suffered to pass all guards and sentinels which officers are permitted to do. [This book has never been found!]

*The road to glory is a patriot army and a free country is thus open to **all**. This order is also to have retrospect to the earlier stages of the war, and to be considered as a permanent one.*

The Badge of Military Merit was the first decoration given in America and the second in the world. On 22 February 1932, on the anniversary of George WASHINGTON's two hundredth birthday, the name was officially changed to the Purple Heart.

In April 1942, the War Department amended its policy regarding the issuance of the Purple Heart and eliminated the use of the medal as a meritorious award. On 5 September 1942, the War Department announced that the Purple Heart would now be exclusively awarded for those wounded or killed in action only!

It is evident here that the administration in 1942 was unable to come up with its own unique design for an award given to those who were being wounded or killed in action, so stole General WASHINGTON's thunder, which probably rolled him over in his grave. This incredible award was no longer available to any soldier who performed meritorious service, bringing shame and disgrace to both soldiers and the late General WASHINGTON. One can only hope that General WASHINGTON's ghost will forever haunt them.

Captain John KEMPER was obviously entitled to this award, but being the kind of humble man he was, he never put in for any awards or money for his special service under General WASHINGTON. However, his descendants wanted his distinguished service recognized, since it was retroactive, and forever recorded in history. However, its original intention by General WASHINGTON had been changed two hundred years later, making it extremely difficult, if not impossible, to obtain.

On 30 November 1782, a peace treaty was signed in Paris. The French were upset that this was done without their consent. Benjamin FRANKLIN negotiated and settled things down. Mr. FRANKLIN seemed to have some sort of magical ability in working things out with differences of opinion.

Chapter XXI
Broken Promises

On 10 March 1783, General WASHINGTON's senior officers, camped in Newburgh, New York, planned a march on Congress with swords for broken promises regarding their commitments and obligations to fulfill the much-needed back pay for the Continental Army. Back in 1780, Congress had solemnly guaranteed all Continental officers a pension of half pay for life.

On 15 March 1783, General WASHINGTON maintained his integrity by gathering all his officers and calmly derailed the Continental Army's action against Congress, once again. As this author said at the start of this story, Congress had made many wise decisions during this period of time, but appointing George WASHINGTON as commander-in-chief of the Continental Army and Continental Navy was the most important.

He went on to break up what would have been another military takeover of our country, thereby preserving the democracy we all cherish today; majority rule. Although our government might be molded or modified differently in the future, for now it was a good start. General's Horatio GATES and Israel PUTNAM were among the Continental officers planning an assault on Congress. Whenever General WASHINGTON was on the scene, his very presence alone commanded attention and it was given. However, at this time he lost the respect of his Continental officers for not being there for them, when they were always there for him.

What was not known at the time or made clearly visible throughout history was, General WASHINGTON was the world's first and only congressional general. He always took the side of the Continental Congress over the military as if he was one of them. All attempts by his junior officers to have him removed and replaced with General Horatio GATES or whomever they thought would better suffice, went in vain. There were just too many chiefs and not enough Indians.

Congress was not about to replace one of their own; they had molded General WASHINGTON to their liking. General WASHINGTON never showed respect for his officers by addressing them by their rank, but in fact, always addressed them by sir or Mr. in all correspondences. Even after the Revolution, when our new country was getting organized, George WASHINGTON did not pick one of his Continental officers to run with him when he ran for the presidency, even though he supposedly grew close to them every day at camp. He in fact, chose John ADAMS, a member of Congress. He never allowed the military to be ranked over members of Congress.

Unlike the Congress of today's America, which is officially elected, the Continental Congress of 1775-1783 was merely a group of men. They were respected men, delegates in their own states' territory, who were banded together to form an inherent power, self-appointing themselves into the position of making decisions on behalf of the colonists and the army. They had no lawful jurisdiction to do so. They were a group of rebels fighting against the Crown, which 65 to 75 percent of the population favored.

Because the Continental Congress in reality had no authority, this meant that any and all resolutions that they wrote were worth less than the paper on which they were written. The resolutions themselves were very effective and were what was needed if, indeed, they could have been backed up like they would be in today's Congress. The system they molded later became law, when they officially acquired the power to do so and is still in use today.

The Continental Congress had no authority to enforce the resolutions, nor was there any way they could be held accountable for not fulfilling them. They were under false pretenses and only looked like they were accomplishing something. They had good intentions and most of their decisions were indeed worthy. At times, however, they were forced by circumstances to go against their better judgment, definitely not favored by the colonists, and seized what was needed for the good of the Continental Army, which in the long run benefited everyone.

On 11 April 1783, Congress officially declared an end to the Revolutionary War. Now, all Americans, who truly deserved and could claim this title, could start rebuilding their lives. The only colonists who were true Americans were the ones who broke away from the British control and fought in and supported the American Revolution. Many Continental soldiers returned to their homes with empty pockets, but were happy to be home to start a new life in a newly established country that was now their own.

The 65 percent who did not fight and remained here were granted the title Americans, by the true Americans, even though they had never earned it by fighting for it. Although we celebrate the birth of America as beginning with the signing of the Declaration of Independence on 4 July 1776, America was not officially a nation of its own until Congress declared an end to the Revolutionary War on 11 April 1783.

By 29 April 1783, lands of the Loyalists went up on the auction block for sale. They were once the ones who had everything to lose. Now they were losing everything; they had put their faith in the wrong army. Over one hundred thousand Loyalists, in fear for their lives, fled America to British-controlled locations like Canada, Haiti, the Caribbean Islands and England.

The Tories/Loyalists and neutralists had truly believed that the British were going to win the war, and they might have if not for the French assistance. Now, they had nowhere to hide, so they had to run. There was nowhere in America for these kinds of people for they were deceptive and treacherous.

In May 1783, after Colonel Daniel and his brother Captain Jacob KEMPER had been successful in organizing the Society of Cincinnati, as founding members, they held their first meeting. At this meeting they rallied to have General WASHINGTON elected to be their first president general. All in attendance agreed with the KEMPER brothers. On this same date, their brother Captain John KEMPER was discharged from the Continental Army, but had to continue to clear up accounts for his sister, Maria Sophia MORTON, with General WASHINGTON and the Continental Congress.

Both Daniel and Jacob tried to coax their brother Captain John KEMPER into aiding them in organizing the Society of Cincinnati. However, Captain KEMPER was tied up settling affairs for their late brother-in-law, John MORTON, with both General WASHINGTON and Congress. He was successful, and Congress ordered all loans, plus interest, to be paid to Mr. MORTON's widow, Maria Sophia (Kemper) MORTON.

This settlement by Congress enabled Mrs. MORTON and her family to live a comfortable life, in addition to providing a decent education for her children. Her son Jacob MORTON became a major general in the US Army. In later years, her other son, John MORTON Jr. (1765-1835), ended up giving a declaration of his memory of his uncle, Colonel Daniel KEMPER's service during the American Revolution.

On 13 June 1783, the main contingency of the Continental Army was disbanded; however, many of the troops who wanted to stay in the military became part of the regular army. Many complained for back pay but never received it. The navy, likewise, dismantled its war ships in preparation for peace. When most leaders in history become incredible conquerors, they cannot stop fighting. They start executing their officers who made them what and who they are, when they differed in opinion.

Conquerors—like Alexander the Great (356 BC—323 BC), Mark ANTONY and Cleopatra, Constantine the Great (AD 272—AD 337), Napoleon BONAPARTE, and Adolph HITLER—could not stop conquering. They all ended up being the cause of their own demise. General George WASHINGTON did not go out to conquer new lands; he was a defender. When peace was negotiated, the war was over, and he surrendered his sword. He became the father of what would become one of the most powerful countries on earth. *"He who defends his country and people is God blessed!"*

On 24 June 1783, Congress, under as much fear from the Continental Army veterans as it had been when General HOWE captured Philadelphia, once again had to flee America's capital for safety in Princeton, New Jersey. Congress, who had no money to pay the Continental soldiers during the American Revolution, were in worse shape now. The amount of debt owed the Continentals had accumulated to a huge amount of uncountable hundreds of thousands. They had no income during the Revolution other than running off paper money on the press.

The money they ran off would be pretty much the same as a group of men in today's society, breaking off and doing the same thing. Anyone can design his or her own money, but it will be unrecognized and worthless, as Monopoly game money; easy money is never easy. Congress could only now begin taxing the people of their new country, thereby creating its first real revenue as a nation.

On 25 November 1783, a cold, frosty, but clear and brilliant morning, the British evacuated the city of New York. Captain John KEMPER's cousin, Major Sebastian BEAUMAN, commandant of artillery, under General Henry KNOX, who had been the last to evacuate New York City upon the British invasion, was now the first to enter the city on the British evacuation. He gave the order to haul down the British flag and hoist the American flag on the Battery before the British even left the harbor.

They released a roar of artillery on the Battery bolstering the raising of the American flag. As the British looked back as their ships left the harbor, the skyline was filled with fireworks surrounding the American flag. The cheers were as loud as the fireworks; a new age had begun. After the British evacuated, all factions against the rebel resistance faded away into obscurity and dissipated. Now our new nation could move forward.

After the British had evacuated New York City, refugees who had fled the city in fear started slowly returning. Eliza HOPPER, along with her mother, Anna, and sister Maria (Polly), likewise, returned. Her sister Anna (Anny) had already been married to John VAN NORDWYK. The city was in shambles from the British occupation and evacuation, so everyone had to start to rebuild their lives all over again.

On 4 December 1783, General WASHINGTON said farewell to some of his officers at Fraunces Tavern on Broad Street in New York City. This meeting took place in the long room on the second floor. However, General WASHINGTON had lost the respect of most of the officers of the Continental Army back in March in Newburgh. He did not know more than a half of a dozen men in the room. The rest just wanted to claim that they were there at his final farewell.

He was seen with tears in his eyes as he said, *"With a heart full of love and gratitude, I now take leave of you, I most devoutly wish that your latter days may be as prosperous and happy, as your former ones have been glorious and honorable."* Colonel Benjamin TALLMADGE dressed this farewell up years later in his memoirs because he could empathize with General WASHINGTON.

Now that General WASHINGTON had announced his final departure, other Continental officers began to follow suit. Captain John KEMPER was asked to meet with his brothers Captain Jacob and Colonel Daniel KEMPER, as well as Colonel Alexander HAMILTON, for a private celebration at City Tavern in Philadelphia.

After Captain KEMPER entered the tavern, he looked around to find his brothers and Colonel HAMILTON over in a secluded corner, under dim lamplight. They all had smiles on their faces. John immediately cocked his head to the left, while clinching his right fist diagonally and as if striking an invisible object, acknowledging an incredible victory. John's brothers and Colonel HAMILTON returned the striking fist acknowledgement with glee. Many other private celebrations took place around the country.

Over the next few years, all records like those kept by the clothier-general James MEASE, proving all the thousands owed to Continental officers, mysteriously disappeared. The disappearance of these records wiped out not only the amount of thousands owed each of the officers, like Colonel Daniel KEMPER, but of utmost importance, the proof of their service and history as well. The clothier-general's department was the only department in which Colonel Daniel and Captain John KEMPER's service would have been recorded. All Continental officers who knew these brothers' involvement personally were passing on rapidly.

The quartermaster, commissary, and clothier departments served all regiments of the Continental Army. The officers' records of the contribution to the history of the birth of America were now gone. Only the records of General George WASHINGTON and his senior staff remained intact. The documents of the lower-ranking officers were scarce. Since Captain John and Colonel Daniel KEMPER served directly under General WASHINGTON, their involvement and backing from the top brass and statesmen as well were more difficult to erase, nevertheless they tried.

Now that the Congress declared that the Revolution was over, our country could begin to forge itself as a new nation. Alexander HAMILTON became its first secretary of the treasury. The War Department began collecting all military records on the Revolution. Although the Revolution was over, for Captain John KEMPER, it would never be over! In the upcoming pension years, he was forced to relive it over and over and over again!

In the upcoming pension years, civilians got their revenge against Captain KEMPER in an uncanny way. They prevented him from getting the rightful amount of pension as captain and wagon master. They stripped him of his rank of captain, claiming that his service as wagon master was, in fact, civilian; therefore, he was ineligible to receive a pension. They demoted him from lieutenant in the United States Navy, back to midshipman. This damage was just the beginning.

After the Revolution, Captain KEMPER, like his close friend and comrade from Philadelphia and Valley Forge, Colonel Alexander HAMILTON, maintained strong military ties. He continued his service in the American Army; then Colonel HAMILTON sent him, under sealed orders, to Hudson, New York. Another friend and comrade from Valley Forge, Captain Anthony MAXWELL, joined him a few years later. Even though John moved upstate, he always stayed in close contact with his older and closest brother, Colonel Daniel KEMPER, through letters and occasional visits.

In mid-December 1783, President George WASHINGTON was elected as the first president general of the Society of Cincinnati. By this time, most all Continental officers were together again. General Marquis De LAFAYETTE was honored in bestowing upon Colonel Daniel KEMPER the Badge of the Society of Cincinnati. This honor was in remembrance of the day when

Colonel KEMPER was responsible for saving his life at the Battle of Brandywine. President WASHINGTON approved.

On 23 December 1783, General George WASHINGTON resigned his position as commander-in-chief before General Thomas MIFFLIN, president of Congress. He then went home a private citizen subject to politicians he neither respected nor admired. After King George III heard of General WASHINGTON returning to Mount Vernon as a private citizen, he gasped, *"If he does that, he will be the greatest man in the world!"* King George knew what it took to become the world's greatest man, but did not have the stuff to do it himself. He was not about to sacrifice his power of a king to become a private citizen; no king ever had. In retrospect, King George admired General WASHINGTON, who always treated his enemies with respect and never held grudges.

Chapter XXII
When Johnny comes Marching Home
(The Forage Master)

Captain John KEMPER and his childhood sweetheart, Eliza HOPPER had spent many years apart and the only means of contact they had had was through correspondence. The many letters they had written back and forth were delivered by Mr. MARTIN. He was "the Post" (mail carrier) and a family friend. His route was between Philadelphia and New Brunswick. For personal reasons for the family he had gone as far as the in-laws, the MORTONS in Basking Ridge, New Jersey. Eliza often received updates on John's endeavors from his sister, Maria Sophia (Kemper) MORTON.

Eliza had spent many countless hours and days wondering if John was safe. She had been informed by his sister Maria Sophia (Kemper) MORTON that the ship *Hector*, which John had embarked on, had gone out to sea and had not returned to port in Philadelphia. John was then considered missing in action and the status of his well-being was unknown. The worry and wait was unbearable. She drove her mother, Anna, crazy with her worry and anxiety. She wondered if her dream of John being her husband would ever happen. She had grown into a, beautiful young woman and, more than ever, wanted John to see her now.

Colonel Daniel KEMPER was obliged by military standards and protocol never to reveal more intelligence than was necessary for the protection of his brother and fellow Continental officers. This was a terrible struggle for Colonel KEMPER—to be between his family and the loyalty to his country. Neither Eliza nor his parents, nor anyone for that matter, could be told anything different. Everything was kept in an elite circle of Continental officers. He could not even put them at ease.

On 10 January 1784, John wrote to his childhood sweetheart, Elizabeth (Eliza) HOPPER, who, by then, was all grown up, that by February he would be coming home. Eliza was ecstatic about John's homecoming and had innocently spread the news throughout the area. Civilians, on the other hand, had plans of their own for Captain KEMPER's homecoming. Now they knew he was on his way.

On 15 February 1784, after the American Revolution, Captain John KEMPER returned home to New York City, which had a population of about twenty thousand. He, like many others returning home found their homes and businesses occupied by Tories/Loyalists. He was greeted by angry Tories/Loyalists throwing vegetables, fruits, and eggs at him, yelling, *"Forage-Master!"* Captain KEMPER had acquired quite a reputation during his feats for the Continental Army. Word had spread far and wide, *"There was no master like the forage-master, Captain John KEMPER!"*

It was also well known that he hated Tories/Loyalists as he considered them soldiers and puppets of the British Empire. Captain KEMPER never killed any Tories, but he never showed them any favor either. They were ignored and never tolerated in his company.

Captain KEMPER had become a target of Loyalists for all he had done to keep the army alive at the civilians' expense. From Philadelphia to New York City, Captain KEMPER had become hated as General WASHINGTON's man who did his dirty work. Captain KEMPER had to seek employment through those who favored the Revolution, like new businesses of the city of New York being started by retiring Continental soldiers.

Loyalists who had owned everything and were hoping to have the Americans as slaves after the Revolution, were now about to lose it all for their support of the Crown. There was no longer an army left to protect them; they had evacuated and fled to England, taking many Loyalists with them.

Upon his return, Captain **KEMPER** and Eliza realized that the time and distance they had been apart had not diminished their feelings for each other but, instead had strengthened their love and devotion. They immediately started making preparations for their marriage. During this period of time, Eliza noticed a change in John and commented to him, *"John, before you joined the army, you were so full of life, happy-go-lucky. Now you seem to have changed, more serious; what happened?"*

John replied, *"I see the world differently now, Eliza; war has a way of opening your eyes to reality, letting you know how precious life really is."*

He continued, *"During my time as a prisoner of war, I witnessed personally how both the British army and navy commanders were ruthless in their treatment and cruelty of American prisoners. When stories of murder and torture of your fellow comrades come to you in stories or rumors, it is typical to wonder how accurately they really are, until you become personally involved."*

John closed by saying, *"General WASHINGTON, who knew about the cruelty the British treated the American prisoners with, never took revenge and treated the British prisoners with kindness and humanity. That had to be tough."*

All their correspondences through the Revolution were later passed down to their daughter, Elizabeth **KEMPER**, who had been named after her mother, Elizabeth (Eliza) **HOPPER**. If not for having passed everything down to their daughter, everything would have been lost forever. Elizabeth later transcribed all her father's journals and other papers and books from German to English but kept the originals for nostalgia.

John had moved to 3 Partition Street in New York City. It was away from the hustle and bustle of the city and close to the Hudson River, where John grew up as a young man. In addition, it was just about two miles south of his parent's estate in Greenwich; if they ever needed help, he was close by. John's whole family was sorry about the loss of John MORTON but was grateful that the war was over and everyone else had returned safely. Everyone got together joyously to make plans for their future. First, John had to get with his sister, Maria, privately.

John had been holding on to some personal effects for Mr. MORTON during the Revolution that he now turned over to his sister, Maria Sophia (Kemper) MORTON. John sat down with Maria and told her many of the business involvements he had with her husband, General WASHINGTON, and Congress, of which she knew only some. He then remarked, *"You know sis, if someone had been thrown overboard, then history would surely have changed, and the family would never have gotten the chance to meet such a great man."*

Maria softly smiled and said, *"Thanks John!"*

John told his sister that the British needed to interrupt Mr. MORTON's financing of General WASHINGTON and the Continental Congress. They did not know that he would not be home, nor that it would end up in his death; and unfortunately, nor did they care. They got the goose that laid the golden eggs. Although Congress made sure that his business continued to function, it was definitely not the same without him at the head of it, and had no intentions of cheating his family.

Unfortunately, General WASHINGTON and the Continental Congress, unlike their own, unintention-ally overlooked her husband's safety. They took him for granted and, like many, did not realize what they had until it had been lost. Because he was not military or congressional, it was easily overlooked. However, in trying to right their wrong, they made sure that his family received all the monies due him, plus interest.

In addition, Mr. MORTON, besides entertaining General WASHINGTON personally at their home, gave many contributions of valuable commodities to General WASHINGTON, Congress, Captain KEMPER, and his wagon train, for which there was no charge. John was the go-between. Furthermore, Mr. MORTON had continued his prospects during John's stint in the US Navy. He did the best he could do without his wagon transportation; Mr. MORTON knew the circumstances.

Captain KEMPER closed by stating: *"Mr. [John] ADAMS once told me that Congress viewed Mr. MORTON as the Goose that laid the Golden Eggs. General WASHINGTON thought of him as a man who could heal a whole army and keep it going against all odds, providing hope and proving what good could come from gold. I rather think of my brother-in-law as a man whose heart was so big, that it weighed him down heavily."*

Congress had made sure that Mr. MORTON's widow, Maria and their family received all compensation due them from her husband's extraordinary loans, plus interest. Again, John had been the go-between to make sure all settlements were complete. This was one of the few exceptions that Congress made to pay its debts, besides paying General Marquis DE LAFAYETTE $200,000. Mr. MORTON's and Mr. LAFAYETTE's accounts were the main ones they felt obliged to settle. Mr. MORTON was the main financial ingredient to the success of the Revolution.

John continued, *"One of the many valuable lessons in life and humanity Mr. MORTON taught me was when he told me, 'The most important deeds, treasures and assistance would come from good friends and loved ones.' They would see what you needed to continue on your path and get the job done without ever asking for anything in return." In fact, he said, 'you will never know they were doing it until after it is finished.' Mr. MORTON gave much more than he ever received in return."*

This discussion into Mr. MORTON's importance during the Revolution helped give closure to Maria's loss. Maria thanked John for sharing a little insight into the mechanics of the Revolution that very few others knew went on. Maria told John, *"My husband liked working with you and wanted you to come into business with him after the Revolution."*

John replied, *"I know, he told me, I would have liked that. He was like a candle light that could never be blown out. I miss Mr. MORTON dearly."*

Maria softly smiled and said, *"I do too."*

She then once again softly smiled and said, *"It looks like the baby in the family became a giant in the Revolution."*

John slowly lowered his head then looked back up at his sister and replied, *"My older sister, the one with all the wisdom. But, I am not really a giant, just fortunate enough to be placed in the right position to be of use for a good cause."*

Maria then exclaimed, *"More likely, the right man, in the right place, at the right time in the history of the birth of America, much like General WASHINGTON."*

John once again lowered his head then looked back up at his sister and said, *"Only someone in the family could be so kind to make that sort of comment."*

Maria replied, *"One good remark deserves another. General WASHINGTON and Lord STIRLING was just a couple of the many who stopped by with their blessings on my husband's fate. You go now and stay in touch."*

She then looked intensely at John and said, *"Listen John, there is something I need to get off my chest. When we sent notice to Eliza that you had finally escaped and returned safely home, she was so excited she stole that horse and carriage. She was fortunate that it was from friends of the family who later married in; otherwise, the outcome could have been much different."*

After John contemplated his sister's concerns, knowing that the subject was going to pop up sooner or later, he warmly responded, *"I know, Sis, like you I found out afterwards; Eliza called it a loan. I contacted the VAN NORTWICKS and offered to pay them any compensation for whatever losses they felt were due them. They just commented that, at first, when they found their horse and carriage missing, they thought hoodlums had taken it. After they found out it was Eliza and her reasons, after she had returned their property, they understood and let it ride."*

John then abruptly addressed his sister, *"Sis, I am going to have to move, there are too many Loyalist still around that would love to have my head. I was ambushed just the other day, but was able to narrowly make my escape by jumping into the river; however, they got my horse."*

Maria chuckled. *"I heard; poor Eliza. That is what you get for naming a horse after your childhood sweetheart; everyone wants your girl."* John chuckled.

John chuckled and said, *"Like our grandfather, I always wanted to keep her in my heart and on my mind. I often spoke to the horse as if it were Eliza."*

Maria said, *"I bet she got special treatment, too."*

John warmly nodded, *"Oooooh yeah!"*

Maria said, *"Good, there is nothing wrong with that."*

John said, *"You know, Sis, when I lost my horse, I learned something new in life."*

Maria said, *"What is that, John?"*

John said, *"When you lose something that is part of you, rather human or animal, a part of you goes with it."*

Maria said, *"Yes it does."*

She then softly asked, *"Where are you going to go now, John?"*

John said, *"Colonel* [Alexander] *HAMILTON seems to think he will have a task for me to assist in, upstate. They are starting a new city and want to name it after the explorer, Hendrick HUDSON* [ca.1568-1611], *who discovered the Hudson River."*

He went on, *"They are creating a city for ex-Revolutionary soldiers to settle at a location called Claverack Landing. There are still some details that need to be worked out. Colonel Hendrick VAN RENSSELAER* [1742-1814] *is working on it now. It will be sort of like a get-a-way from the larger cities like, New York and Philadelphia. There, we will be able to break away from the resentment in our home towns and have a chance at a new start in life."*

Maria then closed by saying, *"You go now and stay in touch."*

They smiled, embraced, kissed each other on the cheek and said their good-byes.

As John was leaving, Maria added her feelings, *"John I am so glad that you were the go-between in settling my husband's accounts between General WASHINGTON and Congress; however, I never believed, for one moment, that they would ever try to cheat our family."*

John said, *"They did not!"*

Continually not being able to leave each other's company, Maria said, *"You know John, our mother* [Maria Regina], *although always singing with such a sweet and lovely voice, constantly brings sad tidings and melancholy to all of us, including her grandchildren."*

John said, *"I know, she constantly relives her memories, both good and bad, which continue to consume and haunt her. The songs of Zion that she sings in our native language* [German], *always carried her memories swiftly back across the great ocean to Germany. She never did leave the homeland."*

After John and Maria said their good-byes, John went to his childhood sweetheart, Eliza **HOPPER**, to discuss starting a family and planning their future.

Eliza said to John, *"Honey, you know, you are so different than your father."*

John replied, *"And my father is so different from his. You know the old saying, 'Like father, like son,' I feel is incorrect. I feel it is more accurate to say, 'Like father, like daughter, like mother, like son.'"*

He continued, *"My father* [Jacob], *other than having his hereditary military commanding rights being passed down on Stahleck Castle from his father, was never military. While his father* [Johann], *my grandfather, was a full colonel in the Prussian wars. He served two Kings and an Emperor. Now I ask you, how different can a father and son be? We all have different paths and destinies we must follow."*

Eliza softly grinned, acknowledging John's answer.

He closed by saying, *"My father could have joined the Imperial Army, but he did not. His destiny was to come to a new land, America. By doing so, he prepared a new path for his children to decide their own destinies. It would have ended up entirely different if my parents had stayed in Germany. History has been changed and for the better for all."*

On 24 February 1784, as recorded in family Bible records, John KEMPER became a building contractor. It was ordered by the committee of audit accounts that *"John KEMPER be paid for glaziers work on public lamps and to the goal and Almshouse* [hospital] *for the city of New York."* He remained in the city until 1786, when he moved to Hudson, New York.

On 12 May 1784, the clerk ordered a bond to pay John KEMPER in full for his account of glazing at city hall and lamps. John stayed closely involved with the city.

On 15 July 1784, John and Eliza decided on taking a horseback ride through the country. As they walked to the stables to get the horses, John asked, *"Where would you like to go, baby?"*

Eliza replied, *"Anywhere, why not start at your father's tavern for old times' sake, then your old tree fort, the Eagle's Nest, at the edge of the swamp?"*

John said, *"Good idea, but how are you going to ride a horse in a dress?"*

Eliza said, *"Let me show you, help me up."*

John helped Eliza up on her horse and she positioned herself sideways.

Eliza said, *"This is the way a lady rides a horse."*

John smiling away lowered his head and shook it from side to side and said, *"That is the first time I heard that one. However, I doubt that you would be able to out run a British raiding party, riding side-saddle."*

Eliza responded, *"You do not know that. You have not seen this young lady ride a horse since we were kids."*

John's smile slowly faded away, and he said, *"Has it been that long?"*

Eliza replied, *"John, you have been a way at war for a very long time."*

John looked up at the sky as a hawk hovering above was screeching and caught his attention. He slowly said, *"It did not seem very long. During the Revolution, somehow, time just seem to rush by. I still cannot believe that it is all over, and yet now, now it seems like so long ago. How can that be?"*

Eliza said, *"I don't know, honey. I never could understand why men always have to fight. If it is not in war, then they are fighting each other in taverns."*

John patted Eliza on her side hip and said, *"Enough of this, let us take that ride."*

John leapt up on his horse, and they slowly trotted toward Kemper's Tavern.

After they arrived at the tavern, it appeared so desolate, having survived time. They both stood dazed for a moment, quenched in old memories. Eliza said. *"I can still see Madam Ursula."*

John replied, *"So can I, I saw her throughout the whole war."*

Eliza turned to John and asked, *"What do you mean?"*

John said, *"Her fortune telling on my future haunted me throughout the Revolution, and still does."*

Eliza said, *"Her predictions seemed so sound; I wonder what ever happened to her."*

John said, *"I wonder, maybe the British got her; she was a beautiful woman, they would have ravished her."*

Eliza said, *"That seems sad, maybe she got away with the rest of the refugees like my family, when General WASHINGTON ordered evacuation."*

John responded, *"Maybe. I can still see someone dancing on the bar; who could that be?"*

Eliza burst out laughing, *"I have no idea, just some dizzy gal hoping to have her fortune told."*

Eliza's laughter turned silent, and she asked John, *"What ever happened to Lone WOLF? Your letters were filled with him."*

John took in a deep breath, and slowly exhaled, *"I suppose they were. I had to discharge him, along with the rest of my army just before I joined the navy. He went galloping north up Front Street in Philadelphia, heading back towards the Hudson Valley Region. I never did see him again. I miss him a lot."*

Eliza, agreeing with John, said, *"He was kind of a colorful character. I can still remember when he recommended to your father that he serve me a whiskey so that I could grow fast."*

Now John burst out laughing, exclaiming, *"Oh my God, I forgot all about that."*

Eliza continued, *"You may have, but I most assuredly did not."*

John continued, *"He brought me a lot of laughs, both at camp and on the trail. Now Bouncing BEAR, you did not meet him, but he was another one of my Indian scouts. Both he and Lone WOLF just could not get along. I had to keep them separated so that they would not try to kill each other; and that was not easy to do. I had to be constantly on my guard."*

Eliza, after a moment of thinking to herself, she said, *"You know, John, when we were kids, I used to hope that you would teach me things, but you never did."*

John replied, *"I had to wait for you to grow up, remember?"*

Eliza said, *"Some wait for people to grow up to teach them, some do not. Some think the younger you are when you learn something, the better you become."*

John said, *"Listen sweetheart, when I was a young man I had other things on my mind."*

Eliza then said, *"Like a hornet's nest?"*

Now, John burst out laughing again, *"Take it easy on me, I was just a young man out exploring the world and trying to understand it."*

Eliza then said, *"You know, John, I am not a little kid any more, I am all grown up."*

John said, *"It must have been the whiskey!"*

Eliza said, *"I'll give you a whiskey. You are lucky your father's tavern is not opened, I would go in there and grab a bottle and christen you with it."*

John then said, *"Sorry, Red!"*

Eliza said, *"Do not call me Red, I am a strawberry blonde, as she pulled her fingers slowly down through her curls laying over her chest."*

John said, *"Ooooooooooooooooops."*

Eliza then said, *"You know, honey, when we were kids, I used to look into your sparkling blue eyes and think I was heaven-bound."*

John quickly cut in, *"Alright, alright, I know where this is leading, Miss green eyes."*

Eliza was smiling profusely as John cut her off, knowing on what she had intended for the finish. There was something special that happened to them when they were kids; it was considered their childhood secret and nobody else's.

John continued, *"Since the Revolution is over, let us go and see if the fort still stands."*

Eliza said, *"Now that is a good idea! Maybe we can do some things in the fort that we never could before. After all, young people only do what comes naturally."*

While smiling and softly laughing, John said, *"Alright, alright, let us go."*

Eliza said, *"Dear, I am trying to be romantic!"*

John said, *"I know, I know. Let us first see what shape that fort is in. It is funny how time changes everything."*

On 8 December 1784, it was ordered that Mr. Recorder issue warrants on the treasurer to pay John KEMPER's two accounts in full; one for repairs of lamps and one for the glaze works for the city hall and barracks.

In 1785, Jacob and Maria Regina KEMPER returned to New York City and settled in a house close to their daughter Maria Sophia MORTON. Maria Sophia had returned to the city in 1783, after the death of her husband, John MORTON, in Basking Ridge, New Jersey, and after peace was concluded. John got together with his brother's, Daniel and Jacob, and sister Maria, to welcome their parents back to the city.

After Jacob and Maria Regina got situated, their father, Jacob started things out by saying, *"You have all served our top leaders in establishing our new country as your grandfather had served two Kings in Prussia and an Emperor. If he could have been alive to witness this moment in time, he would have been as proud of all of you as we are."*

Maria added to the conversation by saying, *"It is good that the family can finally reunite after such a long war. All the pain and uncertainty of what the final moment would result in is finally settled; and we are all content."*

Maria Sophia's daughter, Eliza Susan, then rolled out a silver platter filled with coffee, punch, hors d'oeuvres, and other refreshments for the family. After everyone was taken care of, Eliza began playing her piano softly at a low tone so as not to drown out the family conversations, but bring comfort. Maria Regina, being delighted with hearing the German songs that had been maintained in the family, hummed along with the music.

At this family gathering, both Daniel and John announced their wedding plans to the family. Maria started by saying to John, *"Since Eliza has met her part of the pact, can we now assume that you are going to meet yours?*

John said, *"Yes you can."*

Maria continued, *"Since you are now going to be marrying into Royalty, and Eliza is going to be making you her King, how does your family address you now, as 'Your Majesty?'"*

While softly smiling and lowering his head, John responded, *"Maria, since you, Daniel and our parents have always instilled in me the importance of following my own path and destiny in life, you can all address or call me anything you want."*

Maria said, *"Well now, let us just settle for addressing you as either our loving brother, uncle or son."*

John warmly replied, *"Good enough."*

John was marrying into royalty. Eliza had descended from the Scandinavian kings and queens of Denmark, Sweden, Norway, Poland, and all the Eastern European countries. She also descended from Lady Godiva (980-1067) and the emperors of the Byzantium Empire in Constantinople and the Holy Roman Empire, under Charlemagne (742-814).

Her lines then descended from the Carolina kings and the Roman Empire, on down from Augustus Caesar of Rome and Mark ANTONY, through both of his wives, Octavia and Cleopatra, and the pharaohs of Egypt; and Alexander "the Great."

She also descended from Pompey "the Great,' of Rome, Herod "the Great (73BC-4BC)," king of Judea; and Zenobia, Julia Aurelia (ca.240-aft.274), Warrior Queen of Palmyra. Her lines of royalty were as plush as could be.

On 11 April 1785, it was ordered that Mr. Mayor issue his warrant on the treasurer that John KEMPER be paid for repairing city lamps.

On 22 April 1785, Hudson had been incorporated as a city to include territory in the boundaries of the Stockport Creek on the north, the Claverack Creek on the east, the north line of the Manor of Livingston on the south and the Hudson River on the west. Colonel Henry J. VAN RENSSELAER was elected part of the committee that used their influence to get Hudson incorporated by New York State. Hudson was being set up as a retreat for revolutionary soldiers from all over the country.

On 20 May 1785, Captain John KEMPER and his childhood sweetheart, Elizabeth Ann HOPPER, along with his brother

Colonel Daniel KEMPER and Elizabeth MARIUS (1753-1803), celebrated a double wedding in New York City. At this time, their father, Jacob, passed the family Bible on to Daniel, while he gave his father Johann's grand sword to his namesake, John.

In June 1785, James MEASE died suddenly in Philadelphia. His executors confiscated all of James MEASE's records. This included Daniel KEMPER's set of books, which he had given to James MEASE accounting for monies of *"$6,600 and odd dollars"* owed to him. MEASE was working on settling Daniel's account when his untimely death occurred.

Out of all the clothier-generals who came and went during the course of the American Revolution, James MEASE is the only one who stayed on long after the Revolution and died at that post. Mr. MEASE's deputy clothier-general, Charles YOUNG, likewise stayed on.

After Mr. MEASE died, his clerk and deputy clothier-general in Philadelphia, Charles YOUNG, sent for Daniel, informing him that Mr. MEASE had suddenly died and that he should return to Philadelphia as soon as he could. Upon Daniel's return, he found that his books had been confiscated by Mr. MEASE's executors. Repeated requests to the executors from Daniel to return his set of books went completely ignored.

On 13 July 1785, it was ordered Mr. Mayor issue his warrant on the treasurer that John KEMPER be paid for painting constables staves and glazing lamps.

On 15 February 1786, John KEMPER, who lived at 3 Partition Street in New York City, was listed as an engine man in Engine Company #No. 3; and fireman in Fire Hose No. 3. In the course of putting out many fires in the city, John picked up many of the fire-fighting skills.

On 19 April 1786, John KEMPER was listed as a vice in Fire Hose No. 3. Shortly thereafter, he was noted as removed (transferred or moved to a new locality). In this case, he was sent on a mission by Colonel Alexander HAMILTON to Hudson, in Upstate New York. They still maintained strong military ties. Their friendship since the days at Kemper's Tavern stood strong as well. The city had been named after Hendrick HUDSON, who had discovered the Hudson River.

Chapter XXIII
Mission to Hudson, New York

Colonel HAMILTON sent a dispatch to Captain KEMPER to meet both him and his brother, Colonel Daniel KEMPER at the place that their father used to keep on Broadway. This meeting was to take place on the twenty-sixth of April 1786 at 1:00 pm. Here they would discuss certain matters and be given final instructions on what to do when he reached Hudson, before his departure from the city.

It was at this time there was a parting of the brothers. While Daniel remained in the city, Colonel Alexander HAMILTON needed Captain KEMPER to go on another mission upstate, to Hudson, New York. He gave Captain KEMPER a letter of recommendation and sealed orders to deliver to Colonel Henry J. VAN RENSSELAER in Hudson.

On 26 April 1786, the skies were heavily overcast, storm clouds were coming in, but everyone was dressed for the rains. Captain KEMPER and his wife, Eliza, stepped into their horse and carriage to head for the old abandoned Kemper's Tavern in Spring Garden, across from St. Paul's Chapel on 209 Broadway.

After their arrival, both Daniel and Alexander were waiting for John. They all paused for a moment, as if looking back through a window of time, at all the good times at Kemper's Tavern. Crowds could be seen and cheers could be heard coming from the tavern as they raised and clanked their glasses. Dancing and laughter was taking place in the back room. Other crowds were outside in back by the pit. Madam Ursula was still telling her fortunes, while Eliza was dancing on the bar, swishing her skirt from side to side.

Although everything that was taking place was in absolute serenity and ghostly form, it was as if the good times were happening all over again. Everyone had their own private memories of Kemper's Tavern. Everyone was so young, where had time gone?

John stepped down from his horse and carriage to join both Alexander and his brother Daniel, who were hurdled under the overhead where Madam Ursula used to tell her fortunes. Eliza and their military escort stayed back while the officers discussed business. Then the rains came and grew heavier with time, and fog started to develop.

Colonel HAMILTON started out, *"This is where our friendship began, John."* John remarked, *"Yes, I remember."* Colonel HAMILTON continued, *"Since the KEMPERS are the first friends I made when I came to New York to attend King's College, I thought it was appropriate that we should all meet here before your departure from the City."*

John answered, *"Yes, it is, the time we spent here in our youth seems just like yesterday, and seems like it went on for so many years."* There is little else recorded in Eliza's diary on this event, other than what her husband had told her, as all she could hear was mumbling.

In moving upstate to Hudson, John and his wife, Eliza (Hopper) KEMPER, received a two-man military escort in their two-horse carriage. Before stepping into the carriage, Captain KEMPER erected his pole flag of thirteen stars and stripes in the metal clamps on the right side of his carriage. Since the Revolution, and thereafter, Captain KEMPER never went anywhere without his country's flag.

In their horse and carriage, they rode along the scenic route following the eastern side of the Hudson River. As they rode along, both John and Eliza looked from the left to the right at the vast wilderness as a bald eagle flew high above, screeching. It was as if they were in a fairy-tale wonderland. Then Eliza said, *"John it is so beautiful!"*

John replied, *"Yes it is."*

Eliza said, *"And, it is all ours."*

John said, *"Yes it is."*

Along the way, they stopped at the Wagon-Wheel Tavern overlooking the Hudson River to rest up their horses and get a bite to eat. The guards sat at a separate table so John and Eliza could have privacy. As they sat on the river deck, John noted that their new country had a vast wilderness ready to be explored and settled. He was ready to start a family. In his possession were the sealed orders from Colonel Alexander HAMILTON, which were to be delivered to Colonel Henry J. VAN RENSSELAER.

Eliza got up from her seat and went over to the railing of the deck to look out over the vast Hudson River Valley. There was a moose that had slowly strolled into the shallows of the river, among the Lilly pads, to get a drink. As Eliza looked in awe, she said, *"It is so beautiful, Honey, the River is so pure you can just dip your cup into it and have a drink of water."*

John said, *"Yes we can."*

Eliza said, *"We are in a pristine land."*

John said, *"Yes we are."*

Eliza said, *"Do you think it will stay this way?"*

John said, *"I hope so, Baby; I truly hope so. It is going to take a lot of love and caring; I only hope we do not start taking things for granted."*

Eliza then returned to the table to sit down with her husband.

While John and Eliza were discussing how beautiful the Hudson Valley was, all of a sudden, — bang! At the sound of a rifle going off, John, being alarmed, quickly turned by instinct to catch the sight of the tavern keeper lowering his rifle after shooting a lion sunbathing on the woodshed.

After hearing the gunshot, the moose being startled trampled off. The innkeeper, in regards to his actions, simply stated, *"They prowl the area and grab our children; I have to protect our residents and our customers."* The landscape was indeed beautiful, but deadly as well.

As things calmed down, John mumbled, *"There is your lion, Lone WOLF."*

Eliza looked back at John and said, *"What was that?"*

John replied, *"Nothing, just thinking out loud."*

In Rhinebeck, they had a room waiting for them at the Beekman Arms. The innkeeper told them to take their horses and carriage out back to the parking lot. The stables were there where their horses could be given forage and watered, while their carriage was tied up. *"Thieves are everywhere,"* the innkeeper exclaimed. *"They come around like rats; you never know they have been here until you find something missing."*

Their next stop would be Hudson.

The following morning, Captain KEMPER's escort prepared his team of horses and carriage. After John helped Eliza climbed in, his guards mounted, and they headed for Hudson.

After arriving in Hudson, Captain KEMPER turned over Colonel Alexander HAMILTON's sealed orders to Colonel

Henry J. VAN RENSSELAER. Colonel VAN RENSSELAER informed Captain KEMPER that he had received a dispatch that he would be arriving. He told John to stay in close contact and that he would be sending for him once everything was in place.

On 12 October 1786, John and Eliza KEMPER had a daughter, Sophia Susan (1786-1880), born in Hudson, New York. She was named after John's sisters, Maria Sophia, wife of John MORTON, and Susan, wife of Dr. David JACKSON of Philadelphia. She was also named after John's grandmother, Sophia, who remained in Germany when the family moved to America. Whenever John and Eliza gave one of their children two names, they always tried to name them after two family members.

On 6 November 1786, John KEMPER donated eight shillings to the construction of the Christ Church, which took place at Second and State Street, Hudson, New York. John also brought his fire-fighting skills with him and helped start Fire Hose number one in the city of Hudson.

On 14 April 1787, according to the Annual Report of the State Historian, Captain KEMPER was appointed captain in Company Number Six over Captain Thomas LEE (1739-1814). Captain LEE was demoted to KEMPER's vice (subordinate) and later declined the position, possibly because his feelings were hurt. Although Colonel VAN RENSSELAER's regiment was filled, he made an exception to the rule and made room for John.

Captain LEE was formerly a captain of the Eighth Company, Fifth regiment of the New York Continental Line. This was more like a military transfer from a post that Captain John KEMPER held in New York City in Colonel Alexander HAMILTON's regiment, rather than just a re-enlistment in the army.

Something else was going on during this period of time; out of all the appointments in the Annual Report of the State Historian, Captain KEMPER's given name is the only one left blank. Was something else intended for him but forgotten or deliberately failed to be filled in?

On this same date of 14 April 1787, Elisha JENKINS (1765-1848) was appointed a lieutenant. Elisha became a good friend of Captain KEMPER's during his service in Colonel Henry J. VAN RENSSELAER's regiment. He went on to become a colonel, secretary of the State of New York, vice-chancellor of the regents of the University of New York State, New York State comptroller, mayor of Albany, New York, and member of the New York State Assembly; and later he became a presidential candidate in 1840.

When the Pension Law was passed by an act of Congress on June 7, 1832, Colonel JENKINS signed a voucher verifying Captain John KEMPER's service during the American Revolution, which was clear and well-known to anyone who had served with him or had been his friends and neighbors.

On 17 September 1787, the Constitution of the United States was written to replace the Articles of Confederation made back in 1777. Laws and rights were continually being upgraded to accommodate the rapid growth of the new nation. Alexander HAMILTON signed for New York State.

In April 1789, all of New York City and outlying areas started to prepare for the inauguration of George WASHINGTON. The KEMPER family was doing the same; John's wife, Eliza, was nine months pregnant and due any day. Eliza told John that she would be just fine in the hands of friends and family and told him to take a sloop down to the city to join his family for the inauguration.

After John arrived in the city, the women went off to themselves and so did the men. Daniel, John and their father, Jacob all related their excitement. Jacob started things out by saying, *"It is so incredible that my children have played a major role in serving directly under our commander-in-chief, and now first president to be in a new country that is all ours."*

Daniel replied, *"It is because of our good upbringing, Dad."* Everyone proudly smiled.

Daniel went on to ask John, *"How is Anthony [MAXWELL]?"*

John replied, *"Just fine, our families have become very close, especially our wives."*

Daniel continued, *"I still remember the drumming out of Lieutenant Frederick ENSLIN at camp [Valley Forge] by the entire Continental Army, Anthony sure knew how to get everyone's attention, especially General WASHINGTON's."*

John answered, *"That incident still pops up and we laugh about it frequently."*

However, Anthony said, *"It was not so funny at the time."* When Anthony had accidentally walked in on them and reported the incident to his superior, he did not think of Lieutenant ENSLIN lying about the act, fearing the consequences. After Lieutenant ENSLIN filed charges against Anthony and had him arrested for slandering his good name, he feared he was going to be court-martialed.

Colonel Aaron BURR, who was president of the court-martial proceedings, interviewed Private John MONHORT, who confessed, saying that *"Lieutenant ENSLIN used his rank to intimidate him into submission."*

After Colonel BURR reported the results of his investigation to General WASHINGTON, His Excellency then ordered the release of Ensign MAXWELL and to start the court-martial proceedings for Lieutenant ENSLIN.

Daniel then inquired, *"Anthony then went on to become captain did he not?*

John answered, *"Yes he did, and he fought in most all of the battles from the beginning of the Revolution until he retired in 1781. Anthony married Eva, daughter of Captain Hendrick PLATNER (1745-1825). Hendrick was in the 8th Albany County regiment during the Revolution. Both are members of our officers' club up in Hudson among other Revolutionary soldiers."*

Jacob interjected by saying, *"Let us join the rest of the family."*

On 30 April 1789, George WASHINGTON delivered his first inauguration address in New York City, after being elected the first uncontested president of the United States of America. Eliza Susan MORTON's (1774-1850) mother, Maria Sophia, had asked her daughter to record her memoirs of this historical event, much the same as her Uncle John KEMPER had during the Revolution under General WASHINGTON. Eliza started recording,

> *The ceremony took place in the old Federal Hall, as it was afterwards named, which stood in the center of four streets. I was on the roof of the first house on Broad Street, which belonged to Captain PRINCE, the father of one of her school companions; and so near to President WASHINGTON, I could almost hear him speak.*

While Eliza was on the rooftop, Daniel, John and the rest of the family stood in the back of the crowd, not being able to get closer. Daniel softly nudged John in the left side of his ribs, while pointing at their niece on the rooftop, recording the inauguration. Daniel then said, *"Now she has the birds-eye view."*

John replied, *"Yes, she does. I wonder if she can hear anything, we surely cannot."*

Daniel then commented, *"I do not know, but we will ask her when the family gets together after the inauguration."*

John continued, *"You know Dan, during the Revolution, all civilians hated General WASHINGTON and we were the only ones close to him. Now, they surround him and we cannot get close."*

Daniel replied, *"I know, time changes everything. Everyone loves a winner. Now that we have won the war, everyone wants to be close to him and all those who were part of it."*

Eliza continued recording,

> *"The window and roofs of the houses were crowded; and in the streets the throng was so dense that, it seemed as if one might literally walk on the heads of the people. The balcony of the hall was in full view of this assembled multitude. In the center of it was placed a table; with a rich covering of red velvet; and upon this, on a crimson velvet cushion, lay a large and elegant Bible. This was all the paraphernalia for the August scene. All eyes were fixed upon the balcony; where, at the appointed hour, Washington entered, accompanied by the* [Robert R. Livingston] *Chancellor of the State of New York, who was to administer the oath; by John Adams, the Vice-President; Governor* [George] *Clinton* [1739–1812]*; and many other distinguished men.*

> *By the great body of the people, he had probably never been seen, except as a military hero. The first in war was now to be the first in peace. His entrance on the balcony was announced by universal shouts of joy and welcome. His appearance was most solemn and dignified. Advancing to the front of the balcony, he laid his hand on his heart, bowed several times, and then retired to an armchair near the table. The*

populace appeared to understand that the scene had overcome him and was at once hushed in profound silence.

After a few moments, Washington arose, and came forward. Chancellor [Robert R.] Livingston [1746–1813] read the oath according to the form prescribed by the Constitution; and Washington repeated it, resting his hands on the Bible. Mr. [Samuel] Otis [1740–1814], the Secretary of the Senate, then took the Bible to raise it to the lips of Washington, who stooped; and kissed the book.

At this moment, a signal was given, by raising the flag upon a cupola of the Hall, for a general discharge of the artillery of the Battery. All the bells in the city rang out a peal of joy, and the assembled multitude sent forth a universal shout. The President again bowed to the people, and then retired from a scene such as the proudest monarch never enjoyed. Many entertainments were given, both public and private; and the city was illuminated in the evening.

After the inauguration, the family, like so many others around the city, got together to discuss their future. While in the family gathering, Daniel said to John, *"Jacob and I were two of the founding members of the Society of Cincinnati, why do you not join? George WASHINGTON is president general of the Society now and, like us, knows you personally; there would not be a problem."*

John answered, *"I know, thanks, Dan. I still remember when you and Jacob tried to get me to help you start the organization, but I had other things to attend to for our sister* [Maria Sophia (Kemper) MORTON]. *However, I now belong to the officers' club up in Hudson and I would not be able to attend the meetings down here anyway."*

Dan slowly sighed and said, *"I understand, but you still could become a member."*

John replied, *"Maybe another time, I have to get home to my wife, she is due any day. As far as an officers' club is concerned, I will always remain a member. Other veterans are the only ones who are familiar with military service and understand the hardships of war."*

After George WASHINGTON became president of the United States, he began organizing the structure of government for civilian control. His vice president, John ADAMS, a former member of Congress, assisted in every way. They made sure that the military would never be able to threaten the civilian-constituted authority ever again. There were never any other significant accomplishments by President WASHINGTON during his two terms in office.

On 2 May 1789, after John arrived back in Hudson, Eliza was having his son, whom they named John Jr. He was named after John's grandfather, Colonel Johann (John) KEMPER, his brother-in-law, John MORTON and himself, thereby continuing the naming tradition and this time, knocking out three birds with one stone. This son died young, before 1807, at which time they then had another son and named him John, so as to keep the name in the family.

After John returned to Hudson, he continued his membership in the officers' club. This was a private club organized for Revolutionary veterans. John continued to meet other soldiers who served in the Revolutionary War, besides those he served with, including Captain Anthony MAXWELL (1754-1825), Captain Abraham VAN BUREN (1737-1817), Captain Hendrick PLATNER (1745-1825), Captain Diel ROCKEFELLER (1730-1811), Lieutenant William ROCKEFELLER (1750-1793), and Lieutenant Nathaniel (Nathan) ROWLEY (1762-1850) who all became close friends. They all met and shared their Revolutionary stories. Captain John KEMPER, along with all the rest, except

Captain MAXWELL, served under Colonel Henry J. VAN RENSSELAER at one time or another.

Sergeant John HARDICK (1752-1843) who lived close by, likewise, became a close friend. Mr. KEMPER introduced Mr. HARDICK to his wife, Eliza's sister, Mary (Polly) HOPPER (1770-1848), who was then living with her mother, Anna, and stepfather in Claverack. They fell in love and started planning for their marriage.

Sergeant HARDICK (who was in Captain Casper HUYCK's [1742-?] company), Lieutenant John UPHAM (in Colonel Robert VAN RENSSELAER's [1740-1802] regiment), Lieutenant Colonel Henry J. VAN RENSSELAER, and General Horatio GATES fought with them at the Battle of Saratoga.

On 6 November 1789, John's mother Maria Regina (Ernst) KEMPER passed on in New York City. John had originally arrived in Hudson in a horse and carriage with a military escort of two soldiers. He now used a sloop to ply back and forth from Hudson to the city (New York) as it was a faster means of travel so that he and his wife could attend his mother's funeral with the rest of his family.

However, the waters were starting to get frigid, and he could not stay too long. His father, Jacob, and brother Daniel met him at the docks with a horse and carriage, then they headed up the road to Greenwich, where they lived. John had oil paintings of his parents that he passed down in the family, many of which have been faded or torn over the past hundred and eighty years, but a good artist could breathe new life into an old oil painting, by simply repainting it.

John also had an oil painting of his grandfather, Colonel Johann KEMPER, in front of his castle, with its twelve towers bolting up into the sky. Stahleck Castle was built on a huge cone of rock about a thousand feet above Bacharach. The Colonel chose this studio setting for his oil painting. In this painting, the Colonel appears to have been about forty-five years of age. This painting, likewise, was passed down in the family and is still in this author's possession today (2016).

After the funeral, John's sister, Maria Sophia MORTON, removed their father to her house for his comfort and care during the final years of his life. He had previously gone blind while living in Germantown so she would read his German books and newspapers to him. His privations were alleviated by the attention of his children and grandchildren. Maria's daughter, Eliza Susan MORTON had her piano placed in an apartment adjacent to theirs, so that her grandfather could hear her sing and play whenever he pleased. During his final years he was patient, sensible and resigned.

The following morning, Daniel took John and Eliza in his horse and carriage back to the docks to catch a sloop back to Hudson. They embraced and said their good-byes.

Before boarding, John closed by saying, *"You know Dan, you have always been there for me since I was a young boy and all through the Revolution; you have always been my hero!"*

Dan then answered, *"And I will be there until the end."*

John and Eliza then boarded the sloop. As the sloop headed north up the Hudson River, John slowly waved, while watching his brother get smaller and smaller as the sloop sailed north. Eventually, Daniel faded into obscurity.

On the sloop ride back to Hudson, Eliza, looking up at John, who stood five foot nine inches tall, with blond hair and piercing blue eyes, while playing with the button on his shirt, said, *"Honey, I love you so much."*

John, looking down at Eliza, who stood five foot two inches tall, with radiant strawberry-blond hair and piercing green eyes, answered, *"I love you too, baby."* Eliza was of pure Dutch descent on her father's side.

One of the stories passed down in the family from John and Eliza was that Germany and Holland were once one country controlled by one family. Eventually the family divided their kingdom, while one brother took the mainland, which was Germany, he named his descendants VON, and the other brother took the lowland, which was Holland, and named his descendants VAN.

Eliza then asked John if she could ask him a question and get a serious answer; *"Have you ever loved someone so intensely that they gave you goose bumps and made you quiver with pure joy?"*

John answered, *"Absolutely!"*

Eliza excitedly replied, *"Really? Who?"*

John answered, *"My flag!"*

Eliza started pounding on John's chest, *"That is not a person. I'm trying to be romantic."*

John then replied, *"So am I, like you, I love my country and its flag. There will never be any others like it in the world. Most importantly, we would have no future without our country."*

Eliza continued, *"It is always our flag, why can you not just think of me once in a while and our family? I think we should name a son after your Uncle John MORTON."*

John replied, *"I agree; he so loved me and our cause. I also feel we should name a son after your father, my brother, Matthew and Uncle Mattheus [ERNST], knocking out three birds with one stone."*

Eliza responded, *"I would like that, I was only twelve when my father died; I never really got a chance to know him, we take so much for granted."*

On 21 March 1790, John HARDICK and Polly HOPPER got married at the Dutch Reformed Church in Claverack. Captain John KEMPER and his wife Eliza (Hopper) KEMPER attended with their brother-in-law, John, and his wife, Anny (Hopper) VAN NORDWYCK.

On 17 April 1790, John KEMPER's mentor in Congress, Benjamin (Ben) FRANKLIN, to whom he had credited for unconditionally helping General WASHINGTON, passed on. Captain KEMPER's world of yesterday, that he knew so well and took for granted, slowly faded away as time moved on.

On 10 August 1791, Captain William *"Bloody Bill"* CUNNINGHAM got his just rewards! He was hung in England for the crime of forgery. Ironically, the gallows finally claimed him, but not before he gave a full death confession of all the inhumane treatment of American prisoners and the thousands of brutal murders he committed while provost marshal in New York City. Death confessions are the most trusted and accepted, because the truth could no longer hurt the guilty party.

On 3 April 2005, E. (Everette) Howard HUNT Jr. (1918-2007) started his deathbed confession, vindicating a US government/ CIA team involvement in the assassination of President John F. KENNEDY. He named such key participants as Vice President Lyndon Baines JOHNSON (1908-1973), assisted by J. (John) Edgar HOOVER (1895-1972), who gave orders to a CIA-led hit-team code-named *"the Big Event"* and helped guide the Warren Commission's lone gunman cover-up. This confession by a top CIA official proved conclusively that Lee Harvey OSWALD (1939-1963) was set up exactly as he had claimed, as a patsy. Our CIA was a *"Mission Impossible"* agency.

James FILES (1942-?), who was sent from Chicago by the Mafia, was the actual one who got the head-shot on President KENNEDY with his fireball. He was stationed behind the wooden fence on the grassy knoll. The CIA had a couple of hit teams, one stationed in the rear of KENNEDY's moving vehicle, and one stationed in the front. The two in the front were captured on a photo taken at the time, but had to be enlarged in order to see more detal. One was dressed as a police officer (called badge man), while the second stood alongside him wearing a construction helmet. James FILES was released from prison on parole in May 2016, but not for killing the President.

Sometime in the early 1790's, Daniel and his brother, Jacob KEMPER, had a difference of opinion at the Society of Cincinnati. Daniel took the side of the rest of the members, where Jacob disagreed. Neither one would give in. Since Daniel out ranked his brother, and since all officers present, like General Marquis DE LAFAYETTE, served closely with Daniel during the American Revolution, they all sided with him.

Because of this difference of opinion, Jacob felt that his brother had abandoned him. He decided to separate himself from the family and went out on his own. Jacob never forgave Daniel and never reunited with the family. It was as if he held the whole family to blame. Since Jacob was no longer in touch with the family, when he died young in 1800, the rest of the family did not find out until after the fact. Therefore, his actual death date was never known.

On 30 August 1791, in view of the scarcity of water in Hudson, the council resolved that, *"John KEMPER be appointed to take the pump-break and upper box from the public pump, and, at the hour of 6 in the morning, at 12 at noon, and at 5 in the evening of each day, go with, or deliver to the hands of some careful persons to be carried to the pump; that each of the citizens applying for water may have an equal proportion; and that said break and box shall not be delivered at any other times of the day until a constant supply of water shall be found in the pump."*

On 10 October 1793, Captain John KEMPER and his wife Eliza, had a son, Charles Morton, baptized at the Zion Lutheran Church in Athens, Greene County, New York. This son was named after John's dear friend Charles YOUNG and his brother-in-law, John MORTON. Charles Morton KEMPER (this author's line of descent) ended up serving in the War of 1812 and married Catherine MAXWELL (1794-1832).

Catherine was the daughter of Captain Anthony MAXWELL, who was a very close, dear friend of Captain KEMPER's during the American Revolution. Anthony knew personally of Captain KEMPER's dedication and hardships while at Valley Forge. He shared in his sufferings and volunteered as an ensign in foraging excursions under Captain KEMPER's command.

Anthony served in Colonel William MALCOLM's regiment and fought in all the battles with General George WASHINGTON. Anthony also served under Major General Marquis DE LAFAYETTE (1757-1834) and in the Indian Wars in Western New York under General John SULLIVAN (1740-1795). He also served under Brigadier General William MAXWELL (1733-1796), General Nathanael GREENE (1742-1786), Colonel Aaron BURR, Colonel Aaron OGDEN (1756-1813), Colonel Oliver SPENCER (1736-1811), Lieutenant Colonel Goose VAN SCHAAIK (1736-1789), and Colonel Phillip VAN COURTLANDT (1749-1831). Most of Anthony's service to our country was achieved in combat.

During the Valley Forge encampment, Anthony was an ensign. Whenever Captain John KEMPER needed volunteers to go out on foraging excursions and acquire food and clothing for the troops at camp, Anthony was always one of the first to volunteer. During these desperate times of dire need of food and clothing for the Continental troops, John and Anthony became very close, dear friends. So close, in fact, that after the Revolution, when

John had moved up to Hudson, New York, he later called on Anthony to join him as a confidant in a local project in which he was involved. Their families later intermarried.

In addition, John, after taking a beating from the pension department in the final days of his life, was unable to afford a plot of his own and was offered a space in Captain Anthony MAXWELL's family plot in the Hudson City Cemetery. This action was ordered by Captain Anthony MAXWELL's widow, Eva (Platner) MAXWELL, daughter of Captain Hendrick PLATNER.

Continental and revolutionaries were a family that stuck together to the end. If anyone suffered shame, their comrades stood by their sides. Just like when Reverend CALDWELL and his wife, Hannah, were murdered. The only problem was, other than John's brother, Colonel Daniel KEMPER, most all other Continental officers had died, so they were unable to come behind Captain KEMPER.

John's daughter, Elizabeth KEMPER, named after her mother, comforted her father in the final days of his life, especially in his pension years. After her promise to never marry until she won her father's case, she ended up filing the first lawsuit against the pension department after her father's death, for as far as her pocketbook carried her. Elizabeth died an old maid and in tears, as her father had. Was it really possible that all her father's service in the birth of America was going to be erased forever? Elizabeth had to make sure all the family history was passed down in the family, hoping that someone would come along who had the resilience to carry on the fight. This author did just that!

On 17 April 1794, John KEMPER, who had brought his fire-fighting skills with him from New York City, headed a team of firemen appointed by the City of Hudson to superintend Fire Engine Number One. Since Hudson's first fire in 1793, at which time they had no fire department, things quickly got out of hand.

Now, they had the right man for the job, Mr. KEMPER, who had a history of firefighting skills from the big city of New York. He would teach the fundamentals of firefighting to the interested parties of the city of Hudson. Its residents were grateful.

The Hudson City legislature *"resolved, that two houses be erected over the two wells—on that in Second Street and in the Main Street—for the reception of fire engines, and that the said wells be made convenient for the supply of water."*

The Main Street house was soon afterward removed *"to the corner lot of the late Justus VAN HOESEN [1742-?], and that the committee cause a sufficient covering to be made for the other engine on some part of the Market Square, under superintendence of John KEMPER and Paul DAKIN [1761-1822]."*

In 1794, Captain KEMPER's niece, Eliza Susan, daughter of John and Maria Sophia (Kemper) MORTON, was a very fascinating and highly cultivated woman. She possessed a charming voice and played the piano, much like Eliza HOPPER when singing and playing the harpsicord.

It was during her visit to Boston that, meeting at the house of a mutual friend while singing and playing the piano, Ms. MORTON captivated the heart of Mr. Josiah QUINCY (1772-1864), and within a week, after steady courtship, Mr. QUINCY asked for her hand in marriage; they were then engaged.

On 15 August 1794, John's father, Jacob KEMPER passed away in New York City at eighty-five years old. Jacob left this plane with a happy heart, having had three sons who served as officers in the Continental Army. Jacob's immigration to the colonies proved fruitful, for his children served in *the birth of America,* in a big way. Colonel Daniel and Captain John KEMPER served directly and faithfully under their commander-in-chief, General George WASHINGTON. They both contributed greatly to its success.

Once again, John and his wife returned to the city (New York) to attend his father's funeral. This time his brother Daniel and his wife, Elizabeth, picked them up at the docks in their horse and carriage. John's sisters and cousins were all in attendance.

They rode out of the city (New York) on the road to Greenwich, which was two miles north of New York, where the family had lived. Their father, Jacob, originally purchased this home, which was on a lease from Trinity Church back when they were kids. As John stepped down from the carriage after it had stopped, he began to look around. Everywhere he looked, old memories popped up of when he was growing up.

The high bank of the Hudson River, fringed with trees, where the house was situated, commanded an extensive view of that noble river; the grounds were ornamented with trees and scrubs and a fine hawthorn hedge. As John looked down the road to the City (New York), he could see a ghostly figure of his father step into a carriage and ride down the road to attend his tavern. John and his brother, Daniel's sister, Maria Sophia (Kemper) MORTON, and his cousins Washington MORTON (1776-1810) and John MORTON Jr. (1765-1835), likewise, lived on the KEMPER estate.

Lush wilderness and swamps, however surrounded Greenwich; in later years, this would all change. When the family let the lease expire, this estate was leveled and divided into city lots; and Morton Street marked the site of John MORTON Jr.'s house. In years to come, the lush wilderness and swamps would be cleared, and the city of New York would end up swallowing the whole island and become the largest city in America.

John was beginning to foresee the future; everyone wanted to live in the new land and become Americans. How could their family have done so right in building a new country, which the rest of the world would envy? Daniel moved back to the city of his birth, New Brunswick, New Jersey. Cities were being built everywhere across America and America continued to grow in size. Would there ever be any end to progress?

On 30 August 1794, John KEMPER's niece, Eliza Susan, was now living with her husband Josiah QUINCY in Boston, Massachusetts. Still grieving over her beloved grandfather's death, she placed his obituary in the Boston paper.

In 1796, Colonel Daniel KEMPER befriended a French artist by the name of Charles Balthazar Julien Feavret DE SAINT-MEMIN, who had fled France from the French Revolution. Being impoverished, Daniel took him in his home to tutor his children in French. During this period of time, since he was an artist, he painted portraits of Colonel Daniel KEMPER, his wife, Elizabeth (Marius) KEMPER, his sister, Maria Sophia (Kemper) MORTON, his niece, Eliza Susan (Morton) QUINCY and her husband Josiah QUINCY.

He also had paintings done of his nephews Washington MORTON and John MORTON Jr. All these paintings are in the Corcoran Gallery of Art in Washington, DC By this time, all of Daniel's children had moved away so were unavailable for oil paintings. Even though his brother Jacob lived close by, he still maintained his distance from the family. All these paintings are no longer on display but, in fact, are in storage in the basement to make room for newer paintings done of new statesmen. All these oil paintings were done at home and not at a studio where you get dressed up for.

On Sunday, 25 June 1797, Major William DUNLAP (1754-1838) took passengers to Bellevue on a sightseeing tour. After the Revolution, the Kemper's Tavern had become a tourist attraction as the place where it all began. In 1775, in the back room was where Jacob KEMPER welcomed Continental officers to set up New York City's first recruitment center. Anthony MAXWELL would become one of the first recruits, and later became good friends with Captain John KEMPER. While Major DUNLAP drove them in his horse and carriage past Kemper's tavern, he explained, *"This is the place* [Jacob] *KEMPER used to keep."*

In 1769, Jacob KEMPER had set up his tavern at Spring Garden on Broadway, not realizing it was not going to be just another tavern. Twenty-eight years later, it still stood, although quiet and desolate. All that could be heard or seen was, the breeze blowing leaves around. Ex-Continental soldiers would often come by to grab a memory of the past. All that could be heard or seen were ghostly figures of Madam Ursula, the wooden Indian, the knight in shining armor next to the hearth of the fireplace, and the noise of crowds of people having fun and raising a glass or two, cheering.

Major DUNLAP then recorded that he called on Miss [Eliza] MORTON, Captain John KEMPER's niece and singer, who was much pleased with Maria's song in his opera (the music). Since the tavern days, Major DUNLAP had become good friends with various members of the KEMPER family. Memories remained strong with all those who attended Kemper's Tavern.

Mr. DUNLAP's opera was named Sterne's Maria. Some of these diary entries were published in the New York Genealogical and Biographical Record and stored in the New York Historical Society. Major DUNLAP was an officer in the Continental Army and well acquainted with the family and, like many other Continental soldiers, had spent time at Kemper's Tavern before the British took possession of the city. Now he was going back in time.

On 7 October 1797, John KEMPER's nephew, Washington MORTON (1776-1810), married Cornelia Lynch SCHUYLER (1775-1808), daughter of General Philip SCHUYLER (1733-1804) of Albany, New York and sister of Elizabeth (1757-1854), wife of Colonel Alexander HAMILTON. John sent his congratulations and said, *"I am going to have to contact my friend the Colonel [Alexander HAMILTON] to let him know that, we are getting closer all the time."*

On 26 April 1798, John and Elizabeth (Eliza) KEMPER had a daughter, Elizabeth, born in Hudson and named after her mother. Elizabeth would go on to record her families' history. Her diary became a valuable and significant reference for the defense of her father in the fight in having his pension and military status restored. She would be the hero to carry on his fight and pass his records down in the family. It would take seven generations before another family member would carry on the battle.

Over 150 years later, it would help win her father's case and have his service under General George WASHINGTON restored. Her diary is a historical tribute to the birth of America and is still cherished by her family today. Without her diligence, so much knowledge would have been lost forever.

In June of 1799, Captain Anthony MAXWELL's father-in-law, Captain Henry PLATNER, was convicted of forgery and sentenced for life in state prison. As we have learned, Revolutionary officers and their families stuck together. As luck would have it, Colonel Morgan LEWIS (1754-1844), quarter master-general during the American Revolution, who beat out Vice President Aaron BURR for the governorship in 1804, now as the governor of New York State, pardoned him on 10 June 1806.

On 6 December 1799, John and Eliza KEMPER had a son, Matthew (1799-1824), born in Hudson, New York. He was named after Eliza's father, John's brother, and his uncle Mattheus ERNST, knocking off three birds with one stone. Matthew served as a seaman of New York State and, while at sea, died young. Matthew had been impressed with his father's sea service and wanted to follow suit. He is described on his seaman's protection certificate filed in New York City, dated 10 May 1824, as being twenty-four years old, 5 foot 4 1/2 inches tall, with a dark complexion, born in Hudson, New York.

On 14 December 1799, General George WASHINGTON, retired first President of the United States, member of the Masonic Order and lifetime president of the Society of Cincinnati, passed on at Mount Vernon, Virginia. He only had a bad cold, but during this period of time, doctors believed that by bleeding someone the sickness would be released with the process. Nine pints of blood were drained from George WASHINGTON. After all the battles and wars he survived, he ended up dying by his own caretakers, the ones who loved him most.

George WASHINGTON's wife, Martha, in accordance with his will, freed 124 of his slaves. He stipulated that his estate was to pay for their care for decades. Martha's ninety-four slaves went back to her descendants upon her death in 1802. Also, in accordance with a previous agreement between her and George, Martha burned all their correspondences with each other. Only three letters between them escaped being destroyed.

After reading about George WASHINGTON's death, John KEMPER's daughter, Elizabeth, recorded in her diary that her father's heart dropped, he bent his head in sorrow, and then replied, *"So many secrets died with that man."* Her father further commented, *"Some things are just better left buried."*

No leader in world history had lost more battles than George WASHINGTON, yet he went on to become the Father of what would become one of the most powerful countries on earth. Its progress would not develop because of rage, hatred or jealousy, but in fact, goodness and the willing to help feed and protect other countries, no matter how big or small.

As a eulogy to George WASHINGTON's character, it is important to note how honorable a gentle-man he was. He never held grudges against people or officers who spoke, disagreed, conspired or tried to remove him from office. George WASHINGTON had ordered the execution of Loyalists who were found guilty of treason by helping the enemy. However, he did not include his former slaves who joined the Loyalists and fought for the Crown against him. In fact, he went even further by granting his slaves their freedom upon his death. As written in his will, he also allowed them to live off his estate for decades to follow. He held higher standards for the military than he did for civilians.

On 26 December 1799, at George WASHINGTON's funeral, Congress selected Major General Henry LEE to give his eulogy, and he said, *"First in war, first in peace, and first in the hearts of his countrymen."* The news of George WASHINGTON's death had a profound affect around the world. Even the British, showing respect, ordered their flag to be lowered to half-mast on its entire navy fleet. Napoleon **BONAPARTE** of France ordered a ten-day requiem (mass for the dead).

On 26 December 1799, *"the Hudson Council having received certain accounts of the death of our illustrious beloved, General George WASHINGTON and being desirous of testifying their sorrow in the most public manner do resolve that the citizens be immediately notified to repair to the City Hall to form a procession to the Presbyterian Meeting House where suitable prayers will be made by the Reverend Mr. SAMSON and an eulogy will be spoken by Mr. GILBERT on the solemn occasion."*

The procession moved in the following order:

"Captain Nicholas HATHAWAY's [ca. 1773-1815] *company of infantry, with arms reversed and music muffled and shrouded.*

> *Recorder and orator.*
> *Common Council, two and two.*
> *The Reverend Clergy.*

Officers of the late Revolutionary Army, including Captain John KEMPER and Captain Anthony MAXWELL, both of whom served with General WASHINGTON at Valley Forge.

> *Other officers, civil and military.*
> *Citizens, two and two."*

The minute the guns were fired by the artillery, the bells of the city were tolled, all places of business were closed and a vast concourse of citizens, wearing badges of mourning and with deepest grief, assembled at the church to listen to the solemn eulogy. He would never be forgotten and even death would never erase him from history.

On 8 November 1800, an alarm went off in Washington, *"Abracadabra, poof!"* Smoke began to bellow into the sky from an office building in Washington, DC, the War Department. Most all of the revolutionary records that had been collected went up in flames. There was a lot of controversy going around in our country during this particular period in our history. Veterans claimed that their new civilian-constituted authority had committed this act with malice, preventing them from being able to prove their service to their country and file a claim for back pay.

On 23 December 1800, Maria Sophia (Kemper) MORTON's son John MORTON Jr. wrote a letter to his aunt Susan (Kemper) JACKSON in Philadelphia, Pennsylvania. This letter was sent from Alexandria, DC In his letter, he stated,

> *On the 19th he had gone to Mount Vernon with Mr. DANDRIDGE to visit General WASHINGTON's widow, Martha WASHINGTON.*

> *Upon arriving, they found that the Cameron Run Stream had been swelled by heavy rain the preceding night. They decided to dash through and got soaking wet. When they reached the door, Old Frank, General WASHINGTON's mulatto servant, greeted them. Old Frank recognized Mr. MORTON right away. Having witnessed their plight, conducted them to their chambers, lit a brisk fire and soon got them situated.*

> *They then received a most flattering reception from Mrs. Martha WASHINGTON. Colonel Tobias LEAR [1762–1816], former personal secretary to*

President WASHINGTON, had come to dine on Sunday. Mrs. WASHINGTON though altered by years and evidently lost at times in melancholy thought, displayed great fortitude.

"They then received a most flattering reception from Mrs. Martha WASHINGTON. Colonel Tobias LEAR [1762-1816], former personal secretary to President WASHINGTON, had come to dine on Sunday. Mrs. WASHINGTON though altered by years and evidently lost at times in melancholy thought, displayed great fortitude."

Mr. John MORTON Jr. went on to say that, *"he had seen Mrs. Abigail ADAMS in Alexandria, while on his way to Mount Vernon. She had invited him to dine with President John ADAMS and herself today, but was prevented by indisposition."* Still, after all this time, the MORTON's family was still warmly welcomed by leading heads of state for all their father had done for General WASHINGTON, the Continental Congress, and the American revolutionary cause.

On 27 March 1801, John KEMPER was listed as one of the first vestrymen for the Christ Church in Hudson, New York, as recorded in the history of Columbia County. John continued serving as a vestryman until 1803.

Sometime, around 1802, bounties were put up on lions that were prowling around towns from the woods and forest which they normally inhabited. One man was found eaten alive off a roadside just outside of Claverack. His bloody trail was found from the roadside leading into the woods. He was so badly mangled that he could never be identified.

John KEMPER and Anthony MAXWELL participated in these lion hunts. There were thousands of lions that inhabited the woods and forests that surrounded the towns. They were sneaking up on children and road travelers, grabbing them by surprise. Something had to be done. John and Anthony's wives, Eliza and Eva, were just terrified that their husbands might not return home.

Anthony had a Beagle that he named "Malcolm" after his colonel. This small dog would accompany the hunt so that the men could not be sneaked up on by the cats. The prime area of cat attacks where John and Anthony were concentrating their hunt was around the towns of Claverack, Ghent, Kinderhook, Gallatin and Germantown.

While John's wife, Eliza, and Anthony's wife, Eva, sat around the table having coffee, John and Anthony were looking over the map where all the cat attacks were. Anthony said, *"Just like old days, huh John?"*

John replied, *"Yes it is my friend, yes it is. It seems that wherever we reside, there will always be predators to contend with. We will always have to locate and eliminate them. The problem is, we often become too relaxed and comfortable in civilization and forget about predators who never forget about us."*

Anthony said, *"There are far more thousands of lions in the woods and forests surrounding our towns than there were ever British. We could never eliminate them all."*

John said, *"More like hundreds of thousands, and the deer population for hunting, by both man and lions, is down because of it. They are hungry. They must now extend their hunting grounds; and, just like all predators, they must compete for their game. Let us at least try to make a dent in their population."*

Eliza said, *"Without you guys, that little doggie would be a cat snack."*

John said, *"That is what teamwork is all about, protecting one-another from predators."*

Anthony said, *"With Malcolm by our side, no cat stands a chance."*

Eva said, *"Oh, you guys are just impossible."*

Eliza asked, "Why does man always have to have a gun?"

John answered, "without it we would not progress in civilization."

Up until this point, Anthony's Beagle, who seen his rifle on the table alongside of their map, and being familiar with the preparation for a hunt, had been eagerly wagging his tail. After they folded up the map, Anthony grabbed his rifle and said, "Are we ready Malcolm?"

The Beagle ran around in circles, excitingly barking, as if he was chasing his tale. John and Anthony then went outside, as John stuck their map in his saddlebags. They kissed their wives, said their goodbyes and mounted their horses. On the rear of their saddles, their camping gear was rolled up. As they started on their journey, with Malcolm running alongside, their wives were wildly waving and yelling, "Good luck guys, please come home!"

On 19 October 1803, Colonel Sebastian BEAUMAN died in New York City. Colonel BEAUMAN had married Captain John KEMPER's cousin, Anna Gertrude WETZELL (1751-1786), who had died from complications in childbirth in 1786. Captain KEMPER served with Captain BEAUMAN at Valley Forge, where they shared many of the good times and bad times that tested men's souls.

When Captain KEMPER would have lunch with his brother, Colonel Daniel KEMPER, they would have Captain BEAUMAN join them as part of the family circle. Likewise, when Captain KEMPER was delivering supplies to General WASHINGTON's army at West Point, he would stop in to see Captain BEAUMAN and Lieutenant Anthony MAXWELL, as they were stationed there. Soon after, Captain BEAUMAN was promoted to major.

On 12 July 1804, Major General Alexander HAMILTON died in New York City from a bullet wound in the stomach, suffered from an illegal duel with Vice President Aaron BURR the day before. Elizabeth KEMPER recorded in her diary, *"Whenever my father would read in the newspaper of a former Continental officer passing on, he would reply, another comrade in arms goes under."* Then comment on his personal dealings with those officers. Today was no different, he responded by saying that, *"Aaron BURR was a despicable individual; he was not the best soldier, but he was not the worst either. He killed a good and honorable man, a very dear friend and comrade in arms."*

Captain KEMPER continued to voice his distaste for Aaron BURR:

> *Lieutenant Colonel BURR never did any heroics during the Revolution, which would gain favor from General WASHINGTON and earn his blessing. That is why he was never promoted to full colonel. He was a fill-in when Colonel MALCOLM was absent or on another assignment.*

> *Colonel BURR was content with staying in the background while everyone else did the dirty work. He never appeared to be crazy about the Revolution, he just seemed to exist, like a bump on a log; I never could understand why he joined. After the Revolution he got involved in politics, which credentials were less demanding than the military, besides having Revolutionary status which gave him recognition.*

He then closed by saying,

> *Even Ethan ALLEN gathered a bunch of men together and called them the "Green Mountain Boys." He then took his men and attacked Montreal; he was quickly captured and held prisoner for years.*

He eventually became an American status symbol. General WASHINGTON later negotiated for his exchange, and because of his heroics gave him the rank of colonel, without any military experience whatsoever. If Colonel BURR could have mimicked these heroics, or those of Lord SRIRLING, who sacrificed himself to save General WASHINGTON and the Continental Army, he could have gone places in the Army.

From 1804 through 1825, little was recorded on Captain KEMPER. All we know for sure is that, during the 1820s John turned over his dress sword to his son, Charlie, who served in the War of 1812. Charlie later joined many of his children who had settled in Westport, Connecticut, and became an auditor. John turned his service sword over to his son John, Jr. John's brother, Daniel turned over his dress sword and service sword to his son, Bishop Jackson KEMPER (1789-1870), who later settled in Nashotah, Waukesha County, Wisconsin.

Daniel also made sure his son, David Jackson, received the KEMPER family Bible. The KEMPER family, although at great distance from one another, still stayed in close contact through correspondences; the Revolutionary bond was strong. It was as if the family still was not finished celebrating their victory. They were very much enjoying the fruits of their families' participation in the Revolution.

On 20 February 1806, John and Anny (Hopper) VAN NORTWYK had a daughter, Eliza Kemper VAN NORTWYK, born in Claverack, Columbia County, New York. Eliza was named after Anny (Hopper) VAN NORTWYK's sister, Eliza (Hopper) KEMPER, wife of Captain John KEMPER. John and Anny VAN NORTWYK had moved upstate to Claverack to be near their family. Anny had talked her husband into visiting Hudson so she could be near her sisters, Eliza KEMPER and Polly, wife of Sergeant John HARDICK.

Afterward, John and Anny (Hopper) VAN NORTWICK returned to New Brunswick, New Jersey, where they lived out their lives. Some of their older children stayed in Hudson, living close to their KEMPER in-laws. Some would join Captain John KEMPER's son, Daniel in settling in Wayne County, New York, named after General Anthony WAYNE. John and Ann brought their youngest daughter, Eliza Kemper VAN NORTWICK back with them to New Brunswick, New Jersey.

On 24 June 1807, after their previous son John, Jr. had died young, John and Eliza had another son, whom they again named John KEMPER Jr. (1807-1862). This was a common practice in this era. This son survived to marry Elizabeth (Eliza) MORRIS (1808-1842). They only had one daughter, Elizabeth KEMPER (1833-?), named after both John's wife and mother, Elizabeth (Eliza Hopper) KEMPER.

In 1814, Captain KEMPER's daughter, Sophia Susan, who he named after his sisters, Maria Sophia and Susan KEMPER, married Horace WILLARD and had a son they named Jackson Morton WILLARD (1813-1888). She named him after her two uncles, Dr. David JACKSON, who married her Aunt Susan KEMPER; and John MORTON, who married her Aunt Maria Sophia KEMPER. Captain KEMPER always told his children, *"We must keep the MORTON name alive for all that he did in the Birth of America."*

On 23 March 1815, Captain John KEMPER's son, Charles Morton, after courting Anthony MAXWELL's daughter, Catherine for months, fell in love and got married. Both sides of the family had become so close because of their parents having served together during the American Revolution. The wedding was held at the Reformed Church in Claverack. Both sides of the family attended the wedding.

During the reception, Anthony and John sat down together. Anthony said, *"You know John, this marriage kind of bonds our families together forever."*

John answered, *"Yes it does, but it did not take a marriage to make our bond strong."*

Anthony continued, *"I still remember when we caught the British buying supplies from that farmer on one of our foraging excursions and you left everyone in their underwear."*

John burst out laughing, *"I do too; and we both know they do as well."*

Anthony added, *"We had some good times together, John."*

John replied, *"Yes we did Anthony, yes we did."*

Anthony finished, *"You know, John, the best thing that ever happened to me during the Revolution, was meeting you at your father's tavern."*

John looked softly at Anthony and responded, *"Back at you my friend, back at you!"* Anthony softly grinned and bowed his head.

In the 1820s, Captain KEMPER's disabilities from being tortured on the various prison ships, by the provost marshal, Captain William "Bloody Bill" CUNNINGHAM in New York City and in Mill Prison, England, finally caught up with him. John paid dearly for his mission for his country. John's brother Colonel Daniel KEMPER, because of his old age, could not get around anymore without his cane. Both were experiencing the discomforts of old age, but the worst would later happen to both of them and it would have nothing to do with their disabilities.

Also in 1820 Washington IRVING (1783-1859) released his novel, *"The Legend of Sleepy Hollow,"* along with IRVING's companion piece, *"Rip Van Winkle."* Anthony MAXWELL's wife, Eva (Platner) had purchased the stories to read in the comfort of her living room, near their fireplace. As she was reading, familiarity kept jogging her memory.

Then she said to her husband as he was resting in his easy chair, *"Honey, what was that story you told me about the Headless Hessian?"*

Anthony inquired, *"You mean when the Hessian was decapitated at the Battle of White Plains by our cannonball?"*

Eva answered, *"Yes! That is it."*

Anthony responded, *"His head was splattered all over the battle field, then his comrades rushed his body off and later buried him at Sleepy Hollow, Why?"*

Eva answered, *"Well, apparently he comes out of his grave every Halloween and haunts Sleepy Hollow in search of his head."*

Anthony replied, *"Whaaaaaaaaat?"*

Eva then held up the cover of the book to show her husband.

Anthony's eyes opened wide, and then he said, *"Let me see that book!"* Anthony started reading then said, *"I have to go see John [KEMPER]!"*

Eva said, *"Why not our daughter Catherine and our son-in-law, Charlie Morton KEMPER?"*

Anthony answered, *"Because Charlie's father was in the Revolution with me and knows this story personally, I will be right back."*

Eva sighed, *"Do not forget my book!"* Anthony then ran outside, mounted his horse and rushed over to his friend, comrade and in-law, Captain John KEMPER's home.

After he arrived, he rapidly knocked on the door and Eliza answered, *"Welcome Anthony!"*

Anthony replied, *"I have to see John!"*

Eliza yelled out, *"Hoooney!"*

Anthony quickly rushed by her and said, *"John! Look at this book!"*

John being puzzled by all the excitement slowly took the book and looked at the cover. He then looked up at Anthony who said, *"Now read the page I left book marked for you in the book."*

John opened the book and began to read then said, *"Oh my God! Where did you get this book?*

Anthony answered, *"Eva bought it at the book store, not realizing what it was about."*

"You know, John," Anthony continued, *"I was right there on that hill with Colonel MALCOLM when our cannon ball decapitated that Hessian."*

John responded, *"I remember, you have told me the story dozens of times. Furthermore, my brother Daniel and I were at the same battle, but in different locations. He has related this same story to me many times as well."*

After briefly reviewing the book, John stated, *"You know, Anthony, the Headless Horseman has been haunting Sleepy Hollow for years. They have finally written a story about it."*

Anthony replied, *"I know, that is why I am here."*

John then looked up at Anthony and said, *"I want to buy a copy."*

Anthony added, *"I do too."*

John said, *"You already have this one."*

Anthony replied, *"Nooo! This is Eva's."*

John said, *"Okay, let us go to the book store and order two copies, then."*

Anthony said, *"I have to return this one to Eva."*

John called, *"Eliza! Take this book back to Eva; we are going to the book store."*

Eliza inquired, *"What is going on, guys?"*

John answered, *"Meet us over at Anthony's; we will explain everything when we get back."*

In September 1824, General Marquis DE LAFAYETTE arrived in New York City. Since his arrival had been announced, a deputation (delegation) from Hudson had waited on him there tendering him the hospitality of the city and soliciting the honor of a visit from him, which invitation was politely accepted. General LAFAYETTE was getting used to this kind of invitations wherever he traveled throughout the country.

After leaving New York City, General DE LAFAYETTE traveled up the North River (Hudson) on board the steamer, *James Kent*, commanded by Commodore Samuel WISWALL (1773-1837). His old friend Colonel Henry B. VAN RENSSELAER (1742-1813), who served under him during the Revolution, pulled up in a small boat next to the *Kent*. He then got on board and they embraced each other. The Marquis then proceeded to Clermont mansion in Columbia County, New York, where they passed the night in festivity.

There the Marquis was met by a committee from Hudson with General Jacob Rutsen VAN RENSSELAER (1767-1835) and

James FLEMING (1762-1835), who were accompanied by the Hudson City guards, the Scottish Plaids and the Hudson brass band. The middle of the following day the company reached the wharf in Hudson, where General Marquis De LAFAYETTE entered a carriage drawn by four superb horses, escorted by the military and a great procession of citizens all under the direction of Colonel Charles DARLING as marshal of the day. The marquis continued to bow to the great crowds assembled for his purpose, a custom that he acquired from General WASHINGTON.

As he descended from his carriage, he was limping from the wound he received from the Battle of Brandywine, nearly a half of a century ago. At the courthouse he was welcomed by Mayor Rufus REED, Esq. (1788-1869), who presented him with a great number of Revolutionary veterans, including Captain John KEMPER and Captain Anthony MAXWELL, both of whom served with General LAFAYETTE at Valley Forge, during the times that tried men's souls.

At the Allen's Hotel, where the reception was being held, above the chair honor (chair of honor), hung a flower border inscription in the words, *"We bow not the head, we bend not the knees, but our hearts, LAFAYETTE, we surrender to thee."*

On 25 May 1825, Captain Anthony MAXWELL died at Hudson, New York. He was a very close, dear friend of John's from Valley Forge, and his son, Charles' father-in-law. Little did John know that in the upcoming pension years, he would be offered to be interred in, Anthony's family plot. However, something else would happen in the family to deter that.

On 18 January 1826, John KEMPER lost his childhood friend and then wife of forty-one years, Elizabeth (Eliza Hopper) KEMPER, in Hudson, New York. Suddenly, John felt all alone and empty inside. Why was the world still turning? All the family attended her funeral and she was interred in the Old Hudson City Cemetery, on a hill overlooking the city of Hudson. After the service was over, while sobbing in tears, John asked to be alone with Eliza one last time, as he tried to say goodbye.

The family had ended up so poor all they could afford was a wooden board cross, with carved name and dates. The end result would be the same for John KEMPER when he passed on. In later years, his fifth generation great-grandson, this author, presented documentation to the federal government that yielded a monument in Captain KEMPER's honor. Likewise, this author erected a monument of his own in his honor. Both are erected in the Old Hudson City Cemetery.

Sometime in the year 1826, after his wife's death, John KEMPER of Hudson, New York, wrote a letter to Peter H. KEMPER (1780-1853) of Virginia. In this letter, John gave a brief history of his KEMPER line in Germany. John stated, *"His father, Jacob KEMPER, was born in Bacharach* [Germany], *a fortified town on the Rhine* [River], *of which his father, Colonel* [Johann] *KEMPER, was a military commander or governor, the office being hereditary in the male line of the family."*

It is unclear how this letter came about. Either John saw a newspaper story making reference to Peter KEMPER, or Peter had contacted John for information on his line of descent from the KEMPER family. The editor of Eliza Susan QUINCY'S memoirs accidentally received a copy of John's letter from her in 1878. Eliza still had this letter from her uncle John KEMPER, long after his death.

At the time John KEMPER had written this letter to Peter H. KEMPER in Virginia, he was sixty-nine years old. His memory was beginning to fade; he stated that his grandfather Colonel Johann KEMPER was military commander or governor of Bacharach. The fact is, as recorded early in the KEMPER family Bible records, Colonel Johann KEMPER was not only hereditary military commander of Stahleck Castle, but because of his wealth, status and rank under Frederick William I *"the Great*

Elector" and Frederick I, king in Prussia, as well as Leopold I, emperor of the Holy Roman Empire, was commissioned governor of Bacharach by the Emperor, himself.

John stated that, the town of Bacharach, where his father, Jacob was born, was situated a mile above Kaub. It was fortified with walls and twelve towers. Above a huge cone of rock stood the castle of Stahleck, connected to Bacharach by two fortified walls. It was well known for its fine wines which were sold throughout Europe.

The town of Bacharach was named after, the Alter of Bacchus Dionusia, the wine God. His worship had extended over the entire Greek and Roman world, 222-204BC. The Alter of Bacchus in the Rhine could be seen at low tide. Bacharach is surrounded by massive vineyards, and is still celebrated for its fine wines to this very day, 2016.

There was a difference of opinion on the birth place of John's father, Jacob KEMPER. John's niece, Eliza Susan (Morton) QUINCY, claimed he was born in Kaub. This author believes she confused her mother's birth place with that of her grandfather's. This author's German researcher checked both locations and there were no records in either town of Jacob's birth.

John KEMPER also stated that, since all officers under Frederick William I, "the Great Elector" and Frederick I, king in Prussia, were noblemen, he must have been a man of rank (social and financial standing) as well. Later descendants in the 20th century would capitalize on this phrase by John KEMPER, adding "VON" to the KEMPER name, inferring nobleness.

The fact, stated by John in this letter to Peter H. KEMPER, was that his grandfather's name was Colonel Johann KEMPER, not VON KEMPER. Furthermore, from early family Bible records and conversations carried on by both Captain John and his brother Colonel Daniel KEMPER refer to the same.

The fact is that, Jacob KEMPER's wife, Maria Regina, daughter of Reverend (Johannes?) ERNST and Maria Ursula, lady of rank is where that verbiage got scrambled in the family. Therefore rank came on the ERNST side of the family, not KEMPER.

Back during this period of time, as well as during the American Revolution, whenever anyone wanted to retain a copy of their letter, they had to rewrite the exact same letter all over again. When John's niece, Eliza S. QUINCY, contacted Uncle John for any history he could remember of the family, John sent his copy of his letter he had written to Peter H. KEMPER in Virginia, feeling that it would remain safe with the family.

After John's death, his daughter, Elizabeth KEMPER, likewise wrote to all members of the family, including her cousin Eliza S. QUINCY, requesting their memories on the role their parents played in the Revolution. Elizabeth needed to collect all the factual documentation she could in order to reconstruct an accurate history of her father's life during the American Revolution.

Now that America was settling down and strengthening itself as a nation, the generals would get all the glory. Towns and counties throughout the thirteen states were being named after them. Across the river from Hudson, which Captain KEMPER now called home, was named Greene County, after General Nathanael GREENE. Further west was named Wayne County, after General Anthony WAYNE, and so on and so forth throughout the states.

Emigration was flooding the shores of America from Europe. Along with the good came some bad. Monsters and traitors from other countries could migrate to America and call it home. If they committed a crime in this country, they would be protected by the Constitution of the United States and be provided with a jury of their peers.

Technology was rapidly growing. Trains and train stations were being built everywhere for speedy transportation throughout the states. One train station was built in Hudson, New York. Captain KEMPER looked on as the station was being built, and could only imagine, "where is America going now?"

Chapter XXIV
The Pension Years
(Deception and Death Lurks!)

On 9 April 1832, Colonel Daniel KEMPER addressed Congress for his pension, submitting an accounting of what happened to the records in the clothier-general's department. He stated that he had left his books in Philadelphia with James MEASE, clothier-general, showing $6,600 and some odd dollars owed him.

Then Charles YOUNG deputy clothier-general, contacted Daniel that Mr. MEASE had died suddenly and that he should return as soon as he could. When Daniel finally returned, Mr. MEASE's executors had confiscated his books and never turned them back over to him so that he could prove his claim. His submission is recorded in the journals of the United States Senate and Congress.

Colonel Daniel KEMPER also gave certificates proving his service in Major General Charles SCOTT's (1739-1813) brigade; as a member of the Society of Cincinnati and deputy clothier-general; from Brigadier General Andrew LEWIS (1720-1781); General Nicholas FISH (1758-1833); Colonel Richard VARICK (1753-1831), recording secretary for General George WASHINGTON and president of the Society of Cincinnati; and the late venerable Colonel Marinus WILLET (1740-1830).

Daniel was awarded $600 pension as a colonel to be paid semi-annually. It is to be noted here that Colonel KEMPER served under the intelligence chief General SCOTT, including sitting in on court-martials. There were many other intelligence connections with both him and his brother John KEMPER. Throughout history, so many have been over looked. Now that we are able to easily access historical information over the Internet, historians and other researchers alike can now go back through a window of time and re-analyze what really happened.

Colonel Daniel KEMPER's credentials were impeccable. Daniel had stayed in the New York City area, in the nest of Continental officers, while his brother John moved upstate to Hudson, New York. Daniel and John's brother, Captain Jacob KEMPER, who served in Lieutenant Colonel Ebenezer STEVENS' (1751-1823) Third Artillery in the New Jersey Line, likewise, stayed in the New York City area. Jacob also had been a founder of the Society of Cincinnati, along with his brother Daniel. They are both listed as original members (OM).

1. The Pension Law of 1832 is enacted

On 7 June 1832, the Pension Law was passed by an act of Congress enabling all Revolutionary veterans who were still alive the chance to obtain a pension for their service to their country. This windfall finally allowed veterans to obtain some compensation, while at the same time collecting and recording the history of the birth of America from the veterans who had lived through it. There was a new generation of Americans who knew little to nothing about the beginnings of their country. They wanted to obtain all records that could be recovered. This new generation was hungry for the knowledge, while the old went out of their way to deliberately destroy it. The vast majority of soldiers who had served in the American Revolution had since passed on.

The regulations read,

> *This law has been construed to extend, as well to the line, as to every branch of the staff of the Army, and to include under the terms "Continental Line," "State troops," "militia," and "volunteers,"*

all persons enlisted, drafted or who volunteered and who were bound to military service, but not those who were occasionally employed with the army upon civil contracts, such as Clerks to Commissaries and to Store Keepers, &c, Teamsters, Boatmen, &c. Persons who served on board of private armed vessels are also extended from the benefits of the law, as well as persons who turned out as patrols, or were engaged in guarding particular places at night, and were not recognized as being in actual military service.

It continued on to say,

"Every applicant will produce the best proof in his power. This is the original discharge or commission; but if neither of these can be obtained, the party will so state under oath, and will then procure, if possible, the testimony of at least one credible witness, stating in detail his personal knowledge of the services of the applicant, and such circumstances connected therewith, as may have tendency to throw light upon the transaction.

"This law has been construed to extend, as well to the line, as to every branch of the staff of the Army, and to include under the terms "Continental Line," "State troops," "militia," and "volunteers," all persons enlisted, drafted or who volunteered and who were bound to military service, but not those who were occasionally employed with the army upon civil contracts, such as Clerks to Commissaries and to Store Keepers, &c, Teamsters, Boatmen, &c. Persons who served on board of private armed vessels are also extended from the benefits of the law, as well as persons who turned out as patrols, or were engaged in guarding particular places at night, and were not recognized as being in actual military service."

It continued on to say,

> *"Every applicant will produce the best proof in his power. This is the original discharge or commission; but if neither of these can be obtained, the party will so state under oath, and will then procure, if possible, the testimony of at least one credible witness, stating in detail his personal knowledge of the services of the applicant, and such circumstances connected therewith, as may have tendency to throw light upon the transaction."*

This would be the method veterans, like Captain KEMPER, would need as all their service papers were confiscated when they became prisoners of war. Other proofs of Captain KEMPER's service were confiscated by the executors of James MEASE, clothier-general of the Continental Army and later mysteriously disappeared. Since most of the remaining revolutionary records were destroyed in the Washington fire, Captain KEMPER could now bring forth witnesses to testify as to his service to our country but there were not a lot of witnesses still alive.

On 23 June 1832, Captain John KEMPER's son Charles Morton's wife, Catherine MAXWELL died because of complication of childbirth after delivering their daughter Emeline (1832-1832), who likewise died shortly thereafter. Catherine was only thirty-eight years old. Catherine and her daughter were interred in the Old Hudson City Cemetery in her father Anthony MAXWELL's lot. Both sides of the KEMPER and MAXWELL family attended the funeral.

On 20 July 1832, John KEMPER's son Daniel, who was living right next door to him, helped his father and sister Elizabeth into his horse and carriage. John sat upright while holding his crutches in front of him. As they rode through the city of Hudson on their way to the courthouse, friends and neighbors waved sporadically. Everyone knew of Captain KEMPER and of his special service under General WASHINGTON.

Mr. KEMPER held the highest respect by leading statesmen and citizens of the community. They also knew well of his stories during the Revolution and always looked forward to hearing them repeated. They also knew about the new pension law that had been enacted and where Mr. KEMPER was headed, to the Hudson City Courthouse to make his declaration in order to obtain a pension. Finally, some were going to be rewarded for their service during the Revolution.

After their arrival at the courthouse, John sat down with Daniel and Elizabeth by his side and declared,

> *He was born in the city of New York in September 1756"* [actually 1757]. That, *"In August 1777, being then in Philadelphia, he entered into the service of the United States under Charles YOUNG, Deputy Clothier under James MEASE, Clothier General— This Deponent was Wagon Master, and received a Captain's pay and rations, and was engaged in convoying the wagons and other Transports from the Public Stores to the Army—He was in that service when the British entered Philadelphia, and had at that time, upwards of one hundred wagons under his command, with a Lieutenant's Guard to protect the Transports.*
>
> *"He was in that service till the spring after the British evacuated Philadelphia. While in this service, he was at several times sent on foraging excursions."* This deponent further says, *"In explanation of the above mentioned service, that his special duty was to superintend the Convoy and of Clothing from the Public Stores at Philadelphia and Lancaster, to General WASHINGTON's Head Quarters at*

> *the Park* [Valley Forge]*; and that he had* [General]
> *WASHINGTON's* **'special protection'** *against the*
> *interference of any other officer with his wagons;*
> *that he was in such service from Aug. 1777 till the*
> *spring of 1779, being about eighteen months, when*
> *he was discharged by said Charles YOUNG.*

Please note that, Captain KEMPER stated that Charles YOUNG verbally discharged him from the clothier department but, in fact, never received a written discharge, which was normally required. Therefore, his service in the Revolution remained intact. He was just going through a transfer. However, no one caught this at that time. Unbeknownst to Captain KEMPER, his friend and comrade Charles YOUNG, deputy clothier-general under James MEASE, was still alive. He was born the same year as Captain KEMPER in 1757 and died in the same year as well, 1842.

It is to be noted here that John KEMPER, in his declaration, spoke in the same language as George WASHINGTON, having been by his side first-hand. Those taking the declarations of veterans during this period of time were unfamiliar with the language spoken by revolutionaries. This was something very important missed by the men of the War Department. Both Giles F. YATES (1798-1859) and Commissioner James L. EDWARDS scrutinized it, YATES, on behalf of Captain KEMPER, while EDWARDS deliberately abused it.

John, in gentlemanly fashion used wording in his declaration that downplayed the importance of his orders of fulfillment by a *"military acquisition,"* given to him by Colonel Alexander HAMILTON. This was in response to an emergency dispatch he had received from General WASHINGTON.

Captain KEMPER used the words *"transporting public stores"* instead. This phrase came back to haunt him in later years when he found out he was being cheated out of the correct amount of pension to which he was entitled. Captain KEMPER was reluctant in describing his military acquisition of the capitol of Philadelphia, fearing that civilians would take it the wrong way.

He then entered the service of the state of Pennsylvania, in the Corvette Ship named Gen. [Nathanael] Greene, in capacity of first Midshipman and laid her cruise out which was six months. This Corvette was Commanded by Capt. [James] MONTGOMERY [1749–1809], Samuel CARSON First Lieutenant, Jacob DEHART Second Lieutenant.

In the spring of 1780, he entered the Brig "Fair American," Capt. Stephen DECATUR [1752–1808], and went a cruise of six months. This was a Brig of sixteen guns.

He then entered the brig Hector of fourteen guns, Captain James SLOVER, and the day after sailing, the Hector was captured by the British Frigate, 'Iris' and the crew carried prisoners to New York.

This deponent and others were confined aboard the old Jersey Prison Ship, and from there transferred by order of Admiral [Sir George Bridges] RODNEY, to the Provost [marshal] and thence came by Yarmouth to England and confined at Mill-Prison in Plymouth. Here he was confined until the spring of 1781, when he escaped and got home just after the taking of [General Lord Charles] CORNWALLIS.

And this deponent further declares that he has no Documentary evidence, having lost all his papers when taken prisoner; that he knows of no person whose testimony he can procure, who can testify to said service.

As Daniel was driving his father and sister Elizabeth home after filling out his declaration, he asked his father, *"Dad, since both Charlie and John* [Junior] *received one of your Revolutionary swords, do you have any plans for you pistols that you carried during the Revolution?"*

John turned to his son Daniel then replied, *"Yes I do!"*

Daniel nonchalantly offered a soft nod, excepting his decision even though he did not know what it was. He then turned to focus on steering the horse and carriage.

John continued, *"I was intending on handing them over to you. I am so glad you reminded me, I almost forgot. I have them in my chest at home. When we arrive, I will dig them out for you. I do not believe I will need them anymore. The Revolution is over."*

Daniel's eyes lit up like stars, as if asking, *"How did you know I was interested?"* Instead, replied, *"Thank-you father. I will treasure them always."*

On 22 September 1832, Captain KEMPER's sister, Maria Sophia MORTON, widow of the late *"Rebel Banker"* John MORTON, passed on in New York City. Every time John turned around, someone in the family, or someone with whom he served with in the Revolution, was going under. John sent a letter to his nephew, Major General, Jacob MORTON (1761-1836), offering his deepest condolences to the family and begged for their forgiveness in being unable to attend his beloved sister's funeral. John explained that, his own disabilities and his difficulty in getting around on crutches had imprisoned him close to home.

All of a sudden, Madam Ursula appeared out of a mist in John's vision. He assembled his thoughts on her predictions of some of his friends and loved ones passing on within a short time frame. Flashbacks of Madam Ursula continued to haunt him.

On 24 November 1832, Justice Josiah W. FAIRFIELD (1802-1878) called John KEMPER back into the Columbia County Courthouse, informing him that the pension department had claimed that they never received his application for a pension forwarded to their office on 20 July 1832. Therefore, it was necessary for him to fill out a new application.

John KEMPER personally appeared in the open court and now sat before the Justices of the Justices Court of the City of Hudson, County, aforesaid, with his daughter Elizabeth. John KEMPER, a resident of said city, aged seventy-six years, who, being duly sworn according to law, did on oath make the following declaration in order to obtain the benefits of the Act of Congress passed 7 June 1832:

> *That he was born in Sept. of the year 1756* (actually *1757) at the City of New York. That he resided in said city to the opening of the Revolution. That in the month of August of the year 1777, he went to Philadelphia & there was appointed Wagon Master, under Col. MEASE, Clothier General of the Army. That his brother* [Colonel] *Daniel KEMPER was Deputy Clothier at the Park or Headquarters* [Valley Forge], *& Col. Charles YOUNG was Deputy at Philadelphia. That he served as said Wagon Master, receiving a Captain's pay and rations, and the same for his horse till about May of the year 1779, making one year & nine months.*

> *That he left Philadelphia on the afternoon of Sept. 25 (the day before the British entered said city) with upwards of a hundred wagons under his command, laded with clothing & cloths. He had a "Captain's guard" to convoy said wagons to Headquarters* [General WASHINGTON's camp in Potsgrove]. *That he received his orders of march from Colonel*

> *[Alexander] HAMILTON at Walnut Street in said*
> *city; the cloths convoyed to Lancaster.*
>
> *He always had a protection from against detention*
> *from any other officers of General WASHINGTON.*
> *While the British lay at Philadelphia, his route was*
> *from Lancaster to Headquarters [Valley Forge] &*
> *after said British evacuated said city, the stores were*
> *carried back again, [to Philadelphia] & there he*
> *served till said expiration of one year & nine months.*

Once again, Captain KEMPER downplayed the importance of his role as wagon master. He neglected to inform the pension department of his true mission: to confiscate all food, clothing, cattle, and horses, including those of the residents of Philadelphia, so that the British could not gain possession of them as they had done in New York City. This was a military acquisition, at gun point, of all supplies in the city of Philadelphia, ordered by both, General WASHINGTON and Colonel HAMILTON. Captain KEMPER was concerned about civilian reaction to a military acquisition.

During this period of time in our history, so much coverage had been given to the thousands of Americans who were slaughtered in the British prisons. Captain KEMPER decided to concentrate his efforts on his suffrage as a prisoner of war, after being captured, while serving in the US Navy. He also neglected to inform the pension department of his true mission in the US Navy; he could not, because it was top secret! Therefore, he had to camouflage his service as a prisoner of war.

> *In May of 1779, immediately after quitting the army,*
> *he joined the navy of Pennsylvania. He entered the*
> *ship 'General [Nathanael] GREENE,' Capt. [James]*
> *MONTGOMERY, as first midshipman & served six*
> *months, & was discharged in November of same year.*
> *During this service, he was cruising on the coast.*

It is important for the reader to pause here for a moment. In the above paragraph of Captain KEMPER's second declaration, he stated, *"**Immediately** after quitting the army, he joined the navy of Pennsylvania."* This part of his declaration clearly shows that, before he left the Continental Army, he had planned to join the US Navy.

Is this what General WASHINGTON had planned for Captain KEMPER's next mission, when he summoned him to his residence in Philadelphia? Generally, whenever an officer's tour of duty ended, he would re-enlist for another six-month tour in the same duty, maintaining the same rank. No officer is going to voluntarily demote himself unless instructed to do so for a specific mission with no penalties.

Captain KEMPER's position under General WASHINGTON was too important for just a six-month tour or demotion; that is why he had a one-year and nine-month tour before being discharged. Now, he was being sent on a new mission at sea but needed to learn the ropes of a seaman first. This appeared to follow the normal procedures of a recruit and enlistment.

> *In the spring of 1780, he entered the Brig 'Fair American,' Capt. Stephen DECATUR, as a volunteer & served as such, for six months cruising all the time.*

Every six-month tour, John KEMPER's rank went up; now, he was just one rank under lieutenant.

> *Again in the spring of the year 1781, he entered the Brig "Hector," Capt. James SLOVER, as lieutenant. Sailed from said Philadelphia in the morning & was taken prisoner about 9 o'clock, same night by the British Frigate "Iris" [formally the USS Hancock]. He was taken to the city of New York & imprisoned in the Old Scorpion. From thence he was transferred with the other Iris prisoners on board the*

'Old Jersey.'—He with 71 other officers were then transferred thence to the "Provost," under [Captain William] CUNNINGHAM, Provost Marshall, where he was confined three weeks.

Then by the command of Admiral [Sir George Bridges] RODNEY, they were removed to the 'Old Yarmouth' [sixty-four-gun ship] & conveyed to England & confined at Mill Prison. They sailed from New York to England in November of 1781. In the spring of 82, he escaped from prison, obtained passage to the West Indies & from thence to Philadelphia where he arrived in November of the year 1782; making it one year and nine months absence.

And he further declares that in all said time, he was in actual service of the United States four years six months. And he further declares that he always served as a volunteer & in the grades above set forth, and never received any written discharges—When taken prisoner, he lost all his papers [confiscated when captured] & has no documentary evidence. That the only record of his age is memory & tradition—That since the Revolution, he has resided sometime at New York [City] & the last 46 years at Hudson aforesaid.

Once again we need to concentrate on Captain KEMPER's statement, *"Never received any written discharges."* Therefore, he was never discharged but, in fact, was preparing for his next station. He recorded that, *"immediately after he left the clothier-general's department, he joined the navy in Philadelphia."*

It was all part of the plan by General WASHINGTON and Colonel TALLMADGE. He was launched into the heart of the British Empire to locate targets; would he find them? Would he come home alive?

That he can find no living witnesses of his said service & must refer the Department to John W. EDMONDS [1799–1874], Recorder of said Hudson [Presiding Justice of the Supreme Court]; Joseph D. MONELL [1781–1861], Clerk of this County; Elisha JENKINS [1765–184], Vice Regent of the Union City of this State, & others of his neighbors who can testify as to his character for truth & veracity & his reputation as a soldier of the Revolution—

"That he is not personally acquainted with any clergyman of this city, there being none of his crew resident here, of his acquaintance. And he would also refer the Department to the Hon. Martin VAN BUREN, who can testify as to the same facts as the other persons referred to—

John ended by directing the courts to the Honorable Martin VAN BUREN (1782-1862), who testified to the veracity of Captain John KEMPER's declaration of his service to our country during the American Revolution. Martin VAN BUREN ran for vice president along with incumbent President Andrew JACKSON (1767-1845) that same year. After he served the vice president term, he ran for and became the eighth president of the United States (1837-1841).

Martin VAN BUREN's father, Abraham (1737-1817), was a captain in the seventh Albany County regiment, which marched to join General Horatio GATES at the Battle of Saratoga. Abraham had become friends with Captain KEMPER at the officers' club after he moved upstate to Hudson, NewYork. They all shared in each other's stories and revolutionary experiences.

Abraham had introduced Captain KEMPER to his family, and they had visited each other in one's or the other's home over the years. Martin VAN BUREN, when he was a state senator, served with Dr. William Henry DOLL (1775-1829) of the New York

State assembly, who had married Captain KEMPER's cousin Sophia BEAUMAN (1773-1848), daughter of Colonel Sebastian BEAUMAN (1739-1803) and Captain KEMPER's first cousin, Anna Gertrude WETZELL (1751-1786).

Captain KEMPER had served with Colonel BEAUMAN at Valley Forge and brought supplies to him when he was at West Point, New York. Whenever Captain KEMPER would bring supplies to General WASHINGTON's camp, he would always stop in to see close friends and family, like Colonel BEAUMAN and Lieutenant Anthony MAXWELL. These men were always in the battlefront, and he never knew when or if he would see them again.

When Senator Martin VAN BUREN (1782-1862) was not visiting Dr. William DOLL at his home, he would often have him over for dinner, along with Captain KEMPER and Colonel Elisha JENKINS in his home in Kinderhook, New York. Captain KEMPER described Mr. VAN BUREN's home as a large grand estate with a beautiful Dutch house. It lay just south of the village of Kinderhook, off the main road to Albany. New York. According to Elizabeth, her father told her how peaceful it was at Mr. VAN BUREN's home. He liked that it was surrounded by woods and away from the hustle and bustle of the city. It was like a walk in the park.

The court obtained vouchers for John's service from the Honorable Martin VAN BUREN, United States senator, New York State attorney general, governor of New York State, chairman of the United States Committee on Judiciary, secretary of state under President Andrew JACKSON (1767-1845); Colonel Elisha JENKINS (1765-1848), secretary of New York State, vice-chancellor of the regents of the University of New York State, New York State comptroller, mayor of Albany, New York, member of the New York State Assembly, and was a presidential candidate in the election year of 1840. He also served with Captain John KEMPER in Colonel Henry J. VAN RENSSELAER's regiment.

Other important figures stepped in: John's brother Colonel Daniel KEMPER, aide-de-camp to General George WASHINGTON, deputy clothier-general of the Continental Army, special-assistant aide at the Battles of Germantown and Monmouth, saved General Marquis DE LAFAYETTE's life, recipient of the Badge of the Society of Cincinnati by General Marquis DE LAFAYETTE; John Worth EDMONDS (1779-1874), presiding justice of the Supreme Court, New York State Assembly (1831-1832), New York State Senate (1832-1835), son of General Samuel EDMONDS, who grew up with Captain KEMPER in New York City and served with him at Valley Forge; Joseph D. MONELL (1781-1861) surrogate judge, New York State Assembly, clerk of Columbia County and Gayer GARDNER (1778-1849) a merchant in Hudson.

After the Honorable Martin VAN BUREN had filled out his voucher of Captain John KEMPER's service, he stopped by to see John at his home. Mr. VAN BUREN knocked on John's door and John replied, *"The door is open."*

Mr. VAN BUREN opened the door and walked in. He replied, *"Good to see you, John. I just finished up at the courthouse giving my voucher of your service; everything is set. Enjoy your well-earned pension for your service to our country, it has been a pleasure that I was able to assist."*

John said, *"Thanks, Mr. VAN BUREN, it was just formalities that needed to be followed."*

Mr. VAN BUREN responded, *"Yes, I know; I need to get back on the campaign trail now so, I will leave you with my best wishes. No need to let me out I know the way."*

"Nonsense," John said, *"I need some exercise anyway."*

Visits by old friends, either business or otherwise, were always welcomed by John. He was at the age where any day could be the final day.

John used his crutches as a brace to stand and followed Mr. VAN BUREN to the door. Mr. VAN BUREN shook John's hand, got into his carriage, waved goodbye and rode off. Mr. KEMPER raised his right crutch in the air acknowledging Mr. VAN BUREN's wave. He watched as Mr. VAN BUREN's carriage faded away in the distance. He slowly turned and went back into his house. Whenever politicians were running for office in Hudson, they always stopped by for his support.

Elizabeth recorded in her diary that her father had informed her of what Colonel Elisha JENKINS had told him after filling out his voucher for John's service. Colonel JENKINS informed the pension department that everyone knew personally of Captain KEMPER's service. He also declared that all Captain KEMPER's friends were members of the officers' club in Hudson, which membership was filled with officers of the Revolutionary War. He continued that everyone knew of his sealed orders from Colonel Alexander HAMILTON to Colonel Henry VAN RENSSELAER. If anyone ever knew what was in the orders, it was never recorded in Elizabeth's diary.

This small amount of information that Colonel Elisha JENKINS recorded for the War Department would never have been known about if not for Elizabeth recording it in her diary. Colonel JENKINS also signed a certificate at the Hudson City Courthouse, stating, *"John* [KEMPER] *served precisely as stated in his declaration!"* The pension department was in sole possession of Colonel JENKINS's voucher. This voucher was one of the many documents alluded to that had subsequently disappeared. Colonel JENKINS was also a member of the officers' club in Hudson.

John W. EDMONDS was well acquainted with Captain John KEMPER's service through his father, General Samuel EDMONDS (1760-1825). General EDMONDS grew up in New York City with Captain KEMPER. After the war broke out, he joined the Revolution from Rhode Island. During the Revolution, he continued as friends with Captain KEMPER. After Colonel

Alexander HAMILTON sent Captain KEMPER to Hudson (formerly Claverack Landing), General EDMONDS followed. John EDMONDS made this information clear in his voucher of Captain John KEMPER's service.

All these statesmen had become close, dear friends of John KEMPER's, over the years. Upon receiving Captain John KEMPER's declaration and the supporting vouchers of his service, the pension department threw in a monkey wrench; they falsely claimed that they never received his declaration. They requested that John re-submit another declaration. As we read between the lines, the pension department was looking for a variance that might affect the veracity of his statement. This is not an unusual request from a government agency that wants to verify the authenticity of a claim to the benefits they are offering.

It is not likely that the pension department requested a second voucher from the Honorable Martin VAN BUREN, Colonel Elisha JENKINS, or John W. EDMONDS, presiding justice of the Supreme Court. They knew better than to question these top heads of state, which could open a can of worms. Neither did they contact them for clarification. Their vouchers mysteriously disappeared for reasons that will be made clear shortly. John was blinded by his love for our country having played a major part in its birth and having had no clue about what was happening to him.

This declaration is pretty much the same as the first with the following exceptions. John stated in his first declaration that, he had left Philadelphia on the afternoon before the British captured and occupied said city, with over a hundred wagons under his command and a *'lieutenant's guard'* to protect the transports. In his second declaration, he stated that it was a *'captain's guard.'* He also added additional important details to his service. John stated that *"he received his 'orders of march' from Colonel* [Alexander] *HAMILTON on Walnut Street, in Philadelphia."* Wow! Bingo!

If the pension department had done what they were supposed to and looked into General George WASHINGTON's papers, which they had easy access to right there in Washington, they would have found out that General WASHINGTON had, in fact, sent an emergency dispatch to Colonel Alexander HAMILTON, warning him that *the British Army commanded by* [Major] *General Sir William HOWE was marching toward Philadelphia with 15,000 troops.*

It ordered Colonel HAMILTON to Philadelphia to *"find who he trusted to evacuate said city and to have all the supplies of the stores cleared out with everything that could be carried, before the British got possession of the city."* Or more likely, as Commissioner EDWARDS admitted, *"he had examined everything in the reach of his department,"* but kept all the details to himself. Commissioner EDWARDS considered the pension department his, and no one was going to upset his apple cart.

It is to be noted here that out of all the captains Colonel Alexander HAMILTON had become familiar with, including Captain Henry *"Light Horse Harry"* LEE, Captain John KEMPER was his number 1 choice—the one who he trusted most. Captain KEMPER was a real gentleman, non-confrontational, and whenever a job needed to be done, he would always be there early.

Colonel HAMILTON had become close with Captain KEMPER at Kemper's Tavern and while at Philadelphia, including having good times at City Tavern. In addition, he knew that General WASHINGTON had become fond of Captain KEMPER since the crossing of the Delaware.

Furthermore, Colonel Alexander HAMILTON never issued **"orders of march"** to civilians. This was a military order given to military personnel only. Civilians would not be familiar with military protocol! Only another Continental officer would have known of this order. At this point, President George WASHINGTON had already passed on and Major General

Alexander HAMILTON had been killed in an illegal duel with Vice President Aaron BURR on 12 July 1804. HAMILTON's death left Captain John KEMPER the last Continental officer left alive to personally know of this order. Why did the pension department not see this, or did they? What shadows and mysteries lurked in the darkness here?

John KEMPER continued to add more important details in his second declaration of his service to our country. He added, *"His brother, [Colonel] Daniel KEMPER, was deputy clothier-general of the Continental Army"* (one of his superior officers). John further added, *"He was also a prisoner on the Jersey and Scorpion Prison Ships."* John stated, *"He was in actual service of the United States for four years and six months, and one year nine months as a prisoner of war."* If the pension department had asked more precise questions, they would have gotten a household full of information. Questions are more easily answered than trying to guess what someone is looking for.

On 26 November 1832, Justice Josiah Woodbury FAIRFIELD of Hudson, New York, responded to the Honorable James L. EDWARDS, commissioner of pensions, claiming that John KEMPER's application for a pension forwarded to his office on 20 July 1832 never arrived. Then J. W. FAIRFIELD stated that *"he could not understand what possibly could have happened to it but a new application has been sent."* How would Commissioner EDWARDS know of an application forwarded on that date when there was no correspondence alluding to it? Hmm, suspicious?

J. W. FAIRFIELD continued by saying, *"This new application is in accordance with your rules and regulations, which I hope is all satisfactory, for reasons I have mentioned to the Secretary of the Navy,"* Levi WOODBURY (1798-1851), appointed by President Andrew JACKSON on 23 May 1831. *"I am desirous that these papers might be examined and acted upon, out of regular course. In making those suggestions to the secretary, and in expressing this wish to you, I trust I am actuated by pure motives, 'with no interest to transgress any of your rules and regulations'."*

What J. W. FAIRFIELD was making reference to, was the Honorable Martin VAN BUREN's voucher of Captain John KEMPER's service during the American Revolution. The Honorable VAN BUREN was currently running for vice president of the United States, along with incumbent President Andrew JACKSON. What Justice FAIRFIELD was trying to do was to avoid what could become a sticky situation, especially if Commissioner EDWARDS were to say that Martin VAN BUREN was incorrectly understood when he vouched for Captain KEMPER's service.

On 30 November 1832, after the pension department received John's second declaration informing them that his brother, Colonel Daniel KEMPER, was deputy clothier-general, they contacted him for his voucher of his brother, John's service.

On 13 December 1832 in New Brunswick, New Jersey, John's brother Colonel Daniel KEMPER responded to the secretary of war's request to give a voucher regarding his brother John's service. Daniel replied, *"Your favor of the 30th last, I had the honor to receive on the third instant, and should have paid earlier attention to its contents, had my health permitted."*

It is the sincere belief of this author that although Daniel was now 83 years old and probably not in the best of health, he got a quick letter out to his brother John. He asked him for some details on his deployment so that he could best assist him. The naming of all the officers who were in Mill Prison with his brother John was just too perfect and thoroughly documented in the British archives. It is not likely that Daniel could have remembered all of them. Daniel was trying to give a credible account of his brother's life during the American Revolution. At one time, everything was crystal clear to him; but now, time had disrupted his memory.

During this period of time, so much attention was being devoted in the press to the countless thousands of prisoners who had been slaughtered in the British prison ships and under the Provost Marshal Captain William "Bloody Bill" CUNNINGHAM in New York City. Colonel Daniel KEMPER thought by concentrating on John's naval service and as a prisoner of war, he would finally be able to help his brother get what was rightfully his. Or so he thought! Because of Daniel's own declining health, he was getting around in a wheeled rocking chair.

After the pension department went through the same routine with Daniel claiming that they did not receive his voucher, it also is this author's firm belief that Daniel referred back to his brother, John's letter. In his second voucher, he added that *"after his brother's health was restored, he again went back to Philadelphia and entered into the service under General* [John Peter] *MUHLENBERGH in a fort* [Mifflin] *on the Delaware River."* However, it is possible that Daniel did remember this icon on his own, as both he and his brother, John, did march with him, along with General WASHINGTON, through the streets of Philadelphia, and both served with him at Valley Forge.

On 18 April 1833, in New Brunswick, New Jersey, Colonel Daniel KEMPER, now 84 years old, responded to the secretary of war's letter that they never received his voucher of his brother John's service during the American Revolution. Daniel stated that he was responding to the pension department's request of 15 April 1833. Like everyone else, he did not know what was really going on. He trusted that the pension office was being truthful and not deceptive. Times had truly changed.

He began by informing the pension department, that he was afflicted with the debilitated state of body and mind last winter. He feared that he would no longer be able to give an accurate account of his brother's service, but did his best. This voucher is severely scrambled. Daniel did the same as he did in his first voucher and put John's naval service before his duties as wagon master. He went on to explain that *"when my brother made his escape to the Jersey shore, John was able to find his way to my house to recover."*

"After his recovery," Daniel stated, *"John returned to Philadelphia in the spring of 1782 and served under General* [John Peter] *MUHLENBERGH in a fort* [Mifflin] *on the Delaware River."* However, John clearly stated in his declaration that, *"After his escape he arrived back home in November 1781, just after the surrender of General* [Lord Charles] *CORNWALLIS at Yorktown* [19 Oct. 1781]. *After a brief recovery, he again returned to Philadelphia in the same month and year, November 1781."*

Therefore, it is more accurate to say that early in November of 1781 was the time he entered into the service under General MUHLENBERGH, a friend and comrade whom he marched through the streets of Philadelphia with and served with at Valley Forge. So you can see how badly scrambled Daniel's second voucher is. To see the original document, visit this author's album National Archives on Facebook. Daniel closed by saying that *"His brother, John, is a perfect cripple and cannot get around without his crutches, cannot attend to his business and is supported by his children."*

Upon receiving Colonel Daniel KEMPER's second declaration, the pension department stated in their own records that *"because the timetable was moved up, they were not able to use it to support John's declaration."* This is not true! They could have done the same thing that this author did and what anyone else can do: extract all the data from Daniel's declaration, without changing any of the language, and then place all the information back in proper chronological order. Bingo! You end up with a nice supportive voucher of Captain John KEMPER's service during the American Revolution. In fact, eight years later, the pension department did use, from both John's and his brother Daniel's declarations, one part against him but never used any information on John's behalf; how convenient.

Daniel stated in his voucher, *"His brother, John, joined and did duty with the militia in New Jersey."* Daniel is referring to the fact that on 15 September 1775, all three brothers—Daniel, Jacob, and John—joined the Minute Men of the New Jersey Line of Captain Adolphus WALDRON's militia of King's County Light Horse. Captain WALDRON was German and a friend of the family. That is why all three brothers joined his company. This initial service at the start of the Revolution, likewise, is covered in the KEMPER family Bible; however, for some unknown reason, John never claimed this part of his service in his declaration.

Jacob KEMPER later became captain and did duty in the Continental Line of New Jersey for the entire duration of the American Revolution. This was a revolutionary family, whose enlistments were encouraged and supported by their brother-in-law John MORTON and their parents, Jacob and Maria Regina KEMPER, a military family from Germany, who had been the hereditary military commander of Stahleck Castle, Bacharach, Germany.

Daniel went on to state that *"John then went to Philadelphia, was on an armed vessel when he was captured and transferred to the prison ship, Jersey. John then made his escape to the Jersey shore and made his way to Daniel's house, where he recovered."* Daniel continued that *"John then returned to Philadelphia and entered the ship, General Green, as a midshipman for a six-month cruise. Then John was recaptured by the British Brig, Iris, and carried to New York."* Daniel continued to try to recollect his memories the best he could; time had wiped out so much.

Daniel continued by saying, *"But after some time, he was with many others, Comd MANLEY, Capts CAMP* [John KEMP], *CUNNINGHAM, TALBOT, SLOVER, BARNEY and others, were taken on shore and confined in the Provost guard house in the city, under* [Captain William] *CUNNINGHAM. And from thence they were sent on an old British ship of war, and sent to England*

and confined in the Mill Prison, charged with piracy and rebellion on the high seas. They were severely treated for a long time."

Even though the other officers named by Daniel to have served with his brother, John, were out of sequence in order of event, all these officers are 100 percent documented in the British Prison records to have been confined with Lieutenant John KEMPER in Mill Prison, England. There was one mistake on the spelling of the name CAMP because of the similar pronunciation; its actual spelling was KEMP, representing John KEMP. It is pretty incredible that Daniel could remember all these officers. This could have happened one of two ways. One, Daniel knew personally of his brother John's mission to locate certain targets, specifically certain officers or two, he had a letter from his brother refreshing his memory by listing them.

Daniel continued by saying, *"After a long time, he with another, effected their escape and got on board a ship bound to the island of Jamaica. When they arrived, and after some time, he again effected his escape on shore and was concealed by a colored women, until he was convey'd on board an American vessel and arrived once more on his native shore, but very much reduced by his hard usage. - After he had recovered his health and strength toward spring, he went again to Philad, was in the fort [Mifflin] on the Delaware River with Genl MUHLENBERGH, was afterwards employed by Mr. MEASE, Cloth<u>r</u> Genl, and appointed Wagon Master, and engaged in transporting the **public stores** from the city [Philadelphia] to Lancaster. He continued in that employ to the close of the Revolution."*

So as you can see, Daniel's voucher is out of sequence and severely scrambled, especially since he was the deputy clothier-general of the Continental Army. But once again, if you extract all the data without changing any of the language and place it all back in proper chronological order, you do not have a bad voucher from a very old man in his mid-eighties. What Daniel was trying hard not to do here was show privilege for his brother; however, in the later pension years, he would be forced to tell the truth, that he procured his brother John's appointment. With all the years that had gone by, Daniel had done the best he could. Would it be enough?

For those of us who are veterans, we are well familiar with friends and family who sometimes join us in the military. We are often given different deployments and may not always know of all the details, but since we are close to them and share in our stories, we can give a fairly good account of their service. The accuracy, of course, depends a lot on our age. Those of us who are veterans always do our best to help those whose service we know of personally.

On 1 May 1833, after all documents were thoroughly investigated and given credence, Lewis B. CASS (1782-1866), secretary of war, who was appointed by President Andrew JACKSON on 1 August 1831 and James L. EDWARDS (1787-1862), commissioner of pensions, who had been appointed by President JACKSON on 3 March 1833, signed a voucher entitling John KEMPER to receive a pension as captain and conductor of transport teams and midshipman in the army and navy of the Revolution. New wording had to be entered into this new certificate when it had to be forged years later.

What was unknown at the time was even though Captain John KEMPER's service under General WASHINGTON was verified, along with General WASHINGTON's special protection of him, riddles filled the War Department heads. Eventually, after Captain KEMPER found out he was being cheated out of a large portion of his pension, they ended up canceling and holding it hostage in hopes of finding out what the special protection was for. Would they be successful?

This special protection would end up being the heart of all inquiries throughout the entire pension years. Fraudulent claims would be made by the pension department in hopes of shaking loose the true meaning for General WASHINGTON's special protection of Captain John KEMPER.

In later years, these records would have to be forged, but only after they could re-acquire Captain KEMPER's original certificate, which they did by manipulating Captain KEMPER's agent, Mr. YATES, into returning it for the promise of a new certificate. However, they forgot to include the new certificate and forged the old one.

This newly forged certificate recorded entitled him to receive $216 per annum during his natural life, commencing on 4 March 1831 and payable semi-annually on the fourth of March and the fourth of September every year. What was unknown by John at the time was that as captain and wagon master in the Continental Army under General George WASHINGTON, he was supposed to have been receiving $480 semi-annually. Furthermore, there were additional monies due as lieutenant in the US Navy.

But something is dreadfully wrong here! John did not catch it until several years later when other veterans at the officers' club in Hudson, New York, including his brother Colonel Daniel KEMPER and brother-in-law Sergeant John HARDICK, who had married John's wife, Elizabeth's sister, Polly HOPPER (1770-1848), brought it to his attention. Up until this point, Daniel had not known that his brother was being underpaid; when he found out, he was enraged and advised his brother to put in for the correct amount.

Sergeant John HARDICK, likewise, was a pensioner of the American Revolution, having served in Captain Jacob PHILIPS's (1746-1807) company in Colonel Robert VAN RENSSELAER's Eighth Albany County Regiment. His regiment marched to join General Horatio GATES at the Battle of Saratoga and was present for the surrender of General John BURGOYNE. Besides being a good friend and brother-in-law, he was Captain John

KEMPER's neighbor, living in the second ward of the city of Hudson. *A storm is brewing!*

John KEMPER headed to the Hudson City Courthouse to see James ROWLEY (1790-1858), a friend of the family; John had joined the officers' club with his father, Lieutenant Nathaniel ROWLEY (1762-1850), when he moved upstate. Nathaniel was a young boy when he had joined the Revolution and had served in Captain Ebenezer CADY's (1743-1816) company, in Colonel William B. WHITING's (1731-1796) Eighth Albany County Regiment. Colonel Henry J. VAN RENSSELAER was the lieutenant colonel. Lieutenant ROWLEY had marched with Captain CADY's company to join General Horatio GATES at the Battle of Saratoga. All were present for the surrender of General John BURGOYNE.

On 4 October 1835, Colonel Benjamin TALLMADGE died at Litchfield, Connecticut. Captain KEMPER's daughter, Elizabeth, was at a newsstand in Hudson when she caught sight of an article regarding Colonel TALLMADGE. Remembering that her father had mentioned his name frequently over the years, she bought the article and took it home with her. After arriving home, Elizabeth said, *"Dad, there was an article on Colonel TALLMADE at the newsstand which I purchased."*

John inquired, *"What does it say, honey?"*

Elizabeth answered, *"That he had just died in Litchfield, Connecticut. a few days ago, and throughout the years gave thanks to the many members of his spy ring who were 'un-trumpeted' and 'unknown' who helped secure victory against the British."*

John nervously asked, *"Does he mention any names?"*

Elizabeth answered, *"I do not think so."*

Her father said, *"Make sure!"*

After Elizabeth finished the article, she replied, *"No!"*

Elizabeth's father, seemingly calmer, replied, *"First of all, it was not Colonel TALLMADGE's spy ring, but in fact, General WASHINGTON's. Colonel TALLMADGE, like the rest of us, was given a position that General WASHINGTON trusted us with. He should not be tooting his own horn, nor should he be revealing, acknowledging or implying any intelligence secrets of our country. If he had done this when General WASHINGTON was around, he would have been court-martialed."*

"Colonel TALLMADGE appears to be glorifying his own name, implying that everything was top secret except him. Thereby proving, in his own words, that everyone involved in intelligence was more important than he was, which is more accurate to say. All intelligence officers die invisible and unknown; unless, of course, they have other intentions in mind for themselves, like being remembered for something."

On 17 December 1835, after a constant influx of complaints to Congress, of revolutionary veterans struck off the rolls, they enacted a resolution requiring the War Department to furnish a statement of all veterans pensioned for their services during the American Revolution who were struck off the roll. Later, Captain KEMPER would become a member of this roster, after he had made the same mistake others had made, discovering he was being underpaid and put in for an increase.

On 24 February 1836, James L. EDWARDS, commissioner of pensions, and the Honorable Lewis CASS, secretary of war, submitted a list of pensioners struck off the roll to the Honorable James K. POLK (1795-1849), speaker of the House of Representatives. The list numbered in the hundreds. Can you imagine all those veterans in the final years of their lives being erased from the rolls and thus being left desolate? Shortly thereafter, Lewis CASS suddenly bailed out as secretary of war, leaving much speculation and his post vacant before his term ended. He did not stick around long enough to train the later incoming secretary of war Joel R. POINSETT (1779-1851).

These records showed that when many of the pensioners put in for an increase, for one reason or another, their pension was canceled. It appears that these veterans were sporadically targeted as not to bring notice to the numbers of them and in different localities so that they could not compare notes or join forces. It looked like a conspiracy to get at the veterans' money, knowing that they neither had the means or time left in life to discover or contest what was going on. Captain KEMPER's case was uniquely different and lingered on to the present time, 1987.

On 8 December 1836, John KEMPER's nephew, Major General Jacob MORTON (1761-1836), died in New York City. John sent his condolences and asked his widow, Catherine (1767-1849) to please forgive his inability to attend his funeral as he could barely get around with his crutches because of his own disabilities.

On 7 March 1837, President Martin VAN BUREN appointed Joel Roberts POINSETT secretary of war. He served until 5 March 1841. He was not trained by the previous Secretary of War, so he was unacquainted with what was about to happen with Captain John KEMPER's case or what had been going on with any other veterans. He was totally in the dark. After he found out about Captain KEMPER's pension being canceled without being informed of the reason, he ordered the agent Commissioner EDWARDS to answer their inquiries.

2. Who Has Been Dipping into Captain Kemper's Pension Money? Inquiry into Being Underpaid in His Pension for Five Years

On 5 July 1837, James ROWLEY of Hudson, New York, wrote to James L. EDWARDS, commissioner of pensions, in Washington, DC. He stated,

> *John KEMPER has been informed that he is entitled to a larger pension under the act of 1832 than he is currently receiving for his duties as wagon master during the Revolutionary War. Under the act of Congress passed May 1779, a Wagon Master shall receive $80 per month [$480 semi-annually] & one ration per day & $10 per month [$60 semiannually] substances [totaling $540 semiannually]. He requests the proper procedures to go through to obtain that increase.*

Up to this point, John had been underpaid for five years for his services as a captain and wagon master in the Continental Army and as a lieutenant in the United States Navy. John's rank and service had been changed in the original records in the pension office of the War Department from what he had stated in his declaration without anyone knowing of it. All requests were ignored by the pension department. At this point, by ignoring him, Commissioner EDWARDS might have hoped Captain KEMPER would forget about it and let it ride.

Captain KEMPER then contacted his brother, Colonel Daniel KEMPER, answering his repeated requests on how things were going. He informed his brother that his inquires had gone continually ignored by the pension department for the past two years. We had paved the way for the good and the bad. Daniel advised his brother John, that something very funny was going on here and further advised him to seek an agent providing legal representation and that he would back him 100 percent. As one of his brother's superior officers, he was confident he would be able to vindicate him.

Daniel closed in his advice to his brother by saying, *"John, we are not amongst our own anymore. All those running our country never went through the hardships and sufferings we went through for its existence; we are on our own now. There is no more General WASHINGTON to protect us. I understand many other*

Revolutionary veterans from the New York area [New York City] *have had their pensions cancelled. Something very fishy is going on here, but I cannot put my finger on it."* Daniel was unaware that his brother's case would become the longest in American history.

3. John Kemper Contacts New York State Agent, Giles F. Yates

On 20 April 1839, after being ignored for two years, Captain KEMPER went in again to see James ROWLEY at the Hudson City Courthouse. He advised John to write to the New York State agent for Veterans Affairs, Giles Fonda YATES (1798-1859), surrogate and counselor at law of Schenectady, New York.

John wrote Agent YATES,

> *"I wish you would the next time you go to Washington—attend to my application for an increase of pension. I am satisfied that I do not get as much as I am entitled to. Let me know what papers, if any, you wish me to furnish you.*

> *Yours—Jno KEMPER*

Agent YATES started setting up procedures to represent John, but he had no idea how different this case would be and that it would cost him over ten years of his lifetime. Likewise, John had no idea that this pension battle would take up all the final years of his life and be the cause of his death.

What Captain KEMPER did not know was that Commissioner EDWARDS had a surprise in store for him in the event he took this action any further. That surprise was about to happen to the shock and disbelief of all. Captain KEMPER's friends and neighbors would rally to his side while the halls of Congress went into shock. Then members of Congress would join in on Captain KEMPER's side. John's brother, Daniel, who was being taken care of by his daughter, Jane, likewise, rallied to his brother's side. Daniel felt he was partially to blame after advising his brother to take legal action to obtain what was rightfully his.

On 23 April 1839, Giles F. YATES, counselor at law, wrote James L. EDWARDS, commissioner of pensions, requesting a re-examination of John KEMPER's papers with a view of getting his stipend increased. Up until this point, John KEMPER had been underpaid for seven years, and all requests for the past two years had been ignored. The debt owed by the pension department continued to increase dramatically.

However, now a New York State agent was involved and James L. EDWARDS was furious! During this period of time, James L. EDWARDS was untouchable. Even all the members of Congress who came behind Captain KEMPER had no power to do anything but request an inquiry. Agent YATES was captivated profoundly by Captain KEMPER's part as a founding father in the birth of America and represented his dignity profusely!

In August 1839, Captain KEMPER's niece, Eliza Susan (Morton) QUINCY, took a trip. She crossed the Hudson River from New York City to Jersey City, New Jersey. From there she went by railroad to Morristown, New Jersey, and there took a carriage to visit her childhood hometown of Basking Ridge, New Jersey.

She passed the night at Somerville then went on traveling bad roads but beautiful country to New Brunswick. She sent her servants to inform her uncle Daniel KEMPER of her arrival and that she would visit him in the afternoon. Mr. KEMPER, who was ninety years of age, still had his faculties. Eliza recorded, *"He was one of the most noble looking old men she ever saw; his sight and hearing perfect. He was delighted to see me,"* and said, *"I see your mother in you!"*

Eliza's uncle Daniel had visitors—his daughter, Jane KEMPER (1788-1872), and granddaughter, Elizabeth Marius (1824-1898), daughter of his son, Bishop David Jackson KEMPER (1789-1870), of Nashotah, Wisconsin. Daniel had everything pleasant around his residence. However, Daniel never informed his niece what troubles her Uncle John was going through. If Eliza's description of her uncle Daniel is correct, why were his records at the pension office making him look feeble-minded?

He was fond of the cultivation of flowers and took Eliza into his garden. He showed her the stone house on Albany Street where her grandparents had resided and where he was born in 1749. As a reward for his service as colonel in the army of the Revolution, he received a lucrative office from General WASHINGTON and was appointed head of US Business and Custom House Service in New York City (1795-1807) and was treated by the citizens of New Brunswick with great respect.

4. Pension Is Canceled!

On 4 September 1839, the semi-annual date when John was to receive his pension came, but the money never arrived. He waited and waited and waited, but still there was no notification. He finally contacted the agent in Albany, New York for paying pensions. The agent informed John, *"His pension had suddenly been cut off without notification or reason, and* [the agent] *does not know what to think of it."* John, being confused, went to see James ROWLEY, commissioner of deeds at the Hudson City Courthouse, to inquire as to what could possibly have gone wrong.

On 23 September 1839, James ROWLEY of Hudson, New York, wrote to James L. EDWARDS. He tried to bring notice that John KEMPER was old, feeble, frail, and terribly disappointed with having his pension for his service to our country discontinued. Mr. ROWLEY requested an explanation for the suspension so that John could be properly represented.

James ROWLEY related Captain KEMPER's disappointment,

> *"John Kemper has been notified by the agent for paying pensions in Albany* [New York], *that his pension has been suspended for reasons, not stated and Mr. Kemper feels very disappointed. And as his pension has been his main support, he being old and infirm, wishes me to ask you for the reasons for the suspension of his pension. So that if it is possible to give him an opportunity of being heard in answering, or explaining whatever the objections may be. My own personal acquaintance with Mr. Kemper is such that I know him to be considered here, an honorable poor man and has been a citizen of our place for more than thirty years past. I am with much respect your obedient servant—James Rowley.*

James ROWLEY's letter to James L. EDWARDS, commissioner of pensions was, intercepted by his superior, Joel R. POINSETT, secretary of war. Not knowing what was going on in the previous administration, Mr. POINSETT immediately looked into John KEMPER's records. After examining them, he personally responded to James ROWLEY, of Hudson, New York.

On 28 September 1839, Joel R. POINSETT, Secretary of War, responded to James ROWLEY's inquiry, stating,

> *"In answer to your letter of the 23rd, inst. I have to inform you that I know of no reason for not paying the pension of John KEMPER. He was paid up to the 4th of March last, and I have given no order whatever to stop his pension. The Agent* [James L. EDWARDS] *should have given notice to Mr. KEMPER in writing, and assigned a reason for not paying him. I have written to the Agent on the subject.*

Secretary of War Joel POINSETT had no way of knowing about the *trickery* Commissioner EDWARDS was pulling for his defense. Mr. POINSETT later took Commissioner EDWARDS at his word, claiming that Captain KEMPER served under a civil contract and was not entitled to a pension and backed off the issue. It is truly amazing how Commissioner EDWARDS was able to quickly doctor up Captain KEMPER's records, in sighting new meaning in the wording of his declaration, which had already been proven, without being held accountable and providing evidence.

In retrospect, whenever a veteran's pension was canceled because of fraud, as implied by Commissioner EDWARDS, charges would have had to be brought against all those involved who gave vouchers and testimony of Captain John KEMPER's service. Vouchers and witnesses like those from President Martin VAN BUREN, Colonel Elisha JENKINS, Colonel Daniel KEMPER, and John W. EDMONDS, presiding justice of the Supreme Court. This never happened! In fact, all these vouchers and testimonies are now missing but alluded to in many other correspondences.

On 5 October 1839, after receiving an order from Joel POINSETT, Secretary of War, to comply with the proper procedures for suspending veterans' pensions, EDWARDS answered James ROWLEY's inquiry regarding his applicant, John KEMPER. In this letter, Commissioner EDWARDS stated that,

> *"In answer to your enquiries respecting the suspension of John KEMPER's pension, under the act of 7 June '32, I have to state that, the reovy* [recovery] *documents of Genl. WASHINGTON recd* [record] *since the admission of his claim furnished a very strong presumption that the allowance to him as Wagon Conductor in the Dept. of the Clothier General is not warranted - He alleged and was allowed a service of 18 mo from Aug 77 to spring 79 as Wagon Conductor engaged in transporting clothes from the Depots to the Head Quarters."*

It also stated that,

> *"There is 'a return of the Depy Wagon Ms [Master] General—Wagon & Sub Conductors now present with the army on 1st Feby 78' on which his name is not borne - This in connexion with the source whence he alleges he recd. his employment or as he terms it, appointment, furnishes strong evidence that his service of superintending the teams employed in transporting the clothing of the army from the Depots of the Clothier Genl. To the Head Quarters was under civil contract—And therefore afforded no groun[ds] for a claim."*

First of all, John KEMPER was appointed captain and wagon master in August of 1777, while in Philadelphia; not on the first February 1778, when the entire Continental Army was stationed at Valley Forge. This author doubts that there was very little activity at all on this date in the deputy wagon master general's department; and if there was, it would only have been someone newly appointed.

Furthermore, the clothier-general's department never employed civilians to carry on military operations, such as delivering supplies, other than providing them to the army at reasonable prices as ordered by the Continental Congress. Nor were civilians allowed to know where headquarters for the Continental Army were set up. Civilians were, during this period of time, treacherous and naturally incompetent. They supported the Crown, not the Revolution, and turned General WASHINGTON's whereabouts into the British on every chance that they got.

Commissioner EDWARDS continued, *"He [John KEMPER] should state in deta[il] the circumstances under which he was appointed—The responsibilities of his duties to whom he was admenable for the faithful discharge of them—How the Teams*

& Teamsters were procured & paid and how & under what circumstances he left the service" —

Commissioner EDWARDS finally did what he was supposed to, but only because he was ordered to do so by his immediate supervisor, the secretary of war, Joel POINSETT. However, EDWARDS had everyone answering to him instead of him answering the original inquiry about why he canceled the pension: *"Why was Captain John KEMPER underpaid for his service as captain and wagon master in the Continental Army and lieutenant in the US Navy?"* Mr. EDWARDS continued to dodge all documentation and references from the beginning to the end of this case.

EDWARDS continued, *"He was allowed for 6 mo as midshipman in the Pa Navy which carried his alleged service to 24 mo. The maximum of the act 7 June '32—He also alleged 2 other terms in the Pa Navy which it may be important to him to establish if the 18 mo as Wagon Conductor should be finally disallowed—The proof of his rank & service as Midshipman & of the public character of the ships in which he sailed should be drawn from the office of the Secy of Pa. To whom a brief of the cruises should be submitted as necessary data for conducting his examination -"*

Commissioner EDWARDS was fully aware that he was the only one who had all declarations and vouchers backing Captain KEMPER's case. However, he slipped and made a couple of mistakes here, but nobody caught it. First, he used the word *"enquiries,"* admitting that he had two or more that he had not answered, until ordered to do so by Joel POINSETT, secretary of war. Secondly, he used the word *"suspended,"* which means that it was not officially canceled! Thirdly, he alluded to the possibility of it being re-instated by using the phrase, *"If Wagon Conductor should finally be disallowed."* He was also softly preparing him for the possibility that it might not be allowed.

Before making a final decision, Commissioner EDWARDS was being cautious, waiting to see if anyone was going to come up with anything other than what he had already collected. He was not about to share anything with Captain KEMPER's attorney. Furthermore, he refused to acknowledge what was recovered in General WASHINGTON's documents so that he could not be challenged. He refused to furnish or acknowledge those documents, thereby leaving everyone in the dark as to what he was referring.

John's brother Colonel Daniel KEMPER made the reasons for the lack of supporting documents perfectly clear in his declaration to the United States Senate and United States Congress on 9 April 1832. In this declaration, Daniel stated that *"after the sudden death of James MEASE [June 1785], clothier-general of the Continental Army, his executors confiscated all his records, in addition to Daniel's books."*

Therefore, Daniel and anyone else in the records of the clothier-general's department could no longer prove the thousands of dollars in debt owed them, since the records had disappeared. These records are the only ones that would have borne both Captain John and Colonel Daniel KEMPER's names. Commissioner EDWARDS knew about this declaration but kept silent. To see these original documents, please view this author's Facebook album, National Archives.

On 9 October 1839, after James ROWLEY received Commissioner EDWARDS's letter, he called John KEMPER into the courthouse. He transmitted EDWARDS's wishes for a supplement to his original declaration; John sighed with relief, then replied, *"Is that all he wanted? All he had to do was ask me, he did not have to cut off my pension."* Commissioner ROWLEY had John fill out a supplemental declaration putting together a more detailed account of his service to our country, answering all Commissioner EDWARDS' requests.

Supplemental Declaration

In this declaration, John stated,

"My appointment as captain and wagon master was procured by my brother Daniel, who was an aide to General WASHINGTON. He was also a colonel and appointed deputy clothier-general by James MEASE."

"In early August of 1777, he was requested by his brother to head to Philadelphia and report to the wagon-master general's department. Once there, he was appointed captain and wagon master by James YULE [1755-1832], deputy wagon-master general. He received a captain's pay of $40 per month, along with his rations, and the same for his horse."

"He was ordered to receive one hundred and fifty wagons by General WASHINGTON, himself. This order came through Colonel HAMILTON from his temporary head-quarters on Walnut Street in Philadelphia. He was given an automatic clearance through all guards and sentinels and was to report directly to General WASHINGTON."

"His waggoneers [teamsters] were ordered to be paid $15 per month, but since the Continental dollar was worthless, he was ordered to pay them with certificates, which were supposed to be redeemable for cash in the future. Although the waggoneers were disgruntled about their means of pay, we all had our orders."

"He was responsible for suppling General WASHINGTON and the army as long as he was in this department. His original headquarters for supplying the army was in Philadelphia, until the

British captured said city. He then serviced General WASHINGTON and the army from Lancaster, while his wagon train was camped in the wilderness at Conestoga Creek."

"He was primarily stationed in Philadelphia, under James MEASE and his deputy clothier-general, Charles YOUNG. Whenever he was at camp [General WASHINGTON's headquarters], *he was given assignments either by his brother* [Daniel] *or General WASHINGTON. At all times, he maintained General WASHINGTON's special protection from any interference of his command or detention by superior officers."*

"Three days prior to the British capturing Philadelphia, he was given emergency orders from Colonel HAMILTON to transfer all stores from Philadelphia to Lancaster, before the British occupied said city. He then received his orders of march from Colonel HAMILTON on Walnut Street."

"After he had loaded up all his wagons with the stores from the city, he lined them up, heading north on Front Street. He then left Philadelphia one half day before the British captured said city, with a captain's guard [Continental Dragoons] *to protect the transports. He headed toward General WASHINGTON's headquarters in Potsgrove; Colonel HAMILTON accompanied him."*

"After the British had evacuated Philadelphia in June of 1778, he escorted members of congress back to the city, where he reset up headquarters."

"On many occasions, depending on the importance of the transports, his brother [Daniel], Captain

[Henry] LEE, Colonel HAMILTON, General LAFAYETTE and/or General WASHINGTON accompanied his wagon train.

In the spring of 1779, General WASHINGTON was restructuring the clothier-general's department. He made the states responsible for supplying clothing and other supplies for the regiments they had put together."

"In Mid-May of 1779, he was released by Charles YOUNG deputy clothier-general in Philadelphia. He immediately joined the navy at the docks on Front Street in Philadelphia."

Commissioner ROWLEY then advised John that it was best that they give everything to his attorney, Giles F. YATES, for him to handle from this point on. Commissioner ROWLEY closed by requesting John to keep him informed. He inferred that he had other connections that could help. Also, that all his friends and neighbors, who knew his service well, were behind him.

What was not known at that time, other than by the family and personal friends, was that James ROWLEY was a personal friend of John KEMPER's family. James's father, Nathaniel ROWLEY, was a lieutenant in Colonel Robert VAN RENSSELAER's Eighth Albany County Regiment in which, at the time, Henry J. VAN RENSSELAER was a lieutenant colonel.

As a fellow revolutionary soldier, Lieutenant ROWLEY had joined the officers' club in Hudson, New York, and knew Captain KEMPER and his service personally. Besides meeting at the club with him, they often visited in one or the other's home, sharing their war stories. James had grown up knowing Captain KEMPER's service through his father; what he did not know was what was now happening or why—no one did. All he could do was to advise the KEMPER family on how to proceed.

5. Agent Yates Battles Pension Department to restore and Increase Captain KEMPER's Correct Amount

On 12 October 1839, once Giles YATES received John's supplement and true reason his pension was suspended, he prepared a letter to James L. EDWARDS. In this letter, he included John KEMPER's supplement and an analogous case to John KEMPER's by the name of Zaddock HEDDEN (1742-1786). YATES had received this name from a colleague of his, Mr. S. SPENCER in New York City. Giles had sent Agent SPENCER a copy of John KEMPER's case and asked if he had any cases analogous to it? Mr. S. SPENCER sent Agent YATES a copy of HEDDEN's case.

Agent YATES would use HEDDEN throughout the entire history of John KEMPER's case. However, letters, declarations and vouchers backing John KEMPER started to disappear at the pension department. If they had not been alluded to in other correspondences, they might never have been known about, other than in the family.

On 22 October 1839, after being ignored by Commissioner EDWARDS, Captain John KEMPER's New York State agent, Giles F. YATES launched a major assault against James L. EDWARDS, commissioner of pensions. *"Since Mr. John KEMPER's pension has been suspended, he has made several appeals to me, to see him righted."* Giles cited some documents from both General WASHINGTON's papers in the office of the secretary of state and the Journals of the Continental Congress (5 March 1779 and 10 November 1780).

> *Mr. KEMPER, although not rich, has ever sustained the highest character for integrity and veracity. The story of his service as Conductor of wagons, or Wagon Master 18 months and for more than 6 months as a midshipman in the Pennsylvania Navy, he has repeated to his friends and acquaintances years ago, and before the pension law of 1832 was*

passed, as many of his neighbors, or those who were such formerly, can testify. The statement, therefore, of his services, as set forth in his declaration, being in accordance with the uniform statements of Mr. KEMPER on this subject.

Besides, his character and statements are vouched for and confirmed by gentlemen worthy of the highest credit [President Martin VAN BUREN; Colonel Elisha JENKINS, secretary of state; Colonel Daniel KEMPER, aide-de-camp to General WASHINGTON and deputy clothier general of the Continental Army; John W. EDMONDS, presiding justice of the Supreme Court]. *Now it does seem to me, that by disallowing his pension granted once upon an admission of these statements. His own truth and that of his codeponents and avouchers, is called in question!*

How much more did Attorney YATES know about top statesman who supported John KEMPER? Was he being coached by them or their representatives on the side?

Mr. KEMPER, as I understand the matter, was pensioned for the 24 months services above alluded to. I feel of the correctness of my impression, that at the time Mr. KEMPER's pension was allowed, the rates of payments were less than they now are, and that the rate of offices such as he held, was not fully settled. Knowing the course you had adopted in analogous cases in which I was the agent, I had reason to hope for a similar decision in the case of Mr. KEMPER, and made my application in his behalf accordingly—Not having the most remote idea, that the proof in the case could not in any respect be considered defective.

The claim of Mr. KEMPER was admitted on his oath, and that of his brother, who was at the time the service was rendered, assistant Clothier General to James MEASE, Clothier General of the U. States, as I discovered in examining in the WASHINGTON papers in the office of the Secretary of State, and the Journals of Congress. Mr. KEMPER, therefore, produced as competent a witness as could have been had as to the facts in the case, and more over it seems it was all evidence called for to establish the claim.

The objection seems to be that if Mr. KEMPER was employed in the army at all, it was in the transport service under civil contract, by which a charge is cast upon Mr. KEMPER & his brother & their avouchers as before alluded to. With a view to meet this objection, I have made a careful examination of the case. Mr. KEMPER served under the direction of the Clothier General aforesaid and the Commander-in-Chief [General George WASHINGTON himself] was engaged in carrying clothing to the army, and at the time when its safety, and the safety of the country in fact, depended upon the faithful discharge of the duties assigned to such officers. See General WASHINGTON's letter on the subject of the Character of men to be appointed to fill offices of that description. The Quarter Master Genl, the Commissary Genl & the Clothier Genl, and their Deputies acted together. See Journals of Congress March 5, 1779.

The Quarter Master General, the Com: Gen. & Clothier General, and such of their deputies as they shall appoint, be and they are hereby authorized & in the line of their respective departments. & now it is to be supposed that either department, would have had regularly in its employment a Wagon Master entrusted with public property to an immense amount for a year and a half, and all that time under civil contract!

Besides, these departments or rather the heads of them did not enter into civil contracts unless empowered to do so by law. In a case where ox teams were to be substituted for horses if thought unofficial to the service, the Com: in Chief, was authorized by law to direct the Quarter Master to that effect. [See journal 10 November, 1780.] *Again, if a civil contract had to be entered into, it would have been made with A. B.* (about) *as a private individual & not as an officer.*

If Mr. KEMPER then served under the direction of the Clothier General & it is unreasonable to expect to find his name on the roll of any Deputy Wagon Master, even if the few rolls of that description hitherto found, could be relied upon as perfect. Which it is notorious is far from being the case. In the whole of the WASHINGTON papers, which I have examined faithfully, I cannot find more than two or three of these rolls.

I have found a few rolls of naval officers in the Treasury Department [register's office] *but none among the WASHINGTON papers; and have now turned my attention to the examination of documentary proof to establish KEMPER's naval service, which alone, unless I very much misjudge the matter, would entitle him to all the pension he formerly received. Whether such proof is or is not to be found in your department, we are not informed. I feel bound to solicit a reexamination of the claim.*

Giles also stated that *"all of John KEMPER's neighbors can testify to his service in the American Revolution, of which they have known about all of their lives."* Giles further stated, *"The technologies of language in describing his offices by the various agents who handled his case, are not obnoxious to suspicion, and cannot without an imputation cast upon his character, which is, without reproach, be gainsay."*

Mr. YATES was interpreting Mr. EDWARDS's conduct as responding to language given by Captain KEMPER's vouchers, but he was dead wrong! Commissioner EDWARDS was guarding his back for misappropriating thousands of dollars in funds that were supposed to have been going to Captain KEMPER over the past seven years. Much forgery and destruction of records would have to follow.

More importantly, he would have to re-acquire Captain KEMPER's original certificate awarding him for his service as captain and wagon master in the Continental Army; how could he do that? Mr. EDWARDS would have to make minor concessions, while still staying in control.

In the correspondence above, Agent YATES states, *"Besides, his character and statements are vouched for and confirmed by gentlemen worthy of the highest credit."* How did attorney YATES know about the vouchers of these top statesmen and know that EDWARDS knew? He had not seen these vouchers! Did John have him contact officers of the Hudson City Courthouse, Commissioner James ROWLEY and Josiah W. FAIRFIELD? Was he just trying to make reference to these statesmen, letting EDWARDS know that he knew about John KEMPER's plight, without implicating them further?

On 26 November 1839, Giles F. YATES sent yet another correspondence to James EDWARDS, continuing to plead Captain John KEMPER's case. He stated that, *"He [Yates] is in possession of a correspondence from John's brother,* [Colonel]

Daniel KEMPER, asst. clothier-general [of the Continental Army and aide-de-camp to General WASHINGTON], *giving his 'affidavit' that his brother John was a 'wagon master' & that he served under him."* Daniel, who is ninety years old now, continued by saying that, *"he also recollects his brother serving as a midshipman in the navy, but can no longer remember the particulars."* He further declared that *"his revolutionary papers and documents were destroyed when taken prisoner."*

In closing, Giles replied, *"In the absence of these, it has been usual in your department to receive as competent & conclusive (& should to be) the testimony of* officers *under whom the applicant served. In this case, Daniel KEMPER* has given *his affidavit, and I cannot possibly conceive what sound objection there can be to the reestablishment & allowance of the claim, with the increased allowance to which John KEMPER is entitled & which others who* held the same rank now receive.*"* Since Agent YATES had provided the pension department with evidence from John's superior officer under whom the applicant served, he thought the case was closed.

On 30 December 1839, James L. EDWARDS, commissioner of pensions, replied to Giles F. YATES's letter of November 26 last. James continued to impugn Giles's documents, continuing to prove that he was un-reproachable and untouchable. He clearly stated,

> *"In the case of John KEMPER, it is apparent from the character of his service & from the several statements of his brother's* [Colonel Daniel KEMPER], *that he was an employee in the transport service under the Qr. Master Genl—And was not one of the 'Deputies' to which the resolution of Congress quoted by you refers—A large portion of these were attached to the Dept. of the Clothier Genl and engaged under civil contract as well in procuring the materials and converting them into clothes & as in transporting*

> *them to the points required by the stations of the*
> *public force—Upon a close examination of the*
> *case, I think it is clear that he is not entitled as a*
> *'Conductor of Transport teams' as he terms his office*
> *or as Wagon Master agreeably to your designation.*

Please note that Commissioner EDWARDS admitted to several statements given by John's brother, Colonel Daniel KEMPER. Daniel confirmed in his letter read at his brother, John's funeral, that he had written many correspondences to both Commissioner EDWARDS and Giles YATES. All these correspondences are now missing. Where could they have gone and what could they have contained?

Although Giles YATES was very competent in all the research he had done in Washington, DC on Captain KEMPER's case, he unintentionally missed something very important. In a resolve of Congress dated 26 November 1777, it was ordered that *"clothing supplies be supplied to officers and soldiers of the Continental Army out of 'public stores.'"*

If Agent YATES had not missed this, he would have been able to shut down Commissioner EDWARDS permanently, regarding his contention that the language used by both Colonel Daniel and Captain John KEMPER, regarding transporting public stores, was proof of civil service. This was a congressional order; there were no other means of obtaining these supplies. Commissioner EDWARDS's ignorance of proper protocol for classifying veterans made him incompetent to fulfill his office—a disgrace, a danger to veterans, to humanity, and to all of America of which he represented!—a sad commentary in American history!

Furthermore all wagon masters, when filing for a pension, filled out their declaration of transporting *"public stores"* the same way. Why Giles YATES did not find these, is unknown. One in particular was John MC CARROLL (1757-1834), who had filled out a declaration to obtain a pension on 5 February 1832.

In his declaration Mr. MC CARROLL stated that *"he was born 13th Mar. 1757, that his tour of service was rendered in Pennsylvania and he was stationed with others at Doylestown to protect the supplies for Valley Forge from across the Delaware [River]. The British were at this time at Philadelphia and the American Army under WASHINGTON lay at Valley Forge . . . Shortly after this last term of service he went out with his wagon and teams hauling 'public stores' for one year part of the time under Samuel COX [1759-1839], wagon master."*

Commissioner EDWARDS continued to capitalize on the language he liked best and rejected all contrary evidence regardless of its authenticity. This was Commissioner EDWARDS's sole grounds for claiming civil service rather than military, besides General WASHINGTON's ***"special protection,"*** inferring that he needed to protect him because he was civilian.

The fact is, there was no other way of obtaining, or means of transporting, supplies to the newly formed Continental Army other than from the public stores, as ordered by Congress. The army still needed to get organized. For Commissioner EDWARDS not to know about this, in his position, during this period of time, just was not possible!

Most importantly, Captain KEMPER had responded to direct, emergency orders from both General WASHINGTON and Colonel Alexander HAMILTON to clean out all the stores in Philadelphia so the British could not gain possession of them. This was a mandatory military acquisition, not civilian!

Elizabeth KEMPER recorded in her diary,

> *"My father has been totally confused with what is going on with Commissioner EDWARDS and the Pension Department. They have vouchers from his friend and comrade, Colonel Elisha JENKINS stating he was appointed lieutenant on the same*

date her father was appointed captain in Colonel Henry VAN RENSSELAER's regiment, and that he knew personally of his letter of recommendation from Colonel Alexander HAMILTON to Colonel Henry VAN RENSSELAER.

Also, President Martin VAN BUREN gave his voucher before becoming president of his personal knowledge of John KEMPER's service during the Revolution quoting many examples, including mentioning some of his friends who also were friends of John KEMPER's, like Colonel Elisha JENKINS and likewise knew personally of his service and/ or served with him." Mr. VAN BUREN had also added that, *"His father* [Captain Abraham VAN BUREN (1737–1817)] *belonged to the same officer's club as Captain KEMPER and Colonel Elisha JENKINS in Hudson, N.Y.*

Elizabeth noted,

"In addition, the presiding Justice of the Supreme Court, John Worth EDMONDS, signed a voucher with his knowledge and the knowledge of his father, General Samuel EDMONDS as well, in regards to Captain John KEMPER's service.

On 10 January 1840, John **KEMPER** wrote to James L. **EDWARDS**, commissioner of pensions. John wrote,

"I was several years ago allowed a pension for my services in the war of the Revolution. In the past summer, an application was made on my behalf for a reexamination of my papers with a view of having my pension increased. Should I on such reexamination be found entitled thereto, and if not, I was content

to continue to receive the amount which had been awarded me.

On the s[ai]d application for such examination and as I verily believe without due consideration of sufficient cause, my name was stricken from the roll of Pensions.

In writing to as[c]ertain the reason for it, I was informed that my name had been stricken off without authority and thereupon I applied for my usual six months pay last fall when the Pension agent told me he had received another letter from you stating that the first order to have my name stricken off was correct. This result was very unexpected to me & likewise very una[cc]ountable. And I still think there must be some misapprehension as I most assuredly was in the service of the United States as stated in the papers now on file in your office.

The above application, alluded to by Captain KEMPER, in which he had applied for his usual six month's pay last fall, is now missing, along with so many other documents alluded to. After Mr. KEMPER's application had been received by Commissioner EDWARDS, he again wrote another letter to the agent for paying pensions in Albany, New York. That agent then contacted Mr. KEMPER that Commissioner EDWARDS had written him a second letter, informing him that his previous action on canceling his pension was correct and no reinstatement, under any conditions, was possible at this time.

Captain KEMPER continued, *"Several months have now elapsed since my name was stricken from the roll, and I am desirous that you would in person take this matter into your own hands as soon as you can, believing that if you do so you will be satisfied that my name ought to be again placed upon the roll."* If Captain KEMPER had known that Charles YOUNG, deputy clothier-general under

James MEASE, was still alive, all he would have had to do was get Mr. YOUNG's confirmation of his service and separation from the Continental Army and this case would have been permanently closed!

> *I do not wish to trouble the **President of the United States** [Martin VAN BUREN], who is one of my **vouchers** & **witnesses**, nor any of my other friends [Colonel Elisha JENKINS and John W. EDMONDS] to intercede in an off in which is properly cognizable before you & should be decided solely by you!*

Very Respectfully Yours—Jno Kemper

This letter was the only one left intact by which Commissioner EDWARDS did not feel threatened. All previous correspondences between Captain KEMPER and the pension department, of which there were many, are now missing. Mr. KEMPER had continually elaborated on his service in the wagon master department in detail. Captain KEMPER is still under the belief that Commissioner EDWARDS will do right by him. He does not understand the psychology of what Mr. EDWARDS is pulling. Psychology did not come into focus until the twentieth century by Sigmund FREUD, M.D. (1856-1939).

Commissioner James L. EDWARDS continuously ignored this letter, along with all previous correspondences from Captain KEMPER. For some unknown reason, Commissioner EDWARDS was unable to face Captain KEMPER on any terms, including correspondences, at least the few that were left on file. Commissioner EDWARDS was solely responsible for all negative action taken against Captain KEMPER. There was never any indication that anyone else was ever involved from the pension department or War Department. What was really going on here? What was EDWARDS afraid of? What was he really trying to hide? Why had he targeted Captain KEMPER?

Elizabeth KEMPER recorded in her diary, *"My father had many correspondences with Commissioner EDWARDS over the years, in which he claimed, Commissioner EDWARDS was fishing for some answers on something he found in WASHINGTON's papers on his service under him; and he was not going to get it, even at the cost of his pension, but never said what it was."* Where are all these correspondences?

On 29 January 1840, Giles F. YATES addressed James L. EDWARDS once again, informing him, *"I understand that, Mr. [Martin] VAN BUREN, the President of the United States interested himself in behalf of Mr. KEMPER when he applied—and you had all the evidence called for in the case and allowed his claim. I have on previous occasions referred to the claim of Mr. Zaddock HEDDEN of the City of New York, and I know from what S. SPENCER, Esq. of that city told me, that Mr. HEDDEN received a full pension as a Wagon Master, and upon less direct evidence than has been adduced in the case of KEMPER."*

Please note that in Giles YATESs' reference above he had *"on previous 'occasions' referred to the claim of Zaddock HEDDEN."* The word occasions is plural, meaning two or more; there are no previous correspondences on file in the pension department mentioning Zaddock HEDDEN or Captain KEMPER's supplement. Where are they? Where were they filed? Or, were they filed? So many documents proving Captain KEMPER's service have gone missing.

He (YATES) then informed him (EDWARDS) of some new details John KEMPER had given him on his appointment. He reported that *"Mr. KEMPER was appointed captain and wagon master by James YULE [1755-1832], deputy wagon master general, and while engaged as a wagon master, received $40 per month until 1779, when the depreciation of the currency was such that he was paid at the rate of $60 per month."* Most Continentals received no pay, as it was just a figure of their worth put on paper. *"Mr. KEMPER had the rank of captain. Mr. KEMPER prefers a claim* *as a midshipman also."* Why did Captain KEMPER allow himself to be demoted from lieutenant to midshipman?

Giles continued, *"Now unless there was fraud practice in obtaining the pension of Mr. KEMPER, I cannot see upon what grounds his pension was suspended. If there was fraud practice in getting the pension, I wish you to say so at once, that the persons who were engaged in riding the old gentleman, may be prepared to meet the charge."* This powerful statement went ignored by Commissioner EDWARDS.

This was reference to President Martin VAN BUREN, Colonel Elisha JENKINS, Colonel Daniel KEMPER and John W. EDMONDS, who were just a few of John's vouchers. Commissioner EDWARDS held a presidential appointment, and if this action had been presented to President Martin VAN BUREN, Commissioner EDWARDS could have just as quickly and easily been replaced as he was appointed. For the life of this author, it is not clear why Mr. YATES did not do this.

John was now eighty-three years old, and by this time over 95 percent of everyone who fought in the American Revolution had passed on. All the highest-ranking Continental officers—like General George WASHINGTON, Major General Alexander HAMILTON, General Marquis DE LAFAYETTE, General John SULLIVAN, General *"Mad"* Anthony WAYNE, General John MUHLENBERGH and Colonel Henry J. VAN RENSSELAER (all of whom Captain KEMPER had served or was directly involved with)—, had passed on.

Back during the American Revolution, there was not one officer who did not know who Captain John KEMPER was. He was the brightest star in the sky, the one that kept them alive at Valley Forge, through his transporting of supplies from Lancaster to General WASHINGTON's headquarters at Valley Forge. He was also sent on many foraging expeditions when supplies got low at Lancaster.

Some of the other Continental officers that Captain John KEMPER was directly involved with at Valley Forge and while bringing supplies to the Continental Army at their various camps and headquarters, were Lieutenant Colonel John LAURENS, aide-de-camp; Major General Baron Frederick Wilhelm VON STEUBEN, inspector general; Major General Nathanael GREENE, quarter master general; Brigadier General William MAXWELL; Colonel Elias BOUDINOT, commissary-general of prisoners; Brigadier General Count Casimir PULASKI; Quartermaster-General, Major General Thomas MIFFLIN, aide-de-camp; Colonel Tench TILGHMAN, aide-de-camp; and many others.

There were no more witnesses to call on. Besides his brother, Colonel Daniel KEMPER, President Martin VAN BUREN, Colonel Elisha JENKINS and John W. EDMONDS, Captain John KEMPER was on his own. Agent YATES did not have access to any of these declarations or vouchers to compare his arguments to, as they were in the sole possession of the pension department. Commissioner EDWARDS was not about to share anything with Agent YATES that would help to bring this case to a resolution. Also, note that Commissioner EDWARDS ignored all references to President VAN BUREN's voucher and never claimed it proved civil service.

In fact, James L. EDWARDS, commissioner of pensions, in all the years of correspondences on this case never once brought up President Martin VAN BUREN's voucher of Captain John KEMPER's service during the American Revolution. EDWARDS had deliberately avoided all references to President VAN BUREN throughout the entire history of this case. Or, if there had been any correspondences, they all must have been destroyed for his protection. All Mr. YATES had, was a copy of Captain KEMPER's supplement. Mr. EDWARDS's stubbornness had made Captain KEMPER's the longest unresolved and ongoing case in American history!

It is the sincere belief of this author that Commissioner EDWARDS was petrified that Giles F. YATES might contact President Martin VAN BUREN personally; therefore, Commissioner EDWARDS did not want anything negative said about the president left on record. Commissioner EDWARDS also knew that his department was in sole possession of President VAN BUREN's voucher. He could only hope that this case never made it further to any other office than his own.

6. Congressional Involvement

On 4 February 1840, Congressman Aaron VAN DER POEL (1799-1870) got involved. He wrote James L. EDWARDS, enclosing pension papers of James (Jacobus) BARHGTE/BARHYTE (1762-1841), stating, *"Mr. YATES is deeply impressed with the case resemblance to John KEMPER."* The congressman continued by saying, *"Since Mr. KEMPER is one of my constituents, I hope that he will receive a favorable consideration at your hands."*

On 17 February 1840, James L. EDWARDS, commissioner of pensions, responded to Congressman Aaron VAN DER POEL's letter. James stated,

> *"In answer to that part of your letter of the 4th, instant, which relates to the case of John KEMPER and the act of 7 June 1832, and to which the letter of Mr. YATES enclosed in yours refers, I have the honor to refer you to the enclosed copy of my letter of this date to your colleague, Congressman [John] ELY [1774–1849].*

> *The reference to the case of Zaddock HADDEN in the letter of Mr. YATES as analogous to John KEMPER, is not borne only by the facts— HADDEN was a wagon master in the staff of the New Jersey Line and was verified by the late Colonel*

> *[Aaron] OGDEN—John KEMPER was engaged in superintending the transportation of clothes under the clothier genl.*

On 17 February 1840, James L. EDWARDS, commissioner of pensions replied to Congressman John ELY of the sixth instant. He stated,

> *John KEMPER's case has again been thoroughly examined and no reason is perceived for not adhering to the decision heretofore communicated to his attorneys—his own description of his duties and employment under YOUNG and MEASE of the clothier department as a wagon master to superintend the transportation of clothing as also in the statement of his 'brother who was a D.y. [deputy] Clothier,' furnishes evidence that he was one of numerous employees attached to the Department of the Clothier Genl engaged under civil contract, as well as procuring the materials and converting them into clothes as in transporting them to the stations occupied by the public force.*

Commissioner EDWARDS incorrectly reported that Captain KEMPER transported to the public force, when, in fact, John transported from the public stores to the army, as was usual. There was no other location to transport supplies from, until Captain KEMPER started a military warehouse from military acquisitions acquired from the public stores, as ordered by General WASHINGTON.

> *The fact stated by him viz: that he carried General WASHINGTON's **'protection'** against any interference of other officers, corroborates the conclusion that his duties were not rendered under a regular appointment of the Qr Master Genl, which is necessary to entitle him to a pension for*

*that employment—It may here be remarked, that it
has not been shown that he held the grade of Wagon
Master by the tenure of a commission or tantamount
instrument as required by the rules. Even if it could
be proved that he was a component part of the staff
as required by the rules & articles of war, the grade
could not be allowed upon the present proof.*

It is time for our readers to focus on one word, in particular, in the above paragraph, *"regular!"* Commissioner EDWARDS stated, *"The fact stated that he carried General WASHINGTON's **'protection'** against any interference of other officers, corroborates the conclusion that his duties were not rendered under a 'regular' appointment."* Commissioner EDWARDS was finally 100 percent correct, and he knew it. This service was just not a *"regular appointment"*; his service was a *"special appointment"* by General WASHINGTON.

It would seem inconceivable that General WASHINGTON would only have someone bound merely by contract, rather than someone bound by military tradition, customs, and most importantly, jurisdiction. General WASHINGTON had no authority over civilians; therefore, civilians were not subject to military protocol. Hence, civilians could commandeer all supplies and deliver them to wherever they wanted, with no threat of answering to the military.

General WASHINGTON would never, under any circumstances, jeopardize the fate of his Continental Army, and his country, by placing a civilian in this most highly respectable military office. Furthermore, if he had allowed a civilian at this post, he would have had to fear mass desertions and mutiny by his subordinates. Civilian were, during this period of time, treacherous and naturally incompetent. Although General WASHINGTON respected the civilian-constituted authority, he did not appreciate them interfering in military affairs.

Throughout the entire history of this case, Commissioner EDWARDS was trying to manipulate from Captain KEMPER and Attorney YATES, what that *"special protection"* was for. It was *"top secret,"* and Captain KEMPER was not about to reveal it, not even at the cost of losing his pension. That is why General WASHINGTON picked Captain KEMPER; he was loyal, was tough as nails, and could not be broken! Captain KEMPER did not need to tell any secrets in order to boast his importance or ego.

It took this author a lifetime to finally figure out what General WASHINGTON's *"special protection"* from the interference and detention from all his other officers was likely for. This author will divulge that information at the close of this story, for those who were not able to figure it out by that time.

"The other part of his claim as midshipman will not be objected to." Commissioner EDWARDS had confused quarter-master-general with clothier-general. Has he, all of a sudden, lost his focus, or did he ever have it? Perhaps he is just getting nervous that he will be caught in his deception. You accept all of an applicant's declaration, or you accept none, not parts being manipulated for one's selfish grudge just because of an inquiry of being underpaid. Had Captain KEMPER accidentally uncovered a conspiracy to steal veterans' pension money—men who were in the final days of their lives?

You either tell the truth or you are a liar, not a small part of each, to fulfill a one-way ticket against one of America's first 100 percent, disabled American veterans. John gave his all in the birth of America, so people like Commissioner EDWARDS could have a job—for what, to work against the veteran? He was supposed to have been there to protect them and provide comfort in their final days.

For it to be suggested by the pension department that half of John KEMPER's service was civilian and the other half military was absurd. This was another important point that nobody caught at that time. Either you were military or you were not! Please note that Commissioner EDWARDS acknowledged John's brother and superior officer, Colonel Daniel KEMPER as being deputy clothier-general in the Continental Army!

Daniel signed an **affidavit** stating that his brother John was a **wagon master** and served under him. This affidavit, along with many other sound-documented proofs submitted by Giles F. YATES over the years, is now missing—a mystery! All evidence proving Captain KEMPER's service in the Continental Army had to be destroyed by Commissioner EWARDS. Wagon master only came with the rank of captain, a military appointment! If not for Mr. YATES alluding to this affidavit and Colonel Daniel KEMPER informing his brother's family he had given it, it would not be known about.

It also is the firm belief of this author that one of the reasons that Commissioner EDWARDS might have decided to settle on partial navy service, was because Justice Josiah W. FAIRFIELD (ca. 1803-1878) had contacted Levi WOODBURY (1778-1851), secretary of the navy, personally regarding Martin VAN BUREN's voucher on Captain John KEMPER's service. President Andrew JACKSON then appointed Secretary WOODBURY secretary of the treasury on 1 July 1834. To view this letter, see Secretary of the Navy Levi WOODBURY's correspondences at the National Archives in Washington, DC.

It also is interesting how Commissioner EDWARDS had no problem accepting Captain KEMPER's declaration, along with his vouchers from President Martin VAN BUREN, Colonel Elisha JENKINS Colonel Daniel KEMPER and John W. EDMONDS, until Captain KEMPER found out that he was underpaid. Where was his money going? When Captain KEMPER had his attorney, Giles F. YATES, inquire into the discretion, everything changed immediately. Commissioner EDWARDS continued to accept his oath in his declaration in its entirety, backed up by all of John's supporting vouchers, manipulating the meaning and capitalizing on two points of interest, having *"General WASHINGTON's 'protection' and transporting **public stores.***"

Commissioner EDWARDS now claimed that this wording was proof of civil service, not military, and therefore, ineligible to receive a pension. There were no civilian wagon masters! It is sometimes shocking how those in power manipulate words just because their pride and dignity have been shaken—leaving no recourse! However, something else was going on here, Commissioner EDWARDS had been caught with his hands in the cookie jar. What had he been doing with Captain KEMPER's money?

On 24 February 1840, Giles F. YATES launched another major assault against James L. EDWARDS, commissioner of pensions, quoting from General George WASHINGTON's papers and the journals of the Continental Congress. This letter turned out to be the most important in the twenty years (1832-1852) of correspondences on this case. In this letter, he confused John's brother Captain Jacob KEMPER, who was an officer on the Continental Line of New Jersey and died young in 1800, with John's other brother, Colonel Daniel KEMPER, who was aide-de-camp to General WASHINGTON and deputy clothier-general of the Continental Army.

Jacob actually did service as captain of artillery through the entire duration of the war. Now Agent YATES was beginning to lose focus on which of the brothers was who, because he did not have copies of the vouchers. It is not clear from whom Attorney YATES picked up the name of the third brother, either Daniel or John. However, Captain Jacob KEMPER had died in 1800 and, therefore was unable to play any part in the pension years.

Agent YATES began,

> *Sir: I have been favored with the perusal of your letter of the 17th inst., respecting the suspension of the pension of John KEMPER.*
>
> *On the first examination of this claim, all the evidence required was furnished. It was admitted on the oath of the applicant, and his brother a Deputy Clothier General under whom he served . . . it is said he was only one of the numerous employees attached to the department of the Clothier General engaged under civil contract & as to the fact stated by him that he carried Gen: WASHINGTON's protection against any interference of other officers, and which is said to corroborate the conclusion that his duties were not rendered under a regular appointment of the Quarter Master General, which appointed it is adjudged is necessary to entitle him to a pension for that appointment—I hope I will be excused if I again observe.*

Giles continued to pick apart Commissioner EDWARDS's fixation on General George WASHINGTON's **"special protection"** from detention and interference by all his other officers with Captain John KEMPER's command, which he claimed was proof of civil service. Giles continued to point out, *"that the applicant served under the <u>Clothier</u> General & Gen. WASHINGTON, the Commander-in-Chief, and not <u>exclusively</u> or principally under the <u>Quarter</u> Master General. What sort of interference he carried Genl WASHINGTON's protection from, I am not informed, & of course cannot judge of its bearing on the case.—Yet let this be as it may, I cannot see how the fact of his having the <u>protection</u> of the Commander in Chief can warrant the conclusion, that he was not <u>regularly</u> appointed a Wagon Master."*

Let us pause for a moment and concentrate on the paragraph above. YATES stated that, *"what sort of interference he* [John KEMPER] *carried General WASHINGTON's **protection** from, he* *was not informed.”* Nor did he speculate that he was going to find out for him. This was an application by Captain KEMPER for a pension for his service to our country, not his ***“secret service!”***

Were Captain KEMPER and YATES now trying to cover up this secret he and General WASHINGTON had together with the Continental Congress? Did Captain KEMPER slip in his declaration when he stated he held General WASHINGTON’s *“special protection”* from the interference of all other officers with his command? What was really going on here? What was Commissioner EDWARDS really trying to find out here, a top-secret organization perhaps, within the inner circle of government, of which he was not entitled?

7. Giles F. Yates’s Summary

Giles summarized by saying,

> *“He* [John KEMPER] *held an exceedingly important & highly responsible office, and was engaged in carrying clothing to the army, when its safety & the safety of the country depended upon the faithful discharge of the duties assigned to officers of that description.* [See General WASHINGTON’s letter on the subject of the character of men to be appointed to fill such offices.]

> *It was not the Quarter Ms Genl alone, under whose direction such officers were appointed & served. The Quarter Ms Genl, the Clothier General & Commissary General or their deputies acted together. See Journals of Congress 5th March 1779.*

> *Now it is to be supposed, that either department would have regularly in its employment, & for eighteen months, an officer entrusted with public property to an immense amount, and all that time*

too, under civil contract? Besides, these departments or the heads of them did not enter into civil contracts unless empowered to do so by law. Even in a case where ox teams were to be substituted for horses, the Commander in Chief could not do so until authorized by law to direct the Quarter Ms to that effect. See Journal of Congress Nov. 10, 1780.

Again, if a civil contract had been entered into, it would have been with A.B. and not with a Wagon Master. I cannot help thus again to advert to what I conceive to be strong points in opposition to the decision you have lately seen fit to make, and which is so much at variance with your first solemn adjudicate variance with your first solemn adjudication in the matter. I have done only what I conceive to be my duty, and do not under the circumstances expect, nor can I consistently demand a reversal at your hands.

Giles F. YATES finally figured out that no matter what sound-documented evidence he sent Commissioner EDWARDS, he could no longer count on a favorable decision, which was solely at his hands. However, Agent YATES refused to give up and, over the next several years, continued to solicit congressional support.

There were never any civilians under General WASHINGTON's command! Civilians were, during this period of time, treacherous and naturally incompetent; there were so many Tories/Loyalists serving the Crown. General WASHINGTON and Congress would not jeopardize its fate on an undisciplined person filled with treachery.

Giles went on to refer Commissioner EDWARDS to the Journals of the Continental Congress of 5 March 1779, in which it showed that the quartermaster-general, clothier-general and commissary-general or their deputies acted together.

If Commissioner James L. EDWARDS had been reputable he would have looked into the Journals of the Continental Congress as well as General WASHINGTON's papers. He would have discovered one of the reasons General WASHINGTON had to issue *"special orders of **protection"*** from the interference of any of his other officers with Captain John KEMPER's command. The rank that came with wagon master was captain; therefore, a major or colonel could and did confiscate their supplies and use them for their own purpose in whatever regiment they represented. The other part of the reason could not be discussed.

The other part of General WASHINGTON's protection for Captain KEMPER for any intelligence, would never be available to Commissioner EDWARDS, under any circumstances. Is this really what Commissioner EDWARDS was trying to find out, something that would never be any of his business? He rode on General WASHINGTON's *"special protection"* of Captain KEMPER's service for the entire history of this case; was he trying to pressure someone into giving in at the cost of losing his pension?

This information is made clear in General WASHINGTON's papers and the Journals of the Continental Congress. Other officers constantly interrupted the quartermaster, clothier-general and commissary departments and confiscated their goods. Captain KEMPER was a new gun on the ship, in command of General WASHINGTON's special convoy of 150 wagons and the only main line of support for the entire Continental Army.

General WASHINGTON had to prepare for his welcome and protection before Captain KEMPER took office. In addition, something else was happening here. John told his family that Ben (Benjamin) HARRISON was the one he was responsible for reporting to in Congress—reporting to for what? Benjamin HARRISON was a member of the Committee of Secret Correspondence, conducting undercover operations for the Continental Congress and General WASHINGTON. Are there any other mysteries?

Once General WASHINGTON issued his *"orders of protection"*, Captain KEMPER was able to bring all storage and forage supplies directly to General WASHINGTON for proper distribution. It is highly speculative that General WASHINGTON took this action on the advice of his senior officers. Most importantly, John was able to get any *intelligence* directly to the commander-in-chief, without interruption. This action was made clear by General WASHINGTON himself! More importantly, Captain KEMPER had automatic clearance through all guards, sentinels and superior officers. He was either escorted or a path was cleared directly to General WASHINGTON, while being saluted by senior officers.

On 10 March 1840, James L. EDWARDS, being so frustrated over Captain KEMPER's case, realized that he was going to have to retrieve Captain KEMPER's original certificate awarding him for his service as captain and wagon master. He knew he was not going to be able to do this unless he offered something for its return. In this correspondence he did just that. Since this letter was filled with deception, treachery, deceit, and trickery, after it was successful, it also had to be destroyed. It would be incriminating if left on record. The only reference of its content is contained in the following response by Attorney YATES.

He thought by offering a partial re-instatement that everyone would be satisfied, he was dead wrong! This case would continue on for another ten years and help to retire Mr. EDWARDS. Congressional involvement continued to increase as well. When answers were not satisfactory, the pursuit continued.

On 10 March 1840, Commissioner EDWARDS wrote to Giles F. YATES saying,

> *Sir, before a certificate can be issued in the case of Jno KEMPER for his services as midshipman Pa navy agreeable to yours of 24 inst it will be necessary to cancel the certificate he now holds—It should therefore be returned to this office.*

On 24 March 1840, Giles F. YATES responded to a communiqué from James L. EDWARDS, commissioner of pensions, relating to the case of John KEMPER, dated 10 March instant. Giles stated, *"To receive a pension for his services as midshipman, would be tantamount to receiving no pension at all, or would be worse than receiving no pension at all. If be allowed as such for only six months, the period he was allowed for before. It would take more than twice the period of his natural life still unspent, to enable him to realize the amount necessary to refund the over-payment."* Commissioner EDWARDS, who sat at his desk, truly believed he was invincible. He knew Captain KEMPER's records could not be changed without his approval.

Giles went on to say,

> *I refer you again to the case of Zaddock HEDDEN [1757–1840], as analogous to Mr. KEMPER's. Mr. HEDDEN was verified as a wagon master by Colonel [Aaron] OGDEN [1756–1839] and John KEMPER was verified as a wagon master by Jacob KEMPER. Mr. OGDEN was not a superior officer in the same department, but Mr. Jacob KEMPER was, therefore, the case of John KEMPER has better evidence to verify it than Mr. HEDDEN.*

> *If I am mistaken (which I am certified I am not) in supposing that Mr. OGDEN did not serve in the same department with Mr. HEDDEN, and as a superior officer, then the cases are exactly analogous. In ascertaining the amount of pension that will be allowed Mr. KEMPER, he will return his certificate.*

(In the above correspondence, Giles continued to confuse John's brother, Colonel Daniel KEMPER, with his other brother, Captain Jacob KEMPER.)

On 25 April 1840, James L. EDWARDS, commissioner of pensions, responded to Giles F. YATES, Esq., of Schenectady, New York. He stated,

> *In reply to yours of 24th last received 6th instant respecting the case of John KEMPER, I have to remark that the account of his employment given by his brother (to which you refer as affording a proof equally author stative* [expressing a state or condition] *with that by which the service of Zaddock HEDDEN as a wagon master was established by Colonel* [Aaron] *OGDEN) taken in connection with his own statement, constituted the grounds upon which the department decided that he was acting under a civil appointment. His declaration shows three terms as a midshipman amounting to 18 months and the department will not require him to refund. His stipend will be $108 per annum.*

Giles F. YATES had poured his heart out on this case, making it both the longest case and the longest unresolved case in American history. He had missed something very important here; because he did not have copies of the declarations and voucher—the pension department had everything! Commissioner EDWARDS stated that *"John served three six-month terms as a midshipman amounting to 18 months."*

The fact is, John KEMPER spent one six-month term as a midshipman, one six-month term as a volunteer (one rank under lieutenant), and over one year as a lieutenant in the United States Navy, comprising of over two years' naval service. British prison records back up this information after the British frigate *Iris*, captured Lieutenant John KEMPER on 11 September 1780, and it is just as clearly stated in John's declaration.

A midshipman was a person in training to become an officer. After a year in training, John had well earned his rank as lieutenant. After his capture, Lieutenant KEMPER was shuffled around to various prison ships off the Island of Manhattan. He was then transferred to the provost marshal in New York City, prior to being transferred to Mill Prison, Plymouth, England, on 11 January 1781, along with seventy other officers. At the time of Lieutenant KEMPER's escape and arrival back home in November 1781, just after the surrender of Lieutenant General Lord Charles CORNWALLIS at Yorktown on 19 October 1781, he had served fourteen months as a naval officer.

In this author's lifetime, he has never heard of an American veteran who had served his country and, was captured and made a prisoner-of-war and afterward demoted in rank by his country. To this author's knowledge, this is the only case in American history. James L. EDWARDS, commissioner of pensions, did not have the power or authority to promote or to demote, yet, he did just that to Lieutenant John KEMPER. He took away John's rank of lieutenant and demoted him back to midshipman. Nobody caught this at the time because they were concentrating on his service as wagon master under General WASHINGTON and, once again, they did not have a copy of John's declaration for comparison.

On 14 August 1840, Giles F. YATES, Schenectady, New York, responded to James L. EDWARDS, commissioner of pensions by stating, *"I send enclosed Mr. John KEMPER's old certificate for which you promised in your last communication to me on the subject, to substitute a new one."*

Whatever happened to this correspondence from the pension department, demanding the return of the old certificate, remains a mystery! *"Although the stipend now awarded him is less than he conceives himself entitled to, he will accept it until he furnishes proof that he was a regular wagon master, and entitled as such to the same pay as Zaddock HEDDEN, and others whose cases have been admitted on poorer proof."*

It is time for our audience to pause again. Commissioner EDWARDS was so excited and shook up about receiving Captain KEMPER's original certificate that he messed up big-time! He obviously sent Captain KEMPER his new certificate but forgot to record it in his file for August 1840. Instead, he over-anxiously forged the original document on file for the year 1832 so as not to show the discrepancy in money that he should have been receiving. He forgot about adding the new certificate. No one caught this mistake except this author, because no one had access to these veterans' records that are available now.

Since the forged document has Secretary of War Lewis CASS's signature on it, when he was out of office, it appears that he was somehow involved. However, it is possible that Commissioner EDWARDS went to Mr. CASS and claimed that a mistake had been made on an earlier certificate for one of our veterans, which had to be corrected and needed his signature, since he was in office at the time the mistake was made.

Whenever anyone tells the truth, the story is pure; however, whenever anyone tells a lie or commits fraud, they can never get their story straight. He removed the original certificate naming Mr. KEMPER as captain and wagon master and joining the US Navy as a lieutenant in Philadelphia, Pennsylvania. He then doctored it up, changing the original to reflect a conductor of teams and midshipman, since Mr. KEMPER had accepted his offer until he was able to supply more evidence on his case. Commissioner EDWARDS would not have had to change the certificate had he not been trying to cover up his fraudulent conduct.

Commissioner EDWARDS had fought tooth and nail to get that original certificate back; now he no longer had to worry about anything. Once again, no one knew, except Mr. EDWARDS, what was on file in the pension office or that any records had been changed. Conductor of teams with no rank was a must change for the records to account for the low pay Captain KEMPER was receiving.

In addition, his rank as lieutenant in the US Navy, likewise, had to be reduced to midshipman to account for the low pay. Mr. KEMPER's proof of being a lieutenant in the US Navy was in Great Britain, of which he had no access to at the time. In later years, Great Britain became stout allies of the United States and started releasing British prison records of American naval officers. Whatever method Mr. EDWARDS used to manipulate the secretary of war, Lewis CASS into signing the new certificate is unknown, unless he was involved in the pension fraud.

On 10 September 1840, Giles F. YATES, Schenectady, New York re-contacted James L. EDWARDS, Esq., commissioner of pensions. Giles stated, *"At the risk of being deemed obstructive . . . I beg leave to refer you to the records found in the State Department at Washington [DC]—In the book labeled 'Wagon Department' and for the Year 1778, the name of James YOUNG is recorded as a wagon master-general and James YULE as a deputy wagon master-general. These facts compared with his statements, will I trust suffice to convince you that Mr. [John] KEMPER's account is to be relied on."*

Mr. YATES just was not getting the full picture here: No matter what good, sound documentation he sent to the pension office, Commissioner EDWARDS continued to refuse to credit it.

On 17 September 1840, James L. EDWARDS, commissioner of pensions, continued to be obstinate and replied, *"In answer of yours of 10th instant, referring to the records of the State Department, to show that James YOUNG was a wagon master-general, that John KEMPER received his appointment from him as established by the evidence, I have to state that this claim has heretofore been fully examined and upon all the proofs within the reach of the department it has been decided that he held no military appointment in the staff of the Revolutionary Army—This conclusion is warranted by his own and his brother's statements of his duties and employment and confirmed by the relation in which he stood to the army requiring protection against impressments."*

This new word, *"impressments,"* manipulated as a contention by Commissioner EDWARDS, was a ruse; Captain KEMPER clearly stated in his declaration that, *"General WASHINGTON's 'protection' was from detention and interference from any of his other officers with his command."* Here we have yet, another manipulation of words.

This order allowed Captain KEMPER to get all forage, transport supplies and intelligence, without interruption, directly to General WASHINGTON for proper use or distribution. Furthermore, no civilians were able to, nor had the need to, organize a convoy of 150 wagons. This was a military operation, ordered and organized by General WASHINGTON that he would not have trusted to any civilians of whom he had no control. It was completed by August 1777, in preparation for war against the mightiest army and navy on earth, on whose empire the sun never set. What chance would they have? General WASHINGTON never asked that question!

For it to be implied that civilians, during this period of time, were in greater need and possession of huge convoys of wagons for the purpose of supplying goods to some local farmers or townspeople than the Continental Army on the march was purely preposterous. If farmers or merchants in a city, like Philadelphia, were in need of replenishing goods or supplies, which had been depleted through sales, the same measures were taken back then as are used today in the twenty-first century. An individual wagon delivered whatever was needed for that particular store, whether food or hardware, etc.

Today, if supermarkets or department stores are in need of supplies, they have an individual truck deliver what supplies are needed at variable intervals. Stores like Wal-mart, do not wait until they are totally sold out to stick up a sign saying, "Sorry, people, our store is closed until our convoy of a 150 trucks re-supply it." No business can afford to do that. Nor can any business afford 150 trucks, which was equivalent to 150 wagons back then.

Commissioner James L. EDWARDS's statement, *"John KEMPER's claim has been fully examined upon all proofs in reach of the department,"* is the ***"magic bullet!"*** It is the firm belief of this author that Commissioner EDWARDS collected all documents, including General George WASHINGTON's on Captain KEMPER's special service under him, along with President Martin VAN BUREN's, Colonel Elisha JENKINS's, and John W. EDMONDS's vouchers, hiding them in a file box in a concealed location, accessible only to him. Since he had collected everything, there was nothing left for anyone else to find in support of Captain KEMPER's claim, or was there? Could he have missed something?

Then after Captain KEMPER's death, which Commissioner EDWARDS knew would happen sooner than later, and when it was safe to do so, he disposed of all supportive documents. That is the reason for all the missing records and links alluded to in the many correspondences at the National Archives, but why? What did Commissioner EDWARDS find in General WASHINGTON's papers that he felt was so important that it was better that the rest of the world should never know about it? Who else was involved in this investigation? Is there someone in the background giving Commissioner EDWARDS orders, or is he acting alone, making himself judge and jury?

On 22 October 1840, Giles F. YATES of Schenectady, New York, responded to Commissioner EDWARDS,

> *Your letter of the 17th Sept. alt. in reference to the case of John KEMPER, under the act of 7th June 1832, has suggested to my mind a few thoughts, which*

I wish to have placed on file with the other views, representations and arguments on the claimant's side of the question—This I wish more for the sake of having the 'issue joined' fairly between us than because I expect to effect a change in your last decision in the premises.

Giles YATES went on to provide new documentation on the duties of a wagon master and argued against Commissioner EDWARDS's continued reference to a *"civil contract!"*

You state in the letter above referred to, that none of the proofs within the reach of the department show that he held a military appointment, and this you say, appears from his own & his brother's statements of his duties. But is it not in proof that he held a commission? Take this fact in connection with his circumstantial statement relative to his superior officers who appointed him, his duties as an exclusive transporter of clothing in his particular department, and compare this with the fact that by a resolve of Congress that, The Quarter Master General furnish means of transporting clothing dep. and that a careful wagon master or conductor, shall be appointed who shall procure with the clothing & if the clothing is damaged or deficient, the wagon master to be tried by a court-martial.

A person employed to 'transport clothing' under civil contract, would hardly be subjected to martial law.

This is conclusive congressional evidence that the Continental Congress would not tolerate a civilian at this post. Furthermore, the Continental Congress employed the Continental Army as defense of our land, not civilians.

Giles closed giving reference to a resolve of Congress passed in May 1777, volume 3, page 187, *"The pay of a wagon master or conductor of wagons, was fixed at $40 per month, and afterwards increased, doubtless as a consequence of the depreciation of the currency."* which clarifies Captain KEMPER's claim of the amount of pay grade he received.

On 9 September 1841, Congressman Robert MC CLELLAN (1806-1860) got into the act. He sent James L. EDWARDS some papers Giles F. YATES had turned over to him for an increase in pension for John KEMPER of Hudson, New York.

On 10 September 1841, James L. EDWARDS, commissioner of pensions, responded to Congressman Robert MC CLELLAN's inquiry; James replied;

> *I have the honor to return you the letters in the case of John KEMPER, a pensioner under the act of 7 June 1832, enclosed with yours of the 9th instant—They afford no evidence in the case— His pension was erroneously adjusted at first and was subsequently reduced to its present rate after repeated examinations and a long correspondence with Mr. YATES, upon every consideration which he could adduce to obtain a higher rate—the only question at issue was whether his employment in the Clothier Department in charge of teams was under a staff appointment or not—The department has decided, and now repeats the decision that he never held a staff appointment under military obligations.*

Bang! Another *"magic bullet!"* Commissioner EDWARDS finally, without realizing it, admitted that Captain John KEMPER was a *captain and wagon master in the Continental Army.* Commissioner EDWARDS collected all proofs on Captain KEMPER's service during the American Revolution in reach of his department. Included in such proofs were General WASHINGTON's papers, in which it stated that he served exactly as stated in his declarations. There was only one thing missing from Captain KEMPER's battle with the pension department—Eliza!

The only question, according to Commissioner EDWARDS, was whether it was under a staff appointment. John's brother and superior officer, Colonel Daniel KEMPER, aide-de-camp, signed an affidavit stating that his brother John was a captain and wagon master in the Continental Army, that he himself helped procure. Since Commissioner EDWARDS admitted collecting everything, again, there is nothing left for anyone else to find. It appears that during this period of time, no one was familiar with military protocol, and Commissioner EDWARDS banked his career on that.

8. The Gray Stone of Valley Forge

Sometime prior to John's death, faced with fortitude and fearing that darkness was headed his way once again, John returned to Valley Forge with a wagon on one last mission, to pick up the stone he used to sit on while planning his next mission. This gray stone always reminded Captain KEMPER of the gray days at Valley Forge and no matter how dark the days could be, there was always light at the end of the tunnel as recorded in Elizabeth KEMPER's diary. To this very date of July 2016, this stone still sits at the intended grave site for John in the family plot of his friend and comrade, Captain Anthony MAXWELL at Hudson, New York.

John's daughter, Elizabeth KEMPER, recorded in her diary, *"It breaks my heart to watch my father stumble and shake in his crutches, and flooding himself in tears, unbelieving that his country has abandoned him after all he had done for its birth."* In the evening in her father's final days, after her chores were done, Elizabeth would listen to her father's stories making sure she recorded all his *"memoirs"* in her diary for prosperity.

Elizabeth quietly walked into her father's room as he was staring out his window. She asked, *"What are you thinking about, Dad?"*

Her father sighed heavily and replied, *"Memories, honey, just memories; it seems like just yesterday, I was so strong, so young and wild. I dealt personally with the most powerful leaders of our country. They are now all gone, yet in my memory they are still alive. My grandfather, Colonel Johann KEMPER, did the same with the leaders of Prussia, Frederick William I "the Great Elector," and his son, Frederick I, King in Prussia, as well as Leopold I, Emperor of the Holy Roman Empire. Where has time gone? Why must all good things come to an end, while evil continues to flourish?"*

She recorded that when her father would peer out his window in anger of his dealings with the pension department, he would often, in anger, instinctively reach for his sword, which was no longer there. Remembering, he would slowly return his hand to his right side, as if helpless. He would then flip open his pocket watch, which still held the picture of his childhood sweetheart and wife, Eliza HOPPER. John turned to Elizabeth and said, *"After I have passed on, I would like you to have my gold pocket watch with your beloved mother's picture in it."*

Elizabeth bowed her head, and tears dripped down her face.

She recorded everything he could remember, including his childhood stories, prior to the Revolution. She would read the newspapers to her father under the soft flickering light of a lamp to break the monotony and comfort him. Oftentimes, he was concerned about what comrades in arms had passed on; however, by this time, most all of them were already gone.

One night, while a storm was brewing outside, as the sleet and rain sprayed against the window, Elizabeth's father suddenly spoke out, even though they were not discussing anything, *"I wonder what my grandfather would have done if his pension was cancelled, knowing what service he rendered for his country to earn it? For the good of all, some things can never be told."*

He then said, *"Once when I was in Philadelphia, General WASHINGTON informed me that, some things must die with the Revolution."* He went on to say that *"even Congress told him to keep everything in a tightly-knit circle and trust no one but a few that you know have proven themselves to you."*

Elizabeth continued writing as her father continued on about his grandfather.

> *"When my grandfather was receiving his pension, his King and all he served with were still alive. When he passed on, his king made sure that my grandmother continued to receive his pension. My leader and all who I served with have been long gone. All I have left is my brother* [Daniel] *who personally served with me through most of my service. It is not so much the money, even though it is all I have to live on, but my self-esteem is breaking down."*

> Dad had placed a bird feeder outside his bedroom window years ago. He loved to watch the various colored birds, like blue jays and cardinals, come to feed and sing. Even though Dad knew that the bluebirds did not frequent the feeders, but instead stayed hidden in the thickets away from people, he could not figure out why he was not seeing them even at the edge of the tree lines anymore. He is in fear that we are losing them.

> He would often say, *"You very seldom see a bluebird anymore but once you have, you never forget it. It is such a beautiful burst of bright blue, much like the burst of a beautiful rainbow, then bang! It is gone. All that is left is a beautiful memory, much like the*

Revolution. Once you have reached rock bottom, and you figure nothing could ever get worse, you eventually find out you were dead wrong."

As my father gazed out his bedroom window he softly nodded his head, which was common when he was in deep thought. Then, from out of nowhere, Dad said, *"I know why you do not see bluebirds anymore; it is because General WASHINGTON is gone."*

This was confusing to Elizabeth, but she recorded it as such.

Her father then replied, *"As I look out the window it is like a vision into the past, I can see everything as clearly as if it happened yesterday."*

Elizabeth inquired, *"What do you mean, Dad?"*

Her father replied, *"The Revolution, I can see everything as clearly as if it happened yesterday."*

Her father then closed by saying, *"I am sorry, sweetheart only another veteran will know what I mean."*

Elizabeth then said, *"Dad, I know I am not a very good looking woman, most men never take a second look and move on. I feel like my cousins, Jane* [1788-1872] *and* [Phoebe] *Eliza* [1791-1873] (Uncle Daniel KEMPER's daughters). *Look at Charlie's* [KEMPER's] *sister-in-law, Jenny* [Jane Matilda MAXWELL (1820-?)]; *she has always had so many guys chasing her."*

Her father replied, *"Honey, it does not matter! When the beauty is gone, all that remains is the heart to be judged. You have a heart of gold; very few women can match it."*

Elizabeth, *"I bowed my head with a smile, Dad always had a way to boost my morale when I was feeling low, especially since I was trying to relieve some of his own sorrow. How much longer was I going to be able to enjoy his company? I feel that time is not on my side. What can I do to help my father?"*

In another part of her diary, Elizabeth wrote, *"My father has been under great stress lately in his battle with the Pension Department. It is aging him so fast, he does not seem to care to want to live anymore; he sometimes talks to himself, I fear the worst!"* Dad said, *"How can Commissioner EDWARDS imply he does not know who I am; everyone knows who I am! I should not have to explain myself, over and over time and again."*

John closed by saying, *"The way the War Department is treating me, I wonder if there will be any Americans left alive living in our country. Like the Egyptians, someone ought to write a book on the disappearance of the Americans. We turned all our power over to everyone who had nothing to do with establishing our country. Will there be any Americans left, standing proud, to carry the torch?"*

Elizabeth bent her head in sorrow, afraid to answer, and thinking, *"Everyone who knew Dad are dead and buried, except Uncle Dan."* Neither did she know that her brother Charles Morton KEMPER's namesake, Charles YOUNG, who had discharged her father from the Continental Army, was still alive.

> Dad peered out the window and said, *"Why does it take so long for the sun to set?"*

> Elizabeth added, *"Although it is summer, the nights seem longer and the days seem colder. The birds no longer come to my father's windowsill; there is a kind of silence and stillness in the air, as if something is about to happen, like a calm before the storm."*

The missing link, John's departed wife, Eliza, was waiting for John to finish his business, once again.

9. Captain John KEMPER Dies in Battle!

On 11 August 1842, Captain John KEMPER died at Hudson, New York of a broken heart at eighty-five years old. Un-trusted by his country, which he trusted, un-believed by his country, which he believed in, and tormented by the agonies of a falsely concocted claim, John had given his final hour in his battle with the pension department. John had received only one-fifth partial pension for two years before he passed on. Commissioner James L. EDWARDS knew he would outlast him.

Attached to the wall on the right side of the entrance to his home, Captain KEMPER had hung the flag of forty-six stars. He had personally witnessed the growth of our country from thirteen to forty-six states. He would not witness the continued growth but knew it was not done growing. His pride and honor of participating in the birth of America was well-known to his friends, neighbors, and family.

In August 1842, Elizabeth KEMPER had a family meeting with her sister Jane (Jenny) and her husband, Samuel CROSSMAN. They decided that their father should be buried in a family plot, so they bought a small lot number 50 in section 1-A of the Old Hudson City Cemetery. Captain John KEMPER was the first family member interred in this lot. Two months later, Samuel and Jenny's daughter, Maria Regina (1841-1842), died at ten months old from teething. She was interred at the foot of her grandfather, John KEMPER's grave.

Maria Regina was named after Elizabeth and Jenny's grandmother, Maria Regina (Ernst) KEMPER. Samuel and Jenny CROSSMAN had another daughter, whom again they named Maria Regina CROSSMAN (1846-1925). They then had a son whom they named after Elizabeth and Jenny's uncle, Colonel Daniel KEMPER; thus, Daniel Kemper CROSSMAN (1845-1892). John KEMPER's daughter, Jenny CROSSMAN, alone, ended up having more descendants than her uncle Colonel Daniel KEMPER had by both of his wives.

Three years after John KEMPER's death, Samuel and Jenny CROSSMAN lost their son-in-law, William H. STEEN (1814-1845), at thirty-one years old of consumption (tuberculosis). He was interred to the right of John KEMPER, who had been buried in the first plot. In 1867, Elizabeth KEMPER passed on; since the plot next to her father was already taken by Mr. STEEN, she was interred to his right.

John was not interred until 30 August 1842 in the Old Hudson City Cemetery. Elizabeth had spent all her money on her attorney, Nicholas CARROLL, in the first suit against the pension department for her father. The only marker she could afford was a wooden cross of boards, with his name and dates carved in. This, of course, is long since gone. The gray stone brought back from Valley Forge had been put in Captain Anthony MAXWELL's lot at a location originally planned for John's burial.

Captain John KEMPER's cause had become perpetual and lingered on. For the next ten years, in an earnest attempt to have Captain KEMPER's reputation and service restored, battles against the pension department were propelled by, attorneys, statesmen, members of Congress, family, friends and neighbors to bring about a resolve.

After hearing Captain John KEMPER's name for twenty years, Commissioner James L. EDWARDS finally had had enough and resigned his office. He had opened a can of worms he could not close. He had taken all the beating he could take and passed the torch on to the new incoming commissioner of pensions, James E. HEATH (1812-1870).

10. The Day the Liberty Bell Stopped Ringing

In one of Elizabeth's final entries into her diary, she recorded,

"My father had a small model of our 'Liberty Bell' that he used to ring daily whenever he needed something, like coffee; mom and I use to race each other to see what he needed. This day . . . the bell stopped ringing. Goodbye Daddy, I love you so much! I am so sorry you will not rest in peace. But, I will pick up where you left off."

In this entry, you can see where Elizabeth's tears had dried and stained the pages of her diary. However, she was not about to sacrifice her heart, she was planning on carrying on her father's battle for him. She had saved her pennies and sold everything she could without her father knowing what she was doing.

Elizabeth added a later entry, she wrote, *"All my life I was used to hearing my father ring the Liberty Bell; I took so much for granted. I did not realize that it entered a permanent mental thought into my mind. Every day now, I imagine I hear my father ringing the Liberty Bell. I quickly run to his room to see what he needs, but he is not there."*

Elizabeth, in closing down her diary entries stated, *"All my life my daddy always told me something very special, but it never meant more to me than it does now."* He always said,

"When evil surrounds you, when everything seems hopeless and people and families are sacrificing everything, including their lives for freedom and human rights, there is always a spark of humanity

that remains. With a small amount of kindling, it can be re-ignited." He would say, *"George WASHINGTON was the spark that kept America's hopes alive and never stopped looking for that kindling. In my final days on this plane, I will always remember . . . the Revolution!"*

In finishing, Elizabeth states: *"After my mother passed on, Dad would often look out one of the window's in our home and say 'In my dreams, all my friends and loved ones are still alive, going merrily on their way, as if in Heaven. I can clearly see them as I remember them, young and happy, fearing nothing. Most importantly, I am always in their presence, if only for a short while.'"*

Chapter XXV
Captain John Kemper's Papers
(bits and pieces)

After John KEMPER's death, Elizabeth went through her father's things in tears as she went about cherishing old memories. She began to tidy up his room with the intention of keeping everything exactly the way he liked it, when all of a sudden, she accidentally bumped the wall when moving the bed and knocked a board loose, exposing a hidden compartment. Inside was an old flat box filled with what appeared to be old letters and two leather-bound bindings; they were entitled *"Wagon Master"* and *"US Naval Affairs."*

Like her father's journals, everything was written in German. Elizabeth later transcribed all these records, as all their family had been moving ahead with the English language, leaving their native German language behind.

As she went through her father's papers, she had found something she never knew about before, what appeared to be scrambled and mixed messages from a second journal. There were constant references to "the three roses" and "the bluebird." Elizabeth then remembered that her father always told her that his favorite bird was a bluebird. However, this bird was not singing. Short phrases like "mixed drinks, the soft sea breeze after the storm, or going out for candy." There were many words and phrases, but no explanations as to what they meant. Nothing seemed to flow, as in telling a story, and this was one story that her father definitely had not told her about or the rest of the kids. Elizabeth's mind went blank and began to wander. What did this all mean?

As Elizabeth continued going through the box of correspondences and notes, she found other references of *"There is a pigeon in the area,"* and *"I must find some peanuts."* Still another reference stated, *"This pigeon must come home";* however, this was no homing pigeon. All these letters were dated from the late 1770s to the mid-1780s. Still, other references were made about going to see *"the bluebird, Ben or the honeycomb."* More specifically, *"the bee or bees would return to the honeycomb."*

Why would her father be talking this way or doing these things in the middle of a war? Something was definitely puzzling here. Something just did not make sense! Just when Elizabeth thought she had come to know her father so well, she found out she did not know this other side of him at all! Why would he have kept this from her? Why did he have them hidden in the wall? What could possibly be in these records that he did not want anyone else to know about?

Elizabeth stopped and thought for a moment; this was the reason her father did not want us kids rummaging through his room when he was not around. He did not want anyone accidentally finding these records. Did Mom know?

At the funeral, all of John KEMPER's friends, neighbors, children and grandchildren were present, including John Jr. (1807-1860), who was recently widowed. His wife, Eliza MORRIS, died in child birth back in February while they were living in Kinderhook, New York; Charlie (1793-1869), (named after Charles YOUNG); Daniel (1803-1875), (named after uncle Daniel KEMPER), and his wife, Betsey KEMPER (1805-1865); Sophia (1786-1880), (named after John's sisters, Maria Sophia and Susan), and her husband, Horace WILLARD (1781-1846); Jane (Jenny) (1805-1892) (Elizabeth's closest sister), and her husband, Samuel CROSSMAN (1801-1874).

Although John died on 11 August 1842, he was not interred until 30 August 1842. This author and genealogist has researched thousands of cases, and in each one, after they died, they were interred within two to three days. On rare occasions during the winter, they might be buried a few days later; however, most cemeteries have special tools for cutting through the frost layer to get to the soft dirt underneath. Something was going on here; this was nineteen days later, in a very hot time of the year. John's body must have been put on ice to allow for the family to pick out and finish paying for their own family lot to bury their father.

Elizabeth pulled out Uncle Dan's letter to read it to the family, *"Please accept my deepest condolences for my brother's passing. Also, please excuse my inability to attend my brother's funeral, because of my own age and disabilities. Especially, since he had made many trips visiting me in both the city* [New York] *and at New Brunswick* [New Jersey]. *I can still hear my family announcing his arrival, the 'wagon master' is here!"*

Colonel Daniel KEMPER went on to say, *"I have written so many correspondences to both the Pension Department and my brother's agent, Giles YATES, including giving an affidavit, regarding my brother's service. I cannot understand what possibly went wrong here. I understand that your family intends on fighting this action until the end. I can only promise that I will be by your side to restore my brother's reputation, dignity and integrity until my last breath I take in this world. The only problem is my age and mental capacity; I have forgotten far too much that I wish I could remember. Some of my brother's service under General WASHINGTON cannot be told."*

John KEMPER had enjoyed sitting around the fireplace listening to his father Jacob, tell the heroic stories of his grandfather Colonel Johann KEMPER during the Prussian wars. His eyes opened wide whenever Jacob mentioned his father serving under Frederick William "the Great Elector," and Frederick I, king in Prussia. John's grandfather served under the leaders of a country; would it be possible for him to do the same?

Now that John had passed on, his children and descendants would tell stories of his heroics and the injustice that followed him to his grave. The stories would continue for generations until they reached this author. After putting everything together and thoroughly documenting all events, this author decided to return to Washington for a resolve. The effort was successful.

General George WASHINGTON, a master of illusion, concealed Captain John KEMPER's true identity and position under his command. Maintaining his *"special protection"* of Captain John KEMPER's command seemed to suffice as an answer for his importance to the rest of the Continental officers. They were the only ones who really seem to know who he was, but remained a mystery!

Because of the position he held as head of General WASHINGTON's special convoy and only main line of support, as well as wagon master in the clothier-general's department, everyone was satisfied. However, when Captain KEMPER started using his wagon train on foraging excursions, delivering arms and ammunition and food stuffs the army was grateful but started getting confused and then suspicious. Captain KEMPER was supposed to be with the clothier-general's department.

However, Colonel Daniel KEMPER, aide-de-camp to General WASHINGTON, had made it perfectly clear that John's appointment in the clothier-general's department was a *deception.* In reality, John KEMPER would be under the *direct command and control of General WASHINGTON himself.* Likewise, his other contact would be *Colonel Alexander HAMILTON,* aide-de-camp and intelligence officer. The suspicion surrounding Captain KEMPER's service seems to imply that he might have been among one of America's first *"top secret agents,"* though never stated so directly. Continued involvement with other intelligence officers over time seemed convincing.

Why is Captain KEMPER the only officer in American history to hold his commander-in-chief's *"special protection"* from detention or interference by senior officers? Why had Captain KEMPER constantly repeated to his family, friends, and neighbors that Ben (Benjamin) HARRISON (head of intelligence covert operations for the Continental Congress and General WASHINGTON) was his favorite member to report to in Congress?

Why did Colonel Alexander HAMILTON, another intelligence officer, have to meet with John KEMPER and his brother, Daniel at City Tavern after his escape? What *"certain circumstances"* did they need to discuss over a couple of glasses? What was attorney YATES aware of that he needed to work around and keep confidential? Why is this case the longest in American history? Captain KEMPER's official capacity remains shrouded in a cloud of mystery—and is still unknown!

John's daughter Elizabeth, named after her mother, had vowed never to marry until she saw her father's case won. At the Hudson City Courthouse all of John's children signed over their interest to their sister, Elizabeth KEMPER because she had lived with their father and took care of him. Battles with the pension department were about to be restarted. In preparation for the battles, she started detailing the stories her father had passed on to her. She contacted her aunt Susan, widow of the late Dr. David JACKSON of Philadelphia and sister of her father. Elizabeth just lived simply and frugally. She also sold everything she could dispose of in order to help finance her planned lawsuit.

Elizabeth contacted her uncle Dan (Colonel Daniel KEMPER) for everything he could remember on her father's service. She asked him if he knew anything about the papers she had found hidden in her father's room. His reply to her was, *"I know nothing of them, but it is best that you destroy them so that they do not fall into the wrong hands."* She also collected all the stories from her brothers, sisters, nieces, and nephews, as well as her cousins, children of Uncle Daniel; and children of her Uncle John MORTON and Aunt Maria Sophia (Kemper) MORTON.

Special interests were given to her cousin Eliza Susan (Morton) QUINCY because of her memoirs she had written. She was the wife of Josiah QUINCY, mayor of Boston, Massachusetts, state senator, US Congressman, a graduate of Harvard and president of Harvard University (1829-1845). Elizabeth needed all they could remember being told by their parents.

Some remembered the same stories but recalled them differently, while others remembered some that the others did not. She also collected stories from her neighbors and veterans of the officers' club in Hudson, New York. Elizabeth left no stone unturned.

Elizabeth was in heavy correspondence with two of her cousins, Jane and Eliza KEMPER, daughters of Uncle Daniel. Jane and Eliza were living with their brother Bishop David Jackson KEMPER in Nashotah, Waukesha County, Wisconsin. One of the things in common with these three cousins was that none of these women ever married. Both of these ladies sent Elizabeth everything they could remember their father, Daniel, telling them about their uncle John KEMPER besides what they could remember about him from his visits when they were growing up.

She also contacted her cousin, her father's niece, Eliza Susan (Morton) QUINCY, daughter of John's sister, Maria Sophia (Kemper) MORTON, in Quincy, Massachusetts. Eliza wrote back,

> *"My Dear Elizabeth, I was so deeply saddened by your letter. Poor Uncle John, I am so sorry I do not know a lot about his service. My father, who served with your father during the Revolution, as you know, died when I was a young girl of eight. I remember some stories from my brother, [General]*

Jacob [MORTON], who, as you know, died only a few years ago.

Our Uncle Daniel [KEMPER] spoke about him frequently when we lived near him in the city [New York]. All I can remember from what my brother told me was that our father had Uncle John deliver many supplies and other transports during the Revolution with his army and wagons that he had paid for out of his own money. I cannot remember if this was okayed by [General] WASHINGTON or not, or if Uncle John did it on the side to help my father. I would like to think it was a special favor, but they were all so close to [General] WASHINGTON.

I also have a correspondence from Professor John Melchior KEMPER, of Leyden, Holland. He was a descendent of Philip, your father and my mother's father, Jacob's older brother. Boy! This is becoming a tongue twister. In this letter he states that, when his 'grandfather, Johann KEMPER died in 1712, he was only ten years of age and knew very little other than he came from lower Germany.' His maternal line he knew. He was hoping that I could fill him in on some of the details I was trying to find out myself. Uncle John appeared to know the most on the history of Colonel Johann KEMPER, as he was named after him, was his hero and the one he tried to model his own life after.

Everyone in the family always knew this, as my mother said, "John always bolstered of his grandfather, Colonel Johann KEMPER all of his life." She also said that, she is not sure how but, John acquired his sword and all the oil paintings of Colonel KEMPER done in Germany with Frederick 'the Great Elector' and Frederick I, king in Prussia. Josiah and I would pay anything to have copies of those oil paintings made.

I have been collecting our family history and the part that they played in the Revolution for many years. I have also recorded in my memoirs Uncle John's hardships, during his service in the Navy. My mother inspired me to do my memoirs much like my Uncle John had done in his books during the Revolution under General WASHINGTON. Now, those records I would love to see. I also have a copy of a letter Uncle John sent me years ago, that he had sent to a Peter [H.] KEMPER in Virginia. In this letter it detailed the early history of our family in Germany and the ownership of Stahleck Castle. You should already have all these.

As I recall, Peter descended from either a brother or uncle of your father and my mother's grandfather, Colonel Johann KEMPER. Apparently Colonel KEMPER came from a large family of about 15 children. According to Uncle John, Peter descended from one of those lines. You must remember, Elizabeth, during this period of time I was trying to find out all I could about my father [John MORTON], since he died when I was only a child. Much the same way you are trying to do about your father.

If you only knew what it is like to be raised without a father, but hear so many stories about him. All of the stories told by the family just never seemed to be enough. My mother [Maria Sophia] told me that both my father and yours became so close that, they quickly became known as the "Johnny-in-laws." I will make copies of everything I have acquired for you; however, there is quite a lot, so it is going to take me some time. Once again, there is not a lot on just your father, but the entire family history.

Back during this period of time, the only way to make copies of any writings was by hand; there were no copy machines. General WASHINGTON had hordes of copies of his letters made, which is why over half are not in his own hand writing, but his secretary's. It is amazing he had any time left for the war. However, many of his dispatches were left in the hands of recipients and either passed down in the family, published or lost over time.

Some had to be deliberately destroyed. Most of the records of the American Revolution were destroyed deliberately and some by accident; the real reason may never be known. All the best history of the Revolution was kept in secret journals by the Continental Congress, of which they believed only they were worthy of and the general public should never know about. Many of the real heroes of the Revolution were lost because of this mass cover-up. Eliza S. QUINCY continued,

When I lived in the city [New York] near Uncle Daniel, he often spoke about his brother as they were both so close. As you also know, both uncles, Daniel and John were close to and directly under General WASHINGTON. When we were kids we all wanted to know about the Revolution, but sometimes it was just so hard to get Uncle Daniel to discuss certain subjects, especially about your father. It was as if they had something special together that they did not want or could not share with anyone. Most inquiries were in vain.

I do remember one thing but I am not sure that it means anything. On one of the trips Uncle John made down to visit his brother, Daniel and my mother [Maria], I accidentally walked in on them when

they were talking about something to do with three roses and the bluebird. After Uncle John returned to Hudson, I asked Uncle Daniel what that was about," and he nervously replied, *"Something to do with a present my brother either gave or received during the Revolution."*

Whenever Uncle John visited, it was like a small treasure, because he lived upstate and we very seldom got to see him, unlike Uncle Daniel who lived close by. Whenever Uncle John would visit my mother, he would always say, "I came here to hear the beautiful voice of my niece and listen to her play the piano; however, if I am unable to, I guess I will just have to leave." Uncle John always knew how to put a smile on my face.

One night when I was singing and playing a lullaby for him, as he was resting in our comfort chair, I got so involved that I lost track of time. When I caught myself and looked up, Uncle John had fallen to sleep with a smile on his face. I covered him with a quilt then went to bed with a smile on my face. Poor Uncle John, I am so distressed for your loss.

Your Loving Cousin,
Eliza S. Quincy

For some unknown reason, out of all the family members Elizabeth contacted for her upcoming suit against the pension department, this is the only correspondence that remained intact. She never mentioned Eliza as one of her closest or favorite cousins, whereas she did mention Jane as her closest sister.

After Jon KEMPER passed on, his spirit was still alive in so many family, friends and neighbors. They all lined up behind his daughter, Elizabeth, to take on Commissioner EDWARDS and the pension department.

After her father's death, Elizabeth moved in with her sister and brother-in-law, Samuel and Jane CROSSMAN, taking care of their house for her keep. She moved with them from Hudson, New York, to Van Vorst, New Jersey, and finally settled in Litchfield, Connecticut, where she eventually died. While in Litchfield, Elizabeth and Jenny visited Benjamin TALLMADGE's gravesite. For some strange reason, they felt that part of their father was buried with him. Elizabeth was interred in the CROSSMAN family plot, lot 50, section 1-A, in the Old Hudson City Cemetery, Hudson, New York.

Over succeeding generations, various family members removed some parts of these stories to read, to study or to share with other friends and family. When they were returned, they were often put back in the wrong order, having been shuffled like a deck of cards. It was up to this author to restructure this time line to the best of his ability, according to the author's life-long research on events that took place during the American Revolution.

At the end of Elizabeth's diary were batches of mismatched pages that contained phrases and scrambled language. These were part of the materials found concealed in her father's hidden compartment after his death. She felt that they belonged with her father's journals, somehow, but she was not sure where.

Neither Elizabeth nor this author could figure out where they fit into John's story. Some of this language was, *"There is a pigeon in the area; I need to find some peanuts."* This note was addressed to someone named *"Ben."* Was it really a bird he wanted to feed or was it code for something? Was the "Ben" referring to Benjamin FRANKLIN, head of intelligence for the Continental Congress, or Benjamin TALLMADGE, intelligence chief? Or was it referring to Benjamin HARRISON, member of the Committee of Secret Correspondence and chairman of the

Board of War, as well as covert operations? Riddles continued to follow one after another.

This author went through the same difficulties in placing the family history in chronological order that John KEMPER's daughter, Elizabeth, underwent. In relating the stories, many of the family members could not remember the dates the events took place. However, this author had more resources available like the National Archives records, microfilm and the Internet for quick reference. However, so many of the pages were mixed up and out of sequence, not having been either numbered or dated. In addition, there were some pages that were missing. One page would be going thoroughly into a subject, while no page could be found to finish it.

One recording related how he [Captain John KEMPER] tried to mend things between His Excellency and Mr. MEASE. Another was with his brother [Daniel], who likewise asked him to try and fix things between His Excellency and Mr. MEASE.

Since Captain KEMPER was stationed in Philadelphia, along with James MEASE and his deputy clothier-general, Charles YOUNG, in addition to the Continental Congress, he was in the middle of everything. Furthermore, his brother-in-law, John MORTON, continued his gold raising business for General WASHINGTON and the Continental Congress from this city.

Still another recording separate from anything and seemingly belonging nowhere stated, *"His Excellency was a big man, but his body was out of proportion to his size."*

In addition, Elizabeth did not know what to do with the new papers she had found of her father's, but she knew better than to turn them over to the pension office of the War Department. Whom could she talk to about this, besides her uncle Daniel, where everything would remain safe, her new attorney?

One important part of one of General WASHINGTON's correspondences to Colonel Alexander HAMILTON, which corroborates Captain John KEMPER's recollection of his duties, dated 22 September 1777, states: *"When no more supplies can be drawn from public magazines, then resources would have to be obtained from private citizens' stock, in order to maintain the army."*

Colonel HAMILTON passed this dispatch and order from General WASHINGTON onto Captain John KEMPER to fulfill.

Chapter XXVI
The Battle Rages on!

On 20 March 1843, Giles F. YATES of Schenectady, New York, once again put in for an increase in John KEMPER's pension to include his service as wagon conductor. Because he had no copy of John's declaration, he confused the time line, placing his naval service ahead of his service as wagon conductor, much the same way John's brother, Colonel Daniel KEMPER, aide-de-camp, did in his old age. Mr. EDWARDS never corrected any wrong information, allowing them to believe any misconceptions for his own purpose and enjoying the wrong information being put on record.

Giles started out,

> *"Mr. John KEMPER has heretofore applied for an increase of his pension. Instead of an increase, it was stopped all together. After protecting against such treatment, you allowed him the service he had claimed as midshipman. He is undoubtedly entitled to a pension for all the service deserved in his declaration, but if I understand his statement, the service as midshipmen is supported by no particle of such direct proof as that in the grade of Wagon Conductor.*
>
> *It has been intimated in your communication on the subject, that the service as Wagon Conductor was under **civil contract,** but it is clear from his own statement that he was not during the period referred to, engaged for one moment under civil contract. His*

brother [Colonel Daniel KEMPER] *held an office of considerable importance in the army as may be seen by the Journals of Congress, &* ***actually assisted in procuring Mr. [John] KEMPER's appointment as Wagon Conductor.***

After many correspondences with John's brother, Daniel, Agent YATES went on to inform Commissioner EDWARDS of the closeness of the two brothers and underscored it. Mr. EDWARDS was ignoring all proof, while continually asking for more.

Captain KEMPER was a wagon master; the title of wagon conductor meant the same as used on both sides during the entire twenty years of correspondences on his case (1832-1852). Both these titles were used interchangeably.

Agent Giles went on to say, *"Mr. KEMPER is known, if not to the late Secretary of War,"* [John ARMSTRONG Jr. (1758-1843], of Red Hook, New York, appointed on 13 Jan. 1813 by President James MADISON (1751-1836)], *"to many of the secretary's friends as a highly respectable and worthy citizen, and it is hoped, that his former pension will be restored to him."* Agent YATES had received John ARMSTRONG's name from Captain KEMPER, prior to his death, but did not know where or how to use it to his advantage for his defense, so he decided to throw it in at this point to make sure it was put on record.

John ARMSTRONG Jr. was a lieutenant, then major in the Continental Army of Pennsylvania during the American Revolution and had become close friends with Captain KEMPER. After the Revolution, John ARMSTRONG settled in Red Hook, just south of Hudson, New York. His friendship with Captain KEMPER continued to grow over the years, including visits to each other's home. He was just one of the many honorable statesmen and friends of Captain John KEMPER.

Agent Giles stated,

> *It was no easy matter getting the appointment of Wagon Conductor. The pay was considerable, and it was a highly respectable station . . . and the pay too, was that of a captain of infantry.*

> *I am aware that one objection to allowing the claim, or rather restoring the amount of the stipend, is that there is no documentary proof of Mr. KEMPER having been Wagon Master. Thus, the highest grade of evidence is not required in every case, and the next in rank, to wit the **affidavit** of a superior officer,* Mr. [John] *KEMPER's brother* [Colonel Daniel KEMPER aide-de-camp to General George WASHINGTON, and Deputy Clothier General of the Continental Army] *has been adduced."*

Giles F. YATES was an attorney at law and not a psychologist; therefore, he was responding the only way he knew how, in law. What Agent YATES was unfamiliar with was the psychological aspects of why Commissioner EDWARDS was responding the way he was. John KEMPER's inquiry into the correct amount of pension he should have been receiving had gone ignored by Commissioner EDWARDS for over two years. He had hoped that Mr. KEMPER would have forgotten about it.

This gave Commissioner EDWARDS plenty of time to consider his alternatives and tactics in his part of the cover-up, if pursued. Now Captain KEMPER had an attorney and the Secretary of War, Joel R. POINSETT, had ordered him to answer and give reasons for his actions. Commissioner EDWARDS felt that his authority was challenged. He was ready to assert his arrogance and demonstrate that the final decision was his, right or wrong!

On 1 April 1843, Captain John KEMPER's life-long friend, the Honorable John ARMSTRONG Jr. died in Red Hook,

New York, at eighty-five years old. As Giles F. YATES had stated in his previous correspondence to James L. EDWARDS, commissioner of pensions, *"Mr. KEMPER was not only a friend with the late secretary of war, but with his friends as well."* As most of us already know, friends become friends of friends! Agent YATES was making reference to former secretary of war John ARMSTRONG Jr., and feeling that EDWARDS would be more understanding, since he was under the current secretary of war.

On 12 April 1843, James L. EDWARDS responded to Giles F. YATES' continued effort to restore Captain John KEMPER's full pension. He stated,

> *"In the case of John KEMPER to which you have so often called the attention of the Dept. without any additional proof, you are referred to the previous correspondence in which you have been repeatedly informed why his claim as Wagon Conductor has been rejected. So far from his brother's testimony or any proof on file establishing his appointment & service in any military staff, his own statements with that of his brother's, show conclusively that [he] held a civil employment in the army. It is unnecessary in such case, to burthen the office with repeated letters when you are informed that proof is required.*

How can you send additional proof without sending repeated letters? Giles had stated in a previous correspondence *"that he had done what was asked and supplied a **'affidavit'** from John's superior officer, his brother, Colonel Daniel KEMPER,"* John's only superior officer left alive. If you are not part of the solution, then you are part of the problem! EDWARDS was definitely not part of the solution. However, Commissioner EDWARDS was starting to break down, as Captain KEMPER's case continued to go on relentlessly for many years to follow. Captain KEMPER's body may be deceased, but his spirit lives on.

In jogging one's memory, James L. EDWARDS, commissioner of pensions, continued to refuse to acknowledge all old and new documentation, with which Giles F. YATES repeatedly flooded his department. Constant repetition of good, sound documentation continued to be wasted. It remained ignored by Commissioner EDWARDS. Commissioner EDWARDS was a pure *"hypocrite,"* as defined in Webster's dictionary! He should have been turned over to the president of the United States and removed from office. It is still a query as to why Agent YATES did not do this.

Additionally, at the beginning of the Revolution, Daniel, in his 24 July 1777 letter, told John that *"his appointment in the clothier-general's department was just a 'ruse'* [to deceive], *and that he would be under the direct command and control of the Commander-in-Chief, George WASHINGTON, himself."* Further he said, *"He was going to hold General WASHINGTON's 'special protection' from any interference or detention from any of his senior officers."* John was indeed appointed wagon master and had 150 wagons and 320 men under his command.

The appointment in the clothier-general's department was the front or cloak and dagger for something special that General WASHINGTON had planned for John. Daniel did not elaborate on it further, but told John he would get full details when he met in Philadelphia with General WASHINGTON, Alexander HAMILTON, Benjamin TALLMADGE, Benjamin HARRISON himself, and a couple of other members of Congress but was not yet sure of their identities.

On 17 April 1843, at Hudson, New York, John KEMPER's brother-in-law, Sergeant John HARDICK, likewise a pensioner of the American Revolution passed away at ninety-one years old. Mr. HARDICK also stood by his brother-in-law through the final days of his life and then joined him.

On 5 December 1843, at Hudson City Courthouse, Elizabeth KEMPER signed over power of attorney to Nicholas CARROLL (1815-1887), attorney-at-law in the City of New York and Washington, DC In the document she signed, she gave her attorney the power *"to ask, demand and institute such proceedings as to him should seem proper to recover all or any arrears of pension monies now due from the United States for an account of services rendered by the said John KEMPER in his lifetime, and to receive the same and in all things necessary to the recovery thereof as fully to act as I, myself, might or could do."* Elizabeth KEMPER's heart was just as broken as her father's.

The commissioner of deeds who recorded Elizabeth's power of attorney was James ROWLEY, the same person who took her father's supplement declaration. Mr. ROWLEY also had written a letter to the War Department, questioning why John KEMPER's pension was cut off without giving him a chance to defend himself. He then referred John to his state agent, Giles F. YATES, Esq. He now gave Elizabeth KEMPER one of the best attorneys in the country, Nicholas CARROLL, who had offices in both New York City and Washington, DC.

Elizabeth turned over to Nicholas CARROLL copies of all records compiled by her—from her uncle Dan (Colonel Daniel KEMPER, aide-de-camp to General WASHINGTON), her cousins, her brothers and sisters, and neighbors—regarding her father's service. She also elaborated on how Commissioner EDWARDS had manipulated the original certificate away from her father that had been awarded to him as captain and wagon master, after the pension law was enacted. This was the first law suit against the pension office of the War Department in American history. The battle raged on.

On 30 July 1844, Nicholas CARROLL, attorney-at-law, after spending several months researching Captain John KEMPER's and other wagon masters' cases, in addition to confirming all Captain KEMPER's family's, friends' and neighbor's stories, contacted James L. EDWARDS, commissioner of pensions, in Washington, DC. Nicholas enclosed power of attorney from Elizabeth KEMPER, one of the children of John KEMPER, deceased, formerly of Hudson, Columbia County, New York. He enclosed several cases analogous to John KEMPER's. All these documents submitted to the pension department by Mr. CARROLL, are now missing, but alluded to in other correspondences.

Nicholas went on to say, *"John KEMPER was a 'conductor of teams' during the war of the Revolution and was pensioned under the Act of 1832 at $216 per annum. He also performed other services as set forth in his declaration. He was pensioned at the rate of $320 for full service as 'conductor' when he was entitled to be pensioned at the rate of $480—The object of this application is to procure the arrears due his heirs from the 4 Mar. 1831 until his death* [11 August 1842]*."*

On 26 October 1844, after considerable time researching the multiple cases, Nicholas CARROLL had sent him supporting John KEMPER's case; Commissioner James L. EDWARDS responded giving reasons for some of the cases Mr. CARROLL had sent him, at least those left on record. He commented *"that the claim of John KEMPER as conductor has been elaborately contested heretofore and in his lifetime and deliberately upon mature deliberation rejected."* James went on to explain another case, *"That it was inferred from his silence that all was satisfactory to him."*

To see references to these original documents, please view this author's album, National Archives on Facebook, where everything is in chronological order. These documents supplied by Mr. CARROLL, like many others, including the vouchers of President Martin VAN BUREN, Colonel Elisha JENKINS, and John W. EDMONDS, presiding justice of the Supreme Court, which were alluded to by the justices of the court of Hudson,

New York, as well as Giles F. YATES, have since disappeared; one continual mystery after another!

The letter of 26 October 1844, is as such:

Commissioner EDWARDS continued,

> *In the case of Hezekiah RIPLEY (1748–1836), decd, there is a misconception as to the length of his service as asst. Commissary which by the certificate of Saml GRAY (1751–1836), was 9 mo. & estimated by RIPLEY himself as 10 months—The half pay of all the services rendered by him agreeably to his own statement which cannot now be question, has been paid to his children. The proofs of the date of the marriage in the case of Asenah HOTCHKISS is not as conclusive as it should be—but the wagoners under Jo[na]than PARKER (1754–1815) were hired at 15$ per mo. While the enlisted Teamster recd soldiers pay only—There were a number of Conductors in the Commissary & Qr Mr Genl Depts. Engaged in procuring & transporting supplies in Con: at that period of the war, who were under contract & consequently were not regarded as entitled to pensions—*

Commissioner EDWARDS was a master in manipulation of words.

> *The state of the business in this office will not admit of correspondence with more than one person in the same case & not paper is presented in the case of Avery DOWNER (1762–1854) whose claim has been heretofore rejected to raise a doubt as to the propriety of that decision so as to justify & require a re-examination.*

It is to be noted here that because of Captain KEMPER's case ending up being the longest in American history, and because they were answering to so many statesmen and attorneys on his case, which was never ending, they changed their rules and stated, *"This office will not admit of correspondence with more than one person in the same case."* The pension department had taken such a beating and battering over the years, they had to make a new law so as to prevent it from ever happening again. This new rule adopted has been followed to this very day. It should have been called, *"The Captain John KEMPER rule!"*

As Commissioner EDWARDS continued, *"The claim of John KEMPER as Conductor has been elaborately contested heretofore & in his life time and deliberately upon mature deliberation rejected."* Commissioner EDWARDS continued to give the impression that everything was legit and was looked at fairly, when in fact, it was the opposite! There was a constant cover-up going on, while many correspondences, documents and vouchers supporting Captain KEMPER's service, disappeared.

> *In the case of Abraham F. URMAN, the documents filed by him show his appointment to have been 'Issuer of Forage to an asst. Depy Forage Master' and he was allowed the full pay of the highest warrant officer of the line, and it is inferred from his silence, was satisfactory to him—If it can be shown that he received more than 10$ per mo.—The increase will be allowed.*

Please note that the original letter sent by Attorney Nicholas CARROLL making reference to all the cases analogous to Captain John KEMPER's is now missing. All that remains are the cases left on file that the pension department had not felt threatened by; everything else is long gone!

On 6 August 1847, in New Brunswick, New Jersey, John's brother Colonel Daniel KEMPER, aide-de-camp and deputy clothier-general, died at ninety-eight years old. Daniel was the last Continental officer who had anything to do with the birth of America to pass on. All that was left were the memories of those who left their stories behind—stories that have touched our hearts. Daniel, after advising his brother, John, to seek legal representation to obtain the increase for the proper amount of his pension he should have been receiving, stood behind him until the very end of his own life.

Most of the memories and stories died with their children; some, like this author's family, because of the deep impact, were carried on from generation to generation. Daniel stuck by his brother John to the very day John died, then he continued to defend his honor and dignity until the last breath he took in this world, as he had promised in his letter, read at his brother's funeral. Daniel was interred at Christ Church in New Brunswick, New Jersey, where he had been a member most of his life.

Chapter XXVII
Who would be Remembered?

Who would be remembered? Monuments were erected for some like General George WASHINGTON, General *"Mad"* Anthony WAYNE, General Marquis DE LAFAYETTE, General John MUHLENBERG, General Casimir PULASKI, General Alexander HAMILTON, General Nathanael GREENE, General Baron Wilhelm VON STEUBEN, John HANCOCK, and Benjamin FRANKLIN, while John only received a wooden cross.

Of all the officers who served in the Continental Army and the Continental Navy, including General George WASHINGTON, the KEMPER's had the most royal military history. Their grandfather, Colonel Johann KEMPER, served faithfully for two kings and an emperor. He was wounded fourteen times in battle and had a dress uniform covered in medals.

All these founding fathers were personal acquaintances, friends, comrades and family of Captain John KEMPER. He had laughed, had cried, and had fought by their sides, from General WASHINGTON on down. John KEMPER ended up being the only founding father who received just a wooden cross. He was put on the back burner and buried in the archives as if he never existed.

Others, like Captain John KEMPER, because of higher rank or a brighter star over-shadowed them, over time would become insignificant. During the American Revolution, Captain KEMPER was the brightest star in the sky that the Continental Army deeply depended on to bring food and clothing for their survival. For some strange reason, it was easy to forget about him afterward. Some things will never be known about. Afterward, the country consisted of a new generation of Americans who took everything for granted and who were never deeply involved in the past or the historical reason or how they have been able to enjoy the liberties afforded them.

On 18 May 1848, in New York City, New York, John's friend, voucher, and comrade in Colonel Henry J. VAN RENSSELAER's regiment in Hudson, New York, Colonel Elisha JENKINS, died at seventy-nine years old.

On 20 July 1848, Congressman James S. WILEY (1808-1891) contacted the pension department inquiring why John KEMPER was not paid the full amount of his pension for his service during the American Revolution. Agent YATES was still involving members of Congress for a resolution for Captain KEMPER's case. There were many others unsatisfied with the action taken by the pension department against Captain KEMPER. They stood in the shadows, afraid of action being taken against them and pushed for a resolve.

On 25 July 1848, the pension department responded to Congressman James S. WILEY's inquiry. *"In answer of your letter of the 20th instant in the case of John KEMPER, deceased, I have the honor to inform you, that he was placed on the pension roll under the Act of 7 Jun. 1832, at $216 per annum, on the 1 May 1833, and was reduced to $108 on the 14 Sept. 1840."* What happened to Commissioner EDWARDS's new rule that his office would not admit to more than one person on the same case? It appears that Commissioner EDWARDS was afraid to apply it to the very person who was responsible for having had it made.

Commissioner EDWARDS continued, *"He* [John KEMPER] *has been paid up to the 11 Aug. 1842, the day of his death, as appears from the books of the third auditor of the Treasury. The letter of the aledgemood* [this word does not exist in English dictionaries but is an exact transcription from the original documents in the National Archives. Did he mean allege-mood?], *herewith returned.*"

On 10 August 1848, the pension department responded to yet another correspondence from Congressman James S. WILEY, which is now missing. They stated, *"I have the honor to inform you that my letter of the 25ᵗʰ last, contains full information in the case of John KEMPER, deceased, to which decision the department adheres."* Agent YATES continued his push on members of Congress to keep Commissioner EDWARDS in check. Commissioner EDWARDS was not about to concur with anyone. He was making it clear, rather right or wrong, that he was the one in charge.

Giles F. YATES had become quite a fan of John KEMPER's and gave the best ten years of his life trying to win his case. It was as if John was either his brother or father. What possible facts could he have known about that made him fight so hard for so long? He appeared to have known many facts of Captain KEMPER's service, personally; but had to beat around the bush in an attempt to bring about a resolve. Were his hands tied as to what he could reveal? There appeared to be some sort of relationship in words unspoken, as with an associate. For the next two years, things seemed to have settled down, or if there were any further correspondences, they are now also missing.

On 27 November 1850, after Commissioner James L. EDWARDS resigned his position, President Millard FILLMORE (1800-1874) appointed James E. HEATH commissioner of pensions. Mr. HEATH was feeling his oats and was excited about fulfilling his new post; he did not realize that he was walking blindly into a shooting gallery where he would become the next target.

Commissioner EDWARDS briefed Mr. HEATH on Captain KEMPER's ongoing case, which had been disputed for the past eighteen years. He informed him that his service was civilian and they are trying to claim military. Mr. HEATH, already biased, had no clue on what the former Commissioner EDWARDS had pulled or what he was involved in. He instinctively backed the pension department's former decision on John KEMPER's claim.

On 25 December 1850, Wheeler H. CLARK (ca. 1812-1884), commissioner of deeds, of Hudson, New York, wrote to (Captain) Henry Hayden SYLVESTER, Esq. (1808-1898), informing him this:

> *A portion of John Kemper's children wish me to see if an increase of pension can be obtained. John Kemper obtained a pension as teamster and midshipman under the Act of 1832.*
>
> *He resided in this city. The commissioner of pensions struck Kemper from the rolls, but sub-sequently, restored him for his services as midshipman alone, refusing to allow anything for his services as conductor or captain of teams.*
>
> *I wish you to look into Kemper's papers to see if Kemper ought to have been pensioned for his services as teamster.*

So many years have passed since John KEMPER had left this plain, but his spirit still remains strong, yet unsettled in a resolve to all those who knew him. Is there anything possible in the future that can be done to correct this injustice?

The declaration reads,

> *On this 29 May 1851 . . . [John KEMPER's daughter] Elizabeth Kemper, a resident of Van Vorst in said county of Hudson [New Jersey] . . . in order to obtain an increase in pension in the case of John Kemper, deceased under the Act of Congress passed June 7, 1832. That she is the Administratrix . . . .*

That John Kemper . . . died . . . on the eleventh day of Aug. 1842 in Columbia County, N.Y., that at the time of his death, he left no widow, and the following are the only children . . . viz- Sophia Willard, Daniel Kemper, Charles Kemper, John Kemper, Jane G. Crossman and Elizabeth Kemper (this Declarant)... In support of this claim this Declarant refers the Pension Department to evidence on file in the office and to such other evidence as may be furnished by her agent, Wayatentius of Albany, N.Y., or by his substitute.

This author/genealogist researched the name WAYATENTIUS and found that it did not exist anywhere on the planet Earth in any period of time, from the beginning of mankind until present. Was this his real name, and was he a real person? WAYATENTIUS was the one Elizabeth had faith in and to whom she gave him copies of all the records she had put together on her father's service from John's neighbors, all members of her family, including her uncle Daniel and his children, Jane and Eliza KEMPER, who were her first cousins. She had hoped that he would do something with her father's case; if he did, there is no record of any action taken by him. He was no Giles F. YATES for sure!

Elizabeth categorized all the records she received from her family, naming who contributed what. Some of these records were lost while being passed down in the family, but are given reference to in Elizabeth's diary. She had entitled her collection on her father, *"The Birth of America!"*

Elizabeth passed down all the family records to her favorite niece, Mary (Marion) Ann (Kemper) MILLER (1816-1877). Marion had loved her grandfather John KEMPER dearly. Marion had attended her grandfather's funeral and relayed many of the stories that the rest of the family likewise remembered, especially about Benjamin FRANKLIN.

John had told the family constantly over the years, *"Benjamin FRANKLIN was one of the greatest supporter of Congress, General WASHINGTON and the Continental Army."* He said, *"He was always calm, composed and collected, and always in a position to make a difference."* How would he know all this when Mr. FRANKLIN was in Paris for nine years? He also said, *"Ben was the one who had done the most for the Continental Army and America politically."* Furthermore, he said that *"his kite flying and his discovery of electricity was one of his smaller contributions."*

Marion had gone one step further than the rest of the family; she had named a son Benjamin Franklin MILLER, after one of her grandfather's mentors. She also named a son John, after her grandfather. Likewise, she named a daughter exactly after her grandmother, Elizabeth (Eliza) (Hopper) KEMPER. Marion, in turn, left all the family records to her only surviving son, Benjamin (Ben) Franklin MILLER. Ben left all the family records to his only child, Minnie Florence WILCOX, who in turn left all the family records to her only child, this author's grandfather, Basil Gaul Knickerbocker WILCOX. Basil was named after Colonel Edward Linus GAUL (1837-1894), friend of his father, Frank Eugene WILCOX (1860-1914).

Basil had seven children, but in the late 1960s during the final years of his life, he only mentioned this author's mother, Dianthus (Dolly) May PROPER. For some strange reason, only known to the immediate family, Basil had become disappointed in the rest of his children.

On 11 December 1851, Esquires FRENCH and SYLVESTER contacted James E. HEATH, commissioner of pensions. They brought to his attention a package of new documents that England released on John KEMPER regarding his capture while serving on the brig *Hector*, when he was carried to New York City on 7 June 1781 and imprisoned in various British prisons in New York City, before being transferred to Mill Prison, Plymouth, England, and up to his escape.

They stated that *"this list was pulled from the English papers, in the Pennsylvania Packet with the dates of April 23, 30, May 21, 25, June 15, 18, and December 1782. These documents can be found in Colonel Peter FORCE's [1790-1868] Library of this city [Washington, DC]. Admitting this proof, a full pension of $144 cannot be denied."*

On 22 March 1852, James E. HEATH, commissioner of pensions, responded to FRENCH and SYLVESTER's letter of 11 December, last. He declared that *"relative to the case of John KEMPER, you are informed that we cannot decide upon the testimony relied upon to establish the orders to an increase of his pension until it is submitted to this office."* Captain John KEMPER had now been dead for ten years. If any further action was taken on any of these last correspondences, the records are now missing. It is quite clear that these last entries called for a reply and a resolve. There appear to be more mysteries?

Also, please note that the dates here, from 11 December 1851 to 22 March 1852, allow time to verify the new claim before responding to KEMPER's new defense. There is no way this new evidence would not have been submitted. Where is it? What else is missing? It appears that all important documents supporting and giving reference and credence to Captain KEMPER's defense, had been plucked out.

Fortunately, there are many correspondences eluding to most of those documents, proving that they once existed—a sad commentary in American history. Unfortunately, there were probably just as many documents destroyed along with the correspondences alluding to them. In addition, thankfully, John's daughter, Elizabeth KEMPER, foretold the story and recorded everything in her diary for posterity, as she collected the history.

Chapter XXVIII
General Washington's
"Top Secret Agent"?

It was not the author's original intent to delve into this realm of John KEMPER's service for the United States of America in any capacity other than what it was originally believed to be. However, while researching, the evidence kept growing stronger and leading in an opposite direction from what this author thought it should have been. Although the following evidence is highly suggestive, it leads to absolutely nowhere!

It is no longer a secret that, General WASHINGTON was deeply involved in secret intelligence committees. This was the beginning of army intelligence, which has blossomed into the strength that it holds today! Our country is safer because of it. This was the seed from which our Federal Bureau of Investigation (FBI), Central Intelligence Agency (CIA), and National Security Agency (NSA) grew.

General George WASHINGTON could not possibly win the war solely on *"battle power,"* by any means. To that end, General WASHINGTON relied heavily on his trusted, specially designated officers and aides to help him gain intelligence and assist him in conducting intelligence operations. One of General WASHINGTON's main intelligence officers was Colonel Alexander HAMILTON and his personal friends, Colonel Daniel and Captain John KEMPER. He liked a closely knit web in intelligence and called it family, the best means of trusting the success of an organization.

In 1776, General WASHINGTON found it necessary, because of intelligence failure at the Battle of Long Island, to specify an *"elite detachment"* dedicated to reconnaissance. These specially handpicked trusted officers were sent on a variety of covert operations, far too dangerous and too vital for regular troops to handle. *"They were to report to him directly!"* Intelligence officers held the rank of captain or higher. Because of a congressional resolution, *some officers' names were so top secret their names were never revealed!*

From 1777 on, it appears that many of these covert operations took place from Captain KEMPER's wagon-train camp. General WASHINGTON often went to Captain KEMPER's camp with the excuse of picking up supplies with such officers as Generals LAFAYETTE, WAYNE, MUHLENBERG, and Colonels HAMILTON, Daniel KEMPER, and TILGHMAN. General WASHINGTON often had an escort by Captain Henry *"Light Horse Harry"* LEE and his Continental Dragoons. They would all meet in Captain KEMPER's officers' tent, while guards were posted outside. Was all this top brass and guards really needed just to pick up supplies?

In 1778, General WASHINGTON appointed Brigadier General, Charles SCOTT, *"intelligence chief."* As we know, Colonel Daniel KEMPER served in General SCOTT's brigade, had many direct involvements with General SCOTT, including sitting in on court-martials ordered by General WASHINGTON. Daniel had been the go between, linking General SCOTT and his brother, John KEMPER.

In the summer of 1778, Benjamin TALLMADGE, captain of a troop in the Second Continental Light Dragoon Regiment joined General SCOTT's brigade. Here we go again, the intelligence circle.

In the fall of 1778, Benjamin TALLMADGE was appointed intelligence chief and like Captain KEMPER, started reporting directly to General WASHINGTON. As one of the founders of the first organized espionage operations, he was heavily involved in the American Revolution as part of the secret service. In many of Elizabeth's entries, it was noted her father refers constantly to reporting to Ben.

Originally this was thought to be Benjamin FRANKLIN, but he was in Paris for nine years from 1776-1785. All that was left were Colonel Benjamin TALLMADGE and Benjamin HARRISON, who were both part of the secret intelligence espionage ring. However, Captain KEMPER kept everything silent about them. In later years secrets leaked out about Colonel TALLMADGE, when he started to toot his own horn. However, Captain KEMPER was never part of those leaks.

For the security of the missions and operatives themselves, it was necessary for General WASHINGTON to have ordered that, *"the names of persons cannot be inserted."* Congress resolved that *"withholding the names of the persons they have employed, or with whom they have corresponded."* Benjamin HARRISON was definitely part of this operation.

Why did Captain John KEMPER, throughout the entire American Revolution, never have any financial problems? Was his captain's pay being supplemented from another source, besides his brother-in-law, John MORTON, which he never could reveal?

Daniel, on orders from General George WASHINGTON, offered John KEMPER, by letter, his appointment as wagon master in the clothier-general's department, explicitly telling John that, *"your appointment is a ruse."* In actuality, John *"would be under the direct command of General WASHINGTON, himself and maintain his **'Special Protection'** from any interference of his other officers."* This letter was addressed to *"The Eagles Nest"* and not signed by Daniel but, in fact, Dan, and it was to be burned. Utmost secrecy was already underway.

It appears that General WASHINGTON and the Continental Congress used Colonel Daniel KEMPER as a go-between, between them and his brother, John, to divert suspicion away from his true purpose.

Ben HARRISON, who was standing outside Independence Hall watching as the grand parade approached, pointed his finger in the direction of Colonel Alexander HAMILTON, Colonel Daniel and Captain John KEMPER, offering a soft, warm nod. The three returned the soft nod. Words unspoken, what was this all about? Was this the Ben who participated in their meeting with General WASHINGTON? Was this a nod of approval or a nod implying that "now our plan or journey begins"?

Captain KEMPER was ordered by General WASHINGTON to always fill Congress in on any progress, hardships or needs of the army. Wherever Congress was, became Captain KEMPER's home base of operations for the Continental Army. He was the only military security for Congress and his wagons and teams could immediately transport them to safety if necessary.

Captain KEMPER is the only officer in American history to have carried a *"shield of protection"* by his commander-in-chief, General WASHINGTON, from detention or interference from any superior officers. Its purpose was to make sure that any supplies, correspondences, or intelligence from Congress, or other sources that Captain KEMPER carried, got directly to General WASHINGTON without interruption. General WASHINGTON always kept everything *"top secret"* between him, Colonel TALLMADGE, and Captain KEMPER. He always sent his orders to Captain KEMPER sealed, because the contents, if intercepted, could jeopardize the fate of all the Continental efforts and the people involved. Who really was Captain John KEMPER?

Because General WASHINGTON had lost faith in the clothier-general, James MEASE, he decided to give Daniel more power.

Out of all his top brass, General WASHINGTON authorized his trusted aide, Colonel Daniel KEMPER, to deliver all his orders to the three main departments of the Continental Army. He had Daniel KEMPER deliver all his orders to the clothier-general, commissary-general, and quarter master-general.

In the spring of 1779, after General WASHINGTON was confident that his smaller regimental wagon-train would suffice, he no longer needed a huge convoy of wagons and Captain KEMPER was released. General WASHINGTON was untying Captain KEMPER's hands so that he could use him elsewhere. Note that he was being released, not discharged.

In his 25 April 1779 letter to General WASHINGTON, Timothy PICKERING (1745-1829) informed General WASHINGTON that he had sent orders to the clothier general to reserve for Colonel Thomas PROCTOR's (1739-1806) and Colonel Thomas HARTLEY's (1748-1800) regiments a said number of shirts, over-alls and blankets and that the rest in reserve be forwarded to camp.

He also informed General WASHINGTON that Colonel John MITCHELL (1741-1816) had purchased 1,700 blankets that would be forwarded to camp as soon as possible. He also notified His Excellency that he could depend on 4,500 pair of shoes posthaste.

Timothy PICKERING, having heard from Mr. MEASE that he had expressed to" *Mr. KEMPER to buy shoes, immediately,"* conjecturing that there are an additional 1,000 pair available for purchase from the currier, Henry GUEST (1742-1807). He continued that Samuel Allyne OTIS (1740-1814) and Colonel David HENLEY (1748-1823) per their letter dated 1 April, 1779 had sent 7,000 ready-made frocks, 20,000 pairs of overalls and various other clothing.

In May 1779, Captain John KEMPER, after being released because he was no longer needed in the capacity of wagon master, immediately joined the United States Navy, in Philadelphia, Pennsylvania. This was believed to be because the revolutionary blood was flowing in his veins. In actually, General WASHINGTON was sending him on yet another planned mission.

Generally, everyone stays within the branch of service to which they have become accustomed and with which they are most comfortable and familiar, either the army or navy, usually not both. However, both General WASHINGTON and Congress made exceptions to the rule; Captain Silas TALBOT was another one of them.

Commodore John MANLEY, who commanded the USS *Hancock*, was captured by the British and transported to Mill Prison, England. After the USS *Hancock* was captured, the British changed its name to HMS *Iris*. While under this new name, it captured the ship Hector while Lieutenant John KEMPER was on board. This appeared to be a coincidence, but Commodore MANLEY was the person General WASHINGTON and the intelligence committee wanted Lieutenant KEMPER to locate and verify the status of, if still alive.

After John escaped from Mill Prison and returned back to his brother Daniel's home in Morristown, Daniel returned to inform John that he was with General WASHINGTON, General John MUHLENBERG, and Colonel Alexander HAMILTON when he received news of his escape and safe return. Colonel HAMILTON, after sending wishes for a rapid recovery, said, *"He will be glad to share a glass or two at City Tavern, like days of old; on him"* because *"he needs to go over 'certain circumstances' of which we are both familiar."*

In a correspondence to John KEMPER, General WASHINGTON stated, *"We have lost many a good soldier in your absence; a good friend of ours, the Count had passed on as heroically as any soldier could in combat, just prior to your capture."*

How was General WASHINGTON privy to John's capture just after the count's death? Had General WASHINGTON unintentionally slipped in his letter to John, as he had in his letter to his cousin Lund WASHINGTON, just after the fire in New York City?

It appeared that Captain KEMPER was sent on board the *Hector* deliberately to be captured, so that he could infiltrate the heart of the British Empire and its prison system. General WASHINGTON with Benjamin TALLMADGE, chief of intelligence, planned John KEMPER's capture by the British.

John was looking for officers who went missing in action, who General WASHINGTON suspected had been captured and now were prisoners. He was searching for someone of interest to General WASHINGTON and the intelligence committee. He was hoping to make contact with them as he made his *"tour"* of the British prisons, as a prisoner, from New York to England.

After John's recovery, he returned to service under General MUHLENBERG retaining his rank as captain. It appears as if things were status quo during this service under General MUHLENBERG. Was this assignment staged as John appears to have gone invisible once again? There was no recorded activity. Why? John is not seen or heard from again until he returned home after the Revolution to New York City in February of 1784.

His service under General MUHLENBERG would not have been known, if not for Colonel Daniel KEMPER's declaration and Elizabeth's diary entry. Captain KEMPER was operational here, but what he was doing was not recorded. Elizabeth noted that his tour of duty appeared to have been to stand ready to protect Philadelphia from British vessels coming up to attack, even though the Revolution was winding down.

In moving upstate to Hudson, John had in his possession the sealed orders from Colonel Alexander HAMILTON that he was to deliver to Colonel Henry VAN RENSSELAER. After Captain KEMPER turned over the sealed orders, he was told *"to stay in close contact and that he would be sending for him once everything was in place."* Does this sound like another special assignment? What was it that needed to be *"put in place?"* After he was appointed captain in Company 6 of Colonel VAN RENSSELAER's regiment, he again went invisible. Why?

Elizabeth KEMPER recorded in her diary, *"My father had many correspondences with Commissioner over the years,"* in which he claimed, *"Commissioner EDWARDS was fishing for some answers on something he found in WASHINGTON's papers on his service under him; and he was not going to get it,"* but never said what it was.

Where are all these correspondences? What was really going on here? What did EDWARDS feel Captain KEMPER was hiding? Commissioner EDWARDS found something that was incomplete and wanted answers. However, none was forthcoming, nor was he worthy of any beyond John's application for a pension for services stated and rendered.

Commissioner EDWARDS, time after time through the whole history of this case, kept hitting on the words *"special protection,"* not knowing for sure in what Captain KEMPER was involved. It frustrated him that Captain KEMPER would not divulge that information, which only motivated Commissioner EDWARDS more.

Commissioner EDWARDS acknowledged the verification of Captain KEMPER's service as stated in his declarations. Because he did not know who knew what, Commissioner EDWARDS twisted the information constantly, hoping that he could trip up John, Daniel or Mr. YATES. He wanted them to reveal the precise details of Captain KEMPER's special service and the necessity to have General WASHINGTON's *"special protection"* from interference and detention by all his other officers.

He reminded them that this was not a regular appointment. He was so obsessed that he kept digging for years. Commissioner EDWARDS never stopped riding the verbiage of *"special protection"* and transporting *"public stores,"* like a cowboy rides a bucking bronco strictly for show, wondering if and when he would be thrown off. John would not reveal this information, even if it meant that he never would get his pension restored. This loyalty is why General WASHINGTON trusted him.

John told his family that Ben (Benjamin) HARRISON was the one he reported to in Congress on various bouts for General WASHINGTON. Benjamin HARRISON was a member of covert operations for the Continental Congress and General WASHINGTON. Are there any other mysteries? Now as more information has come to light, we can begin to see that these scrambled messages were probably coded messages dealing with intelligence matters.

John was involved with officers who were in the various secret committees, which wrote in various coded systems like his own. Mr. HARRISON operated from the halls of Congress in conjunction with General WASHINGTON on procedures of interest regarding foreign alliance and covert operations.

Colonel Daniel KEMPER once said, *"Some of my brother's service under General WASHINGTON cannot be told!"* General George WASHINGTON, a master of illusions, concealed Captain John KEMPER's true role, which implied that he was among one of America's first *"top secret agents!"* How would he keep this illusion from dissipating?

Maintaining his *"special protection"* of Captain John KEMPER's command seemed to suffice as an answer for his importance to the rest of the Continental officers, because of the position he held as master wagon master in the clothier-general's department. He was the main line of support for the whole Continental Army. However, Colonel Daniel KEMPER, aide-de-camp, had made it perfectly clear that his appointment in the clothier-general's department was a *ruse*. In reality, he would be under the *direct command and control of General WASHINGTON himself*. Likewise, his other contact would be Colonel Alexander HAMILTON, aide-de-camp and intelligence officer.

Why is he the only officer in American history to hold his commander-in-chief's *"special protection"* from detention or interference by all of his other officers? If all the other officers and aides were more important than Captain John KEMPER, then why was Captain KEMPER the only officer to maintain General WASHINGTON's *"special protection"*? Why did most of the officers have monuments while Captain KEMPER's grave was simply marked with a wooden cross and a plain gray rock that he put there himself?

Why did Colonel Alexander HAMILTON, another intelligence officer, have to meet with John KEMPER and his brother Daniel at City Tavern after John's escape for a couple of glasses and discuss *"certain circumstances"*?

What was Mr. YATES aware of that he needed to work around and keep confidential? Why is this case the longest in American history? Captain KEMPER's official capacity, shrouded in a cloud of mystery is still unknown!

As a closing note, it is to be remembered that Giles F. YATES spent over ten years of his life on John KEMPER's case. He had spent more time in Washington, DC, on Captain KEMPER's case than all of his others combined. It is hard to believe that he did not know more than he could reveal. It appeared that he was forced to work around Captain KEMPER's direct involvement in the Revolution in order to avoid revealing what the *"special protection"* was about.

Even though Mr. YATES replied to Commissioner EDWARDS that, *"As to what he* [John KEMPER] *held General*

WASHINGTON's 'special protection' from, he is not informed." It is most likely, that he was. What had Mr. YATES learned about John's service that made him work so hard, for so long, to have his pension increased to captain and wagon master for General WASHINGTON and the Continental Army?

Since General WASHINGTON's *"special protection"* of Captain John KEMPER's service was the prime topic of discussion over the twenty years history of his case (1832-1852), it would have been important to go over it thoroughly with Captain KEMPER. Commissioner EDWARDS never seemed to let it rest and it appeared as if he was trying to pry more details from Daniel and John KEMPER and Giles F. YATES.

However, all efforts were in vain: they would not give any more information on that subject alone and simply avoided the issue. Had John accidentally slipped when filling out his declaration, not realizing he was opening a can of worms? Why did Mr. YATES feel that General WASHINGTON's *"protection"* of Captain KEMPER's command from the interference or detention by his senior officers was too important and delicate to be revealed to the War Department?

1. Statesmen Involved with John KEMPER

Honorable Martin VAN BUREN, United States senator, New York State attorney general, governor of New York State, chairman of the United States Committee on Judiciary, Secretary of State under President Andrew JACKSON; Colonel Elisha JENKINS, Secretary of New York State, vice-chancellor of the regents of the University of New York State, New York State comptroller, mayor of Albany, New York, member of New York State Assembly; John's brother Colonel Daniel KEMPER, aide-de-camp to General George WASHINGTON, deputy clothier-general of the Continental Army, special assistant aide at the Battles of Germantown and Monmouth, receiver of the Badge of the Society of Cincinnati by General Marquis

DE LAFAYETTE; John Worth EDMONDS, attorney-at-law, presiding Justice of the Supreme Court, New York State Assembly (1831-1832), New York State Senate (1832-1835); Joseph D. MONELL (1781-1861, attorney-at-law, New York State Assembly, supervisor city of Hudson, surrogate judge and county clerk; Gayer GARDNER (1778-1849), town assessor, city clerk and a merchant in Hudson.

John ARMSTRONG Jr. was a lieutenant then major in the Continental Army of Pennsylvania during the American Revolution and had become close friends with Captain KEMPER. Major ARMSTRONG was aide-de-camp to General Hugh MERCER and General Horatio GATES.

After the Revolution, John ARMSTRONG settled in Red Hook, just south of Hudson, New York. His friendship with Captain KEMPER continued to grow over the years. He became brigadier general in the United States Army, secretary of the army, secretary of war under President James MADISON, served in the War of 1812, became a United States senator, United States minister to France, and was on the cabinet of President James MADISON, one of the many honorable statesmen and friends of Captain John KEMPER.

All these leading statesmen maintained close ties with Captain John KEMPER after his revolutionary service. Why? Was there another reason other than the new city of Hudson that kept all these men together? Were all these men still not finished with their service to our country? Why is there no paper trail leading to Captain KEMPER other than in vouchers, declarations, and being tracked down by Attorney Giles F. YATES? Captain KEMPER's membership in the Hudson officer's club tied him to all revolutionary officers and statesmen of the area. All who were not soldiers wanted to be connected to those who gave birth to America.

2. Possible Explanations of Some of Captain KEMPER's Mixed Messages

The Bluebird—General George WASHINGTON

The Three Roses—Colonel Daniel KEMPER, Colonel Alexander HAMILTON and Captain John KEMPER

The Honeycomb—The Continental Congress

A Bee—A member of Congress

Bees—All members of Congress

Queen Bee – Benjamin FRANKLIN/Benjamin TALLMADGE/Benjamin HARRISON???

Pigeon—A target (HMS *Iris*, object or person?)

Peanuts—Supplies

Candy—Money (Gold?)

Fleas—Investigators/annoying?

Mixed Drinks—Confusion

Calm after the Storm—Status after a battle

A soft sea breeze after the storm—Everything achieved, ready to come home

Horse has a broken leg—To be disposed of

Gun powder—Explosive

Certain Circumstances—Conditions/status

Barrel of Laughs—Foolish/foolishness

Bear Trap—Entrapment/capture

Fly trap—Sure capture

Mouse trap—Trip someone up

Lost at Sea—Imperiled/endangered/confused

In the Cupboard—Hidden away

Curtains—Cover/being covered

A boat in dry dock—Something not yet ready

Pillow—Comfortable

Salt water—Everywhere

Fish on the line—Chance of catching a target

Cheese and crackers—A snack or past time

Continental dollar—Something that was not in good shape/or worthless

Moon light—Travel by night

One for the road—Final point of departure
Bumble bee—Scary or for show
Hornet—An aggressive officer/or scouting party
The lampshade—A cover up
The cobbler—One who makes something (plan?)
The dollhouse—a location to set things up?

This author had originally thought that *"The Three Roses"* had meant, General Marquis DE LAFAYETTE, Count Casimir PULASKI, and Captain John KEMPER (the three whom General WASHINGTON had brought on board in the month of August 1777), especially since General LAFAYETTE had accompanied Captain KEMPER on so many runs. However, Count PULASKI had gone down to Georgia and died in combat in 1779. Therefore, the only three other possibilities were, Colonel Alexander HAMILTON, Colonel Daniel KEMPER, and Captain John KEMPER, the three who rode together in the grand parade and returned a warm nod to Ben HARRISON when they had reached Independence Hall. This might have been an acknowledgment that their journey was about to begin.

Chapter XXIX
Author's Summary

Giles Fonda YATES, as a New York State representative of Veterans Affairs, surrogate and counselor-at-law, was fully aware that it was his duty to supply sound documented evidence to support veterans' service. He had spent his career doing this. What he did not expect was to have all his honorable hard work with which he flooded the office of the secretary of war over the years, be evaded by James L. EDWARDS, commissioner of pensions, for personal reasons. This was a new experience for Agent YATES and it just did not make any sense!

The final days of Captain John KEMPER's life turned out to be as tenuous as the days at Valley Forge and during his captivity by the British. This time it was more painful; the very country that he loved and adored, fought for, and for which he had sacrificed everything caused it. When thousands had deserted, Captain KEMPER had stayed on, trying to hold the army together, trying to make peace with himself and his Maker. Fortitude was his blanket; to fail was not an option!

This was a new generation of Americans who knew little of how they came to be, other than through stories passed down. Here they had had the opportunity to captivate the very essence of a Continental officer who was part of the very beginnings of how America started. Here was an officer who had served directly under the commander-in-chief and dealt personally with all of General WASHINGTON's senior officers. He laughed, cried and suffered with them, through all the good and bad times. Now he would join them, but only in the memory of his family, friends and God.

Instead of trying to undermine Captain KEMPER for claiming the proper amount of money that was owed him and inquire of him many of his memories under his commander-in-chief and his senior officers at Valley Forge, they could have acquired a treasure trove of historical facts in the birth of America. They could have found out many of his experiences with his senior officers.

They could have discovered all of Captain KEMPER's routes of supply to General WASHINGTON and the Continental Army at their various camps and headquarters throughout our country during its early history—the hardships endured in the process of fulfilling these missions. All they had to do was ask the proper questions instead of trying to cheat him. But ... they were not overly concerned with the history of the birth of America and all those who had sacrificed everything for its existence. This was the only and the last chance they would get to acquire this information.

Finally, they could have learned about some of General WASHINGTON's periods of desperation and hardships and the Continental Army's suffering and needs. Commissioner EDWARDS, whose pride had been damaged and whose scandalous affairs had been almost exposed, was more concerned about winning wrong, rather than losing things right!

In 1888, all revolutionary records were transferred to the Department of State. Up until this point, not much emphasis or concern had been placed on preserving or giving permanent housing to what records there were left on the American Revolution. The American outcry wanting to know how America got started had been increasing over the years. The current administration was trying to preserve what little was left, instead of trying to destroy or cover up evidence of service, as had been done in the past.

On 27 July 1892 (27 stat 275) and 18 August 1894 (28 stat 403), Congress authorized the transfer to the War Department of all military records for the Revolutionary War period then in the custody of other executive branch departments. These military records were transferred between 1894 and 1913 from the departments of State, the Interior and the Treasury.

After the Department of Interior had received the revolutionary pension records for their branch, Bureau of Pensions, they came across Captain KEMPER's case. After initially going over his case, they commented, *"Even if service as wagon master was not military and under civil contract, it was important duty and should be included in any history of his case."* They went on to say, *"He could not have escaped home from imprisonment in 1781 in his statement, according to his own calculations as to the lengths of various services and his brother's statements moved up the accounts of his various tours so that they could not be considered."*

Although the investigation done by the Bureau of Pensions in the Department of Interior was competent, it was incomplete. Records later released by Great Britain, after they had become an ally of the United States, proved conclusively that Lieutenant John KEMPER was, in fact, captured by the British frigate *Iris* and taken to Mill Prison, Plymouth, England, as a bartering chip to be exchanged for British officers who had been captured by the Americans. Their records also verified that Lieutenant KEMPER had escaped in 1781. He had arrived home just after the surrender of General Lord Charles CORNWALLIS in Yorktown, on 19 October 1781.

On 20 February 1899, Ethan Allen HITCHCOCK (1835-1909) was, appointed US Secretary of Interior (1899-1907) by President William McKINLEY (1843-1901). Secretary HITCHCOCK started re-organizing the Bureau of Pensions in the Revolutionary War records department. He had his staff make up the first form, 3-525 just for this occasion. By 1900, this task was completed and he ordered one form to be put into each soldier's file, listing his name, rank and tours of duty during the American Revolution, for future easy reference.

This was the most comprehensive form ever put together by any department that held the Revolutionary War records. None of the forms were dated for a very good reason; form 3-525 was developed in 1900, while the pensioners served during the 1700s. This form is still in use to this day. After that, all revolutionary records were transferred back to the War Department.

As all revolutionary records started accumulating at the War Department, William Howard TAFT (1857-1930), secretary of war (1904-1908), ordered all revolutionary records to be categorized. At that time, all revolutionary, Civil War and interim-war veterans' records were reviewed, consolidated, condensed and re-evaluated. Once again, Captain John KEMPER's disturbing case popped up, sticking out like a sore thumb. Something was definitely wrong here! Another comprehensive investigation was ordered, once again.

On 4 August 1906, after Captain KEMPER's case was thoroughly re-investigated and given credence by the department, it was ordered by William H. TAFT, secretary of war, that his records be corrected and he be given back his status as wagon master in the Continental Army and service confirmed as midshipman in the US Navy. Captain KEMPER's honor and integrity, which had been wrongfully taken from him, was now partially restored by the very department that had taken it. In 1912, William H. TAFT became the twenty-seventh president of the United States.

Captain KEMPER's service as wagon master in the Continental Army was partially re-instated by a department head, who had no personal grudges or alternative motives against Captain KEMPER. His rank of captain had not been returned, but this author won that back in 1986. His rank of lieutenant in the US Navy was recognized by the Veterans' Administration in a correspondence dated 27 February 1935, by Adelbert D. HILLER (1893-1946), executive assistant to the administrator of the Veterans' Administration, Brigadier General, Frank Thomas HINES (1879-1960).

This correspondence is labeled, John Kemper, S. 13621, BA-J/ MLB. In this correspondence Mr. HILLER stated, *"In August 1777, he* [John Kemper] *went to Philadelphia and was there appointed wagonmaster under James MEASE, Clothier General of the Army, stationed at Philadelphia, was sent out on several foraging excursions and was discharged in the spring of 1779."*

Mr. HILLER went on to explain John KEMPER's naval service, *"In May 1779, he* [John Kemper] *entered the sea service of the state of Pennsylvania, as first midshipman on board the corvette ship, "General Greene"* [named after General Nathanael GREENE], *Captain Montgomery, and served six months cruising along the coast. In the spring of 1780, he went on board the brig, "Fair America", Captain Stephen Decatur, as a volunteer and served six months. In the spring of 1781, he entered the brig, "Hector", Captain James Seloover, served as a lieutenant; the day after sailing from Philadelphia, the Hector was captured by the British frigate, "Iris", he was carried to New York, imprisoned there and in Mill Prison at Plymouth, England, until the spring of 1782, when he made his escape, obtained passage to the West Indies, and from there to Philadelphia where he arrived in November, 1782."*

There were a few mistakes made in this correspondence by A. D. HILLER. One, he stated that John Kemper, in the spring of 1780, went on board the brig *Fair America*. Actually, the name of the ship was *Fair American*. Second, he stated that, in the spring of 1781, he entered the brig, *Hector*, under Captain Seloover. Actually it was in November 1780, under Captain SLOVER. Three, he stated that, he [John Kemper] was imprisoned in Mill Prison, England, until the spring of 1782. Actually it was the spring of 1781 (verified by British prison records). Four, he stated that, he [John Kemper] arrived in Philadelphia in November 1782. Actually, it was in November 1781, right after the surrender of, Lord Charles CORNWALLIS in Yorktown, in October 1781; as clearly stated by Captain KEMPER.

Too bad Captain **KEMPER**, his family and Giles F. **YATES** were not still alive to see justice served! Captain **KEMPER** had been dead for ninety-three years, yet fireworks still went off whenever anyone reviewed his case. Captain John **KEMPER**'s case, which had become the longest ongoing case in American history, still brought tears. What went wrong and why was the constant question.

Most of Captain John **KEMPER**'s revolutionary service of that he gave to our country over 240 years ago had been buried in the National Archives. Anyone could have obtained copies of these records if they had a name to look for. If not for Captain **KEMPER** being an ancestor of this author, besides his story and oil paintings being passed down in the family, his records might have remained buried forever. For the first time, the world will know the true story on the birth of America—what went right and what went wrong. How the very country that was created from it, would end up erasing as much of its history that could be collected; all for a very good reason.

1. Author's Pedigree Chart

Captain John KEMPER-Elizabeth Ann HOPPER
(1757-1842) | (1764-1826)
Charles Morton KEMPER-Catherine MAXWELL
(1793-1869) | (1794-1832)
Mary Ann KEMPER-Abraham MILLER
(1816-1877) | (1816-1882)

Benjamin Franklin MILLER-Anna Catherine VAN
BENSCHOTEN
(1840-1922) | (1842-1914)
Minnie Florence MILLER-Frank Eugene WILCOX
(1863-1925) | (1860-1914)
Basil Gaul Knickerbocker WILCOX-Bertha Bogardus COX
(1888-1968) | (1882-1953)
Dianthus May WILCOX-Donald Brooks HACKEL
(1920-1985) | (1925-1984)
Gordon Rodney PROPER (named after step-father)
(1949-?)

2. Author's Page

Gordon R. PROPER, after fourteen years of documenting Captain John KEMPER's service, took two weeks to prepare his letter to the United States Veterans Administration. Director Willa V. ROBUCK (1926-1996) permitted this author to supply data proving Captain John KEMPER's case, allowing justice to prevail. This author sent a five-page correspondence accompanying a large package of documents proving Captain John KEMPER's case. Nan L. NAVE (1935-2001), of Director ROBUCK's staff, handled the confirmation and re-evaluation.

There is now a department solely for handling memorial affairs, and rightfully so; it is no longer the pension department. Likewise, if a veteran's pension is discontinued, an appeal goes to a separate committee and not back to the ones responsible for stopping the pension payments. Now, there is no longer a way for an individual to hold personal grudges against an inquiry, especially when they are at fault.

What would be more startling in the growth of America is what would happen in the future. By the year 2016, America would seemingly start to build pressure like a volcano ready to explode. The heart of America would start being torn apart from within; proving conclusively, that one condition that all Americans are forced to live under, can never possibly succeed in harmony! If this volcano erupts, thousands of lives could be lost needlessly.

Edward **GIBBON** (1737-1794), wrote one of the world's greatest documented histories on "The Decline and fall of the Roman Empire." One of the things that was happening in the Roman Empire, which the American Empire was modeled after, is happening in the American Empire today. Does that mean that America will fall like Rome?

One of the main differences between the Roman and the American Empires is, Rome was a nation that depended on conquering other nations, and forcing them to their will. The American Empire is one of defense, not only of us, but of smaller helpless nations that are vulnerable to larger evil nations.

When you become a major world power, you become a target for all evil and jealous nations. Sometimes that jealously leaps over to allied nations as well, fracturing our trust. If good comes to worst, who will we be able to count on?

One hidden misunderstanding of another nation this author would like to bring to the surface, Russia is not our enemy! They have been constantly on defense throughout its history, as well. There was the Napoleon invasion, then the German invasion, who was an ally. In both world wars they have been our ally! Russia's main advantage, at this time in history, is its strong leader, Vladimir Putnin, who is not only wise, but patient.

Russia has the world's largest land mass, which is desperately needed by one nation on earth, an allied nation. This nation has the world's largest population. They have recently prepared for doubling their population growth by allowing its citizens to go from having one child, to having two. Will Russia be prepared for another invasion by yet another ally? Will we be there for them as they were for us?

Author Gordon R. Hackel with World Renowned Chinese Professor of Art Lefu Gu

3. Author's letter to the Veterans' Administration

July 14, 1986

Willa V. Robuck, Director
Office of Administration
Veterans Administration
810 Vermont Ave. N. W.
Washington, D.C. 20420

Dear Mr. Robuck:

The contents of this package, as I discussed with Nan Nave over the phone, is to provide your department with the documentation proving, that John KEMPER was, in fact, appointed captain in company number six of Colonel Henry J. VAN RENSSELAER'S regiment. As you know, when a veteran re-enlists with a certain number of years, he is guaranteed an equivalent of the rank of which he held when he left that particular branch of the service. Please note, that John KEMPER was appointed captain over Captain Thomas LEE, who was demoted to KEMPER'S vice and later declined; possibly because his feelings were hurt. Surely, Colonel VAN RENSSELAER would not have appointed a civilian over a captain and his subordinates without having prior military status. In addition, the military <u>never</u> plugged a civilian contractor into a military chain of command.

Note, that on page 136 of the Military Minutes of the Annual Report of the State Historian, that Captain KEMPER'S given name is left blank. I contacted the Office of the Secretary of State, who informed me, that my copies were accurate transcriptions of the original ones. They could only speculate, that the person involved was intending on going back to fill in the first name but forgot. However, they said, that if the Veterans Administration would like a copy of the original, all they have to do is write to: Secretary of State, Miscellaneous Records Section, Albany, N.Y., requesting a copy of the Council of Appointments Minutes for April 14, 1787; vol. one, page 108; series A, 1845.

But, as you can see on page 4 of the History of Christ Church, Hudson, N.Y., that John KEMPER donated eight shillings on Nov. 6, 1786. Also, on page 257 of the index of the 1790 Census of New York State, there are only two KEMPERS in the entire state; John, who appears in Hudson on page 66; and Daniel who appears in New York City on page 131. On pages 66 and 67 of the 1790 Census of Hudson, I also have highlighted Colonel Henry VAN RENSSELAER and some of his other officers, who lived in Hudson with Captain John KEMPER. In addition, John states in his declaration given in 1832 that, he had lived in Hudson 46 years.

I also have provided you with documentation proving, that 24 other officers who were appointed in Colonel VAN RENSSELAER'S regiment, were in fact, officers who served in the Revolutionary Army. I can further document over a hundred other cases of military appointments in the Annual Report of the State Historian, who, likewise, were soldiers who served in the Revolutionary Army of other regiments and states. The research I must perform to verify this is unimportant if it will help this case. Hudson also is the only city in America of which can boast, of being founded and settled by Revolutionary soldiers from all over the country. Therefore, I have provided your department with a couple of interesting historical perspectives.

P.O. Box 1249 • Hudson, New York 12534-0310

Willa V. Robuck, Director
Page 2
July 14, 1986

On May 1, 1833, Lew CASS, Secretary of War, and James L. EDWARDS, Commissioner of Pensions, after John KEMPER'S case had been thoroughly investigated and given credence, signed a voucher entitling John to receive a pension for his services as conductor of transport teams and a midshipman in the army and navy of the Revolution. As you know, a voucher is signed as a document serving as proof that the terms of a transaction have been met. If the rules or regulations change seven years or so down the road, it really doesn't matter; unless, of course, some witnesses or documents are brought forth to prove fraud was involved. However, this was never the case, and if it had been, then there would have had to have been charges brought up against Martin VAN BUREN, eighth president of the United States, and Colonel Elisha JENKINS who were a couple of John's vouchers. Furthermore, Elisha JENKINS had been appointed a Lieutenant on April 14, 1787, in Colonel Henry VAN RENSSELAER's regiment the same date of which John was appointed captain. Elisha only knew John KEMPER as a soldier of the Revolution, and further declared, that John served precisely as he stated in his declaration and signed a certificate saying so! (See enclosed documents.)

In 1837, after being advised that he was entitled to a larger pension, John applied for an increase. Upon his application finally being reviewed, two years after he originally applied, his pension was suspended all together! Not informed of the reason at first, he later learned that it was due in large part to the fact, that the commissioner in the Pension Office contended that his service was of *"civil contract"* and not a military appointment; therefore, making him ineligible to receive a pension. KEMPER clearly stated: *"... if my pension increase was not allowed, I was content with being constrained to the amount which had been awarded to me."* But what made KEMPER furious, made his blood run red was, when they advocated that his service was civilian and not military! This assault on his credibility and integrity, seven years after it had been thoroughly investigated and given credence, struck a demoralizing blow to his pride and honor.

The Pension Department, however, was unyielding in it contentions, the crux of the department's contentions were based on *"technicalities of language"* and ironically his *"special protection"* from interference of other officers. Then Pension Department contended that this was protection from *"impressments"* and not from interference as he clearly stated, Furthermore, the Pension Department never attempted to justify their claim, they only expressed sentiments after coming under pressure to allocate the proper adjustments to John's pension, for his service as wagon master for the Continental Army. Nevertheless, the Pension Department couldn't come up with any documentation to verify their claim other than, words and words are often, manipulated by those in power.

For it to be suggested that half of John KEMPER'S service was civilian and the other half military is ludicrous. The authenticity of John's declaration, however, is overwhelming, and I can venture to attribute his honesty for merely being a true Revolutionary American partisan. Captain KEMPER'S service was both genuine and meritorious, but the element of fear was now being injected into KEMPER once again; this time, not by his enemy,

P.O. Box 1249 • Hudson, New York 12534-0310

Willa V. Robuck, Director
Page 3
July 14, 1986

but by the country he fought for. John's brilliant dedication and moment of triumph, which it took him years to give, was now being swept away in a few short months. There was little indication that the Pension Department would show kindness or humanity or the civil virtues in general.

The question of John's service being either military or civilian, can be settled now, once and for all; for if this office was filled by a civilian, then all his supplies scheduled for the army, would have been able to have been commandeered by the civilians. General WASHINGTON would never, under any circumstances, jeopardize the fate of his Continental Army and his country, by placing a civilian in this most highly respectable and important office. Furthermore, if General WASHINGTON had allowed a civilian at this post, he would have had to fear mass desertions and mutiny by his subordinates. Civilians were, in this period of time, treacherous and naturally incompetent. WASHINGTON respected the civilian constituted authority, but didn't appreciate them interfering in military affairs. If you cannot respect my philosophy, please feel free to contact John O. MARSH, Jr., Secretary of the Army, for I feel that he is as educated and competent on early American Government and military affairs as I am.

The Pension Department's concept of the duties of a wagon master seemed confused seven years after the fact. Their sentiments changed only when it had been brought to their attention, that they had committed a serious blunder, underpaying KEMPER for his duties as wagon master in the Continental Army. Military wagon masters served the army; <u>civilians did not</u>, other than selling their goods by contract to the army. Hence, this was the extent of civilian dealers and agents, to obtain supplies so that the army could pick them up and deliver them to base. Furthermore, civilians were not sent out on military operations, such as, **foraging in the countryside**. It would seem inconceivable that General WASHINGTON would only have someone bound merely by contract, rather than someone bound by military tradition, costume and, most importantly, jurisdiction.

Nan Nave asked me: ***"What regiment did John KEMPER serve in at Valley Forge?"*** The Department of the clothier general and the quartermaster and commissary departments were <u>never</u> regimented. These departments were organized to serve the regiments (see WASHINGTON's papers and the Journals of the Continental Congress). If KEMPER had been assigned to a regiment, only that regiment would have received his supplies. Furthermore, a regimental wagon master only had 10 to 15 wagons under his command. John KEMPER'S office was much higher than a regimental wagon master, for he was Continental which enhanced his prestige, and the reason why he had over a hundred wagons under his ***"command"*** and maintained General WASHINGTON's ***"special protection."***

Purchase of goods or supplies by the clothier general, quartermaster and commissary departments were primarily by contract with civilian dealers and agents. In addition all these departments were <u>military</u> and responsible for transporting <u>commissary</u> stores.

P.O. Box 1249 • Hudson, New York 12534-0310

Willa V. Robuck, Director
Page 4
July 14, 1986

When these contracts were broken by, the civilians, it was a forager's duty to obtain, by force if necessary, the provisions from dealers or civilian contractors, who refused to sell their products to the American Army.

Since the forage and commissary departments were so mismanaged, resulting in an absence of any detailed account of those who served in them and in what capacity; compounded by the fact that virtually all records for the clothier general's department disappeared after the sudden death of James MEASE, clothier general of the Army, genealogists and historians alike must research the circumstantial evidence to support each claim. In John KEMPER'S case, this can be done from the detailed account of his two declarations, from other records obtained and histories concerning those he served under.

John KEMPER would not be properly classified again until August 4, 1906, when all Revolutionary, Civil War and interim-war veterans' records were reviewed, consolidated, condensed and re-evaluated. It was at this time that he, as a matter of historical perspective and reference, was <u>again</u> classified *"Continental, N.Y.,"* recognizing his ***"military service"*** as a wagon master. But, this time they played it safe and never signed a voucher honoring Captain KEMPER, nor did they record the evidence, which led them to their reconciliation.

The dazzling display of John's resilience after twice being taken a prisoner of war, speaks for itself. Giles F. Yates, who represented John, effected the restoration of John's pension for his 18 months of sea service; however, this was only after the Pension Department had held it hostage, to accept it or receive nothing. YATES also, most eloquently and conclusively represented him regarding his service as wagon master. Although presenting analogous cases for which pensions were granted for other wagon masters and a variety of other substantial points, YATES was not successful.

John wrote a letter to the Pensions Department saying: ***"... I served as I have stated! ... And one day he hoped to prove his service."*** But John KEMPER would not see the matter resolved in his lifetime, for a couple of years later he died with a broken heart; un-trusted by his country which he trusted, un-believed by his country which he believed in, and tormented by the agonies of scrupulous affairs. The Pension Department had instilled upon KEMPER almost as much mental fatigue as his formidable adversaries. KEMPER'S daughter, Elizabeth, who cared for him in his old age, and pursued the matter after his death, died an ***"old maid."***

Colonel Daniel KEMPER and I made the same mistake in patronizing John for his service in the American Revolution. We both concentrated our efforts on John's, naval service, not realizing our country would not commemorate his service because of his monumental hardships and great sufferings he endured for its existence. I have since redirected my efforts toward Captain KEMPER'S greatest contribution of all, his service as wagon master for the Continental Army. It is this war that was fought for the birth of our nation that outweighs al others.

P.O. Box 1249 • Hudson, New York 12534-0310

**HUDSON & MOHAWK VALLEY
GENEALOGICAL RESEARCH CENTER**
*Collecting, Preserving, & Publishing,
Histories, Documents, Manuscripts & Legends*

Willa V. Robuck, Director
Page 5
July 14, 1986

No other time in American history has our entire nation and its army been tested more severely for its endurance. No unsung hero of any other war has ever had the responsibility and fate of his entire country and its army in his hands as Captain KEMPER did. If Captain KEMPER is given as the definition of an unsung hero, then, there can be no others.

Though this information is provided as a footnote to John KEMPER'S story, *"which is currently being co-authored,"* I also would hope that it would inspire the United States Veterans Administration, in conjunction with the Office of the Secretary of the Army, to give an honorable, commensurable review of Captain John KEMPER'S case and properly recognize his unstinting service to our great nation. It is confounding when one considers the twists of fate, ironies and misunderstandings characterizing this story. We, of course, are hoping for a happy ending prior to publication; however, if we are unable to obtain it, we'll just have to hope for it after publication.

It is not my intention to misinterpret the goodwill of your department or defy its purpose, nor is it plausible for me to retract from my intent, for I am compelled to bring to a resolve and restore the credibility and integrity of one of America's finest officers, Captain John KEMPER. God has granted me the wisdom to take the appropriate measures necessary in order that I may accomplish my task, and I feel competent that I will succeed. Captain KEMPER was wronged and he <u>must</u> be righted.

I have not addressed our country with a gun, nor have I taken any hostages in order to gain attention, I have not injured anyone, nor have I taken anyone's life. Yet, the terrorist who practice these measures get all the attention of the world; and I, who have handled things intellectually, with my country, for my country, and for an American who served it, obtain very little recognition. We would all like to be considered the great heroes of our country, particularly if we participated in its birth. It is easier for us to attack, be jealous or hostile, resentful, hateful and deceitful, than it is to be kind, show love, compassion and understanding, summarized by our delusions of grandeur. Why is it so difficult for our government to admit when it has committed a dreadful error? Why must they be so reluctant to conciliate this case?

I look all around me and witness all America and its alliances celebrating our liberty, but how many really know the true story of how it succeeded? It only seems fitting that recognition of KEMPER'S important service, occur at this point in our history. I implore you to consider this case.

Warm Regards,

Rev. Gordon R. Proper, D.H.L.
President

Enclosures

P.O. Box 1249 • Hudson, New York 12534-0310

4. Veterans Administration's letter to Author

Department of Memorial Affairs   Washington D.C. 20420

OCT 0 6 1986

In Reply Refer To: 42
MI# 86 12 00366
KEMPER, John

Reverend Gordon R. Proper
Hudson and Mohawk Valley
  Genealogical Research Center
Post Office Box 1249
Hudson, New York 12534-0310

Dear Reverend Proper:

I am pleased to inform you that we have completed our review of the documentation submitted with your letter of July 14 and found it to be sufficient evidence of Revolutionary War veteran John Kemper's military service.

The marker is being ordered from a Government contractor, who will advise you of the cost for the additional inscription, VALLEY FORGE, requested to appear on the headstone. This inscription item is not provided at Government expense. It is suggested, upon receipt of the contractor's invoice, that payment be made without delay because the headstone cannot be manufactured until payment is received.

We regret the circumstances that caused a delay in approving your application and hope you will be pleased with the headstone.

Sincerely,

KENNETH L. McCONOUGHEY in the absence of
Director Monument Service

"America is #1—Thanks to our Veterans"

After a three-month re-evaluation—VICTORY!!! Capt. KEMPER's case is finally won. John KEMPER's Service—A Historical Injustice Made Right!

JOHN
KEMPER
CAPT
CONTINENTAL LINE
REVOLUTIONARY
WAR
SEP 29 1757
AUG 11 1842
VALLEY FORGE

Acknowledgments

This author owes a great many thanks to the many people who helped and supported this event through the initial repeal of John KEMPER'S pension denial, and through the years since then to this point where this story is finalized. There are some names of persons who helped that, because of their position in state and federal government, I cannot list—they know who they are. There were others who were behind the scenes dedicating their time and drumming up additional support. They were content with being in the back ground rather than being upfront on stage. My deep sense of gratitude goes out to all, and if by chance I have missed mentioning someone, it is not done so intentionally, as there were so many. It is with warm regards that, I thank-you.

- President Ronald W. Reagan, (1911-2004)
  - John G. Grimes (1936-?) *
  - GS-15 (Top Secret Clearance)
  - director of National Security telecommunications
  - served in US Air Force
  - deputy assistant secretary of defense under Richard (Dick) Cheney
  - deputy assistant secretary for counterintelligence & security countermeasures 1980-1984
  - senior director White House situation support staff 1984-1990
  - nominated by President George W. Bush on 17 June 2005

- Lieutenant General Clarence E. McKnight, Jr. (1929-?) *
  - GS-15 (Top Secret Clearance)
  - graduate of West Point

- • commander of US Army Signal Corps, Fort Gordon, Georgia.
- • member of the Joint Chiefs of Staff
- • author of *"From Pigeons to Tweets"*

- William (Bill) B. Bogardus (1927-?) ***
  - • GS-15 (Top Secret Clearance)
  - • assigned to the Defense Communication Agency in Washington, DC.
  - • took part in the planning and subsequent establishment of the Defense Commercial Communications Office (DECCO)
  - • in charge of the office that processed orders to the commercial companies to affect their installation, in total or in part.
  - • founder and civilian director of United States Army Commercial Communications Office (USARCCO) in charge of leasing all government communications around the world for the Department of the Army and for the president, as specially ordered by the Joint Chiefs of Staff. His rating was by an army colonel of the United States Army Strategic Communications Command located at Fort Huachuca, Arizona. Then start, He reported to the commanding general, either a major general or lieutenant general, at Scott AFB, Ill.
  - • was awarded the Department of the army Decoration for Meritorious Civilian Service
  - • has been credited with saving the US government over $40 million.
  - • is in "Who's Who in Finance and Industry"
  - • author of Dear Cousins (descendants of Anneke Jans by her two husbands, Rolef Jansen and Rev. Everardus Bogardus), of which this author contributed greatly to.

- Major General Gerd S. Grombacher (1923-2006)
  - • USACC commander
  - • Served in WW II, Korea, and Vietnam

- Colonel John Edwards (1920-1998)
  - veteran of WWII, Korea, Viet nam
  - national junior Vice Commander of the American Ex-prisoners of War

- Lieutenant Colonel George T. Dolan, Jr. (1930-2006)
  - in charge of bombing and navigational operations in North Vietnam

- Willa V. Robuck (1926-1996) **
  - director of the Veterans Administration in Washington, DC
  - Nan L. Nave (1935-2001)*, staff that handled the re-evaluation and verification of John KEMPER's service, for the Veterans Administration in Washington, DC

- Everett Alvarez, Jr. (1937-?) *
  - deputy Administrator of Veterans Affairs, Washington, DC
  - US Navy commander
  - First US pilot to be downed and detained during the Viet-Nam War
  - eight years as a prisoner of war
  - awarded the Silver Star, two legions of merit, two Bronze Star Medals
  - the distinguished Flying Cross, two Purple Heart medals & the Lone Sailor Award

- Gerald B. H. Solomon (1930-2001) ***
  - United States congressman

- Alfonse D'Amato, Esq. (1937-?)
  - United States senator

- Daniel Patrick Moynihan (1927-2003)
  - United States senator

- Samuel S. Stratton (1916-1990)
  - United States congressman
  - member of the Armed Services Committee

- Jack F. Kemp (1935-2009)
  - United States congressman
  - United States secretary of Housing and Urban Development Committee

- Mario Matthew Cuomo (1932-2015)*
  - governor of New York State
  - Leslie Mann (1958-?)*, regional representative to Governor Mario M. Cuomo

- Jay P. Rolison, Jr., Esq. (1929-2007) **
  - New York State senator

- Clarence (Larry) D. Lane (1921-1998) **
  - New York State assemblyman

- Tito M. Grenci (1928-?) ***
  - sergeant of arms New York State senate
  - New York State Senate and former body guard to Governor Nelson Rockefeller (1908-1979)

- George R. Sharpe *
  - chairman of the Columbia County Board of Supervisors

- William (Bill) H. Bywater (1944-?) *
  - international president IUE-AFL-CIO

- Sal T. Ingrassia (1929-?) *
  - president, District 3 IUE-AFL-CIO

- California State University of Social Sciences
  - Presenters of the Scholarly Research Award
    - Amanda Mott, Ph.D., professor of social sciences
    - N. Roger Coombs, Ph.D., dean, Fellow of the Royal Society, London
  - Signers of the Meritorious Graduate and Man-of-the-Year Award 1999-2014

- • Rev. Magnus Churchill, MA, MG, president of the institute
  - • Albert Flagg Rawlinson, J.D., honorary doctor of humane letters
    - • chancellor of the institute
  - • Amanda Mott, Ph.D., professor of social sciences
  - • N. Roger Coombs, Ph.D., dean, Fellow of the Royal Society, London

- • Timothy (Timmy) D. Hotaling (1960-?) **
  - • head of investigations for New York State DMV
  - • the one who helped write this author's five-page letter which won Captain Kemper's case with the Veterans Administration
  - • US Air Force veteran

- • Joseph L. Bruno (1929-?)
  - • New York State senator
  - • majority leader of New York State Senate

- • Edward I. Koch (1924-2013)
  - • mayor of New York City
  - • member of the US House of Representatives

- • John (Jack) Francis Welsh (1935-?)
  - • chairman and CEO of General Electric

- • Seth Grenci (1960-1999)
  - • bodyguard for David Rockefeller (1915-2017)—owner of Chase Manhattan bank and retired head of the— Trilateral Commission
  - • Columbia County, New York deputy sheriff

- • Richard (Dick) A. Wannemacher Jr. (1948-?)
  - • national service officer of the Disabled American Veterans
  - • served US Navy
  - • Viet-nam War veteran

- William (Bill) G. Hoffman (1912-2001) **
  - chairman, PTS Conference Board IUE-AFL-CIO

- Allison (Al) J. Andrews (1951-?) *
  - commander, Millerton Post of the American Legion, Columbia County, New York
  - past commander Dutchess County American Legion

- Michael (Mike) Clunis (1943-2013)
  - Columbia County commander of the American Legion
  - served US Air Force
  - Viet-nam War Veteran
  - chief of police Stratton Veterans Administration Hospital, Albany, New York

- Leonard (Lenny) W. Peluso (1915-2004)
  - Dutchess County Commander of the American Legion

- Albert E. Schermerhorn (1923-1986)
  - DAV commander of Columbia County Chapter #No. 194

- Darwin (Doc) H. Medick (1928-1987)
  - WWII veteran
  - past Dutchess County commander of the American Legion
  - color guard detail of Dutchess County, New York

- Donald Rice (1929-2010)
  - Dutchess County Veterans' Affairs Officer

- Kenneth (Ken) H. Wilber (1947-?)
  - supervisor, town of Ghent, New York
  - Columbia County treasurer

- Michael (Mike) Yusko Jr. (1947-?)
  - mayor of Hudson, New York

- Bishop Neal R. Coombs Ph.D. (1927-?) **
  - dean of students California State Institute of Social Science
  - mentor

- Jacqueline A. Schrom (1953-?) **
  - Industry Resource Center administrative assistant

- Professional Insurance Agents, a membership-based trade association representing professional independent property/casualty insurance agents, providing focused legislative voice, information, education, and networking opportunities.

- Brian Johnson, B.S. (1957-?)
  - Kira Web Design and Hosting
  - US Marine veteran

- Rev. Ernest (Ernie) Smith (1922-2014) *
  - organizer for Governor Samuel Tildon's monument

- Ralph P. Melino *
  - chairman of the NYS Sons of the American Legion former State Department vice-commander

- James (Jimmy) W. Clifford, Sr. (1937-2011) *
  - president, Local 327, IUE-AFL-CIO

- Larry (Angelo) Markessinis (1922-2020) *
  - superintendent, Hudson City Cemetery

- Herman (Herm) G. Harrington (1924-2007) *
  - chairman of national internal affairs for the American Legion.
  - past commander of New York State American Legion master of ceremonies (MC)

- James M. Leffler (1943-?)
  - national service officer of the Military Order of the Purple Heart (M.O.P.H.)

- Ellen D. Kiehl, Ph.D. (1946-?) *
  - contributing editor

- John J. Faso, Esq. (1952-?) *
  - New York State Assembly minority leader

- Glenn E. Warren
  - New York State assemblyman

- Theodore (Ted) H. Snow (1949-?)
  - investigator, New York State Attorney General's Office
  - director of religious education for the Department of Defense
  - chaplain, having served Army Pacific, Okinawa, Japan;
    intelligence center at Fort Huachuka, Arizona
    and the national training centers at Fort Irwin, California
    and Fort Benning, Georgia
    Marine Viet nam veteran

- Clovis Hunter Brakebill (1920-2002)
  - president general of the National Society of the Sons of
    the American Revolution

- Robert L. Harring (1933-?)
  - general manager of L&B Furniture Industries Inc.

- Lance Reed Miner (1941-?)
  - attorney-at-law, brother of Roger Miner appointed to the
    Supreme Court by President
    Ronald Reagan

- Paul Proper (1930-2018)
  Columbia County Sheriff

- Gary Owens (1949-?)
  - executive representative of General Electric's field
    marketing,
    who flew all around the world for Jack Welsh & General
    Electric

- Captain James J. Dolan, Jr. (1930-2006)
  - chief of police and Hudson Police Department

- William C. Worrall (1936-?)
  - owner and publisher of Keyboard World Magazine
  - in Who's Who in Music and Musicians, Cambridge, England International

- Samuel Ketam (Tiger Sam)
  - New York State commander, American Legion

- John Brodowski (1922-2016)
  - Owner of Johnny's Ideal Printing, Hudson, New York

- Joe White
  - world power lifter

- Ronald (Ron) Anderson
  - union organizer IUE-AFL-CIO

- Michael F. Troy (1944-?)
  - Hudson City Clerk

- Vance G. Smith (1957-?)
  - head of shipping for L&B Corporation
  - drummer for Wallstreet

- George Gordon (1943-2019)
  - world historian

- LeFu Gu (1938-?)
  - World-renowned Chinese professor of art

- Edward (Eddie) D. Gibbons (1929-2006)
  - superintendent of Highways, Ghent, New York

- Benay Britton (1973-?) and Lisa Foronda (1973-?)
  - vocalists from Ravena-Coeymans-Selkirk High School

- Perry (1947-?) and Susan (1963-?) Peters

- Rowles Studio of Hudson, New York

- Benjamin E. Cantele (1932-2008)
  - owner of Cantele Monuments, Mellenville, New York

- Michael Moore, (1976-?)
  - Controls checkout team leader for Atlas Corporation (Video editing)

- Jackson (Joe) Kemper (1942-)
  - (Descendant of Col. Daniel Kemper (1749-1847) and Descendant of Major General Peter Muhlenberg (1746-1807), member of the Society of Cincinnati and in possession of the Kemper family Bible from the early 17'00's in Germany.

- Sharon Dowling Kemper (1947-?)
  - (contributed confirmation and verification of early Kemper records from the Kemper Family Bible)

For their life-long support of this project:

- Gwendolyn (Gwen) Lane (1917-1992)
  - aunt

- Harold Wilcox (1912-1979)
  - uncle

- Roberta (Bobbie) Castang (1930-?), Carol Owens (1928-?)
  - who are/were more like sisters than cousins

- Linda A. (Wilcox) Mc Daniel (1945-2007)
  - beloved sister

- Jeffrey Rhodes (1969-?)
  - nephew

- served in the US Air Force
- trained troops for the Iraq War

*   Those who made things happen beyond imagination. They gave so much extra and never asked for anything in return.

Sources Consulted

1840 Census of Pensioners

American Advertiser Newspaper (Fishkill, N.Y.)

AmericanRevolution.org

An Apostle of the Western Church: Memoir of the Right Reverend Jackson

Ancestry

Annual Report of the New York State Historian

Council of Appointment Minutes for April 14, 1787; vol. 1, page 108; series A, 1845

Biographies in Naval History

Biography of Commodore Joshua Barney

Captain Anthony Maxwell's Pension Records

Captain John Kemper's family Bible records

Captain John Kemper's declaration

Captain John Kemper's pension records

Captain John Kemper's journals

Captain John Kemper's papers (mixed messages)

Captain John Kemper's book *Wagon Master*

Captain John Kemper's book *US Naval Affairs*

Colonel Aaron Burr's notes

Colonel Daniel Kemper's affidavit

Colonel Daniel Kemper's declarations

Colonel Daniel Kemper's letters

Colonel Daniel Kemper's pension records

Colonel Daniel Kemper's voucher

Columbia County Historical Society

Correspondences of John Hancock

Court Records of the Hudson City Courthouse

Daughters of American Revolution Magazine, Febebruary 1917, volume 50

Daughters of the American Revolution Records (DAR)

DAR Patriot Index
Elizabeth Hopper's diary
Elizabeth Kemper's diary
Elizabeth Kemper's memoirs
Federal Census, US
General Society of Mayflower descendants
General Braddock's Expedition
gwpaper.virginia.edu/history/faq/washington
Historical Register of Officers of the Continental Army (by Francis B. Heitman)
Historical Society of Somerset Hills, N.J.
History of Christ Church, Hudson, N.Y.
History of Colombia County, N.Y.
History of Dutchess County, N.Y.
History of New York City
History of the First New Hampshire Regiment in the War of the Revolution (by Frederick Kidder)
Hopper Family in America
Hudson City Newspaper Records, Hudson, N.Y.
Iconography of Manhattan Island (IN Phelps Stokes)
Journals/diaries of Lieutenant James Mc Michael
Journals/diaries of Captain John Kemper
Journals/diaries of prisoners on the *Jersey* prison ship
Journals/diaries of prisoners under the Provost Marshal, Captain William Cunningham
Journals/diaries of soldiers at Valley Forge
Journals/diaries of wagon masters
Journals of the Continental Congress
Journals of Major Samuel Shaw (1754-1794) (by Samuel Shaw and Josiah Quincy)
Journals of General William Heath
Kemper family Bible records
Lafayette's memoirs
Letters of John Adams
Letters of Benjamin Franklin
Letters of Colonel Alexander Hamilton
Letters of Francis Hopkinson

Letters between Francis Hopkinson and General George
 Washington (1777-1789)
Letters of General John Sullivan
Library of Congress
Litchfield Historical Society
Long Island Historical Society
Lossing's field book of the Revolution
Marblehead Museum and Historical Society
Mariners of the American Revolution
Masonic Order Records
Memoirs of Colonel Sebastian Beauman (cousin to Captain
 Kemper)
Memoirs of the Life of Eliza S.M. Quincy (niece of Captain
 Kemper)
Memoirs of Major General (William) Heath
Microfilm of prisoners of Mill Prison, England
National Archives Prologue Magazine
National Archives Washington, DC
New York Genealogical & Biographical Records (NYG&B)
New York Historical Society
New York in the Revolution (by Berthold Fernow)
New York in the Revolution (by James A. Roberts)
New York State Archives, Albany, NY
Papers of George Washington
Papers of Johan Jost Petrie
Papers of Sebastian Beauman
Papers of Timothy Pickering
Pension Records of wagon masters (National Archives)
Pensioners of Revolutionary war struck off roll
Platner Family in America
Records of the Clothier Generals Department
Records of the Dutch Reformed Church, New York City, NY
Records of the Hudson City Cemetery, including interments
Records of the Lutheran Church, New York City, NY
Records of the Zion Lutheran Church, Athens, Greene
 County, NY

Records of the Reformed Church, Germantown, Columbia County, NY
Records of the Reformed Church Claverack, Columbia County, NY
Register Star newspapers, Hudson, NY (1801-1869)
Secretary of the navy, Levi Woodbury's correspondences
Ship passenger lists (from Holland to Philadelphia, PA.)
Sons of the American Revolution Records (SAR)
Society of the Cincinnati Records
Tallmadge, Colonel Benjamin (autobiography)
The Book of Heroes: Great Men and Women in American History
The Brick Academy (newspaper)
The French Alliance and the Winning of American independence (by Edward Ayres,
Jamestown-Yorktown Foundation Historian)
The Greatest Street in the World (Stephens Jenkins)
The Palatine Families of New York 1710 (by Henry Z. Jones)
The Society for the History of Germans in Maryland
The Transactions of the Rockefeller Family Association for Five Years
Tracing the History of the Slave Cemetery
United States Department of State, Washington, DC
United States Department of War, Washington, DC
United States Pension Department, Washington, DC
Washington: Lessons in Leadership
Washington's papers
Wikipedia encyclopedia

Index

Alexander, Madam Mary (Sprat) (1691-1760) 76

Alexander, William "Lord Stirling" (1726-1783) 24, 69, 76, 77, 86, 111, 121, 160, 163, 169, 194, 266, 274, 279, 280, 372. See also Stirling, Col. and Gen. Lord

Allen, Ethan (1738-1789) 66, 258, 414

Allen's Hotel 421

Andre, Major John (1750-1780) 304

Antonius, Marcus (Mark Antony) (83BC-30BC) 106, 107, 127, 128, 362, 382

Aorson, Captain Aaron (1740-?) 67

Armbruster, Eugene L. (1865-1943) 315

Armstrong, Senator, John, Jr. (1758-1843) 524, 525, 526, 551

Arnold, Maj. Gen. Benedict (1740-1801) 96, 263, 270, 271, 272, 301, 306, 312

Attorneys-at-Law/Esq.
  Carroll, Nicholas, Esq. (1815-1887) 507, 528, 529, 531
  Edmonds, John Worth (1799-1874) 440, 475, 551
  Edwards, James L., Esq., (1787-1862) 450
  French, Esq. 538
  Heath, James E. Esq. (1812-1870) 507, 535, 538, 539
  Jay, John Esq., (1745-1829) 92
  Monell, Joseph Dewight (1781-1861) 438, 440, 551
  Reed, Rufus Esq., (1788-1869) 421
  Spencer, S. Esq. 467, 478
  Sylvester, Henry Hayden, Esq., (1808-1898) 536
  Wayatentius, Esq 537
  Yates, Giles Fonda, Esq., (1798-1859) 456, 554

B

Barhgte (Barhyte), James (Jacobus) (1762–1841) 481

Barney, Captain Joshua (1759-1818) 324, 327, 328

Battles in the French and Indian Wars
  Fort Necessity 16
  Monongahela River 16, 17, 18

Battles/Rome
  Actium (2 September 31BC) 106, 107, 127

Battles/Sieges in Germany
  Belgrade (8 September 1690) xxvi
  Belgrade (30 July-6 September 1688) xxvi
  Bonn (October 1689) xxvi
  Buda (78 day siege-27 July 1686) xxv
  Buda (109 day 1st siege-30 October 1684) xxv
  Kaiserworth (17-22 June 1689) xxvi
  Marsaglia (4 October 1695) xxvi
  Mohács (12 August 1687) xxv
  Munkacs (14 January 1688) xxv
  Neerwinden (29 July 1693) xxvi
  Slankamen (19 August 1691) xxvi
  Steinkirk (24 July 1692) xxvi
  Vienna (11 September 1683) xxiii
  Zenta (11 September 1697) xxvi

Battles/Skirmishes/Expedition of the American Revolution
  Assunpink Creek (2 January 1777) 68
  Battle of Little Big Horn (25-26 June 1876) 91
  Brandywine (11 September 1777) 68, 145, 170, 173, 200, 209, 366, 421
  Brooklyn (27 August 1776) 58, 77, 78, 85, 88
  Cooch's Bridge (3 September 1777) (skirmish) 171

D

E

Edmonds, General Samuel (1760-1825) 440, 441, 475

Edmonds, Senator John Worth (1799-1874) 440, 475, 551

Edwards, James L. (1787-1862) vi, 309, 431, 444, 450, 453, 454, 457, 458, 459, 467, 472, 475, 477, 478, 480, 481, 482, 486, 490, 491, 492, 493, 494, 496, 498, 500, 506, 507, 526, 527, 529, 535, 554, 566

Ely, Congressman John (1774-1849) 482

Emperors
Leopold I (1640-1705), Holy Roman Emperor xxii, xxiv, xxv, xxviii, xxix, xxx, xxxi, xxxiii, xxxiv, xxxv, xliv, 274, 423, 502

Empires
Holy Roman Empire xxii, xxiii, xxv, xxviii, xxxi, xliv, 274, 382, 423, 502
Ottoman Empire (Turks) xxv

England/city
London 23, 93, 580, 581
Plymouth 251, 324, 432, 494, 538, 556, 558

Ensigns
Crawford, William (1722-1782) 16
Kemper, Jacob (1753-1800) v, xxxviii, xxxix, xlii, xlvi, 2, 3, 4, 6, 8, 11, 12, 13, 18, 20, 26, 28, 58, 73, 80, 96, 124, 157, 231, 252, 330, 361, 400, 403, 405, 406, 422, 423, 424, 427, 448, 486, 492
Maxwell, Anthony (1754-1826) 41, 59, 80, 95, 110, 122, 125, 131, 174, 223, 233, 241, 252, 253, 277, 289, 365, 395, 401, 402, 405, 407, 409, 411, 413, 416, 418, 421, 429, 439, 501, 507
Scott, Charles (1739-1813) 16, 120, 137, 160, 426, 541

Enslin, Lieutenant Frederick Gotthold (1740-?) 252, 254

Ernst, Anna Maria (Bomper) (1708-ca.1780) 59, 185, 190

Ernst/Ernestin, Maria Ursula (1685-aft.1752) xxxviii, xlv, 14

Ernst/Ernest, Reverend [Johannes?] (ca. 1683-1752) xxxviii, 1, 424

Ernst, Johanna Catharina (1719-aft.1784) 14

Ernst, Johann Mattheus/Mathias (1706-1780) xlvi, 1, 5

Ernst, Maria Christina (1722-1811) 12

Ernst, Maria Regina (1712-1789) xxxviii, xxxix, xlii, xlvi

Ernst, Mattheus/Mathias (1706-1780) xlvi, xlvii, 1, 2, 3, 5, 7, 12, 407

Erskine, Lieut. Gen. Sir William (1728-1795) 116

Explorers
Hudson, Hendrick (ca.1568-1611) 374, 384

F

Fairfield, Justice Josiah Woodbury "JW" (1802-1878) 445

FBI/Federal Bureau of Investigation 138, 540

Fenno, Lieutenant Ephraim (1734-1820) 95

Ferguson, Henry Hugh (1747-?) 251

Files, James (1942-?) 400

Fillmore, President Millard (1800-1874) 535

Fish, General Nicholas (1758-1833) 426

Fister, Captain Henry 67

Flagler, Catharina 9

Flagler, Margaretha/Grietje (Dopp) (1692-1764) 9

Flagler, Philip Solomon (1701-1766) 9, 11, 12, 13

Flagler, Zacharias (1726-1799) 11

I

Q

R

Y

About the Author

Reverend Gordon R. Proper, DHL, MG

This author is *"blood related"* to both Captain John KEMPER and General George WASHINGTON.

Gordon Proper was born in 1949 in Hudson, New York, was raised in Selkirk and attended Ravena-Coeymans-Selkirk High School (RCS).

He started working in investigations for Pacific International Investigators in Long Beach, California, from June 1966 and to July 1995. He also worked for their branch office, Pacific International News Service, out of Las Vegas, Nevada, and continued in this capacity as a major investigator until 1994.

Although there were hundreds of cases, a couple of the most memorable were the following: 1. the murder on President Richard NIXON's Western White House lawn in Oceanside, California: and 2. the death of Charles Milles MANSON Jr./ aka Jay WHITE on 29 June 1993, aged thirty-seven years, which took place 151 miles east of Denver, Colorado, while driving in his car.

It was up to this investigator to interview Charles's mother, Rosalie WHITE, who was a waitress at the Imperial Hotel. By the time I got there, Rosalie (Rosie), had already left for the scene of her last son's tragic death. She told other waitresses that her son had died in a car accident. However, he was distraught over the possible release of his father, Charles M. MANSON, from prison, and decided to shoot himself in the head. We were paid to do this investigation by the *Star Newspaper.*

He is the author of Washington's Master Wagon Master Captain John KEMPER's historical coverage –*ONCE UPON A TIME IN THE AMERICAN REVOLUTION!*